IMPORT⌇NT.

W9-AWN-792

HERE IS YOUR REGISTRATION CODE TO ACCESS
YOUR PREMIUM McGRAW-HILL ONLINE RESOURCES.

For key premium online resources you need THIS CODE to gain access. Once the code is entered, you will be able to use the Web resources for the length of your course.

If your course is using **WebCT** or **Blackboard**, you'll be able to use this code to access the McGraw-Hill content within your instructor's online course.

Access is provided if you have purchased a new book. If the registration code is missing from this book, the registration screen on our Website, and within your WebCT or Blackboard course, will tell you how to obtain your new code.

Registering for McGraw-Hill Online Resources

TO gain access to your McGraw-Hill web resources simply follow the steps below:

(1) USE YOUR WEB BROWSER TO GO TO: **http://www.mhhe.com/dominick8**

(2) CLICK ON **FIRST TIME USER**.

(3) ENTER THE REGISTRATION CODE* PRINTED ON THE TEAR-OFF BOOKMARK ON THE RIGHT.

(4) AFTER YOU HAVE ENTERED YOUR REGISTRATION CODE, CLICK **REGISTER**.

(5) FOLLOW THE INSTRUCTIONS TO SET-UP YOUR PERSONAL UserID AND PASSWORD.

(6) WRITE YOUR UserID AND PASSWORD DOWN FOR FUTURE REFERENCE. KEEP IT IN A SAFE PLACE.

TO GAIN ACCESS to the McGraw-Hill content in your instructor's **WebCT** or **Blackboard** course simply log in to the course with the UserID and Password provided by your instructor. Enter the registration code exactly as it appears in the box to the right when prompted by the system. You will only need to use the code the first time you click on McGraw-Hill content.

Thank you, and welcome to your McGraw-Hill online Resources!

 **Higher Education**

* YOUR REGISTRATION CODE CAN BE USED ONLY ONCE TO ESTABLISH ACCESS. IT IS NOT TRANSFERABLE.

0-07-297124-X T/A DOMINICK: THE DYNAMICS OF MASS COMMUNICATION, 8/E

MCGRAW-HILL
ONLINE RESOURCES

REGISTRATION CODE

IELY-BU7P-0MY5-51D1-5N4L

THE
DYNAMICS
OF MASS
COMMUNICATION

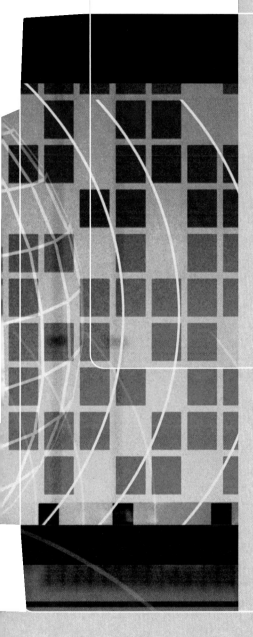

EIGHTH EDITION

THE DYNAMICS OF MASS COMMUNICATION
Media in the Digital Age

Joseph R. Dominick
University of Georgia, Athens

Boston   Burr Ridge, IL   Dubuque, IA   Madison, WI   New York
San Francisco   St. Louis   Bangkok   Bogotá   Caracas   Kuala Lumpur
Lisbon   London   Madrid   Mexico City   Milan   Montreal   New Delhi
Santiago   Seoul   Singapore   Sydney   Taipei   Toronto

The McGraw·Hill Companies

THE DYNAMICS OF MASS COMMUNICATION: MEDIA IN THE DIGITAL AGE

Published by McGraw-Hill, a business unit of The McGraw-Hill Companies, Inc., 1221 Avenue of the Americas, New York, NY, 10020. Copyright © 2005, 2002, 1999, 1996, 1994, 1993, 1990, 1987, 1983 by The McGraw-Hill Companies, Inc. All rights reserved. No part of this publication may be reproduced or distributed in any form or by any means, or stored in a database or retrieval system, without the prior written consent of The McGraw-Hill Companies, Inc., including, but not limited to, in any network or other electronic storage or transmission, or broadcast for distance learning.

Some ancillaries, including electronic and print components, may not be available to customers outside the United States.

This book is printed on acid-free paper.

1 2 3 4 5 6 7 8 9 0 VNH/VNH 0 9 8 7 6 5 4

ISBN 0-07-288579-3

Publisher: *Phillip A. Butcher*
Sponsoring editor: *Phillip A. Butcher*
Developmental editors: *Thom Holmes/Cynthia Ward*
Editorial coordinator: *Marcella Tullio*
Senior marketing manager: *Leslie Oberhuber*
Lead media producer: *Erin Marean*
Senior project manager: *Christina Thornton-Villagomez*
Production supervisor: *Janean A. Utley*
Senior designer: *Gino Cieslik*
Lead supplement producer: *Marc Mattson*
Manager, Photo research: *Brian J. Pecko*
Art editor: *Emma C. Ghiselli*
Permissions editor: *Frederick T. Courtright, The Permissions Company*
Cover interior design: *Amanda Kavanagh*
Typeface: *10/12 Palatino*
Compositor: *Black Dot Group*
Printer: *Von Hoffman Corporation*

Library of Congress Cataloging-in-Publication Data

Dominick, Joseph R.
    The dynamics of mass communication : media in the digital age / Joseph R. Dominick.—
8th ed.
        p. cm.
    Includes index.
    ISBN 0-07-288579-3 (softcover : alk. paper)
    1. Mass media. I. Title.
P90.D59 2005
302.23—dc22

2004040179

www.mhhe.com

>> **For Meaghan and for Carole**

» About the Author

Joseph R. Dominick received his undergraduate degree from the University of Illinois and his Ph.D. from Michigan State University in 1970. He taught for four years at Queens College of the City University of New York before going to the College of Journalism and Mass Communication at the University of Georgia where, from 1980 to 1985, he served as head of the Radio-TV-Film Sequence. Dr. Dominick is the author of three books in addition to *The Dynamics of Mass Communication* and has published more than 30 articles in scholarly journals. From 1976 to 1980, Dr. Dominick served as editor of the *Journal of Broadcasting*. He has received research grants from the National Association of Broadcasters and from the American Broadcasting Company and has consulted for such organizations as the Robert Wood Johnson Foundation and the American Chemical Society.

>> Brief Contents

>> Contents

> PART II   Media   85

Chapter 4
Newspapers   86

Chapter 5
Magazines   120

> PART III   Specific Media Professions   317

> **PART IV**   **Regulation of the Mass Media   383**

Chapter 15
Formal Controls: Laws, Rules, Regulations   384

Chapter 16
Ethics and Other Informal Controls   418

>> Boxed Features

Critical/Cultural Issues

These boxes illustrate the diverse perspectives of those who use the critical/cultural paradigm discussed in Chapter 2.

Decision Makers

Some of these names will be more familiar than others, but all of the people profiled in these boxes have had a significant impact on contemporary mass media.

Ethical Issues

Figuring out the right thing to do is sometimes difficult, as these boxes illustrate.

Media Probe

These boxes provide additional illustrations, examples, and background to topics mentioned in the text.

Media Talk

Need a good discussion starter? These boxes refer to segments on the accompanying CD that introduce important issues in mass communication.

Media Tour

Get a first-hand look at how various media operate and hear media professionals discuss significant concerns in their fields. These boxes are also keyed to the accompanying CD.

Social Issues

New developments in mass communication raise new concerns. These boxes explore how the mass media operate in a social context.

Soundbyte

These brief boxes illustrate the unusual, the ironic, and the offbeat things that sometimes occur in the media world.

>> Preface for the Eighth Edition

The dictionary defines *dynamics* as those forces that produce change in any field or system. Given the events of the last few years, during which both external and internal forces have caused waves of change throughout the media, the word *dynamics* in the title of this book has never been more appropriate.

In the short interval between the seventh edition and the current edition, the United States suffered a devastating terrorist attack, carried out military operations against Afghanistan and Iraq, experienced a meltdown in the dot-com industry, and felt the effects of an economy in a tailspin. All of these external events had significance for mass communication. In addition, important developments occurred within the mass media industries themselves:

- The recording industry, plagued by the effects of file-sharing programs such as Kazaa, took the unprecedented step of suing its potential customers for downloading music.
- Cell phones were being used by 160 million Americans.
- Journalists were embedded with military units during Operation Iraqi Freedom.
- The convergence mergers of AOL and Time Warner and Vivendi and Universal turned sour.
- More and more TV stations converted their signals from analog to digital.
- The number of people in the United States with broadband connections to the Internet increased to more than 35 percent.

Not surprisingly, these developments made the task of updating a book on the mass media more difficult. This difficulty was compounded by the nature of an introductory course in mass communication. Typically two groups of students enroll in such a course. One group is considering a career in the media and is interested in the changing operations and structures of the mass communication industries. Those in the other group are not planning to be media professionals and are interested in becoming intelligent, informed, and critical consumers of media content. One of the original goals of *Dynamics* was thus to present a current and thorough treatment of the various media topics that would be useful to aspiring professionals while offering enough scholarly substance to encourage the development of media literacy among consumers of mass communication. The changes reflected in the eighth edition also had to be tailored to serve the needs of both groups.

Keeping up with political, social, cultural, and technological developments is important for those who aspire to be media professionals since they may directly influence the tasks they perform in the future. Advances in technology create some new career opportunities and erase others; the changing economic and business conditions influence how practitioners create and distribute media content; current events pose new ethical and professional dilemmas.

These changes also have significance for those who will end up in other professions. After reading this latest edition, such students will not be surprised when advertising text messages start showing up on their cell phones or when newspaper publishers offer them free custom editions to get them into the newspaper reading habit. They will understand what HDTV is all about and whether they should be concerned about the social impact of violent video games. In short, keeping abreast of media developments will help them become informed media consumers.

 ## WHAT IS NEW TO THIS EDITION

The new material in the eighth edition can be grouped into several main themes:

- *The continuing digital revolution:* Chapter 3 (*Historical and Cultural Context*) introduces information about cell phones, PDAs, and other mobile wireless communication devices that may usher in more milestones in the evolution of human communication. Chapter 4 (*Newspapers*) examines how newspapers are integrating their online editions with their traditional print versions and discusses the current trend toward requiring consumers to register or pay before being granted full access to their sites. Chapter 5 (*Magazines*) looks into the growing trend toward custom magazines and digital delivery, and Chapter 6 (*Books*) examines the slow development of e-books. The developments in the electronic media—digital TV, HDTV, digital radio, digital music, and digital movies—are discussed in Chapters 7 through 10.

- *The evolution of the Internet:* Chapter 1 discusses how the most successful activities on the Internet (e-mail, file sharing, online auctioneering) are manifestations more of machine-assisted interpersonal communication than of traditional mass communication. The chapter suggests that the idea of the Internet as primarily a mass communication medium should be rethought. Not surprisingly, Chapter 11 (*The Internet and the World Wide Web*) has undergone a major overhaul and features updated sections on spam, broadband, wireless fidelity, streaming Web video, and the Evernet, the Internet's next stage of evolution.

- *The transformation of traditional media by the Internet:* Chapter 4 (*Newspapers*) analyzes how the Internet is being used to attract younger readers. Chapter 8 (*Sound Recording*) examines peer-to-peer file-sharing programs and the way they are reshaping the recording industry. Chapter 14 (*Advertising*) investigates new developments in online advertising.

- *The changing business environment:* Chapter 1 now contains an extended discussion of the multidimensional concept of *convergence*. Each of the media chapters contains the latest information on mergers, acquisitions, and the effects of uncertain economic conditions.

- *Issues in the practice of journalism:* The catastrophic events surrounding September 11 presented unprecedented challenges and problems for the media. Material in Chapter 2 (*Perspectives on Mass Communication*) discusses how the media performed under these difficult conditions and how the audience used the media to keep informed during a time of crisis. Chapter 12 (*News Gathering and Reporting*) examines a different set of issues—those that arose during the coverage of Operation Iraqi Freedom.

- *New pedagogical features:* Each chapter now starts with a list of objectives that ideally will help students concentrate on the important points of each chapter. In addition, chapters now end with an *Internet Resource* section that is divided into three parts. The first part directs students to the book's *Online Learning Center,* where they can review each chapter, take practice quizzes, and find suggestions for further reading and other activities. The second part makes use of McGraw-Hill's *PowerWeb* site, listing additional readings relevant to each chapter and providing questions that instructors can use to start discussion on issues raised by the readings. The *PowerWeb site* also contains links to articles that provide current information on a variety of media topics. The third section lists websites relevant to that chapter that students can explore.

Further, two new types of boxed inserts are keyed to the CDs that accompany the text. The first, *Media Talk*, refers to NBC News video segments on issues related to the text. Instructors can use the videos and accompanying questions as discussion starters. The second, *Media Tours*, features a look inside *Vibe* magazine, the WSEE television station, the WKNE radio station, and *The Record* newspaper. These segments are the next best thing to taking a field trip to a media company. In each Media Tour, media professionals, among them the Director of Photography at *Vibe*, the VP for Internet at *The Record*, the morning DJ/station manager at WKNE, and the News Director at WSEE-TV, discuss their jobs, the operation of their companies, and the challenges facing their industries. Instructors can use these segments as a general introduction to selected media chapters.

 ## THINKING INSIDE THE BOX(ES)

As in past editions, the boxed inserts in each chapter provide background material, present further examples of topics mentioned in the text, and raise issues for discussion and consideration. The eighth edition contains more than 90 new or updated boxes including the *Media Tours* and *Media Talk* already mentioned. As before, the issue-oriented focus has been maintained in constructing these boxes. Forty-six such boxes spotlight pertinent ethical, social, or critical/cultural issues related to topics such as the Jayson Blair affair at the *New York Times*, the coverage of rape in the sports pages, the morality of music file sharing on the Internet, and the problems of maintaining objectivity while covering a war.

The *Media Probe* boxes take an in-depth look at subjects that have significance for the various media. Some examples are interactive television, the increasing obtrusiveness of commercials, and violence in video games.

The *Decision Maker* boxes profile individuals who have made some of the important decisions that have had an impact on the development of the media. Examples include Al Neuharth, Catherine Hughes, Steven Spielberg, and Ted Turner.

As before, *Soundbytes* are brief boxes that highlight some of the ironic, offbeat, and extraordinary events that occur in the media.

 ## ORGANIZATION

Another of the original goals for *Dynamics* was to produce a book with scholarly depth that students would not dread to pick up. Ideally, the organization and writing style of this edition help meet that goal.

As in previous editions, Part I (*The Nature and History of Mass Communication*) presents the intellectual context for the rest of the book. This part expends a good deal of effort comparing and contrasting mass communication with other types of interpersonal communication. This analysis is even more important today now that the Internet continues to raise questions about the definition of *mass communication*. Part I also introduces two perspectives commonly used to understand and explore the operations of the media: functional analysis and the critical/cultural approach.

A study of history can reveal much about the behavior of current media institutions, and the introductory course may be the only exposure that students have to media history. Accordingly, the book gives more emphasis to this topic than is found in many introductory textbooks. Specifically, the concluding chapter of Part I takes a macroanalytic approach, tracing the general history of media from the development of language to the cell phone explosion. Further, each media chapter opens with a specific history of that particular medium that identifies the forces that have shaped its evolution.

Part II represents the core of the book. Chapters 4 through 11 examine each of the major media. This edition puts increased emphasis on the interrelationships among the various media: Newspapers and magazines have print and electronic editions; movies appear on tape and DVDs; radio and TV stations have websites and stream their signals over the Web. Recognizing this trend toward the blurring of distinctions, the book is no longer divided into sections labeled *Print* and *Electronic* media. Part II is simply called *Media*, and each chapter stresses the growing symbiosis among the mass communication industries.

The organization of each of the chapters in Part II follows a similar pattern. Each chapter starts with a brief history of the medium's beginnings leading up to how it is coping with the digital age. This is followed by a section on the defining characteristics of each medium and a discussion of the industry structure.

The book continues to emphasize media economics. Since the major mass media in the United States are commercially supported, it is valuable for students to appreciate where the money comes from, how it is spent, and the consequences that arise from the control of the mass media by large organizations. Mergers, consolidations, convergence, and divergence all have a great impact on what we see and hear. Thus, every media chapter has a section on the bottom line and its impact. Finally, each chapter in Part II concludes with a look at the audiences that each medium attracts and a discussion of career prospects.

Part III (*Specific Media Professions*) examines three specific professions closely associated with the mass media: news reporting, public relations, and advertising. As in Part II, each chapter in Part III begins with a history, examines the structure of that particular profession, discusses key issues in the field, and ends with a consideration of career prospects.

Part IV (*Regulation of the Mass Media*) examines both the formal and the informal controls that influence the media. These are complicated areas, and the book makes the information as accessible as possible. Technical legal language is kept to a minimum, and the primary focus is on the substantive issues. The chapter on formal controls examines such areas as the First Amendment, covering the courts, defamation, and special rules that apply to the electronic media. The chapter on informal controls looks first at media self-regulation and then at theories of individual ethical behavior.

The concluding section (Part V, *Impact of the Media*) continues to emphasize the social effects of the mass media. Some introductory texts give the impression that the effects of the media are unknown or simply matters of opinion. Granted, there may be some disagreement about the effects, but thanks to an increasing amount of research in the field there is much that we do know. Moreover, as informed members of our society, we should have some basic knowledge of the effects of the media on our society and across the globe.

Once again, the writing style is informal and accessible. Whenever possible, points are illustrated with examples from popular culture with which most students will be familiar. Technical terms are boldfaced and defined in the glossary. The book also contains a number of diagrams, charts, and tables that should aid understanding.

IN A SUPPORTING ROLE

>> Media World CD-ROMs

Each new copy of *The Dynamics of Mass Communication*, eighth edition, comes with a two-CD-ROM set. The CDs contain five video segments in an exclusive series called *Media Tours*. The first four segments offer an insider's look at the operations and issues facing an actual newspaper, magazine, radio station, and TV station. The fifth *Media Tour* segment takes a look at how the Internet is affecting media business, as professionals address such questions as "Is the Web profitable?" and "Is the Internet a threat to you?" Also on the CDs are 15 *Media Talk* segments, in which NBC journalists discuss current issues with media experts.

The CDs also contain study help in the form of quizzes that students can take to check their mastery of chapter content. These CDs add another dimension to students' experience of the course and can serve as lecture launchers for instructors. They are fully integrated with the text; for details, see the inside front cover.

>> Online Learning Center, www.mhhe.com/dominick8

The book-specific website is divided into materials for instructors and for students. The instructor's material is password protected, and the password is available to adopters through McGraw-Hill's sales representatives. All students have free access to the student resources.

The instructor resources consist of

- a teaching guide, incorporating all text supplements, written by Rebecca Ann Lind, of the University of Illinois at Chicago;
- detailed chapter summaries, written by Susan Bachner, an educational consultant; and
- PowerPoint slides for each chapter, written by David Stockton, an educational media developer.

The student resources consist of the following useful review tools written by Susan Bachner for students based on content in the text:

- practice tests,
- media timelines,

- learning objectives,
- chapter main points,
- key terms and crossword puzzles,
- suggestions for further reading, and
- an online glossary.

>> PowerWeb: An Online Database of Readings and Resources, www.dushkin.com/powerweb

PowerWeb is a password-protected premium content website that serves as a companion anthology and media news resource. Passcards for instructors and students are packaged inside every new copy of *Dynamics*, eighth edition. The *PowerWeb* site includes

- articles on mass communications issues, refereed by content experts,
- real-time news on mass communication topics,
- weekly course updates,
- interactive exercises and assessment tools,
- student study tips,
- Web research tips and exercises,
- refereed and updated research links, and
- daily news.

>> Instructor Resource CD-ROM

Instructors are provided with a CD-ROM containing exclusive content to help them organize class sessions and administer tests. The content consists of the following:

- **Computerized test bank:** Written by Rebecca Ann Lind, of the University of Illinois at Chicago, this computerized test bank features all new questions that are now page referenced to the text. It is available in both Windows and Macintosh formats.
- **PowerPoint slides:** Created by David Stockton, an educational media developer, these all new PowerPoint slides can be used by instructors in class presentations and by students for review. They are available on disk and at the Online Learning Center.

ACKNOWLEDGMENTS

Once again, I would like to thank all of those instructors and students who have used the first seven editions of this book and who were kind enough to suggest improvements. Several colleagues deserve special mention. Drs. Scott Shamp, Patricia Priest, and Rebecca Lind were kind enough to provide guidance and material for this edition. Students working on their Ph.D.s usually do not have a lot of free time, but Federico de Gregorio, Amanda Hall, Rita Van Sant, and Kevin Williams managed to put together original material for this edition. Moreover, thanks to Cheryl Christopher for help with logistics; to Meaghan Dominick whose knowledge of popular music never ceases to amaze me; to Ron, Aimee, and

Aidan Douglass for demonstrating the latest digital technologies; and finally to Carole Dominick for her organizational skills and for putting up with my general crankiness during the revision process.

And, as always, I would like to thank all of the reviewers who offered helpful and insightful suggestions for improvement:

Meta G. Carstarphen—Gaylord College of Journalism and Mass Communication

Joseph L. Clark—University of Toledo

Mike Eberts—Glendale Community College

Robert M. Ogles—Purdue University

Joseph A. Russomanno—Arizona State University

James B. Weaver, III—Virginia Tech

Clifford E. Wexler—Columbia-Greene Community College

Thanks also to Susan Bachner, Rebecca Ann Lind, and David Stockton for their work on the supporting materials on the text's website.

And, finally, a big thanks to all of those at McGraw-Hill for all their help on this edition: to Phil Butcher who has been supporting this book for the last 20 years or so; to Cynthia Ward for her sedulous editing efforts and helpful suggestions; to Thom Holmes for strategic guidance and tactical help; to Christina Thornton-Villagomez for yet again handling the myriad details of getting the book into print; to Brian Pecko for digging up some really good pictures; to Emma Ghiselli for screen captures; to Leslie Oberhuber for marketing efforts; and to Gino Cieslik for the design of the eighth edition.

Finally, I will repeat myself yet again. The media are a vital force in our society; I hope this book helps us understand them even better.

Joseph R. Dominick

Your Guided Tour

Chapter-Opening Previews

Chapter objectives and vignettes draw students in and help them concentrate on the important points of each chapter.

12

NEWS GATHERING AND REPORTING

This chapter will prepare you to

- describe the qualities that characterize news;

- identify the three main types of news stories;

- distinguish the role of the gatekeeper among broadcast, print, and online news;

- recognize the wire services that provide national and international news;

- discuss the strengths and weaknesses of broadcast, print, and online journalism; and

- explain how the Internet and new digital media have changed news reporting.

In early April, during the opening days of Operation Iraqi Freedom, those watching CNN were able to see live pictures of the Third Infantry Division as it raced toward Baghdad. Embedded reporter Walter Rodgers told viewers that his unit had been under attack for nearly two hours. As he was talking, the camera showed scenes of tanks rumbling by, burning vehicles by the side of the road, and columns of black smoke in the distance. Viewers were able to see this real-time portrait of war thanks to advances in digital technology that have transformed the way reporters cover breaking news events.

In Rodgers's case, a small digital camera captured the images that were then compressed and sent via videophone to a satellite that relayed the live pictures to CNN. Other reporters plugged their microphones and digital cameras into a suitcase-sized device that used a built-in global positioning system to find the nearest communications satellite. Some correspondents shot digital video footage that was edited on a laptop computer and then sent via e-mail or

NBC's David Bloom was one of hundreds of reporters embedded with U.S. military units during Operation Iraqi Freedom. Bloom later died from a blood clot that blocked an artery in his lungs, a condition aggravated by his working conditions in the field.

Media Tour INSIDE *VIBE*

Select the magazine media tour (CD 1, Track 1) on the CD-ROM that accompanies this text. The first part provides a look at the magazine's operations, and the second part features the staff discussing a wide range of issues.

The original strategy was for *VIBE* to be another *Rolling Stone* but with different music. *VIBE*'s timing was good: Hip-hop, one of the primary music styles covered in the magazine, was just gaining popularity among both African-American and white youth. As a result, the magazine was successful in attracting readers. Its circulation grew from about 100,000 in the early 1990s to 800,000 in 2002.

1. How does the business side of a magazine influence the editorial side?
2. What kind of companies might advertise in *VIBE*?
3. How do cultural trends play into the success of a magazine such as *VIBE*?
4. If you were the publisher of *Rolling Stone*, *VIBE*'s biggest competitor, how would you respond to *VIBE*'s success? How, if at all, would you change your magazine?

Media Tours

Keyed to the companion CD-ROM, these boxes offer focus questions for viewing video tours of different media companies.

Media Talk

Also keyed to the companion CD-ROM, these margin notes offer focus questions for viewing NBC News videos related to chapter topics.

MEDIA TALK

Why Is the U.S. Viewed So Poorly in the Arab World?

CD 2, Track 18, 2:32
This interview with *New York Times* reporter and Middle East expert Thomas Friedman was conducted in 2002. In the wake of the Iraq War and the continuing violence in Israel, how successful has the United States been in getting its message across? How could the United States improve its image in the Arab world?

Ethical Issues

These boxes challenge students to think critically about ethical issues specific to mass communications industries.

Social Issues

New developments in mass communication raise new concerns. These boxes explore how the mass media operate in a social context.

of a clock radio that sits on top of a TV set and a handheld device that resembles a TV remote-control unit. Demographic data are gathered from each household member, and then each is assigned a number. While watching TV, each family member is supposed periodically to punch in his or her number on the handheld device to indicate viewing. People Meters can be used to tabulate all viewing—network, syndicated shows, and cable—and can even tabulate VCR playbacks. There are about 5,000 households in the Nielsen People Meter sample, and usable data are obtained from more than 90 percent of the meters. The sample is replaced every two years. The People Meter service is not cheap. Networks pay millions of dollars annually for the service.

Nielsen is also testing other systems. The most ambitious plan uses a passive meter and remote image recognition. Families agreeing to participate in this

Critical/Cultural Issues

These boxes illustrate the critical/cultural studies approach to mass communication in action.

Decision Makers

Profiles of people who have had a significant impact on contemporary mass media.

Media Probes

Additional illustrations, examples, and background to chapter topics.

Soundbytes

These sidebars illustrate the unusual, the ironic, and the offbeat things that sometimes occur in the media world.

The Digital Age

Every media chapter has a special section detailing how that industry is being transformed by the Internet and digital technologies.

This is not to say, however, that all industrial ads should be stodgy and dull. In recent years, several ad agencies specializing in business ads have introduced warmth, humor, and creativity into their messages. The philosophy behind this movement is that businesspeople are also consumers and that they respond as consumers to business and trade ads. For example, Teddi, a California company that makes women's sportswear, placed special cover wraps on hundreds of copies of *Forbes* magazine that went to clothing retailers. The wraps featured Teddi clothes with headlines such as "As seen in *Cosmo*. Cosmopolis, Washington," or "As seen in *Harpers*. Harper's Ferry, West Virginia."

CAREER OUTLOOK   ADVERTISING

After a couple of hard years, the advertising business showed signs of recovery in 2003, but employment prospects looked only a little bit brighter. Employment at U.S. advertising agencies was down more than 16 percent from 2000 as was employment in other advertising sectors of the media. Long-term prospects are tied to the general economy; a rebound will mean more advertising jobs.

>> **Entry-Level Positions**

A job applicant must make some basic decisions early in his or her professional training. Probably the first decision is whether to concentrate on the creative or the business side of the industry.

The creative side, as mentioned earlier, consists of the copywriters, art directors, graphic artists, photographers, and broadcast production specialists who put the ads together. Entry-level jobs include junior copywriter, creative trainee, junior art director, and production assistant. In most of these positions, a college degree in advertising or the visual arts is helpful, with a secondary concentration in marketing, English, sociology, or psychology also a benefit. Good Web skills are also a plus.

The business side of the industry offers careers as account executives, media planners, market researchers, or business managers. Proper preparation for these careers includes extensive course work in both advertising and business, with particular emphasis on marketing. Common entry-level positions in these fields are assistant media buyer, research assistant, junior account executive, or account service trainee.

>> **Upward Mobility**

Opportunities for advancement in advertising are excellent. Outstanding performance is rewarded quickly, and many young people progress swiftly through the ranks. Beginning creative people typically become senior copywriters or senior art directors. Occasionally, some may progress to creative director, the person in charge of all creative services. On the business side, research assistants and assistant buyers can hope to become research directors and media directors. Account trainees, if they perform according to expectations, move up to account executives and later may become management supervisors. The climb to success can occur rapidly; many agencies are run by people who achieved top status before they reached age 40.

Career Outlook

These sections offer a realistic view of entry-level positions and the prospects for upward mobility within eleven media industries.

FIGURE 7–1
Division of AM and FM Audiences

1972	1984	2002
AM 28% / FM 72%	AM 30% / FM 70%	AM 29% / FM 72%

■ AM   ■ FM

The new law caused an avalanche of buying and selling of radio properties, and some stations were sold several times in a single year. In a typical year before the act, about $2 billion was spent on radio acquisitions and mergers. In 1996, the number hit $14.4 billion. That figure was eclipsed the next year when $15.3 billion was spent. New radio giants sprang up almost overnight. The radio industry became even more consolidated as a few large group owners dominated the industry.

On the programming front, talk became the hottest format on AM radio, thanks to the success of such performers as Rush Limbaugh, Dr. Laura Schlessinger, Tom Joyner, and Howard Stern. The trend toward format specialization continued on FM as stations recognized that attracting as little as 2 to 3 percent of the audience was enough to keep them profitable.

A weak economy and the demise of the dot-com companies hurt radio's advertising revenue at the start of the new century. After several years of prosperity, many radio stations cut back on expenses and laid off employees.

The radio industry today is more concentrated than ever. The business is now dominated by just a few big companies. As noted at the beginning of this chapter, Clear Channel is the biggest player in the industry with stations in 190 radio markets. This increasing trend toward consolidation has caused much controversy.

RADIO IN THE DIGITAL AGE

Radio continues to creep into the digital age. Thousands of radio stations have Websites and many now offer streaming audio. For the most part, these sites are used primarily to supplement the on-air station and its traditional analog signal. There are signs, however, that things are speeding up.

Radio talk show host Sean Hannity. His syndicated program reaches about 12 million people.

>> **Terrestrial Digital Radio Broadcasting**

The technology for broadcasting a digital radio signal has been around for years, and several countries already have digital

systems in operation. Digital radio has moved slowly because traditional analog radio is doing just fine and broadcasters have seen no need to disrupt a profitable situation. In addition, radio broadcasters wanted a system that is compatible with existing analog signals so that current radio receivers can pick up the analog signals while new receiving sets can pick up the digital signal. Broadcasters got their wish in the late 1990s, when an **IBOC** (in-band, on-channel) system was developed.

In 2003, several large radio broadcasters announced that they would begin digital radio broadcasting by 2004. Using an IBOC system developed by the iBiquity Digital Corporation, about 100 stations were set to offer the new system in large markets including New York, Los Angeles, and Chicago. The digital signal can be received at the same spot on the radio dial as the analog signal, but it has much better sound quality. A digital signal of an FM station sounds as good as a CD, and a digital AM signal sounds as good as a traditional FM station. In addition, the static and pops normally heard on an AM station disappear. This improvement could have a significant impact on AM radio formats, and many could switch from talk to music to take advantage of the better sound quality.

In order to hear the clearer sound, consumers will have to shell out about $300 for a radio set that gets both the analog and digital signals or about $100 for a digital-only receiver. The new digital sets will also contain new features. A text display can present the latest traffic and weather information as well as display the name of the song and the artist when music is playing

>> **Satellite Radio**

Two companies now offer a direct-from-satellite-to-car radio digital service. XM radio, launched in 2001, offers 70 music channels, half of them commercial free, and 30 news and talk channels for a monthly fee of about $10. Subscribers can also add the Playboy Radio Channel (presum-ably to listen to the articles) for an additional charge. Sirius Radio launched a similar service in 2002 with 60 commercial-free music

Full Range of Chapter Review Material

Clear, concise chapter summaries, key terms lists, and review questions provide students with essential study materials.

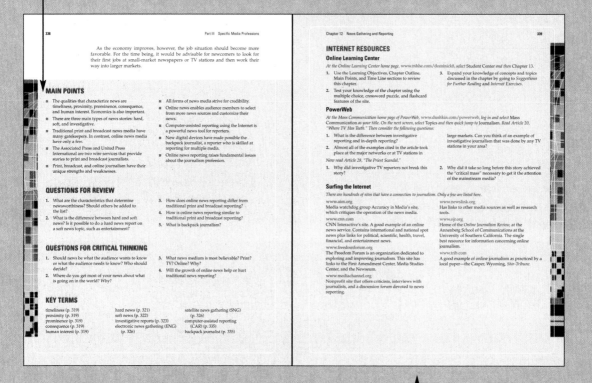

As the economy improves, however, the job situation should become more favorable. For the time being, it would be advisable for newcomers to look for their first jobs at small-market newspapers or TV stations and then work their way into larger markets.

MAIN POINTS

- The qualities that characterize news are timeliness, proximity, prominence, consequence, and human interest. Economics is also important.
- There are three main types of news stories: hard, soft, and investigative.
- Traditional print and broadcast news media have many gatekeepers. In contrast, online news media have only a few.
- The Associated Press and United Press International are two wire services that provide stories to print and broadcast journalists.
- Print, broadcast, and online journalism have their unique strengths and weaknesses.

- All forms of news media strive for credibility.
- Online news enables audience members to select from more news sources and customize their news.
- Computer-assisted reporting using the Internet is a powerful news tool for reporters.
- New digital devices have made possible the backpack journalist, a reporter who is skilled at reporting for multiple media.
- Online news reporting raises fundamental issues about the journalism profession.

QUESTIONS FOR REVIEW

1. What are the characteristics that determine newsworthiness? Should others be added to the list?
2. What is the difference between hard and soft news? Is it possible to do a hard news report on a soft news topic, such as entertainment?

3. How does online news reporting differ from traditional print and broadcast reporting?
4. How is online news reporting similar to traditional print and broadcast reporting?
5. What is backpack journalism?

QUESTIONS FOR CRITICAL THINKING

1. Should news be what the audience wants to know or what the audience needs to know? Who should decide?
2. Where do you get most of your news about what is going on in the world? Why?

3. What news medium is most believable? Print? TV? Online? Why?
4. Will the growth of online news help or hurt traditional news reporting?

KEY TERMS

timeliness (p. 319)
proximity (p. 319)
prominence (p. 319)
consequence (p. 319)
human interest (p. 319)

hard news (p. 321)
soft news (p. 322)
investigative reports (p. 323)
electronic news gathering (ENG)
(p. 326)

satellite news gathering (SNG)
(p. 326)
computer-assisted reporting
(CAR) (p. 335)
backpack journalist (p. 335)

INTERNET RESOURCES

Online Learning Center

At the Online Learning Center home page, www.mhhe.com/dominick8, *select* Student Center *and then* Chapter 13.

1. Use the Learning Objectives, Chapter Outline, Main Points, and Time Line sections to review this chapter.
2. Test your knowledge of the chapter using the multiple choice, crossword puzzle, and flashcard features of the site.
3. Expand your knowledge of concepts and topics discussed in the chapter by going to *Suggestions for Further Reading and Internet Exercises.*

PowerWeb

At the Mass Communication home page of PowerWeb, www.dushkin.com/powerweb, *log in and select* Mass Communication *as your title. On the next screen, select* Topics *and then quick jump to* Journalism. *Read Article 20, "Where TV Has Teeth." Then consider the following questions:*

1. What is the difference between investigative reporting and in-depth reporting?
2. Almost all of the examples cited in the article took place at the major networks or at TV stations in

Now read Article 28, "The Priest Scandal."

1. Why did investigative TV reporters not break this story?

large markets. Can you think of an example of investigative journalism that was done by any TV stations in your area?

2. Why did it take so long before this story achieved the "critical mass" necessary to get it the attention of the mainstream media?

Surfing the Internet

There are hundreds of sites that have a connection to journalism. Only a few are listed here.

www.aim.org
Media watchdog group Accuracy in Media's site, which critiques the operation of the news media.

www.cnn.com
CNN Interactive's site. A good example of an online news service. Contains international and national spot news plus links for political, scientific, health, travel, financial, and entertainment news.

www.freedomforum.org
The Freedom Forum is an organization dedicated to exploring and improving journalism. This site has links to the First Amendment Center, Media Studies Center, and the Newseum.

www.mediachannel.org
Nonprofit site that offers criticism, interviews with journalists, and a discussion forum devoted to news reporting.

www.newslink.org
Has links to other media sources as well as research tools.

www.ojr.org
Home of the *Online Journalism Review,* at the Annenberg School of Communications at the University of Southern California. The single best resource for information concerning online journalism.

www.trib.com
A good example of online journalism as practiced by a local paper—the Casper, Wyoming, *Star-Tribune.*

Springboards for Discussion and Research

Critical thinking questions based on the text and Internet resources engage students with issues affecting them as consumers and future professionals.

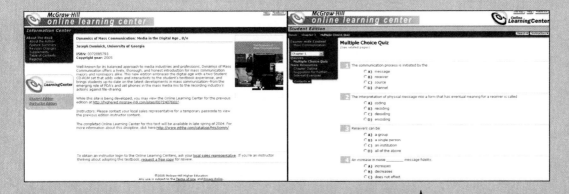

Online Learning Center, www.mhhe.com/dominick8

This book-specific website features practice tests, media timelines, learning objectives, chapter main points, key terms and timelines, suggestions for further reading, and an online glossary. For the instructor, the password-protected area of the website offers a teaching guide, detailed chapter summaries, and PowerPoint slides.

Powerweb: Online Database of Readings, www.dushkin.com/powerweb

Use the passcard insert to access this premium-content website, which serves as a companion anthology and media news resource.

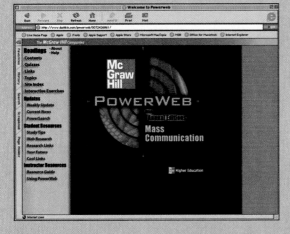

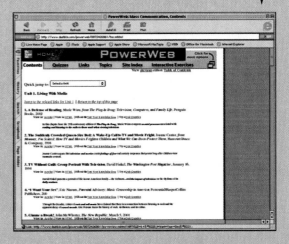

Media World CD-ROMs

This 2 CD-ROM set for students, packaged with the book, features videos and study tools that enhance the text.

CD1 contains five exclusive Media Tour videos that provide an inside look at the day-to-day operations and issues facing real media organizations. CD 1 also includes chapter quizzes to help students evaluate their mastery of chapter concepts.

CD2 contains fifteen Media Talk videos from the NBC News archives. In these segments, media experts give their opinions on matters of current debate and controversy.

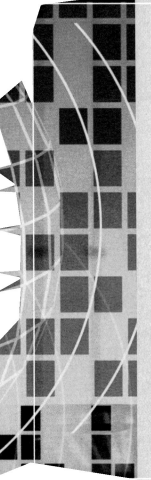

THE NATURE
AND HISTORY
OF MASS
COMMUNICATION

COMMUNICATION: MASS AND OTHER FORMS

This chapter will prepare you to

- recognize the elements of the communication process;

- understand the different types of communication settings;

- identify the function of gatekeepers;

- describe how the Internet has changed mass communication;

- explain the various types of mass media convergence; and

- explain the implications of disintermediation on the media.

Had you been surfing the Web on January 25, 2003, you might have been mildly perplexed that it was taking longer than normal to load some popular Websites. Had you been aware, however, of what was actually causing the slowdown, you would have been extremely concerned. The slowdown was due to an Internet worm called "Slammer," a worm that demonstrated how it might be possible to take down the whole Internet in just 15 minutes.

It started in a computer, probably somewhere in Asia, when someone sent a tiny piece of code, just a few lines long, to a computer hooked to the Internet. The code was a worm, a self-contained program that can replicate and send copies of itself to other machines on the network. (Note that a worm is not a virus; a virus attaches itself to some other program, like an e-mail attachment, and its spread depends upon people opening the attachment. A worm is self-sufficient; it doesn't need any human help. Also, note that a worm can contain a virus.)

Unlike the destructive and annoying SoBig worm that clogged up e-mail inboxes during the summer of 2003, Slammer wasn't aimed at home computers. It was far more threatening. The worm burrowed itself into a piece of Microsoft software called SQL Server

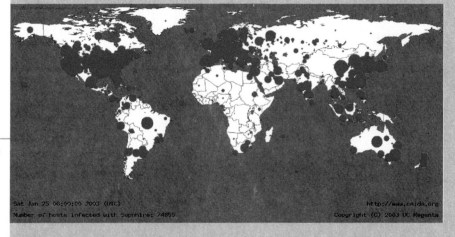

This map shows the spread of the Slammer word 30 minutes after its release. The bigger the circle, the more computers that were affected.
From www.cs.berkeley.edu~weaver/sapphire/.

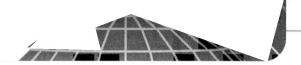

2000, a database program that many companies use to build their network server applications. It exploited a flaw in the software that allowed it to clog up and eventually shut down the entire system; hence, its name *SQL Slammer,* or just *Slammer* for short.

When Slammer first got into a computer it started looking for other computers to infect by generating random IP addresses (these are four sets of numbers that identify computers hooked to the Internet, such as 10.200.122.144). When it infected a vulnerable computer, that computer also started sending out messages. An avalanche effect occurred quickly. Thousands of infected computers were sending so many messages back and forth, as many as 10,000 messages per second, that they clogged the system.

In the United States, companies that relied on the Internet to carry data felt the effects. Bank of America customers could not withdraw money from any of the bank's 13,000 ATMs. Some Continental Airlines flights were canceled when the airline's online reservations center could not process requests. Some investment banks in New York City found that their e-mail was no longer working. In Washington state, the computers connected to the 911 emergency number ran so slowly that dispatchers started taking notes with pencil and paper.

The results were worse in Asia and Europe. In South Korea, people couldn't access the Internet for hours. Japan and India reported similar problems. People in Finland had trouble placing phone calls.

By the time the weekend was over, more than 200,000 computer servers had been infected. Five of the 13 Internet "root" servers, the computers that contain the databases that translate names such as "weather.com" into machine-readable num-

bers, were overwhelmed by the traffic. The total cost to clean up after the worm was about $1 billion.

Still, it could have been worse. Slammer hit on a weekend, a low traffic period. Had it struck on a Monday, the worm might have shut down the entire Internet. Big investment firms would have been paralyzed; 911 numbers would have been useless; the travel industry would have ground to a halt. In addition, Slammer was easily controlled. The worm didn't write itself to a hard drive but simply resided in a computer's memory. Turning the machine off and then installing a patch killed the worm. Finally, Slammer wasn't malicious. It didn't destroy files or capture passwords or credit card numbers; it simply replicated itself over and over again. Had Slammer carried a mean and nasty virus embedded in its code, the outcome might have been disastrous.

>> Warhol Worms

Even more frightening is how fast Slammer traveled through the Internet. Computer experts estimated that the worm was doubling in size every nine seconds after it first appeared. After three minutes, Slammer was scanning for vulnerable servers at a rate of more than 55 million scans per second. Within 10 minutes, Slammer had affected 90 percent of all vulnerable computers.

Many scientists warned that Slammer was the forerunner of a "Warhol worm." Pop artist Andy Warhol once remarked that in the future everybody would be famous for 15 minutes. A Warhol worm would become famous, or perhaps infamous, because it would spread fast enough to infect the entire Internet in 15 minutes. Is such a feat possible? A research paper from the University of California published in 2001 suggests how it might happen.

Rather than using Slammer's technique of generating random IP addresses, a true Warhol worm would first target vulnerable computers with extensive connections to the Internet. Once these machines were infected, the worm would replicate itself and look for others. After 15 minutes, more than a million key computers would be contaminated. What if a deranged individual or terrorists attached a malicious virus to this hyperfast worm? It's possible that the whole Internet would grind to a halt. The damage would be incalculable. Software designers and computer security experts face a neverending battle to safeguard the system from such threats.

Communication between people is fragile. Technological advances have increased the speed and reach of human communication but, as the Slammer example illustrates, communication can become even more fragile when machines are involved. The following examples may not be as disturbing as the Slammer incident, but they are no less illustrative:

■ Thanks to a glitch, a computer at a Michigan hospital sent a letter to 8,500 former patients informing them that they were dead.

■ In Sweden, a computer error accidentally changed the amount of a government check for a woman's monthly child support from about $322 to $10 billion, a sum that's more than the Gross Domestic Product of Bolivia. When the woman notified the bank about the error, the bank sent her flowers and thanked her for not cashing the check.

■ In a Canberra, Australia, shopping center, someone tampered with public weight and body mass machines. Instead of printing out for users cherry messages such as "Happy New Year" and "Best Wishes for the Future," the machines printed out insults such as "You weigh 200 pounds, you fat pig" or "Get off the scale. You're hurting me."

■ A man got a bill from his gas company for $3.7 trillion. When he ignored it, the company threatened to take him to court if he didn't pay the full sum immediately. It turns out that a computer glitch accidentally confused the 13-digit property reference number with the amount due.

■ Some lucky travelers were able to book a room at New York's swank W Hotel for $25 rather than the normal $259 nightly rate when an employee accidentally loaded an incorrect room rate into the hotel's computer. (That's not the first time a computer slipup has helped consumers. The website for Hilton Hotels mistakenly offered rooms for $0 a night at some of their U.S. hotels. A mistake by United Airlines on their Website let tourists fly round trip to Europe for less than $30. Both Hilton and United honored the incorrect rates.)

Even with low-tech devices, human communication often goes awry:

■ A London bank sent out 15,000 letters promoting its new telephone help line. Unfortunately, there was a typo in the phone number and everybody who dialed the wrong number was connected to a sex chat line.

■ An Atlanta radio station released a Christmas CD with songs by popular artists. The CD label was supposed to say that the proceeds from sales of the CD were to be used to "fight illiteracy." Regrettably, the station distributed 10,000 of the CDs with a label that said that the proceeds were to be used to "fight illliteracy."

- In April of 2003, Peter Jennings, the anchor of ABC *World News Tonight*, informed viewers that Federal Reserve Chairman Alan Greenspan was in the hospital "with an enlarged prostate." The typist who was preparing the closed-captioned text that accompanied the newscast hit a couple of wrong keys and wrote that Greenspan was in the hospital "with an enlarged prostitute."

- In Miami, a T-shirt manufacturer printed shirts for the Spanish-speaking community to commemorate the pope's visit to the city. Rather than reading, "Ví el papa" (I saw the pope), the shirts read, "Ví la papa" (I saw the potato).

Despite their apparent lack of similarity, these illustrations share certain elements common to human communication. They serve as a starting point for an examination of the difference between mass and other forms of communication.

THE COMMUNICATION PROCESS

At a general level, communication events involve the following:

1. A source.
2. A process of encoding.
3. A message.
4. A channel.
5. A process of decoding.
6. A receiver.
7. The potential for feedback.
8. The chance of noise.

Figure 1–1 depicts the communication process. We will refer to this figure as we examine the process more fully.

>> Transmitting the Message

To begin with, the **source** initiates the process by having a thought or an idea that he or she wishes to transmit to some other entity. Naturally, sources differ in their communication skills ("Garçon, I will have du Boeuf Haché Grillé au Charbon de Bois" versus "Gimmeahamburger"). The source may or may not have knowledge about the receiver of the message. As I write these lines, I have only a general notion about the kinds of people who will read them, and I have absolutely no idea what you'll be doing while you're reading them (that's probably for the best). Sources can be single individuals, groups, or even organizations.

Encoding refers to the activities that a source goes through to translate thoughts and ideas into a form that may be perceived by the senses. When you have something to say, your brain and your tongue work together (usually) to form words and spoken sentences. When you write a letter, your brain and your fingers cooperate to produce patterns of ink or some other substance that can be seen on paper. Encoding in a communication setting can take place one or more

FIGURE 1–1

**Elements of the
Communication
Process**

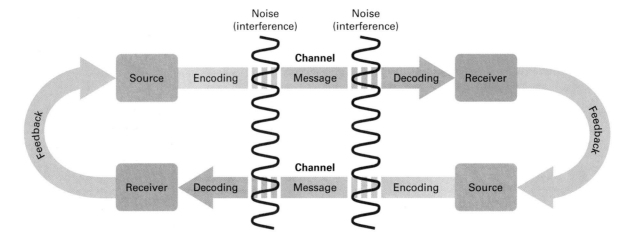

times. In a face-to-face conversation, the speaker encodes thoughts into words. Over the telephone, this phase is repeated, but the phone subsequently encodes sound waves into electrical energy.

The **message** is the actual physical product that the source encodes. When we talk, our speech is the message. When we write a letter home, what we put on the paper is the message. When a television network presents *Frasier* or *ER,* the programs are the message. Human beings usually have a large number of messages at their disposal that they can choose to send, ranging from the simple but effective "No!" to something as complicated as Darwin's *On the Origin of Species.* Messages can be directed at one specific individual ("You turkey!") or at millions (*People* magazine). Messages can be cheap to produce (the spoken word) or very expensive (this book). Some messages are more under the control of the receiver than others. For example, think about how hard or easy it is for you to break off communication (1) in a face-to-face conversation with another person, (2) during a telephone call, and (3) while watching a TV commercial.

Channels are the ways the message travels to the receiver. Sound waves carry spoken words; light waves carry visual messages. Air currents can serve as olfactory channels, carrying messages to our noses—messages that are subtle but nonetheless significant. What kind of message do you get from someone who reeks of Chanel No. 5? Of Brut? Of garlic? Touch is also a channel (e.g., braille). Some messages use more than one channel to travel to the receiver. Radio signals travel by electromagnetic radiation until they are transformed by receiving sets into sound waves that travel through the air to our ears.

>> Receiving the Message

The **decoding** process is the opposite of the encoding process. It consists of activities that translate or interpret physical messages into a form that has eventual meaning for a receiver. As you read these lines, you are decoding a message. If you are playing the radio while decoding these lines, you are decoding two messages

Regulating the Olfactory Channel

Bend, Oregon, recently passed a city ordinance banning anybody who gives off a "grossly repulsive odor" from getting on a city bus.

simultaneously—one aural, one visual. Both humans and machines can be thought of as decoders. The radio is a decoder; so is a videotape playback unit; so is the telephone (one end encodes and the other end decodes); so is a film projector.

A single communication event can involve many stages of decoding. A reporter sits in on a city council meeting and takes notes (decoding); he or she phones in a story to the rewrite desk where another reporter types the story as it is read (decoding). The story is read by an editor (decoding). Eventually it is printed and read by the audience (decoding). What we said earlier about encoding also applies to decoding: Some people are better at it than others. Many of you will not be able to decode "¿Dónde está el baño?"; others will. Some people are able to read 1,500 words a minute; others struggle along at 200.

The **receiver** is the target of the message—its ultimate goal. The receiver can be a single person, a group, an institution, or even a large, anonymous collection of people. In today's environment, people are more often the receivers of communication messages than the sources. Most of us see more billboards than we put up and listen to more radio programs than we broadcast. The receivers of the message can be determined by the source, as in a telephone call, or they can self-select themselves into the audience, as with the audience for a TV show. It should also be clear that in some situations the source and receiver can be in each other's immediate presence, while in other situations they can be separated by both space and time.

>> Feedback

Now let us examine the bottom half of Figure 1–1. This portion of the figure represents the potential for **feedback** to occur. Feedback refers to those responses of the receiver that shape and alter the subsequent messages of the source. Feedback represents a reversal of the flow of communication. The original source becomes the receiver; the original receiver becomes the new source. Feedback is useful to the source because it allows the source to answer the question "How am I doing?" Feedback is important to the receiver because it allows the receiver to attempt to change some element in the communication process. Communication scholars have traditionally identified two different kinds of feedback—positive and negative. In general terms, positive feedback from the receiver usually encourages the communication behavior in progress; negative feedback usually attempts to change the communication or even to terminate it.

Consider the following telephone call:

"Bambi?"

"Yes."

"This is Harold. I sit in front of you in econ class."

"Are you the one who keeps scratching your head with a pencil?"

"Gee, I never noticed it. I guess I do it unconsciously. Say, I was wondering if you would like to have coffee with me sometime after class."

"Are you kidding?"

Click.

Negative feedback. The original receiver terminated the message. Here is another conversation:

"Bambi, this is Rod."

"Oh, hi, Rod. Has your leg healed up from the last game yet?"

"Yeah."

"How are your classes going?"

"I can't get econ."

"I'll be over in 20 minutes to give you some help. OK?"

"OK."

Click.

Positive feedback. The original receiver encouraged the communication.

Feedback can be immediate or delayed. Immediate feedback occurs when the reactions of the receiver are directly perceived by the source. A speech maker who hears the audience boo and hiss while he or she is talking is getting immediate feedback. On the other hand, suppose you just listened to the latest CD by a popular group and decided it wasn't very good. To communicate that evaluation to the source, you would first have to find out the company that distributed the CD, find a mailing address, phone number, e-mail address, or website address. You would then have to send your feedback via the appropriate channel. If you got your message through to the company, it would still have to be passed on to the group, a process that might take several days or even longer.

>> Noise

The last factor we will consider is **noise.** Communication scholars define *noise* as anything that interferes with the delivery of the message. A little noise might pass unnoticed, while too much noise might prevent the message from reaching its destination. There are at least three different types of noise: semantic, mechanical, and environmental.

Jewel may sing about intuition but what she and other performers really want is positive feedback.

Semantic noise occurs when different people have different meanings for different words and phrases. If you ask a New Yorker for a "soda" and expect to receive something that has ice cream in it, you'll be disappointed. The New Yorker will give you a bottle of what is called "pop" in the Midwest. An advertising copywriter penned the following slogan for a cough syrup company: "Try our cough syrup. You will never get any better."

Noise can also be mechanical. This type of noise occurs when there is a problem with a machine that is being used to assist communication. A TV set with a snowy picture, a pen run-ning out of ink, and a static-filled radio are all examples of mechanical noise.

A third form of noise can be called environmental. This type refers to sources of noise that are external to the communication process but that nonetheless interfere with it. Some environmental noise might be out of the communicator's control—the noise at a restaurant, for example, where the communicator is trying to hold a conversation. Some environmental noise might be introduced by the source or the receiver; for example, you might try to talk to somebody who keeps drumming his or her fingers on the table.

As noise increases, message fidelity (how closely the message that is sent resembles the message that is received) goes down. Clearly, feedback is important in reducing the effects of noise. The greater the potential for immediate feedback—that is, the more interplay between source and receiver—the greater the chance that noise will be overcome.

 COMMUNICATION SETTINGS

>> Interpersonal Communication

Having considered the key elements in the communication process, we next examine three common communication settings, or situations, and explore how these elements vary from setting to setting. The first and perhaps the most common situation is **interpersonal communication,** in which one person (or group) is interacting with another person (or group) without the aid of a mechanical device. The source and receiver in this form of communication are within each other's physical presence. Talking to your roommate, participating in a class discussion, and conversing with your professor after class are all examples of interpersonal communication.

The source in this communication setting can be one or more individuals, as can the receiver. Encoding is usually a one-step process as the source transforms thoughts into speech and/or gestures. A variety of channels are available for use. The receiver can see, hear, and perhaps even smell and touch the source. Messages are relatively difficult for the receiver to terminate and are produced at little expense. In addition, interpersonal messages can be private (whassup?) or public (a proclamation that the end of the world is near from a person standing on a street corner). Messages can also be pinpointed to their specific targets. For example, you might ask the following of your English professor: "Excuse me, Dr. Iamb, but I was wondering if you had finished perusing my term paper?" The very same message directed at your roommate might be put another way: "Hey, Space Cadet! Aren't you done with my paper yet?" Decoding is also a one-step process performed by those receivers who can perceive the message. Feedback is immediate and makes use of visual and auditory channels. Noise can be either semantic or environmental. Interpersonal communication is far from simple, but it represents the least complicated setting.

>> Machine-Assisted Interpersonal Communication

Machine-assisted interpersonal communication (or technology-assisted communication) combines characteristics of both the interpersonal and mass communication situations. The growth of the Internet and the World Wide Web has further

Microsoft's Bill Gates uses machine-assisted communication to get his point across at the annual meeting of the World Economic Forum. *(Raymond Reuter/Sygma)*

blurred the boundaries between these two types of communication. This section concentrates on those situations that are closer to the interpersonal setting. The next section examines how the computer and the Internet have redefined many of the features of mass communication.

In the machine-assisted setting, one or more people are communicating by means of a mechanical device (or devices) with one or more receivers. One of the important characteristics of machine-assisted interpersonal communication is that it allows the source and receiver to be separated by both time and space. The machine can give a message permanence by storing it on paper, magnetic disk, or some other material. The machine can also extend the range of the message by amplifying it and/or transmitting it over large distances. The telephone, for example, allows two people to converse even though they are hundreds, even thousands, of miles apart. A letter can be reread several years after it was written and communicate anew.

A tremendous variety of modern communication falls into this category. Here are some diverse examples of machine-assisted communication:

1. E-mail allows people to send messages across the country in a matter of seconds.
2. People get money from automatic teller machines by inserting a magnetic card and following the machine's instructions.
3. The Sports Nightmare Reminder Service allows you to torment sports fans you don't like. For a small fee, the service will mail an unmarked envelope to whomever you choose with news clippings of a particular team's biggest loss.
4. Telephone companies offer 900 or 976 lines, over which, for a fee, people can hear recorded horoscopes, erotic fantasies, or information regarding the latest Elvis sightings.

The source in the machine-assisted setting can be a single person (as in the e-mail example) or a group of people (as in the Sports Nightmare example) who may know the receiver (e-mail) or not have firsthand knowledge of the receiver (the automatic teller example).

Encoding in this setting can be complicated or simple, but there must be at least two distinct stages. The first occurs when the source translates his or her thoughts into words or symbols. The second occurs when one or more machines encode the message for transmission or storage. When you speak on the telephone, for example, you choose and pronounce your words (stage one), and a machine converts them into electrical impulses (stage two).

Channels are more restricted in the machine-assisted setting. Whereas interpersonal communication can make use of several channels simultaneously, machine-assisted settings generally rely on only one or two. E-mail, for instance, relies on sight; a phone call uses electrical energy and sound waves.

Messages vary widely in machine-assisted communication. They can range from messages that can be tailor-made for the receiver (such as e-mail) or limited to a small number of predetermined messages that cannot be altered once they are encoded (the automatic teller can't comment on your new haircut). Messages in this setting can be private or public and relatively cheap to produce.

Decoding can go through one or more stages, similar to the encoding process. Reading a letter requires only one stage, but reading e-mail requires two: one for the computer to decode electrical energy into patterns of light and dark and another for your eyes to decode the written symbols.

The receiver in this setting can be a single person, a small group, or a large group. Receivers can be in sight of the source or out of view. They can be selected by the source (as with a phone call) or self-select themselves into the audience (taking a pamphlet from somebody on the street).

Feedback can be immediate or delayed. A band playing at a concert will hear the audience applaud following a song. A band that provides streaming audio of a new song on its website might have to wait for days to see if people liked it. In many situations, feedback is limited to one channel, as in a phone conversation. In some situations feedback can be difficult if not impossible. If the automatic teller gives you a message that says, "Insufficient funds," you cannot tell it, "I just made a deposit this morning. Look it up."

Noise in the machine-assisted setting can be semantic and environmental as in interpersonal communication, but it can also be mechanical. Interference with the message might be due in part to difficulties with the machine involved.

In the future, machine-assisted communication will become more important. New mobile media, such as cell phones, personal digital assistants, and laptop computers will become more and more popular and continue to expand the scope and impact of personal communication (see Chapter 3). The Internet may come to function more as an aid to interpersonal communication than as a mass medium (see Chapter 11). Finally, the differences between machine-assisted communication and mass communication will continue to blur.

>> Mass Communication

The third major communication setting is the one that we will be most interested in. The differences between machine-assisted interpersonal communication and mass communication are not that clear. **Mass communication** refers to the process by which a complex organization with the aid of one or more machines produces and transmits public messages that are directed at large, heterogeneous, and scattered audiences. There are, of course, situations that will fall into a gray area. How large does the audience have to be? How scattered? How heterogeneous? How complex must the organization be? For example, a billboard is constructed on a busy street in a small town. Obviously, this would qualify as machine-assisted communication (a machine was used to print the billboard), but is this example better defined as mass communication? An automatic letter-writing device can write thousands of similar letters. Is this mass communication? There are no correct answers to these questions. The dividing line between machine-assisted interpersonal communication and mass communication is not a distinct one.

The line is even less distinct when the Internet and the World Wide Web are considered. Take an e-mail message, for example. It can be addressed to one person, much like machine-assisted interpersonal communication, or it can go to thousands, a situation closer to mass communication. Or take the case of a chat room where one person might be communicating with dozens of others. If two people want more privacy, they can move to a "private" room, a situation that resembles machine-assisted interpersonal communication. On the other hand, feedback in the chat room is limited, a feature of mass communication. The usual clues from personal appearance, tone of voice, and gestures are not present.

Source   Until the advent of the Internet and the Web, the source in the traditional mass communication situation was typically a group of individuals who acted in predetermined roles in an organizational setting. In other words, mass communication was the end product of more than one person's efforts. For example, think about how a newspaper is put together. Reporters gather news; writers draft editorials; a cartoonist draws an editorial cartoon; the advertising department lays out ads; editors lay out all these things on a sample page; technicians transfer this page to a master; other technicians print the final paper; the finished copies are given to the delivery staff; and, of course, behind all this is a publisher who has the money to pay for a building, presses, staff, trucks, paper, ink, and so on. This institutional nature of mass communication has several consequences that we will consider later in this book.

The advent of Internet-based mass communication changes this situation. Thanks to the World Wide Web, one person can become a mass communicator. The full implications of this change may take some time to become clear.

For both traditional and Internet-based mass communication, the source usually has little detailed information about its particular audience. The author of a website has little detailed information about the individual people who visit the site. Traditional mass media may have collective data, but these are typically expressed as gross audience characteristics. The newspaper editor, for example, may know that 40 percent of the readers are between 25 and 40 years old and that 30 percent earn between $20,000 and $50,000, but the editor has no idea about the indi-

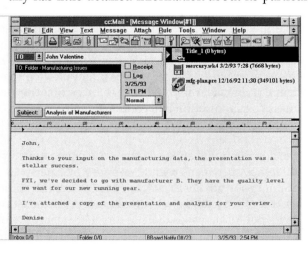

E-mail is fast and environmentally friendly; it uses no paper and vehicles burn no gasoline delivering the message. It is no wonder then that American businesses send billions of e-mail messages every year. *(Courtesy Lotus Development Corporation)*

vidual tastes, preferences, quirks, or identities of these people. They are an anonymous group, known only by summary statistics.

Encoding/Sending   Encoding in mass communication is always a multistage process. A film producer has an idea. He or she explains it to a screenwriter. The writer goes off and produces a script. The script goes to a director, who translates it for the camera. Cinematographers capture the scenes on film. The raw film goes to an editor, who splices together the final version. The film is copied and sent to motion picture theaters, where a projector displays it on the screen, where the audience watches it. How many examples of encoding can you find in that oversimplified version of moviemaking?

Mass communication channels are characterized by the imposition of at least one, and usually more than one, machine in the process of sending the message. These machines translate the message from one channel to another. Television makes use of complicated devices that transform light energy into electrical energy and back again. Radio does the same with sound energy. Unlike interpersonal communication, in which many channels are available, mass communication is usually restricted to one or two.

Decoding/Receiving   Messages in mass communication are public. Anyone who can afford the cost of a newspaper or a CD player or a TV set can receive the message. Additionally, the same message is sent to all receivers. In a sense, mass communication is addressed "to whom it may concern." Of all the various settings, message termination is easiest in mass communication. The TV set goes dark at the flick of a switch, an automatic timer can turn off the radio, the newspaper is quickly put aside. There is little the source can do to prevent these sudden terminations other than bullying the audience ("Don't touch that dial!") or trying to stay interesting at all times ("We'll be back after these important messages").

Mass communication typically involves multiple decoding before the message is received. The CD player decodes patterns of light waves into sound waves for our hearing mechanism. The TV receiver decodes both sight and sound transmissions.

Receiver   One of the prime distinguishing characteristics of mass communication is the audience. First, the mass communication audience is a large one, sometimes numbering in the millions of people. Second, the audience is also heterogeneous; that is, it is made up of dissimilar groups who may differ in age, intelligence, political beliefs, ethnic backgrounds, and so on. Even in situations where the mass communication audience is well defined, heterogeneity is still present. (For example, consider the publication *Turkey Grower's Monthly.* At first glance, the audience for this publication might appear to be pretty homogeneous, but upon closer examination we might discover that members differ in intelligence, social class, income, age, political party, education, place of residence, and so on.) Third, the audience is spread out over a wide geographic area; source and receiver are not in each other's immediate physical presence. The large size of the audience and its geographic separation both contribute to a fourth distinguishing factor: The audience members are anonymous to one another. The person watching the *CBS Evening News* is unaware of the several million others in the audience. Lastly, in keeping with the idea of a public message, the audience in mass communication is self-defined. The receiver chooses which film to see, which paper to read, which

Encoding at the movies. Director John Singleton sets up a shot in *2 Fast, 2 Furious*. A motion picture goes through several stages of encoding before it gets to the audience: idea, story, script, filming and editing.

website to visit, and which program to watch. If the receiver chooses not to attend to the message, the message is not received. Consequently, the various mass communication sources spend a great deal of time and effort to get your attention so that you will include yourself in the audience.

Feedback   Feedback is another area where there are differences between interpersonal and mass communication. The message flow in mass communication is typically one-way, from source to receiver, and feedback is more difficult than in the interpersonal setting. The growing popularity of the Internet and the World Wide Web has made feedback somewhat easier, but there are still situations in which sending feedback to the source takes a great deal of effort. Suppose, for example, you were offended by the content of a TV program. You might call the station immediately. If you got through, you would probably be referred to the network if what you saw was a network show. You could choose to call the network (a long-distance call for most), in which case you would probably reach a receptionist, who would suggest you put your complaint in writing or send an e-mail message. Alternatively, you could search for the network's website and find a place to post your comments. In any case, you would not be sure how long it would take for your message to be read, and you might never know if it was read by anybody associated with the program. Systematic, large-scale feedback gathered by media companies is even more delayed since it is typically gathered by an outside organization, such as Nielsen Media Research for television and the Audit Bureau of Circulations for newspapers.

Noise   Finally, noise in the mass communication setting can be semantic, environmental, or mechanical. In fact, since there may be more than one machine involved in the process, mechanical noise can be compounded (watching a scratchy copy of an old film on a snowy TV set).

Table 1–1 summarizes some of the differences among the three communication settings that we have talked about.

>> Defining Mass Media

In the broadest sense of the word, a *medium* is the channel through which a message travels from the source to the receiver ("medium" is singular; "media" is plural). Thus in our discussion, we have pointed to sound and light waves as media of communication. When we talk about mass communication, we also need channels to carry the message. **Mass media** are the channels used for mass communication. Our definition of a mass medium will include not only the mechanical devices that transmit and sometimes store the message (TV cameras, radio

TABLE 1–1

Differences in Communication Settings

		Setting		
		Interpersonal	**Machine-assisted interpersonal**	**Mass**
Element	**Source**	Single person; has knowledge of receiver	Single person or group; great deal of knowledge or no knowledge of receiver	Organizations or single person; little knowledge of receivers
	Encoding	Single stage	Single or multiple stage	Multiple stages
	Message	Private or public; cheap; hard to terminate; altered to fit receivers	Private or public; low to moderate expense; relatively easy to terminate; can be altered to fit receivers in some situations	Public; can be expensive; easily terminated; same message to everybody
	Channel	Potential for many; no machines interposed	Restricted to one or two; at least one machine interposed	Restricted to one or two; usually more than one machine interposed
	Decoding	Single stage	Single or multiple stage	Multiple stages
	Receiver	One or a relatively small number; in physical presence of source; selected by source	One person or a small or large group; within or outside physical presence of source; selected by source or self-defined	Large numbers; out of physical presence of source; self-selected
	Feedback	Plentiful; immediate	Somewhat limited; immediate or delayed	Highly limited; usually delayed
	Noise	Semantic; environmental	Semantic; environmental; mechanical	Semantic; environmental; mechanical

microphones, printing presses), but also the institutions that use these machines to transmit messages. When we talk about the mass media of television, radio, newspapers, magazines, sound recording, and film, we will be referring to the people, the policies, the organizations, and the technology that go into producing and distributing mass communication. A **media vehicle** is a single component of the mass media, such as a newspaper, radio station, TV network, or magazine.

In this book we will examine eight different mass media: radio, television, film, books, sound recordings, newspapers, magazines, and the Internet. Of course, these eight are not the only mass media that exist. Billboards, comic books, posters, direct mail, matchbooks, and buttons are some other kinds of mass media one could choose to examine. The eight types of media we have chosen, however, have the largest audiences, employ the most people, and have the greatest impact. They are also the ones with which most of us are most familiar.

TRADITIONAL MASS MEDIA ORGANIZATIONS

Since a large portion of this book will examine the institutions that are in the business of mass communication, it will be to our advantage to consider some common characteristics that typify mass communicators. This task has been made more complicated by the emergence of the computer and the Internet as communications media. Internet mass communication is distinctly different from the traditional forms of mass communication. We will first explore the salient characteristics of traditional mass communicators and then examine how communication on the Internet has blurred the established definition of mass communication sources. Here are the traditional defining features:

1. Mass communication is produced by complex and formal organizations.
2. Mass communication organizations have multiple gatekeepers.
3. Mass communication organizations need a great deal of money to operate.
4. Mass communication organizations exist to make a profit.
5. Mass communication organizations are highly competitive.

>> Formal Organizational Structure

Publishing a newspaper or operating a TV station requires control of money, management of personnel, coordination of activities, and application of authority. Accomplishing all these tasks requires a well-defined organizational structure characterized by specialization, division of labor, and focused areas of responsibility. Consequently, traditional mass communication is the product of a bureaucracy. As in most bureaucracies, decision making takes place at several different levels of management, and channels of communication within the organization are formalized. Thus, many of the decisions about what gets included in a newspaper or in a TV program, for instance, are made by committees or groups. Further, decisions are made by several different individuals in ascending levels of the bureaucracy, and communication follows predetermined and predictable patterns within the organization. This results in end products that seldom resemble the original idea of the creator.

>> Many Gatekeepers

Another important factor that characterizes the traditional mass communicator is the presence of multiple **gatekeepers.** A gatekeeper is any person (or group) who has control over what material eventually reaches the public. Some are more obvious than others, such as the editor of a newspaper or the news director at a TV station. Some gatekeepers are less visible. To illustrate, imagine that you have the

Ruben Studdard and Clay Aiken, the 2003 finalists on *American Idol,* perform a song with 2002 winner, Kelly Clarkson. The producers of the program capitalized on *Idol's* appeal to young viewers to get the gatekeepers at Fox to air the series.

world's greatest idea for a TV series, an idea that will make *ER* and *Friends* look mediocre. You write the script and mail it off to Universal Studios in California. A clerk in the mailroom judges by the envelope that it is a script and sees by the return address that it has come from an amateur writer. The clerk has been instructed to return all such packages unopened with a note saying that Universal does not consider unsolicited material. Gate closed.

Frustrated, you decide to go to Los Angeles in person and hand deliver your work. You rush to the office of Universal's vice president in charge of production, where a receptionist politely tells you that Universal never looks at scripts that are not submitted through an agent. Gate closed. You rush out to a phone booth and start calling agents. Fourteen secretaries tell you that their agencies are not accepting new writers. Fourteen closed gates. Finally, you find an agent who will see you (gate open!). You rush to the agent's offices, where he or she glances through your script and says, "No thanks" (gate closed). By now the point is probably clear. Many people serve as gatekeepers. In our hypothetical example, even if an agent agreed to represent you, the agent would then have to sell your script to a producer who, in turn, might have to sell it to a production company which, in turn, might have to sell it to a network.

In the newsroom, an assignment editor decides whether to send a reporter to cover a certain event. The reporter then decides if anything about the event is worth reporting. An editor may subsequently shorten the story, if submitted, or delete it altogether. Obviously, gatekeepers abound in mass communication. The more complex the organization, the more gatekeepers that will be found.

>> Large Operating Expenses

It costs a large sum of money to start a mass communication organization and to keep it running. Recently, the Gannett Company bought 21 newspapers from the Thomson Corporation for $1.13 billion. Cable TV company Comcast paid $53 billion to acquire AT&T Broadband in 2002.

Once the organization is in operation, expenses are also sizable. In the late 1990s, it cost approximately $4 million to $5 million annually to run a small daily newspaper (one with a circulation of about 35,000 to 40,000). A radio station in a medium-sized urban market might spend $700,000 annually in operating expenses. A TV station in one of the top 10 markets might need more than $10 million to keep going. Only those organizations that have the money necessary to institute and maintain these levels of support are able to produce mass communication.

Media economics have contributed to another trend that made itself evident at the end of the decade: consolidation of ownership. Companies that have strong financial resources are the likeliest to survive high operating expenses and are better able to compete in the marketplace. Consequently, by 2000 a number of global media giants had emerged to dominate the field. Table 1–2 lists these "megamedia" companies. The names listed in the table will turn up frequently in succeeding chapters.

>> **Competition for Profits**

In the United States, mass communication organizations exist to make a profit. Although there are some exceptions (the Public Broadcasting System, for example), most newspapers, magazines, record companies, and TV and radio stations strive to produce a profit for their owners and stockholders. And while radio and television stations are licensed to serve in the public interest and newspapers commonly assume a watchdog role on behalf of their readers, if they do not make money, they go out of business. The consumer is the ultimate source of this profit. When you buy a CD or a movie ticket, part of the price includes the profit. Newspapers, TV, magazines, and radio earn most of their profits by selling their audiences to advertisers. The cost of advertising, in turn, is passed on by the manufacturers to the consumer. The economics of mass communication is an important topic, and we will explore it later in this book.

Since the audience is the source of profits, mass communication organizations compete with one another as they attempt to attract an audience. This should come as no surprise to anyone who has ever watched television or passed a

TABLE 1–2	Company (home country)	2002 revenue (in billions)*
Global Media Giants	1. Time Warner (United States)	$41.8
	2. Vivendi Universal (France)**	31.1
	3. Walt Disney Co. (United States)	25.3
	4. Viacom (United States)	24.6
	5. Sony (Japan)	19.9***
	6. Bertelsmann (Germany)	19.4
	7. News Corp. (Australia)	17.5
	8. Comcast (United States)	12.5

*To give some perspective to these data, General Motors' revenue for the same period was $186 billion; General Electric's was $130 billion.

**General Electric, parent company of NBC, acquired Vivendi's media assets in 2003.

***Includes revenue from only media sources.

magazine stand. The major TV networks compete with one another to get high ratings. Millions of dollars are spent each year in promoting the new fall season. Radio stations compete with other stations that have similar formats. Record companies spend large sums promoting their records, hoping to outsell their competitors. Daily newspapers compete with weeklies and with radio and television. Motion picture companies gamble millions on films to compete successfully. This fierce competition has several consequences, and we will return to this topic time and again.

THE INTERNET AND MASS COMMUNICATION

The emergence of the Internet has created a new channel for machine-assisted and mass communication. (Chapter 11 offers a more detailed look at the Internet.) As we have seen, e-mail and chat rooms are examples of machine-assisted communication via the Internet. The World Wide Web brings the Internet into the realm of mass communication and reverses the traditional pattern of one-to-many communication. Websites offer everybody the *chance* to become mass communicators; mass communication is never guaranteed, but the potential is there.

This situation is possible because the Internet brings down the cost of mass communication to a level at which almost anybody can afford it. A single individual can create and maintain a website for a relatively small sum. The affordability of this channel can make anybody an electronic publisher with access to a potential audience of millions, thus creating a whole new type of mass communicator.

These new Web communicators represent exceptions to the five characteristics of mass communication sources listed on page 17. First, websites can be produced by single individuals; there is no need for a large staff. Second, many websites bypass gatekeepers, a circumstance that has both positive and negative consequences. (On the one hand, individuals have the freedom to post whatever they want to without fear that somebody will censor or change the content. On the other hand, there's no guarantee that what is made available is accurate or worthwhile. Rumors, conspiracy theories, and truly tasteless content abound on the Net. There are no editors to sort out the credible from the bizarre or to distinguish merit from trash.) Third, as already noted, start-up and operating costs for websites are not typically expensive. Fourth, although many companies have started websites to make a profit, many others have no such motivation. Some websites apparently exist to serve the public or to gain attention and prestige for their owners. Fifth, competition for an audience may be typical of many commercially sponsored websites, but there are many others for which competition is not a factor.

It should be pointed out that just because the Internet gives everybody the chance to become a mass communicator doesn't mean that everybody who puts up a website is automatically engaging in mass communication. If nobody visits the website, no mass communication takes place. The fact that Uncle Harold publishes a Web page does not necessarily mean that Uncle Harold is on the same level as Time Warner as a mass communicator. True, both Uncle Harold and Time Warner face the same challenges—creating Web content that people want to see, persuading them to visit the site, and convincing them to return—but Time Warner has far more resources with which to meet the challenges. In short, the potential to be a mass communicator exists for everybody, but actually becoming one is difficult.

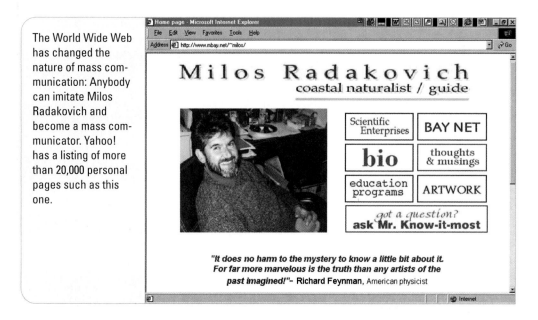

The World Wide Web has changed the nature of mass communication: Anybody can imitate Milos Radakovich and become a mass communicator. Yahoo! has a listing of more than 20,000 personal pages such as this one.

In addition, the Internet seems to be evolving into more of an interpersonal than a mass medium. There are, of course, many websites that fit the criterion of traditional mass communication (CNN.com, ESPN.com, usatoday.com), but consider the operations that have been most successful on the Internet (e-mail, instant messages, eBay, weblogs, file-sharing a la Napster and successors). All of them are not so much examples of mass communication as they are examples of machine-assisted interpersonal communication involving targeted communications between single individuals or among small groups of people. In addition, none of them was started by a big media company; they grew thanks to the efforts of individuals.

Many media professionals have predicted that traditional mass media content (TV, movies, recordings, newspapers) will eventually converge into digital formats and be delivered into the home via the Internet, making the Net the single most important channel of mass communication. This prediction may come true someday, but for the moment most Americans don't go online to get their news or to watch TV shows and movies. They go online to communicate with others. Take the terrorist attacks of September 11, 2001. Most Americans learned about the attacks from TV and followed events on that medium rather than going online. They used the Internet to send e-mail to friends, family, and coworkers and to enter chat rooms, looking for comfort and consolation from other people (see page 36).

Whatever its ultimate use, the Internet has prompted mass communication scholars (and textbook writers) to rethink conventional definitions and categories of mass communication. This new channel has also necessitated fresh models to describe the mass communication process, a topic that we will turn to next.

 MODELS FOR STUDYING MASS COMMUNICATION

Figure 1–1 outlined the elements present in the general process of communication. When we want to talk about mass communication, however, we need to construct a new model that adequately represents its distinctive features. The following dis-

FIGURE 1–2

Traditional Mass
Communication Model

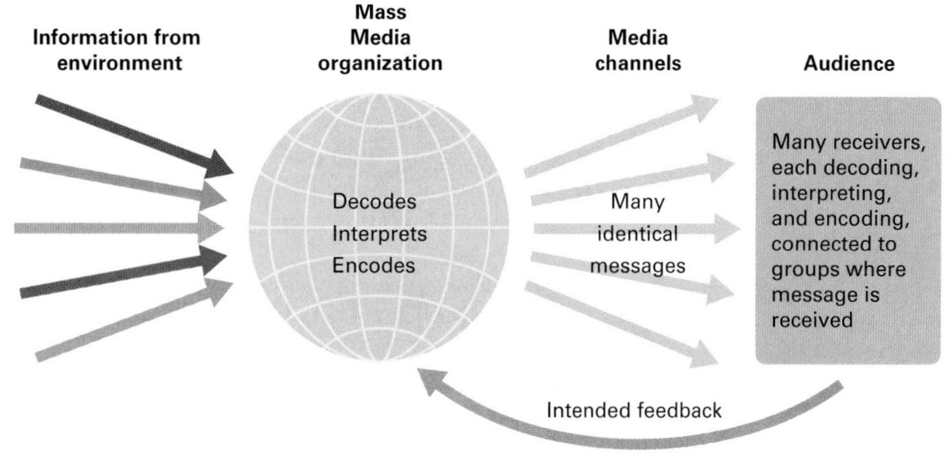

cussion introduces two models of the process. The first (Figure 1–2) applies to the traditional mass communication situation, while the second (Figure 1–3) is a new model for describing Internet mass communication.

The traditional representation of mass communication represented in Figure 1–2 is adapted from an early model described by Wilbur Schramm.[1] Although a half century old, it still illustrates the main concepts. Let's begin our discussion at the far left of the model and work toward the right. Information from the environment (both news and entertainment) is filtered through a mass media organization (newspaper, TV network, movie studio, recording company, etc.) where it is decoded, interpreted, and encoded. In other words, the media organization serves as a gatekeeper. Of all the possible CDs that a recording company could release, only a few are noted, interpreted as potential hits, and reproduced in large numbers. At a newspaper, reporters cover potentially newsworthy events and then encode a story. In turn, the story is reviewed by editors who decide if it should make it through the gate and into the newspaper.

Once through the gate, the message is reproduced many times over and sent through the appropriate channel. A recording company, for example, produces a large number of CDs that are sent to retail outlets or directly to consumers. Hundreds or thousands of copies of a newspaper are printed and distributed to subscribers.

The far right side of the model represents the receivers, or the audience. The model suggests that these audience members are not just passive recipients of messages. They decode, interpret, and encode messages themselves. In addition, audience members are not isolated from one another. They are connected to groups, such as family, peers, and coworkers, in which the messages they receive from the media are talked about, reinterpreted, and often acted upon. Some audience behavior (buying a product, subscribing to a paper, watching a TV show) is observed by the media organization and is used as feedback to help shape future messages. There is little direct interaction between sources and receivers. All in all,

[1]Adapted from Wilbur Schramm, *The Process and Effects of Mass Communication* (Urbana, IL: University of Illinois Press, 1954).

the Schramm model represents the traditional few-to-many world, where only those sources that can afford to do so publish and distribute information to everyone else.

In contrast, Figure 1–3 is a rough attempt to represent Internet communication, a new arrangement that makes possible several different levels of communication: one source communicating with one receiver (e-mail); one source communicating with many receivers (CNN.com); a few sources communicating with a few receivers (chat rooms, weblogs); and many sources communicating with many receivers (eBay).

Note that in this simplified model, content is provided not only by organizations, but also by individuals. In this circumstance, there are no organizational gatekeepers. A single individual performs the decoding, interpreting, and encoding functions. Also note that Figure 1–3 is not a one-way model. Communication doesn't proceed from left to right but flows inward. The traditional mass communicator no longer necessarily initiates the process. Instead, it is possible for the receiver to choose the time and manner of the interaction. Suppose you wanted to find out what happened in a game involving your favorite baseball team that

FIGURE 1–3

Internet Mass Communication Model

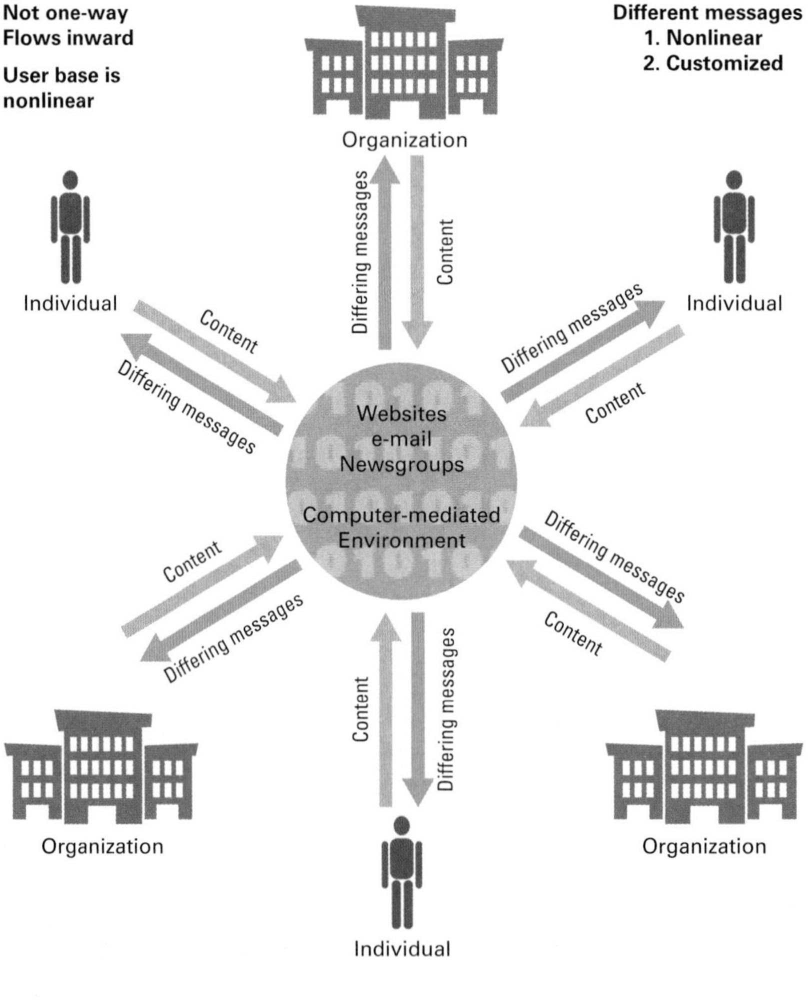

Not one-way
Flows inward

User base is
nonlinear

Different messages
1. Nonlinear
2. Customized

Organization

Individual

Individual

Differing messages

Content

Differing messages

Content

Websites
e-mail
Newsgroups

Computer-mediated
Environment

Content

Differing messages

Content

Differing messages

Content

Differing messages

Content

Differing messages

Organization

Organization

Individual

went into extra innings and finished late at night. With the traditional media, you would have to wait for a newspaper to be published or wait for your favorite TV station, cable network, or radio station to report the score. With the Internet, you could visit a sports news website and find the information immediately. Furthermore, if you wanted to know more, you could visit your team's website for more details and check message boards for the reactions of others to the outcome. In short, the audience member has more control of the process.

Another area of contrast between the traditional and Internet models is that the messages that flow to each receiver are not identical. For example, you have many different choices about what you can use as your starting page when you access the Internet. In addition, it's possible to customize the information you receive. Excite, for example, offers many different configurations that allow you to choose specific sports scores, news headlines, stock market reports, weather forecasts, and entertainment news. Each receiver can customize the information that he or she receives. Some writers have characterized the traditional mass communication model as a "push" model (the sender pushes the information to the receiver), whereas the Internet model is a "pull" model (the receiver pulls only the information that he or she wants).

Moreover, in the traditional model, many messages proceed in a linear manner. A newspaper, for instance, is designed to be read from page 1 to page 2, and so on. A book is designed to be read from Chapter 1 to Chapter 2. Thanks to **hypertext,** a means of presenting information in which text, sounds, images, and actions are linked in a way that allows you to jump around among them in whatever order you choose, the receiver no longer has to start at the beginning to find the information he or she wants.

Finally, Figure 1–3 shows that both individuals and organizations are linked through a computer-mediated environment. This makes interaction and feedback much easier. The online magazine Slate.com, for example, has a site labeled "Enter the Fray," where readers can comment on stories in the magazine. This environment allows people and organizations to be linked in unprecedented ways, in totally new forms of interaction. The auction site eBay joins buyers and sellers all over the world. The newsgroup humanities.classics brings together people who were probably never aware of one another and lets them talk about Descartes and Wagner. The Internet links producers and customers and makes e-commerce possible (see Chapter 11). All in all, the new model, incomplete as it might be, suggests a new way of conceptualizing communication in the age of the Internet.

 ## THE FUTURE OF MASS MEDIA SEGMENTATION

The past two decades have seen a basic change in the mass communication process: It's become less mass oriented and more selective. In the 1930s, for example, almost everybody tuned their radios to *Amos 'n' Andy.* Today the top-rated network radio show gets about 2 or 3 percent of the audience. In the 1950s, virtually everybody watched Milton Berle on TV. The typical top-rated shows would attract about 45 percent of all TV households. Currently, top-rated shows get about 20 percent of the audience, thanks to competition from cable; broadcast networks such as Fox, the WB, Paxnet, and UPN; VCRs; video games; and the Internet.

In the 1940s and 1950s, general-interest, mass circulation magazines, such as *Life, Look,* and *Collier's,* were popular. Today *Reader's Digest,* the most widely read general-interest magazine, is down from its all-time high of 18.4 million readers in 1977 to about 12 million in 2002. In 1960, about 75 percent of the adult population read a newspaper. In 2003, that figure was down to about 50 percent.

What we are seeing is the fractionalization, or segmentation, of the mass audience. What are the forces behind this fundamental change? First, today's audiences are different. There has been an increase in one-parent families. In many households both spouses bring home paychecks. Time has become a scarce commodity, and much of it is devoted to commuting, working, and child raising. All this means less time devoted to the media, and when audience members do spend time with the media, they look for content geared to their special interests. Second, the emergence of new media, such as DVDs, cable TV, the Internet, and direct broadcast satellites, has given today's consumers more media to choose from. Consequently, the audience for any one media vehicle is divided into smaller and smaller segments. Finally, manufacturers and service organizations have turned from mass to target marketing. This has led to an era in which Americans now have more choices than ever before. Large movie theaters with a single screen have given way to 12- or 14-screen multiplexes. Instead of having a handful of radio stations, most big cities now have a couple dozen. There are magazines for seemingly every demographic and special interest group. Back in the 1960s, most households could get just four TV channels. Now most get more than 100.

Does all this mean that *mass communication* is no longer a meaningful term? Should this book be titled *The Dynamics of Segmented Communication?* Well, not quite yet. First, the definition of *mass communication* given earlier still applies. Complex organizations still use machines to transmit public messages aimed at large, heterogeneous, and scattered audiences. Audiences are still large (even a flop TV show can reach four million households), scattered, and heterogeneous enough to justify using the term *mass communication.* Second, the channels of mass communication are unchanged, although there are more and more mass media using these channels: about 13,000 radio stations today compared with half that number a couple of decades ago, more than 3,000 new magazines in the last decade, a record number of TV stations, and so on. The messages sent by these mass media through the channels of mass communication have become more specialized. Magazines, newspapers, radio, TV, and websites are aiming their content at more defined audience niches, in part to meet the demands of advertisers and in part because it's more cost-efficient. Consequently, it's harder for any one media vehicle to reach a large number of audience members. Nonetheless, the potential is still there for the right message in the right medium to transcend the limits of specialized content and to attract a mass audience in the broadest sense of the term. This happened, for example, with *Roots, Who Wants to Be a Millionaire, Titanic,* and the coverage of the September 11 attacks. Obviously, although the content of the media has become more specialized, the potential for reaching a mass audience still exists.

>> **Convergence**

The dictionary defines *convergence* as the process of coming together or uniting in a common interest or focus. Convergence is not a new idea (some past examples are sporks, clock radios, and brunch), but the word has enjoyed renewed popularity in the last few years and has become the centerpiece in discussions about future trends in mass communication. It is a difficult term to discuss, however, because it has been used to refer to several different processes.

At one level, it refers to **corporate convergence.** This trend started in the 1980s with *synergy.* Companies that were content providers such as movie studios and record labels acquired distribution channels such as cable TV. As digital technologies emerged, synergy turned into *convergence,* a vision of one company delivering every service imaginable.

The biggest example of corporate convergence was the 2001 merger of "new media" AOL with "old media" Time Warner. At the time, the merger looked like a good idea. Nearly 60 percent of American households had a computer, and everybody had a TV. The convergence enthusiasts envisioned a future in which each household would have a high-speed broadband connection to the Internet that provided interactive TV, movies on demand, online magazines, e-mail, and Web surfing. Time Warner had the content with its magazines, movies, and TV shows, and AOL had the pipeline into more than 20 million homes. The merger, however, proved disastrous as the company's stock dropped more than 60 percent in the years that followed. It got so bad that "AOL" was officially dropped from the company name in 2003.

In France, Vivendi bought "old media" Universal Music and Universal Studios along with a French pay-TV service to go with its "new media" telecommunication and data transmission networks. As in the Time Warner–AOL merger, the convergence of old and new media didn't live up to expectations, and by 2003 Vivendi had sold its music and entertainment assets to General Electric, parent of NBC. Finally, old media company Bertelsmann spent about $90 million trying to resurrect Napster as a legitimate online music service, a venture that eventually failed.

Why didn't corporate convergence work? One reason was technical. Americans were slow to adopt the high-speed broadband connections needed for convergence to occur. Another reason was bad timing. The mergers occurred shortly before Internet-related stocks went into a tailspin, drying up potential capital for advancing the process. A third had to do with misreading consumer psychology. Just because somebody connects to the Internet through AOL doesn't necessarily mean that he or she wants to watch CNN or Warner Brothers movies or read *Time* magazine. There's no fundamental relationship between content and distribution channels. Will corporate convergence reemerge as a viable business model in the future when more Americans are connected to the Internet via broadband? Maybe, but for now the trend in corporate circles seems more toward divergence than convergence.

The trend toward more mass media and more specialized content seems irreversible. Several consequences of this movement, however, bear scrutiny. To begin, the traditional media, whatever their shortcomings, did provide a national agenda for society and helped define a national consensus. They focused the attention of the nation and mobilized its resources. The fireside chats of Franklin Roosevelt, for example, were credited with helping the country survive the hardships of the depression. Could such a phenomenon take place in the 21st century? Douglas Cater is a media critic who was among the first to question whether media specialization was beneficial to society. In a 1973 *Wall Street Journal* article, Cater posed the fundamental question "What happens when each minority group listens to its own prophets? When there are no more Walter Cronkites each evening to reassure us that despite its afflictions the nation still stands?"

Mass communication scholar Wilson Dizard described the traditional mass media as a kind of social "Elmer's glue" that bound people together (see the discussions on "Linkage" and "Transmission of Values" in the next chapter). Communication researcher Gladys Gantley in a 1991 *Washington Quarterly* article speculates that the growth in the number of specialized and personalized media might have political repercussions. Increased access to a greater range of information could serve as a democratizing force, but there might be a downside: "[If] [s]pread to millions of individuals throughout the world, each literally following his or her own agenda, such power could remove the glue of social cohesion. . . . Power to the people could mean that nobody is in control."

Neil Postman, in his provocative book *Amusing Ourselves to Death,* suggests another troubling possibility. The proliferation of media and messages could result in a flood of trivialized content that distracts us from the key social issues of the day. We might, as his title suggests, amuse ourselves to death.

Another type of convergence is **operational convergence.** This occurs when owners of several media properties in one market combine their separate operations into a single effort. For example, in Florida, WFLA, the *Tampa Tribune,* and TBO.com operate a converged news department. In Lawrence, Kansas, convergence occurred when the Lawrence *Journal-World* combined the news reporting functions of the paper, the paper's website, and its local cable news channel. All in all, it is estimated that there are about 50 examples of this kind of convergence currently underway. If cross-media ownership rules are relaxed, this trend may accelerate.

The advantages of this type of convergence are obvious. It saves money because rather than hiring a separate news staff for each medium, an operation can have the same reporters produce stories for the paper, Website, and TV operation. In addition, each medium can promote its partners. The TV newscast can encourage readers to visit the website or the print newspaper.

There are, of course, disadvantages as well. Reporters require additional training to master various media. This has generated some controversies among print reporters who are not eager to become "backpack journalists" (see Chapter 12) and carry around video cameras and audio recorders as part of their reporting tools. Further, many critics worry that converged operations mean fewer independent and diverse forms of journalism. Some conclude that, although operational convergence may be good for the media companies, it may not be good for consumers. In any case, the jury is still out on the merits of operational convergence.

Finally, there is **device convergence,** combining the functions of two or three devices into one mechanism. Examples of this trend are numerous. Laptop computers play DVDs. Many Personal Digital Assistants are combination computers and cell phones. Some cell phones incorporate digital video cameras. Experts predict that eventually there will be one information appliance in the house that combines the functions of a TV set with those of a computer. Of course, the fact that two functions can be merged in a single device doesn't mean that consumers will snap it up. In addition, if convergence results in a piece of equipment that is too complex to operate, not much is gained.

>> Disintermediation

This rather ungraceful, tongue-twisting word refers to the process whereby access to a product or a service is given directly to the consumer, thus eliminating the intermediary, or "middleman," who might typically supply the product or service. The Internet and the World Wide Web have created a ubiquitous and easily accessible network over which buyers and sellers make direct contact. The Internet has already provided several examples of **disintermediation.** Travelers bypass travel agents and book airline tickets directly online; traders bypass brokers and purchase stocks directly online; consumers bypass salespeople and buy insurance online. (Some businesses have more to fear from disintermediation than others. It's unlikely that consumers will bypass restaurants because of the Internet.)

Disintermediation is of obvious concern to mass media organizations. Those media that can easily be distributed over the Internet are the first to feel its effects. Take sound recording, for example: An artist can use the Web to distribute a CD directly to consumers. The recording company, distributor, and retailer are no longer needed in the process. Or consider book publishing: An author can put a book directly on a website for readers to download, thereby bypassing publishing companies and bookstores altogether.

Other mass communication organizations that do not have the immediate fears of the recording and publishing industries will have to face the implications of this phenomenon. For example, audience members can listen to radio on the Web; local stations are no longer necessary. Before long, movie fans will be able to download current full-length films onto DVDs. Will motion picture theaters become obsolete? The chapters in Parts Two and Three of this book will have more to say about disintermediation and its impact on the various media.

MAIN POINTS

- The elements in the communication process are a source, encoding process, message, channel, decoding process, receiver, feedback, and noise.

- The three types of noise are semantic, environmental, and mechanical.

- The three main settings for communication are interpersonal, machine-assisted interpersonal, and mass communication.

- Each element in the communication process may vary according to setting.

- *Mass communication* refers to the process by which a complex organization, with the aid of one or more machines, produces public messages that are aimed at large, heterogeneous, and scattered audiences.

- Traditionally, a mass communicator was identified by its formal organization, gatekeepers, expensive operating costs, profit motive, and competitiveness. The Internet has created exceptions to these characteristics.

- New models have been developed to illustrate Internet mass communication.

- Communication content has become more specialized in the past 40 years, but the channels of mass communication still have the potential to reach vast audiences.

- The recent history of mass communication contains examples of corporate, operational, and device convergence.

- The Internet makes possible disintermediation, eliminating the intermediary, or middleman. This phenomenon has implications for many media.

QUESTIONS FOR REVIEW

1. What are the eight elements in the communication process?
2. What are the three types of noise?
3. Compare and contrast interpersonal communication with machine-assisted interpersonal communication.

4. How has the Internet changed the characteristics of the sources of mass communication?
5. What is the difference between a "push" and a "pull" model of mass communication?

QUESTIONS FOR CRITICAL THINKING

1. What's the most embarrassing communication breakdown that's happened to you? Analyze why it happened. Semantic noise? Environmental noise? Mechanical noise?
2. Keep a media diary for a day. Tabulate how much of your time is spent in interpersonal, machine-assisted interpersonal, or mass communication. What conclusions can you draw?

3. What are some of the shortcomings of the communication models in Figures 1–2 and 1–3? Are there some elements that are missing?
4. Disintermediation is becoming more common as more people use the Web. Can you find additional examples? Are there some mass media that won't be affected by this trend? Do you think this is a positive or negative development?

KEY TERMS

source (p. 5)
encoding (p. 5)
message (p. 6)
channels (p. 6)
decoding (p. 6)
receiver (p. 7)
feedback (p. 7)

noise (p. 8)
interpersonal communication (p. 9)
machine-assisted interpersonal communication (p. 9)
mass communication (p. 11)
mass media (p. 14)

media vehicle (p. 15)
gatekeepers (p. 16)
hypertext (p. 23)
corporate convergence (p. 25)
operational convergence (p. 26)
device convergence (p. 26)
disintermediation (p. 27)

INTERNET RESOURCES

Online Learning Center

At the Online Learning Center home page, www.mhhe.com/dominick8, *select* Student Center *and then* Chapter 1.

1. Use the Learning Objectives, Chapter Outline, Main Points, and Time Line sections to review this chapter.
2. Test your knowledge of the chapter using the multiple choice, crossword puzzle, and flashcard features of the site.

3. Expand your knowledge of concepts and topics discussed in the chapter by going to *Suggestions for Further Reading* and *Internet Exercises.*

PowerWeb

At the Mass Communication home page of PowerWeb, www.dushkin.com/powerweb, *log in, select* Mass Communication *and on the next screen select* Topics.

1. Under "Gatekeeping," read Article 19, "You Can't Report What You Don't Pursue." Then answer the following questions: How is self-censorship an example of gatekeeping? Can the audience ever be aware of how much self-censorship exists? What impact will increasing media consolidation have on self-censorship?

2. Under "Internet," read Article 26, "The Real Computer Virus." Recall that Chapter 1 mentioned that one feature of Internet communication is the lack of gatekeepers. In addition to the examples mentioned in this article, can you think of any examples of false information that first appeared on the Internet and made its way into legitimate mass media channels? Is there any way to prevent this from happening?

Surfing the Internet

Listed here are sites that deal with interpersonal and mass communication.

http:excellent.com.utk.edu/JMCE/
The home of *Journalism and Mass Communication Educator,* a periodical that examines instruction, curriculum, and leadership in mass communication education.

http:pertinent.com/
A website that lists articles on various aspects of interpersonal communication, including business communication skills.

www.digital-convergence.org
The latest research on and experiments about convergence sponsored by the Convergence Center at Syracuse University.

http://www.tcpd.org/McCain/Handouts/NotNet.pdf
Site that contains several examples of the disintermediation phenomenon.

2

PERSPECTIVES ON MASS COMMUNICATION

This chapter will prepare you to

- understand the differences between the functional approach and the critical/cultural approach to studying mass communications;

- explain the value of each approach in the analysis of the mass communication process;

- describe the five functions mass media perform for society;

- explain uses-and-gratifications analysis;

- recognize the dysfunctions of mass communication; and

- understand the concepts of *meaning, hegemony,* and *ideology.*

People study mass communication for a variety of reasons. Scholars study it to better comprehend the process and to develop theories that explain and predict how the media operate. Critics study mass communication to offer insights about its influence and to suggest improvements. Media consumers study mass communication to become media literate, to be able to understand the elements involved in the mass communication process, and to analyze and critically evaluate information presented in the mass media.

No matter what the reason for study, it is helpful to use a **paradigm** (a model or pattern that a person uses to analyze something) to guide the way we think about the mass communication process. A paradigm is useful for several reasons:

1. It provides us with a consistent perspective from which to examine mass communication.

2. It generates concepts that are helpful in understanding media behavior.

3. It helps us identify what is or is not important in the process.

There are many paradigms that we could use to study mass communication. This chapter will introduce two that provide different ways of looking at media and society. The **functional approach** emphasizes the way that audiences use

American soldiers in action near Tikrit during Operation Iraqi Freedom. Media coverage of the war was subject to lengthy analysis by professionals, critics and scholars.

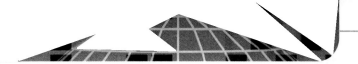

mass communication and the benefits people receive from media consumption. A second paradigm, which many have labeled the **critical/cultural approach,** examines the underlying power relationships in media exposure and stresses the many meanings and interpretations that audience members find in media content. (Chapter 18 introduces a third paradigm for examining mass media effects.)

A recent example highlights the differences between these two approaches. Operation Iraqi Freedom began on March 19, 2003, with more than 70 million Americans tuned to TV to follow the first air strike of the war. For approximately the next six weeks, media reporting of the war dominated the headlines. The 24-hour news channels began nonstop coverage. Their ratings increased from 300 to 500 percent. TV cameras located in Baghdad gave viewers ringside seats as missiles and bombs exploded in and around the Iraqi capital. News reporters "embedded" with military units provided unprecedented eyewitness coverage from the front lines. Ex–military officers and other pundits offered their analysis of why the war was or was not going well. Near the end of the battle in Baghdad, local residents assisted by U.S. Marines pulled down a statue of Saddam Hussein in front of TV cameras. The increased news coverage continued after major hostilities were declared over.

A person using the functional analysis model would want to know why people watched the coverage and what gratifications they received. Did the coverage link Americans from all parts of the nation? Why did Americans choose one news source over another? Did they believe what the pundits were telling them? This was the first war fought during the Internet age; how did Americans use this medium during this conflict?

A critical/cultural researcher would be interested in other elements of the process. During the struggle many newscasters wore American flag pins, and some channels incorporated the American flag into the graphics they used to introduce war coverage. Did these gestures have an influence on the objectivity of the coverage? What is the appropriate relationship between patriotism and journalism? Did the corporate ownership of the major American media play a role in news coverage? Did the media downplay and underreport the antiwar demonstrations that occurred around the world? Did the embedded reporters become cheerleaders for the Pentagon?

All in all, this event could serve as the springboard for many disparate avenues of inquiry. This chapter will first examine functional analysis and then look at the critical/cultural approach.

 ## FUNCTIONAL ANALYSIS

In its simplest form, the functional approach holds that something is best understood by examining how it is used. In mass communication, this means examining the use that audiences make of their interactions with the media.

By way of introduction here are some actual responses given by college students to two questions:

1. Why do you watch TV?
   - I like to watch when there's nothing else to do.
   - I like to vegetate sometimes.
   - I don't like eating alone.
   - It's easier to do than jog.
   - Television keeps me informed and entertained and it beats the hell out of studying.
   - It makes up for the newspaper I fail to read.
   - I watch TV to be entertained. Also, if the TV is on my girlfriend's mother thinks we're watching it.

2. Why do you go to movies?
   - Because movies take you to La-La Land, a fantasy place.
   - Movies are a good place to take a date.
   - To escape the everyday doldrums of life.
   - My boyfriend works at a movie theater and I get in for free.
   - I need an escape and movies are more socially positive than drugs.
   - I like to sit in the dark with sticky shoes.
   - I like the popcorn and the Jordan Almonds.
   - Movies are a fantastic way to be entertained while with a geek-me-out date.

Responses such as these, varied though they are, have led to several generalizations about the functions that media have for a society and for its individual members. This section will focus on cataloging and describing those functions.

>> The Role of Mass Communication

Maybe the best way to appreciate the role that mass communication plays in our society would be to imagine what it would be like if, all of a sudden, the whole system never existed. How would we find out what was on sale at the local supermarket? How would we know Britney Spears's current love interest? (Would there *be* a Britney Spears?) How could we find out what was happening in the Middle East? How could we avoid the traffic jams during rush hour? How would we spend our evenings? Obviously, the mass media are a pervasive part of our lives. Just how pervasive might become clear if we charted the various functions the media perform for us. Before we do this, however, we need to realize that different media have different primary uses. Not many people, for example, listen to records to find out the latest news or read the newspaper while driving their cars. Moreover, different groups of people use the same mass media content for different reasons. History professors, for example, might read articles in scholarly journals in order to keep up with their profession. Others who pursue history as a hobby might read the same journals in order to relax and be diverted from their normal routine.

One more qualification needs to be mentioned before we begin examining the functions and uses of mass communication. It is possible to conduct this analysis on at least two different levels. On the one hand, we could take the perspective of a sociologist and look through a wide-angle lens to consider the functions performed by the mass media for the entire society (this approach is sometimes called **macroanalysis**). This viewpoint focuses on the apparent intention of the mass communicator and emphasizes the manifest purpose inherent in the media content. On the other hand, we could look through a close-up lens at the individual receivers of the content, the audience, and ask them to report how they use mass media (this approach is called **microanalysis**). Sometimes the end results of these two methods are similar in that the consumer uses the content in the way that the source intended. Sometimes they are not similar, and the consumer uses the media in a way not anticipated by the mass communicator—a phenomenon noted by both the functional and critical/cultural paradigms. Let's begin our analysis by using the wide-angle lens.

>> Functions of Mass Communication for Society

For a society to exist, certain communication needs must be met. These needs existed long before Gutenberg bolted together his printing press and Morse started sending dots and dashes. Primitive tribes had sentinels who scanned the environment and reported dangers. Councils of elders interpreted facts and made decisions. Tribal meetings were used to transmit these decisions to the rest of the group. Storytellers and jesters entertained the group. As society became larger and more complex, these jobs grew too big to be handled by single individuals. Throughout the following discussion we will examine the consequences of performing these communication functions by means of mass communication as opposed to interpersonal communication. Furthermore, there may be instances in which these consequences are undesirable from the point of view of the welfare of the society. These harmful or negative consequences are called **dysfunctions.** We will consider some of these as well. Lastly, these functions are not mutually exclusive. A given example might illustrate several different categories.

Surveillance   **Surveillance** refers to what we popularly call the news and information role of the media. The media have taken the place of sentinels and lookouts. The size of this surveillance apparatus is impressive; in 2002, more than 90,000 people were employed in news-gathering jobs in radio, television, newspapers, news magazines, and wire services. The output is also substantial. The four major national television networks provide approximately 600 hours annually of regularly scheduled news programs. CNN provides a 24-hour news service to cable subscribers. Fox and MSNBC offer similar services. Many radio stations broadcast nothing but news. Newsmagazines reach nearly 10 million people. Approximately 1,500 daily newspapers and 7,500 weeklies also spread the news. On any given day, approximately 50 million to 60 million Americans are exposed to mass-communicated news. About 90 percent of the American public report that they receive most of their news from either the electronic media or newspapers.

The surveillance function can be divided further into two main types. Warning, or **beware, surveillance** occurs when the media inform us about threats from terrorism, hurricanes, erupting volcanoes, depressed economic conditions, increasing inflation, or military attack. These warnings can be about immediate threats (a television station interrupts programming to broadcast a tornado warning), or they can be about long-term or chronic threats (a newspaper runs a series about air pollution or unemployment). There is, however, much information that is not particularly threatening to society that people might like to know about. **Instrumental surveillance** has to do with the transmission of information that is useful and helpful in everyday life. News about films playing at the local theaters, stock market prices, new products, fashion ideas, recipes, and teen fads are examples of instrumental surveillance.

Note also that not all examples of surveillance occur in what we traditionally label the news media. *People* magazine and *Reader's Digest* perform a surveillance function (most of it instrumental). Smaller, more specialized publications such as technical journals also perform the job of surveillance. In fact, the surveillance function can be found in content that is primarily meant to entertain. HBO's "Sex and the City" performed a surveillance function for fashions and designer footwear.

What are some of the consequences of relying on the mass media to perform this surveillance function? In the first place, news travels much faster, especially since the advent of the electronic media. It took months for the news of the end of the War of 1812 to travel across the Atlantic. In contrast, more than 90 percent of the U.S. population knew about the terrorist attacks of September 11, 2001, within two hours of the events. The beginning air strikes in Operation Iraqi Freedom were reported on television minutes after they happened. Speed sometimes leads to problems. Inaccuracies and distortions travel just as fast as truthful statements. During its coverage of September 11, CNN mistakenly reported an attack on the Capitol building in Washington, D.C. During Operation Iraqi Freedom, several news media erroneously reported that coalition forces had been attacked with Scud missiles.

The second consequence is a bit more subtle. In prehistoric times, if war broke out, it was fairly simple for people to find out about it: A stranger would appear and belt you with a club. The world of early men and women was small and easily surveyed. All of it was within the range of their eyesight, and seldom did it extend over the next hill. Today, thanks to the mass media, there are no more hills. Our world now extends well beyond our eyesight, and we can no longer observe all of it directly. The media relay news from environments beyond our immediate senses that we cannot easily verify.

Much of what we know about the world is machine-processed, hand-me-down information. News is prescreened for us by a complex arrangement of reporters and editors, and our conception of reality is based on this second-generation information, whose authenticity we do not usually question. For example, human beings have allegedly walked on the moon. Millions saw it—on TV. Not many saw it in person. Instead, we took the word of the TV networks that what we were seeing was fact, not fiction. However, some people feel that television staged the whole thing somewhere in Arizona as part of a massive, government-inspired

This public-service campaign is an example of the warning function of the media. *(Tony Freeman/Photo Edit)*

DESIGNATED DRIVER
Don't leave the party without one.

GANNETT OUTDOOR

publicity stunt. The same phenomenon occurred in 1997 with the Pathfinder landing on Mars. There were still some people who thought the pictures received from Mars were fakes. The point is this: In today's world, with its sophisticated system of mass communication, we are highly dependent on others for news. Consequently, we have to put a certain amount of trust in the media that do our surveillance. This trust, called **credibility,** is an important factor in determining which news medium people find the most believable. We will discuss the concept at length in Chapter 12.

The widespread use of the Internet for news does not change this basic idea. The stories posted on cnn.com or other news-oriented websites have been screened by several reporters and editors. Other websites that deal with news, such as the Drudge Report, may not have a layer of editors, a circumstance that may affect the sites' credibility. Information that is spread through e-mail and by lesser-known websites may be especially suspect. In the aftermath of the September 11 attacks, many people opened their e-mail to find a picture of a tourist atop the World Trade Center with an approaching plane in the background. The picture was later exposed as a hoax, but many people were fooled into believing it. Whether the news is filtered or unfiltered, we still have to decide how much faith we invest in the media that provide it.

On the dysfunctional side, media surveillance can create unnecessary anxiety. During the summer of 2002, the news media carried reports of an asteroid on a collision course with the Earth that would hit the planet in February of 2019. Here is a sample headline: "Killer Asteroid. Earth Must Act Now to Avoid Armageddon." Subsequent calculations revealed that the asteroid would miss the Earth by a comfortable margin.

The fact that certain individuals or issues receive media attention means that they achieve a certain amount of prominence. Sociologists call this process **status conferral.** At the basis of this phenomenon is a rather circular belief that audiences seem to endorse. The audience evidently believes that if you *really* matter, you will be at the focus of mass media attention, and if you are the focus of media attention, then you *really* matter. Knowing this fact, many individuals and groups go to extreme measures to get media coverage for themselves and their causes so that this status-conferral effect will occur. Parades, demonstrations, publicity stunts, and outlandish behavior are commonly employed to capture airtime or column inches. In the early 1990s, the Ku Klux Klan staged a march in Washington, D.C. Only about 40 people participated in the march, but it still garnered the group extensive coverage on TV and in the print media.

Just after Christmas, 2002, a representative of a company called Clonaid called a press conference to claim that the company had created the first human clone. As it turned out, Clonaid was sponsored by the Raelians, a cult that believed that life on earth was started by aliens from a UFO. In addition, Clonaid offered no independent corroboration of its claim, no DNA tests, no description of methods, no mother, and no cloned baby. Nonetheless, the media scrambled to cover the event, and CNN even carried the news conference live, thus conferring status on a group that probably did not deserve it and further confusing the public about the controversial practice of cloning.

Interpretation   Closely allied with the surveillance function is the interpretation function. The mass media do not supply just facts and data. They also provide information on the ultimate meaning and significance of events. One form of

The events of September 11 provide vivid examples of many of the functions that the mass media serve for society. One type of media surveillance—warning surveillance—informs the audience about immediate threats. The Associated Press carried word of the first plane crash into the World Trade Center seconds after it happened. CNN's first report of the crash came at 8:49. By 8:55, just seven minutes after the crash, each of the major broadcast and cable news networks had live shots of smoke billowing from the tower's top floors. Local radio stations cut away from music and talk shows and broadcast live reports from the scene. Millions of people stayed glued to their TV sets for the rest of the day. That evening, it was estimated that more than 75 million people tuned into the four broadcast networks prime-time coverage of the events. Millions more watched on the all-news cable networks. Despite some lapses, most people gave the media high praise for their coverage.

But as the chapter points out, warning surveillance can tell us about two kinds of threats: immediate, as was the case with the World Trade Center attacks, and long-term. It is in this latter category that the media's performance has come under perhaps valid criticism. After the attacks, many Americans were puzzled about why anybody would hate this country enough to perpetrate this kind of a tragedy. Most of us had little knowledge of terrorist cells or radical Islamic extremists. In a special episode of *The West Wing,* produced as a response to the attack, one of the characters asked the question that most Americans were asking: "Why does everybody hate us?" One of the reasons we had to ask that question might have been that the media did not do an adequate job alerting us to this long-term problem. Coverage of international news has declined; overseas bureaus have been closed. The news media have shown a tendency to concentrate on scandals, sex, celebrities, and the sensational rather than the complicated issues of our new global society. What were the media covering before September 11? The Gary Condit scandal. Shark attacks. The West Nile Virus. One study found that between January 1 and September 10, 2001, the three major TV networks devoted a total of only 58 minutes to news about

terrorist organizations and Osama bin Laden. The Gary Condit story received three times as much coverage. (In their defense, the media reply that this is what the audience wants. Their experience suggests that the public does not read or watch international news. So perhaps we also share some of the blame.)

Many groups use extreme measures to get media coverage for themselves and their causes. The terrorists involved in the September 11 attacks had lived in the United States. They were doubtlessly familiar with the habits and practices of the news media. No one will ever know for sure, but it seems that the attacks were planned, in part at least, with media coverage in mind. It seems plausible that the hijackers knew that, once the first tower was attacked, news coverage would be intense. For maximum impact, they might have timed the second attack on the World Trade Center so that it would be carried on live TV.

Further, as already mentioned, the mass media present their audiences with hand-me-down information since the news is usually prescreened by editors and other gatekeepers. It is necessary to qualify this assertion a bit. Much of the time during the September 11 attacks, journalists and the audience experienced events simultaneously as they were unfolding. We saw the events in real time, with little need for reporters to describe what was going on. In a sense, we were all eyewitnesses.

The linkage function was also plainly visible on September 11. Throughout the day people huddled around what ABC correspondent Peter Jennings called "the national campfire." The media, especially TV, fostered a sense of national community that had not been experienced for a long time.

The media can transmit the values of a society. This function was also demonstrated in the attack's aftermath. The American flag was featured prominently in news coverage. The major TV news channels adopted red, white, and blue symbols to accompany their news coverage. The new wave of patriotism that swept over the country was reinforced and strengthened by the media.

interpretation is so obvious that many people overlook it. Not everything that happens in the world on any given day can be included in the newspaper or in a TV or radio newscast. Media organizations select those events that are to be given time or space and decide how much prominence they are to be given. Stories that ultimately make it into the paper, on the newscast, or on a media organization's Website have been judged by the various gatekeepers involved to be more important than those that did not make it.

Another example of this function can be found on the editorial pages of a newspaper. Interpretation, comment, and opinion are provided for the reader as an added perspective on the news stories carried on other pages. A newspaper might endorse one candidate for public office over another, thereby indicating that, at least in the paper's opinion, the available information indicates that this individual is more qualified than the other.

Interpretation is not confined to editorials. Articles that analyze the causes of an event or that discuss the implications of government policy are also examples of the interpretation function. Why is the price of gasoline going up? What impact will a prolonged dry spell have on food prices? Radio and television also carry programs or segments of programs that fall under this heading. An editorial by Daniel Schorr or by the manager of the local TV or radio station is an example. TV documentaries are others. When the president broadcasts a major political address, network correspondents usually appear afterward to tell us what the president "really said." During Operation Iraqi Freedom, military experts offered their interpretations of recent events and provided the audience with their opinions concerning the progress of the war.

Interpretation can take various forms. Editorial cartoons, which originated in 1754, may be the most popular form. Other examples are less obvious but no less important. Critics are employed by the various media to rate motion pictures, plays, books, and records. Restaurants, cars, architecture, and even religious services are reviewed by some newspapers and magazines. One entire magazine, *Consumer Reports,* is devoted to analysis and evaluation of a wide range of general products. Political "spin doctors" try to frame the way media cover news events in a way that is positive for their clients.

The interpretation function can also be found in media content that at first glance might appear to be purely entertainment. The comic strip *Dilbert* reflects a certain viewpoint about corporate America. *Martha Stewart Living* sends a message about what constitutes the "good life." Various interpretations of attitudes toward gays and lesbians are found in Dr. Laura Schlessinger's radio program and in the TV series *Will and Grace.*

Commentator Bill O'Reilly offers his interpretation of current events during his show on the Fox News Network

What are the consequences of the mass media's performing this function? First, the audience is exposed to a large number of different points of view, probably far more than they could come in contact with through personal channels. Because of this, a person (with some effort) can evaluate all sides of an issue before arriving at an opinion. Additionally, the media make available to the individual a wide range of expertise that he or she might not have access to through interpersonal communication. Should we change the funding structure of Social Security? Thanks to the media, a person can read or hear the views of various economists, political scientists, politicians, and government workers.

There are, however, certain dysfunctions that might occur. First, there is no

One of the criticisms leveled at the media's coverage of Operation Iraqi Freedom concerned how analysts and so-called pundits assessed the progress of the war. Government officials and other observers charged that these media experts were the victims of drastic "mood swings," as their analysis moved from positive to negative and back to positive in a matter of days.

In the early days of the war, the mood was intensely optimistic. Analysts were impressed with the "shock and awe campaign" promised by the Pentagon, and the military forces made significant early gains. Both TV and newspaper commentators concluded that the war would be over quickly. Some even described it as a "cakewalk."

Then American forces ran into opposition. Several Americans were taken prisoner, and the Arab satellite network Al Jazeera broadcast pictures of the bodies of U.S. soldiers. In addition, a sandstorm and stretched supply lines slowed the military advance.

All of a sudden, the tone of coverage changed drastically. Retired generals serving as TV analysts proclaimed that the battle plan was flawed, that there were too few troops on the ground, that the absence of an attacking force from the north would prolong the war for several months, and that the campaign was launched at the wrong time. The word *quagmire,* was resurrected from the Vietnam era and applied to the present.

Only a couple of days later, organized opposition lessened, the advance picked up steam, and in a short time Baghdad was captured. Analysts changed their tone once again and praised the operation.

This flip-flopping probably did little to enhance the analysts' credibility. It also illustrates several lessons about media interpretation in the digital age. First, the competitive demands of 24-hour news coverage increase pressure on analysts to jump to conclusions, to say something dramatic, or to make grandiose pronouncements simply to have something exciting to talk about. Second, events move faster than analysts can analyze. The rapidly changing modern battlefield makes it difficult for anyone to reach informed conclusions. Finally, media analysts need to be more thoughtful and discerning in their interpretations. In the beginning of the war, it appeared that many had uncritically accepted the Pentagon's optimistic assessments. As the going got tougher, analysts seemed to endorse the charges of those critical of the campaign without analyzing the validity of the criticisms. In sum, news consumers are entitled to informed interpretation from the media, not just snap judgments.

guarantee that interpretations by media experts are accurate and valid. After the merger between Time Warner and AOL was announced, a writer for the *New York Times* called it a "triumph of the Internet as an irresistible force in business," another expert called it "a new economic era for the TV industry," and a third said it was "a true digital media company. . . . That's why I'm going to hold on to that stock." So far, at least, it seems that these interpretations were flawed.

Second, there is the danger that an individual may, in the long run, come to rely too heavily on the views carried in the media and lose his or her critical ability. Accepting without question the views of the *New York Times* or Rush Limbaugh may be easier than forming individual opinions, but it might lead to the dysfunctional situation of audience passivity and of people allowing others to think for them.

Linkage   The mass media are able to join different elements of society that are not directly connected. For example, mass advertising attempts to link the needs of buyers with the products of sellers. Legislators in Washington may try to keep in touch with constituents' feelings by reading their hometown papers. Voters, in turn, learn about the doings of their elected officials through newspapers, TV, radio, and websites. Telethons that attempt to raise money for the treatment of certain diseases are another example of this **linkage** function. The needs of those suffering from the disease are matched with the desires of others who wish to see the problem eliminated.

Another type of linkage occurs when geographically separated groups that share a common interest are linked by the media. Publicity about the sickness known as Gulf War Syndrome linked those who claimed to be suffering from the disease, enabling them to form a coalition that eventually prompted government hearings on the issue.

The best examples of linkage, however, are the various websites, newsgroups, and chat rooms on the Internet. The online auction site eBay, for example, links people who have items to sell with people who are looking for items to buy. A person in California looking to sell an Alex Rodriguez rookie baseball card might be linked with a buyer in Maine, a linkage that would have been much more difficult without the Internet. Match.com bills itself as the place where "You are just a few clicks away from meeting thousands of interesting, intelligent, and successful singles just like you!" WebMD offers subscribers various "communities" where they can share stories about their medical conditions.

The linkage function is present in other media as well. The magazine *Gambling Times* allows a person interested in games of chance to be linked to others with a similar interest. Cell phones link parents with children. Sports talk radio joins people with a common interest in athletics.

The media can create totally new social groups by linking members of society who have not previously recognized similar interests in one another. A concrete example occurred in 2003 when the FCC voted to ease media ownership restrictions. Media coverage of the event helped build an unlikely coalition of opposition groups including the National Rifle Association, Black Voices for Peace, and the American Civil Liberties Union.

On the other hand, this linkage function may have harmful consequences. In 2002, it was estimated that there were more than 300 hate sites on the Internet. Terrorists can use these sites to spread hate propaganda and to recruit new members. Some websites provide password-protected online discussion groups in which veteran terrorists can persuade new members to join their cause.

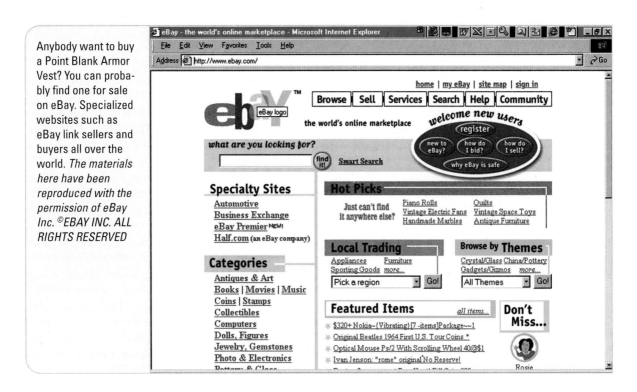

Anybody want to buy a Point Blank Armor Vest? You can probably find one for sale on eBay. Specialized websites such as eBay link sellers and buyers all over the world. *The materials here have been reproduced with the permission of eBay Inc.*

Contributed by Federico de Gregorio

Strode saw him when he was off adventuring one day alone. He kept trying to help the kid, but the kid just seemed a magnet for trouble. Eventually Strode brought him home to Rithwic where I met him for the first time. I was wary of the kid at first—he had been training as a mage, but something was not right with his studies. I sent him off to do some research alone for a bit and after a day or so he came back to me with greatly improved magic skills. I was glad I could help the kid and I told him I'd be happy to answer any questions or give him advice on magic any time. I didn't think I'd hear from him again.

Online Diary of Tzantali of Rithwic, a.k.a. Lydia Blatter

The preceding scenario is a fairly typical one in the land of Massively Multi-Player Online Role-Playing Games (MMORPGS). But what are MMORPGs anyway? At a very basic level, they are video games played over the Internet that link together players from all over the world.

MMORPGs are unique in that they must be played online. So in addition to purchasing and installing the game, one must also register for an account that will allow the game to be played at all. Further, players have to pay to be linked to others. Virtually every single MMORPG today requires a subscription fee for access (typically around $15 per month).

MMORPGs link together many people. Although there are not any official criteria, as a rule of thumb any game that allows fewer than 5,000 players at the same time is not considered massively multi-player. Many of the most popular MMORPGs, such as *EverQuest, Ultima Online,* and *Dark Age of Camelot,* often have upwards of 80,000 people playing simultaneously at any given time. Read the previous sentence one more time. Eighty thousand people is larger than many towns in the United States and some countries in the world. And that is only in one game. There are around 60 active MMORPGs running, with many more being developed.

Although they are called *games,* a frequent description used by people who play MMORPGs is "community." While it is possible to play such games without communicating with anyone, it is extremely difficult to be successful doing so. From communication comes protection, support, feuds, friendships, weapons, and opportunities. Several recent studies have shown that people who regularly play MMORPGs usually cite, as reasons to play, the social linkage aspects over "winning" at the game.

Such games raise interesting questions about what it means to be part of a community, what it means to be sociable, or even what it is to be a friend. Many players report building lasting relationships with people who live thousands of miles away but whom they have never actually met in person. MMORPGs have been the scenes of funerals, celebrations, protests against war, and even weddings. These social interactions often continue outside of the games themselves. There are hundreds of Web pages devoted to particular games (and even specific groups within the games) where people come together to ask questions, seek advice, share experiences, gather information, and gossip about other players. In short, the game has linked them together.

Transmission of Values The transmission of values is a subtle but nonetheless important function of the mass media. It has also been called the **socialization** function. *Socialization* refers to the ways an individual comes to adopt the behavior and values of a group. The mass media portray our society, and by watching, listening, and reading, we learn how people are supposed to act and what values are important. Consider the images of an important but familiar concept as seen in the media: motherhood. The next time you watch television or thumb through a magazine, pay close attention to the way mothers and children are presented. Mass media mommies are usually clean, loving, pretty, and cheerful. Ivory Snow laundry detergent typically adorns the packages of its products with a wholesome-looking mother and healthy child smiling out across grocery aisles. (Incidentally, the company was embarrassed a few years ago when one of their clean-scrubbed, all-American types went on to star in X-rated films.) The Clairol company sponsored an ad campaign that featured the "Clairol Mother," an attractive and glamorous female who never let raising a child interfere with maintaining her hair. When they interact with their children, media mothers tend to be positive, warm, and caring.[1] Consider these media mommies drawn from TV: Marge Simpson, Debra Barone (*Everybody Loves Raymond*), Rachel Green (*Friends*), Lorelei Gilmore (*The Gilmore Girls*), Lois (*Malcolm in the Middle*), and even Sharon Osbourne. All are understanding, reasonable, friendly, and devoted to their children.

These examples show that the media portray motherhood and child rearing as activities that have a positive value for society. Individuals who are exposed to these portrayals are likely to grow up and accept this value. Thus, a social value is transmitted from one generation to another.

Sometimes the media consciously try to instill values and behavior in the audience. Many newspapers report whether accident victims were wearing seat belts at the time of impact. In 1989, TV writers voluntarily agreed to portray alcohol usage more responsibly in their programs and include references to designated drivers whenever possible. The next time you watch current TV shows, see if you can find anyone smoking a cigarette. The health concerns regarding smoking have prompted it to virtually disappear from prime-time TV. (When Whoopi Goldberg's character in her 2003 sitcom was portrayed as a smoker, she received heavy criticism from anti-smoking groups.)

There are probably countless other examples of values and behavior that are, in part at least, socialized through the media. Let us examine some of the consequences of having the mass media serve as agents of socialization. At one level, value transmission via the mass media will help stabilize society. Common values and experiences are passed down to all members, thereby creating common bonds among them. On the other hand, values and cultural information are selected by large organizations that may encourage the status quo. For example, the "baby industry" in this country is a multimillion-dollar one. This industry advertises heavily in the media; it is not surprising, then, that motherhood is depicted in such an attractive light. To show mothers as harried, exhausted, overworked, and frazzled would not help maintain this profitable arrangement.

Mass media can also transmit values by enforcing social norms. In 2003, news reports surfaced about a Department of Defense program that created a futures market in which investors could bet on when terrorism would occur, when a war might break out, and when assassinations might happen. Members of Congress labeled the plan "sick" and "ghoulish," and mounting public opinion against the concept caused it to be shut down.

Not every attempt by the media to enforce social norms is successful. In an effort to combat binge drinking by college students, several campuses launched media campaigns designed to show that excessive alcohol consumption was not as widespread or normal as many college students might think. The idea behind the campaign was to show college students that most of their peers drink only moderately or less, thus reducing pressure on students to drink to excess. A report released in 2003, however, found no drop in student binge drinking on university campuses that used a social norms media campaign in their prevention efforts.

TV and Socialization   Of all the mass media, television probably has the greatest potential for socialization. By the time an individual is 18, he or she will have spent more time watching television than in any other single activity except sleep.

---

[1]OK, Mrs. Costanza, George's mother on "Seinfeld," might be an exception.

A prime-time program that is popular with young people might draw an audience of six million 6 to 11 year olds. Because of this wide exposure, several writers have warned of possible dysfunctions that might occur if television became the most important channel of socialization. For instance, since so many TV programs contain violence, it has been feared that young people who watch many violent programs might be socialized into accepting violence as a legitimate method of problem solving. In one survey among grade schoolers, heavy TV viewers were more likely than light TV viewers to agree with this statement: "It's almost always all right to hit someone if you are mad at him or her." Or another possibility is that the pervasiveness of television violence will encourage fearfulness about the "real world." One study, for example, found that children who were heavy TV viewers were more fearful of going out at night than were light TV viewers. We will discuss this topic at greater length in Chapter 18.

Surveys about television have indicated that this medium can also function as a source of knowledge about occupations. For example, during the 1970s, the two most common occupations held by leading female characters in prime-time TV were those of homemaker and law enforcement officer. No other occupation came close to these two in frequency of portrayal. If she had no other sources of countervailing information, a girl growing up in this decade might have been socialized into believing she had two career choices when she grew up: to get married or to become a cop.

Finally, it has been argued that for many years the image of minority groups transmitted from one generation to the next by the mass media reflects the stereotypes held by those in power: white, Anglo-Saxon, Protestant males. As a result, Native Americans and black Americans endured many years during which Native Americans were seen as savages who murdered civilized whites, and blacks were depicted in menial and subordinate roles. These stereotypes were slow to change, partly because it took a long time for members of these minority groups to influence the workings of large media organizations.

Entertainment   Another obvious media function is that of entertainment. Two of the media examined in this book, motion pictures and sound recordings, are devoted primarily to entertainment. Even though most of a newspaper focuses on the events of the day, comics, puzzles, horoscopes, games, advice, gossip, humor, and general entertainment features usually account for around 12 percent of the content. (If we considered sports news as entertainment, that would add another 14 percent to this figure.) Television is primarily devoted to entertainment, with about three-quarters of a typical broadcast day falling into this category. The entertainment content of radio varies widely according to station format. Some stations may program 100 percent news, while others may schedule almost none. In like manner, some magazines may have little entertainment content (*Forbes*), while others are almost entirely devoted to it (*National Lampoon*). Even those magazines that are concerned primarily with news—*Time* and *Newsweek,* for example—usually mix some entertaining features with their usual reporting.

The scope of mass media entertainment is awesome. By late 2003, approximately 70 million people in the United States had paid money to see *The Lord of the Rings: The Two Towers.* About 80 million people watched the last episode of *Seinfeld.* The comic strip *Doonesbury* is read by 18 million people. Eight million people bought copies of *Harry Potter and the Order of the Phoenix*. Norah Jones's album *Come Away With Me* sold seven million copies. In a typical month, about five million people read (or at least look at) *Playboy*.

The importance of the entertainment function of mass media has grown as Americans have accumulated more leisure time. The workweek has decreased from about 72 hours at the turn of the 20th century to the current 40 hours.

Troubadours, storytellers, court jesters, and magicians fulfilled the entertainment function in the centuries before the media. What are the consequences of having this task now taken over by mass communication? Clearly, the media can make entertainment available to a large number of people at relatively little cost. On the other hand, entertainment that is carried by the mass media must appeal to a mass audience. The ultimate result of this state of affairs is that media content is designed to appeal to the lowest common denominator of taste. More programs that resemble *Survivor* and *Jerry Springer* will find their way to TV than will opera performances. Newsstands are filled with more imitators of *Playboy* than imitators of *Saturday Review*. We are more apt to see sequels such as *Star Trek VIII, Wes Craven's New Nightmare,* and *Lethal Weapon VII* than we are to see *Much Ado About Nothing II* and *More King Lear*. Rock stations outnumber classical stations 20 to 1.

One other consequence of the widespread use of media for entertainment is that it is now quite easy to sit back and let others entertain you. Instead of playing baseball, people might simply watch it on TV. Instead of learning to play the guitar, an adolescent might decide to listen to a tape of someone else playing the guitar. Critics have charged that the mass media will turn Americans into a nation of watchers and listeners instead of doers.

>> How People Use the Mass Media

It is probably clear by now that statements made about the functions of mass communication in society could be paralleled by statements about how the media function at the level of the individual. Consequently, we will now focus on how the individual uses mass communication (in other words, we are moving from macro- to microanalysis). At the individual level, the functional approach is given the general name of the **uses-and-gratifications model.** In its simplest form, the uses-and-gratifications model posits that audience members have certain needs or drives that are satisfied by using both nonmedia and media sources. This discussion will be concerned more with media-related sources of satisfaction. The actual needs satisfied by the media are called *media gratifications*. Our knowledge of these uses and gratifications typically comes from surveys that ask people questions about how they use the media (much like the questions at the beginning of this chapter). Several researchers have classified the various uses and gratifications into a four-category system:

1. cognition;
2. diversion;
3. social utility; and
4. withdrawal.

Cognition   Cognition is the act of coming to know something. When a person uses a mass medium to obtain information about something, then he or she is using the medium in a cognitive way. Clearly, the individual's cognitive use of a medium is directly parallel to the surveillance function at the macroanalytical level. At the individual level, researchers have noted that two different types of cognitive functions are performed. One has to do with using the media to keep up with information on current events, while the other has to do with using the media to learn about things in general or things that relate to a person's general curiosity. Several surveys have found that many people give the following reasons for using the media:

- I want to keep up with what the government is doing.
- I want to understand what is going on in the world.
- I want to know what political leaders are doing.

These reasons constitute the current-events type of cognitive gratification. At the same time, many people also report the following reasons for using mass media:

- I want to learn how to do things I've never done before.
- I want to satisfy my curiosity.
- The media make me want to learn more about things.
- The media give me ideas.

These statements illustrate the second type of cognition—using the media to satisfy a desire for general knowledge.

Diversion   Another basic need of human beings is for diversion. Diversion can take many forms. Some of the forms identified by researchers are (1) stimulation, or seeking relief from boredom or the routine activities of everyday life; (2) relaxation, or escape from the pressures and problems of day-to-day existence; and

The aftermath of an explosion on a bus in downtown Jerusalem. One of the types of cognition is awareness of current events. Many people turn to the media for breaking news, such as the continuing violence between Israelis and Palestinians during 2003

(3) emotional release of pent-up emotions and energy. Let us look at each of these gratifications in more detail.

Stimulation Seeking emotional or intellectual stimulation seems to be an inherent motivation in a human being. Psychologists have labeled these activities "ludic behaviors"—play, recreation, and other forms of activity that seem to be performed to maintain a minimum level of intellectual activity. Many people report that they watch, read, or listen simply to pass the time. The media have taken advantage of this need to avoid boredom in many creative ways. Ted Turner has started an airport TV channel that beams news and commercials to passengers in airline terminals. Some airlines provide audio and video entertainment during long flights. Supermarkets have grocery carts with video screens that display the latest bargains. Some restaurants and coffeehouses have computers on their tables to allow customers to surf before they sup. There are now special magazines that are distributed only to doctors' waiting rooms. Advertisements are now found on walls and the backs of stall doors in rest rooms.

SOUNDBYTE

What . . . no Metallica?

Researchers who study the diversion function of the mass media focus on the process by which people seek rewarding media content. No less important is the opposite process: avoiding those forms of entertainment people cannot stand. For example, an Illinois high school teacher was looking for a way to cut down on the number of students who were kept after school as punishment. He started playing Frank Sinatra albums during detention. School behavior improved dramatically.

Relaxation Too much stimulation, however, is undesirable. Psychological experiments have indicated that human beings are negatively affected by sensory overload, in which too much information and stimulation are present in the environment. When faced with sensory overload, people tend to seek relief. The media are one source of this relief. Watching *Friends* or reading *People* magazine represents a pleasant diversion from the frustrations of everyday life. The choice of material used for relaxation might not always be apparent from surface content. Some people relax by reading articles about Civil War history; others read about astronomy or electronics. Still others might relax by listening to serious classical music. The content is not the defining factor, since virtually any media material might be used for relaxation by some audience members.

Emotional Release The last manifestation of the diversion function is the most complex. On the one hand, the use of the media for emotional release is fairly obvious. For instance, the horror movie has had a long history of popularity in America. Starting with *Dracula* and *Frankenstein* and continuing through *The Creature from the Black Lagoon*, *Them*, and *The Thing* right up to *Nightmare on Elm Street*, *Friday the 13th*, *The Ring*, and *Scream*, people have sat in dark theaters and screamed their lungs out. Tearjerkers have also drawn crowds. *Broken Blossoms*, *Since You Went Away*, *The Best Years of Our Lives*, *Terms of Endearment*, *Dying Young*, and *Titanic* have prompted thousands, perhaps millions, to cry their eyes out. Why do audiences cheer when Seabiscuit wins? Probably because people enjoy a certain amount of emotional release. People feel better after a good scream or a good cry.

On the other hand, emotional release can take more subtle forms. One of the big attractions of soap operas, for example, seems to be that many people in the audiences are comforted by seeing that other people (even fictional people) have

Teens love to be terrorized—at least at the movies. Eighty percent of the audience for slice-and-dice films, such as the *Nightmare on Elm Street* series, is under the age of 21. In addition, the terror audience is almost always evenly split between males and females. This is not coincidental; slasher and splatter films are popular date movies. Apparently they serve an important function for their young audience. As one teenager, quoted in a recent issue of *Seventeen,* put it, "Sometimes you feel weird or self-conscious holding onto a guy's hand on the first date but this way you can just grab him." Said another teenage girl, "Guys like to take you to horror movies, hoping you'll be real afraid and need them to comfort you." Said a third, "You can get all rowdy with boys and jump into their lap."

Scientific studies seem to confirm that horror films are performing a social function for teens. In one experiment at the University of Indiana, female college students were paired with male confederates of the researchers. One male was instructed to remain silent while the couple watched a scene from a horror movie. A second male confederate acted wimpy, saying, "Oh my God" at the gory scenes and generally acting afraid. The third male confederate acted macho, showing no signs of fear and shouting, "All right!" during the gory scenes. Another condition in this experiment paired males with female confederates who acted the same ways.

The results? Males enjoyed the horror film most when they were paired with the females who acted afraid. In contrast, females enjoyed the film most when paired with the macho males. The researchers concluded that horror movies encourage traditional gender-specific ways of behavior for both men and women, a conclusion supported by the preceding quotes from teen moviegoers.

troubles greater than their own. Other people identify with media heroes and participate vicariously in their triumphs. Such a process evidently enables these people to vent some of the frustrations connected with their normal lives.

Emotional release was probably one of the first functions to be attributed to media content. Aristotle, in his *Poetics,* talked about the phenomenon of **catharsis** (a release of pent-up emotion or energy) occurring as a function of viewing tragic plays. In fact, the catharsis theory has surfaced many times since then, usually in connection with the portrayals of television violence. Chapter 18 contains a discussion of research that has dealt expressly with the catharsis notion.

Social Utility   Psychologists have also identified a set of social integrative needs, including our need to strengthen our contact with family, friends, and others in our society. The social integrative need seems to spring from an individual's need to affiliate with others. The media function that addresses this need is called **social utility,** and this usage can take several forms. First, have you ever talked with a friend about a TV program? Have you ever discussed a current movie or the latest record you heard on the radio? If so, then you are using the media as **conversational currency.** The media provide a common ground for social conversations, and many people use things that they have read, seen, or heard as topics for discussion when talking with others. There is a certain social usefulness in having a large repository of things to talk about so that, no matter where you are, you can strike up a conversation and be fairly sure that the person you are talking to is familiar with the subject. ("What did you think of the Super Bowl?" "How did you like *American Wedding?*")

Social utility is apparent in other instances as well. Going to the movies is probably the most common dating behavior among adolescents. The motion picture theater represents a place where it is socially acceptable to sit next to your date in a dark room without parental supervision. In fact, many times the actual film is of secondary importance; the social event of going out has the most appeal.

Other people report that they use the media, particularly TV and radio, as a means to overcome loneliness. The TV set represents a voice in the house for peo-

Many theatergoers found emotional release cheering for the underdog Seabiscuit in the movie of the same name.

ple who might otherwise be alone. Radio keeps people company in their cars. In fact, some viewers might go so far as to develop feelings of kinship and friendship with media characters. This phenomenon is called a **parasocial relationship,** and there is some evidence that it actually occurs. For example, in one study done during the 1970s that examined parasocial relationships between the audience and TV newscasters, more than half the people surveyed agreed with the statement "The newscasters are almost like friends you see every day."

Withdrawal   At times, people use the mass media to create a barrier between themselves and other people or activities. For example, the media help people avoid certain chores that should be done. Children are quick to learn how to use the media in this fashion. This hypothetical exchange might be familiar:

"It's your turn to let the dog out."
"I can't. I want to finish watching this program. You do it."

In this case, attending to mass media content was defined as a socially appropriate behavior that should not be interrupted. In this manner, other tasks might be put off or avoided entirely.

People also use the media to create a buffer zone between themselves and other people. When you are riding a bus or sitting in a public place and do not want to be disturbed, you bury your head in a book, magazine, or newspaper. If you are on an airplane, you might insert a pair of earphones in your ears and tune everybody out. Television can perform this same function at home by isolating adults from children ("Don't disturb Daddy. He's watching the game") or children from adults ("Don't bother me now; go into the other room and watch *Sesame Street*").

Content and Context   In closing, we should emphasize that it is not only media content that determines audience usage, but also the social context within which the media exposure occurs. For example, soap operas, situation comedies, and movie magazines all contain material that audiences can use for escape purposes. People going to a movie, however, might value the opportunity to socialize more than they value any aspect of the film itself. Here the social context is the deciding factor.

It is also important to note that the functional approach makes several assumptions:

1.   Audiences take an active role in their interaction with various media. That is, the needs of each individual provide motivation that channels that individual's media use.

2.   The mass media compete with other sources of satisfaction. Relaxation, for example, can also be achieved by taking a nap or having a couple of drinks, and social utility needs can be satisfied by joining a club or playing touch football.

3.   The uses-and-gratifications approach assumes that people are aware of their own needs and are able to verbalize them. This approach relies heavily on surveys based on the actual responses of audience members. Thus, the research technique assumes that people's responses are valid indicators of their motives.

A great deal of additional research needs to be done in connection with the uses-and-gratifications approach. In particular, more work is needed in defining and categorizing media-related needs or drives and in relating those needs to media usage. Nonetheless, the current approach provides a valuable way to examine the complex interaction between the various media and their audiences.

 ## CRITICAL/CULTURAL STUDIES

The functional approach relies on empirical methods common to the social sciences. Researchers who use this approach ask people questions and tabulate their results or enumerate characteristics of media content. In contrast, critical/cultural researchers use a more qualitative and humanities-oriented approach. This perspective takes a macroanalytic outlook and examines such concepts as ideology, culture, politics, and social structure as they relate to the role of media in society. Some background on this school of thought may be helpful.

>> **History**

Most scholars suggest that the beginnings of the critical/cultural model can be traced to the Frankfurt School during the 1930s and 1940s. The Frankfurt School was a group of intellectuals committed to the analytical ideas of Karl Marx. (Keep in mind that we are discussing Marxism as a philosophical system and an analytical tool. Marxism as a political and economic system has fallen on hard times of late.) In simplified terms, the core of this Marxist approach was that the best way to understand how a society worked was to examine who controlled the means of production that met the basic needs of the population for food and shelter. Marx noted that many Western countries had adopted a system of industrial capitalism in which mass production created wealth for the capitalists—the ones who owned the factories where the goods were produced. Mass production ensured that the basic needs of a society were met, but at a cost: tension between the haves (the wealthy) and the have-nots (the workers who worked in all those factories). In other words, the capitalist system exploited the working class and guaranteed their domination by the wealthy. Because capitalists were interested in creating more capital (or wealth), they had a vested interest in ensuring that the system stayed in place. Marx suggested that life would be better for all if some other, more equitable system of sharing wealth were in place.

The members of the Frankfurt School extended Marxist analysis into the cultural life of a society. They noted that, just as big firms controlled the production of economic goods, other big companies controlled the production of cultural goods. The radio industry, motion picture studios, newspaper and magazine publishers, and later the television business all adopted the capitalist model of production. According to the Frankfurt School, the culture industry exploited the masses just as capitalists did. They published and broadcast products based on standardized formulas that appealed to the mass audience and at the same time glorified and promoted the capitalist culture. For example, during the depression of the 1930s, Hollywood did not make films that advocated a different economic or political system. Instead, the studios churned out glitzy musicals and comedies that portrayed common people who get a break and make it big despite bad economic times. The television sitcoms of the 1950s showed well-off families content with their lives in the suburbs: Ozzie and Harriet never agitated for a new economic system.

Much of the writing of members of the Frankfurt School was designed to show the exploitative character of mass culture and how the culture industry helped destroy individuality by promoting the social dominance of large corporations. The object of the critical theory espoused by these writers was resistance to this mass culture and exploitation. The media were so powerful and pervasive, however, that critical resistance to these forces was nearly impossible. The media continued to reinforce the status quo.

The viewpoint of the Frankfurt School was criticized for being pessimistic and gloomy and for underestimating the power of the audience. Nonetheless, this perspective caused many to analyze the impact of the media industries on the political and economic life of a society and to use interdisciplinary theories and methods in their investigations.

The next important stage in the development of the critical/cultural approach took place in Great Britain during the late 1950s and early 1960s. Scholars at the Centre for Contemporary Cultural Studies at Birmingham University noted that members of the British working class used the products of mass culture to define their own identities through the way they dressed, the music they listened to, their hairstyles, and so forth. The audience did not seem to be manipulated by the media, as the Frankfurt School argued; instead, the relationship was more complicated. Audience members took the products of mass culture, redefined their meaning, and created new definitions of their self-image.

This emphasis on meaning was reinforced by studies of film and television. A theory developed by British film critics suggested that cinematic techniques (camera angle, editing, imagery) subtly but effectively impose on the audience the meanings preferred by the filmmaker.

This theory was later amended to acknowledge that, although films and TV shows could try to impose their preferred meanings on people, audience members were free to resist and come up with their own meanings of what they saw. For example, although the dominant theme in a documentary about efforts to control

During the Depression, most Hollywood films refrained from making social or political statements about the bad times. Instead, films like *The Gay Divorcee,* shown here, suggested that things were fine and that, with a little luck, everyone could afford the good life portrayed in the film.

pollution might be how hard industry is trying to control the problem, some in the audience might see the program as nothing more than an empty marketing gesture by big companies.

Important to the cultural studies group were the values that were represented in the content. Again drawing from Marx, the group noted that the values of the ruling class became the dominant values that were depicted in mass media and other cultural products. Marx analyzed dominant values in economic terms, but the cultural studies scholars extended the perspective to class, race, and, with the growth of feminist studies, gender. In Britain, and later in the United States, the dominant values that were represented were those of white, upper-class, Western males. The media worked to maintain those values by presenting versions of reality on TV and films that represented this situation as normal and natural, as the way things should be.

The audience, however, was not passive. The dominant values may have been encoded in complex and subtle ways (much critical/cultural research is aimed at describing and analyzing these subtle depictions), but viewers can supply their own meanings to the content (much critical/cultural research tries to catalog how various audience members interpret content in different ways). One of the classic studies examined how the audience made sense of a British TV program, *Nationwide*. One group of viewers seemed to accept the dominant message of the program that British society was harmonious and egalitarian; another group "negotiated" their own, somewhat different interpretation; and a third group, young blacks who were not part of the mainstream, rejected it altogether.

The critical/cultural approach gained prominence in the United States during the 1970s and 1980s and was adopted by communication researchers and scholars engaged in feminist studies. Like Marxist analysis, feminist analysis saw inequalities in the way that wealth and power were distributed in society. Marx, however, argued that this inequality stemmed from industrial capitalism; feminist scholars suggested that it stemmed from male domination of women in society (sometimes referred to as *patriarchy*). Feminist critics examined how the media and other forms of culture strengthened the oppression of women. Advertising, for example, might suggest that the proper (or natural) place for a woman is in the home or that looking good is the preferred way for women to achieve success.

Not all critical/cultural scholars, however, emphasize power relationships. James Carey, for example, contended that researchers should study how communication creates, maintains, or modifies a culture. He argued that it was valuable to look upon communication as a ritual—how it draws people together and how it represents a sharing of beliefs. Someone interested in the ritual role of mass communication, for instance, might examine the cultural meanings of men gathering to watch *Monday Night Football* and how this rite illustrates the social bonds that help maintain society. Other critical/cultural scholars have examined how cultural myths are embodied in mass communication. A myth is an expressive story that celebrates a society's common themes, heroes, and origins. Studying the way popular media programs utilize the collective myths of a culture might help us understand their success. *Star Trek,* for example, has spawned a cult following, four TV series, and upwards of a half-dozen movie sequels. A mythic analysis of the TV show suggests that it draws upon myth deeply rooted in American history—the myth of the frontier where a wagon train heads hopefully into uncharted and potentially dangerous territory in search of better horizons. Note that the *Star Trek* prologue describes space as "the final frontier," the *Enterprise* takes the place of the wagon train, Klingons take the place of hostile Indians, and Kirk becomes the wagon master while Spock serves as scout.

As is probably obvious by now, the critical/cultural perspective is multidimensional and encompasses a wide variety of topics and analysis methods. It is difficult to summarize the important notions of such an eclectic approach, but the ones listed next have general relevance.

>> Concepts

Like most other specialized ways of examining the audience, critical/cultural studies has developed its own specialized vocabulary. We will examine some of the key terms.

Cultural studies, naturally enough, broadens the study of mass communication to encompass the notion of **culture.** Culture is a complex concept that refers to the common values, beliefs, social practices, rules, and assumptions that bind a group of people together. Hence, it is possible to identify a street culture or an Asian American culture or even a college student culture.

Culture is studied through the practices and texts of everyday life. A **text** is the object of analysis. Texts are broadly defined. They can be traditional media content such as TV programs, films, ads, or books, or they can be some things that do not fit into the traditional category, such as shopping malls, T-shirts, dolls, video games, and beaches.

Texts have **meaning,** the interpretations that audience members take away with them from the text. In fact, texts have many meanings; they are **polysemic.** Different members of the audience will make different interpretations of the same text. Some may interpret it the way the source intended; others may provide their own unique meanings.

Ideology is contained in texts. Broadly defined, an ideology is a specific set of ideas or beliefs, particularly regarding social and political subjects. Mass communication messages and other objects of popular culture have ideology embedded in them. Sometimes the ideology is easy to see. Commercials, for example, illustrate the belief that consumption is good for you and for society. Other times the ideology is more subtle and harder to detect.

Hegemony has to do with power relationships and dominance. In the United States, for example, those who own the channels of mass communication possess cultural hegemony over the rest of us. Groups with political and economic power extend their influence over those groups who are powerless or at the margins of society. Hegemony, however, is not based on force. It depends on the dominated group's accepting its position as natural and normal and believing that the status quo is in its best interest. Media rules, regulations, and portrayals all help the dominant class present the status quo as customary and desirable. Hegemony creates the positions of the superior and the inferior. This division is unstable and continuously being negotiated through interpretations of meaning.

A couple of examples will illustrate how these concepts are used in the critical/cultural approach. One critical/cultural study used the long-running TV show *60 Minutes* as its text. The analysis found predictable themes and formulas in the program. One common type of *60 Minutes* segment can be interpreted as the classic American detective story. Somebody, maybe a business that is ripping off consumers, is committing a crime. The *60 Minutes* reporters have to hunt down clues and gather information. They may sneak in a hidden camera to catch the wrongdoers in the act. The reporters become the heroes; the evildoers are the villains. The story is eventually resolved, and those who were committing the bad deeds are exposed or brought to justice.

This seems to be a meritorious service to the public. But upon closer inspection, this kind of *60 Minutes* story seems to be reinforcing the hegemony of the dominant class. Note that these stories go after companies or businesses that have violated some basic values of American capitalism: "Thou shalt not cheat the customer"; "thou shalt not promise more than thou canst deliver." The stories never question the basic ideology that capitalism is good for you. Instead, they imply that life would be fine if we could just expose all those companies that do not play by the rules of free enterprise and bring them back into the fold. Further, note how the program stands up for the little person. The reporters are our friends and champions. Everything is fine with the system, and CBS can continue to make money from selling ads in a top-rated program. It is easy for an audience member to come away with an interpretation that simply reinforces the economic and social hegemony of the powerful.

A second example concerns arcade video games as a text. These games are typically played by a relatively powerless segment of society—younger teenagers. Nonetheless, these players can find a meaning in the games that lets them resist, for a rather short time, forms of social control, allowing them to form their own cultural identity. The arcade games, for instance, reverse the traditional relationship between machine and machine operator. In industry, the two work together to produce some commodity. In the arcade, the player plays against the machine. The idea is to consume, not to produce.

Playing arcade games is regarded by some with a certain amount of disapproval; some games are violent, and others have mature themes. There is also the view that game playing is just a waste of time, and this disapproval on the part of *non*players probably plays a role in the games' attraction to those who *do* play. In addition, the joystick or steering wheel offers the player a direct means to control his or her environment, something that may not be possible in much of everyday life. These factors may account for the continuing popularity of this type of entertainment. Nonetheless, a closer look suggests that, although video games allow the player some freedom of cultural interpretation, the games still work to reinforce the dominant ideology—the social values contained in the games are the common ones in society. Arcade players get a chance to blow away monsters, aliens, drug runners, thugs, and other assorted bad guys; there is no opportunity to show disfavor with the prevailing social norms. And, of course, many of those quarters from the arcade go back to the video game companies, which maintain their economic hegemony and make more games that teens can play to make them feel as though they are resisting the dominant ideology while they are actually supporting it.

This book presents a series of boxed inserts that illustrate the critical/cultural approach and demonstrate the range and diversity of critical/cultural topics. For example, in Chapter 5 you will find a critical/cultural analysis of *YM* magazine; in Chapter 6 an analysis focuses on Oprah's book club.

Some friction exists between those who choose the traditional effects or functional approaches and those who adopt the critical/cultural approach. This discord seems unnecessary since these various paradigms ask different questions about media and society and use different tools to look for answers. In addition, each approach can learn from the others. No technique is somehow better than the rest. All are useful in the quest to understand the complicated relationships between mass communication and its audience.

MAIN POINTS

- Functional analysis holds that something is best understood by examining how it is used.

- At the macro level of analysis, mass media perform five functions for society: surveillance, interpretation, linkage, transmission of values, and diversion. Dysfunctions are harmful or negative consequences of these functions.

- At the micro level of analysis, the functional approach is called *uses-and-gratifications analysis*.

- The media perform the following functions for the individual: cognition, diversion, social utility, and withdrawal.

- The critical/cultural approach has its roots in Marxist philosophy, which emphasized class differences as a cause of conflict in a society.

- The critical/cultural approach suggests that media content helps perpetuate a system that keeps the dominant class in power. It also notes that people can find different meanings in the same message.

- The key concepts in the critical approach are text, meaning, hegemony, and ideology.

- Although they are different approaches, both functional analysis and critical/cultural studies can be valuable tools for the analysis of the mass communication process.

QUESTIONS FOR REVIEW

1. What is the difference between macroanalysis and microanalysis?

2. What is a dysfunction? What are some examples?

3. What is status conferral? How does it work?

4. What is meant by the uses-and-gratifications approach? What are its assumptions?

5. What are the key terms in the critical/cultural approach?

QUESTIONS FOR CRITICAL THINKING

1. Compare and contrast the functional approach and the critical/cultural approach. How does each view the audience? How does each view the media?

2. Compare your own reasons for watching TV and going to the movies with those that appear at the beginning of the chapter. Are there any similarities?

3. Can you find any more current examples of status conferral? Linkage? Media dysfunctions?

4. As mentioned in the text, one of the assumptions of the uses-and-gratifications approach is that people can verbalize their needs. Suppose this assumption is false. Is the uses-and-gratifications approach still useful?

5. Using the critical/cultural viewpoint, can you detect ways that the media preserve the current political and economic status quo?

KEY TERMS

paradigm (p. 30)
functional approach (p. 30)
critical/cultural approach (p. 31)
macroanalysis (p. 32)
microanalysis (p. 33)
dysfunctions (p. 33)
surveillance (p. 33)
beware surveillance (p. 33)
instrumental surveillance (p. 33)

credibility (p. 35)
status conferral (p. 35)
linkage (p. 38)
socialization (p. 40)
uses-and-gratifications model
    (p. 43)
catharsis (p. 46)
social utility (p. 46)
conversational currency (p. 46)

parasocial relationship (p. 47)
culture (p. 51)
text (p. 51)
meaning (p. 51)
polysemic (p. 51)
ideology (p. 51)
hegemony (p. 52)

INTERNET RESOURCES

Online Learning Center

At the Online Learning Center home page, www.mhhe.com/dominick8, *select* Student Center *and then* Chapter 2.

1. Use the Learning Objectives, Chapter Outline, Main Points, and Time Line sections to review this chapter.

2. Test your knowledge of the chapter using the multiple choice, crossword puzzle, and flashcard features of the site.

3. Expand your knowledge of concepts and topics discussed in the chapter by going to *Suggestions for Further Reading* and *Internet Exercises.*

PowerWeb

At the Mass Communication home page of PowerWeb, www.dushkin.com/powerweb, *log in and select* Mass Communication *as your title. On the next screen, select* Topics. *Read Article 6, "Can TV Improve Us?" Then answer the following questions:*

1. How does the designated driver campaign mentioned in the article illustrate the transmission of social norms function of the mass media?

2. The article also mentions an episode of *Felicity* in which the title character researched birth control methods. How does this relate to the surveillance and socialization functions of the media?

Surfing the Internet

The following are useful sites that are related to the material in this chapter. In addition, scan some of the newsgroups on the net to see some of the special-interest topics that bring people together.

http://eserver.org/theory/
Page contains links to works using the critical/cultural approach in many disciplines.

www.aber.ac.uk/media/sections/gen08.html
Site containing links to articles that discuss the uses-and-gratifications approach.

www.cyberdiva.org/ccsol/
Home of the Critical and Cultural Studies interest division of the National Communication Association.

www.uky.edu/~drlane/capstone/mass/uses.htm
A discussion of the various approaches and models used to analyze the role of media in society.

www.cultsock.ndirect.co.uk/MUHome/cshtml/index.html
A useful summary of the uses-and-gratifications approach with good examples.

3

HISTORICAL AND CULTURAL CONTEXT

This chapter will prepare you to

- describe the major events and general trends in media history;

- recognize the milestones in the development of human communication;

- understand the role that these advances played in prompting significant changes in our culture and society;

- learn that the emergence of new communications advances changes but does not make extinct those communications that came before; and

- understand that each advance in communication increases our power to convey and record information.

This modern-day storyteller keeps alive the oral culture of our ancestors and introduces another generation to the art of verbal communications.

The historical and cultural contexts of media are important because history tends to be cyclical. This fact has been apparent for centuries. Many ancient civilizations relied on storytellers to hand down the history and culture of their civilization so that they might learn from the past. The same is true for modern society. Knowing what happened many years ago might help us understand what is going on now. For example, when radio first started in the 1910s and 1920s, its future was uncertain. Many thought radio would compete with the telephone and telegraph as a means of sending messages from point to point, while others saw radio's future in aviation, providing radio beacons for aircraft.

The first organization to recognize radio's importance was the military; the Navy led the way during World War I. After the war, as interest in the new medium increased, a totally new function emerged. Radio was used to broadcast information and entertainment to a mass audience. Many individuals and organizations scrambled to make use of this new means of communication: the telephone company, newspapers, businesses, and even universities. None had any clear idea how radio broadcasting would pay for itself. Eventually, the radio industry became a commercial medium, dominated by big business, that in fewer than 10 years reached an audience of 50 million. Radio

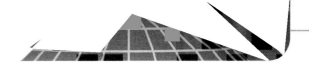

changed America's news and entertainment habits and became a medium whose influence on popular culture is still being felt.

Compare radio's development with that of the Internet, which was started by the Department of Defense to improve military communication. When first developed, the Internet was envisioned as a means of point-to-point communication. It gained popularity through the efforts of scientists and amateur computer enthusiasts. When the World Wide Web and newsgroups offered a place where anyone could post messages and reach a large potential audience, businesses, educational organizations, government agencies, and individuals all scrambled to stake out a site. Everybody is currently trying to figure out how to make websites profitable. Will the Web eventually become primarily a commercial medium dominated by big business? Will it change the way we get our news and entertainment? What sort of cultural impact will it have? History may help us answer these questions.

You have probably heard the old joke about the guy who was annoyed because he couldn't see the forest because of all the trees, or couldn't see the blizzard because of all the snow, or couldn't see the city because of all the tall buildings (you probably get the idea by now). Well, sometimes it can be hard to see history because of all the names, places, dates, and events. Consequently, this chapter steps back and takes a broad view of media history, emphasizing major events and general trends. It also provides additional background information by examining communication in the days before mass communication developed.

Specifically, this chapter discusses seven milestones in the development of human communication: language, writing, printing, telegraph and telephone, photography and motion pictures, radio and television, and digital media. A potential eighth milestone is the advent of wireless handheld media. (See Figure 3–1.) It is hoped that this overview of the historical and cultural context of mass communication will supplement and make more meaningful the specific histories of the various media presented in Parts II and III of this book.

 LANGUAGE

Our prehuman ancestors must have had some means of communication, probably nonverbal—maybe using gestures and body movements—and then eventually developed verbal communication using a spoken language. But why? Why didn't humans continue to depend on nonverbal communication and use their mouths just for eating and breathing? Such a scenario is certainly possible. Hearing- and speech-impaired people do this. What made spoken language superior? The truth is that we're not sure. Several theories have been advanced to explain the phenomenon. One theory notes that sign language is not very effective in the dark. If prehistoric humans were to be successful while hunting or moving about at night, they had to work out other means of communicating. Charles Darwin argued that language superseded gesture because language left both hands free to work with tools or handle weapons. Whatever the reason, early humans talked rather than gestured. *When* they started talking is another question that is hard to answer. Some scholars think the inception of verbal communication dates back hundreds of thousands of years; others suggest it developed around 40,000 B.C.

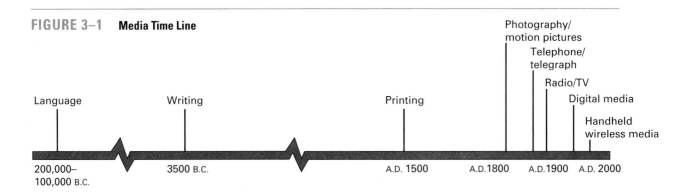

FIGURE 3–1   **Media Time Line**

How exactly did language develop? Again, nobody knows for sure. There are some picturesque theories (see Soundbyte, "You Don't Say"), but none seems entirely adequate. What is fairly certain is that language was a tremendous factor in the advance of early civilization. For example, hunting became more efficient since directions could be given to coordinate the hunt (directions to a better place to camp could be reported to others in the tribe). Further, a more defined social power structure emerged, as the strong could issue commands to the weak. Instructions for making tools or utensils could be passed on to others. Language helped develop conceptual thinking and provided a means to manipulate ideas, transmit culture, and deal with abstractions. The birth of language marked a major development in the history of the human race.

Our ancestors developed an oral culture—one that depended upon language and the spoken word. Such a society (several examples still exist today) is tremendously dependent on memory. Much of the history, beliefs, and folklore of the culture is transmitted by individuals who memorize great amounts of information and recite it to those in the next generation who, in turn, pass it on to their offspring. This has several implications. Because there is a limit to what a person can remember, the growth of knowledge and information in such a society is slow. Further, there is the risk that an advance or breakthrough will not be remembered well enough to be transmitted. The Incas, for example, apparently made great strides in architecture that were lost because the oral tradition was too fragile to preserve them.

As humans developed further, so expanded the variety of food-gathering means: Farming reduced the need to roam over large territories to seek food. Instead, small agricultural villages developed. As more and more people settled in villages and towns, it became harder to rely on the oral tradition to fulfill communication needs. Efficient farming needed a means to keep track of when to plant crops. It was also helpful to have records of who owned the domesticated animals that were part of the village. As the village's population grew, it was useful to monitor what belonged to each family. This need to keep more detailed, permanent, and accessible records was probably the impetus behind the next great communications revolution—writing.

 # WRITING

Two problems had to be solved before a system of writing was invented. The first had to do with deciding what symbols were to be used to represent spoken sounds or ideas. The second involved selecting the surface on which to write the symbols.

>> Sign Writing versus Phonetic Writing

The first problem was solved in two ways. One early symbol system might be called *sign writing,* in which each symbol was based on a picture that resembled the thing it stood for. Thus, a circle with wavy lines radiating from it might stand for the sun, while a series of wavy lines stacked on top of each other might stand for water. One early form of this style of writing developed in Sumeria (present-day Iraq) about 3500 B.C. A second, more familiar example developed in Egypt a few hundred years later and came to be known as *hieroglyphics.* The most durable form of sign writing blossomed in China about 2000 to 1500 B.C. This method required learning thousands of different pictographs that represented various objects and actions.

The second type of writing system was based more on sound than signs. A group of letters, called an **alphabet,** was used to symbolize each of the sounds that make up a word. The Phoenicians are generally credited with having developed the alphabet being used to write this sentence. The Phoenicians were sea traders, and their invention gradually spread across the Mediterranean to Greece, where a standard alphabet of 24 letters was constructed. The epic poems of Homer were put into written form about 800 B.C. Later, the Romans modified the Greek alphabet into the 26 letters that are now standard in English. The alphabet was a more efficient way of writing than the pictographs used by the Egyptians and Chinese. For example, a computer keyboard with 47 keys can easily write any sentence in English complete with numbers and all punctuation marks. To do the same in the Chinese pictograph system would require about 9,000 keys. Eventually, even the pictographs used by the Egyptians evolved into an alphabet based on sounds.

>> Clay versus Paper

The problem of selecting a writing surface was solved in various ways. The Sumerians used soft clay tablets and a wedge-shaped tool to record their pictographs. Clay was inexpensive and durable (many of the Sumerian clay tablets still exist today). On the other hand, tablets were not very transportable, and it was difficult to make fine lines and delicate markings in clay. The Egyptians made papyrus from a plant that grew in the Nile region. Strips of papyrus were woven together, soaked, and pounded together into a flat surface that was polished with a rock until smooth. Hieroglyphics were painted or scratched on the papyrus with a brush or a pen. The Greeks wrote on parchment, made from treated animal hides. Parchment was more durable than papyrus but much more expensive to manufacture. Sheets of parchment or papyrus could be stitched together into long scrolls. It was the Chinese who developed the writing surface that was to become the standard—paper. Mixtures of rags, tree bark, and other fibrous materials were soaked in tubs, pounded with mallets, pressed into sheets, and left to dry in the sun. The resulting paper had many advantages: It was lightweight, cheap, and easy to write on. Moreover, sheets of paper could be stacked and bound together, producing what we today would recognize as a book. The Chinese were making paper by about A.D. 100, but it took nearly another thousand years before paper became widely used in Europe.

>> Social Impact of Writing

The arrival of writing carried with it several consequences for early society. In the first place, it created a new division in society. Before writing, almost everybody had about the same degree of communication skills if they could speak and hear. But not everybody could read and write. Those who could had access to information not available to the rest of the population. And, as is usually the case, with greater access to information comes greater access to power. This power was concentrated in the rulers and the scribes who served the ruler. In Egypt, for example, only privileged children, who would later become priests or government scribes for the pharaohs, were taught to read and write.

Second, writing helped make possible the creation of empires. Writing made organization easier. Tax collection records could be kept more efficiently, as could the accounts of payments. An army could be established and paid regularly. Written orders to commanders simplified administration. Writing helped develop trade and increased a country's treasury. Although it is difficult to say what role writing played in its development, it is probably no coincidence that the first Egyptian dynasty under Menes (the ruler who united upper and lower Egypt and established a capital at Memphis) came into being about the same time as the Egyptians were developing their hieroglyphics. Additionally, writing helped establish and maintain both the Greek and the Roman empires. Note that this is not to say that writing caused empires to develop; other political, economic, and social conditions had to be present as well. But it is probably safe to say that writing made it *easier* for these empires to come about.

A third, more subtle, effect had to do with the nature of knowledge itself. For the first time, it was possible to preserve and nourish a permanent body of knowledge. Before writing, the transmission of knowledge from one generation to the next was hampered by the limits of human memory and distortion. Knowledge that was written down, however, could be stored. The Greeks established the Great Library at

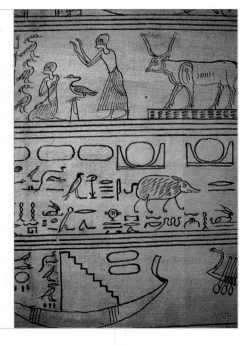

Early forms of picture writing such as this were developed in Sumeria and Egypt about 5,000 years ago.

The growth of international travel and global marketing has started a trend back toward pictographic communication, a method that cuts across languages. Airports all over the world, for example, have adopted a common pictograph system with symbols that denote baggage claim, rest rooms, ground transportation, and the like. Many products also use pictographs to convey information. See if you can identify what the following pictographs represent. (Answers are below.)

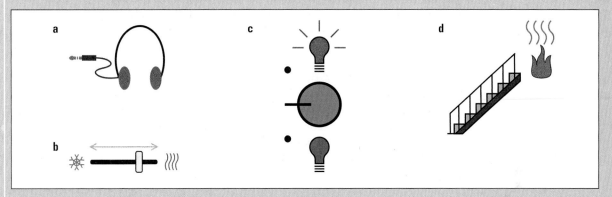

(a) headphone plug; (b) defroster in car; (c) power switch; (d) fire escape.

Alexandria around 311 B.C., which eventually contained about a half-million scrolls. Scholars from all over the Greek world came to Alexandria to use the library and to further increase the store of knowledge.

Finally, writing made it possible to develop a consistent and enduring code of laws. Before the written word, legal decisions were made by local judges representing the particular village or community where they were located. There was no general, overarching, impersonal body of law on which decisions were based. With writing, law became tangible in the establishment of codes that transcended locale and individual circumstances. The first great legal document in history, the Code of Hammurabi, was written in Sumeria around 2000 B.C.

>> **The Middle Ages**

The Roman Empire came to an end around the sixth century and was followed by the feudal period in Europe. By this time, books were becoming more numerous but were far from common. Early books were copied by hand by scribes, a long and laborious process. As Christianity spread through Europe, bookmaking became centered in monasteries, where monks, writing on parchment in individual carrels, would carefully copy and illustrate the most important religious books of the period. Sometimes the original was garbled in the process since spelling varied widely from place to place, and many authors used abbreviations known only to them. The resulting volumes were treated as works of art and were closely guarded; some were even chained to keep them from being taken from the monastery. Another problem with many of the early books was that, once written, they disappeared forever in the monastery's library because there was no way for others to find them. Books were placed on the shelf in the order in which they were acquired by the library. There was no filing according to subject or author. Scholars had to depend on the librarian's memory to find anything. (Umberto

Eco's 1980 novel, *The Name of the Rose,* provides a fascinating description of a medieval library.)

As trade increased throughout medieval Europe, the need for information grew. Merchants needed to keep track of financial information and to document the various currencies in circulation. The idea of a university probably originated in India and North Africa and eventually spread to Europe. The University of Paris was founded around 1150. Oxford began holding classes in the same century. As the feudal system gave way to strong, centralized monarchies, governments needed more information to help collect taxes and defend their borders. Lawyers needed to record the outcomes of legal cases. All this demand helped move the process of bookmaking away from the monastery and into lay society. Writing shops, or *scriptoria,* opened all across the continent. The copying business was helped by the widespread introduction of paper, which had finally made its way into Europe from China. Books copied on paper were cheaper than books on parchment, but they were still expensive. If you wanted a copy of a book in the early 14th century, for example, you would have to hire a scribe; negotiate a price; decide on the ink color, binding, and illustrations; and then wait, maybe as long as a year, for the book to be produced.

Demand for books still outran supply, however, and there were not enough scribes to handle all the work. Consequently, the scribes were able to charge even higher fees, and books became even more a medium of the elite. Economic and social progress seemed to have hit a roadblock.

This problem was solved around 1450 with the invention of the printing press and movable type, the third of our communication milestones.

PRINTING

The invention of printing is actually a story of many inventions. One of these was the development of paper by the Chinese. China was also responsible for the development of block printing—character outlines were carved out of a block of wood, and the raised parts were inked and pressed against a piece of paper. The oldest surviving block-printed book was published in 868. The Chinese also perfected a system of movable type, first using clay and later blocks of wood for individual characters. The Koreans were experimenting with movable metal type by the beginning of the 15th century.

The next major invention occurred in Germany, where Johann Gutenberg is generally credited with developing a printing press that used movable metal type. Gutenberg published his famous Bible around 1453, and his new printing method quickly spread across Europe. Only 30 years after Gutenberg's Bible appeared, there were printing presses in more than 110 towns in western Europe alone. The total increase in the number of books available in Europe is impossible to calculate, but it is probably safe to say that by 1500 there were hundreds of times more books available than in 1450. As books proliferated, their cost went down. Although still expensive, books were no longer the exclusive possession of the very rich. The printed book could now be afforded by those who were simply relatively prosperous.

The consequences of the printing revolution are so far-reaching and extensive that it is impossible to discuss all of them. Most scholars seem to agree, however, on the most significant results.

Johann Gutenberg was a wine connoisseur as well as a metallurgist. His design for the printing press was borrowed from a similar device used in wine making.

>> Effects of the Gutenberg Revolution

The printing press facilitated the development of vernacular (everyday) languages across the European continent. Most of the pre–printing press, hand-lettered books had been written in Latin—the language of the Catholic Church and of higher education. Reading these works therefore required the knowledge of a second language, which restricted the type of people who might use them to the educated elite. Many early printers, however, recognized that a broader market for their books would be available if they were published in French, German, or English. Many printers also felt closer ties to their home country than to the Church, further encouraging the printing of books in native languages. This trend had other consequences. Bodies of information now became more accessible to more people, further encouraging the growth of literacy, and, in turn, prompting more books to be published. Finally, the use of the vernacular probably helped prepare the wave of nationalism that swept Europe in succeeding centuries.

The printing press played a role in the religious upheaval that swept Europe in the 16th century. Before the press, those clerics who disagreed with the doctrines and policies of the church had limited channels for expression. Handwritten copies of their views were few, had limited circulation, and could easily be censored or confiscated by authorities. The situation was forever changed after Gutenberg. Theologian and religious reformer Martin Luther's writings were translated from Latin into the vernacular, printed as pamphlets, and distributed all over Europe. It has been estimated that it took only a month for his famous Ninety-five Theses (the ones he nailed to the church door in Wittenberg, Germany) to be diffused across Europe. One of his later pamphlets sold 4,000 copies in a month. Despite efforts by the church to confiscate and burn Luther's writings, the Reformation movement continued. In addition, the printing of the Bible in the vernacular meant that individuals now had direct access to the core of their religious belief system. The Bible could now be read directly and interpreted individually; there was no need for clerical intervention. This increased access to information further weakened the power of the Catholic Church, and helped the spread of Protestantism.

Moreover, the arrival of printing speeded up the publication of scientific research. Although it would still be considered agonizingly slow today in an era of e-mail and the Internet, printing a book of scientific findings took far less time than it did when manuscripts were handwritten. Printing also ensured that identical texts would be read by scientists in different countries and helped them build on the work of others. Galileo and Newton made their contributions to science in the 17th century, after advances in 16th-century printing.

The printing press even helped exploration. The efforts of the Vikings are little known, due in part to the fact that they explored during a time when it was difficult to record and publicize their exploits. Columbus visited America after printing developed, and his deeds were widely known in Europe a year after his return. Printed accounts of the discoveries of early explorers found a ready audience among those eager to find wealth and/or bring religion to the New World. Many early developers published glowing (and sometimes overly optimistic) accounts of life in the new lands, hoping to promote investments and help business. The journeys of the early voyagers were helped by printed books that contained navigational and geographic information about the Americas.

Further, the printing press had a profound effect on the growth of scholarship and knowledge. Whereas access to handwritten textbooks was difficult, university students now had printed texts. (Think how hard it would be to take this course if everybody in the class had to use just one textbook.) As the number of books increased, so did the number of students who studied at a university. Literacy increased further. Interest in the classical works of Greece and Rome was revived as they appeared in printed books that were read by many. Books based on the scholarship of other countries appeared. The advances in mathematics made by the Indians, Muslims, and Arabs were disseminated. Without the printing press, the Renaissance of the 16th century might not have occurred.

Finally, the printing press led to the development of what we would today call *news*. As will be discussed in Chapter 4, early newspapers sprang up in Europe at the beginning of the 17th century. These early publications were primarily concerned with foreign news. It wasn't long, however, before these early papers focused on domestic news as well. This development did not sit well with some early monarchies, and government attempts to suppress or censor news content were not unusual. It took until the end of the 17th century to establish the notion of a press free of government control (more on this topic in Chapter 4). The early newspapers made government and political leaders more visible to the public and helped create a climate for political change in both Europe and America.

>> Technology and Cultural Change

Before leaving this topic, we should note that it is easy to ascribe too much significance to the printing press. It is easy to assume that the printing press was the prime mover behind all the effects mentioned. Such a view is called **technological determinism**—the belief that technology drives historical change. A more moderate position suggests that technology functions with various social, economic, and cultural forces to help bring about change. Printing did not cause the Reformation, but it probably helped it occur. And vernacular languages were growing in importance before Gutenberg, but his invention certainly helped them along. In any case, the birth of printing marks the beginning of what we have defined as *mass communication*, and it is certainly a momentous event in Western history.

The next centuries brought further refinements to printing. A metal press was developed by the late 1790s; steam power to drive the press was added shortly thereafter. Advances in printing technology helped usher in the penny press, a truly mass newspaper (see Chapter 4). A better grade of paper made from wood pulp came into use in the 1880s, about the same time as the Linotype machine, a device that could compose and justify a whole line of metal type. Photoengraving brought better visuals to the paper in the 1890s, as did the development of halftone photography a few decades later. Hot metal type gave way to photocomposition and offset printing in the 1970s and 1980s, and the computer ushered in an age of relatively cheap desktop printing a few years later. Printing has changed a great deal over the years, but its consequences are still much with us.

The next two communication milestones occurred during what many have called the age of invention and discovery, the period roughly encompassing the 17th, 18th, and 19th centuries. The reasons behind the many achievements of this period are several. The great explorations of previous centuries had brought different cultures together, and scholars were able to share ideas and concepts. Further, there was a change in the way people generated knowledge itself. The traditional authority of the Catholic Church was eroding, and intellectuals looked less to revelation as a source of knowledge and more toward reason and observation. Philosophers such as Bacon, Descartes, and Locke argued for systematic research based on what the senses could perceive. In addition, scientific societies in Italy, France, and Great Britain helped advance the frontiers of knowledge. And, as already mentioned, the printing press helped distribute news of current discoveries to all, prompting others to achieve new breakthroughs. Whatever the reasons, these three centuries saw such advances as Galileo's use of the telescope and the notion of a heliocentric solar system; the theory of blood circulating through the body; Newton's theory of gravitation; the roots of modern chemistry; electricity; and the discovery of microscopic bacteria. Inventions came along at a dizzying rate: the steam engine, the locomotive, the plow, the internal combustion engine, the automobile, the sewing machine, the dynamo, and a host of others. Not surprisingly, the field of communication also saw major developments, as the next two milestones demonstrate.

CONQUERING SPACE AND TIME: THE TELEGRAPH AND TELEPHONE

It is appropriate that we spend some time discussing the telegraph and telephone, two related technologies that presaged many of the features of today's media world. For instance, the telegraph harnessed electricity; it demonstrated the technology that would eventually be used in radio. It was also the first medium to use digital communication (dots and dashes). The telephone, with its interconnected network of wires and switchboards, introduced the same concept now at the core of the Internet: Everybody was linked to everybody else.

>> Development of the Telegraph

It is difficult for people raised in an age of cellular phones, CNN, fax machines, e-mail, and the Internet to appreciate the tremendous excitement that greeted the development of the telegraph. Before the appearance of the telegraph in the early 19th century, messages could travel only as fast as the fastest form of transportation (with some minor exceptions). A messenger on horseback would clop along at around 15 to 20 miles an hour. A train carrying sacks of mail could travel about 30 miles in an hour. The fastest form of message transportation was the carrier pigeon, which could cover more than 35 miles an hour. Then along came the telegraph, which sent messages traveling over wires at the almost unbelievable speed of 186,000 miles per second, the speed of light itself. No wonder that, when it first appeared, the telegraph was described as the great "annihilator of time and space." It was the first device that made possible instantaneous point-to-point communication at huge distances. It was also the forerunner of what we today might call, to use an overworked cliché, the *information superhighway.*

The technology necessary for the telegraph dates back to the discovery of electricity. Many early inventors realized that electricity could be used to send messages simply by varying the time the current was on and off. Experiments with early versions of the telegraph (*telegraph* comes from Greek words meaning "to write at a distance") were performed in the late 1700s. By the 1830s and 1840s workable telegraph systems had been developed in England and in the United States.

Samuel Morse was the principal force behind the creation of the telegraph in America. His device consisted of a sending key, a wire, and a receiver that made marks on a paper tape in concert with changes in the electrical current. Later versions let the operator read messages by listening to the clicks made by the receiver and did away with the paper tape. To simplify message transmission, Morse developed a code consisting of dots and dashes that is still in use today.

Morse demonstrated his device in the late 1830s and eventually received a grant from the government to continue his work. He constructed a line between Baltimore and Washington, D.C., and opened the nation's first telegraph service with the famous message, "What hath God wrought?"

>> Cultural Impact of the Telegraph

Public reaction to the new machine was a combination of awe and amazement. The telegraph wires that swayed between poles were called *lightning lines.* The early telegraph offices set out chairs so that spectators could watch as messages came in from distant cities. Some people refused to believe the new invention worked until they traveled to the source of the telegraphic message and verified it with the sender. Some were afraid that all that electricity flowing around above them posed a danger to their health, and they refused to walk under the wires.

SOUNDBYTE

Skeptic

Some were skeptical about the benefits of the telegraph. Maine might be able to talk to Texas, but, as Henry David Thoreau pointed out, what if Maine and Texas have nothing important to talk about?

Despite these fears, the telegraph grew quickly and the lightning lines quickly crisscrossed the nation. By 1850 almost every city on the expanding Western frontier could communicate with every other city. Maine could talk to Texas at the speed of light. By 1866 a cable had been laid underneath the Atlantic Ocean, linking Europe and America. Four years later, the overland wires and undersea cable carried more than 30 million telegraphic messages (telegrams).

The telegraph was changing communication at about the same time another invention was changing transportation—the railroad. Interestingly, the telegraph wires generally followed the railroad tracks, and station masters were often the first telegraphers. The telegraph made it possible to keep track of train locations and coordinate the complex job of shipping goods to various parts of the country—particularly to the West. The telegraph helped the train bring settlers to the frontier and played a role in the country's westward expansion.

The conduct of war was changed by the telegraph. Troops could be mobilized quickly and moved, usually by railroad, in response to tactical and strategic developments. The significance of the telegraph for the military was demonstrated many times during the Civil War.

Morse's invention had an impact on commerce as well. It sped up communication between buyers and sellers, reported transactions, and organized deliveries.

Alexander Graham Bell demonstrates a later version of his telephone for representatives of the business community. Bell and his colleagues eventually received 30 patents for telephone-related inventions.

Instant communication brought about standard prices in the commodity markets. Before the telegraph, the price of corn varied with local market conditions and might be several dollars cheaper in Chicago than in St. Louis. After the telegraph connected all markets, local variations were evened out.

Further, as we will discuss in more detail in Chapter 4, the telegraph greatly enhanced the newspaper's ability to transmit news. Information from distant places had previously taken weeks to reach the newspaper office. With the telegraph and Atlantic cable, even news from Europe could make the next day's edition. Newspaper publishers were quick to recognize the potential of this new device and used it heavily. Many incorporated the word "Telegraph" into their name. The telegraph also helped the formation of news agencies, or *wire services* as they were also called. The Associated Press made great use of the expanding telegraphic service to supply news to its customers. Finally, the telegraph changed the style of reporting. Since the early telegraph companies charged by the word, news stories became shorter. Rather than wordy, reflective, and interpretive reports, scoops, breaking news, and the bare facts began to characterize news reports after the telegraph.

>> Government and Media

The telegraph also set the precedent for the relationship between the government and large media companies. In many other countries, since the telegraph was used to deliver messages, it seemed an extension of the post office, and the government agency that assumed responsibility for the postal service also administered the telegraph. This model was not followed in the United States. Although some in the government endorsed a federal takeover of the telegraph system, the prevailing sentiment was in favor of private, commercial development. By the end of the 19th century, telegraphic communication was dominated by a large company, Western Union. As we shall see in later chapters, other mass media—motion pictures, radio, television—were also developed as private rather than government enterprises and were dominated by one or more large companies.

>> A Change in Perspective

Another consequence of the telegraph was subtler and harder to describe. In some ways, the telegraph changed the way people thought about their country and the world. By erasing the constraints of space, the telegraph had the potential to function as an instant linkage device (see Chapter 2) that tied people together. Morse wrote how the telegraph would make a neighborhood of the whole country. A Philadelphia newspaper, shortly after the successful demonstration of the device, wrote that the telegraph destroyed the notion of "elsewhere" and made everywhere "here." The paper declared the telegraph would "make the whole land one being." An article in a magazine of the period was even more expansive:

The telegraph "binds together by a vital cord all nations of the earth." It may not be too much of an overstatement to contend that the telegraph introduced the notion of a global village that was to be popularized a hundred years or so later by Marshall McLuhan. It created a sense of unity among Americans and encouraged them to think in national and international terms.

The telegraph was joined by a companion invention, the telephone. Like the Morse invention, the telephone also conquered time and space and had the added advantage of requiring no special skills, such as Morse code, for its use. It transmitted the human voice from point to point. There was some confusion over the precise role the telephone would play in society, but eventually the notion of linking phone users by wires and the development of the switchboard made it possible to connect one place with many others. This arrangement helped it become a fixture in businesses and homes across the nation. The telephone made private communication easier to achieve. It was now possible for people to converse away from the watchful eyes of parents, bosses, and other authority figures. Finally, like the telegraph industry, the telephone industry would also be dominated by a large corporation, AT&T, which would eventually gain control of Western Union.

In sum, the telegraph and the telephone enabled people to communicate over vast distances in what we now call *real time* and had far-reaching impact on the political, economic, and social development of the United States and the rest of the world. We will discuss this impact in detail throughout the book. In many ways, it is still making itself felt today.

CAPTURING THE IMAGE: PHOTOGRAPHY AND MOTION PICTURES

The telegraph and the telephone drew upon advances in the science of electricity. The next communication advance we will examine could not have occurred without advances in the field of chemistry.

>> Early Technological Development

Two things are required to permanently store an image. First, there must be a way to focus an image on a surface. Second, the surface must be permanently altered as a result of exposure to the image. The first requirement was fulfilled in the 16th century with the creation of the camera obscura, a dark chamber with a pinhole in one wall. The light rays that entered the chamber through the small hole projected an image on the opposite wall. The second requirement took longer to achieve. In the 1830s, two Frenchmen, Joseph Niepce and Louis Daguerre, experimented with various substances that changed upon exposure to light rays. Silver iodide provided the best results, and Daguerre sold this discovery to the French government. An English scientist, William Fox Talbot, working at about the same time as Daguerre, refined the process by capturing his images on paper in the form of negatives, permitting copies to be made. Other advances quickly followed, including the use of flexible celluloid film. George Eastman's company introduced the Kodak box camera in the 1890s with the slogan "You press a button. We do the rest." The Kodak was designed for the mass market. Amateur photographers simply loaded a roll of film in the camera, pressed the button, and sent the film off to Kodak to be developed, printed, and returned to the photographer.

There were several long-range consequences of these technological advances. Early photos (called *Daguerreotypes*) required long exposure times, making them particularly suitable for portraits, for which the subject could remain still. These early portraits provided a way to preserve and humanize history. Our images of George Washington, for example, are from paintings that show him in an idealized manner, usually in noble poses making him appear distinguished and powerful. Our images of Abraham Lincoln, however, come from the many photographs that were taken of him during his term in office. The early photos, done around 1860, showed him in flattering poses. The later photos, taken after years of war, showed a man grown visibly older, with lines creasing his forehead and tired eyes.

>> Mathew Brady

The Civil War was the first American war to be photographed. Before the camera, the public's view of war was probably shaped mostly by paintings and etchings that showed magnificent cavalry charges and brave soldiers vanquishing the

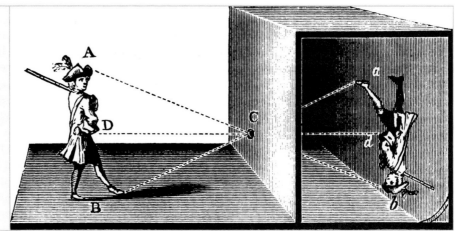

In the camera obscura, a small opening containing a lens produces an inverted and reversed image of an object. Many artists used the camera obscura to help them draw precise images of people, landscapes, and buildings.

Mathew Brady's famous 1864 photo of a war-weary Abraham Lincoln. Part of this portrait was later used on the five-dollar bill.

enemy, not the horror and the carnage of combat. Mathew Brady persuaded the U.S. government to give him access to the battlefield. (Brady apparently thought the government would cover the costs of his venture, but his expectations were never met, and many of his photos were lost. See Media Probe, "Mathew Brady and His War Photos.") Because early photography was not able to capture action scenes, Brady was limited to photographing scenes of the aftermath of a battle. These images, however, were powerful enough. In 1862, Brady's colleagues photographed the battleground at Antietam just two days after the battle and before all the dead had been buried. The resulting photographs were the first to show the actual casualties of war. When the photos went on view in a New York gallery, they caused a sensation. The carnage of battle was revealed to all. As Oliver Wendell Holmes remarked, "Let him who wishes to know what war is like look at this series of illustrations." A hundred years later, other communication advances would bring scenes of horror from the Vietnam War directly into American living rooms.

Photography had an impact on art. Now that a means had been developed to preserve realistic images, artists were free to experiment and develop different ways of portraying the world. Again, although it is hard to say how much of a role photography played in influencing painting, the impressionist, postimpressionist, and cubist schools of painting came to prominence at about this same time. At the other end of the spectrum, photography itself became a fine art, as virtuosos such as Alfred Steiglitz, Margaret Bourke-White, and Edward Steichen created masterpieces of graphic reproduction.

>> Photography's Influence on Mass Culture

One did not have to be an artist, however, to take pictures. Everybody could and did. Advances in film and camera technology put cameras in the hands of the masses. Ordinary people took photos of significant people, objects, and events: marriages, new babies, new cars, pets, vacations, family reunions, proms, and so on. Photo albums quickly became a part of each family's library. Photography enabled each generation to make a permanent record of its personal history.

Advances in the printing process, such as halftone photography, made it possible for photographs to be published in magazines and newspapers. By the beginning of the 20th century, dozens of illustrated dailies and weeklies were published in the United States. This development created a new profession—**photojournalism**—and changed America's conception of news. Photojournalism reached new popularity in the 1920s when the pace of life increased, and many innovations cropped up that promised to save time for the consumer—lunch counters for fast meals, express trains, washing machines, vacuum cleaners, and so forth. When it came to news reporting, the biggest time-saver was the picture. Readers could look at photos more quickly than they could read the long text of a story. As a consequence, printed columns decreased and space devoted to pictures increased, helping popularize the tabloids and picture magazines such as *Life* (see Chapter 5).

Photojournalism had more subtle effects as well. First, it changed the definition of *news* itself. Increasingly, news became that which could be shown. Accidents, natural disasters, demonstrations, and riots were natural photo opportunities. This visual bias in news reporting continues to be a topic of concern even today. Second, as photo historian Vicki Goldberg put it, photography created "a communal reservoir of images." Certain historic events were fixed forever in the minds of the public by their photos: the fiery crash of the *Hindenberg,* the young girl screaming over the body of a dead student at Kent State, the smoking remains of the World Trade Center, the toppling of the statue of Saddam Hussein in Baghdad. All of these images have been etched permanently on the national consciousness.

>> ## Pictures in Motion

The technology behind photography led to the development of another way to capture an image. The goal behind *this* new milestone, however, was to capture an image in motion. Chapter 9 details the early history of the motion picture medium and traces how it evolved from a series of toys into a giant entertainment industry. It is significant that this new medium evolved while three significant trends were occurring in the United States. The first was industrialization. The Industrial Revolution, which began in the early 19th century, continued into the 20th century. Production and manufacturing both increased significantly. Along with industrialization came the second trend, urbanization, as people moved into the cities to be near the plants and factories where they could find jobs. In the United States, one-fourth of all Americans lived in an urban area by 1914. The third trend was immigration. About 25 million people immigrated into the United States between 1871 and 1914, and most of them wound up in cities where they went to work in manufacturing plants.

The culmination of these trends was the creation of an audience that was drawn to the new medium of motion pictures. The first movie houses sprang up in the

Some news photos, such as this one of the ruins of the World Trade Center, are forever etched in the national consciousness.

cities. They were called *nickelodeons*, storefronts that had been turned into makeshift theaters, with uncomfortable benches or folding chairs for the audience, a tinkling piano, and poor ventilation. Nonetheless, nickelodeons were big hits among the newly arrived immigrants. By 1910 there were more than 10,000 of these nickelodeons around the country, and film exhibitors and filmmakers quickly recognized that there was a market for filmed entertainment. The motion picture business had started. Film eventually moved to plusher theaters and tried to appeal to the middle class, but it left its mark on the immigrant population. Many learned the customs and culture of their new country from nickelodeons.

>> Motion Pictures and American Culture

The long-range impact of the motion picture lay mainly in the areas of entertainment and culture. As the demand grew for feature-length films, only very large companies were able to come up with the money needed to pay production costs. As will be noted in Chapter 9, these large companies came to dominate the production, distribution, and exhibition of movies. Today's film industry is controlled by global conglomerates that still follow many of the patterns established in the 1920s.

Movies forever altered America's leisure time. Vaudeville soon died out. Going to the movies became an important social activity for the young. Saturday afternoons that once were spent going to parks and friends' houses were now spent inside a darkened theater.

The movies became a major cultural institution. Photography and the mass-appeal newspaper had made it easier for people to recognize and follow the fortunes of their favorite celebrities, but motion pictures raised this process to a new level. Hollywood produced cultural icons, the movie stars. The popularity of motion pictures was based on their appeal to all social classes. Unlike serious drama, opera, and ballet, which appealed to the elite, movies attracted the masses. The movies helped bring about the notion of a popular culture, a phenomenon whose benefits and liabilities are still being debated.

In 1915, American poet Vachel Lindsay published *The Art of the Moving Picture.* This volume signaled the beginnings of a new popular art form. Lindsay's book was the first of many serious attempts to develop a theory of film. Although a popular entertainment form that blended business and art, film soon became a topic worth serious study, a trend still with us today as evidenced by the many universities that teach film as part of their curricula.

The cultural influence of television is sometimes subtle. Shows, such as cable network TLC's "Trading Spaces," revived interest in home remodeling and interior design.

important source of socialization among children and that TV programs inspire antisocial and other undesirable behavior. (Chapter 18 reviews the evidence for these assertions.)

Although the telegraph was the first to be called the "great annihilator of time and space," it appears that television might be a better candidate for that title. Audiences have seen TV pictures live from Baghdad, Earth's orbit, the moon, and Mars (well, as live as they can be from a place so far away). In fact, today's TV viewer expects to see live reports of breaking stories, no matter where they are; no place seems far away anymore.

Photography was credited with creating a reservoir of communal experience. Television, however, has widened and deepened that reservoir. For example, televised images of President Kennedy's funeral, the *Apollo 11* moon landing, the *Challenger* explosion, and the planes striking the World Trade Center have all been indelibly impressed upon the national consciousness.

THE DIGITAL REVOLUTION

In his book *Being Digital*, Nicholas Negroponte, director of MIT's Media Laboratory, summed up the digital revolution as the difference between atoms and bits. Traditionally, the mass media delivered information in the form of atoms: Books, newspapers, magazines, CDs, and videocassettes are material products that have weight and size and are physically distributed. Negroponte maintains that this is rapidly changing: "The slow human handling of most information in the form of [recorded music], books, magazines, newspapers, and videocassettes is about to become the instantaneous transfer of electronic data that move at the speed of light." In short, atoms will give way to bits.

As an example, consider the difference between e-mail and traditional paper mail. In the traditional system, a letter must be placed in an envelope with a postage stamp and given to the U.S. Postal Service, where employees sort it and from which they transport it and deliver it a few days later to its recipient. E-mail needs no paper, no postage, and no delivery by postal carriers. It is a series of bits of information that travels electronically and is delivered in seconds rather than days. With e-mail, the same message can be copied a thousand times and sent to a thousand different people much more quickly and cheaply than with paper mail.

At the risk of oversimplifying a rather complicated topic, we can describe **digital technology** as a system that encodes information—sound, text, data, graphics, video—into a series of on-and-off pulses that are usually denoted as zeros and

All the communication milestones discussed in this chapter changed the way information was stored or transmitted. Starting with the printing press, they all expanded the scope of human communication by making it possible for people to share information with other people in other places or at other times. This achievement prompted a rather optimistic attitude toward the social benefits of the media. The text points out how the telegraph was viewed as a force for morality, understanding, and peace. Both radio and TV were touted as means of bringing education, high culture, and refinement to the masses. Cable TV was supposed to bring new forms of entertainment to minority groups and open the way for two-way TV that would aid the democratic process by making possible electronic polling. None of these things has yet come to pass. Nonetheless, the Internet, with its ability to connect everybody to everybody, is currently being touted as an information revolution that will affect society as deeply as the printing press. Whether this will happen is a matter of debate, but for now it might be useful to ask if new communication technologies automatically carry with them social benefits. Have they been liberating or constrictive?

A number of social critics have pointed out that new communication media expand the potential for freedom of expression and have greatly enlarged the scope of human culture. The cost of sending messages over long distances has dramatically decreased. Thanks to the telegraph, telephone, and Internet, people can do business, socialize, and argue with people all over the world. The new media have made information available to all. And, if information is power, the new media will empower more individuals. New means of communication make it easier for democracy to function. Film,

radio, and TV have opened up new art forms and patterns of entertainment.

Others suggest a different interpretation. The new communication media have spurred the growth of large conglomerate owners whose main goal is profit, not cultural enrichment. Further, new communication media create an overload of information, some of it overpowering and pervasive, such as commercials, junk e-mail, and telemarketing. The information made available by the new technologies may be neither interesting nor useful nor profound, and it may interfere with people's attempts to identify the truly significant.

Moreover, although technological advances—such as the telegraph, telephone, and Internet—have expanded the scope of communication, is any of the communication worthwhile? Check out any chat room and you will probably find that much of the communication consists of greetings, good-byes, flirting, and "how-are-you's." Newsgroups exchange recipes, talk about sports, review cigar brands, and discuss other information that most could live without. How much real dialogue actually occurs? Is it possible to have a meaningful conversation with people whom you can't see and who may not even be who they say they are? The new media have done little to promote political participation. Voter turnout in the United States continues to decline, and political apathy continues to increase. Most people would probably stay at home and watch TV instead of going to a political forum. Further, many critics would argue that the new media have provided little that is new and fresh in the arts and entertainment. Expanded TV channels have brought us more of the same.

In sum, advances in communication media have the potential for both positive and negative consequences.

---

ones. Once digitized, the information can be duplicated easily and transported at extremely low costs.

As will be discussed in Chapter 11, the computer was the first device to use the digital system to process information. The innovation quickly spread to other media. Digital technology makes possible the special effects now common in motion pictures and television as well as digital audio, digital video, digital photography, and digital equivalents of newspapers, magazines, and books.

The development of the Internet meant that computers could send digital information to all parts of the globe. All of a sudden, a new distribution medium was available that permanently changed the media environment. In short, digital technology and the Internet triggered a revolution in the way information was stored and transmitted. As a result, the traditional mass communication media found themselves in uncharted waters and had to figure out how they were going to cope with this drastic development. Newspapers, for example, used to exist only on paper (atoms). Now they exist in both paper and digital form (bits). Big recording companies used to distribute music on tape or on disk (atoms). Napster and other music-sharing sites proved that individuals could download music files (bits) from other

The World Wide Web is ephemeral. The average life of a Web page is 100 days. After that it is changed or it simply disappears. Is it possible to maintain an archive of information for a medium that is constantly shifting?

Brewster Kahle thinks so. He has invented the Wayback Machine, the first large-scale attempt to preserve a record of the ever-changing Internet. (The Wayback Machine is named after a time-traveling device made famous in an old cartoon series from the *Rocky and Bullwinkle* show.) Every 60 days since 1996, the Wayback Machine has taken a snapshot of the World Wide Web and stored it in its memory files. As of 2003, the Wayback Machine had stored more than 10 billion pages of Web history, the equivalent of a library with 3,000 miles of shelf space or five times the size of the Library of Congress.

Why would anybody want to do that? In the first place, it produces a valuable record for future historians. The Wayback Machine contains records of now defunct dot-coms, such as online grocer WebVan or the crime site APBnews.com. An individual can also check out the early Website of amazon.com or the home page of the suicide cult Heaven's Gate. Second, it creates a significant reference source. Important research papers often become unavailable if a researcher leaves a university and his or her Web pages are deleted. Politicians who make promises on their old campaign websites can be held accountable. The Wayback Machine even has an archive of material relating to September 11. Finally, it is fun. Fans can check out the Websites of dozens of bands that have long since evaporated or examine trailers of past movies. People can go back a few years and look at their old personal pages.

The Wayback Machine is easy to use. A visitor simply types in a URL and a date range and begins surfing. Apparently, there are many people who are interested in rummaging around old digital content. The Wayback Machine received more than a million visitors in its first week.

individuals on the Internet, totally bypassing the recording companies. The chapters in Parts II and III of this book discuss how the media are adapting to the digital age.

The digital revolution, of course, has had profound impact not only on the mass media, but also on other institutions. It has, for example, transformed business. Even companies that deal in atoms rather than bits have found that they have had to devise whole new marketing and distribution schemes to capitalize on the new digital age. It is not possible (yet) to have a tennis racket physically delivered over the Internet, but you can go online, search the various sporting goods sites for bargains, and order one that appeals to you. The Postal Service or a package delivery company, however, still has to deliver the racket (atoms) to you. The importance of this new form of buying and selling has added a new noun, *e-commerce,* to the global vocabulary.

The digital revolution marked some historic milestones in 2003. More digital than conventional film cameras were sold. The dollar value of DVD rentals outpaced VHS tape rentals for the first time. The top money-making film of the summer, *Finding Nemo,* relied heavily on digital technology for its special effects. Cable TV and electronics companies announced plans for a "plug and play" device that would allow digital TVs to connect directly to cable without a set-top converter box, a development that would accelerate the transition to all-digital TV.

The potential social and cultural implications of the digital age are considerable, but there are primary considerations. First, many of the creative arts have embraced digital technology. Sculptors, graphic artists, musicians, and painters now produce digital creations.

Second, the notion of community may have to be rethought. In the past, people developed friendships based on local geography. The digital world of the Internet makes possible virtual communities based on shared needs and interests rather than locale. African Americans, for example, no matter where they live, who visit websites such as NetNoir, BlackVoices, and BlackPlanet can make friends, discuss relevant issues, and connect to African American culture and lifestyles.

Third, consider what the digital age might mean for politics. A huge amount of political information—party platforms, candidates' positions, and texts of speeches—is available in digital form on the Web. Ideally, this should result in a better-informed electorate. Moreover, fund-raising is going digital. During his campaign for the 2004 Democratic presidential nomination, Governor Howard Dean raised the bulk of his money online. The confusion and bitterness surrounding the results of the 2000 presidential election in Florida prompted many to call for a system of online voting. Indeed, the Internet raises the possibility of true direct democracy. Our current representative democracy was conceived in part as a solution to the practical problem that all the people could not be physically present in one place to debate and vote. The Internet now makes it possible for computer owners to debate and cast a ballot at home. Do we still need representatives? Should we institute "digital democracy"?

Finally, there is the problem of the "digital divide." Access to digital information is not equal. About 70 percent of middle-class homes have Internet access, compared with about 35 percent of lower-income homes. Viewed from a global perspective, the divide is much wider. As of 2003, only about 10 percent of the world's population was connected to the Internet, mostly in the developed countries. In the future, those who have access to information will have more access to power than those who do not. Will this digital divide translate into more serious social, economic, and political divisions?

THE NEXT REVOLUTION? WIRELESS HANDHELD MEDIA

More than 160 million Americans had cell phones in 2004. More than 50 million carried around laptop computers, and another seven million had **personal digital assistants (PDAs).** All of these devices share common characteristics:

- They are linked together using wireless technology.
- They are portable and make it possible for people to access information no matter where they are.
- They are interconnected and allow individuals to hook into the worldwide phone network or to the Internet.
- They combine features of mass communication and interpersonal communication.

These devices will eventually merge into one device that combines the functions of cell phone, computer, still and video camera, pager, and PDA, another example of device convergence mentioned in Chapter 1. In fact, some prototypes of these gadgets are already on the market.

These new media have the potential to transform drastically traditional media and alter American culture. Some of these effects are already apparent. Wireless media have already changed the practice of journalism. The cell phone and laptop have replaced the pencil and notebook as the principal tools of the trade (see the section on the Backpack Journalist in Chapter 12). Reporters can now send text, audio, and pictures from the field using these new devices.

Further, many mass media organizations are using wireless media to distribute their content. Subscribers to ESPN Wireless can download scores, standings, latest news, and a summary of games in progress to their phones or PDAs. The BBC offers news summaries to those who subscribe to its mobile service. Content from the *New York Times* digital edition can be downloaded to pagers, cell phones, PDAs, and laptops.

Wireless mobile media have taken on some of the surveillance functions of mass media mentioned in Chapter 2. The newest generation of cell phones allows users to take a still picture and post it on the Web in seconds. Imagine millions of Americans walking around with video-equipped cell phones. When breaking news occurs, people on the scene can take video and still photos before the media arrive. This phenomenon is already happening in Japan, where video-equipped phones are more common. In the future, we might all become reporters.

Wireless mobile media have already had an impact on American culture. Cell phones link parents and children. A recent survey estimated that by 2004, about 75 percent of all teenagers will have access to a cell phone, and 50 percent will own their own. The increasing number of teens with cell phones is due in part to parents who want their children to be prepared in the case of an emergency or who want to check up on them when they are out of the house. To a family in which parents are on the go because both hold jobs and children have to get to soccer or gymnastics practice, a cell phone may seem indispensable to keep everyone on schedule. This new phenomenon is called **mobile parenting.**

Being linked to people also makes life easier. If you are late, you can call or send a message over your PDA alerting those who are waiting for you. If you are lost, you can call for directions. If you are buying groceries for dinner, you can check to see if people want fish or chicken. There are many other examples, but the words of one 17 year old pretty well sum it up: "With my cell phone I can order pizza from anywhere." This use vividly illustrates how mobile wireless media are serving the linkage function of communication; thanks to the Internet and the cell phone network, everybody can be linked to everybody.

Mobile media have "softened" the concept of time. Cell phones have made lateness more socially acceptable. You have probably experienced this scenario several times. You are supposed to meet a friend at a restaurant at eight. At two minutes after eight, your friend calls you on your cell phone and says he is in his car only a couple of miles away and should be there in 10 minutes. If you are in contact, can you really be late?

Like most media revolutions, wireless mobile media have a downside. It is now known that the September 11 terrorists coordinated their movements by cell phone. The protesters at the 1999 World Trade Organization meeting in Seattle organized their sometimes violent demonstrations using cell phone text messages. Driving and handheld media don't mix. As everybody is aware by now, people talking on cell phones can be annoying. Most professors are not amused by cell phones ringing during lectures. Mobile media cost money. If it turns out that only the rich can afford these devices, the "digital divide" between rich and poor will only increase.

 ## CONCLUDING OBSERVATIONS

In 1981, Tony Schwartz, a telecommunications expert, published *Media: The Second God*. One section of the book titled "Communication in Year 2000" described how the communication landscape would look in the 21st century. Looking at Schwartz's book today, one is impressed with the accuracy of his predictions regarding media that already existed in 1981. There is, however, no mention of the computer as a communication device, the Internet, or cell phones. This prompts some observers to suggest that it is difficult to predict when totally new communication technologies will emerge and how they will evolve. They may have impacts that we, at the moment, cannot even fathom.

What lessons can we draw from the milestones in the development of human communication? First, it is difficult to predict the ultimate use of a new medium. When the telegraph was invented, many thought that it would have profound effects on the world order. Since nations of the world were linked by the telegraph, it was predicted that misunderstandings would cease, prejudices would vanish, and peace would reign. Things did not quite go in that direction. Alexander Graham Bell suggested that the telephone be used as a means of communication among the various rooms in a house or that phones be sold only in pairs, linking only two specific points, such as a person's office and home. Others thought the phone would serve as a sort of wired radio. When radio first started, most thought it would be used as a substitute for telegraph or telephone communication. It took a while for the idea behind broadcasting to develop. Will our predictions about the ultimate future of the Internet be any more accurate?

Second, it appears that the emergence of a new communications technology changes *but does not make extinct* those advances that came before it. The telegraph and the telephone did not kill the printed word; nor did film, radio, TV, and the Internet. Television did not make radio extinct, but it did cause a major change in the way the medium was used. Likewise, the computer, the Internet, and mobile media will probably not cause any of the traditional media to evaporate, but they will probably change the way we use these "old" media.

Figure 3–1 (see page 58) is a time line that displays when each of the eight milestones occurred. A quick examination of the figure makes clear that the pace of communication innovations has accelerated. It took humans dozens of centuries to get from language to writing. The jump from writing to printing took about 5,000 years. The telegraph and telephone cropped up only 300 years later, followed quickly by photography and motion pictures. Radio was invented only a few years after that, as was TV. The computer followed on the heels of television. In fact, a person born in 1900 and who lived 100 years (an accomplishment becoming increasingly more common) would have lived through three milestones: film, radio/TV, and computers. Each advance in communication increases our power to convey and record information, and each has played a role in prompting significant changes in our culture and society. It is becoming difficult to digest fully the impact of one communication medium before another comes on the scene.

MAIN POINTS

- Seven milestones in the evolution of human communication are language, writing, printing, telegraphy and telephony, photography and motion pictures, radio and television, and digital media. Wireless handheld media may become an eighth milestone.

- Language led to the development of an oral culture in which information was passed on by word of mouth from one generation to another.

- The invention of an alphabet and a usable surface made writing possible. Writing created a social division in society. Those who could read and write had access to more information than those who could not.

- Writing helped create and maintain empires as well as make storehouses of information, such as libraries, possible.

- Printing made information available to a larger audience. It helped the development of vernacular languages, aided the Protestant Reformation, and contributed to the spread and accumulation of knowledge.

- The telegraph and telephone were the first media to use electricity to communicate. They marked the first time the message could be separated from the messenger. The telegraph helped the railroads move west and permitted the newspapers to publish more timely news. The telephone linked people together in the first instance of a communication network.

- Photography provided a way to preserve history, had an impact on art, and brought better visuals to newspapers and magazines. Motion pictures helped socialize a generation of immigrants and became an important part of American culture.

- Radio and television broadcasting brought news and entertainment into the home, transformed leisure time, and pioneered a new, immediate kind of reporting. Television has an impact on free time, politics, socialization, culture, and many other areas as well.

- The digital revolution changed the way information was stored and transmitted and made e-commerce possible.

- In general, it is difficult to predict the ultimate shape of a new medium. New media change but do not replace older media. The pace of media inventions has accelerated in recent years.

- The next communication milestone might be the move to wireless handheld media.

QUESTIONS FOR REVIEW

1. What is the difference between writing based on signs and writing based on an alphabet?

2. Why was the telegraph labeled "the great annihilator of time and space"?

3. What exactly is the "communal reservoir of images" created by photojournalism? Can you think of other examples of images that are forever fixed by photographs?

4. What digits are used in digital technology? Why could the telegraph be considered the first digital device?

QUESTIONS FOR CRITICAL THINKING

1. Printing was known in China for a long time before Gutenberg appeared. Why wasn't there a social revolution in China as there was in Europe when printing appeared?

2. Suppose Henry David Thoreau (see page 66) were alive today. What do you think he would say about the Internet?

3. Many people would argue that, of all the communication media discussed in this chapter, television has had the greatest impact on society. Do you agree?

4. When the Internet was first developing, the term *information superhighway* appeared frequently in news stories about it. Now that the Internet has been around for a while, news stories rarely contain that term. Why is this so?

5. Do you own a PDA or cell phone? If yes, how have they changed your life?

KEY TERMS

alphabet (p. 59)   photojournalism (p. 70)   personal digital assistants (PDAs)
technological determinism (p. 64)   digital technology (p. 77)   (p. 80)
                                                                                  mobile parenting (p. 81)

INTERNET RESOURCES

Online Learning Center

At the Online Learning Center home page, www.mhhe.com/dominick8, *select* Student Center *and then* Chapter 3.

1. Use the Learning Objectives, Chapter Outline, Main Points, and Time Line sections to review this chapter.

2. Test your knowledge of the chapter using the multiple choice, crossword puzzle, and flashcard features of the site.

3. Expand your knowledge of concepts and topics discussed in the chapter by going to *Suggestions for Further Reading* and *Internet Exercises*.

PowerWeb

At the Mass Communication home page of PowerWeb, www.dushkin.com/powerweb, *log in and select* Mass Communication *as your title. On the next screen, select* Topics *and then jump to* Advertising. *Read Article 42, "Inventing the Commercial." Then answer the following questions:*

1. As the text points out, TV became popular during an age of relative prosperity. Suppose this had not been the case. Would advertising agencies have been just as influential in the development of TV programming had TV been developed during the Depression of the 1930s? Why? Why not?

2. On a general level, how did early TV advertising influence American culture?

3. Check out the picture of the Keds Cheerleaders that accompanies the article. How would such a group look today?

Surfing the Internet

Here are some sites that provide information on media history. Some of the sites mentioned in Chapters 4 through 11 are also of relevance here.

http://jefferson.village.virginia.edu/albell/
homepage.html
Home page of Alexander Graham Bell. The site reconstructs Bell's path to the invention of the telephone.

http://mediahistory.umn.edu
The best all-around site for media history. Contains an extensive time line, other net links, book reviews, articles, archives, chat boards, and pages on the history of specific media.

www.archive.org
Home of the Wayback Machine mentioned in Media Probe, "Archives in the Digital Age." Surf the Web the way it used to be.

www.cln.org/themes/history_film.html
Links to many sites that contain information about film history.

www.gutenbergdigital.de
Gutenberg's Bible on the Web.

www.jls.palo-alto.ca.us/virtualmuseum/ushistory/
morse
Page devoted to Samuel Morse and telegraphy. Contains diagrams of early telegraphs and a Morse code alphabet.

MEDIA

4. NEWSPAPERS

This chapter will prepare you to

- describe the challenges newspapers face in today's digital age;

- recognize the conditions that had to exist before a mass press could come into existence;

- understand the significance of the penny press;

- explain the features that define both online and print renditions of newspapers;

- understand the function of the Audit Bureau of Circulations (ABC); and

- identify the various methods newspapers are using to gain readership.

Have you read a newspaper other than the campus press today? If you are like most people in your age group, your answer to that question is probably "no." A couple of generations ago about one of every two 18 to 30 year olds read a newspaper. Today the ratio is closer to one in four. In the digital age young people increasingly get their news from the Internet and cable TV and less and less from newspapers. Publishers are fully aware of this and the problem it creates for the future of the industry—which leads us to Chicago and the color red.

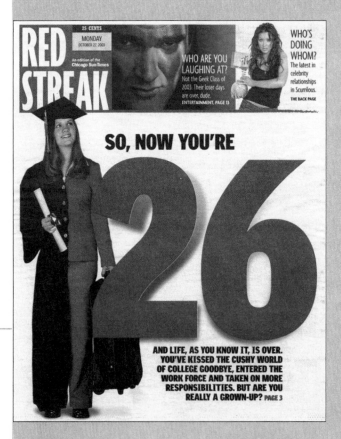

In an attempt to reach younger readers, the *Chicago Sun-Times* distributed thousands of free copies of its 20-something oriented *Red Streak*.

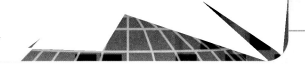

In late 2002, not one but two new tabloid newspapers were launched to reach this group of nonreaders. The venerable *Chicago Tribune* got into the game first when it published *RedEye,* so named because it was aimed at those young people who stay out late. Not to be outdone, the *Chicago Sun-Times* countered with *Red Streak,* the traditional term for the final edition of a newspaper. Both papers hoped that readers of the new tabloids would get into the newspaper reading habit and eventually become readers of the parent papers.

Both red papers emphasized the same content: Many photos along with entertainment news, dating tips, restaurant guides, club notes, and sports, movie, and music reviews. The news stories were shortened versions of articles that appeared in the parent publication. Readers seldom had to turn a page to finish a story. A sampling of recent stories from the two tabloids consisted of "On the Hunt for Some Red Hot Nightlife" and "What Turns You On?" Both papers were geared for speed (the first copy of *RedEye* contained a Top Ten List of reasons to read the paper that included only nine reasons in order to save time), and both put a heavy emphasis on being "cool."

The reaction of media critics was not enthusiastic: "Condescending." "News sliced so thin the servings wouldn't even make a meal for an anorexic." "More interested in celebrities than news." "A fifty-year-old with a graying pony tail trying to talk . . . hip." "News for the 'Dude' generation."

In the long run, of course, it will be readers and not critics who determine the future of these new ventures. Success or failure, *RedEye* and *Red Streak* have illustrated a couple of key lessons about the modern newspaper industry. First, both newspapers were driven more by marketing considerations than by journalism. The papers needed a way to reach the 18 to 34 demographic; market research suggested this was the formula. Second, they showed the extreme measures that newspaper publishers will take to attract a younger audience. Why would anybody spend a lot of money developing a paper for people who do not read newspapers? That would be like beef ranchers trying to sell steak dinners to vegetarians. The answer is simple: The average age of a newspaper reader is 53 and getting older every year. What are the prospects for the newspaper when most of its readers will be dead in 30 years? If the newspaper industry is to survive, it must attract younger readers.

This chapter looks at the history, economics, structure, and future of this industry as it copes with this and other challenges of the digital age.

 ## HISTORY

>> Journalism in Early America

Before we get to the details, it might be helpful to identify some general features of newspapers in early America:

- There were few papers.
- Printers and postmasters did most of the early publishing.
- News was not as timely as it is today.
- The idea of a free press was not endorsed by colonial governments.

Benjamin Franklin became the publisher of the *Pennsylvania Gazette* in 1729, when he was 24 years old. The paper became the most successful colonial newspaper, and Franklin became the best-known colonial journalist and publisher.

In 1690, Boston printer Benjamin Harris published the first American newspaper, *Publick Occurrences both Foreign and Domestick.* One of the items in the paper alleged an affair between the king of France and his son's wife. This news story infuriated the Puritan officials of the colony, and they shut down the paper after one issue. The notion of a free press had yet to surface in America; most colonists believed that a paper had to have royal consent to be published.

Fourteen years later, John Campbell, the local Boston postmaster, published the *Boston News Letter.* Published with royal permission, the paper was dull and lackluster, with many news stories simply reprinted from European papers. Campbell's paper had only about 300 subscribers and never made a profit.

A few years later, another Boston paper, the *New England Courant*, came on the scene. It was published by James Franklin, Ben's older brother, without government permission. Eventually, the elder Franklin's paper got him into trouble with the local authorities, and he was thrown into prison. Ben took over, and the paper prospered under his leadership. Ben eventually moved on to Philadelphia, where he started the *Pennsylvania Gazette,* which boasted such innovations as more legible type, headlines, and a cleaner layout.

Ben Franklin retired from a successful publishing career at the age of 42. During his career, he had started several papers, published one of America's first magazines, run the first editorial cartoon, proved that advertising copy could sell merchandise, and, perhaps most important, demonstrated that journalism could be an honorable profession.

>> The Beginnings of Revolution

Tensions between the colonies and the Crown were rising during Franklin's tenure as publisher, and this controversy sparked the development of the early press. One example of this tension was the trial of John Peter Zenger. Zenger published a paper openly critical of the British governor of New York. The governor threw Zenger into jail and charged him with criminal libel. Zenger's lawyer argued that no American jury should feel bound by laws formed in England, and Zenger was acquitted, striking a symbolic blow for press freedom.

Newspapers grew in numbers during the Revolutionary War, and most were partisan, siding with the colonies or with the Crown. This period marked the beginnings of the **political press,** which openly supported a particular party, faction, or cause.

In 1776, when the Continental Congress adopted the Declaration of Independence, the text of the document was published in the *Pennsylvania Evening Post* on July 6. The next year the Continental Congress authorized Mary Katherine

Goddard, publisher of the *Maryland Journal,* to print the first official copies of the Declaration with the names of the signers attached. Under Goddard's direction, the *Journal* became one of the leading colonial papers during the war. Goddard was one of about 30 women who printed or published colonial newspapers.

>> The Political Press: 1790–1833

The politicization of newspapers did not end with America's victory in the Revolutionary War. Instead, partisan leanings of the press were transferred into another arena—the debate over the powers of the federal government. The participants in this controversy included some of the best political thinkers of the time: Alexander Hamilton, James Madison, Thomas Jefferson, and John Jay. Newspapers were quick to take sides in this debate, and their pages were filled with Federalist or anti-Federalist propaganda. Heated political debate gave way to name-calling and quarreling between these two groups, and the content of many newspapers became colored by volatile and inflammatory language.

At the vortex of this debate between Federalists and anti-Federalists was the Constitution of the United States. Although the original document made no mention of the right of a free press, the Bill of Rights did contain such a provision. The **First Amendment** held that "Congress shall make no law . . . abridging the freedom of speech, or of the press." Thus the idea of a free press, which had grown during the Revolutionary period, became part of the law of the new nation when Congress ratified this amendment in 1791.

Newspapers grew with the country in the first 20 years of the new century. The daily newspaper began in 1783 and grew slowly. By 1800, most large cities had at least one daily paper. By 1820, there were 24 dailies, 66 semi- or triweeklies, and 422 weeklies. These newspapers were read primarily by the upper socioeconomic classes; early readers had to be literate and possess money to spend on subscriptions (about $10 per year or six cents an issue—a large sum when you consider that during those years five cents could buy a pint of whiskey). The content was typified by commercial and business news, political and congressional debates, speeches, acts of state legislatures, and official messages.

Politics was still the main focus of many of the nation's papers, and several papers sent correspondents to Washington to report political news. James Gordon Bennett, whom we shall meet again later, covered Washington for a New York paper. The first woman to achieve recognition as a political journalist was Anne Royall, who published two papers in Washington between 1831 and 1854. Royall was a crusader for free speech and state's rights, and she campaigned against graft and corruption.

During this period, several newspapers arose in response to the needs and interests of minority groups. *Freedom's Journal,* the first of over 40 black newspapers published before 1860, was founded in the late 1820s by the Reverend Samuel Cornish and John Russwurm. Written and edited by blacks, the paper championed the cause of black people by dealing with the serious problems arising from slavery and by carrying news of foreign countries such as Haiti and Sierra Leone that appealed to its black audience.

At about the same time, in 1828, another minority group, the Cherokee Indian nation, published the *Cherokee Phoenix,* written in both Cherokee and English. When the Cherokees were evicted from their home in Georgia and resettled in Oklahoma, a new paper, the *Cherokee Advocate,* was started and continued to operate until 1906. The *Advocate* was revived in the 1970s and now publishes a monthly edition.

Two early examples of the black press: *Freedom's Journal* was started in 1827 by John Russwurm, the first black person to graduate from a college in the United States, and by Samuel Cornish. Cornish later edited *The Colored American,* a paper that had subscribers from Maine to Michigan.

>> Birth of the Mass Newspaper

Several conditions had to exist before a mass press could come into existence:

1. A printing press had to be invented that would produce copies quickly and cheaply.
2. Enough people had to know how to read to support such a press.
3. A mass audience had to be present.

In 1830, the U.S. manufacturing firm R. Hoe and Company built a steam-powered press that could produce 4,000 copies per hour. This and subsequent steam-powered presses that were even faster made it possible to print an extremely cheap newspaper that everybody could afford.

The second element that led to the growth of the mass newspaper was the increased level of literacy in the population. The first statewide public school system was set up during the 1830s. The increased emphasis on education led to a concomitant growth of literacy as many people in the middle and lower economic groups acquired reading skills.

The third element was more subtle and harder to explain. The mass press appeared during an era that historians call the age of Jacksonian democracy, an age in which ordinary people were first recognized as a political and economic force. Property requirements for voting had died out. Every state but one chose presidential electors by popular vote. In addition, this period was marked by the rise of an urban middle class. The trend toward democratization of business and politics fostered the creation of a mass audience responsive to a mass press.

>> The Penny Press

Benjamin Day was only 22 years old when he launched the mass-appeal *New York Sun* in 1833. Day's idea was to sell his daily paper for a penny (a significant price reduction from the six cents a copy for other big-city dailies). Moreover, the *Sun* contained local news, particularly those items that featured sex, violence, and human-interest stories. Conspicuously absent were stodgy political debates. Day's gamble paid off as the *Sun* attracted readers, and the **penny press** was launched.

Others imitated the *Sun*'s success. The colorful James Gordon Bennett launched the *New York Herald* in 1835, which was an even more rapid success than the *Sun*. The *Herald* introduced a financial page, a sports page, and an aggressive editorial policy that emphasized reform.

Another important pioneer was Horace Greeley. His *New York Tribune* appeared in 1841 and ranked third behind the *Herald* and *Sun* in circulation. Greeley used his editorial pages for crusades and causes. He opposed capital punishment and gambling and favored trade unions and westward expansion.

Greeley also supported women's rights. In 1845, he hired Margaret Fuller as literary critic for the *Tribune*. In addition to providing commentary on the fine arts, Fuller wrote articles about the hard lot of prostitutes, women prisoners, and the insane. Greeley's decision to hire Fuller is typical of his publishing philosophy: Like Fuller, he never talked down to the mass audience and attracted his readers by appealing to their intellect more than to their emotions.

The last of the major newspapers of the penny-press era that we shall consider began in 1851 and, at this writing, is still publishing. The *New York Times*, edited by Henry Raymond, promised to be less sensational than the *Sun* or the *Herald* and less impassioned than Greeley's *Tribune*. The paper soon established a reputation for objective and reasoned journalism.

All these publishers had one thing in common. As soon as their penny papers were successful, they doubled the price.

Significance of the Penny Press   At this point, we should consider the major changes in journalism that were prompted by the success of the mass press during the period from 1833 to 1860. We can identify four such changes. The penny press changed

1. the basis of economic support for newspapers;
2. the pattern of newspaper distribution;

Front page of the *New York Sun*: Benjamin Day's reliance on advertising for revenue is illustrated by the several columns of classified ads appearing on the front page.

3. the definition of what constituted news; and

4. the techniques of news collection.

Before the penny press, most of a newspaper's economic support came from subscription revenue. The large circulation of the penny papers made advertisers realize that they could reach a large segment of potential buyers by purchasing space. Moreover, the readership of the popular papers cut across political party and social class lines, thereby assuring a potential advertiser a broadly based audience. As a result, advertisers were greatly attracted to this new medium, and the mass newspapers relied significantly more on advertising revenues than did their predecessors.

Older papers were distributed primarily through the mails; the penny press, although relying somewhat on subscriptions, also made use of street sales. Vendors would buy 100 copies for 67 cents and sell them for 1 cent each. Soon it became common to hear newsboys hawking papers at most corners in the larger cities. Since these papers had to compete with one another in the open marketplace of the street, editors went out of their way to find original and exclusive news that would give their paper an edge.

The penny press also redefined the concept of news. The penny press hired people to go out and look for news. Reporters were assigned to special beats: police, financial, sports, and religion, to name a few. Foreign correspondents were popular. Newspapers changed their emphasis from the affairs of the commercial elite to the social life of the rising middle classes.

This shift meant that news became more of a commodity, something that had value. And, like many commodities, fresh news was more valuable than stale news. Any scheme that would get the news into the paper faster was tried. Stories were sent by carrier pigeon, Pony Express, railroads, and steamships. The Mexican War of 1846 made fast news transmission especially desirable, and many newspapers first used the telegraph to carry news about this conflict. All in all, the penny papers increased the importance of speed in news collection.

>> Newspapers Become Big Business

A new reporting technique emerged during the Civil War as telegraphic dispatches from the war zones were transformed into headlines. Because telegraph lines sometimes failed, the opening paragraphs of the story contained the most important facts. If the line failed during a story, at least the most important part would get through. Thus, the "inverted pyramid" style of reporting was developed.

After the war, from about 1870 to 1900, the total U.S. population doubled, and urban population tripled. Newspapers grew even faster than the population; the number of dailies quadrupled, and circulation showed a fivefold increase. As a result, newspapers became a big business, and some big-city papers were making more than $1 million a year in profits by the mid-1890s. The thriving newspaper business also attracted several powerful and outspoken individuals who had a profound influence on American journalism. We will consider three: Pulitzer, Scripps, and Hearst.

Joseph Pulitzer came to the United States from Hungary and eventually settled in St. Louis. After a string of unsuccessful jobs, he found he had a talent for journalism and turned the *St. Louis Post-Dispatch* into a success. In 1883, he bought the *New York World*. In a little more than three years, Pulitzer increased the paper's circulation from 15,000 to 250,000.

What was Pulitzer's formula for success? Pulitzer stressed accuracy. He also introduced practices that appealed to advertisers: more advertising space and ads priced on the basis of circulation. Moreover, he aimed his paper at the large population of immigrants then living in New York by stressing simple writing and many illustrations. Pulitzer reintroduced the sensationalized news format of the penny press. The *World's* pages carried stories about crime, violence, and tragedy. Finally, Pulitzer endorsed the notion that a paper should promote the welfare of its readers, particularly the underprivileged. Although Pulitzer did not originate the idea, he certainly put it into practice. The paper crusaded against unsanitary living conditions, corrupt politicians, and big business, all topics that gained Pulitzer many supporters among the working class.

Attempts to reach a working-class audience were not confined to the East. In the Midwest, E. W. Scripps started papers in Cleveland and Cincinnati, both growing industrial cities with large populations of factory workers. The Scripps papers featured concisely edited news, human-interest stories, editorial independence, and frequent crusades for the working class. Scripps pioneered the idea of a newspaper chain. By 1911, he owned 18 papers.

Perhaps the best-known of these three newspaper giants, thanks to the film *Citizen Kane,* was William Randolph Hearst. While Pulitzer was succeeding in New York and Scripps was acquiring papers in the Midwest, 24-year-old Hearst was given control of the *San Francisco Examiner,* thanks to the generosity of his wealthy father. Hearst went after readers by appealing to their emotions. Fires, murders, and stories about love and hate were given splashy coverage. Hearst banked heavily on sensationalism to raise his readership level. His strategy worked. The *Examiner* shot to the number-one position.

>> Yellow Journalism

Hearst, like Pulitzer before him, then invaded the big league—New York City. In 1895, he bought the *New York Journal.* Soon, Pulitzer and Hearst were engaged in a fierce circulation battle as each paper attempted to outsensationalize the other. As one press critic put it, the duel between these two spread "death, dishonor and disaster" all over page one. Sex, murder, self-promotion, and human-interest stories filled the two papers. This type of reporting became known as **yellow journalism,** and whatever its faults, it sold newspapers.

The battle between Pulitzer and Hearst reached its climax with the Spanish-American War in 1898. In fact, many historians have argued that the newspapers were an important factor in shaping public opinion in favor of hostilities. When the battleship *Maine* was blown up in Havana harbor, the *Journal* offered a $50,000 reward for the arrest of the guilty parties. Circulation jumped over the one million mark. War was finally declared in April, and the *World* and the *Journal* pulled out all the stops. Hearst chartered a steamer and equipped it with printing presses. He also brought down his yacht and sailed with the U.S. fleet in the Battle of Santiago. The *Journal* put out 40 extras in a single day.

Although the period of yellow journalism was not the proudest moment in the history of the American newspaper, some positive features did emerge from it. In the first place, it brought enthusiasm, energy, and verve to the practice of journalism, along with aggressive reporting and investigative stories. Second, it brought wide exposure to prominent authors and led to some fine examples of contemporary writing. Stephen Crane, Frank Norris, Dorothy Dix, and Mark Twain all wrote for newspapers during this period (1880–1905). Further, yellow journalism

William Randolph Hearst, the successful publisher of the *San Francisco Examiner* and later the *New York Journal,* employed sensationalism (yellow journalism) to win the circulation wars of the late 1800s. He created a major publishing empire consisting of a chain of newspapers, a wire service, and four syndicates.

helped popularize the use of layout and display devices—banner headlines, pictures, color printing—that would go on to characterize modern journalism.

>> The Early 20th Century

From 1900 to 1920, consolidation characterized the newspaper business. Although circulation and profits went up, the number of daily newspapers decreased and the number of cities with competing newspapers dropped by 60 percent. What happened?

First, the cost of new technology—Linotype machines, high-speed presses—proved too expensive for many marginal papers. Second, advertisers showed a preference for the paper with the largest circulation in the market. Smaller-circulation papers saw their revenues shrink to the point at which they could no longer compete. Third, consolidation had increased profits in the railroad, grocery, and hotel businesses, and newspaper publishers decided it could do the same for them. Consequently, newspaper chains—companies that owned several papers—grew quickly. By 1933, six chains—Hearst, Scripps-Howard, Patterson-McCormack, Block, Ridder, and Gannett—controlled 81 dailies with a combined circulation of more than nine million, about one-fourth of all daily circulation.

Appearing with the consolidation trend and enjoying a short but lively reign was **jazz journalism.** At the end of World War I, the United States enjoyed a decade of prosperity known as the Roaring Twenties. The radio, Hollywood, the airplane, Prohibition, and Al Capone all captured national attention. The papers that best exemplify jazz journalism all sprang up in New York between 1919 and 1924. All were characterized by two features: (1) They were **tabloids,** printed on a page that was about one-half the size of a normal newspaper page; and (2) they were richly illustrated with photographs.

The *New York Daily News* debuted first. After a slow start, by 1924 the *News* had caught on. Its tabloid size was easy for people to handle while reading on buses and subways; it abounded with photos and cartoons; and the writing style was simple and short. The biggest content innovation of the *News* and the most noticeable was the lavish use of pictures. The entire front page was frequently given over to one or two pictures, and a two-page photo spread was included on the inside.

>> The Impact of the Great Depression

The Depression had great social and economic impact on newspapers and magazines. During the 1930s, total daily newspaper circulation increased by about two million; the total population increased by nine million. The total income of the newspaper industry, however, dropped about 20 percent in this decade.

When Lyndon Johnson signed the Civil Rights Act of 1964, he invited leaders of the Civil Rights movement to join him in the Oval Office. Only one woman was among the group that witnessed the historic moment—Ethel L. Payne, an African American journalist who had reported on civil rights for more than a decade.

Payne was the granddaughter of slaves. She originally wanted to become a lawyer but was denied admission to law school because of her race. In 1948, she went to Japan to work with African American troops who were stationed there. Two years later Payne showed excerpts from her personal journal about the problems of black soldiers to a reporter for the *Chicago Defender* who was visiting Japan. Her stories became a series in the newspaper and launched Payne into a journalism career.

Based in Chicago, she won awards for her coverage of problems in the African American community. She went to Washington in the mid-1950s to cover the beginnings of the Civil Rights movement. She wrote stories analyzing the historic *Brown* v. *Board of Education* Supreme Court decision. Payne made her presence felt at White House press conferences when she asked President Dwight Eisenhower pointed questions about the lack of progress on civil rights during his administration.

In 1956, Payne covered the arrest of Rosa Parks in Montgomery, Alabama, and the subsequent bus boycott. She reported the big stories of the Civil Rights movement, including the efforts to integrate the University of Alabama, the violence in Little Rock, Arkansas, the confrontation at Selma, Alabama, and the march on Washington in 1965. She was one of the first reporters to interview Dr. Martin Luther King Jr.

In 1966, she traveled to Vietnam to cover African American troops, who were involved in much of the fighting. She later accompanied Secretary of State Henry Kissinger on a six-nation tour of Africa. In 1978, at age 67, she ended her career with the *Chicago Defender* to write a syndicated column. Seven years later she became a leader in the effort to free South Africa leader Nelson Mandela.

Ethel Payne died in 1991. The *Washington Post* published a tribute to her on its editorial page. It praised her for being fair, straightforward, and independent, an assessment probably shared by her millions of readers.

Marginally profitable papers were unable to stay in business, and approximately 66 dailies went under.

Although worsening economic conditions were one cause of the newspaper's decline, more important was the emergence of radio as a competitor for national advertising dollars. From 1935 to 1940, newspapers' share of national advertising revenues dropped from 45 to 39 percent, while radio's share jumped from 6 to more than 10 percent. By 1940, however, thanks to increased revenue from local advertisers, newspaper revenues were back up. Nevertheless, the economic picture was still not rosy, and the number of daily papers declined to 1,744, an all-time low, in 1945.

>> Postwar Newspapers

After World War II, economic forces continued to shape the American newspaper. Some trends of the postwar period were created by advances in print and electronic technology, but others had begun even before the war. For example, the postwar economy forced the newspaper industry to move even further in the direction of contraction and consolidation. Although newspaper circulation rose from approximately 48 million in 1945 to about 62 million in 1970, the number of dailies stayed about the same. There was actually a circulation loss in cities with populations of more than a million, and several big-city papers went out of business. Moreover, the number of cities with competing dailies dropped from 117 to 37 between 1945 and 1970. This meant that about 98 percent of American cities had no competing papers.

In 1945, 60 chains controlled about 42 percent of the total daily newspaper circulation. By 1970, there were approximately 157 chains that accounted for 60 percent of total circulation. Why had the number of chains continued to grow? One factor was the sharp rise in costs of paper and labor. Newspapers were becoming more expensive to print. The large chains were in a position to share expenses and to use their presses and labor more efficiently. Several papers could share the services of feature writers, columnists, photographers, and compositors, thus holding down costs.

The consolidation trend was also present across media, as several media conglomerates controlled newspapers, magazines and radio, and television stations. Black newspapers were also caught up in the trend toward concentration. In 1956, the *Chicago Defender* changed from a weekly to a daily, and its owner, John Sengstacke, started a group of nine black papers, including the Pittsburgh *Courier* and the Michigan *Chronicle*.

Another continuing trend was the competition among media for advertising dollars. The total amount of advertising revenue spent on all media nearly tripled between 1945 and 1970. Although the total spent on newspapers did not increase at quite this pace, the amount spent on television increased by more than threefold. The rising television industry cut significantly into the print media's national advertising revenue.

>> Contemporary Developments

The biggest development of the 1980s was the birth of *USA Today.* Following are some of the innovations sparked by this paper:

- splashy graphics and color;
- short, easy-to-read stories;

- many graphs, charts, and tables; and

- factoids (a *factoid* is a list of boiled-down facts—much like this list).

Many newspapers across the country incorporated these changes into their editions.

The developments of the last 15 years in the newspaper industry can be summarized by four Cs: competition, consolidation, classifieds, and credibility. For several decades the newspaper's chief competitors were radio and broadcast television. Today, however, newspapers must compete not only with their traditional rivals, but also with 24-hour cable news networks and Internet sites. As a result, the competition for advertising dollars is more intense than ever.

The trend toward newspaper consolidation continues. A few big firms dominate the business. Moreover, a 2003 decision announced by the Federal Communications Commission to relax the ban on ownership of same-market newspapers and broadcasting stations could accelerate the trend even more.

Classified ads make up about 40 percent of the typical newspaper's revenue. A growing number of websites are siphoning off some of the money that newspapers would normally take in for classified ads. In 2001, for example, income from classifieds dropped by 35 percent from the previous year. Websites that focus on job seekers, such as Monster.com, have become newspapers' chief competitor for this revenue.

Finally, a 2003 scandal at the *New York Times* involving a reporter who fabricated parts of news stories prompted a "credibility crisis" and led to a period of self-examination at the *Times* and other papers (see "Credibility and the *Times*"). Publishers searched for ways to regain the confidence of their readers and reexamined their fact checking and managerial arrangements so that such an embarrassment would not happen again.

NEWSPAPERS IN THE DIGITAL AGE

The newspaper industry is still experimenting to find the best way to incorporate an online presence in the traditional print edition. All of the results are not in yet, but one thing seems certain: The era of giving the news away for free online is rapidly coming to a close.

>> Online Newspapers

Online papers do not differ from their print counterparts with regard to their primary function. Both gather, evaluate, and organize information. They differ significantly, however, in the way they distribute this news to their readers. Traditional newspapers use paper, ink, presses, trucks, and delivery workers; online papers are transmitted digitally to computers and handheld wireless media.

Online papers have certain advantages over traditional newspapers:

- Printed newspapers are limited by the **newshole,** the amount of news that can be printed in one edition. Online papers have no such limitations. The full text of lengthy speeches, transcripts of interviews, and extensive tables and graphs can be accommodated easily.

- Online papers can be updated continuously. There are no edition deadlines for online papers.

- Online papers are interactive. E-mail addresses, bulletin boards, and chat rooms allow readers to provide quick feedback to the paper. Many have searchable archives and links to other sites.

In 1994 about 20 daily papers had websites. In 2000, more than 1,100 were online. Of the top 150 papers, 148 offered their news online. The Newspaper Association of America's (NAA) website (www.naa.org) contains links to 1,153 online dailies, ranging from *USA Today*, with a print circulation of more than two million, to the *Americus* (Georgia) *Times-Recorder*, with a print circulation of 6,900. Online papers vary tremendously in their size and complexity. Large papers typically have extensive sites that offer more features and content than their print counterparts. Smaller papers may simply post a limited number of stories and classified ads. Weeklies and special-service papers have also branched out into the Web. The NAA's site has links to more than 500 of these sites.

The relationship between the online and print versions of the newspaper varies from paper to paper. Some large papers have made the Web version an autonomous operation, separate from the print side. Many other papers, however, have the Web staff working under the direction of the newspaper's editors.

>> Paid Access

The first newspaper websites contained modified versions of the paper's print edition. Publishers hoped that the sites would generate enough advertising revenue to make the online versions profitable. This did not happen. For most papers, the website was simply a drain on finances and resources.

Faced with this reality, publishers looked for other ways to generate income. One model was to charge a subscription fee to access the online version. The *Wall Street Journal* successfully used this model for years, and several smaller papers have followed suit. The *Albuquerque Journal* and *The Columbus Dispatch*, for example, now charge for content that they used to give away. In the case of the *Dispatch*, a subscriber to the print edition gets free access to the online edition, but nonsubscribers have to pay $4.95 a month.

Many newspapers, however, are reluctant to institute a fee, fearing that it will drive away readers. A 2002 survey estimated that less than 10 percent of online newspapers charge a fee for access. An increasingly popular alternative for newspapers is the registration model. In this arrangement the reader pays for access to the site, not with money but by giving up personal information. Publishers were initially cautious about requiring registration because they thought it would decrease readership. This did not turn out to be the case. The *New York Times*, for example, has more than 10 million registered users. The *Los Angeles Times* had 500,000 people register in the first few months after it adopted the subscription model. The *Dallas Morning News* registered 660,000 people, a number that is higher than the paper's weekday circulation. Revenue generated by the website jumped from almost nothing before registration to almost $1 million.

The typical registration process asks for a reader's age, address, zip code, e-mail address, income level, and hobbies. Publishers can turn this information into added revenue in several ways. First, they can sell customized e-mail lists to advertisers. For example, Travelocity would be interested in purchasing a list of the e-mail addresses of people who check "travel" as a hobby. Second, publishers can promote their own products to readers. The *Los Angeles Times* used its registration data to send targeted e-mails to male sports fans offering them a chance to subscribe to an all-sports e-mail newsletter published by the *Times.* Finally, sales

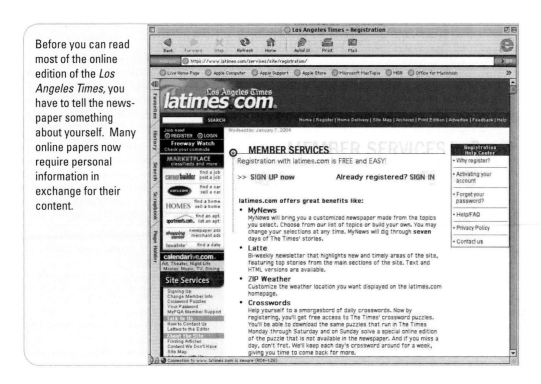

Before you can read most of the online edition of the *Los Angeles Times,* you have to tell the newspaper something about yourself. Many online papers now require personal information in exchange for their content.

staff share registration data with potential advertisers so they know what types of people will see their ads. Given their success so far, look for more papers to ask you to give up personal information before sharing the news with you.

>> Digital Editions

A digital edition of a newspaper is not the same as an online edition. The online edition looks different from the print edition; the online paper has no page numbers, its pages are not divided into columns, it has no top or bottom, the text is printed in a different font from the print version and it does not contain the same ads as the print version. On the other hand, a digital edition offers the same content as the printed newspaper but in a format that can be read on a computer screen.

What are the advantages of a digital edition over an online version? First, a digital edition is more familiar to readers; it has the same design and typography as the print edition. Second, digital editions show where in a newspaper a story was placed, thus giving it some context, something lost in an electronic version. Readers want to know this because, for example, they know that stories on page 14 of the paper are less important than those on pages 1, 2, or 3. Third, digital editions are convenient. They can be downloaded automatically to a personal computer daily without the subscriber having to do anything. Online papers require the user to visit a site for each reading. In addition, once digital newspapers are downloaded, subscribers can take them anywhere. To read an online paper, on the other hand, a person has to be connected to the Internet.

There are, however, some disadvantages. Subscribers need a cable modem or a DSL line for best results. Unlike online papers that are updated several times a day, digital editions are published only once a day, resulting in news that may be hours old. Finally, reading the digital edition requires a great deal of zooming and scrolling that many would find annoying.

Online journalism has raised a host of ethical questions that reporters, editors, and publishers are struggling to answer. Here are just a few:

- *What is the proper separation of news and commerce at a website?* Traditionally, to preserve journalistic integrity, the editorial side of a newspaper was separated from the business side. Online, the boundaries are blurry. For example, a person who reads a book review at the *New York Times* online site can click a button and purchase the book from Barnes&Noble.com. The *Times* gets revenue from each such sale. Is this simply providing an additional service to the reader, or is it a conflict of interest? Can the *Times* be objective when reporting news about Barnes and Noble or its rival Amazon.com? What about an online paper that publishes movie reviews and offers a link to a site where readers can purchase tickets to a local theater online, giving the paper a commission for each online ticket sale? Would the paper ever publish a bad review?

- *If an online paper has links to external sites, is it responsible for the content of those sites?* In a story pointing out the increasing danger of electronic eavesdropping and personal data snooping by private detectives, the *New York Times* online provided links to the websites of the companies that engaged in such practices, seemingly exacerbating the problem. Another online *Times* story about convicted killer Charles Manson contained links to four websites maintained by less-than-credible organizations that proclaimed Manson's innocence. Again, is this simply another online reader service, or is the *Times* providing its audience with dubious and potentially misleading information?

  Some online papers post disclaimers noting that they are not responsible for the content of linked sites, but is this enough to fulfill their ethical obligations to readers? Is it enough for the paper to simply wash its hands and not be responsible for any harm that might come from corrupted information?

- *What ethical obligations do online papers have when it comes to corrections?* A traditional newspaper usually has an explicit policy concerning when and where corrections will be published. Most online papers have no such policy. If they make an error, they will simply correct it when someone points it out, without acknowledging the mistake. Do they owe their readers more?

Despite the downside, nearly 100 papers worldwide publish a digital edition. Most papers, such as the *Spokane Spokesman-Review,* sell subscriptions to both the print and digital editions and close off their websites to those who subscribe to neither. Some of the papers currently available in digital form include the *New York Times,* the *Boston Globe,* and the *Sacramento Bee.*

Expect to see more papers offer the digital edition option. In the first place, it is cheap to produce and has the potential for improving the bottom line. Secondly, the Audit Bureau of Circulations, the organization that certifies newspaper circulation, has announced that newspapers can include paid digital edition subscriptions in their circulation totals.

>> Handheld Media

Newspapers traditionally have been delivered to a place—a person's home or office. In the digital age newspapers are increasingly delivered to a person, thanks to the growing availability of wireless connections to the Internet and the increasing popularity of various handheld information devices: cell phones, personal digital assistants (PDAs), and laptops. One of two Americans, for example, owns a cell phone (for more on wireless handheld media see Chapter 3). These devices are becoming new delivery channels for newspapers. The *Wall Street Journal,* for example, offers financial news to subscribers over their cell phones. *USA Today* provides news updates every 15 minutes over cell phones and PDAs to more than 100,000 customers. The newspaper even delivers video clips to some subscribers with special digital assistants.

In the near future, newspapers may be sending news to **tablet PCs.** These devices weigh only three pounds, are an inch thick, and are about the size of a sheet of regular letter paper. They can display text and graphics and play both audio and video clips. An electronic edition of a paper can be downloaded to a tablet PC in about a minute over a high-speed Internet connection. The pages look like those in a typical print newspaper. Content can be updated during the day. As one industry expert put it, the newspaper delivered to a tablet PC is the first electronic newspaper you can really read in the bathroom.

The advertising and marketing potential of this channel is significant since ads delivered via mobile media reach people near the point of purchase. Checking sports scores on your personal digital assistant? While you are at it why not purchase tickets to a future game? In addition, many young people are heavy users of cell phones and PDAs. This is the same group that has turned away from traditional print newspapers. Handheld media offer publishers one way of reaching this segment of the audience. In sum, look for newspapers to be designed for multiple digital platforms, not just paper. As *New York Times* publisher Arthur Sulzberger Jr. put it, "Newspapers cannot be defined by the second word—paper. They've got to be defined by the first—news."

 ## DEFINING FEATURES OF NEWSPAPERS

Both the online and the print editions of the newspaper share some defining features. First, the newspaper is made up of diverse content. Newspapers contain international, national, and local news. In addition, they feature editorials, letters to the editor, movie listings, horoscopes, comics, sports, film reviews, recipes, advice columns, classified ads, and a host of other material. Their range of content is extensive.

Second, newspapers are conveniently packaged. Both the print and online versions are organized according to content. There are sections devoted to general news, financial news, sports, and entertainment. In addition, each story contains a headline that makes it easy for readers to decide if they want to peruse the rest of the story.

Third, newspapers are local. Reporters cover meetings of the local school board, the city council, and the zoning commission. They cover the local police station and tell about the newest store openings in the local mall. Sports sections cover the hometown Little League and high school teams. Local people with merchandise to sell use the classified ads. Newspapers are the only medium with the resources to report all the neighborhood activities in a community.

Fourth, more than any other medium, the newspaper serves as a historical record. One writer described newspaper journalism as "the first draft of history." The typical paper contains a record of daily events, some profound, some not so profound, that influence our lives. If a person wants to get a sense of what life was like in the 1940s, for example, he or she can flip through some old issues of the paper and see what events were on people's minds, what movies they were seeing, and what products were being advertised.

Fifth, as we have seen, newspapers perform the watchdog role in our society. They monitor the workings of government and private industry for misdeeds and wrongdoings. They alert the public to possible threats and new trends.

Finally, newspapers are timely. News is not useful if it is stale. Recognizing this fact, the largest-circulation newspapers in the United States publish daily and online editions that can break news any time of the day. Getting the news out fast has always been one of the characteristics of the newspaper business.

 ## ORGANIZATION OF THE NEWSPAPER INDUSTRY

The print newspapers that are published in this country are many and varied. They range from *The Wall Street Journal,* a nationally oriented financial daily, to the *Journal of Commerce,* a small financial paper published in Portland, Oregon; from the *National Enquirer* to the *Daily Lobo,* the college newspaper of the University of New Mexico; from the million-plus–circulation *New York Times* to the 6,000-circulation Gallipolis *Daily Tribune* in Gallipolis, Ohio. Obviously, there are many ways to categorize an industry as diverse as this one. For our purposes, we will group papers by frequency of publication (dailies and weeklies), by market size (national, large, medium, small), and by their appeal to specialized interest groups. Table 4-1 shows the top 10 newspapers by circulation and the percent in circulation change between 1999 and 2002.

>> ### Print Dailies

To be considered a daily, a newspaper has to appear at least five times a week. In 2002, there were 1,468 dailies, down slightly from 2000 (see Figure 4–1), and about 7,500 weeklies. Whether a daily or a weekly, the chief concern of a newspaper is its **circulation,** the number of copies delivered to newsstands or vending machines and the number delivered to subscribers. Weekday morning circulation has increased and Sunday circulation has stayed about the same in the last 20 years. Evening circulation, however, has shown a major decrease. As a result, total daily newspaper circulation has declined to approximately 56 million, a figure that dropped steadily between 1965 to 2002 (see Figure 4–2). At the same time, the population of the United States has been growing. Consequently, the ratio of newspapers per household has declined. To illustrate: In 1960, 111 newspapers were sold per 100 households; in 2002, about 55 newspapers were sold

TABLE 4–1

Top 10 Newspapers by Circulation

Although newspaper circulation has declined slightly, there are some pronounced variations.

Paper	1999 circulation (millions)	2003 circulation (millions)	Percent change
1. USA Today	1.67	2.16	+29
2. Wall Street Journal	1.75	2.10	+20
3. New York Times	1.08	1.12	+3
4. Los Angeles Times	1.08	0.95	−12
5. Washington Post	0.76	0.74	−3
6. New York Daily News	0.70	0.73	+4
7. New York Post	0.49	0.65	+32
8. Chicago Tribune	0.66	0.61	−8
9. Newsday	0.58	0.58	0
10. Houston Chronicle	0.55	0.55	0

FIGURE 4–1

**Number of Daily
Newspapers in the
United States,
1870–2001**

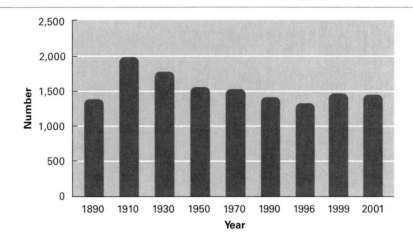

per 100 households. This circulation crunch has not hit all papers with equal force, and this becomes evident when we divide daily newspapers into market groups.

National Newspapers   Only a handful of papers fall into this category. These are publications whose content is geared not for one particular city or region but for the entire country. These papers typically use satellites to transmit images and information to regional printing plants where the papers are assembled and distributed. The newest addition to this category, with a circulation of about 2.2 million, is the Gannett publication *USA Today,* started in 1982. The paper's use of color and graphics and focus on such topics as sports and weather made a significant impact on other newspapers. Other papers with a national edition are the *New York Times, The Wall Street Journal*, and the *Christian Science Monitor.*

Large Metropolitan Dailies   The decline in circulation has hit these papers the hardest. Although the total population of the top 50 metropolitan areas increased more than 30 percent from 1960 to 2002, the circulation of newspapers published in those areas dropped about 45 percent. In addition, the last few years have seen the demise of several well-known big-city papers: the *Indianapolis Star and News,* the *Honolulu Star-Bulletin,* the Memphis *Press-Scimitar,* and the Dallas *Times-Herald,* to name a few. Why the drop in big-city circulation? There are several reasons, including migration from the central city to the suburbs, transient populations, rising costs of distribution, and increased competition from other media, most notably television.

Suburban Dailies   Although suburban communities of between 100,000 and 500,000 residents are home to only 12 percent of total newspapers, they account for about 40 percent of all circulation. Suburban dailies, located in the areas surrounding the larger cities, are experiencing a period of growth. Circulation of these papers grew by about one-third from 1987 to 2002. One reason for this increase is the growth of suburban shopping centers, which have attracted many merchants formerly located in the central cities. To these merchants, suburban papers represent an efficient way of reaching potential customers. In addition, suburban residents are apparently less inclined to go to the city at night for dinner

FIGURE 4–2

**Daily-Newspaper
Circulation, 1980–1999**

(Compiled by author)

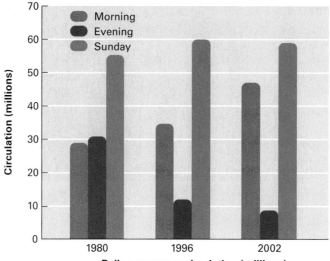

Daily newspaper circulation (millions)

and entertainment, a factor that has cut down newsstand sales of city papers. Perhaps the best-known suburban paper is *Newsday,* aimed at the residents of Long Island. In 2002, *Newsday* had a circulation of about 580,000, making it the eighth largest daily paper in the country.

In a quest to regain readers, large metro dailies have taken on the suburban press on the smaller papers' own turf. Big-city newspapers are putting out more **zoned editions,** sections geared to a particular suburban area.

Small-Town Dailies   This category of newspapers has also made circulation gains. From 1979 to 2002, newspaper circulation in towns with 100,000 or fewer inhabitants grew by 19 percent. Recently, circulation among papers in this category has declined slightly, although dailies in towns with populations of less than 25,000 have shown modest circulation gains. Surveys have shown that readers of these papers perceive the papers to be sources of local information, for both neighborhood news and advertising.

>> Print Weeklies

The number of weekly newspapers in the United States has remained fairly stable at about 7,500 over the last 20 years. The circulation of weeklies, however, has more than doubled for this same period, from 29 million in 1970 to more than 71 million in 2002. Despite this increase in circulation, the rising costs of printing and distribution have made weekly publishers more cost-conscious.

>> Recapturing Readers

No matter what their size or frequency of publication, all print newspapers are faced with the task of maintaining their loyal readers while attracting new ones. Newspaper executives are aware that spending time with the daily paper is no longer the habit it once was. What are some of the things that newspapers are doing to attract readers?

- They are using more color. Readers generally like color, and papers are using it liberally throughout the newspaper. Even the gray and proper *New York Times* and the conservative *Wall Street Journal* have introduced color to their pages.

- They are changing their writing and editing style. Stories are shorter and accompanied by summary decks under the headline or have story-related information in sidebars on either side of the story. Some papers run highlighted synopses within long stories.

- They are changing the content of the paper. Many papers have become less dependent on lengthy stories dealing with local government. Appearing with more frequency are features dealing with lifestyles, fashions, and entertainment and articles usually described as "news you can use" (e.g., "How to Find the Perfect Babysitter," "Best Open-Late Restaurants," and "Managing Your Money").

Many of these efforts are intended specifically to attract the audience segment that has been the hardest to recapture: teens and young adults. Surveys show that at the turn of the century only one in three Americans under 35 regularly read a newspaper. Fifty percent of 18 to 24 year olds do not read a newspaper at all.

>> Special-Service and Minority Newspapers

Special-service newspapers are those aimed at several well-defined audience segments. There are, for example, many newspapers published specifically for the African American community. The African American press in this country has a long history, dating back to 1827. Most early papers were started to oppose discrimination and to help gain equal rights and opportunities. The African American press reached its circulation peak in the 1960s when approximately 275 papers had a circulation of about 4 million. Since that time, the African American press has seen a significant decline in both numbers of papers and circulation.

In 2003, approximately 200 African American papers were publishing in 35 states and the District of Columbia. Although some African American papers were doing well, others were facing financial problems. In general, the problems faced by the African American press stemmed from increasing competition from white-owned papers, decreasing circulation (which made it more difficult to attract

Editors at work in the *USA Today* newsroom. A substantial part of each reporter's and editor's day is spent sitting in front of a computer.

Al Neuharth got into the newspaper business when he was 11 years old and delivered the *Minneapolis Tribune*. At 13, he had a part-time job in the composing room of a local weekly.

After serving in the military, he took a job as a reporter for a paper in South Dakota and later moved to the *Miami Herald*. Neuharth moved up rapidly through the ranks and eventually entered management. In 1960, he was appointed an assistant executive editor of the *Detroit Free Press*. His achievements there brought him to the attention of executives of the Gannett Company, who persuaded him to leave Detroit to manage two of Gannett's papers in New York. Neuharth's success there earned him a promotion to the position of chief of Gannett's operations in Florida. By 1970, Neuharth had become CEO of the company.

His emphasis was on the bottom line. During his tenure, Gannett's annual revenue increased from $200 million to $3.1 billion. Neuharth continued the strategies of his predecessors by acquiring small- and medium-market dailies that enjoyed a monopoly status in their markets and keeping costs down while raising ad rates. Strung by criticism that his papers emphasized profit at the expense of good journalism, Neuharth strengthened the editorial operations of Gannett

Al Neuharth, the man responsible for making Gannett the nation's biggest newspaper.

papers, and by 1980, many had won awards for excellence in reporting.

Neuharth's biggest gamble came in the early 1980s when he decided to use a network of communication satellites and regional printing plants to produce *USA Today*, a national general-interest newspaper. The new paper was greeted with derision by critics, who dismissed it as a "McPaper" that served up flavorless "fast-food" journalism. *USA Today* was an immediate hit with readers, however, and quickly garnered more than a million readers. Advertisers took a little longer to get on board, but the paper eventually turned a profit.

Now most experts agree that, after 20 years on the newsstands, *USA Today* has had a significant impact on the industry. Most newspapers have incorporated color, a splashy page makeup, more charts and graphics, and shorter, more tightly written stories.

Neuharth retired in 1989 to become chair of the Freedom Foundation, an organization dedicated to furthering the cause of a free press in society. He also continues to write a syndicated newspaper column. The *Washington Journalism Review* named him the most influential person in print media for the decade of the 1980s.

advertisers), more expensive newsprint, and criticism from many in the African American community that the papers were too conservative and out-of-date. In an attempt to recapture readership and advertisers, many African American papers have changed their format and editorial focus and have begun to concentrate on local news. In the late 1990s it was estimated that the combined circulation of all African American newspapers was about 2 million, down almost 50 percent from the 1960s. In an attempt to gain readers, many African American newspapers were trying to appeal to upscale readers by emphasizing news about education, medicine, and economics. Many papers added color and updated graphics.

Hispanics are the fastest-growing minority group in America, and the Spanish-language press has grown with them. According to the *National Hispanic Media Directory*, the number of Spanish-language publications has from 232 in 1970 to 550 in 2002. The most prominent Spanish-language daily is the New York City tabloid *el diario/La Prensa*, with a circulation of more than 70,000.

There are many other ethnic newspaper publishers in the United States. Twelve cities have at least one Chinese-language newspaper, and eight cities have papers targeted to Polish Americans.

The best-known member of the Spanish-language press is *el diario/La Prensa*, published in New York City. The paper has a circulation of more than 70,000.

Another special type of newspaper is exemplified by the college press. Although numbers are hard to pin down, as of 2003 there were about 1,500 college papers published at four-year institutions, with a total circulation of more than six million. College newspapers are big business; consequently, more and more papers are hiring nonstudent professionals to manage their operation. Two of the largest college papers in terms of circulation are the University of Minnesota's *Minnesota Daily* and Michigan State University's *State News*, both with circulations of approximately 30,000. College newspapers get high readership scores. One survey noted that about 96 percent of students read at least part of their campus paper.

 ## NEWSPAPER OWNERSHIP

The two most significant facts about newspaper ownership are the following:

1. Concentration of ownership is increasing as large group owners acquire more papers.
2. There has been a decrease in the number of cities with competing papers.

The biggest newspaper group is the Gannett Company with 100 dailies and a combined circulation of about six million. Knight-Ridder Newspapers Inc. controls 31 dailies with about a 3.8 million circulation. Other newspaper chains that own dailies with a combined circulation of more than two million are Advance Publications, Tribune Company, and the New York Times Company (see Table 4–2).

▶▶ The Decline of Competition

Concentration of ownership is not a new trend in the newspaper business. What is new, however, is the dominance of the industry by big group owners. The number of group owners has risen from about 8 in 1900 to approximately 130 in 2003. These 130 groups account for about 80 percent of newspaper circulation.

Coupled with the growth of group ownership is the decline of newspaper competition within single markets. Back in 1923, more than 500 cities had two or more competing daily papers, including 100 that had three or more. By 2003, there were

TABLE 4–2

Biggest Newspaper Groups, 2002 (ranked by revenue)

Name	Number of papers owned	Top paper
Gannett Company Inc.	100	*USA Today*
Knight-Ridder Inc.	31	*Philadelphia Inquirer*
Advance Publications	25	*Cleveland Plain Dealer*
New York Times Co.	11	*New York Times*
Tribune Co.	12	*Chicago Tribune*

only a dozen cities that had independent competing newspapers. In another 12 cities competition was kept alive only through a **joint-operating agreement (JOA).** A JOA is formed, under approval by the Justice Department, to maintain two newspapers in a city when otherwise one would go out of business. Functions of the two papers—circulation, advertising, and production—are combined to save money. Only the editorial staffs remain separate and competitive. JOAs exist between papers in Cincinnati, Tucson, and Birmingham, to name a few examples.

>> The Pros and Cons of Group Ownership

The pros and cons of group ownership and decreasing competition have been widely debated among newspaper executives and press critics. Critics maintain that fewer competing papers means a loss in the diversity of opinions available to the audience. They also claim that top management in group operations places profits above newspaper quality. A newspaper owned by a chain, say these critics, would likely avoid local controversy in its pages to avoid offending advertisers. It has also been charged that chain newspapers are usually under the direction of absentee owners, who may have little knowledge of or concern for local community interests.

On the other hand, those who favor newspaper groups argue that group owners can accomplish certain things that smaller owners cannot. For example, a large group owner can afford to have correspondents and news bureaus in the country's capital, Washington, D.C., and foreign cities—an arrangement too expensive for a small owner to maintain. The chains are also better able to afford the latest technical equipment. Finally, chains have the resources to provide for more elaborate training and public-service programs than those provided by individually owned papers. The validity of each of these arguments depends in great measure on the particular group owner involved. Many group-owned papers are doing excellent jobs. Others may not rate so highly.

PRODUCING THE NEWSPAPER

>> Departments and Staff

The departmental structure and staffing of a newspaper vary with size. All papers, however, are generally divided into three departments: (1) business, (2) production, and (3) news-editorial. The business department is in charge of selling advertising space and building the paper's circulation and revenue through various promotions. As the name implies, the production department

Social Issues   Beware the Blog?

A blog (for Web log) is an online journal replete with fact, opinion, observations, musings, and links to other sites chosen by the author. Blogs exist in a part of cyberspace called the *blogosphere.*

Blogs are a fairly recent phenomenon. There were only a couple dozen in 1999, but their number has since grown quickly thanks to the development of automated publishing systems that make it easy for anyone to start one. Recent estimates put the total number of blogs on the Web somewhere between 500,000 and a million. A new blogger joins the crowd every couple of minutes or so. About five million people read blogs every day.

Most blogs are of interest only to their creators and maybe a couple of friends. Critics call them "soapboxes for the self-absorbed," an "electronic vanity press," or "a self-aggrandizing fad." Despite their faults, blogs have already had a significant effect on journalism and may become even more important in the future.

Most experts agree that blogs became a channel of journalism during and after the terrorist attacks of September 11. People close to the event posted frequent updates on their blogs and provided information and observations that traditional news sources could not offer. September 11 raised the profile of blogs and prompted many in the conventional media to take them seriously.

The power of blogs was demonstrated again in 2003 when Senate Majority Leader Trent Lott made a racially insensitive remark. The mainstream media reported the statement but most then let the story drop. Bloggers, however, kept the story alive by digging into political documents from Lott's past that seemed to echo his current sentiments. It was as if a large team of self-appointed investigative reporters were following the story. Eventually, the major media picked up the bloggers' lead, and the story regained national prominence. Lott was forced to step down.

Bloggers were busy during Operation Iraqi Freedom. Some blogs were compiled by military personnel in the area who offered unedited accounts online. A blogger in Baghdad described day-to-day conditions in the city until the power was knocked out. At a recent technology conference, more than two dozen people blogged the proceedings live and sent digital pictures to thousands of interested people all over the globe, scooping the traditional journalists covering the conference.

Some think that blogs will forever change journalism. Reporter and cybercolumnist Dan Gillmor compared traditional journalism to a lecture: Reporters tell you what they think is important and the audience listens or tunes out. With blogs, journalism is more like a conversation, with the audience taking an active role. Blogging thus represents bottom-up journalism.

Anybody with access to the Internet becomes a reporter and commentator. When a news event occurs, the audience is no longer limited to the news distributed by huge media conglomerates. In an era of increasing media concentration, blogs may represent a way to empower the audience. As Gillmor sums up, blogs add something to the journalistic mix that was missing—the voice of the readership.

Along with their potential, blogs open up new problems. How much credibility can you put into a blogger's report? The information is unfiltered, unedited, and not checked for accuracy. Bloggers are not bound by the two-source rule that professional reporters follow. (A mistake might eventually be caught by other bloggers, but that might take a long time.) In addition, bloggers are not like professional journalists who have no self-interest in the stories they report. Bloggers' self-interest may show through in how they "spin" or color the facts. Further, are bloggers bound by the same ethical rules as journalists? At a recent conference, a speaker asked that his remarks remain off the record. Reporters in the audience honored his request, but several bloggers did not. In the blog era will anything be off the record? Does society need thousands of amateur reporters roaming the streets? Can anything be private anymore?

A good site for those who want to learn more about this phenomenon is www.daypop.com/blogrank. It has links to the 100 most popular blogs.

handles the physical tasks necessary to get the news printed on paper. The most complex department is news-editorial. Note that these two operations—news and editorial—are kept separate by name. The editorial pages contain opinion, while the news pages contain objective reporting.

The managing editor oversees the day-to-day operation of the news department and coordinates the work of the newsroom. The city editor supervises the newspaper's local coverage. He or she assigns reporters to beats (such as city hall or the police) and also directs a staff of general-assignment reporters to handle a variety of stories. The wire editor edits international and national news reported by the

CRITICAL / CULTURAL ISSUES

Rape in the Sports Pages

Contributed by Patricia Joyner Priest, Ph.D.   As a media researcher and an advocate for rape survivors, I have a long-standing interest in how the media cover rape and how people learn about the topic. This is important because, among other things, knowledge—and myths—about rape and its aftermath influences (1) women's assessment of risk, (2) their decision to report the incident, (3) juries' verdicts, and (4) rapists' beliefs that they can get away with the crime. Here's a quick example of the problem: Recently, when I did a search using the key word *rape,* I was dismayed to find that eight of the first ten Web pages listed were porn sites.

Barring some terrible firsthand knowledge, most of us learn about rape from newspaper reports that provide expansive coverage of stranger rapists who commit serial assaults. Acquaintance rape is rarely covered by the press, although women much more commonly are raped by people they know. The one place where reports of acquaintance rape occasionally surface is alongside news of grand slams and touchdowns: in the sports pages. Rapes are reported here because the prominence of people involved in news items is a key factor when editors determine newsworthiness.

There are several troubling aspects of the placement and character of these articles. First, if crime coverage is partly driven by a responsibility to inform people of possible risks, why place reports of rape in a section read less frequently by women? Most troubling is the framing of these stories: The reports cast the *woman* making the claim as the troublemaker, because her allegations threaten the man's—and his team's—future. Sportswriters highlight the suspect's importance to the team with detailed statistics. The articles seem like the kind of handicapping information you might read at a horse race, not sobering indicators of what may be yet another instance of an urgent social problem.

These news stories are formulaic in other ways as well. Denials, often voiced by the man's parents, his defense attorney, and the player himself, are the most salient feature of the initial coverage. While it is *crucial* that the man have his day in court, balance is important, too, so that the sports section does not incessantly promote the insinuation that women who report rape are lying.

It is also common for the coach and teammates to praise the man's character, even though he may have had a history of serious violence. Another frequent theme suggests that the woman has ruined the man's career and life.

It is the woman's reputation, in fact, that is often ruined. Humanizing details about her are rarely provided except to mention negative information such as whether she had been drinking. Instead, she is often portrayed—most prominently by the defense attorney and the alleged assailant—as a prostitute, a "gold digger," a groupie, and a liar.

Statistics indicate the overwhelming odds faced by victims seeking justice. The authors of the book *Pros and Cons* write, "Of the 217 felony sexual assault complaints against college and professional athletes that were reported to police between 1986 and 1995, only 66 ever reached the trial stage. [Of these,] 85% were acquitted."

Women who think of rapists only as strangers who jump out from behind bushes are woefully uninformed about this basic, terrible fact: An acquaintance can get away with rape fairly easily, because the man can claim consent. It is that simple. And it's simpler still for sports heroes, accustomed throughout their lives to special treatment, even—or especially—when they step over the line.

The rare cases that make it to court are usually dropped for lack of evidence. Yet we warn women that resistance might make things worse. And, clearly, many of the suspects would be highly intimidating assailants, even if they do not brandish a weapon.

We rarely perceive these harmful cultural patterns of reporting about and responding to rape, but I've talked to people visiting the United States who are often puzzled by the victim-blaming stance of the public and the press. Perhaps it will help to consider this: What if a man went up to an athlete's hotel room—perhaps because the player said he had to get something or had to use the bathroom—and then the sports star raped *him?* Would we think the man was stupid, naive, or "asking for it"? See how gendered attitudes can shape our thinking, the criminal's behavior (if he knows he will probably get away with it), the response of the criminal justice system, and media coverage?

1. Think about coverage of rape you've seen (or look up some news stories about rapes). To what extent and in what ways do these stories reinforce the problems written about here?

2. If you were a reporter, what types of things do you think you'd want to include in (or exclude from) rape stories?

3. What can we, as consumers and citizens, do to try to change this pattern of reporting about and responding to rape?

major news services, such as the Associated Press. Most newspapers also have one or more staff people who are responsible for preparing the editorial pages.

>> Prepublication Routine

There are two basic sources for news copy: local reporting and wire services. Early in the day the wire editor scans the outputs from the wire machines and flags possible stories for the day's paper. At the same time, the city editor is assigning stories to various reporters, and the managing editor is gauging the available space, the *newshole,* that can be devoted to news in that day's edition. This space changes according to the number of ads scheduled to appear on any one day. The greater the number of ads, the greater the number of pages that can be printed and the larger the newshole.

As the day progresses, reporters file their stories electronically via laptop or desktop computer. These stories are edited and then processed by a design desk. Editors decide page makeup. Photos and graphics are added and pages are put together. The pages are sent to a composing room and then to the press where they are printed and bundled together for delivery.

This routine, of course does not apply to the paper's online version. There is no newshole to worry about; stories can be as long as needed. Some content is rewritten from the print edition while other content is original. Links to full-length documents or other sources can be added as well as audio or video clips. When finished stories are posted to the site, there is no need for a composing room or a press. Updates to stories can be posted continuously or at specific times of the day.

ECONOMICS

Newspapers derive their income from two sources: advertising, which provides about 80 percent of the total, and circulation (revenue from subscriptions and single-copy sales), which accounts for the other 20 percent. Advertising revenue is closely related to circulation since papers with a large circulation are able to charge more for ads that will reach a larger audience.

The newspaper industry went through a period of cost cutting from the mid-1990s to the turn of the century. Staff sizes were reduced, paper sizes were narrowed, and more efficient production techniques were introduced in an effort to keep papers profitable. As a result, the industry was still in good financial health as of 2003. In fact, profit margins were still hovering around the 20 percent mark, compared to about a 12 percent margin for all industries.

Despite this rosy situation, a look at the longer term reveals several potential threats to this prosperity. First and most ominous, newspapers face increased competition for advertising dollars from cable TV, billboards, direct mail, and Websites. Newspapers' share of the total amount of money spent on advertising was 29 percent in the late 1970s. In 2002, that number had slipped to about 20 percent. Second, the number of people who regularly read a newspaper has been dropping steadily for more than 25 years, and the drop is most pronounced among young people, the exact audience that advertisers want to reach. Lastly, as mentioned earlier, although some papers are beginning to make money from their online operations, for many papers the electronic edition still loses money.

On the bright side, newspapers take in circulation and advertising revenues every day, making them good cash-flow businesses. Furthermore, the majority of newspapers enjoy a monopoly in their markets and represent a cost-effective way for advertisers to reach a local community. How long the current prosperity will last, however, is anybody's guess.

>> Advertising Revenue

Advertising revenue comes from four separate sources:

1. local retail advertising,
2. classified ads,
3. national advertising, and
4. prepaid inserts.

Local retail advertising is purchased by stores and service establishments. Department stores, supermarkets, auto dealers, and discount stores are the businesses that buy large amounts of space. Classified advertising, which is bought by local businesses and individuals, is generally run in a special section in the back of the newspaper. Buyers and sellers purchase classified ads for a wide range of products and services. National advertising originates with manufacturers of products that need to reach a national market on a mass basis. The majority of these ads are for automobiles, food, airlines, and Web-based companies. Prepaid inserts, or preprints, are advertising supplements put together by national, regional, and local businesses that are inserted into the copies of the paper. Companies such as Sears and Best Buy frequently use preprints. The paper charges the advertiser for the distribution of the preprints.

Local retail ads account for the most advertising revenue, about 45 percent. Classified ads rank next, accounting for about 36 percent in 2002. This figure is down from about 40 percent in 2000, probably due to the competition from Websites such as Monster.com and others that carry classified ads. The remaining 19 percent of revenue comes from preprints and national ads.

>> Circulation Revenue

Circulation revenue includes all the receipts from selling the paper to the consumer. The newspaper, however, does not receive the total price paid by a reader for a copy of the paper because of the many distribution systems that are employed to get the newspaper to the consumer. The most common method is for the paper to sell copies to a distributor at wholesale prices, usually about 25 percent less than the retail price. Other methods include hiring full-time employees as carriers and billing subscribers in advance. These methods show promise, but they also increase the cost of distribution.

One closely studied factor important in determining circulation revenue is the effect of increased subscription and single-copy prices. In 1970, 89 percent of newspapers were priced at 10 cents a copy. In 2003, none cost less than 25 cents. Most cost 50 cents or more. Sunday papers have shown similar increases. In 1970, the typical price was 25 cents. By

S O U N D B Y T E

Who?

Beat reporters need to know the jargon of the area they cover lest embarrassing things happen. A case in point: A new reporter covering the legal circuit for a Virginia paper did not know that FNU (first name unknown) and LNU (last name unknown) were common abbreviations in Virginia law enforcement. Unaware of this jargon, the newcomer dutifully reported that a Mr. Fnu Lnu had been indicted by a grand jury.

Newspapers are turning to automation to save money. These robot paper movers work for the *Rocky Mountain News.*

2003, it was more than $1.50. The rising price of newspapers has probably had some negative impact on circulation revenue. Several papers have noted a decrease in subscriptions among older, fixed-income residents following a price increase.

>> ## General Expenses

The costs of running a newspaper can be viewed in several ways. One common method is to divide the costs by function:

1. news and editorial costs;
2. expenses involved in selling local, national, and classified ads;
3. mechanical costs, including composition and plate production;
4. printing costs, such as newsprint (the paper), ink, and the cost of running the press;
5. circulation and distribution costs; and
6. general administrative costs, such as secretarial and clerical services and the cost of soliciting for subscriptions.

Some of these costs are variable. For example, printing costs increase as the number of printed copies increases. Distribution costs also increase with circulation size. Other costs are fixed. The expense of sending a reporter to the airport to cover a visiting dignitary is about the same for a paper with a circulation of 10,000 as for one with a circulation of 100,000. This means that the cost of running a newspaper depends somewhat on the size of the paper. For a small paper (circulation about 25,000), general administrative costs rank first, accounting for about one-third of all expenses. The cost of newsprint and ink ranks second, followed by mechanical costs. Total expenses for this size daily run about $3 million to $5 million per year. In the case of a big-city daily (circulation 200,000), newsprint and ink costs rank first, followed by administrative expenses and mechanical costs. On the average, newsprint accounts for about 25 cents of every dollar spent by a paper.

FEEDBACK

>> The Audit Bureau of Circulations

The best-known feedback system for newspapers is that connected with the **Audit Bureau of Circulations (ABC).** During the early 1900s, with the growth of mass advertising, some publishers began inflating the number of readers in order to attract more revenue from advertisers. In an effort to check this deceptive practice, advertisers and publishers joined to form the ABC in 1914. The organization's purpose was to establish ground rules for counting circulation, to make sure that the rules were enforced, and to provide verified reports of circulation data. The ABC audits about three-fourths of all print media in the United States and Canada, about 2,600 publications.

The ABC functions in the following manner. Publishers keep detailed records of circulation data. Twice a year, publishers file a circulation statement with the ABC, which the ABC in turn disseminates to its clients. Once every year, the ABC audits publications to verify that the figures that have been reported are accurate. An ABC representative visits the publication and is free to examine records and files.

In an average year, the ABC's field staff of 90 travels approximately 300,000 miles and spends about 135,000 audit hours in verifying the facts on member publications' circulation. The cost of the ABC's services, about $5 million per year, is financed through member dues and service fees.

In late 2001, the ABC began reporting readership figures along with circulation data for more than 50 newspapers. The new readership report provides demographic information about subscribers, those who buy single copies of a paper, and pass-along readership. This new service provides newspapers with the same type of information as the Nielsen reports for the TV industry (see Chapter 10) and will help them better demonstrate their advertising effectiveness.

>> Newspaper Audiences

As of 2003, approximately 56 million copies of morning and evening papers, either purchased at the newsstand or delivered to the doorstep, found their way into American homes every weekday. Daily newspaper circulation, in absolute terms, has decreased since 1970, as a glance at Table 4–3 shows. The population, however, has been increasing. To reflect this fact and to provide additional perspective, column four of the table presents the ratio of daily circulation to the total

TABLE 4–3

Daily and Weekly Newspaper Circulation

Source: Compiled by author.
*1990 and 2000 figures not comparable to prior years as a result of change in information collection methods.

Year	All daily papers	All weekly papers	Daily circulation per 1,000 adults
1960	58,882,000	21,328,000	475
1970	62,108,000	29,423,000	428
1980	62,201,840	40,970,000	360
1990	62,327,962	56,181,047*	329
2000	55,772,847	70,949,633	287

adult population of the United States (expressed in thousands). As can be seen, daily newspaper circulation is not keeping pace with the overall growth of the population.

The percentage of adults reading one or more papers every day has declined from about 80 percent in the early 1960s to about 57 percent in 2003. The most pronounced decline has occurred in the 18-to-29 and 30-to-44 age groups and among those who have not attended college. The overall drop in daily circulation has been most noticeable in urban areas. As Figure 4–3 shows, newspaper circulation in cities with more than a half-million residents dropped about 24 percent between 1973 and 2000. Conversely, circulation in medium-size towns with populations between 50,000 and 500,000 increased 46 percent. Circulation in smaller communities decreased about 42 percent in the same period.

Why the overall decline? Some have attributed it to the increased mobility of Americans, the increase in single-person households, more expensive subscription and per-copy prices, a general decline in the level of reading ability among young people, and competition from other media.

Print newspapers are losing readers to online media. In 1995, about 4 percent of the U.S. population went online at least once a week to get their news. By 2003, the figure was more than 25 percent. A recent survey by the Pew Research Center found that one in seven Internet users have reduced the amount of time that they spend with daily newspapers. The key demographic group that reads most of its news online is young adults—the same group that reads print papers

FIGURE 4–3

Fluctuations in Daily-Newspaper Circulation by Size of City, 1973–2000

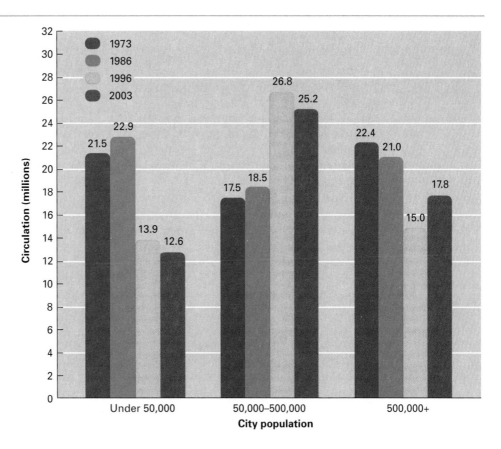

the least. When people go online for news they do not necessarily go to online newspapers. Many visit portals such as Excite or Yahoo; some go to search engines such as Google; while others check CNN.com or a TV network news website.

CAREER OUTLOOK

THE NEWSPAPER INDUSTRY

The newspaper industry is a big employer. In 2003, newspaper employment exceeded 445,000 people. In fact, newspapers now rank among the leaders in the Labor Department's listing of the nation's manufacturing employees. More women are entering careers in journalism. The 2003 workforce was about 48 percent female.

The economic prosperity of the past decade helped improve the job market for those going into the journalism profession. More jobs became available, and average pay increased. Nonetheless, the newspaper industry has historically been one of the lowest-paying media industries. A 1999 survey by the *Columbia Journalism Review* found that entry-level reporters for print newspapers were making between $18,000 and $25,000, ranking them below their counterparts in broadcast and magazine journalism.

>> Entry-Level Positions

A person seeking an entry-level job as a reporter has the best chance of landing a job at a small daily paper or weekly. Starting out at a small paper will give a newcomer experience in several areas of newspaper work, since the division of labor at these papers is less clear. A reporter might also function as a photographer, edit wire copy, and write headlines. One possible way to break into the profession is to secure a summer job or an internship. Additionally, some people break into the profession as proofreaders, rewrite persons, or researchers.

Other entry-level jobs can be found in the business side of the paper. Students who are interested in this type of work should have a background in business, advertising, and economics, along with a knowledge of mass communication. Since advertising is such an important source of newspaper revenue, most newspapers will gladly accept a newcomer who wishes to work in the sales department.

Of course, online newspapers represent a further opportunity. The kinds of jobs that are available are varied and are still being defined: Information has to be filed in the appropriate places, files must be updated, graphics need to be designed, e-mail must be answered, story leads suggested by subscribers need to be checked out, and so forth.

>> Upward Mobility

A person who is selecting an entry-level position in newspapers should consider where the job might lead and how long it will take to get there. In the case of a reporter, upward mobility can come in one of two ways. A reporter can advance by becoming skilled in editing and move up to the position of copyeditor or perhaps state editor, regional editor, or wire editor. The ultimate goal for this person would be the city editor's or managing editor's slot. Other reporters might not wish to take on the additional administrative and desk work that goes with a managerial position. If that is the case, then career advancement consists of moving on to larger-circulation papers in big cities or to increased specialization in one field of reporting.

On the business side, the route for advancement in the advertising department usually leads from the classifieds to the national advertising division. This department works with manufacturers of nationally distributed products and services and plans display advertising for these companies. Those who begin in the circulation department can eventually rise to the position of circulation manager. Ultimately, the top job that can be reached, short of publisher, is that of business manager, the person in charge of the entire business side of the paper.

MAIN POINTS

- Newspapers in colonial America were published with permission of the local government. A free press did not appear until after the Revolution.

- The mass newspaper arrived in the 1830s with the publication of Benjamin Day's *New York Sun*, the first of the penny-press papers.

- The era of yellow journalism featured sensationalism, crusades, and human-interest reporting and introduced more attractive newspaper designs.

- Many newspapers were merged or folded during the early 1900s. Tabloid papers became popular. The trend toward consolidation would continue into the years following World War II.

- There are four types of daily papers: national newspapers, large metro dailies, suburban dailies,

and small-town dailies. Other major types of papers are weeklies, special-service newspapers, and minority newspapers.

- More than 1,000 papers now have online versions.

- Newspaper ownership is characterized by large group owners and declining competition.

- Newspapers are currently enjoying financial prosperity but are worried about competition from online media and declining readership among young adults.

- Newspaper audiences are measured by the Audit Bureau of Circulations. Newspaper readership has declined for the past several decades, with big-city dailies hardest hit by the decrease.

QUESTIONS FOR REVIEW

1. Trace the changes in the definition of *news* from the 1600s to 2000.
2. What are the defining characteristics of newspapers?
3. What are some of the advantages the traditional ink-and-paper newspaper has over the online version? What are some of the advantages the online version has over the print version?
4. What are the main revenue sources for newspapers?

QUESTIONS FOR CRITICAL THINKING

1. Why don't young people read a newspaper? What, if anything, could newspapers do to recapture this audience segment?
2. Has the growth of newspaper group owners helped or hurt the newspaper industry? Has it helped or hurt society?
3. Should newspapers be allowed to own broadcast stations in their markets? Why? Why not?
4. Will the online version eventually replace the print version of a newspaper? Why or why not?

KEY TERMS

political press (p. 88)
First Amendment (p. 89)
penny press (p. 91)
yellow journalism (p. 93)
jazz journalism (p. 94)

tabloids (p. 94)
newshole (p. 97)
tablet PCs (p. 101)
circulation (p. 102)
zoned editions (p. 109)

joint-operating agreement (JOA) (p. 108)
Audit Bureau of Circulations (ABC) (p. 114)

INTERNET RESOURCES

Online Learning Center

At the Online Learning Center home page, www.mhhe.com/dominick8, *select* Student Center *and then* Chapter 4.

1. Use the Learning Objectives, Chapter Outline, Main Points, and Time Line sections to review this chapter.
2. Test your knowledge of the chapter using the multiple choice, crossword puzzle, and flashcard features of the site.
3. Expand your knowledge of concepts and topics discussed in the chapter by going to *Suggestions for Further Reading* and *Internet Exercises*.

PowerWeb

At the Mass Communication home page of PowerWeb, www.dushkin.com/powerweb, *log in and select* Mass Communication *as your title. On the next screen, select* Topics *and then quick jump to* News Reporting. *Read Article 24, "Details, Details" Then answer the following questions:*

1. What is the difference between "narrative" journalism and ordinary journalism?
2. Why don't we see more examples of narrative journalism?
3. How does narrative journalism compare to documentary filmmaking? Are there techniques used by both?

Surfing the Internet

The following are examples of sites that deal with the newspaper industry. All listings were current as of late 2003.

www.cln.com
Creative Loafing Online, a guide to the arts, culture, and entertainment. A good illustration of the nontraditional weekly press.

www.decaturdailydemocrat.com
A good example of a slick online paper published by a small-town daily.

www.naa.org
Site of the Newspaper Association of America, a major industry trade organization. Contains information on newspaper circulation, public policy, and diversity, as well as links to the organization's *presstime* magazine. A hot-link feature allows visitors to see a list of newspapers online in a chosen state.

www.ojr.org
The *Online Journalism Review,* published by the University of Southern California, the best single source for the latest information on Internet journalism.

www.theonion.com
Looks like an authentic online paper but is not.

www.usatoday.com
Colorful site of the national daily *USA Today.* Looks familiar because it is modeled after the paper-and-ink version.

5

MAGAZINES

This chapter will prepare you to

- discuss the characteristics of magazines;

- understand how the magazine industry is divided;

- understand the function of Mediamark Research Inc. (MRI);

- explain how the Internet supplements magazines and expands and enriches the reading experience;

- identify the five main magazine content categories; and

- describe the departments that produce magazines.

When it first started in 1996, *Yahoo! Internet Life (YIL)* was touted more as a lifestyle guide than a technology magazine. It did contain articles about the best Web health and travel sites, product guides, and how-to articles on downloading from the Web, but it also published articles on politics, ethics, style, privacy, and entertaining. The magazine attracted a diverse readership all of whom had one thing in common: They were interested in technology and the Internet. Naturally, high-tech dot-com companies were eager to reach this crowd, and *YIL* grew from a circulation of 175,000 in 1996 to more than a million

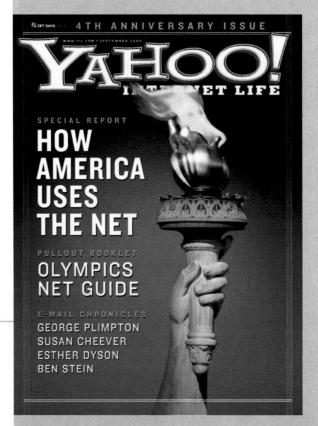

Yahoo! Internet Life started strong but wound up as one of the casualties of the dotcom crash.

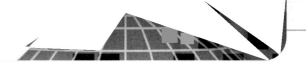

in 2000. Advertising revenue increased from $2 million to more than $63 million in the same time period. By any measure, *YIL* was a success.

Then things started to go sour. The Internet bubble burst. Many of the magazine's dot-com advertisers didn't survive the shakeout. Attempts to increase ad sales to more traditional companies failed because the magazine did not fit a conventional demographic niche. To top it off, a declining economy dried up advertising dollars across all media. Consequently, advertising revenues plummeted, down more than 50 percent in the first six months of 2002. Ironically, the magazine's circulation actually increased during this time, but advertising was the most important part of *YIL's* revenue streams. With little evidence that the advertising market would pick up, the publisher had little choice but to pull the plug. Several other high-tech magazines met the same fate.

The short life of *Yahoo! Internet Life* illustrates some lessons about the modern magazine industry. First, like *YIL,* most magazines now depend more than ever on advertising revenue to keep them afloat. Subscription prices tend to be kept low to increase the readership numbers that advertisers want to see. If advertising dollars flow freely, as they did around the turn of the century, the industry thrives. If advertising dollars are hard to come by, as they were in 2002–2003, then the industry falters. Second, magazines are becoming even more of a specialized medium. Illustrating the degree of specialization in the industry are a magazine for people who have pet ferrets and another for people who own luxury pools (not just normal pools but luxury pools). In *YIL's* case, the magazine's narrow specialization was primarily attractive to a specialized industry. When that industry tanked, *YIL's* audience was too amorphous to attract other advertisers. Finally, despite the failure of many magazines whose content dealt with the Internet, the overall relationship between the magazine industry and the Internet has been favorable. Traditional magazines publish both print and online editions. Many magazines use their digital versions to sell subscriptions to their print counterparts. Some magazine websites sell books, CDs, or other products. In sum, even through poor economic times, magazines have done a respectable job of adjusting to the digital revolution.

This chapter will examine the history, structure, and organization of the ever-changing magazine business.

 ## HISTORY

>> The Colonial Period

In colonial times, *magazine* meant "warehouse" or "depository," a place where various types of provisions were stored under one roof. The first **magazines** printed in America were patterned after this model; they were to be storehouses of varied literary materials gathered from books, pamphlets, and newspapers and bound together under one cover.

It was Ben Franklin who first announced plans to start a magazine in the colonies. Unfortunately for him, a competitor named Andrew Bradford got wind of his idea and beat Franklin to the punch. Bradford's *American Magazine* was published a few days before Franklin's *General Magazine* in 1741. The two publications carried political and economic articles aimed at an intelligent audience.

Both Franklin's and Bradford's magazines were ambitious ventures in that they were designed for readers in all 13 colonies and deliberately tried to influence public opinion; both quickly folded because of financial problems. The next significant attempt at magazine publishing occurred in Philadelphia when another Bradford (this one named William) started the *American Magazine and Monthly Chronicle* in 1757. This publication also contained the usual blend of political and economic articles mixed with a little humor; it was well edited and able to support itself for a year.

As America's political relations with England deteriorated, magazines, like newspapers, assumed a significant political role. Thomas Paine, who, in his rousing pamphlet *Common Sense,* argued for separation from England, became editor of the *Pennsylvania Magazine.* This publication strongly supported the Revolution and was a significant political force during the early days of the war. It became an early casualty of the conflict, however, and closed down in 1776.

All these early magazines were aimed at a specialized audience—one that was educated, literate, and primarily urban. Their overall impact was to encourage literary and artistic expression and to unify the colonies during America's struggle for independence from England.

>> After the Revolution

Magazines popular during the late 18th and early 19th centuries contained a mix of political and topical articles directed primarily at an educated elite. The birth of the modern newsmagazine can be traced back to this period. *Niles Weekly Register,* which reported current events of the time, was read throughout the country.

Politics was also reflected in other magazines of the period. One of the most influential was the *Port Folio,* edited by the colorful nonconformist Joseph Dennie. Dennie's intended audience was a select one; he wished to reach "Men of Affluence, Men of Liberality, and Men of Letters." Although the major thrust of the paper was political, Dennie interspersed travelogues, theater reviews, satirical essays, and even jokes.

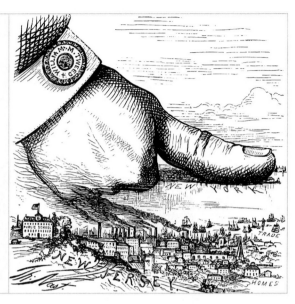

This political cartoon, titled "Under the Thumb," was created by Thomas Nast and appeared in *Harper's Weekly* during the summer of 1871.

>> The Penny-Press Era

While the penny press was opening up new markets for newspapers (see Chapter 4), magazine publishers were also expanding their appeal and coverage. The *Knickerbocker, Graham's Magazine,* and the *Saturday Evening Post,* all established between 1820 and 1840, were written not so much for the intelligentsia as for the generally literate middle classes. By 1842, *Graham's,* under the direction of Edgar Allan Poe, had a circulation of 40,000. The growing social and economic importance of women was illustrated by the birth of *Godey's Lady's Book* in 1830 and *Peterson's* in 1842. These two magazines offered articles on fashion, morals, diets, and health, and printed elaborate, hand-colored engravings in their pages. *Godey's,* under the editorship of Sara Hale, was a pioneer for women's rights and was the first magazine to campaign for wider recognition of women writers. (See Media Probe, "Sara Josepha Buell Hale.")

In 1850, *Harper's Monthly* was started as a magazine that would present material that had already appeared in other sources (rather like the *Reader's Digest,* except that the articles were reprinted in full). *Harper's* also included elaborate woodcut illustrations along with its articles in double-sized issues. *Harper's Weekly* was instituted seven years later and was to become famous for its illustrations of the Civil War. In 1863, this magazine began publishing reproductions of Mathew Brady's war photographs.

The most famous example of the crusading approach of the penny press was the *Harper's Weekly* campaign against the corrupt political administration in New York in 1870. Under the control of William "Boss" Tweed, a group of unscrupulous politicians managed to bilk the city out of approximately $200 million. The editorial cartoons of Thomas Nast were credited with helping bring down this ring.

>> The Magazine Boom

In 1860, there were approximately 260 magazines published in the United States; by 1900, there were 1,800. Why the surge? The primary factors were more available money, better printing techniques that lowered prices, and especially the Postal Act of 1879, which gave magazines special mailing rates. It became possible to aim for a national market on a mass scale, and several magazines set out to do just that.

The most successful of the magazines seeking a mass market was the *Ladies' Home Journal,* founded by Cyrus Curtis in 1881. The first issue, eight pages long, contained an illustrated short story, an article on growing flowers, fashion notes, child care advice, needlework hints, and recipes. Curtis was the first to recognize the potential for national advertising in the magazine industry.

The general crusading spirit of the press spilled over onto the pages of leading magazines of the late 1890s and early 1900s. Theodore Roosevelt dubbed the magazines that embraced this reform movement **muckrakers.** Corrupt practices in big business was the first topic to activate the muckrakers' zeal. *McClure's* ran an exposé of the Standard Oil Company by Ida M. Tarbell. Although it carried the innocuous title "History of the Standard Oil Company," the article was filled with dynamite, for it revealed bribery, fraud, unfair business practices, and violence. Shocking stories on political corruption in big cities and another series on crooked practices in the railroad industry followed Tarbell's initial effort. Other magazines joined in. *Cosmopolitan* published "The Treason of the Senate" in 1906. It followed up with attacks on the International Harvester Company. By 1912, the trend toward crusades and exposés had spent itself.

The beginning of life for *Life:* The magazine's first cover was shot by famous photographer Margaret Bourke-White.

Many of the problems uncovered by the muckrakers had been remedied. Most important, the public had grown tired of the crusades and magazines had to search for other ways to attract readers.

>> Between the Wars

Shifting economic conditions and changing lifestyles in the decades following World War I also influenced magazine development. Three distinct types evolved in the years between World War I and World War II: (1) the digest, (2) the newsmagazine, and (3) the pictorial magazine.

The finest example of the digest genre, *Reader's Digest,* appeared in 1922. Although this magazine reprinted articles that had appeared elsewhere, it first condensed and edited the material so that it could be read by people in a hurry.

The idea of a newsmagazine was not new—examples could be found in the 19th century. *Time,* however, borrowed little from its predecessors. From its beginning in 1923, *Time* based its format on an original concept: the distillation and compartmentalization of news under various departments. Other innovations included the use of the narrative style to report news stories; group journalism produced by the pooling of the efforts of reporters, writers, and editors into anonymous articles; the institution of a large research department; and a brash, punchy, jargonish writing style. The magazine prospered slowly, but by

Time magazine celebrated its 75th birthday in 1998. Henry Luce, its creator, was only 24 years old when he published this first issue.

1930 it was turning a substantial profit. Two imitators, *Newsweek* and *U.S. News,* appeared in 1933.

In the mid-1930s, two magazines, *Life* and *Look,* revived the tradition of the pictorial weekly originated by *Harper's* and *Leslie's. Life* was launched in 1936 and had almost a quarter of a million subscribers before it even had a name. It featured public figures caught in unguarded moments, photo essays, occasional glamour shots, and articles on the arts. In this format, *Life* would live for 36 years (it would reappear in the late 1970s in a totally different format). *Look* hit the newsstands in 1937, just two months behind *Life. Look* lacked the current-affairs emphasis of its forerunner and concentrated more on personalities and features. Over the years, it evolved into a family-oriented magazine. *Look* expired in 1972.

>> The Postwar Period

Magazines of the postwar era reflected publishers' firm belief that the one way to become profitable was to specialize. Increased leisure time created a market for sports magazines such as *Field and Stream, Sports Afield, Golf Digest, Popular Boating,* and *Sports Illustrated.* Scientific advances also generated a resurgence of a popularized version of *Scientific American.*

The rapid expansion of urban communities and urban lifestyles gave rise to many specialized publications. Liberalized attitudes toward sex prompted such ventures as *Confidential* (1952) and the trendsetting *Playboy* (1953). During the 1960s, the rebirth of an interest in urban culture encouraged the rise of "city" magazines, of which *New York* is probably the best example. For the black press, the most significant development in the 1950s was the expansion of black magazines. John Johnson had started *Negro Digest* back in 1942 and used his profits to publish *Ebony,* whose format imitated that of *Life,* in 1945. In the early years of the 1950s, he added *Jet,* a weekly newsmagazine, and *Tan.* These were followed later by *Black World* and *Essence.*

>> Contemporary Magazines

After several years of economic growth, magazines, along with most other media, hit tough economic times in 2002–2003. Increasing costs and declining advertising revenues forced magazines including *Mademoiselle, Working Woman, Talk,* and

Sports Illustrated Women to shut down. Experts were forecasting more lean times before things got better.

Magazines also faced marketing problems. Supermarkets and big discount stores such as Wal-Mart were becoming more selective about the number of magazines they would display on their shelves. Sweepstakes competitions, such as the one conducted by the Publisher's Clearinghouse, have been discontinued because of legal problems. In response, many magazines have offered readers deep discounts in subscription prices. As a result of all these factors, single-copy sales of magazines have continued to decline.

The industry is becoming more volatile. More than 700 new magazines start up every year; only about 40 percent are still in business 12 months later. The biggest circulation successes during the first years of the new century, *Maxim* and *O,* did not even exist in 1995. The current trend in magazine publishing is finding a hot topic and quickly launching a magazine to capitalize on it. When the topic cools, so do the magazines devoted to it. The popularity of wrestling around the turn of the century, for example, inspired the birth of several magazines. When the craze faded, these magazines lost circulation.

The magazine business continues to be dominated by a few big companies that publish best-selling magazines. The top five magazine publishers accounted for nearly 40 percent of the revenue of the entire industry in 2002.

Several magazines, such as *Slate* and *Salon,* appeared in an online-only form. Many traditional print magazine publishers viewed these competitors with apprehension because they feared the online products would take away readers and advertising revenue. As it turned out, they need not have worried. In general, online-only editions were generally money-losing propositions. A few narrowly targeted "e-zines" and some business-to-business publications managed to make a profit, but these were the exceptions. Overall, the Internet turned out to be more of a friend than an enemy to traditional print magazines.

MAGAZINES IN THE DIGITAL AGE

Magazines and other print media face a dilemma when dealing with the Internet. On the one hand, they need an online presence to stay competitive, but on the other hand, if they put the print magazine's content on the Web for free, they risk hurting the print magazine's circulation. Initially, magazines hoped that their websites would bring in additional revenue and attract a new group of online readers that might offset any declines in print circulation. As a result, around the turn of the century many magazines hired large staffs to run online sites, and they made sure that the Web versions had the latest technological bells and whistles to impress visitors.

During 2003–2004 the weakening economy and the failure of the Internet to live up to some of the hype that surrounded it forced publishers to take a second look at their online activities. Many cut back their online staffs and budgets. Websites that featured the latest and "coolest" high-tech tools were scaled down into something more realistic. As of 2004, it seems apparent that print magazines have learned to coexist with the Internet. It is not the threat that they once imagined, nor has it lived up to some of its more optimistic forecasts. In sum, the Internet has become a complement to the traditional print magazine.

CRITICAL / CULTURAL ISSUES

Lessons from *YM*: A Feminist Analysis

YM is one of the most popular magazines aimed at teenage girls, read by almost eight million female teens. A typical *YM* issue contains articles on hair, fashion, cosmetics, dating tips, romance, sexual mores, and advice. A recent issue, for example, contained such articles as "Back to School Beauty and Fashion Blowout," "Guy Truths and Lies: What They Really Think About Fast Girls and Mushy Moments," and "Ten Little Love Lies Every Girl Should Tell."

What are the lessons that *YM* is teaching young females? This was the focus of a 1996 article in the *Journal of Communication Inquiry.* The authors, Margaret Duffy and J. Michael Gotcher, analyzed articles that appeared in *YM* between 1993 and 1995 and found several congruent themes that pictured a consistent view of gender relations: Getting the guy was the most important thing. The authors contend that *YM* portrays a world in which the only power that is available to a young woman comes through seduction, beauty, and fashion and that the magazine further convinces teens that this arrangement is natural and desirable.

Duffy and Gotcher point out that, in general, *YM*'s articles focus on romance, love, and sex—which are intimately linked to fashion, beauty, and cosmetics and to information regarding how to get the guy. For instance, one prominent theme in *YM* is that a girl's power of attraction can be increased by getting the right information. The magazine typically runs articles such as "How Can I Get Guys to Notice Me?" "What Am I Supposed to Wear?" and "How Far Should I Go on a Date?" Answers and advice about these issues come from supermodels, celebrities, doctors, and psychologists. And, not surprisingly, much of the advice concerns products and services that young girls can purchase in hopes of becoming more attractive. The use of credible sources suggests that this information is an important and normal part of everyday life.

Another theme is that wearing the right clothes will provide young women the power they need to attract men. Many photo layouts show young models in mildly suggestive costumes, and accompanying copy stresses the commanding strength that goes with looking good. Some illustrative titles are "Killer Clothes—They'll Knock Him Dead," "Flirty Dresses—They'll Have Him at Your Mercy," and "Totally Touchable Sweaters—Fuzzy Cover-Ups to Make Him Want to Cuddle You." These articles usually include brand names and prices for the clothing items shown. These displays suggest that buying high-priced clothing is the natural way for young women to become happy.

In sum, the authors note that *YM* portrays the pursuit of males as almost the only purpose in life and as an unquestioned good thing to do. Nowhere in the magazine is it suggested that a young woman might find a rewarding life through personal achievements, education, friendship, public service, or other avenues. The world of *YM* provides young women with little information on occupational opportunities (other than modeling) and depicts a world in which success is determined by how well a female meets the needs and expectations of males. Women are shown that they can gain power and happiness by purchasing the right dress or brand of cosmetics or by implementing manipulative strategies recommended in the magazine. Duffy's and Gotcher's article concludes by pointing out that *YM* provides an inadequate range of models for female teens to consult when attempting to find meaning in the world around them.

1. *YM* is aimed at female teens. To what extent are the themes contained in *YM* also present in magazines aimed at adult women (such as *Cosmo* or *Ladies' Home Journal*)?

2. How might this emphasis on attractiveness, trendy fashions, and the pursuit of males affect the self-esteem of young women who are overweight or unable to afford the "right" clothes? What about the self-worth of young teens who are discovering they are lesbians?

3. What responsibilities might the editors of *YM* have to present a more well-rounded, realistic picture of young womanhood?

>> Symbiosis

Almost every major magazine, and many not-so-major ones, has an online counterpart. Magazinesatoz.com contains links to the home pages of more than 1,300 periodicals ranging from *Entertainment Weekly* to *The Profitable Embroiderer.* Most experts agree that it would be difficult to launch a new print magazine without also launching a website. For example, both *CosmoGirl!* and *ChicSimple* debuted simultaneously in print and online.

The print version and the online version of magazines complement each other in various ways. Many magazines, such as *Newsweek,* refer readers to their websites for additional information and longer versions of stories. Visitors to a magazine's home page can subscribe to the print version online. Big media conglomerates use their magazine websites to promote other company holdings. Time.com, for instance, contains banner ads for CNN and a special offer from AOL, both of which are owned by Time Warner.

In addition, Time Warner is using the popular magazines *People* and *Entertainment Weekly* to help AOL. Full-time access to the websites for these magazines is restricted to AOL subscribers and magazine subscribers. A person who buys a copy at a newsstand is given a one-week pass to the sites via a code word printed in the magazines.

>> Additional Revenue Streams

Many magazine publishers have found ways to bring in additional dollars through their websites. Most sell space for banner ads on their sites. Others engage in e-commerce and sell books, DVDs, or CDs that are produced by the parent company. The *Good Housekeeping* home page, for example, contains a link to a page where viewers can order books bearing the Good Housekeeping brand. Another arrangement is for the magazine to make a deal with an online retailer and use the magazine's website to attract customers to the retailer. The magazine makes its money by taking a small percentage of the sales or by charging a flat fee to the retailer. To illustrate, *Modern Bride* has a deal whereby local companies that provide wedding services are listed state by state on its website. Other magazines charge for special services. The online version of *Time* makes its archive of past articles dating back to the mid-1980s available to readers who are willing to pay $2.50 to copy a single article or to pay a monthly subscription fee for unlimited downloads.

>> Digital Delivery

One of the advantages of the digital revolution that became possible only recently is the ability to deliver copies of a magazine in digital form to PCs and laptops. The idea behind digital delivery is that readers like their magazine reading experience exactly as it has been for hundreds of years. Therefore, a digitally delivered magazine tries to duplicate the paper magazine reading experience as closely as possible. Unlike an online magazine, in which a reader can choose from a menu of selected content edited for the Web, a digitally delivered magazine contains all the stories, graphics, fancy layouts, headlines, ads, and even the annoying little subscription cards that a person would find in the print version. Unlike the online version, in which a reader has to scroll to read a story, the digital version is displayed one page at a time, and the pages are displayed side by side as is the case with the print version. The display even simulates page turning.

As of late 2003, a company called Zinio Systems offered digital subscriptions to more than two dozen magazines, including *Business Week* and *Seventeen.* Other companies are exploring ways to deliver magazine content to handheld, wireless devices such as PDAs and IBM's new Tablet PC (see Chapter 4).

Digital delivery offers many advantages. For the publisher, it is much cheaper to deliver magazines digitally than it is to print them on paper and send them through

The home page of zinio.com, where you can subscribe to your favorite magazine in digital form

the mail. In addition, a digital version can contain audio and video files and hyperlinks and can be searched easily. On the downside, not everybody likes to read from a screen, and you cannot stick a digital version of a magazine in your pocket. In addition, subscribers have to download special software to view the magazines. It also takes time to download a magazine, especially with a slow dial-up connection. Magazine executives think that digital delivery will catch on first with scientists and technicians who primarily read high-tech publications at work where they can use high-speed Internet connections to download the material. The success of digital delivery in the general consumer market is still uncertain.

 ## DEFINING FEATURES OF MAGAZINES

The first defining feature of magazines is that, of all the media discussed in this book, they attract the most specialized audiences. There are publications that are designed to reach specific demographic groups (*Modern Maturity, Maxim*); specific occupational groups (*Pointe,* the magazine for ballerinas, or *Builder*); specific interest groups (*Cigar Aficionado, American History*); specific political groups (*National Review, Mother Jones*); specific geographic groups (*Southern Living, Arizona Highways*); and a host of other very specific groups (*Latin CEO*).

The second defining feature is magazines' relationship with social, demographic, economic, and social trends. Of all the media, magazines are most in tune with such trends. As consumer and business needs change, some new magazines emerge, some old magazines cease publication, and others fine-tune their content. The weakening economy forced several magazines, particularly those in the Internet area, out of business in 2002–2003. However, it also prompted many consumers to look for ways to save money, and the magazine industry responded with new publications such as *Chic Simple, Real Simple,* and *Budget Living.* The increased emphasis on security after the September 11 attacks helped launch *Homeland First Response,* and the *Journal of Counterterrorism.*

The third feature is that, as we have seen, magazines can *influence* social trends. Magazines helped fuel the American Revolution. The muckrakers at the turn of the 20th century prompted social reform. In the 1950s, *Playboy* launched the sexual revolution in the United States. In the 1970s, *Ms.* helped usher in the women's movement.

Finally, traditional magazines are packaged in a format that is portable and convenient and that features high-quality print and exceptional graphics. Although online magazines will carve out a niche for themselves, the traditional print magazine will probably be around for a long time.

 ## ORGANIZATION OF THE MAGAZINE INDUSTRY

One of the problems in discussing the magazine industry is deciding what exactly is a magazine. The dictionary defines *magazine* as a "periodical publication, usually with a paper cover, containing miscellaneous articles and often with illustrations or photographs." This definition is broad enough to include *TV Guide,* with a circulation of more than nine million; *Water Scooter,* a magazine for boating enthusiasts; *Sky,* given away to airline passengers by Delta Airlines; *Successful Farmer,* the magazine of farm management; *Go,* distributed to Goodyear tire dealers; *The Journal of Social Psychology; Gloria Pitzer's National Homemakers Newsletter;* and the *Bird Watcher's Digest.* There are around 15,000 to 16,000 magazines published in the United States. Both the number and the diversity of these publications are staggering. For example, *Standard Rate and Data Service (SRDS),* a monthly directory of advertising rates and other pertinent information about magazines, lists 83 automotive magazines, 41 horse-oriented publications, and four periodicals devoted to snowmobiling. There are more than 4,000 magazines sold regularly on newsstands, and the number of new consumer titles continues to rise: more than 700 in 2002. Obviously, classifying the magazine industry into coherent categories is a vexing problem. For our purposes, we will employ two organizational schemes. The first classifies magazines into six main content categories:

A glance at any newsstand will illustrate that consumer magazines fall into major general-interest categories such as sports, health, computers, business, and women's interests.

1. general consumer magazines,
2. business publications,
3. custom magazines,
4. literary reviews and academic journals,
5. newsletters, and
6. public relations magazines.

The second scheme divides the magazine industry into the three traditional components of manufacturing: production, distribution, and retailing.

>> Content Categories

General Consumer Magazines   A consumer magazine is one that can be acquired by anyone, through a subscription or a single-copy purchase or as a free copy. These magazines are generally shelved at the corner newsstand or local bookstore. (Other types of magazines are usually not available to the general public.) These publications are called *consumer magazines* because readers can buy the

At any newsstand find magazines such as *Cosmopolitan*, *marie claire*, and *Glamour*. Now check out the cover lines that preview the articles that appear inside. Chances are you will see lines like "Guys Tell What They Like in Bed," "Sex Secrets of Happy Couples," and "How to Have the Best Sex Ever."

Articles about sex make up a significant part of the content of women's magazines, and the provocative cover lines surely catch the attention of the casual shopper waiting in line at the grocery store. Moreover, it is probably safe to assume that many women (and probably some men) read and believe the content of these articles. The stories themselves are usually filled with analysis and feature quotes from people interviewed by the writer. But how accurate are they?

An article in the March/April 2002 issue of the *Columbia Journalism Review* suggests that, when it comes to sex, these magazines might be embellishing things. The article reports that checking the facts in such articles is not exactly a priority. In addition, some stories are "tweaked" with fake quotes, composite characters, or exaggeration. One common practice is to change the age and occupation of the people quoted to fit the magazine's target market. Thus, a 40-year-old administrative assistant might become a 27-year-old advertising executive in an article. In addition, if the content of the interview is not sexy enough, writers may be asked to go back to sources to ask them to spice up their answers. Journalists consider all of such practices taboo.

Is there any justification for this behavior? Some might argue that the pressures to churn out stories more provocative and sexier than those of the competition makes it easy for writers to cut corners and embellish a little here and there. Others might ask what the harm is. *Cosmopolitan* is not *The New Republic*. Women's magazines are in the business of publishing an entertaining product that is fun to read. Readers should expect a little embroidery. Sex is a fun topic, and articles about it can adopt a nonserious tone.

On the other side of the coin, it should be noted that a casual attitude toward fact checking in sex articles might lead readers to ask if the magazine has the same attitude toward stories on other topics, such as women's health and sex discrimination. In addition, embellished stories might lead some readers, when comparing their own sexual fulfillment to an exaggerated standard, to feel inadequate and frustrated, trying to meet unrealistic expectations. In short, tweaking in stories may not be as harmless as some might argue.

We have been talking about women's magazines. The next time you pass a newsstand, make sure to check out the cover lines on *men's* magazines such as *Maxim* and *Men's Health*. The comparison might be interesting.

products and services that are advertised in their pages. One noticeable trend in the content of consumer magazines is, as mentioned, the movement away from broad, general appeal to the more specialized. *SRDS* lists approximately 50 content groupings of consumer magazines, ranging from "Antiques," with 25 publications, to "Women's," with 92 titles. Some of the better-known consumer magazines are *People*, *Time*, *Reader's Digest*, *TV Guide*, *Sports Illustrated*, and *Woman's Day* (see Table 5–1). Note that consumer magazines can exist in both print and online versions.

Business Publications   Business magazines (also called *trade publications*) serve a particular business, industry, or profession. They are not sold on newsstands, and their readership is limited to those in the profession or business. The products advertised in these publications are generally those that would be purchased by business organizations or professionals rather than by the general public. *Business Publications Rates and Data*, a companion publication to *SRDS*, lists approximately 4,000 titles of business magazines. Most of these magazines are published by independent publishing companies that are not connected with the fields they serve. For example, McGraw-Hill and Penton are two private publishing companies that publish business magazines in a wide variety of areas. Other business publications are put out by professional organizations, which publish them as a service to their members. The degree of specialization of these magazines is seen in the medical field, which has approximately 375 publications serving various medical specializations. Some business publications are called *vertical* because they cover all

TABLE 5–1

Top 10 Consumer Magazines, 2002

Magazine Publishers of America Fact Sheet, available at www.magazine.org.

Title	Circulation (millions)	Percent change from 1999
Modern Maturity	17.4	−15
Reader's Digest	12.0	−4
TV Guide	9.1	−18
Better Homes and Gardens	7.6	0
National Geographic	6.8	−20
Good Housekeeping	4.7	4
Family Circle	4.6	−4
Woman's Day	4.2	−2
Time	4.1	0
Ladies' Home Journal	4.1	−9

aspects of one field. For example, *Pulp and Paper* reports on all segments of the paper mill industry. Other publications are called *horizontal* because they deal with a certain business function, no matter in what industry it exists. *Selling,* for example, would be targeted at salespeople in all industries. Leading business magazines include *Computerworld, Oil and Gas Journal,* and *Medical Economics.* Business publishers are also active in supplying databases and computer bulletin board systems to their clients. Like consumer magazines, business publications can exist in print and online.

Custom Magazines   Custom magazines are published by corporations that try to keep existing customers satisfied while attracting new clients. Some are distributed for free at various business locations; others can be purchased at newsstands. Sony, for example, publishes *Sony Style,* a magazine that promotes its electronic products. Ikea produces *Space,* a lifestyle magazine that also encourages readers to buy Ikea products.

Custom magazines have been around for a while. Airlines have published them for decades, but in the last few years custom magazines have become more visible primarily because businesses have discovered that they are an effective marketing tool. As of 2003, about 30 companies specialize in producing custom magazines, and many of these companies are owned by big advertising agencies that use them as another tool in their advertising efforts for their clients.

Custom publishing flourished during the early part of the century. Although traditional magazines struggled with a weak advertising market, the budgets for custom magazines increased. Circulation for custom magazines has been increasing, with some custom magazines averaging more than 100,000 readers. In addition, some custom magazines have started running ads from other companies. A recent issue of Cisco's *IQ,* for example, contained an ad for luxury watches.

Custom mags present at least two problems for the traditional magazine industry. First, they siphon off advertising dollars from more conventional magazines. If Sony can target its potential customers with its *Style* magazine, it might reduce its advertising buys in *Time, Newsweek,* or other consumer publications. Second, a custom magazine editorial staff may have less independence than a traditional magazine. It would be highly unlikely that a story in Sony's *Style* would say some-

It seemed like a good idea at the time. *McCalls* magazine had been around for 125 years, and the once vibrant publication had become a bit musty. From a circulation peak of about 8.5 million readers in the 1960s, the magazine had dropped to less than half of that number by 2000. Filled with articles about food, housekeeping, and family, *McCalls* was losing about $2 million a month in 2001.

Noting the success of other magazines built around a celebrity, most notably *O, the Oprah* magazine and *Martha Stewart Living,* the *McCalls* publisher thought an alliance with popular talk show host Rosie O'Donnell would be just the thing to put some spark into the fading women's magazine. Thus, the publisher and O'Donnell entered into a deal in which the financial partnership was 50-50, but the publisher maintained editorial control.

Then the bloom came off the rose, so to speak. The magazine began to reflect some of Rosie O'Donnell's concerns about social issues. The first copy of *Rosie* contained a lead story about gun control and some rather racy jokes authored by Rosie herself. In addition, the publisher hoped to emulate Oprah and Martha Stewart by using Rosie's talk show to promote the magazine. However, shortly after the magazine was launched, Rosie quit her talk show. Sales of *Rosie* went into a decline. The conflict intensified further when a new editor was brought in to help turn things around. Rosie and the new editor had serious "creative differences" about the direction of the magazine. Circulation continued to fall. Things got so bad that Rosie eventually wanted her name taken off the magazine. The publisher responded with a lawsuit; Rosie countersued. The magazine was shut down.

The bumpy history of *Rosie* shows what can happen when a publisher hooks up with a celebrity. If the celebrity and the intended market are a good match, such as with Oprah and fans of her show, the magazine will thrive. If they are a bad match, such as the activist Rosie O'Donnell and the generally traditional and conservative readers of *McCalls,* the road will be bumpy. (And, of course, if the celebrity gets into legal trouble, such as happened with Martha Stewart, the magazine will suffer as well.) Hooking up with a celeb can bring rewards, but it also brings risks.

thing negative about Sony products or the company. Be that as it may, it appears that custom magazines will be a more important factor in the years to come.

Literary Reviews and Academic Journals   Hundreds of literary reviews and academic journals, generally with circulations under 10,000, are published by nonprofit organizations and funded by universities, foundations, or professional organizations. They may publish four or fewer issues per year, and a large number do not accept advertising. These publications cover the entire range of literary and academic interests, and they include such journals as *The Kenyon Review, Theater Design and Technology, European Urology, Journalism and Mass Communication Quarterly, Poultry and Egg Marketing,* and *The Journal of Japanese Botany.* Some literary reviews and journals have online versions.

Newsletters   When some people hear the word *newsletter,* they think of a club, PTA, or church bulletin filled with helpful hints. Although these newsletters are important to their readers, we are talking about newsletters typically four to eight pages long and usually created by desktop publishing. They are sold by subscription, and in recent years they have become big business. In fact, there is even a *Newsletter on Newsletters,* published for those who edit newsletters. The coverage area of a newsletter may be broad or narrow. It might deal with one particular business or government agency, or it might report on a business function that crosses industry lines. The *Federal Budget Report,* for example, reports on just the president's budget and appropriations. On the other hand, the *Daily Labor Report* covers congressional actions that have an impact on many industries.

Newsletters are extremely specialized, with small circulations (typically under 10,000) but with high subscription prices. Typical fees are about $200 to $300 a year, but fees of $600 to $800 are not unheard of, and some daily newsletters cost as much as $4,000 annually. Some influential newsletters are *Aerospace Daily, Oil Spill Intelligence Report,* and *Drug Enforcement Report.* In the mass communication area, *Media Monitor* cover events in the print and broadcast industries, and *Communication Booknotes* reviews new books about the mass media. Many newsletters are available online, and some can be delivered to PDAs and other mobile devices.

Public Relations Magazines   These are magazines published by a sponsoring company and intended specifically for one of its publics. An internal public relations (PR) magazine is aimed at employees, salespeople, and dealers. An external PR magazine is directed to stockholders, potential customers, and technical service providers.

These publications typically carry little advertising, apart from promotional items for the sponsoring organization. *Marathon World* and *Target* are among the thousands of PR magazines that are published every year. These publications also have their own professional organization, the International Association of Business Communicators. Most PR magazines exist only in print, but some have online counterparts.

>> Function Categories

A second useful way of structuring the magazine industry is to divide it by function into the production, distribution, and retail segments.

The Production Function   The production phase of the industry, which consists of approximately 2,000 to 3,000 publishers, encompasses all the elements necessary to put out a magazine—copy, artwork, photos, titles, layout, printing, and binding. A subsequent section will describe in more detail how a magazine is produced.

The Distribution Function   The distribution phase of the industry handles the job of getting the magazine to the reader. It is not a simple job. In fact, the circulation department at a large magazine may be the most complex in the whole company. As with newspapers, circulation of magazines means the total number of copies that are delivered through mail subscriptions or bought at the newsstand. There are two main types of circulation. In **paid circulation,** readers pay to receive the magazine, either through a subscription or at the newsstand. Paid circulation has two main advantages. First, periodicals that use paid circulation qualify for lower, second-class postal rates, and paid circulation provides a revenue source to the publisher in addition to advertising. On the negative side, paid-circulation magazines must undertake expensive promotional campaigns to increase subscriptions or to sell single copies. Paid-circulation magazines also have the added expense of collecting subscription payments and record keeping. Most consumer magazines use paid circulation.

The alternative to paid circulation is **controlled circulation.** Controlled-circulation magazines set specific qualifications for those who are to receive the magazine. Magazines that are provided to airline passengers or motel guests are examples. Two advantages of controlled circulation are that publications using it can reach all the personnel in a given field and that these publications avoid the costs of promoting subscriptions. On the negative side, controlled-circulation magazines gain no revenue from subscriptions and single-copy sales. Further, postage for these publica-

Walk by the men's section of any newsstand in the United States and you can see the influence that Felix Dennis has had on magazine publishing. You will see titles such as *Maxim, Stuff, FHM,* and *King* with scantily clad women on the covers and articles with titles such as "Get in Bed with Anna Kournikova," "The Girls of Reality TV," "The Ugliest Brawls in Sports History," and "The Best of E-Mail Pranks."

Before Felix Dennis, men's magazines in the United States were generally of two types: (1) general interest style magazines such as *Esquire* and *GQ* and (2) magazines devoted to a single subject: cars, sports, health, nude women, and so on. The prevailing publishing wisdom was that men would not read a magazine that offered self-help advice. *Men's Health* redefined the category in 1986 when it offered service articles akin to those found in women's magazines, but it was Dennis who totally revamped the category by taking the "lad magazine" concept from Great Britain and introducing it into the United States.

At the risk of oversimplifying, the lad magazine's formula consists of sex, sports, beer, gadgets, clothes, and fitness. The unashamedly heterosexual *Maxim,* for example, seems based on the philosophy that the adult American male is simply an overgrown adolescent. A typical issue contains ample doses of sexy models, frat-boy humor, and man-to-man advice articles. Unlike *Esquire* and *GQ,* says Dennis, *Maxim* is for the man who likes sex better than he likes socks.

Dennis has been quoted as saying that his one talent is that he knows what people want two minutes before they know it themselves, and his past history bears him out. Dennis got into the publishing business in the 1960s when he published an underground magazine in Great Britain. In the 1970s, Dennis published magazines based on current fads, such as Kung-Fu movies, and collectible items from films such as *Star Wars* and *E.T.* In 1985, Dennis published *MacUser* just before Macintosh personal computers became popular. He eventually sold the U.S. edition of the magazine for $25 million, which he used to finance the start of other computer magazines that proved successful, including *Computer Buyer* and *Computer Shopper.* By the mid-1990s, Dennis was the fourth largest publisher in the United Kingdom.

In 1995, Dennis launched the British edition of *Maxim.* Once again, Dennis was able to detect a popular trend. *Maxim* became profitable two years after its launch, about twice as fast as most successful magazines. Flushed with success, Dennis launched *Maxim* in the U.S. market. The magazine quickly developed a readership. By 2002, its circulation hovered around the 2.5 million mark, making it the best-selling men's magazine. The magazine has also spun off a line of furniture and hair grooming products.

Felix Dennis is nothing if not eclectic. Along with his men's and computer magazines, he also publishes *This Week,* a political magazine, and *Evo,* which is devoted to automobiles. In addition, Dennis is the author of a critically acclaimed book of poetry—not what you would expect from the publisher of a lad magazine.

---

tions costs more. Controlled circulation has generally been used by business custom magazines and public relations magazines.

No matter what method is chosen, the circulation of a magazine is an important number. The larger the circulation, the more the magazine can charge for its advertising space.

For a paid-circulation magazine, distributing copies to subscribers is a relatively simple affair. The complicated (and expensive) part of this process is getting subscribers. There are no fewer than 14 methods that are used by magazines to build subscription lists. They include employing cash-field agencies, which have salespeople make house-to-house calls to sell subscriptions directly to consumers; employing direct-mail agencies; direct-mail campaigns sponsored by the publisher; and, finally, what are called *blow-in cards,* those annoying little cards that fall out of a magazine as soon as you open it.

Single-copy distribution to newsstands and other retailers is a multistep process. The publisher deals with only one party, the national distributor. Four national distributors work with the nation's publishers. The national distributor handles from a dozen to 50 or more titles. At least once every month, representatives of the magazine sit down with the national distributor and determine the number of magazines to be distributed for an upcoming issue. The national distributor then delivers the magazines to wholesalers who sell magazines and paperback books within specified areas. In any given month, a wholesaler might receive 500 to 1,000 magazines to distribute to dealers.

The particulars of online magazine distribution, of course, are much different. Online magazines and newsletters can be distributed by e-mail, with "copies" going only to those who request them, or they can exist on a website, where they wait for readers. Whatever the arrangement, online magazines have no need for national distributors or wholesalers.

The tremendous diversity of the magazine industry is illustrated by this magazine display in a bookstore. Magazine publishers compete vigorously for prime space (front row, eye level) in such a display.

The Retail Function   The retailer is the last segment of the industry. The best available figures indicate that there are approximately 140,000 retail outlets in the United States. Of these, the supermarket accounted for 44 percent of all sales in 2002. Supermarket sales have become so important that publishers pay the stores a premium of about $20 per checkout rack to have their titles prominently displayed. When a dealer receives a magazine, he or she agrees to keep the magazine on the display racks for a predetermined length of time (usually a week or a month). At the end of this period, unsold copies are returned to the wholesaler for credit.

 ## MAGAZINE OWNERSHIP

Recent mergers and acquisitions have resulted in a magazine industry dominated by large corporations. Many of the conglomerates (e.g., Time Warner, Hearst) have extensive holdings in other media. Table 5–2 contains a ranking of the top consumer magazine publishers by 2002 revenue and lists their well-known titles.

 ## PRODUCING THE MAGAZINE

>> **Departments and Staff**

The publisher is the chief executive officer at a magazine. He or she is responsible for budgeting, maintaining a healthy advertising position, keeping circulation high, and making sure the magazine moves in a consistent editorial direction. The publisher oversees four main departments:

1. *Circulation:* This department is responsible for keeping current readers satisfied and getting new readers.
2. *Advertising and Sales:* As the name suggests, this department is responsible for selling space in the magazine to potential advertisers.
3. *Production:* This department oversees the actual printing and binding of the magazine.
4. *Editorial:* The head of this department supervises the editorial staff, plans topics for upcoming issues, and helps out with various public relations

TABLE 5–2	Company	2002 revenue (billions)	Well-known titles
Top Consumer Magazine Companies	Time Warner	$4.9	*People, Time, Sports Illustrated*
	Hearst Corp.	$2.2	*Good Housekeeping, Cosmopolitan*
	Advance Publications	$1.9	*Parade, Vogue*
	Primedia	$1.5	*Seventeen, Soap Opera Digest*
	International Data Group	$0.8	*PC World, Computerworld*

activities. The managing editor handles the day-to-day operation of the magazine such as making sure articles are in on time, choosing artwork, and changing layouts.

Some magazines might also have an additional department to handle their online operations, but declining revenues have compelled many publications to incorporate the online function into the departments listed.

>> Publishing the Magazine

Everything moves in cycles. Early magazine publishers were printers as well as writers, but during the 19th century, the production function was divorced from the editorial function. Many magazines have now gone full circle: Computers enable writers and editors to set their words into type and make up pages, reuniting the production and editorial functions.

The first step in all magazine production is preliminary planning and generating ideas for upcoming issues. Once the overall ideas are set, the next step is to convert the ideas into concrete subjects for articles. At this point, preliminary decisions concerning article length, photos, and accompanying artwork are made. Next, the managing editor assigns certain articles to staff writers or freelancers.

The next step involves putting together a miniature **dummy,** a plan or blueprint of the pages for the upcoming issue that shows the contents in their proper order. This phase can now be done electronically, thanks to computer programs that allow editors to view 32 pages at a time.

At about this same time, schedules are drawn up to ensure that an article will get to the printer in time to be included in the forthcoming issue. A copy deadline is set—this is the day the writer must hand in the story to the editor. Time is set aside for editing, checking, and verifying all copy. A timetable is also set up for illustrations and artwork.

Most articles are now written and edited at the computer. Once they are in acceptable form, a computerized typesetter sets the copy in body and display-size type, and the articles are sent to the press or posted on the magazine's website.

John Johnson is the founder of the company that publishes *Ebony* and *Jet.*

ECONOMICS

There are four basic sources of magazine revenue: subscriptions, single-copy sales, advertising, and ancillary services such as e-commerce, custom publishing, and database assistance. This section will concentrate on the first three of these:

subscriptions, single-copy sales, and advertising. At the beginning of this century, the magazine industry was taking in about $29 billion from these sources. Note, however, that this $29 billion is not an accurate estimate of the money that was actually received by magazine publishers. Some of this money went to distributors, wholesalers, and advertising agencies.

The magazine industry was struggling through tough economic times in the early years of the new century. After a record-setting year in 2000, gross industry revenue fell about 4 percent in 2001 to about $29 billion. The industry did not fare much better in 2002. A slow economy, increased competition from the Internet and other media, and the dot-com bust all contributed to the general downturn.

In addition, there were some troubling trends on the horizon. Thanks to deep-discounted subscription offers single-copy sales continued to slide, down almost 12 percent from 1999 to 2003. In addition, total circulation was just about flat for the same period. A glance at Table 5–1 shows that, of the top 10 consumer magazines, only one actually increased its circulation from 1999.

Yet another problem for the industry was a change in the marketing environment. Big retail outlets, such as Wal-Mart, wanted to display on their magazine racks only popular titles that were selling fast. They did not want to clutter up their shelves with magazines that sold only a few copies or took a long time to sell. As a result, it was becoming harder for new magazines to find shelf space. With all the bad news, it was not surprising that many magazine executives were reexamining the business model for their industry.

Another significant trend is the growing importance of advertising in the revenue mix for magazines. In 2002, advertising accounted for nearly 70 percent of the revenue of the top 300 consumer magazines. Subscription revenue makes up about 20 percent, with newsstand sales accounting for the remainder. One result of this growing trend is that magazines prosper along with the general advertising climate. If there is plenty of advertising money going around, magazines will do well. On the other hand, during an ad slowdown as was the case during 2001–2003, magazines will feel the pinch.

Of course, the relative importance of subscriptions, single-copy sales, and advertising varies tremendously from magazine to magazine. *Reader's Digest* gets about 51 percent of its revenue from subscriptions, 46 percent from advertising, and only 3 percent from newsstand sales. On the other hand, *Cosmo* gets 7 percent from subscriptions, about 72 percent from advertising, and 21 percent from single-copy sales, usually at supermarkets. *TV Guide* displays another pattern: 41 percent of its revenue comes from advertising, 47 percent from subscribers, and 12 percent from single-copy sales. To gain some perspective on advertising fees, consider this: In 2003 it cost about $116,000 to run a full-page, black-and-white ad in *TV Guide*. The same ad in *National Geographic* would cost $33,000.

From the perspective of the consumer, it makes sense to subscribe to a magazine rather than to purchase it regularly at the newsstand (see Media Probe, "Do the Math"). From 1996 to 2003, average annual subscription rates actually dropped from about $30 to $24. On the other hand, average cover prices during that same period shot up from $1.71 to nearly $5.

Where does the money go? The typical dollar breaks down approximately as shown in Table 5–3.

Two items included in the manufacturing and distribution category of Table 5–3 have increased at the fastest rate: paper and postage. The cost of coated paper, for example, rose about 20 percent from 1997 to 2000 but leveled off from 2001 to 2004. Postal rates, however, continued to increase.

 ## FEEDBACK

The magazine industry, like the newspaper industry, depends upon the Audit Bureau of Circulations (ABC) for information about who is reading the publication. The ABC audits most consumer magazines and issues a "pink sheet"—so called because its report is printed on pink paper—every June and December. The ABC statement reports the magazine's average paid circulation and the magazine's **rate base.** The rate base is the number of buyers guaranteed by the magazine and is also the number that the magazine uses to compute its advertising rates. Other information in the report includes circulation for each issue in the past six months, state-by-state circulation data, and a report on five-year trends. The ABC also offers a service that tabulates the number of visitors to a magazine's Website.

Another company, Business Publication Audit (BPA), specializes in business and trade magazines. It issues reports similar to those of the ABC, with additional information concerning the occupations of readers who receive controlled-circulation publications.

Although it is helpful to know the total circulation figure for a magazine, that number does not tell the whole story. Circulation measures the **primary audience,** those people who subscribe to the magazine or buy it at the newsstand. In addition, there is the **pass-along audience,** those people who pick up a copy at the doctor's office, at work, while traveling, and the like. **Mediamark Research Inc. (MRI)** provides data

TABLE 5–3	Expense	Amount
Breakdown of a Magazine's Dollar	Advertising expenses	$0.09
	Circulation costs	$0.31
	Editorial costs	$0.09
	Manufacturing and distribution	$0.40
	Other costs	$0.01
	Administration	$0.10

on the total audience for magazines. This company selects a large sample of the magazine-reading audience and conducts personal interviews with individuals to get an exposure score for each magazine. The reports issued by MRI are extremely detailed and encompass many volumes. They contain such specific information as what percentage of a particular magazine's readers make more than $50,000 per year and detailed product-use data, such as how many readers used a headache remedy in the past month. A small portion of an MRI report is reproduced in Figure 5–1.

>> Magazine Audiences

Although data on the audience of a particular magazine are readily available, information about the total audience for magazines is hard to come by, primarily because of the difficulty in defining what qualifies as a magazine. Nonetheless, some figures are available. In 2002, as reported to the Audit Bureau of Circulations, total magazine circulation exceeded 358 million copies. Of these, about 15 percent were bought at the newsstand, while the remaining 85 percent were delivered as part of a subscription. If we examine circulation figures per 1,000 people, as we did with newspapers, we find that magazine circulation has exceeded the growth in the adult population during the 1980s, 1990s, and into 2003.

It appears that almost everybody does some type of magazine reading. In an average month, 94 percent of U.S. adults read at least one copy of a magazine.

FIGURE 5–1

Exercpt from an MRI Report

Copyright © by Mediamark Research Inc.

							TIMES/LAST 7 DAYS							
				ALL				HEAVY & MEDIUM 3 OR MORE				LIGHT LESS THAN 3			
	%	%													
	TOTAL U.S.	A	B %	C %	D		A	B %	C %	D		A	B	C	D
BASE: FEMALE HOMEMAKERS	*000	*000	DOWN	ACROSS	INDEX		*000	DOWN	ACROSS	INDEX		*000	DOWN	ACROSS	INDEX
ALL FEMALE HOMEMAKERS	85323	6628	100.0	7.8	100		4397	100.0	5.2	100		2231	100.0	2.6	100
MONEY	2719	*310	4.7	11.4	147		*214	4.9	7.9	153		*95	4.3	3.5	134
MOTOR TREND	499	*18	.3	3.6	46		*2	-	.4	8		*16	.7	3.2	123
MUSCLE & FITNESS	1109	*99	1.5	8.9	115		*86	2.0	7.8	150		*13	.6	1.2	45
NATIONAL ENQUIRER	11898	1134	17.1	9.5	123		770	17.5	6.5	126		*364	16.3	3.1	117
NATIONAL GEOGRAPHIC	12588	692	10.4	5.5	71		*416	9.5	3.3	64		*276	12.4	2.2	84
NATIONAL GEOGRAPHIC TRAVELER	889	*19	.3	2.1	28		*7	.2	.8	15		*13	.6	1.5	56
NATIONAL LAMPOON	*313	*21	.3	-	-		*21	.5	-	-		-	-	-	-
NATURAL HISTORY	662	*76	1.1	11.5	148		*6	.1	.9	18		*70	3.1	10.6	404
NEWSWEEK	8286	637	9.6	7.7	99		*447	10.2	5.4	105		*190	8.5	2.3	88
NEW WOMAN	3214	*206	3.1	6.4	83		*129	2.9	4.0	78		*77	3.5	2.4	92
NEW YORK MAGAZINE	728	*117	1.8	16.1	207		*87	2.0	12.0	232		*30	1.3	4.1	158
NEW YORK TIMES (DAILY)	1355	*67	1.0	4.9	64		*31	.7	2.3	44		*36	1.6	2.7	102
NEW YORK TIMES MAGAZINE	2087	*159	2.4	7.6	98		*116	2.6	5.6	108			1.9	2.1	79
THE NEW YORKER	1189	*81	1.2	6.8	88		*51	1.2	4.3	83		*43	1.3	2.5	96
OMNI	975	*102	1.5	10.5	135		*47	1.1	4.8	94		*30	2.5	5.6	216
1,001 HOME IDEAS	3610	*315	4.8	8.7	112		*290	6.6	8.0	156		*55	1.1	.7	26
ORGANIC GARDENING	1904	*35	.5	1.8	24		*28	.6	1.5	29		*25	.3	.3	12
OUTDOOR LIFE	1864	*121	1.8	6.5	84		*107	2.4	5.7	111		*6 *15	.7	.8	31

Most read more. One study reported that adults read or look through an average of 10 magazines a month. About 28 percent read a magazine on an average day, and the typical adult spends about 25 minutes daily reading magazines. As far as demographics are concerned, the typical magazine reader is more educated and usually more affluent than the nonreader. Magazine readers also tend to be joiners. One survey found them far more likely to belong to religious, scientific, and professional organizations than nonreaders.

CAREER OUTLOOK

THE MAGAZINE INDUSTRY

>> **Entry-Level Positions**

Most jobs in the magazine industry are found at small publications or at business and trade magazines. In the editorial department, the most common entry-level job is that of editorial assistant. Editorial assistants do a little bit of everything: proofreading, research, replying to authors' letters, coordinating production schedules, filing, indexing, cross-referencing, and answering readers' mail.

Another beginning-level position at some magazines is that of researcher. A researcher spends his or her time pulling together assorted facts and data for staff writers or compiling folders and research notes for articles that are in the planning stage. This particular job requires a general education, skill at using the library, and familiarity with reference books and the Internet.

Many newcomers start out as readers. When articles or stories arrive at the magazine, they are assigned to a reader, who studies them, summarizes them for an editor, and may even make recommendations about what to publish. Some beginners become staff writers. The assignment editor gives the staff writers assignments such as preparing a calendar of upcoming events of interest to the readers or editing a section of helpful household hints.

Newcomers in the circulation department are usually found in the subscription-fulfillment department, where they update subscription lists, send out renewal notices, and handle complaints. Other beginning-level positions in this department are subscription salesperson and assistant to the subscription director or to the single-copy sales manager. In the advertising department, entry-level positions are typically assistants to a staff member. Assistants to an advertising copywriter help prepare copy for leaflets and display cards, compile various reports, and assist in the preparation of direct-mail letters. Assistants to the sales promotion manager compile and verify statistical tables and charts, check promotional materials, handle routine correspondence, and suggest new promotional ideas.

>> Upward Mobility

Career advancement in the editorial department can follow two different routes. Editorial assistants move up the ladder to become assistant editors, usually assigned to a specific department of the magazine. The next step up is associate editor; the next position is senior editor. From there, the person may go on to be managing editor or perhaps even editor in chief.

In the circulation department, the next step up after an entry-level position is into the subscription director's or single-copy sales manager's slot. Advancement from this position consists of moving into the top management ranks by becoming circulation director. For many, the circulation director's job has led to a position as associate publisher or even publisher. In the advertising department, upward mobility consists of moving into the position the newcomer was formerly assisting, such as copywriter or sales promotion manager. Another route upward is to join the magazine's sales staff. Ultimately, the top position to aspire to in the advertising department is that of advertising director, a member of the magazine's top management team. The job of advertising director frequently serves as a springboard to the publisher's position.

MAIN POINTS

- The first American magazines appeared during the middle of the 18th century and were aimed at an educated, urban, and literate audience.
- The audiences for magazines increased during the penny-press era as mass-appeal publications became prominent.
- Better printing techniques and a healthy economy helped launch a magazine boom during the latter part of the 19th century.
- The muckrakers were magazines that published exposés and encouraged reform.
- Magazines began to specialize their content following World War I. Newsmagazines, digests, and picture magazines became popular.
- The magazine industry has used the Internet to complement the print versions of its magazines.

- Magazines are specialized, current, influential, and convenient.
- The magazine industry is dominated by large publishing companies.
- The magazine industry can be divided into the production, distribution, and retail divisions.
- A typical magazine publishing company has several main departments, including circulation, advertising, production, and editorial.
- Magazines get revenues from subscriptions, single-copy sales, and advertising.
- MRI is a company that measures magazine readership.

QUESTIONS FOR REVIEW

1. What are the four defining features of contemporary magazines? Should any other features be added to this list?

2. Why did the general-interest magazines *Look* and *Life* go out of business?

3. How is the magazine industry learning to coexist with the Internet?

4. What are the major departments at a magazine?

QUESTIONS FOR CRITICAL THINKING

1. Are there dangers in having large corporations dominate the magazine publishing industry?

2. *Playboy, Cosmopolitan,* and *Ms.*—three magazines that influenced social trends—all came on the scene before 1980. Are there any more current magazines that have been influential in shaping American culture and society? If not, why not?

3. Is it possible for a magazine to become too specialized? How big does a specialized audience have to be to support a print magazine? A Web-only magazine?

4. Muckraking by magazines never reappeared after its heyday in the early 20th century. Why not?

KEY TERMS

magazines (p. 121)
muckrackers (p. 124)
paid circulation (p. 134)
controlled circulation (p. 134)

dummy (p. 137)
rate base (p. 139)
primary audience (p. 139)

pass-along audience (p. 139)
Mediamark Research Inc. (MRI)
  (p. 139)

INTERNET RESOURCES

Online Learning Center

At the Online Learning Center home page, www.mhhe.com/dominick8, *select* Student Center *and then* Chapter 5.

1. Use the Learning Objectives, Chapter Outline, Main Points, and Time Line sections to review this chapter.

2. Test your knowledge of the chapter using the multiple choice, crossword puzzle, and flashcard features of the site.

3. Expand your knowledge of concepts and topics discussed in the chapter by going to *Suggestions for Further Reading* and *Internet Exercises.*

PowerWeb

At the Mass Communication home page of PowerWeb, www.dushkin.com/powerweb, *log in and select* Mass Communication *as your title. On the next screen, select* Topics, *and then quick jump to* Magazines. *Go to the Advertising topic area* Weekly Update Archives *and choose "The Challenges to Magazines" from the list. After reading the article respond to the following questions:*

1. Will cable television siphon away audiences from consumer magazines? Which magazines would be the most vulnerable? Why?

2. How can magazines best use the Internet?

3. The data mentioned in the article show that the total number of magazines in the marketplace has decreased in the last five years. Suggest some reasons for this downturn.

Surfing the Internet

The following are examples of sites of or related to magazines. All sites were current as of late 2003.

http://money.cnn.com
A cooperative venture between CNN and *Money* magazine, both owned by Time Warner. Note the many interactive financial tools at the site, the way the site encourages online visitors to subscribe to the print magazine, and the cross-promotion between the magazine and CNN.

www.businessweek.com
Note how some of the content on this site of one of the leading business magazines is only available to those who subscribe to the print issue.

www.magazine.org
The site of the major trade association of the industry, the Magazine Publishers of America. Contains statistics, FAQs, press releases, and research reports.

www.magazinesatoz.com
Contains a menu that lets you link to digital editions of more than 1,300 publications. Also has a search engine that enables you to search magazine articles.

www.zinio.com
Provides digital delivery of magazines. Download the software and a sample issue to see for yourself how this process works.

6

BOOKS

This chapter will prepare you to

- understand that books are the oldest form of mass communications;

- recognize the factors that led to the commercialization of book publishing;

- explain how the digital revolution may change the underlying structure of the book industry;

- identify the main parts of the book industry; and

- understand the economics that support the book industry.

April 5, 2002, may be remembered as one of the saddest days in the book industry. On that day Oprah Winfrey announced that she was shutting down the highly influential Oprah's Book Club. The well-known talk show hostess said that it had become too difficult to find books that she felt compelled to share with her audience.

Started in 1996, Oprah's Book Club was without a doubt the most powerful book promotion tool in modern publishing. *The Oprah Winfrey Show* reached an audience of about 25 million Americans every week and was distributed in more than a hundred foreign countries. In the six years of its existence the club recommended more than 40 book titles and all of them became best-sellers. A book that was chosen by the club generally sold an additional 500,000 to a million copies. In a business in which most novels sell less than 30,000 copies, such exposure was a windfall to both authors and publishers. One publishing executive estimated that an Oprah selection was worth at least $2.5 million to the company's bottom line. In addition, when people went to a bookstore to buy an Oprah book,

Bookstores devoted whole sections to the books selected by Oprah Winfrey's Book Club. Oprah recommended 47 books to her members and all of them became instant bestsellers.

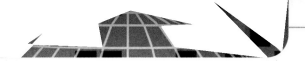

about 75 percent also bought something else. No wonder Oprah's announcement brought tears (figuratively if not literally) to publishers and booksellers everywhere.

In mid-2003, Oprah reconsidered her decision and decided to bring back a variation of her book club. Tentatively called *Traveling with the Classics,* the new club will concentrate more on works by Dickens, Hemingway, and Shakespeare rather than on modern authors. Even with that limitation, publishers welcomed the news. If a book club member went to a bookstore to buy a copy of a book by John Steinbeck maybe he or she might also pick up a copy of a book by John Grisham. In sum, it appears that Oprah will continue to be a cultural force in America for the foreseeable future.

The Oprah saga illustrates some key aspects of the modern book industry. First, books highlight the friction between mass culture and high culture, between critical and popular success. Critics charged that Oprah was trivializing literature by recommending sentimental, popular works of fiction that were primarily aimed at women (see Critical/Cultural

Issues, "Oprah Winfrey Sells Fictional Self-Help to Her Viewers," on page 145). Jonathan Franzen, whose book was an Oprah selection, suggested the choice belittled the literary merit of his novel. Second, books have a synergistic relationship with other forms of media (see Media Probe, "Crossmedia Synergy," on page 160). Books are promoted by many TV shows. In fact, when Oprah's Book Club ended, the *Today* show and *Live with Regis and Kelly,* among other programs, started their own book clubs. Moreover, many magazine publishers also publish books, and books are often made into movies and TV shows. Finally, Oprah's Book Club fit nicely with the current conglomerate ownership in the book industry in which an emphasis on profits encourages the promotion of a few best-selling authors whose success is a big plus to a company's bottom line.

With or without Oprah's help, the book publishing industry will continue to be a major social and cultural force in America. Let us begin our consideration of this industry by taking a brief look at how it has evolved.

 HISTORY

Early books were inscribed by hand and lavishly decorated; many were valued as works of art. Until approximately the 12th century, most books in Europe were produced by monks in monasteries. As noted in Chapter 3, all this changed with the invention of movable type that worked with a printing press.

The invention of movable metal type suitable for printing is generally credited to Johann Gutenberg. Trained as a metalworker, Gutenberg developed a way to cast metal type and to encase it in a wooden mold that could then be attached to a printing press. In about 1455, Gutenberg printed his first book—the Bible. First put on sale at the Great Frankfurt Fair, the book cost the equivalent of three years of wages for the typical laborer of that time period.

Gutenberg's innovations spread quickly throughout Europe. The Protestant Reformation and the writings of Martin Luther spurred the printing of religious books. Printed books appeared in England in 1476. Although book publishing was not considered a socially important force, Henry VIII recognized its potential as a political force and required all printers to obtain government approval before setting up shop.

CRITICAL / CULTURAL ISSUES

Oprah Winfrey Sells Fictional Self-Help to Her Viewers

Contributed by Rita Van Zant   Oprah's Book Club has become the newest self-help narrative to be sold to women to influence their cultural perceptions of themselves. Oprah has created a frenzy in this country by promising her audience that their lives will be markedly improved if they "Get with the Program" and read her fiction selections monthly. Because of her strong belief in the power of individual people to change their circumstances, Oprah feels that if she can get people to start reading books, they will become more self-aware. Using her book club, Oprah has offered her viewers, mainly women, the same "do-it-yourself" remedy for the mind, body, and soul that for years has been prevalent within the self-help industry.

The self-help world is big. During the last 40 years, the number of people who have joined self-help groups and purchased self-help books has grown exponentially. By the early 1990s, self-help discussion groups numbered well over 150,000. One of three adult Americans has purchased a self-help book. Of these, 75 to 85 percent are women. There is a reason for these statistics. The self-help marketing industry tends to toy with the emotions of women who feel inferior or victimized in some way, whether they are staying home caring for their children or seeking a career in the workforce. There is something wrong with them, women are told, but fortunately they can be "cured" by paying for some self-help therapy or buying self-help books. Many women have been exposed to this disease and have paid both financially and emotionally to "cure" it. The profound preoccupation with the self began with the "me" decade of the 1970s, which became the "me-first" decade in the 1980s and became the "why me?" decade of the 1990s. By tapping into this phenomenon of bibliotherapy, Oprah Winfrey has become the most effective promoter of self-help for recovery on television today.

Oprah's Club reflects her New Age philosophy that women are responsible for their behavior and they can fix themselves if they want to intensely enough. In essence, what she says is that women are just not good enough as they are. They are told they must continue to strive for perfection, even though it is never attainable. The bar is always raised. This false paradigm is an important factor in the growth of the self-help market. For years, marketers have created an obsession with the self and made money from it. For example, women are told in various media that they are pathological because they shop too much; then they are told to buy books to learn how to stop shopping. The college-educated, middle-class women who are most likely to take advantage of this help are being told that the habits they have acquired are not normal. Oprah is shrewdly taking advantage of this unquenchable desire of women to become better people.

The Oprah Winfrey Show has become the major representative of a self-help panacea for women today. The anxieties that Oprah feeds her viewers do represent the real problems in our society—but in a twisted way. Many women are frustrated because they are working longer, harder hours both at home and at work with little to show for it except weariness. What Oprah doesn't discuss or even acknowledge is that women cannot solve this problem by themselves. The insistence by Oprah that self-help is the cure-all to the emotional and psychological concerns of her viewers obscures the real problem—that the inequality of the marketplace needs to be changed. Women need to be told they deserve their full share of the economic pie.

When Oprah advocates self-help as opposed to the changing of the hegemonic culture, she is helping the oppression continue. She sells products, not political solutions. Oprah continues to refine the "new woman"—but not necessarily to women's advantage. Thus, women are really settling for a placebo. If Oprah would use her program to rally her viewers to vote as a bloc for women and family issues that would economically benefit them, their lives would change much more dramatically than by reading self-help books.

1. If you were Oprah's producer, how would you suggest she respond to criticisms such as this?

2. Van Zant argues strongly that self-help books are actually harmful to women. To what extent do you agree or disagree with her? Why?

3. Most readers of self-help books are women. What are some self-help books that might be created specifically for men, and what does this tell us about the social construction of gender in our society?

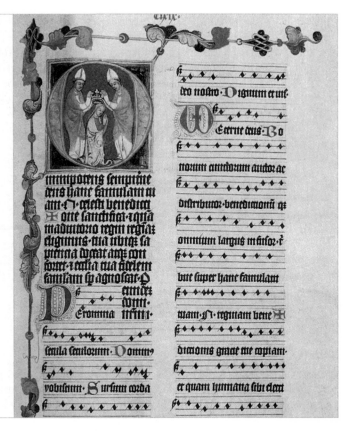

Many early medieval manuscripts, such as this hymn book, were "illuminated" with colorful drawings and graphics.

>> Colonial America

By the early 17th century, book publishers had followed the early immigrants to North America. In 1640, the Puritans in Cambridge, Massachusetts, printed the *Bay Psalm Book*. About 90,000 other titles were to follow it as book publishing took hold in the American colonies. Early publishers functioned as printers and sometimes as authors. One of the early printer-publishers who went on to fame was Benjamin Franklin. His *Poor Richard's Almanack* sold about 10,000 copies a year. Most book content was religious, such as that in *The Practice of Piety* and *Day of Doom*. Sentimental novels, many of them imported from England, also sold well. As the Revolutionary War approached, many book printers turned out political pamphlets. Thomas Paine's *Common Sense* sold 100,000 copies in just 10 weeks.

>> The Penny-Press Era

The change in printing technology and the growth of literacy mentioned in Chapter 4 also helped the book publishing industry. Many of the publishing companies still active today can trace their roots to the early 1800s. Many publishers specialized in professional and educational books, while others addressed their efforts to the general public. Book prices declined and authors such as James Fenimore Cooper and Henry Wadsworth Longfellow became popular, as were the works of English authors. Public education and the penny newspaper created a demand for reading materials. The number of public libraries tripled between 1825 and 1850. Book reading became a symbol of education and knowledge.

The novels of Charles Dickens and Walter Scott were best-sellers during this period, as were books by Herman Melville and Henry David Thoreau. Specialized books also appeared. In the late 1840s, textbooks were profitable, as were reference, medical, and engineering books. The most significant book of the period, however, was probably Harriet Beecher Stowe's *Uncle Tom's Cabin*, published in 1852. It sold 300,000 copies in its first year and was credited with converting many readers to an antislavery position.

>> The Paperback Boom

During the Civil War, soldiers turned to reading to fill the idle time between campaigns. This created a demand for cheap reading materials, and before long a series of paperbacks priced at 10 cents apiece flooded the market. These "dime novels" included the popular Frank Merriwell and Horatio Alger stories. By 1880, about one-third of all the books published in the country were paperbacks, and 15 firms were selling the softbound volumes at prices ranging from 5 cents to 15 cents. Many of the best-selling paperbacks were pirated editions of best-sellers in England and other European countries. By the late 1880s, this problem was so bad that a new copyright law was adopted. The effect of this new law, combined with years of cutthroat competition and price cutting, spelled the end of this era of paperback popularity.

>> The Early 20th Century

The period from 1900 to 1945 saw the commercialization of publishing. Prior to this time, many publishing companies were family-owned and specialized in publishing one particular kind of book. Publishers were a closely knit group, and their dealings with one another resembled what might take place in a genteel private club. Several events altered this situation. First, a new breed of literary agents, concerned with negotiating the best bottom line for their authors, entered the scene. Forced to pay top dollar for the rights to books, the publishing business became more businesslike. Second, many publishing houses expanded into the mass market, publishing popular works of fiction. To compete effectively in the mass marketplace, these publishing houses introduced modern promotion and distribution techniques to the book industry. Third, a depression in the 1890s and a subsequent sluggish economy meant that the book industry was forced to depend more on banks for finance capital. The banks, of course, insisted that the book companies be run with the utmost efficiency, with an eye toward increasing profits. By World War II, all these factors combined to make the book industry more commercially oriented.

The content of popular books was highly variable during this time period. Outdoor adventures written by such authors as Jack London and Zane Grey were popular at the turn of the century. During the Roaring Twenties, light fiction such as *The Sheik* and P. G. Wodehouse's *Jeeves* were best-sellers. Detective fiction by Erle Stanley Gardner (Perry Mason was his hero) and Ellery Queen sold well during the depression. In 1936, two books broke the two million mark in sales, Dale Carnegie's *How to Win Friends and Influence People* and Margaret Mitchell's *Gone with the Wind*.

>> Postwar Books: Paperbacks and Consolidation

Shortly after the end of World War II, new paperbacks published by Bantam, Pocket Books, and New American Library appeared. These books were popular because of their 25 cent price and because new channels of distribution were used

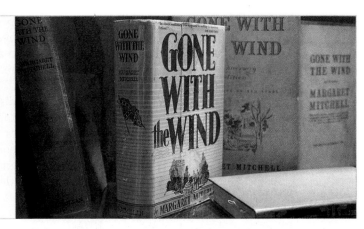

Margaret Mitchell's *Gone with the Wind* was turned down by 25 publishers before Macmillan published it. The book still sells about 50,000 hardcover copies a year.

to market them. Wire racks filled with paperbacks appeared in train stations, newsstands, drugstores, and tobacco shops. A whole new audience was thus exposed to paperbacks. In 1950, the "quality" paperback appeared. These were serious nonfiction or literary classics that found their prime markets in education.

Moreover, expanded leisure time and more disposable income made book reading a popular means of recreation. All in all, the book publishing business looked like a good investment for the future. Consequently, large corporations began acquiring book companies. Between 1958 and 1970, there were 307 mergers or acquisitions of publishing companies. These mergers brought new financial and management resources to the book industry, which helped it stay profitable during the 1970s.

The content of popular books during this period was varied. The first big paperback best-seller following World War II was Dr. Benjamin Spock's *Baby and Child Care.* Other notable paperbacks followed. Mickey Spillane's Mike Hammer was a hard-boiled private eye who appeared in six novels during the 1950s that sold 17 million copies. *Peyton Place,* a novel famous for its racy parts, sold 10 million in paperback. All in all, from 1946 to 1970, paperback sales were dominated by light fiction and an occasional how-to book.

BOOKS IN THE DIGITAL AGE

The digital revolution continues to have an impact on the book industry but not quite the profound impact that was predicted a few years ago. The hottest topic around the turn of the century was the **e-book,** a development that has the potential to reshape the publishing industry.

>> Pixels versus Print

Book publishers have been using digital technology for decades. Authors submit texts in digital form using a word processing program, and publishers edit copy and set type from these electronic texts. The electronic text, however, is eventually transformed into the traditional print-and-ink books that are sent to bookstores and other outlets where consumers purchase them.

In contrast, the e-book is never converted to ink and paper. An e-book consists of three parts: (1) the hardware (portable devices such as laptop computers, PDAs,

The Compaq iPAQ, a battery-powered e-book reader that can hold a dozen books.

and specially designed e-book readers that enable users to read a book); (2) the software (computer programs that control how the text is displayed); and (3) the content (digital material that includes text, images, and even spoken words available in a number of formats that can be downloaded from the Internet).

The potential of the system was demonstrated by the success of a Stephen King novella published exclusively online in 2000. In just three days, a half-million people had downloaded the work. Publishers and book sellers noted with concern that the e-book made it possible for authors to sell and distribute their works directly to consumers, thus bypassing the publisher and retail outlet altogether (another example of the disintermediation concept mentioned in Chapter 1).

>> Will Gutenberg Get the Last Laugh?

As it turned out, publishers' and retailers' fears were unfounded and the e-book revolution never occurred. What happened? In the first place, there was a rush to develop dedicated e-book readers, and many of these devices came to market with poor image quality and a less-than-friendly user interface. As a result, e-books were hard to read. Second, not all formats were compatible with all display devices. Moreover, not enough books were released in e-book form; many consumers did not feel it worthwhile to buy an e-book reading device when so little content was available. In addition, e-books got caught up with the general demise of many high-tech innovations that failed to live up to their hype. The market never materialized.

Consequently, companies that had rushed into the e-book business quickly rushed out. Random House and Time Warner closed their e-book publishing divisions after a little more than a year in operation. The library market was also affected when netLibrary ceased operations. E-book sales slowed to a trickle.

Does this mean we should be writing the obituary of the e-book? Have ink and paper won out? Not necessarily. For the moment at least, it is clear that e-books will have a hard time making it in the mass consumer market, but there are specialized areas in which e-books are gaining popularity. Reference books, for example, are prime candidates for e-books. The huge *Physician's Desk Reference* is now available in a digital form that can be read by doctors from any location on their personal PDAs. Other reference books, such as dictionaries, technical manuals, and encyclopedias, are also prime targets. In e-book form, they can be updated easily and can be linked to other Internet sites. Travelers represent another promising market. People on long trips can download several novels and three or four travel guides to their readers and avoid lugging around copies of heavy books. Finally, it seems likely that e-books will find their way into the college text market. The digital format allows instructors to rearrange chapters and incorporate their own material. From a student standpoint, carrying around a portable e-book reader is probably a lot easier than hauling around a heavy backpack filled with print textbooks. Experts suggest that by 2006 e-books will account for about one-fourth of all textbook sales.

>> Printing on Demand

Another possibility thanks to digitalization is **printing on demand.** This publishing method is a little less radical than that of the e-book. In this approach, traditional publishers are still part of the mix but books are printed and distributed differently.

The way it works is that publishers create a huge database of books in digital form. A customer goes to a bookstore, browses through a catalog, and selects a book. A machine in the bookstore then downloads the book and prints it while the customer waits. Folletts has installed printing-on-demand systems in selected college bookstores across the country. These systems can download and print a textbook in about 15 minutes.

The implications of printing on demand are impressive. Traditional book publishers look for books that will sell enough copies (usually a large number) to make a profit. They then print thousands of books, ship them to bookstores, and hope that most of them are not returned as unsold copies. With printing on demand, however, publishers do not have to guess how many books they should print. They simply print one whenever somebody orders it. This eliminates all the expensive production and shipping costs and guarantees that no books will be returned unsold. Eliminating these costs and the guesswork involved in forecasting demand means that publishers can make money on a book that sells only a

Synergy is the power that a group of individuals or organizations has when they are working together as opposed to working separately. The drive for synergy was behind much of the trend toward convergence among media companies.

Books are natural partners for other media. Many magazine companies take content from their magazines and reconfigure it into book format. For example, Meredith, the publisher of *Better Homes & Gardens* magazine, has published 12 editions of the *Better Homes & Gardens Cookbook*, which has sold more than 30 million copies. *TV Guide* partnered with Crown to publish its 50th anniversary book.

The benefits of this crossmedia synergy are readily apparent. From the magazine's perspective, books are a good way to increase the exposure of the magazine, reuse content for another purpose, and provide another revenue stream. From the book publisher's perspective, the link with a magazine can provide a rich source of available content and instant consumer awareness. *TV Guide*, for instance, has a weekly readership of nine million.

Additionally, magazine and book publishers work together on marketing and promotions. A magazine may run excerpts from a book or give a book publisher discount rates on advertising space. A book's design may be similar to a magazine's and take advantage of established logos.

Books, of course, have long been popular sources for movie content. *Harry Potter* and *The Lord of the Rings* are just the latest examples of this synergy. TV shows have also spun off books. *Star Trek*, for example, inspired a number of books. More recently, a series of books tied in with *Buffy the Vampire Slayer* has sold nearly three million copies. The Fox series *24* offers a vivid example of how books can fit into a company's utilization of synergy. The series is produced by Rupert Murdoch's Fox studios, it airs on Murdoch's Fox TV network, and a book based on the show was recently published by HarperEntertainment, a division of HarperCollins, which is owned by (who else?) Rupert Murdoch.

few hundred copies. This might open up the way for a multitude of special-interest books that would be too expensive to publish with the traditional method.

Moreover, a book title would never go out of print. It would be permanently stored somewhere on a hard drive or disk. Even the most esoteric or obscure titles could be accessed easily.

Printing on demand has yet to make its way into the local bookstore. It was estimated that, as of 2003, printing on demand accounted for less than 1 percent of total book sales. Nonetheless, the technique has gained ground. Much printing on demand takes place between printers and publishers of scientific and medical books, but at least one company, Lightning Source, has made a profit printing trade books. Lightning Source has a digital warehouse of thousands of books, and it prints orders from Amazon.com. As of 2003, the company had printed six million books.

No one is suggesting that the e-book and printing on demand will ever totally replace the traditional ink and paper book. People will still be drawn to the feel and texture of books and the unique experience of reading paper pages bound between covers. Even so, the digital age has already opened up a number of possibilities for the book industry, and even more will become apparent as technology continues to evolve (see Media Probe, "Crossmedia Synergy"). In the future the e-book will become more popular with readers; it will just take it longer to become so than everybody thought.

DEFINING FEATURES OF BOOKS

Books are the least "mass" of the mass media. It took about 40 years to sell 20 million copies of *Gone with the Wind*, but more than 50 million people watched the movie version in a single evening when it came to television. Even a flop TV show

You Really Can't Tell a Book by Its Cover

The publisher of *Married Lust: The Ten Secrets of Long Lasting Desire* faced a unique marketing dilemma. Market research disclosed that husbands and wives liked the book but were reluctant to buy it because they were afraid their children might read it or they would be embarrassed to read the book in a public place, such as on the beach or on an airplane.

The author came up with a novel solution: a reversible cover. On one side is the legitimate cover. On the other side is a nonembarrassing, kid-proof title: *Modern Tactics in Higher Education.* The publisher agreed that no self-respecting kid would ever open a book with that title.

might have 10 million people in its audience, whereas a popular hardcover book might make the best-seller list with 125,000 copies sold. Even a mass-market paperback might sell only about six million copies.

Books, however, can have a cultural impact that far outweighs their modest audience size. *Uncle Tom's Cabin* is credited with helping to change a nation's attitude toward slavery. Dr. Spock and his *Baby and Child Care* altered the way parents brought up their children and became the target of critics who blamed him and his methods for the social unrest of the 1960s. *Silent Spring* changed the nation's attitudes toward the environment.

Finally, books are the oldest and most enduring of the mass media. Gutenberg printed the first book in the 15th century. Public libraries have been around for hundreds of years. Many individuals have extensive collections of books in their own home libraries. People throw away newspapers and magazines shortly after reading them, but most save their books.

 ## ORGANIZATION OF THE BOOK INDUSTRY

The book publishing industry can be divided into three segments: publishers, distributors, and retailers.

>> Publishers

The publishing segment consists of the 2,000 or so establishments that transform manuscripts submitted by authors into books that are sought by readers. Every year these companies publish 50,000 to 55,000 new titles. Book publishing is a highly segmented industry. **Publishers** have developed a classification system for the industry based upon the market that is served. The following are the 12 major divisions suggested by the Association of American Publishers:

1. *Trade books* are aimed at the general consumer and sold primarily through bookstores. They can be hardbound or softbound and include works for juveniles and adults. Trade books include hardcover fiction, nonfiction, biography, cookbooks, art books, and several other types.

2. *Religious books* include Bibles, hymnals, prayer books, theology, and other literature of a devotional nature.

3. *Professional books* are aimed at doctors, lawyers, scientists, accountants, business managers, architects, engineers, and all others who need a personal reference library in their work.

4. *Book club* books at first may sound more like part of a distribution channel than a division of the publishing segment, but some book clubs publish their own books, and almost all prepare special editions for their members.

5. *Mail-order publications* consist of books created for the general public and marketed by direct mail. These are different from book clubs because the books are marketed by the publisher, and customers do not incur any

Books are portable and personal and can be read whenever and wherever it is convenient.

membership obligations in an organization. The Time-Life Company, among others, has marketed books dealing with cooking, home repair, the Civil War, Western history, aviation, World War II, and other topics.

6. *Mass-market paperbacks* are softbound volumes on all subjects that achieve their major sales in places other than bookstores. Typically, these are the books sold from racks in supermarkets, newsstands, drugstores, airports, chain stores, and so on.

7. *University presses* publish mostly scholarly titles or books that have cultural or artistic merit. University presses typically are run on a nonprofit basis, and most of their customers are libraries and scholars.

8. *Elementary and secondary textbooks* are hard- and softcover books, workbooks, manuals, and other printed materials, all intended for use in the classroom. Logically enough, schools are the primary market for these publishers. (This division is also referred to as *elhi* publishers—from *el*ementary and *hi*gh school.)

9. *College textbook* publishers produce texts and workbooks for the college market.

10. *Standardized tests* make up a relatively small segment of the industry. Publishers of these items put together tests of ability, aptitude, interest, personality, and other traits. For example, the Educational Testing Service publishes the Scholastic Aptitude Test and the Graduate Record Exam.

11. *Subscription reference books* consist of encyclopedias, dictionaries, atlases, and the like. They are usually marketed in packages to schools, libraries, and individual consumers.

12. *Audiovisual and other media* consist of tapes, films, slides, transparencies, games, and other educational material for schools and training companies.

Table 6–1 shows the relative importance of each of these segments to the industry. As can be seen, trade, professional, and textbook publishing are the major divisions, accounting for 74 percent of sales.

>> **Distributors**

The Internet has drastically changed the book distribution system. There are now two main channels by which books get to consumers. In the traditional method, the publisher usually ships copies of the book to a wholesaler or distributor who,

	Division	Percentage of sales
TABLE 6–1 **Sales by Publishing Industry Division, 2002**	Trade	26
	Religious	5
	Professional	19
	Book clubs	5
	Mail order	1
	Mass-market paperback	6
	University press	1
	Elhi text	15
	College text	14
	Standardized tests	2
	Subscription reference	3
	AV and other media	3

in turn, sends the books to a retail outlet where consumers can buy them. Online booksellers such as Amazon.com and barnes&noble.com use a different approach. The consumer orders a book from the website, and the book is shipped from the seller's warehouse directly to the consumer, bypassing the distributor and retail outlet. E-books, of course, go directly from publisher to consumer, bypassing everything in between. Figure 6–1 illustrates these distribution arrangements.

>> Retailers

There are more than 20,000 traditional "brick and mortar" bookstores in the United States plus the big online booksellers mentioned. Big chains, such as Barnes and Noble, Borders–Waldenbooks, and Books-a-Million dominate traditional bookselling. In 2002, these four firms took in about $7.8 billion in revenue, with Barnes and Noble in first place with about $3.8 billion in sales. Online retailers were not far behind. Amazon.com ranked third with about $1.9 billion.

Other retail channels include college bookstores and direct-to-consumer booksellers such as book clubs and mail-order sellers.

 ## OWNERSHIP IN THE BOOK INDUSTRY

The book industry is dominated by large conglomerates with interests in other media. The top five companies as of mid-2003 were the following:

1. *Pearson Publishing:* A global media company that is the world's largest educational publisher, with imprints such as Scott Foresman and Prentice Hall. It also owns the Penguin Group of consumer publishing firms (Penguin, Dutton, and Viking) as well as the *Financial Times* business newspaper. Its Pearson Television produces more than 150 programs worldwide, including the hugely popular *Baywatch.* Publishing revenue was more than $5 billion in 2002.

2. *Random House:* Part of the Bertelsmann media empire, which includes interests in 600 companies in 53 countries and is engaged in books,

FIGURE 6–1

**Channels of Book
Distribution**

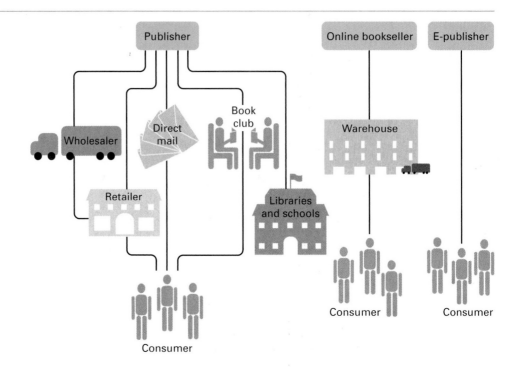

music, magazines, TV, and radio. Bertelsmann also owns 41 percent of
barnes&noble.com plus other Internet holdings. Random House had
about $1.5 billion in revenue in 2002.

3. *HarperCollins:* Rupert Murdoch's worldwide communications company,
which owns HarperCollins as well as 20th Century Fox, the Fox TV network,
and various newspapers and magazines. HarperCollins had revenues of
about $1 billion in 2002.

4. *Simon & Schuster:* Part of the newly merged CBS/Viacom, a conglomerate
that has TV networks, radio stations and a radio network, cable networks,
theme parks, and a TV syndication company. Publishing revenue was $650
million in 2003.

5. *Time Warner Publishing:* Part of the Time Warner company, the biggest media
conglomerate in the world, with an online service, cable systems, magazines,
and TV and radio, movie production, and other interests. The publishing
group includes Warner Books, Time-Life Books, and Little, Brown and
Company. In 2002 it had revenues of about $350 million.

 PRODUCING THE BOOK

>> Departments and Staff

There are four major departments in a typical publishing company: (1) editorial,
(2) production, (3) marketing, and (4) general administration or business.

The editorial department is in charge of dealing with authors. The department is
responsible for selecting manuscripts and preparing them for publication. Some

Jeff Bezos was always tinkering with things. When he was three, he took apart his bed. Eleven years later, he tried to make a hovercraft out of a vacuum cleaner. Sixteen years after that, he tinkered with the way books were sold and totally revolutionized a business by starting Amazon.com.

After growing up in Houston and Miami, Bezos enrolled at Princeton, where he studied computer science and engineering. After a couple of jobs in the financial marketplace, he wound up at a Wall Street investment company. One day in 1993, while doing financial research, he came across a startling statistic: The Internet was growing at a rate of 2,300 percent a year. Bezos recognized the tremendous selling potential of the Net and decided to launch an online business. He reasoned that things that are big mail-order sellers should also do well online. Accordingly, he made a list of the top 20 mail-order products and determined that books would be the best item to sell. A virtual bookstore would have the space to list all the millions of books in print; no brick-and-mortar store could do that. Further, book wholesalers had already produced CD-ROMs that listed all available titles. Bezos recognized that the existing book databases could easily be put online.

Bezos's family and friends invested $300,000 in his idea, and Bezos moved to Seattle, the home of many net-savvy programmers, who would be needed to get the business online. Seattle was also the home of one of the biggest book wholesalers in the country.

Working out of his garage, Bezos created a website that he tested among his friends. It seemed to work well, and Bezos decided to open the site to everybody. But what to call it? He originally wanted to call it Cadabra.com, as in "abracadabra," the magic incantation. When he tried this name out on his laywer, the lawyer thought Bezos said "Cadaver.com" and wanted to know why he would name his site after a dead body. Bezos went back to the drawing board and eventually settled on Amazon.com, after one of the world's longest and most powerful rivers.

The rest, as they say, is Internet history. The company grew quickly. In 1996, Amazon.com had 300 employees. In 2001, it had about 3,000. From a few thousand customers in its first year, it now has more than 20 million in about 150 countries. Sales in 2001 exceeded $2 billion. Its brand name is more recognizable than Burger King or Barbie. Amazon.com has also branched out from books and now sells CDs, toys, electronics, and gifts from its website.

Furthermore, Amazon.com is one of the companies that have defined the Internet economy, where growth seems more important than profits. As of 2000, the company had lost more than $1.5 billion. Nonetheless, its stock was selling at $113 a share. Then reality set in. Like many other dot-coms, Amazon was hit hard by a stock slump in mid-2000, and its stock price dropped 76 percent. Despite this precipitous loss, investors value Amazon at $10 billion, more than Barnes and Noble, Kmart, and J.C. Penney combined. Bezos has recently slashed costs and has projected that the company will turn profitable in the next couple of years.

No matter how profitable or unprofitable Amazon.com may become, one thing is certain: It has helped make pointing and clicking a significant part of Americans' shopping repertoire.

editors specialize in procuring new manuscripts, and others read manuscripts, write reports on them, and recommend acceptance, revision, or rejection. Other editors work with accepted manuscripts, checking grammar, language, and accuracy.

As its name suggests, the production department oversees the physical design of the book. This department is responsible for type style, composition, paper, printing, and binding.

The marketing department supervises sales, promotions, and publicity. The actual type of marketing depends upon the book and its intended audience. Publishers of elhi textbooks sell mainly to school systems. Mass-market paperbacks are sold to retailers who, in turn, sell them to the public. Advertising in trade magazines, television interviews, and reviews in respected publications are common marketing tools.

The business manager at a publishing company is responsible for several functions. One of the most important is accounting. Further, this department prepares budgets and makes long-range financial forecasts. Other responsibilities include dealing with internal personnel policies and supervising the general day-to-day operational needs of the company.

>> **Publishing the Book**

Editors get their books in three ways: through submissions by agents, as unsolicited books sent in by authors, and as book ideas generated by the editor. Most trade manuscripts are submitted through literary agents. Agents are known quantities and will not generally submit manuscripts that they know are unacceptable to the editor. Unsolicited manuscripts are given an unflattering name in the business: "slush." As they come in, these manuscripts are put in the slush pile and eventually read, if the author is lucky, by an editorial assistant. Most of the time they are rejected with a form letter, but every once in a while an author gets through. *The Office Humor Book,* for example, went from the slush pile into five printings. Editors also generate ideas for books. If an editor has a good idea for a book, he or she will generally talk to one or more agents who will suggest likely candidates for the assignment. This is another good reason writers should have agents. In any case, the author typically submits a proposal consisting of a cover letter, a brief description of the planned book, a list of reasons it should be published, an analysis of the potential market, an outline or a table of contents, and perhaps one or two sample chapters. The proposal usually goes to an acquisitions editor and is evaluated. If the publishing decision is favorable, then a contract is signed and the author begins work in earnest.

Editorial work starts as soon as the author submits chapters to the publisher. Editors look at the overall thrust of the book to make sure it makes sense and achieves its original intent. Moreover, the mechanics of the book are checked to make sure that the general level of writing is acceptable, that all footnotes are in order, that all necessary permissions to reproduce material from other sources have been obtained, and that all artwork is present. Eventually, both author and editors will produce a manuscript that is mutually satisfactory.

While all this editing is going on, other decisions are being made about scheduling, designing the interior look of the book, and designing the cover. When everything is in order, the book is printed, bound, and sent to the warehouse to await distribution, or it is distributed online.

 ## ECONOMICS

Despite an economic downturn at the beginning of the century, competition from the Internet, television, changing lifestyles, and continued predictions that reading is a lost art, the book industry still manages to show modest growth. Although 2002 was not a good year for book publishers, more than $26 billion of books were sold, up more than 5 percent from 2001. Thanks to best-sellers such as Hillary Clinton's memoirs and a new Harry Potter adventure, 2003 promised to be even better. Figure 6–2 shows revenue for the industry between 1983 and 2002.

Why do books continue to be popular? First, the population is getting older; the fastest-growing age group is 35 to 49 years old—the age when people buy the most books. Second, people have disposable income to spend on books. Finally, federal and local governments continue to make education a funding priority. Per-pupil expenditures at the elementary and high school levels have increased and are expected to grow in the future, enhancing the market for texts, workbooks, and standardized tests.

At the consumer level, it is obvious that books have become more expensive. In 2003, a copy of *Harry Potter and the Order of the Phoenix* had a list price of $30, while

FIGURE 6–2

**Book Publishing
Revenue, 1983–2002**

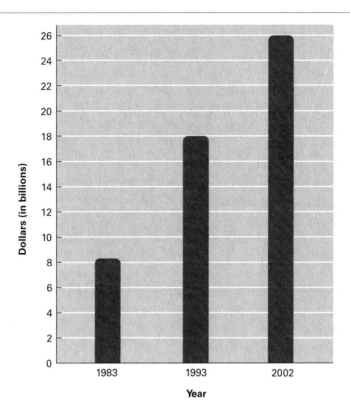

best-selling paperbacks went for $7.99. The high prices have prompted many con-
sumers to buy from discount sellers and the used book market.

A publisher has two main sources of income: (1) the money that comes from
book sales and (2) money from **subsidiary rights** (sales to book clubs, foreign
rights, paperback rights, and reprint permissions). Of these two, the income from
book sales is the most important. It should be noted, however, that the publisher
does not get all the money from the sale of a book. The list price is discounted for
wholesalers and booksellers. These discounts might amount to 40 percent for
many books.

The costs a publisher incures are many. First, there is the cost of manufacturing
the book: printing, typesetting, and paying royalties to the author. These costs are
variable and are tied to the number of books printed. For example, paper costs
would be more substantial on a book with a press run of 20,000 than on one with
a run of 2,000. There are also operating expenses, including editorial, production,
marketing, and general administration expenses. Table 6–2 shows a hypothetical
operating statement for an adult trade hardcover book published by a typical publishing company. The book has a list price of $20 (all numbers are rounded for con-
venience), and 10,000 copies were printed. After a year, 2,000 copies were unsold
and were returned to the publisher for a credit. This means that 8,000 copies were
sold. Allowing a 40 percent discount from the list price leaves the publisher with
revenues of about $12 per book. Multiplying 8,000 by $12 gives us the gross sales
amount: $96,000. From this are subtracted the costs of returns and allowances,
leaving a balance of $77,000 in net sales revenue. Manufacturing costs and author
royalties amounted to $45,400. This sum is subtracted from the net sales to find the

When it first debuted, most authors thought that online bookseller Amazon.com could only help the sales of their books and increase their royalty checks. After all, about 750,000 websites have links to Amazon.com, including many websites maintained by authors and publishers. In 2001, however, Amazon.com began offering links to used books for sale.

As a result, if you were looking for a copy of John Grisham's best-selling novel *The King of Torts* on Amazon.com in mid-2003, you could order a new copy of the book direct from the online bookseller for $16.77. Or you could click on a link and buy from a private seller a "mint condition" used copy of the book for only $7.24. Which one would you pick? If you chose the used copy, what would you do with the money you saved?

Amazon.com's policy of advertising used books on the same screen on which it advertises new copies of a book has enraged authors. Neither authors nor publishers make any money from the resale of a book. Nor are these sales figured into best-seller lists. The Authors' Guild noted that "used" copies of books become available almost immediately, suggesting that many used copies are actually review or promotional copies not intended to be resold.

It makes little difference to Amazon.com if a person buys a new or used copy; the company makes money on the sale of both. In the case of a used book, Amazon collects a 99-cent fee for the sale plus 15 percent of the purchase price.

In 2002, the Authors' Guild, while acknowledging that selling used books is perfectly legal, asked Amazon.com to list its used books on a different area of its website and not on the same screen from which new copies can be ordered. Not only did Amazon ignore the request, but it also began to market used books more aggressively, sending e-mails to people who recently bought books informing them how much they could make by reselling the book on Amazon.com. In response, the Authors' Guild urged all of its members to delink their websites from Amazon.com and relink to its rivals.

Amazon.com argues that selling used books is actually good for authors. The cheaper prices bring in new readers who, in turn, use the money they save to buy new books. Authors counter by suggesting that any money saved will probably go toward buying other used copies. The used-book market will condition consumers to wait for the lower prices on used books.

Interestingly, neither side has any statistics to back up its argument. The Authors' Guild has no data on how much, if at all, used book sales have hurt new sales. Amazon.com has no evidence to show that consumers are using their savings to buy new books.

---

gross margin on sales (the amount that net sales exceeded the cost of sales), in this case $31,600. Table 6–2 also assumes that the publisher sold some subsidiary rights (to a book club or a paperback publisher) and received $6,900 in return. So far, the total income from the book is $38,500 ($31,600 + $6,900). Subtracting the total operating expense of $34,600 from $38,500 yields a net income of $3,900.

These figures, of course, would vary for other publishers and for other segments of the book industry. Profit margins typically varied from 2 to 20 percent during the period between 1999 and 2002. Advances and acquisition rights are two of the big expenses in publishing. For example, Simon & Schuster paid Hillary Clinton an advance of $8 million for her memoirs.

 ## FEEDBACK

The most important form of audience feedback in the book industry is the **best-seller lists** compiled by newspapers such as the *New York Times* and *USA Today* and the trade publication *Publisher's Weekly*. These organizations use slightly different methods to tabulate a rank ordering of the best-selling books, but all involve collecting data from a sample of the various channels of book distribution—chain bookstores, independent bookstores, newsstands, and price clubs—and then assigning various weights to the numbers to come up with the rankings. Making the best-seller list is important since many bookstores automatically order large numbers of all books that make the list. Consequently, appearing on the list can mean added sales for a book.

TABLE 6–2				
Profit-Loss Statement of Trade Hardcover with $20 List Price	Press run	10,000 copies		
	Returned	2,000 copies		
	Gross sales	8,000 copies	@ $12	$96,000
	Returns and allowances			(19,000)
	Net sales			77,000
	Cost of sales			
	Manufacturing			27,700
	Royalties			17,700
	Total cost of sales			45,400
	Operating expenses			
	Editorial			4,500
	Production			1,600
	Marketing and fulfillment			18,500
	Administration			10,000
	Total operating expenses			34,600
	Margin of net sales over cost of sales			31,600
	Other income			6,900
	Net income			3,900

A new feedback tool became available in 2002 with the arrival of BookScan, a new service from the same company that provides sales data for the recording industry. BookScan provides point-of-sale information from the big chain bookstore sellers and from some independent bookstores as well. Companies that subscribe to BookScan can access sales data broken down by subject, format, region, and metropolitan area.

>> Audiences

A book industry survey of readers revealed that two-thirds of all books are purchased by those over 40. Readers under 25 accounted for less than 5 percent of all book sales. Book reading was positively related to income and education. In 2002 about 56 percent of all households in the United States bought at least one book.

THE BOOK PUBLISHING INDUSTRY

Book publishing is a small industry; there are only 70,000 to 75,000 jobs nationwide in the entire business. Consequently, there is a lot of competition for many of the jobs, particularly those on the editorial side.

There are two general areas to pursue in book publishing: editorial and business. Entry-level positions are competitive, and most newcomers typically join a publishing company as editorial assistants. There are numerous clerical tasks to be performed in publishing: answering authors' letters, reading manuscripts, writing reports about manuscripts, checking facts, proofreading, writing catalog copy, and so on. Editorial assistants do these and countless other tasks.

Labor versus Management in Journalism Textbooks

As mentioned in Chapter 2, the critical/cultural approach examines texts, broadly defined. In a paper presented at the 2000 convention of the Association for Education in Journalism and Mass Communication, Dr. Jon Bekken took a more literal approach and examined textbooks, in this case, journalism textbooks, to discover if these texts were instilling a professional ideology in their readers.

Bekken noted that studies of the coverage of business conflicts have generally found that the media cover these disputes from a perspective that does not favor labor or labor unions. For example, labor reporting focuses on the inconvenience strikes cause for consumers rather than on the issues that lead to a strike. Wages rather than health and safety are portrayed as the central concern of labor. In addition, there is a trend toward ignoring labor news altogether. Fewer that a dozen newspapers employ even one full-time labor reporter.

Bekken wondered if these attitudes might have been fostered during a reporter's academic training. He was specifically interested in the way organized labor was portrayed in 29 media writing and reporting textbooks. After performing a critical/cultural analysis, he concluded that the texts marginalized labor, making it seem unimportant. For instance, he noted that some textbooks have exercises that ask students to write articles about layoffs or hiring freezes based on press releases or notes from interviews with corporate or government officials. The subtle lesson conveyed in these exercises is that the important perspectives do not include those of labor. Other texts simply make little or no mention of labor or labor unions despite the fact that many newspaper workers belong to the International Typographical Union, and several newspapers have been plagued by labor-management troubles.

Most texts generally gloss over labor problems in the newspaper industry itself. Health risks such as carpal tunnel syndrome, poor working conditions, and inadequate pay are seldom mentioned. The idea that joining a union might help address some of these issues is not discussed.

Bekken chronicles other examples of how labor is almost trivialized. One textbook devotes as many words to covering labor as it does to covering weddings. Another urges reporters to avoid an antibusiness attitude in their stories and to rely on corporate officials, financial analysts, and government regulators as sources for business news. When textbooks do discuss how to cover labor, their emphasis is on covering strikes, violence connected with strikes, or unfair labor practices.

What are some of the results of the way these texts depict labor? As Bekken says,

> Students carry blind spots towards labor inculcated in their academic training into newsrooms across the country. Editors and publishers have slashed the number of labor reporters. . . . Reporters and editors typically do not look to the labor movement for news—rather they wait for strikes, or include labor in discussions of special interest groups said to dominate the political system.

Bekken ends his analysis by noting that, in recent decades, textbook authors have tried to remove sexist language and pay more attention to cultural sensitivity. Moreover, newer editions of reporting texts have been expanded to cover topics such as religious news and consumer news. Nonetheless, he points out, most journalism textbooks do not do a good job covering that large number of Americans who labor for a living. The fact that many of the students who read these books go on to ignore labor in their own reporting ought not surprise us.

1. What can textbook authors do to try to remove some of the promanagement bias Bekken discovered? How can teachers using these biased books help lessen the books' drawbacks? What can students do to try to raise awareness of these issues in class?

2. If you have taken or are taking a writing/reporting class, look at the text you are using. How and to what extent does it marginalize or trivialize labor?

3. To what extent—and why—does it matter whether such texts avoid discussing labor problems in the media industry or carry a promanagement bias?

Authors such as Amy Tan help promote their books by going on extensive book tours.

The next logical step up the career ladder is to become an assistant or associate editor. These individuals work with senior editors in several different areas: manuscript acquisition, copyediting, design and production, artwork, and so on. Eventually, this path leads to a position as an editor. After getting the necessary experience, editors are promoted to senior editors, managing editors, or executive editors, positions that carry a good deal of administrative responsibility.

On the business side there are several career paths open. Many people start as sales representatives and sell their company's books to the appropriate customers. Sales and marketing experience are so vital to the well-being of the industry that the path to top management usually begins in the sales department. At many companies, presidents and vice presidents are almost always former salespeople with extensive experience in marketing.

It is not always necessary to work for a publishing company to find employment in this area. Many people work as freelance editors, designers, proofreaders, indexers, artists, and photographers. These typically are people who have had some experience and have branched out on their own.

MAIN POINTS

- The book is the oldest form of mass communication. Early books were printed by hand until the invention of movable type and the printing press.

- In early America, publishers were also printers. Books became more popular during the 17th and 18th centuries.

- From 1900 to 1945, the book publishing industry became more commercialized. Continuing consolidation has resulted in a modern book industry that is dominated by a few large companies.

- The digital revolution has yet to have a drastic effect on the book industry. E-books and printing on demand have yet to become important parts of the industry. Despite the slow progress of digital content, there are signs that it is moving forward in specific content areas.

- The book industry consists of publishers, distributors, and retailers. The emergence of online booksellers has changed the way books are sold and distributed.

- Despite some ups and downs, book publishing has been profitable during the past few decades.

QUESTIONS FOR REVIEW

1. How has the content of popular books changed from the 17th to the 21st century?

2. What are the defining features of books?

3. What are the main revenue sources for book publishers?

4. What is the difference between a trade book and a mass-market paperback?

QUESTIONS FOR CRITICAL THINKING

1. With all the talk about declining literacy and complaints that nobody reads anymore, why do book sales keep increasing?

2. Will e-books ever become as popular as traditional ink-and-paper books?

3. What advantages or disadvantages are connected with a book industry dominated by a few big firms?

4. Have books become too expensive? What factors contribute to rising prices?

KEY TERMS

e-book (p. 149)
printing on demand (p. 151)

publishers (p. 153)
subsidiary rights (p. 159)

best-seller lists (p. 160)

INTERNET RESOURCES

Online Learning Center

At the Online Learning Center home page, www.mhhe.com/dominick8, *select* Student Center *and then* Chapter 6.

1. Use the Learning Objectives, Chapter Outline, Main Points, and Time Line sections to review this chapter.

2. Test your knowledge of the chapter using the multiple choice, crossword puzzle, and flashcard features of the site.

3. Expand your knowledge of concepts and topics discussed in the chapter by going to *Suggestions for Further Reading* and *Internet Exercises.*

PowerWeb

At the Mass Communication home page of PowerWeb, www.dushkin.com/powerweb, *log in and select* Mass Communication *as your title. On the next screen, select* Topics *and then quick jump to* Media Use. *Read Article 1, "A Defense of Reading." Then consider the following questions:*

1. This article concludes with the statement ". . . television provides distraction, reading promotes growth." Is it possible for reading to be a distraction and for television to promote growth? Why or why not?

2. How does the Internet relate to this topic? Since much of the content on the Net is text, will it prompt us to read more?

3. What was the last book (not counting textbooks like this one) that you read? Does your own experience support the author's argument that children read fewer books when TV is available to them?

Surfing the Internet

Remember, websites change all the time; some move, some evaporate, and some transform.

www.bookweb.org
The home of the American Booksellers Association, the trade group representing independent bookstores. Contains the current best-sellers list.

www.bookwire.com
Takes a look inside the book business. Includes news, features, and links to other related sites.

www.bisg.org.
Home of the Book Industry Study Group. Provides research information about the industry.

www.publishersweekly.com
The online version of *Publisher's Weekly*, the leading trade magazine. Includes job listings.

7

RADIO

Shortly before 2 A.M. on January 18, 2002, a Canadian Pacific Railway train with five railcars, each carrying 150,000 gallons of anhydrous ammonia, derailed about one mile west of Minot, North Dakota. The railcars split apart, and a deadly toxic cloud spread over much of the town. In an attempt to warn residents, authorities tried to call local radio stations. No one answered the phone. Police finally called station employees at their homes. It took more than an hour before the stations began broadcasting warnings. The poisonous cloud killed one person and sickened hundreds.

All of the six commercial stations in Minot were owned by Clear Channel Communications, a huge media conglomerate that controls more than a thousand radio stations nationwide. In order to save money, big companies generally cut the staff at local stations and depend upon satellite-delivered music to fill airtime. This was the case in Minot. At the time of the spill, all six stations were broadcasting music piped in by satellite; there were no human DJs present at the stations.

People who live in the Great Plains and other rural areas have always

Radio is a mobile medium. Most people listen in their cars during "drive time," early morning and late afternoon.

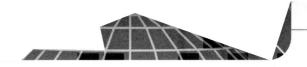

depended heavily on radio for local news. In the past, stations were owned by families that had ties to the community. They broadcast commodity prices, obituaries, and weather alerts. In the last six or seven years, these stations have joined hundreds of others all over the United States that have been swallowed up by big radio companies, such as Clear Channel. As a result, the local quality has for the most part vanished. Corporate headquarters in some other part of the country now make programming decisions. Local news has nearly vanished. Sometimes the DJs people hear are not even at the station but are prerecorded voices delivered by satellite, as was the case in Minot.

Many critics have used the Minot incident as an argument against consolidation in the radio industry. In truth, however, this tragedy cannot be blamed entirely on consolidation and unconcerned media giants. Later investigation showed that there actually was an employee on duty (but not a DJ) during the spill, but technical problems prevented the police from getting through. Nonetheless, it is also true that in 2002 all six Minot commercial stations employed only one full-time newsperson. Had there been three or four independent locally owned stations with their news departments competing against one another on that January night, the news would have gotten out much faster.

The increasing consolidation of the radio industry has overshadowed the effects of the digital revolution. In fact, of all the media discussed in this book, radio is the one that has been least affected by the shift to digital media. There are signs, however, that this situation might be changing. Digital technology may soon change the way we receive radio programs and might even have an impact on the trend toward consolidation. But this is getting ahead of the story. Let us first take a look at how radio got to where it is today.

HISTORY

In 1887, Heinrich Hertz, a German physicist, successfully sent and detected radio waves. Guglielmo Marconi used Hertz's efforts to build a wireless communication device that could send Morse code—dots and dashes—from a transmitter to a receiver. Marconi started a wireless telegraphy company that would play an important part in early radio's development.

Reginald Fessenden and Lee De Forest provided the breakthroughs that would make broadcasting—as opposed to sending dots and dashes—possible. Fessenden, with the help of the General Electric (GE) corporation, built a high-speed, continuous-wave generator that could broadcast the human voice and music. De Forest invented the vacuum tube, originally called the *audion*, which made it much easier to receive radio signals.

The development of early radio was hampered by legal battles over patent rights to various inventions. When World War I broke out, the U.S. Navy assumed responsibility for all relevant patents, and radio made great technical strides during the war.

>> Big Business

After the war, corporate America recognized the potential of radio. A new company, the Radio Corporation of America (RCA), was formed and acquired the assets of the U.S. division of the Marconi Company. Stock in RCA was held by some of the biggest companies of the period: AT&T, General Electric, and

Westinghouse. Note that these companies thought RCA would be in the wireless telegraphy business. Despite the efforts of Fessenden and De Forest, it was hard to envision that broadcasting news and entertainment to the general public could make money.

Some individuals, however, were more prescient. David Sarnoff, an employee of the Marconi Company who later became head of RCA, suggested that one day this new invention would become a "radio music box." Sarnoff himself would be one of the central figures in the development of this new medium.

>> Mass Audience

Frank Conrad, an engineer for Westinghouse in Pittsburgh, tinkered with radio as a hobby. He built a radio transmitter in his garage and started broadcasting recorded music, reporting sports scores, and showcasing the musical abilities of his sons. In a short time, he had attracted an enthusiastic audience of radio fans. A local department store started selling radio sets so that more people could hear Conrad's programs. Westinghouse built a station so that Conrad's signal would be heard by more people. Westinghouse also built the radio sets and received "free" advertising because of its connection with the station. The station, KDKA, signed on in 1920 and is still on the air, making it the country's oldest station.

KDKA was a success. RCA, GE, and AT&T, along with many other companies and organizations, started radio stations. Radio listening became a national craze. By discovering that an audience existed for broadcast programs intended for the general public, radio found the role it would play for the foreseeable future.

>> Better Receivers

Early radio receivers were not user-friendly. They were powered by an assortment of large, bulky, and sometimes leaky batteries. Tuning required patience, a steady hand, and a knowledge of electronics.

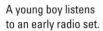
A young boy listens to an early radio set.

By 1926, however, set manufacturers had improved their product. New radios ran on household current, could be tuned with just two knobs, had better antennas, and looked like a fashionable piece of furniture. Between 1925 and 1930, 17 million radio sets were sold, and radio was becoming truly a mass medium.

>> Radio Goes Commercial

One of the curious things about early radio broadcasting was that very little of it was done by broadcasters. The early stations were owned by a polyglot of organizations. WLS in Chicago was owned by Sears, Roebuck (*World's Largest Store*); WGN by the *Chicago Tribune* (*World's Greatest Newspaper*); WSM in Nashville by the National Life Insurance Company (*We Shelter Millions*); and WHB in Kansas City by the Sweeney Automotive and Electrical School.

Radio receivers in the 1930s no longer required a knowledge of electronics to operate. A family could simply sit back and listen.

Early broadcasting was not expensive, and radio station owners figured they got their money's worth through the exposure they received through the station. Before long, however, operating expenses began to pile up, and stations searched for a way to have their stations turn a profit.

Nobody knew quite how to do it. Some felt listeners should send in voluntary contributions; others wanted a tax on radio tubes. It was the phone company that finally came up with a workable plan. AT&T began selling time on WEAF, their flagship station in New York, to anybody who wanted to broadcast a message. The most logical customers for this new service were companies that had things to sell. Thus, in 1922, the Queensboro Realty Company paid $300 for five radio talks that extolled the benefits of living in the country, preferably on a lot bought from the Queensboro Realty Company. Other companies quickly recognized the advertising potential of this new medium and bought time on WEAF and other stations. The problem of financing radio broadcasting was solved—broadcasting would be supported by advertising.

>> Networks

Linking radio stations into a **network** made good economic sense. Rather than having each individual station pay the costs of producing its own program, it was much cheaper for all stations to share the cost of a single program and broadcast the same show on all stations. Moreover, a linked network of stations could give advertisers the ability to reach a larger audience in a wider geographic area.

The first network was the National Broadcasting Company (NBC), a subsidiary of RCA, set up in 1926. NBC actually started two networks. One consisted of stations originally owned by RCA, and another was made up of stations acquired from AT&T when the phone company decided to get out of the broadcasting business. NBC got a competitor when the Columbia Broadcasting System (CBS) went on the air the next year. William S. Paley, whose career with CBS would last into the 1980s, headed the new network.

The two networks grew quickly. By 1937, NBC had 111 affiliated stations, while CBS had 105. Advertisers were spending more than $27 million annually on network radio. It was obvious that the network-affiliate arrangement would persist for some time to come.

Revenues from advertising permitted the networks to hire big-name entertainers. Jack Benny, Ed Wynn, and George Burns and Gracie Allen were all well-known vaudeville entertainers who successfully made the transition to radio. The most successful program, however, was *Amos 'n' Andy*, a comedy starring Charles Correll and Freeman Gosden, two white comedians working in blackface. Although considered racist today, the show was top-rated during the late 1920s and early 1930s, and listening to it became a national habit.

>> ## Government Regulation

Early radio regulation did not anticipate the success of broadcasting. As more and more stations went on the air during the 1920s, interference became a tremendous problem, and the government lacked the authority to do anything about it.

Congress finally acted to resolve this situation by passing the **Radio Act of 1927.** This act set up the Federal Radio Commission (FRC), a regulatory body that would issue licenses and try to clean up the chaos that existed. The commission defined the AM broadcast band, standardized channel designations, abolished portable stations, and moved to minimize interference. By 1929 the situation had improved, and the new radio medium was prevented from suffocating in its own growth.

Thus, by the end of the 1920s, the framework for modern radio broadcasting was in place. It would be a commercially supported mass medium dominated by networks and regulated by an agency of the federal government.

>> ## The Depression: 1930–1940

By most standards, radio was not hit as hard by the Depression as were other industries. In fact, the amount of money spent on radio advertising tripled from 1930 to 1935. Profits may not have been as high as they would have been in better economic times, but the radio industry was able to weather the Depression with relatively little hardship.

"This . . . is London." Edward R. Murrow's famous opening was familiar to millions of Americans who listened to his reports from the British capital during World War II. Murrow went on to a distinguished career in TV journalism.

The most significant legal development for radio during the Depression years was the formation of the **Federal Communications Commission (FCC).** President Roosevelt wanted to create a government agency that would consolidate the regulatory functions of the communications industry. In response to the president's demands, Congress passed the **Communications Act of 1934,** which consolidated responsibilities for broadcast and wire regulation under a new seven-member Federal Communications Commission. Aside from the expanded size of the commission and its increased duties, the fundamental philosophy underlying the original Radio Act of 1927 remained unchanged.

>> ## Birth of FM

In the mid-1930s, Edwin Howard Armstrong, a noted inventor, demonstrated frequency modulated radio, or FM, to his friend David Sarnoff, head of RCA. At the time, Sarnoff was more interested in promoting the development of television and, despite the technical advantages of FM, was not interested in backing Armstrong's creation. Armstrong tried to develop FM on his own. He set up his own transmitter for demonstrations and by 1940 had sold the rights to manufacture FM receiving sets to several companies. Sarnoff offered Armstrong $1 million for a license to his invention, but Armstrong, probably still angry over Sarnoff's earlier rejection, refused. FM's further development was interrupted by the start of World War II.

>> Radio Programs

Depression-era programs reflected a need for diversion and escape. Action-adventure series, such as *The Lone Ranger,* were popular, as were daytime soap operas. Network radio news grew during the 1930s, and live coverage of special events, such as the abdication speech of Edward VIII of England, drew huge numbers of listeners. Broadcasts from Europe on the eve of World War II kept many listeners glued to their radio sets for the latest bulletins. During the war, Edward R. Murrow gained fame through his reports from war-torn London.

>> World War II

Radio did well during the war. The number of dollars spent on radio ads nearly doubled from 1940 to 1945. Helped by a newsprint shortage and an excess-profits tax that encouraged companies to advertise, radio broadcasting outpaced the newspapers as a national advertising vehicle in 1943.

The shape of modern broadcasting would be significantly altered by a court ruling that came in the middle of the war. In 1943, the Supreme Court ruled that NBC must divest itself of one of its two networks. NBC chose to sell the weaker network to Edward Noble, who had made his fortune selling Life Savers candy. Noble renamed his network the American Broadcasting Company (ABC), and by the end of the war, ABC had 195 affiliates and was a full-fledged competitor for the older nets.

>> Innovation and Change: 1945–1954

The nine-year period following World War II was marked by great changes in both the radio and recording industries, changes that ultimately drove them closer together. The development of television delayed the growth of FM radio, altered the nature of network radio, and forced the radio industry to rely on records as the most important part of a new programming strategy.

FM   Despite the fact that FM sounded better than AM, was static free, and could reproduce a wider range of sound frequencies, AM broadcasting had started first and FM had to struggle to catch up. FM had the misfortune of beginning its development at the same time as TV. In addition, because of technical considerations, both FM radio and TV are suited for about the same place in the electromagnetic spectrum, and in 1945, the FCC decided to give the rapidly expanding TV service the space formerly occupied by FM. The commission moved FM "upstairs" to the 88- to 108-MHz band (where it is today), thus rendering obsolete about half a million FM radios.

TV   Of course the biggest change in radio's fortunes came about because of the emergence of television. (Chapter 10 has more to say about the development of TV.) By 1948, it was apparent that TV would take over the mass entertainment function served by network radio. The emergence of TV meant changes in the content, economics, and functions of radio. Although many individuals believe that television cut into the revenues of the radio industry, no such thing happened. In fact, revenues rose steadily from 1948 to 1952 and, after a brief drop from 1953 to 1956, continued to rise. The part of the industry upon which TV did have a drastic effect was network radio. The percentage of local stations with network affiliations dropped from 97 percent in 1947 to only 50 percent by 1955. Network revenue dropped by 60 percent for approximately the same period. Faced with this loss, stations relied more heavily on revenue from ads for local businesses. In short, they redistributed the makeup of their revenue dollar. As TV became the new mass medium, local stations cut back on their budgets; relied more heavily on music, talk, and news; and began searching for a formula that would allow them to coexist with television.

Specialized Formats   By 1956 it was obvious that the networks would no longer be the potent programming source they had been in the past. In that year, radio networks were carrying only about 35 hours of sponsored evening programs each week. Finally, by 1960, all the once-popular evening programs and daytime serials had come to an end. Radio network service was limited primarily to news and short features, usually amounting to no more than two or three hours of time a day.

Local stations soon adapted to this change. Now that they no longer were tied to the networks for the bulk of their programming, the locals were free to develop their own personalities. Most did so by adopting a specialized format, a sound that had distinctive appeal to a certain segment of the audience. The most successful experiment occurred in the Midwest, where a station began monitoring the sales of records and sheet music and playing those tunes that were selling the most. Hence, the Top 40 format was born! Featuring a bright, continuous, and upbeat sound, the format was ruled by the **clock hour,** which specified every element of programming. The success of the Top 40 sound encouraged radio stations to experiment with other specialized formats. By 1964, at least a dozen different formats, ranging from country to classical, had sprung up.

>> Growth and Stabilization: 1955–1990

The number of radio stations continued to grow during these years, from 3,343 in 1955 to more than 7,000 in 1970. More and more stations adopted the Top 40 format, and it very quickly became the format of choice among young listeners—who, as it happened, had a good deal of money to spend on the records they heard played by their favorite disc jockey, or DJ. Since at this time the DJ had control of what songs were played on the air, he or she became the focus of promotional efforts by record companies to gain airplay for their new songs. All too soon this arrangement led to the growth of **payola** (see Media Probe, "Payola"), and a nasty scandal ensured.

The most significant development in radio during the 1970s and 1980s was the successful emergence of FM. By the early 1960s, AM stations were becoming harder to get; it was easier to get an FM license. The FCC passed the **nonduplication rule,** which prevented an AM-FM combination from duplicating its AM content on its FM station for more than 50 percent of the time. Faced with this ruling, FM stations developed their own kind of sound (many went to a rock format) that capitalized on FM's better technical qualities. As a result, the number of FM sta-

In the 1950s, the DJ became an important figure in radio programming. In fact, many became stars in their own right. DJs sent out glossy pictures of themselves to their fans; they appeared at supermarket openings and record hops; they were the emcees at personal appearances by rock-and-roll groups. As the DJs became more influential, they also began to program their own shows. They picked the records that they would play during their shifts.

Record promoters also recognized the tremendous importance of airplay in the marketing of a hit. The more a record was played on the radio, the more it sold. Quite naturally, record promoters and DJs began to develop close ties. In the beginning, the relationship was innocent enough. Promoters would make sure that DJs got the latest releases their companies were offering, and they also put in a good word or two about their companies' products. Competition grew intense, however, and by 1959 about 250 new records were released every week. Some unscrupulous promoters resorted to more than words to advance their records. At first, they would send DJs an elaborate Christmas gift. If that did not work, some even "hired" the DJ as "creative consultant" and paid him or her a fee every month. Others would cut the DJ in on the action and offer to pay a penny to the DJ for every record sold in the market. Eventually, most promoters stopped these charades and simply passed the DJ an envelope filled with money in return for airplay of their company's songs. In 1958 and 1959, record distributors reportedly spent over a quarter of a million dollars in the larger markets on payola.

The news of this illicit business practice did nothing to help the image of rock and roll or of broadcasting. Section 508 was added to the 1934 Communications Act to stop this practice, but it was not altogether successful. New payola scandals broke out in the industry in the early 1970s. At least one record company was accused of offering drugs to station personnel in return for increased airplay, and some concert promoters were accused of offering several monetary bribes. Payola resurfaced in 2000 when 80 program directors at Spanish-language stations were investigated for allegedly taking bribes from Fonovisa Records.

The most recent twist in the payola saga involves independent promoters who charge music labels a fee to promote their records and pay money to radio stations for access to their programmers and playlists. The money involved can be substantial. In large markets the promoters might funnel as much as $300,000 to the stations. Record labels consider this just another promotional cost in getting their songs on radio. This arrangement is perfectly legal since no covert money flows directly from the labels to the stations. Despite its legitimacy, the practice has drawn criticism from several sources. *Rolling Stone* labeled it "legal payola," and congressional leaders found the practice troubling. In response, Clear Channel and other radio group owners announced in 2003 that they were cutting their ties with independent promoters. Nevertheless, payola is one problem that just will not disappear.

tions tripled between 1960 and 1970, and profits began to increase. By 1990, FM accounted for about 90 percent of listening time. Many AM stations switched to a news/talk format in order to stop the audience erosion (see Figure 7–1).

A noncommercial radio network, **National Public Radio (NPR),** went on the air in the early 1970s with an 80-station network. Over the next five years, its number of affiliates doubled, and by 1980 it was reaching a cumulative audience of more than five million people per week. Its most successful programs were its daily news programs *Morning Edition* and *All Things Considered.*

>> The Volatile 1990s

The pivotal event for radio in the 1990s was the passage of the **Telecommunications Act of 1996.** The act was concerned primarily with encouraging competition in the new communication technologies, but the radio industry, through skillful lobbying, was able to include itself in the bill. Only a few sentences in the final version of the act concern radio, but those few sentences had an impact out of proportion to their length. A key provision completely erased the cap on the number of stations a company could own and increased to eight the number of stations a company could own in a single market.

FIGURE 7–1

Division of AM and FM Audiences

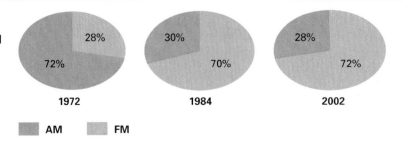

28%
72%
1972

30%
70%
1984

28%
72%
2002

■ AM ■ FM

The new law caused an avalanche of buying and selling of radio properties, and some stations were sold several times in a single year. In a typical year before the act, about $2 billion was spent on radio acquisitions and mergers. In 1996, the number hit $14.4 billion. That figure was eclipsed the next year when $15.3 billion was spent. New radio giants sprang up almost overnight. The radio industry became even more consolidated as a few large group owners dominated the industry.

On the programming front, talk became the hottest format on AM radio, thanks to the success of such performers as Rush Limbaugh, Dr. Laura Schlessinger, Tom Joyner, and Howard Stern. The trend toward format specialization continued on FM as stations recognized that attracting as little as 2 to 3 percent of the audience was enough to keep them profitable.

A weak economy and the demise of the dot-com companies hurt radio's advertising revenue at the start of the new century. After several years of prosperity, many radio stations cut back on expenses and laid off employees.

The radio industry today is more concentrated than ever. The business is now dominated by just a few big companies. As noted at the beginning of this chapter, Clear Channel is the biggest player in the industry with stations in 190 radio markets. This increasing trend toward consolidation has caused much controversy.

 ## RADIO IN THE DIGITAL AGE

Radio continues to creep into the digital age. Thousands of radio stations have Websites and many now offer streaming audio. For the most part, these sites are used primarily to supplement the on-air station and its traditional analog signal. There are signs, however, that things are speeding up.

>> **Terrestrial Digital Radio Broadcasting**

The technology for broadcasting a digital radio signal has been around for years, and several countries already have digital

Radio talk show host Sean Hannity. His syndicated program reaches about 12 million people.

Catherine Hughes, head of Radio One, the nation's largest radio group targeting black listeners, is the first African American woman to head a publicly traded company. Her path to the top was not an easy one.

Hughes started in radio by working in the sales department at Howard University's radio station. Eventually, she became the station's manager. She decided to start her own radio station in 1980 by buying WOL-AM in Washington, D.C. At the time, she was a single mother with limited financial resources. Bank after bank rejected her loan application. She finally found one bank willing to lend her part of the money she needed, and she secured additional backing from a consortium of financiers who specialized in funding black business enterprises.

The station nearly failed. Hughes had her house and car repossessed and even sold some family heirlooms to pay the bills. She actually moved into the station, sleeping in a sleep-ing bag and cooking on a hot plate. She saved programming costs by doing her own talk show. Trying desperately to get advertising, she went door-to-door persuading small retailers to spend $10 for a minute of commercial time. Seven years later, the station finally turned a profit.

Hughes next decided that the time was right for expansion. She noted that African American family income was growing along with its buying power. Taking advantage of relaxed federal ownership regulations, Hughes acquired another 11 stations over the next six years. She took her company public in 1999. Radio One's stock price nearly doubled in the first three months.

In 2002, Radio One was the seventh largest radio broad-caster in the United States based on its revenue of more than $280 million. The company owns 65 stations in 22 cities and programs five channels on the XM satellite radio service. No more cooking on a hot plate for Catherine Hughes.

systems in operation. Digital radio has moved slowly because traditional analog radio is doing just fine and broadcasters have seen no need to disrupt a profitable situation. In addition, radio broadcasters have wanted a system that is compatible with existing analog signals so that current radio receivers can pick up the analog signals while new receiving sets can pick up the digital signal. Broadcasters got their wish in the late 1990s, when an **IBOC** (in-band, on-channel) system was developed.

In 2003, several large radio broadcasters announced that they would begin digital radio broadcasting by 2004. Using an IBOC system developed by the iBiquity Digital Corporation, about 100 stations were set to offer the new system in large markets including New York, Los Angeles, and Chicago. The digital signal can be received at the same spot on the radio dial as the analog signal, but it has much better sound quality. A digital signal of an FM station sounds as good as a CD, and a digital AM signal sounds as good as a traditional FM station. In addition, the static and pops normally heard on an AM station disappear. This improvement could have a significant impact on AM radio formats, and many could switch from talk to music to take advantage of the better sound quality.

In order to hear the clearer sound, consumers will have to shell out about $300 for a radio set that gets both the analog and digital signals or about $100 for a digital-only receiver. The new digital sets will also contain new features. A text display can present the latest traffic and weather information as well as display the name of the song and the artist when music is playing.

>> Satellite Radio

Two companies now offer a direct-from-satellite-to-car radio digital service. XM radio, launched in 2001, offers 70 music channels, half of them commercial free, and 30 news and talk channels for a monthly fee of about $10. Subscribers can also add the Playboy Radio Channel (presum-ably to listen to the articles) for an additional charge. Sirius Radio launched a similar service in 2002 with 60 commercial-free music

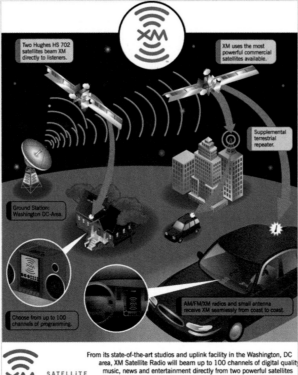

XM radio—digital radio sent directly to your car radio for a fee.

channels and 40 news, talk, and variety channels. Both services offer programming choices that do not exist in broadcast radio. Sirius, for example, offers several channels of alternative rock, several jazz channels, a Broadway show tunes channel, and a channel that features programs from the golden age of radio drama.

Although feedback from early subscribers was overwhelmingly positive, both services found it difficult to attract new customers. By mid-2003, XM had about 500,000 subscribers and Sirius about 100,000. Both companies were experiencing financial difficulties. Part of their problem has been convincing consumers to pay a monthly fee for radio, a service that traditionally has been free. Nevertheless, cable TV faced the same difficulty and successfully overcame it. In any case, the future of satellite radio is still murky.

>> Internet-Only Stations

Satellite radio services target listeners in their cars, but Internet-only stations are competing for audiences who listen to radio at work. Web broadcasters offer dozens of specialized music formats, such as reggae and technorock, with limited commercials. The audiences for most Internet-only stations tend to be small, numbering in the low thousands.

Webcasting was nearly dealt a serious blow in 2002 when the Copyright Arbitration Royalty Panel ruled that Webcasters had to pay a royalty to artists and music labels for use of their songs. The initial royalty rate was so steep that many Web-only radio stations would have been forced out of business. Eventually, Congress gave Webcasters a break when it passed the Small Webcaster Settlement Act of 2002, which allowed some flexibility in how much the Web broadcasters would pay.

Satellite radio and Internet-only stations are interested in attracting audiences that are dissatisfied with traditional radio, and there are indications that quite a few may fit into that category. As the number of commercial minutes per hour has increased on radio stations, listening time has decreased. Since 1990, time devoted to commercials has doubled, and the radio audience has shrunk 12 percent. What demographic group is most turned off by all the commercials on radio? Young people—the group most in demand by advertisers.

DEFINING FEATURES OF RADIO

Radio is portable. Some radio sets, like the Walkman, are small and personal. Others, like the boom box, are big and public. No matter their size, radio sets are easily transported and go everywhere—the beach, sporting events, jogging trails, the workplace. Car radios provide news and entertainment to commuters on their way to and from work. In fact, it is hard to find a place where radio cannot go.

Radio is supplemental. Most radio listening occurs while we are doing something else—driving, working, studying, falling asleep, waking up, cleaning, and so on. Radio rarely is the prime focus of our attention; it provides an audio background for our activities.

Radio is universal. Virtually every household has at least one working radio. In fact, the average house has about six. Almost every car is equipped with a radio. In an average day, about 75 percent of Americans listen to radio.

Radio is selective. Much like the magazine industry (see Chapter 5), the radio industry has become a niche medium. Radio stations choose formats that attract a small, narrowly defined audience that is attractive to advertisers. As mentioned earlier, if a radio broadcaster can find a formula that attracts just 2 or 3 percent of the audience, odds are that the station will turn a profit.

ORGANIZATION OF THE RADIO INDUSTRY

There are more than a half-billion working radio sets in the United States. That works out to about two radios per person. There are about 12,000 radio stations in operation. Thanks in part to an FCC philosophy that encouraged competition, the number of stations grew from about 6,900 in 1970 to about 12,500 in 2000, an increase of 75 percent. To understand how this rapidly growing business is organized, we will examine it from several perspectives: programming, technology, and format.

>> Local Stations, Nets, and Syndicators

Local radio stations operate in cities, towns, and villages across the country. Big cities have many stations. New York City has 95; Los Angeles, 60. Smaller towns may have only one or two. Whitefish, Montana, for example (population 4,000),

The WYNK humvee on a remote in Baton Rouge, Louisiana. Remotes are an important part of promotion for a local radio station.

has five stations. Programming for these stations is provided by networks and by program syndication companies. Technically speaking, the distinction between a net and a syndication service is that all stations on a network carry the net program at the same time, while syndicated programming is carried at different times by the stations. In practice, however, much syndicated radio programming is satellite-delivered and carried simultaneously, and many network affiliates tape net programming and broadcast it later. To make it even more complicated, the traditional networks also offer syndicated programs. Consequently, the distinction between the two services may no longer be meaningful.

Networks were important programming sources during the earlier years of radio. After the emergence of TV, the importance of radio networks diminished, and they provided only news and public-affairs programs to their affiliates.

Network radio staged a mild resurgence during the early part of the century. The leading radio networks were ABC, Westwood One, and Premiere.

Many experts noted that the demand for syndicated shows was still strong in 2003. Rush Limbaugh continued to lead the syndication race while the drive-time shows of the controversial Howard Stern, Don Imus, and Tom Joyner are also popular.

There are about 50 companies that provide syndicated programs of various length. For example, the American Comedy Network offers a library of 640 comedy bits on 13 CDs. The Motor Racing Network supplies coverage of 50 NASCAR races and NASCAR-related features to about 400 stations.

>> AM and FM Stations

Broadcast radio stations are either AM or FM. **AM** stands for *amplitude modulation,* and **FM** stands for *frequency modulation.* As we saw earlier in the chapter, since about 1975 the fortunes of FM radio have been increasing while those of AM stations are on the decline. In 2003, almost three-quarters of listenership went to the FM stations. Keep in mind, however, that some AM stations, particularly those in large markets, are doing quite well. In 2000, AMs were the top-rated stations in Chicago (WGN), San Francisco (KGO), Detroit (WJR), and Boston (WRKO).

All physical factors being equal, radio signals sent by AM travel farther, especially at night, than signals sent by FM. The AM dial on a typical radio set illustrates the precise frequencies in the electromagnetic spectrum where the AM station operates. AM stations are further classified by channels. There are three possible channels: clear, regional, and local. A clear channel is one with a single dominant station that is designed to provide service over a wide area. Typically, these dominant stations have a strong signal because they broadcast with 50,000 watts of power. For example, the 720 spot on the AM dial is a clear channel with WGN, Chicago, the dominant station, operating at 50,000 watts. The 770 position is also a clear channel with WABC, New York, dominant. A regional channel is one shared by many stations that serve fairly large areas. A local channel is designed to be shared by a large number of stations that broadcast only to their local communities.

FM signals do not travel as far as AM, but FM has the advantage of being able to produce better sound qualities than AM. FM radio is also less likely to be affected by outside interference such as thunderstorms. Similar to AM, FM stations are organized in classes. Class C FM stations are the most powerful, operating at 100,000 watts. Class B and Class A stations are less powerful. A glance at the FM dial of a radio reveals that FM stations operate in a different part of the electromagnetic spectrum than does AM. Figure 7–2 is a simplified diagram of the spectrum showing where AM, FM, and television signals are located. The AM versus FM distinction does not apply to digital radio signals.

>> Station Formats

Perhaps the most meaningful way we can organize radio stations is according to their **format,** a type of consistent programming designed to appeal to a certain segment of the audience. A format gives a station a distinctive personality and attracts a certain kind of audience that advertisers find desirable. In fact, the development of radio after 1960 is marked by the fine-tuning of existing formats and the creation of new ones that appeal to people in distinct demographic and lifestyle categories. Most modern stations can offer an amazingly precise description of the kind of listener they want their format to attract. An adult contemporary station, for example, might set its sights on men and women, aged 25 to 45,

FIGURE 7–2

**Simplified Diagram of
the Electromagnetic
Spectrum**

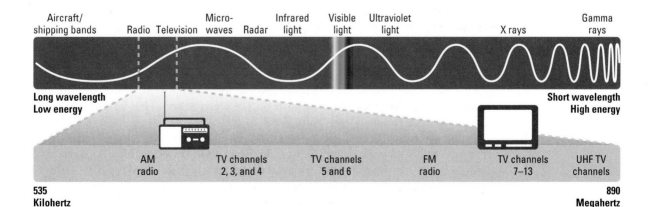

Sometimes it is hard to see new possibilities because we think about things the way we have always thought of them. Such is the case with the radio spectrum. Our current thinking was shaped back in the 1920s when radio transmitters could operate on only one frequency and had to be assigned to a narrow sliver of the radio spectrum so they would not interfere with each other. Accordingly, the spectrum was treated like a piece of scarce real estate that was apportioned by the government through licensing. A piece went to AM radio, a piece to FM radio, and a piece to TV. An even smaller piece went to specific AM or FM stations. Those stations had exclusive rights to broadcast on those frequencies. No trespassers were allowed. The benefit of this system was that we got radio stations that did not interfere with one another; the cost was that the federal government decided who got a license. For the past 80 years or so we have accepted this licensing model as a given; no one has questioned the paradigm.

But that was before digital technology. Today it is possible to build "smart transmitters" and "smart receivers" that use the entire radio spectrum and are sophisticated enough that they do not interfere with one another. To use an analogy, they figure out the best frequency to use the same way that Internet routers figure out the best way to send information across the Net. If one part of the spectrum is busy, the new transmitters simply use another. The interference problem vanishes and with it so does the need for government to dole out spectrum space. In addition, the scarcity problem disappears; the entire radio spectrum is so vast that there is room for everybody to do whatever they want.

This new paradigm, called *open spectrum,* promises to be revolutionary. As far as radio is concerned, it will open up possibilities for more stations. Given the financial and technical resources needed, anybody can start a station. No government approval is needed. Of course, the impact of an open spectrum will spread beyond radio. Increased wireless connectivity, live video delivered to cell phones, and camcorders that can send TV signals to TV sets in other cities are just some of the possibilities. We are at about the same place that Marconi was back in 1896 when he was developing wireless. Marconi could not have predicted what his invention eventually made possible. Similarly, open spectrum might lead to developments we are unable to think of today.

with college educations, making more than $40,000 a year, who read *Rolling Stone,* drive either a BMW or a Volvo, and go to the mall at least twice a week. In our discussion we will cover three basic categories of radio formats: music, news/talk, and ethnic.

The Music Format   Music is the largest category and includes many subdivisions and variations. In 2002 the two most listened-to music formats were Urban, with about 14 percent of all listening time, and Adult Contemporary (AC), with about 13 percent. The Urban format, also called *Rhythm and Blues,* showcases a large number of African American artists and plays rap, hip-hop, and dance music. In mid-2003 some prominent artists featured in the Urban format were 50 Cent, NAS, and Jay Z. The Urban format is aimed at a young audience. In contrast, the main appeal of the AC format is to 25- to 49-year-old females. AC stations are the ones that play "the hits of the 70s, 80s, 90s, and today" with a blend of about 20 percent current and 80 percent older tunes. Some artists whose songs are generally played on the AC format are Celine Dion, Christina Aguilera, and Phil Collins.

Other popular music formats are Top 40 or Contemporary Hit Radio and Country.

Top 40 features a small playlist of hit records in a fast rotation. The Top 40 format has shown a modest increase in listenership in recent years. This format does best with the 12- to 25-year-old age group.

Country stations, as the name suggests, play hit country-and-western singles and employ DJs who are down-home, friendly, and knowledgeable about country music. The country format has two main divisions: (1) traditional country stations that play mainstream classic, twangy country music and (2) contemporary country stations that play more current artists who might use synthesizers and other

Hits by artists such as 50 Cent have made urban contemporary one of radio's fastest growing formats.

modern sounds. A country station's audience still mainly comprises adults from 35 to 55.

Black and Ethnic Formats These formats aim for special audiences that are defined primarily by race and nationality. There are about 175 stations that program for the black audience and about 260 stations that serve the Hispanic audience. Many of the black and Hispanic stations feature urban contemporary music and run news, features, and special programs of interest to their audiences. In addition, about 60 stations have formats aimed at other ethnic groups: Polish, German, Italian, French, Irish, and Greek.

Format Homogenization Radio stations sound pretty much alike no matter where you are. Almost all the major music formats are represented in the large and medium markets, and it seems that every market has its morning "zoo crew"; an AC station that specializes in "the classic hits" of the 70s, 80s, 90s, and today; a modern rock station that calls itself "Power" or "Z" or "Q" something or other; an easy-listening station with a "warm" format that dedicates love songs at night; and maybe even an AM station that specializes in "golden oldies." Even the DJs sound pretty much the same.

There are several reasons for this trend toward homogenization. The most important is the increasing consolidation in the industry. Big radio companies, such as Clear Channel, own stations in all the big markets. What works in one market is likely to work in another. In addition, it is cheaper to program the same music from market to market. Finally, radio has become so competitive that programming decisions are based on the recommendations of program consultants and audience research based on surveys and focus groups. Since the same records are generally tested in all markets and usually score high, the recommendations about what to play are the same from market to market. Not surprisingly, many stations prefer to adopt a "safe" format, one that has worked in other markets, rather than risking a sizable amount of money on a new and untested format.

Voice Tracking One controversial trend in the industry is the rise of **voice tracking** (see Ethical Issues, "Voice Tracking in Radio: Is Anybody There?"). Voice tracking makes use of a single DJ who prerecords song intros, extros, and chatter for music programs on several different stations. The music is mixed in later, and the total program is delivered by satellite to local stations. The biggest advantage of voice tracking is cost cutting; one DJ can do the work that was previously done by several.

News/Talk Format This format is becoming more and more popular on the AM band and accounts for 16 percent of all radio listening time. Some stations emphasize the news part of the news/talk format. National, regional, and local news

It's 11 P.M. Do you know where your radio DJ is?

Thanks to an innovation called *voice tracking,* he or she might be a recorded voice from Los Angeles, Tampa, Norfolk, or Dallas. The concept behind voice tracking is simple enough. A DJ somewhere else records chatter, music introductions, and music recaps. The music itself can be added later. At the local station, this recorded content is mixed together with local weather, traffic updates, promotions, and local commercials. Thanks to computers and satellite distribution, the whole process sounds seamless and most listeners cannot tell the difference.

The growing popularity of voice tracking is also simple: It saves money. Rather than pay six DJs salaries and benefits, a company can pay one DJ to voice track for six shows in six different markets at a substantially lower cost. Since most of a DJ's shift consists mainly of music, one DJ can voice track a four-hour shift in about 30 minutes.

The consolidation of the radio industry has added extra impetus to the voice tracking phenomenon. Clear Channel, the largest owner of radio stations, uses voice tracking in every one of its 255 markets except New York, where union rules make it too expensive. Currently, most voice-tracked programs occur overnight, at midday, and in the evening; most drive-time shows are still live and local.

Executives at Clear Channel and other companies defend the practice as a way of bringing more professional-sounding programming to local markets. From a purely technical perspective, most would agree that the DJs who do voice tracks are smoother and sound more skilled than most local DJs. The production itself is professional and usually error-free. The companies also tout the greater efficiency and savings of the technique.

Opponents cite the fact that voice tracking has put many local DJs out of work. They also note that the philosophy of localism has always been at the heart of the radio industry. Starting in the 1920s, radio stations were licensed to serve the public interest in a local community. Voice tracking is undesirable because it eliminates local talent and severs ties to the local community.

Perhaps a more pertinent ethical argument against voice tracking is the fact that it is based on deception. The audience is not told that its local DJ taped his or her show in some distant city. In fact, voice-tracking DJs go to great pains to make people believe that they are in fact local. They read local newspapers and Internet sites to learn about local events and drop local references into their chatter ("Don't forget the big rock concert at [insert local name here] on Saturday"); they learn about local traffic hot spots to make their traffic intros sound credible ("How's traffic looking on [insert local name here]? Let's get an updated traffic report."); and they might act as if they had attended a local event ("Wasn't that a great game at [insert local sports venue here]? The crowd was something else.").

What do listeners think? Surveys have shown that some feel cheated once they learn that they have been listening to voice tracking and not a live DJ. Others do not seem to care. Many report they listen to hear music and never pay attention to the DJ.

reports are broadcast periodically throughout the day. Sports, traffic, weather, editorials, public-affairs programs, and an occasional feature round out the programming day. News stations appeal primarily to a male audience in the 25- to 54-year-old age category.

The talk format attracts listeners in about the same age group. Common types of programs that appear on stations using the talk format are call-in shows, usually hosted by an opinionated and maybe even abrasive host; interview shows; advice shows; and roundtable discussions. News, weather, traffic reports, and other feature material are blended in with these programs. Unlike the music formats, which do not demand their listeners' close attention, the talk format requires that its audience concentrate on the program in order to follow what is said.

>> Noncommercial Radio

Many of the early radio stations that went on the air during the 1920s were founded by educational institutions. As the commercial broadcasting system became firmly established, many educational stations were bought by commercial broadcasters, and the fortunes of noncommercial radio dwindled. In 1945, with the coming of FM broadcasting, the FCC set aside several frequencies for educa-

Twenty years ago there were about 75 radio stations in the entire country that programmed a talk format. In 2003, there were more than 1,350. Much of that growth has been due to the popularity of conservative talk show hosts such as Rush Limbaugh, Gordon Liddy, and Ken Hamblen. *Talkers* magazine, the leading trade publication of talk radio, lists dozens of conservative talkers in their annual roster of the top 100 talk show hosts in the United States.

Some Democratic politicians have suggested that the conservative voice of talk radio was the driving force behind the Republican midterm gains in the 2002 election. In order to counteract what they perceive to be the growing political clout of talk radio, a group of wealthy Democratic donors announced in early 2003 plans to start AnShell Media, a venture that would finance a liberal talk radio network.

They will not have an easy task. Liberal talk show hosts have not been successful in talk radio. Some have tried. Tom Leykis hosted a liberal talk show for a couple of years but then changed to a format that was more sex-themed. Left-leaning hosts such as Mario Cuomo and Jim Hightower had brief runs as hosts.

Many have speculated on the reasons behind this phenomenon. One theory suggests that conservative talk radio appeals to many people who think the traditional network newscasts and CNN are slanted toward a liberal point of view. A more complicated explanation argues that liberal hosts are not entertaining because they present issues in too much complexity. Conservative hosts, on the other hand, present issues simply and understandably. Yet another viewpoint argues that liberals do not want to offend anybody, which makes for a bland program.

Whatever the explanation, a liberal talk show host faces an uphill battle. The biggest problem is finding major market radio stations willing to gamble on a historically unsuccessful format. Most stations that currently carry a successful conservative show might not want to risk alienating their loyal listeners by scheduling a program with a liberal host.

As of March 2003, the people at AnShell Media were considering a number of possibilities for a talk show host. One name that was at the top of the list was comedian and writer Al Franken, who, not coincidentally, is the author of a book entitled *Rush Limbaugh Is a Big Fat Idiot.* We shall see.

---

tional broadcasting. This action sparked a rebirth of interest in this kind of broadcasting, so that by 2003 there were about 1,900 noncommercial radio stations on the air.

Most noncommercial radio stations are owned by educational institutions or private foundations. Noncommercial radio gets its support from the institutions that own the stations. Ultimately, much of this support comes from tax revenue since taxes support most public educational institutions. Other sources of support are endowments (gifts), grants from foundations or the federal government, and listener donations.

Noncommercial stations are served by National Public Radio (NPR). National Public Radio, founded in 1970, provides program services to about 530 affiliates around the country. Member stations pay a fee based on audience reach and annual budget and receive in return about 50 hours of programming per week. Many of these shows are produced at NPR headquarters; others are produced at NPR stations and distributed by NPR. Probably the best-known NPR programs are *All Things Considered* and *Morning Edition.*

The public radio stations that help support NPR receive financial support from the Corporation for Public Broadcasting (CPB), a private, nonprofit organization funded by Congress. Member stations receive money from the CPB, and those that decide to affiliate with NPR pay some of this money to the network as a fee. NPR also receives grants directly from the CPB. Congress, however, has threatened to cut the CPB's budget, which, in turn, would lead to less money for stations and for NPR. Consequently, many public stations have resorted to underwriting, a practice in which the station accepts money from a person or an organization in return for an acknowledgment on the air. In some cases, these acknowledgments

Journalist Ray Suarez is host of NPR's call-in news program, *Talk of the Nation.*

sound suspiciously like commercials. In contrast, NPR for the most part has resisted the pressure to air these mini-commercials. In 1995, however, NPR relented a bit and allowed underwriters to broadcast brief slogans. At the same time, NPR is trying to raise money in other ways. It has a telephone music ordering service and its own record label, NPR Classics. Public stations and NPR will probably struggle with their money problems for years to come.

The other noncommercial radio network, Public Radio International (PRI), was formerly known as American Public Radio. The Minneapolis, Minnesota, organization is a network that acquires and distributes programming from station-based, independent and international producers. Unlike NPR, PRI does not produce any of its programming but does finance program production at member stations. A noncommercial station can be an affiliate of both NPR and PRI.

 ## OWNERSHIP IN THE RADIO INDUSTRY

As mentioned earlier, the Telecommunications Act of 1996 drastically changed the landscape of the radio industry. The new rules prompted a wave of consolidation that created radio megacompanies. In 1996, there were 5,100 different organizations and individuals who owned radio stations. Six years later that number had dropped to 3,800. By 2003, just two companies, Clear Channel Communications and Infinity Broadcasting, accounted for one-third of the advertising revenue for the total industry.

Table 7–1 is a listing of the top five radio group owners as of 2003. Keep in mind that this list will change as owners continue to make deals. The pace of mergers and acquisitions had slowed by 2003, maybe in part because there are not that many large- and medium-market stations that have not already been acquired by large companies.

The increasing consolidation of radio has alarmed many critics and citizens groups. Congress became interested in the issue in 2003 and, although many legislators spoke out against the dangers of increased concentration, no change was made to the original 1996 legislation.

 ## PRODUCING RADIO PROGRAMS

>> Departments and Staff

The departmental structure of a radio station varies according to its size. Obviously, a small station with five or six employees has a departmental setup different from that of a large station with a hundred-person staff.

TABLE 7–1	Company	Revenue (in millions)
Top Five Radio Group Owners, 2002	Clear Channel	$3,423
	Infinity	$2,187
Data from *Broadcasting & Cable,* September 10, 2003, p. 10.	Cox Radio	$467
	Entercom	$455
	ABC Radio	$425

The two top management positions are the general manager and the program director. The manager has the responsibility for planning and carrying out station policy, maintaining contact with the community, and monitoring program content, audience ratings, and sales information. The program director is responsible for the station's sound. He or she supervises the music or other program material that the station broadcasts and is also responsible for the hiring and firing of announcers and DJs.

The sales department consists of the sales manager and the station's sales force. The news department is responsible for compiling the station's local newscasts and rewriting the wire service reports of national and regional news. The engineering department, under the supervision of the chief engineer, is staffed with technicians responsible for keeping the station on the air and maintaining the equipment.

>> Putting Together a Program

This section will concentrate on how radio programs are produced for the music, talk, and news formats.

Music Format   When the staff of a local station puts together their program, the first step is generally to lay out a **format wheel** (also called a *format clock*), a pie chart of an hour divided into segments representing different program elements. Figure 7–3 is a simplified version of a wheel for a contemporary rock station.

Note that the music is structured to flow from one segment to another. Album cuts and hits from the past are spread around the wheel. Additional wheels would be constructed for the various parts of the broadcast day (i.e., one wheel for morning drive time, another for 10 A.M.–4 P.M., another for evening drive time, and another for 7 P.M.–midnight).

Talk Format   Most of the content of the talk format is produced by the local station. As is the case with the music format, the makeup of the audience is taken into account. During drive time, talk segments should be relatively short and liberally interspersed with news, weather, and traffic reports. The audience for the 10 A.M.–4 P.M. segment tends to be primarily female and, therefore, topics for discussion reflect the interests of that group. The early evening audience is generally younger and contains more males.

Producing a talk show requires more equipment than does producing a simple DJ program. Speaker telephones and extra telephone lines are needed, as well as a delay system. This device gives the talk show moderator a 7- to 30-second delay period during which he or she can censor what is said by the caller. Another important part of the talk show is the telephone screener. The screener ranks the waiting calls by importance, letting the most interesting callers go first, and filters out crank calls or calls from regulars who contact the station too frequently.

All-News Format   The all-news station also works with a programming wheel, similar to that of the music format. Instead of music, however, the news wheel shows the spacing between headlines, weather, news, sports, business reports, and commercials. It also illustrates the **cycle,** the amount of time that elapses before the program order is repeated.

The all-news format is the most difficult to produce. A large staff, consisting of anchorpersons, a managing editor, local reporters, editors, rewrite people, a traffic reporter, and stringers (freelance reporters who are paid per story), is needed. The list of necessary equipment and facilities is also long: radio wire services, sports wire, weather wire, mobile units, police and fire-frequency scanners, short-wave receiver, and perhaps even a helicopter.

 ECONOMICS

After several years of impressive revenue growth, radio's advertising revenue slipped by about 8 percent from the record year of 2000 to 2001. As with other ad-supported media, a slow economy and the loss of dot-com advertising dollars were the main causes of the decline. The downturn was short-lived, however,

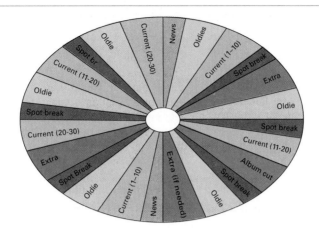

FIGURE 7–3

Format Wheel for a Contemporary Rock Station

as radio income subsequently increased from about $18.4 billion in 2001 to $19.6 billion in 2002, a level just below that of 2000. Part of this recovery was fueled by consolidation as big radio companies offered advertisers greater reach and efficiency for their ad dollars. Another reason was radio's ability to draw upon a wide range of potential advertisers. As the dot-com money dried up, it was replaced by revenue from local and regional businesses.

Most analysts agree that, despite the competition from satellite service and Internet radio, as long as the economy is reasonably healthy, radio's long-term economic prospects are good. The drive-time audience is growing, and average commuting time continues to increase. Radio programming is relatively cheap to produce (most music is supplied free by recording companies) and distribute. Radio also lends itself to target marketing by enabling an advertiser to specialize by age, sex, ethnicity, and lifestyle. The only problem for radio might be its own success. Too much commercial clutter will drive some listeners away.

>> Sources of Revenue

Radio stations earn their money by selling advertising time. The amount that a radio station charges for time is included in its rate card. A typical radio commercial costs several hundred dollars in large cities. The same commercial in a small town might cost only a few dollars.

The radio industry has three sources of income from the sale of commercial time. The first comes from the sale of spots on network programs to national advertisers trying to reach a broad market. The second is the sale of time on local stations to advertisers who wish to reach a specific region (e.g., the Northeast) or a specific type of market (e.g., rural areas). This is called *national spot advertising*. The third source is advertising purchased by local establishments that want their commercials to be heard only in the immediate community. In 2002, each of these sources represented the following amounts of each dollar of radio revenue:

- Network: $0.05
- National spot: $0.17
- Local: $0.78

As the numbers indicate, the overwhelming amount of revenue in radio came from local commercials.

Radio and the Local Community

The philosophy that guided the development of radio in the United States was based on localism. Radio stations were licensed to serve the public interest of those who could hear their signals. Stations were expected to be integral parts of their local communities and responsive to the needs of local residents. The Federal Radio Commission set aside a number of AM channels that were dedicated to lower-power stations serving a particular town. Over the years, other regulations were enacted that favored localism. To encourage the development of roots in the community, owners were required to hold on to stations for three years before they could be sold. Stations had to survey their listeners and ascertain the needs of their community and provide programs to address those needs. Caps were placed on the number of stations one company could own to discourage large corporations from becoming out-of-town station owners with little or no ties to the community. In an effort to assure access for many voices, there were further caps on the number of stations that could be owned in one market.

As pointed out by Charles Fairchild in his article "Deterritorializing Radio: Deregulation and the Continued Triumph of the Corporatist Perspective in the USA," which appeared in a 1999 issue of *Media, Culture and Society,* this localist philosophy is not much with us today. His analysis of changes in the radio industry over the past two decades is a good example of a critical/cultural investigation that focuses on ideology and power relationships in society.

In essence, Fairchild argues that recent changes have removed the connection between a radio station and its local community. He suggests that there are two dominant ideologies in force that compete as definitions of the *public interest.* One, the statist position, conceives of government as the protector of the public interest and an agency that assures that the broadest number of people benefit from the medium. The other, the corporatist view, holds that the market is the best determiner of the public interest. The most economically successful service is the service that succeeds best in the marketplace. In other words, the public interest is what interests the public.

Fairchild notes that the corporatist view has been the dominant model in recent radio operations. Due in part to an active industry lobby and the economic power wielded by large communications corporations, recent changes have almost erased the notion of local service. Following are just a few of those changes: The three-year ownership rule has been dropped; the requirements for ascertaining the needs of the community have been minimized; and perhaps most importantly, the cap on the total number of stations that can be owned has been removed, and the limit on the number of stations owned in a market has been raised to eight.

What are the effects of this change in ideology? The radio industry has become consolidated, with big corporations controlling hundreds of stations. Locally owned stations that had deep roots in the local community have been gobbled up by big companies with headquarters in some faraway city and whose main interest is the bottom line. Consequently, local programming has been reduced in favor of standardized entertainment and news fed from some central location nowhere near the local community. Programming decisions are left to consultants and syndicators who have no local ties whatsoever. Hence, as Fairchild suggests, radio has become "deterritorialized," detached from a community connection.

Fairchild concludes that the corporatist ideology has triumphed: "local radio stations are the objects of unaccountable control from outside local communities and neither the government nor the public have any levers of power with which they can influence broadcasters to provide access to those voices which cannot gain any serious measure of volume elsewhere."

1. What effect might the Internet have on the amount of local news, information, and other services available in any given community? Might the Internet itself have any effect on the relevance or importance of the localism arguments?

2. If the government can deregulate radio, clearly radio can be reregulated. What types of regulations would you like to see that would best serve the public interest, and where would you place the responsibility to ensure that citizens are indeed well served by radio?

3. Who owns the radio stations in your hometown? Compare formats, amount of news, community activities. How do the locally owned stations compare with those that are corporate-owned? Had you noticed a difference before thinking about it now for this class? Does it matter?

>> General Expenses

Expenses in radio are divided into five areas: (1) technical, (2) programming, (3) selling, (4) general administration, and (5) news. Technical expenses include the payroll for the engineering staff and the cost of maintaining and replacing technical equipment. Program costs cover salaries paid to talent, costs of tape and CDs, and music fees paid to the music licensing organizations. Sales costs are made up of the salaries of the sales staff and all the other expenses that go with selling. General administrative expenses include the salaries of all management, secretarial, and clerical personnel; the depreciation of physical facilities; the cost of office supplies; and any interest that is due on loans to the station. News expenses consist of the costs involved in covering local and national stories.

As of 2003, general administration expenses ranked first, accounting for about 40 percent of all expenses. Programming came next, making up about 20 percent of the expense dollar, followed closely by costs associated with sales. News and technical expenses taken together accounted for about 15 percent.

 # FEEDBACK

>> Ratings and Shares

In the radio industry, feedback is provided by ratings conducted by professional research organizations. The major company that measures the radio audience is **Arbitron**. Arbitron surveys radio listening in approximately 280 markets across the United States and reports its results to broadcasters and advertisers.

Within a given market, Arbitron chooses people at random from a listing of all telephone numbers in the market. Individuals who agree to participate in Arbitron's survey are sent a pocket-sized diary to record both in-home and out-of-home listening. Participants are instructed to fill in the diary on a day-to-day basis, noting the time spent listening to radio and identifying the station. Approximately 3,000 to 4,000 of these diaries are mailed in a given market, and Arbitron follows up with several reminder calls to persons in the sample. Nevertheless, only 45 to 50 percent of the diaries are returned in usable form. Figure 7–4 is an example of an Arbitron radio diary. Once the diaries have been returned, Arbitron begins an analysis that typically takes three to four weeks. The end product of this process is a ratings book, which is sent to participating stations.

Measurements of radio and television audiences gathered by the diary method are usually expressed in terms of two related concepts: (1) ratings and (2) share of the audience. A **rating** is simply the ratio of listeners of a particular station to all people in the market. Suppose that in a market with 100,000 people, 20,000 listen to radio station KYYY from 9:00 A.M. to 9:15 A.M. The rating of KYYY would be 20,000/100,000, or 20 percent. A **share of the audience** is the ratio of listeners of a particular station to the total number of radio listeners in the market. For example, again suppose that 20,000 people are listening to KYYY from 9:00 A.M. to 9:15 A.M. and that in the total market 80,000 people are listening to the radio during the same period. KYYY's share of the audience would be 20,000/80,000, or 25 percent. Shares of the audience divide the listening audience among all stations in the market. When they are summed, shares should total 100 percent. Ratings books are important to stations because they are used to establish the rates stations will charge advertisers.

FIGURE 7–4

Sample Arbitron Radio Diary

Arbitron Ratings: Your Radio Ratings Diary. Copyright © Arbitron Ratings Company. Reprinted by permission.

THURSDAY

Time			Station			Place			
	Start	Stop	Call letters or station name *Don't know? Use program name or dial setting.*	Check (✔) one AM	FM	Check (✔) one At Home	In a Car	At Work	Other Place
Early Morning (from 5 AM)									
Midday									
Late Afternoon									
Night (to 5 AM Friday)									

If you didn't hear a radio today, please check here. ☐

In an effort to improve the accuracy of radio ratings, Arbitron and Nielsen Media Research are testing a "peoplemeter" for radio. This new device is designed to be clipped to an individual's clothing. Radio stations encode a special inaudible, unique signal as part of their broadcasts. The peoplemeter "hears" this signal and records the station and the time spent listening. Such a device requires far less effort on the part of respondents.

>> Radio Audiences

There are almost twice as many radio sets in this country as there are people. As of January 2003, there were more than 550 million radio receivers scattered around the United States, with car radios accounting for about one-third of this number. On a typical day at least three-fourths of all adults will listen to radio, and the average person will listen, or at least have the radio on, for about three hours. Most people listen to radio in the early morning when they are getting ready for and driving to work and in the late afternoon when they are driving home. These two "day parts," consisting roughly from 6 A.M. to 10 A.M. and 4 P.M. to 7 P.M., are called *drive time.*

The precise audience makeup for a given station depends upon that station's format. Top 40 stations draw an audience composed primarily of 12- to 24-year-olds, with females outnumbering males by about three to two. Modern rock attracts 18- to 34-year-olds, in about equal proportions of men and women. Beautiful music, classical, and all-news formats generally attract an older crowd, with most of their audience coming from the 45-and-over age group. Country music stations seem to have an across-the-board appeal to those over 25. As a person gets older, he or she tends to evolve out of the audience for one format and move on to another.

WKNE

Select the radio media tour (CD 1, Track 3) on the CD-ROM that accompanies this text. The first part provides a look at the radio station's operations and its various departments while the second segment features the staff discussing some important issues facing the radio industry.

The story of WKNE is typical of many radio stations in that it has changed hands twice in the last few years. It was acquired in the late 1990s by Tele-Media, a company with interests in cable TV, telephone and Internet services. In 2003 the station was sold to Saga Communications, the 18th largest radio group owner in the United States, with 56 stations.

WKNE is also typical of many small-market radio stations. As the clip shows, its personnel often do more than one job and it faces challenges generating advertising dollars in its market.

1. How is consolidation affecting the daily operations of radio stations? What are the positive effects? What are the negative effects?

2. What area of the radio industry is the most lucrative? Which poses the greatest risk? Why?

3. How has the ratio of music and public affairs (news) programming changed over the years?

4. How has computer technology advanced radio programming?

C A R E E R

O U T L O O K

THE RADIO INDUSTRY

About 150,000 people are employed at radio stations and radio networks. The average station employs about 14 full-time people. Competition is tight, but thousands of young people find jobs in radio every year. How does a newcomer gain experience? One good way is to volunteer to work at your college or university radio staion. Try to do as many jobs a possible and learn as much as you can. Another possibility is to arrange for an internship at a local station.

›› Entry-Level Positions

The best place to break into radio is at a small-market station. Small stations hire people who are versatile. A DJ might have to work in sales. A salesperson might have to write commercial copy and produce radio ads. It would be virtually impossible to get this sort of experience at a large station.

Most employment counselors recommend that a beginner take any job that is offered at a station, even if the job is not exactly what you want to do. Once inside the organization, it is easier for you to move to your preferred area.

The two areas in which most entry-level jobs occur are the programming and sales departments. Of these two, the programming area is the more competitive; many people who enter the radio field seem to want jobs as announcers or DJs. Nonetheless, it is possible to find a job if you are persistent and willing to work unusual hours.

The best chance of landing a beginning job in radio can be found in the sales department. Radio stations, especially those in smaller markets, are usually in need of competent salespeople with a knowledge of and an interest in radio. The worst prospects for landing a job are in radio news. Aside from some large-market AM news/talk stations, most stations have drastically cut back their local news staffs.

›› Upward Mobility

For talent, there are two distinct avenues of upward mobility. For DJs, it consists of moving up to larger markets and better time slots. The ultimate goal of most DJs is a drive-time air shift in one of the top 10 markets. In addition, many DJs progress within a station by moving up to the chief announcer's spot and from there to program director.

The sales department offers the best route for upward mobility. Competent salespeople are given bigger and more profitable accounts to service. Some will move up to the sales manager position. From sales manager, many will progress to general manager.

Remember that radio stations are not the only places of potential employment. Program syndicators hire announcers and those experienced in programming music formats. Companies that produce packaged feature programs need producers, writers, and directors.

MAIN POINTS

- Radio started out as point-to-point communication, much like the telephone and telegraph. The notion of broadcasting did not come about until the 1920s.

- The decade of the 1920s was an important one in radio. Big business took control of the industry, receivers improved, commercials were started, networks were formed, and the FRC was set up to regulate radio.

- The coming of TV forced local stations to adopt formats, such as Top 40 or Country.

- FM became the dominant form of radio in the 1970s and 1980s. Sparked by a loosening of ownership rules, a wave of consolidation took place in the industry during the 1990s.

- Radio is moving slowly into the digital age. Satellite radio and Internet radio are two digital services that will compete with traditional radio.

- Radio programming is provided by local stations, networks, and syndication companies.

- Stations have refined their formats to reach an identifiable audience segment.

- The current economic picture of the radio business is positive. Most radio revenue comes from local advertising. Big companies now dominate large-market radio.

- National Public Radio is the best-known public broadcaster.

- Radio audiences are measured by the Arbitron Company using a diary method. The demographic characteristics of the radio listener vary greatly by station format.

QUESTIONS FOR REVIEW

1. What were the key developments during the 1920s that helped shape modern radio?

2. What impact did the Telecommunications Act of 1996 have on the radio industry?

3. What are the defining features of radio?

4. What is the function of a format wheel?

5. How is radio listening measured?

QUESTIONS FOR CRITICAL THINKING

1. What might have happened if radio had developed during the 1930s—the Depression years—instead of the Roaring Twenties?

2. What formats might radio stations have developed if rock and roll had not come along?

3. The radio industry is more consolidated than ever before. Consolidation may have helped radio's

bottom line, but is the listener better served? Why or why not?

4. Listen to the radio stations in your market. Are there audience segments in the market that are not being served?

KEY TERMS

network (p. 169)
Radio Act of 1927 (p. 170)
Federal Communications
    Commission (FCC) (p. 170)
Communications Act of 1934
    (p. 170)
clock hour (p. 172)
payola (p. 172)

nonduplication rule (p. 172)
National Public Radio (NPR)
    (p. 173)
Telecommunications Act of 1996
    (p. 173)
IBOC (p. 175)
AM (p. 178)
FM (p. 178)

format (p. 179)
voice tracking (p. 181)
format wheel (p. 185)
cycle (p. 186)
Arbitron (p. 189)
rating (p. 189)
share of the audience (p. 189)

INTERNET RESOURCES

Online Learning Center

At the Online Learning Center home page, www.mhhe.com/dominick8, *select* Student Center *and then* Chapter 7.

1. Use the Learning Objectives, Chapter Outline, Main Points, and Time Line sections to review this chapter.

2. Test your knowledge of the chapter using the multiple choice, crossword puzzle, and flashcard features of the site.

3. Expand your knowledge of concepts and topics discussed in the chapter by going to *Suggestions for Further Reading* and *Internet Exercises*.

PowerWeb

At the Mass Communication home page of PowerWeb, www.dushkin.com/powerweb, *log in and select* Mass Communication *as your title. On the next screen, select* Topics *and then quick jump to* Radio. *Read Article 48, "Pay for Play," and Article 23, "Blackout on the Dial." Then consider the following questions:*

1. Is "pay for play" ethical? Is it possible for one company, such as Clear Channel, to determine what songs are hits? Are there other ways that new artists can get their recordings exposed to the audience?

2. News is becoming harder and harder to find on radio. Should stations be required to carry news-

casts as part of their public interest obligations? Think about your own listening behavior. What happens when you are listening in your car to music and a newscast comes on? Do you change the station? How big a role does the bottom line play in the decline of radio news?

Surfing the Internet

Websites devoted to radio are about as changeable as the medium itself. With luck, these will still be functioning:

www.otr.com
A site devoted to radio's Golden Age. Listen to clips from kids' after-school serials, radio dramas, and classic comedy shows.

www.cbsradio.com
Home page of the Westwood One radio networks.

www.clearchannel.com
Check out all the media properties of this huge media conglomerate.

www.kisw.com
KISW-FM, a Seattle rock station. Includes local entertainment news, a ticket exchange, and a ski and snow report.

www.npr.org
The home of National Public Radio. In addition to the usual background information, the site has a link to current news and to the *"Public Radio Ethics and Style Guidebook."*

www.rab.com
Home page of the Radio Advertising Bureau. Filled with useful statistics and facts about radio.

8

SOUND RECORDING

They know who you are and what you are doing. And they are going to do something about it.

On April 29, 2003, about 200,000 carefree people were swapping music files on Grokster and Kazaa when all of a sudden an instant message popped up on their screens:

COPYRIGHT INFRINGEMENT WARNING: It appears that you are offering copyrighted music to others from your computer. Distributing or downloading copyrighted music on the Internet without permission from the copyright owner is ILLEGAL. It hurts songwriters who create and

musicians who perform the music you love, and all the other people who bring you music.

When you break the law, you risk legal penalties. There is a simple way to avoid that risk: DON'T STEAL MUSIC, either by offering it to others to copy or downloading it on a "file-sharing" system like this.

When you offer music on these systems, you are not anonymous and you can easily be identified. You also may have unlocked and exposed your computer and your private files to anyone on the Internet. Don't take these

The Recording Industry Association of America (RIAA) is relying on legal means to halt the sharing of music files on the Internet. As of 2004, the RIAA had filed lawsuits against 382 Americans for trading music.

chances. Disable the share feature or uninstall your "file-sharing" software

The message, from the Recording Industry Association of America (RIAA), was the latest weapon used by the RIAA in its battle to stop what it labels *music piracy.* The RIAA has reason to be concerned. Although the industry was successful in shutting down Napster, the first of the file-sharing services, swapping music using Napster successors such as Kazaa and Grokster is more popular than ever, despite continuing industry legal attempts to stifle it. Recording industry revenues continue to decline; industry experts say that music piracy costs the industry more than $4 billion in annual worldwide revenue. It is estimated that about 2.6 billion music files are downloaded every month.

As the warning indicates, recording companies are not sitting still while this happens. The recording industry sued four college students who were sharing hundreds of copyrighted music files for billions of dollars in damages. The students ultimately agreed to stop sharing files and each paid a fine between $12,000 and $17,500. In August 2003, the industry filed an additional 263 lawsuits against other downloaders. If suing the file swappers does not work, recording executives have other weapons at the ready,

some of questionable legality. One technique involves software programs that would surreptitiously invade the computers of music downloaders and do nasty things to them, ranging from freezing their computers for a couple of hours to deleting all of the music files stored on their hard drives. Clearly, the music industry is taking seriously the problem of illegal music sharing.

Programs such as Napster, Kazaa, and Grokster show how technology is influencing the development of sound recording today. In the past, most technological innovations related to the industry had to do with how sound recordings were permanently stored or with the fidelity of the recording. The recording industry profited from these improvements. Witness the change from vinyl to tape in the 1970s and the shift from tape to CDs in the 1980s. Peer-to-peer file-sharing programs, however, threaten to change the way recordings are packaged, marketed, and distributed and have had a damaging effect on the industry's bottom line. Indeed, file-sharing programs have forced the entire industry to reexamine the business model it has followed for more than a century. Let us take a look at the history of sound recording to understand better where Napster and its successors fit in.

HISTORY

Thomas Edison recited "Mary Had a Little Lamb" into a primitive recording machine consisting of a tinfoil-wrapped cylinder, needle, microphone, and crank. It is interesting to speculate what might have happened if Edison had sung the nursery rhyme rather than recited it. Perhaps innovators would have been more aware of the musical potential of this new medium, and the history of the recording industry might have been different. As it was, Edison and others thought his **phonograph,** the name he gave his 1877 invention, might best be suited to recording the spoken word. He eventually tried to sell it to the business community as

The phonograph is just one of Thomas Edison's inventions. His 1877 model was hand-cranked, and the sound waves were preserved as scratches in tinfoil.

an aid to dictation. At the time, the idea of using the phonograph to bring musical entertainment into the home was too wild to imagine.

Edison's phonograph faced new competition when Chinchester Bell and Charles Tainter patented a device called the **graphophone,** in which Edison's foil was replaced by a wax cylinder. In 1887, more competition emerged when Emile Berliner patented a system that used a disk instead of a cylinder. He called his new invention a **gramophone.**

By 1890, three machines that recorded and played back sound were on the market. At about this time, big business entered the picture as Jesse Lippincott, who had made a fortune in the glass-tumbler business, purchased the business rights to both the phonograph and graphophone, thus ending a bitter patent fight between the respective inventors. Lippincott had dreams of controlling the office-dictating market, but stenographers rebelled against the new device, and the talking-machine business fell upon hard times. Strangely enough, relief appeared quickly and financial solvency returned, a nickel at a time, thanks to a new idea: using the phonograph to record music instead of spoken voice.

One of Lippincott's local managers hit upon the idea of putting coin-operated phonographs in the many penny arcades and amusement centers that were springing up all over America. For a nickel, you could listen through a pair of stethoscopelike earphones to a cylinder whose two-minute musical recording had a technical quality that could only be described as awful. Still, these **nickelodeons** were immensely popular, and the demand for "entertainment" cylinders grew. Companies quickly scrambled for a share in the new recording production business.

>> Rivalry

The two decades spanning the turn of the 20th century were a time of intense business rivalry in the recording industry. While the two major companies, the Columbia Phonograph Company and Edison's North American Phonograph Company, fought one another, Berliner's United States Gramophone Company perfected the process of recording on flat disks. Ultimately, Columbia recognized the superiority of the disk and attempted to break into the market by selling the zonophone, its own version of the disk player. As for Berliner, along with machinist Eldridge Johnson, he formed the Victor Talking Machine Company, which had as its trademark a picture of a dog peering into the bell of a gramophone and the slogan "His Master's Voice." Thanks to aggressive marketing, this new company

The 100th anniversary of phonograph recording on a flat disk was 1988. This technology was created by Emile Berliner, an immigrant from Germany, who worked as a stock clerk in a clothing store while investigating the intriguing world of sound amplification and recording. Berliner quickly noted that the cylinders used by Edison had too many disadvantages to be practical. He perfected a way to encode sound on a flat disk that could be easily duplicated by using a master mold, much like pressing waffles in a waffle iron.

His invention was slow to catch on in the United States because of competition from Edison, but it was a success in Europe. Eventually, Berliner introduced to the American market the phonautograph, which he renamed the gramophone. This eventually replaced the cylinder.

In one area, Berliner clearly saw the future. He predicted that prominent singers and performers would collect royalties from the sale of his disks. He was wrong on another count, however. He thought that musicians and artists who were unable to appear at a concert would simply send a record to be played on stage instead.

Berliner also developed the prototype of the modern microphone, and both his inventions—the disk and the microphone—came together when electronic recording was perfected during the 1920s. Even the modern CD owes him a debt. Like his original invention, the CD stores information in a spiral on a flat, rotating surface.

was highly successful and in 1906 introduced the Victrola, the first disk player designed to look like a piece of furniture. By 1912, the supremacy of the disk over the cylinder was established.

On the eve of World War I, record players were commonplace throughout America. A dance craze in 1913 sent profits soaring, a trend that was to continue throughout the war. In 1914, 27 million records were manufactured; 107 million were produced in 1919 following the end of the war. The record industry had entered a boom period.

The boom continued when the years after the First World War ushered in the Jazz Age, a period named after the spirited, popular music of the Roaring Twenties. **Jazz,** which emerged from the roots of the black experience in America, was spontaneous, individualistic, and sensual. Because of its disdain for convention, jazz was widely denounced as degenerate during its early years (about 30 years later, another spontaneous and sensual musical innovation, rock and roll, would also be denounced).

The good times, however, did not last. In the beginning, no one in the record industry regarded radio as a serious threat. Record company executives were sure that the static-filled, raucous noise emanating from a radio would never compete with the quality of their recordings. They were wrong.

>> The Impact of Radio on the Recording Industry

Radio gained popularity in the 1920s, and the recording industry felt the effects. By the end of 1924, the combined sales of players and records had dropped 50 percent from those of the previous year. In the midst of this economic trouble, the recording companies quietly introduced electronic recording, using technology borrowed from their bitter rival, radio. The sound quality of records improved tremendously. But despite this improvement, radio continued to be thought of as the medium for "live" music, and records were dismissed as the medium of "canned" music.

In 1926, the record industry began to market radio-phonograph combinations, an obvious testament to the belief that the two media would coexist. This attitude was also prevalent at the corporate level. In 1927, rumors were flying that the

Victor Company would soon merge with the Radio Corporation of America (RCA). Frightened by this prospect, Columbia, Victor's biggest rival, tried to get a head start by merging with the new (and financially troubled) radio network United Independent Broadcasters. All too soon, however, the record company became disillusioned and dissolved the deal. The much-discussed RCA and Victor merger came about in 1929, with the new company dominated by the radio operation.

>> The Great Depression

The Great Depression of the 1930s dealt a severe economic blow to sound recording. Thomas Edison's record manufacturing company went out of business in 1930. Record sales dropped from $46 million in 1930 to $5.5 million in 1933, and several smaller labels folded. The entire industry was reeling.

In the midst of all this gloom, the recording industry was saved once again by the nickel. Coin-operated record players, called *jukeboxes* (the origin of this term is obscure), began popping up in the thousands of bars and cocktail lounges that sprang up after the repeal of Prohibition in 1933. These jukeboxes were immensely popular and quickly spread to diners, drugstores, and restaurants. Starting in 1934, total record sales began to inch upward; by 1939, sales had increased by more than 500 percent.

>> World War II and After

The record industry did not do well during the war. First, the U.S. government declared shellac—a key ingredient of disks—vital to the national defense, and supplies available for records dropped drastically. Second, the American Federation of Musicians, fearful of losing jobs because of canned music, went on strike. The strike lasted from 1942 to 1944, and, as a result, record sales increased slowly during the war years. However, it was also during the war that Capitol Records embarked on a novel approach to record promotion. The company mailed free records to radio stations, hoping for airplay. This marked formal recognition of a new industry attitude: Radio could help sell records. This new philosophy would revolutionize the recording industry.

During the 1940s, the local record shop was the place to hang out with friends and listen to the latest releases.

In 1948 Columbia introduced the 33⅓ long-playing record (LP). The new disks could play for 25 minutes a side and were virtually unbreakable. Rather than adopt the Columbia system, RCA Victor introduced its own innovation, the 45-rpm extended-play record. The next few years were described as the "battle of the speeds," as the record-buying public was confronted by a choice among 33⅓, 45, and 78 records. From 1947 to 1949, record sales dropped 25 percent as the audience waited to see which speed would win. In 1950, RCA conceded and began issuing 33⅓ records. Columbia won only a partial victory, however. The 45 would become the preferred disk for single pop recordings, and the 33⅓ would dominate album sales. The 78 became obsolete. There were also changes in record players. High-fidelity sets came on the market in 1954, followed four years later by stereophonic record players. Record sales more than doubled during this period.

The mushrooming popularity of television during the 1950s had an impact on both radio and the recording industry. Television took away the big national stars from radio and forced local stations to experiment with new formats in an attempt to keep their audiences. One of the most popular radio formats that emerged was Top 40, a sound that relied on a set playlist based on record sales. The emergence of rock and roll helped the new Top 40 format become popular with a young audience. As we saw in Chapter 7, this young audience had a good deal of money to spend on the records they heard played by their favorite DJs.

>> The Coming of Rock and Roll

Rock had its roots in black rhythm and blues, commercial white popular music, country and western, and jazz. In July 1955, Bill Haley and the Comets moved into the number-one spot on the charts with "Rock Around the Clock." Less than a year later, another performer who would enjoy a far more substantial career came on the scene. "Heartbreak Hotel," recorded by a then relatively unknown Elvis Presley, would stay at the number-one position for seven straight weeks. It was with Elvis that rock and roll first blossomed. Combining a country-and-western style with the beat and energy of black rhythm-and-blues music, Elvis's records sold millions. He appeared on Ed Sullivan's network TV show (from the waist up—Sullivan thought Elvis's pelvic gyrations too suggestive). Through Elvis, rock and roll gained wide recognition, if not respectability.

Presley's success inspired other performers from the country-and-western tradition. Jerry Lee Lewis combined Mississippi boogie-woogie with country music to produce a unique and driving style. His "Whole Lotta Shakin' Going On" sold six million copies from 1957 to 1958.

Elvis Aron Presley sold more than 250 million records, starred in 33 movies, and forever changed American popular music.

Several rock pioneers came from traditional black rhythm-and-blues music. Perhaps the most exciting (certainly the most energetic) was Richard Penniman, or, as he called himself, Little Richard. Except for a period of three months, Little Richard had a record in the Top 100 at all times from 1956 to 1957 (best known are "Long Tall Sally" and "Tutti Frutti"). About the same time, on the South Side of Chicago, Chuck Berry was singing blues in small nightclubs. Discovered by the owner of a Chicago-based record company, Berry was the first artist who paid more than passing

Berry Gordy began as an assembly-line worker in Detroit but ended up as the head of one of the largest black-owned businesses in America. Along the way he also introduced black performers to a wider audience and permanently shaped the evolution of American popular music.

In 1957, Gordy wrote a hit song for R&B artist Jackie Wilson. While Gordy and Wilson were in the studio working on other projects, a group called the Matadors auditioned for Wilson. Although Wilson was unimpressed with their songs, Gordy noticed the potential of their lead singer, a young man named Smokey Robinson.

Berry Gordy Jr. and Motown star Diana Ross.

In the next few years, Gordy continued to write and produce songs for a number of black artists. Unsatisfied with the way his songs were handled by the major record labels, Gordy decided to start his own. He took an $800 loan from his family and in 1959 opened what would later become Motown Records. The company released its first single in 1959 and had its first number-one hit two years later with the Marvelettes' "Please Mr. Postman."

In its early years, Motown appealed primarily to black audiences, but Gordy's strategy was to appeal to both whites and blacks. Motown's advertising slogan was "The Sound of Young America." During the middle 1960s, Gordy's company pioneered the Motown sound, which revolutionized the music industry. Artists such as Stevie Wonder, Marvin Gaye, Smokey Robinson, and Diana Ross and the Supremes became popular with both black and white record buyers. A few years later Gordy introduced the Jackson Five, featuring a young Michael Jackson as lead singer.

In 1988, Berry Gordy was inducted into the Rock and Roll Hall of Fame along with the Supremes, Bob Dylan, and the Beatles. That same year, Gordy sold Motown Records to MCA for more than $60 million. He continued, however, to head Motown's record publishing division and its film and television sections. The sound Gordy created will continue to influence the musical tastes of future generations.

attention to the lyrics of rock and roll. His style would later influence many musical groups, including the Beatles.

>> Rock Goes Commercial

By 1959, through a combination of bizarre events, all the pioneers of rock had disappeared. Elvis had enlisted in the Army. Jerry Lee Lewis had married a 13-year-old girl said to be his cousin and dropped from sight. Little Richard was in the seminary. And Chuck Berry ultimately was incarcerated in federal prison. Thus the way was open for a whole new crop of stars. Economics dictated what this new crop would look and sound like.

Record companies recognized that huge amounts of money could be made from the rock-and-roll phenomenon if it was promoted correctly. Unfortunately, rock and roll had an image problem. In 1959, the record industry was shaken by the payola scandals (see Chapter 7) that, arriving on top of years of bad publicity and criticism that blamed rock and roll for most of society's ills, threatened rock's profitability. Since rock and roll had too much moneymaking potential to be abandoned, the record companies decided to clean up rock's image.

As the 1960s opened, the new look in rock was characterized by middle-class, white, clean-cut, and more or less wholesome performers. Rock stars were young men and women you would not hesitate to bring home and introduce to your parents. On the male side, Ricky Nelson, Bobby Vee, Bobby Vinton, Fabian, Paul Anka, Frankie Avalon, and the Four Seasons were popular. There were fewer examples on the female side. Those who had hits included Annette Funicello, Connie Francis, Brenda Lee, and Lesley Gore. All fit the new image of rock and roll. Consequently, the early 1960s saw few musical innovations. In 1963, however, the music changed again.

>> The British Invasion

Their name was inspired by Buddy Holly and the Crickets, but instead of choosing the entomologically correct "Beetles," the group decided to spell their name "Beatles" (which incorporated the word *beat*). In early 1964, they took the United States by storm. Musically, the Beatles were everything that American

The Beatles have more gold albums—47—than any other group in the history of sound recording.

rock and roll was not. They were innovative, especially in vocal harmony, and introduced the harmonica as a rock instrument. Ultimately, they would change the shape of the music business and American popular culture. The Beatles had seven number-one records in 1964; they held down the top position for 20 of the 52 weeks that year.

Their success paved the way for a veritable British invasion. Most British rock at this time resembled American rock: cheery, happy, commercial, and white. Not surprisingly, some of the first groups that followed the Beatles represented this school (Herman's Hermits, Freddie and the Dreamers, the Dave Clark Five, Peter and Gordon, to name a few). There was another style of British rock, however, far less cheery, as represented by the Rolling Stones and the Animals. This style was blues-based, rough-hewn, slightly aggressive, and certainly not bouncy and carefree.

American artists were not silent during this influx of British talent. Folk music, as performed by Bob Dylan and Joan Baez, was also popular. It was only a matter of time before folk merged with rock to produce folk rock. Soul music, as recorded on the Motown label, also made its mark during the 60s.

>> Transitions

The late 1960s was a time of cultural transition. Freedom, experimentation, and innovation were encouraged in almost all walks of life, and popular music was no exception. Sparked by the release of the Beatles' *Sgt. Pepper* album, a fractionalization of rock began to take place. Several trends of this period are notable. In 1968, Blood, Sweat and Tears successfully blended jazz, rock, and at times even classical music. The Band introduced country rock. The Who recorded a rock opera, *Tommy.* In the

The 1960s was a decade of change in American music. Compare early 1960s recording star Annette Funicello (shown in her Mouseketeer costume) with late 1960s star Janis Joplin.

midst of all this experimentation, commercial formula music was also healthy. The Monkees, a group put together by ads in the newspaper, sold millions of records. Bubble-gum rockers the Archies kept "Sugar, Sugar" at the top of the charts for a month in 1969 (it replaced a song by the Rolling Stones, "Honky Tonk Woman").

Toward the end of the 60s and the beginning of the 70s, rock music became part of the counterculture; in many instances, it went out of its way to break with the establishment. Musically, many of the songs of this era were characterized by the **heavy metal** sound; amplifiers and electronic equipment began to dominate the stage. The artists also broke sharply with tradition. The pioneers in this style of rock were all vaguely threatening, a trifle unsavory, and definitely not the type you would bring home and introduce to the family.

>> Industry Trends: 1970s–1990s

The recording industry enjoyed a boom period during the mid-1970s, resulting in large measure from the popularity of disco. A downturn during the early 1980s reversed itself during the second half of that decade thanks to Michael Jackson's *Thriller* album and a few popular movie soundtracks. The 1990s saw the CD replace tape as the preferred playback medium. Record companies were happy about this since the profit margins on CDs were greater than for tape. As a result, recording industry revenues showed some fluctuation but generally increased during the 90s.

>> The Contemporary Sound Recording Industry

As the new century began, the sound recording industry faced numerous problems. The biggest was the economic threat posed by file-sharing services. The recording industry continued to use legal means to thwart these services, but their popularity kept growing. The industry also responded by setting up its own digital music services with mixed success and by exploring technical devices that would make it more difficult to copy music files. As of late 2003, however, none of these remedies had much impact. As a result, recording companies experienced severe cost-cutting measures and widespread layoffs.

One of the strangest trends in the evolution of popular rock-and-roll music has been a small but persistent genre of records that can only be classified under the somewhat macabre title of "morbid rock." Although its roots probably go back further, it became especially notable in the 1960s. Among the first songs to become a hit was "Teen Angel," the tale of an unfortunate couple whose car stalled on the railroad tracks. Although the young man of the song is smart enough to run like crazy, the young woman goes back to the car to retrieve her sweetheart's high school ring. The train arrives at the same time. End of romance.

Another early example was J. Frank Wilson's "Last Kiss," a tragic tale of a guy and girl out on a date who plow into a disabled car. He survives. She doesn't. End of romance. "Tell Laura I Love Her" told the teary story of a young man who needs money to continue his romance with his lady friend and so resorts to stock car racing to provide extra income. He totals his car and himself. End of romance. "Patches" concerned the romance between a young woman from the wrong side of the tracks and a middle-class young man. Despondent, the young woman drowns herself in the river. At the end of the song, the young man is contemplating the same thing. Even wholesome Pat Boone got into the act with "Moody River," a song that also told the story of two people who throw themselves into the river and drown.

The trend was less noticeable in the early 70s, but a song entitled "Billy, Don't Be a Hero" enjoyed wide popularity. This song was about a boy who goes off to war, against the wishes of his girlfriend, and gets killed. End of romance. (For those who are true fans of this genre, Rhino Records has collected 10 teen tragedy songs ranging from "Last Kiss" to the little-known but nonetheless moving "The Homecoming Queen's Got a Gun." Incidentally, the back cover of the LP doubles as a tissue dispenser.)

The trend resurfaced in 1999 when Pearl Jam's remake of "Last Kiss" went to number two on the charts. Apparently, morbid rock isn't dead yet.

Eminem performs during the 2003 Grammy Awards. Eminem's record label was so worried about file sharing hurting sales, it released his album, *The Eminem Show* nine days early.

In addition, there was growing friction between talent and the leading sound recording companies. Recording artists complained that the companies were understating the number of recordings sold and not paying the artists the appropriate royalty sums. High-profile performers such as Don Henley took to hiring independent companies to audit industry bookkeeping. For its part, the industry contended that artists were properly compensated.

The growing concentration of the recording industry had an effect on what music people heard. The quest for a better bottom line puts the emphasis on turning out CDs that sell big numbers. The music that racks up big sales tends to be predictable and formulaic rather than new and original. Indeed, many observers have blamed the drop in music sales not so much on the Internet but on the lack of any new and compelling musical styles.

Figure 8–1 shows a "family tree" of rock and roll, offering one way of looking at the interrelationships among the genre's many subgenres.

SOUND RECORDING IN THE DIGITAL AGE

As we have seen, throughout most of its history, sound recording used the analog technique. Sound waves were first etched into grooves of a vinyl disc or into rearranged particles on a magnetic tape. In both cases, the recording industry

FIGURE 8–1

The Rock-and-Roll Family Tree, Circa 2004, Greatly Simplified and Somewhat Subjective

If you disagree, draw new arrows and circles.

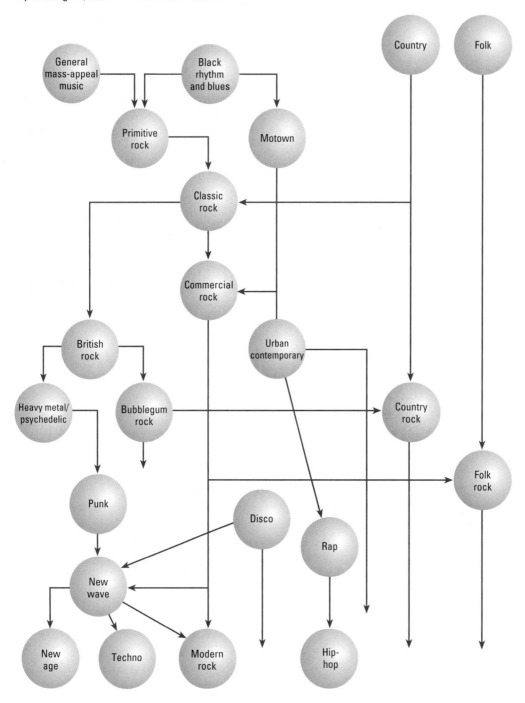

manufactured and distributed the products, discs or tapes, that consumers purchased. The digital technique changed that by encoding music as pure information, a string of binary numbers, from which music could be recovered. As a result, consumers no longer needed to buy the product from the record companies. All they needed were the numbers and their own blank CDs. This development would not have been a problem for the industry as long as there was no efficient way of getting those numbers to the consumer. The development of the personal computer and the Internet, however, made it easy for consumers to download digital information to their home computers.

The recording industry was blindsided by this development. At first recording executives dismissed music downloading from the Internet as something that only a few geeks would be interested in. Then came the overwhelming success of Napster and its progeny. Never had so much music been available to so many for free. The recording industry would be forever changed.

>> The Impact of Peer-to-Peer File Sharing

Explaining to college students how file-sharing programs such as Kazaa and Grokster work is like explaining the Super Bowl to a bunch of pro football players. Both groups are already up to speed. In fact, college students are the single biggest population segment that trades music files. In simplified form, the process works like this: A process called **MP3,** short for Motion Pictures Engineering Group Audio Layer 3, takes digital audio signals (the kind that are encoded on CDs) and shrinks them into small packages that can be stored on a hard drive, downloaded from the Internet, or sent via e-mail. CDs bought at the local retail store can easily be converted to MP3 files and stored on a hard drive.

Once an individual downloads a file-sharing program, such as Kazaa, he or she can use it to search for a given song or artist. The software searches the files of all Kazaa subscribers who are online and displays a list of all the members who have the material. A user simply clicks on one of the locations where the song is stored and downloads it to his or her computer's hard drive. Once copied, the song can be played over the computer's speakers or loaded to an MP3 player, burned to a CD, or shared with others. The total cost to the user is nothing. The revenue to the artist and recording company is also nothing.

File-sharing programs raise many issues, some of them legal (see Chapter 15), some of them ethical (see Ethical Issues, "The Ethics of File Sharing"), some of them economic, and some of them that go to the core of the business model used by the recording industry since its inception. Traditionally, the industry made money from the distribution and sale of the physical product (the tape or disc). When the music is turned into digital bits of information free from the physical product, there is no money to be made. Obviously, the recording industry had to rethink its model.

>> New Business Models

Some recording companies are rethinking how music is marketed and sold. As of 2003, the industry had spent more than $2 billion developing digital music services that could compete with Kazaa, Grokster, and other Napster clones. The major labels spent their money backing two services, MusicNet and Pressplay. Both services worked on the subscription principle. For a monthly fee, a subscriber could download songs, but once a person stopped subscribing, the songs

Recording industry profits slipped about 10 percent from 2001 to 2002 (and 2001 was a bad year). Most experts concede that part of this decrease (some would say most of it) is due to downloading free music. Almost everybody in the recording industry considers downloading songs from file-sharing sites such as Kazaa and Morpheus to be stealing (or *pirating,* as the industry calls it). On the other hand, with few exceptions, people who download music feel quite the opposite.

Every semester I ask my students the following question: Would you go to a store and walk out with a CD without paying for it? Aside from a couple of sarcastic replies, almost all students answer in the negative and concede that taking a CD without paying for it is stealing. I next ask them this: Would you download music from the Internet and share it online without paying for it? Almost everybody answers this in the positive. I then ask them what the difference is between the two situations. Their answers reveal many of the complexities involved in developing an ethical stance about file-sharing programs.

Their rationales for their behavior generally fall into these broad categories:

1. It is acceptable to download and share music because the record companies have been overcharging people for CDs and have been exploiting performers for years (just listen to Courtney Love), and the companies deserve it. File sharing is a righteous protest, just another way to "stick it to the Man," a philosophy first popular during the 1960s.

2. It is acceptable to download and share music because on the Internet all information should be free.

3. It is acceptable to download and share music because most users only download songs that they wouldn't buy anyway so they're not really hurting anybody.

4. Users would pay for their downloads but the record companies haven't found a way to let them do that.

Let us look at each of these arguments from an ethical point of view.

Taken to its logical extreme, the first argument suggests that it is acceptable to steal from any individual company that you think charges too much for its goods or services or somehow mistreats its workers. Would you steal a Buick because you think GM has been pricing its cars too high? Even assuming that the premise about exploiting performers is correct (and it should be noted that many of these "exploited" performers have a pretty impressive lifestyle), is it okay to steal from companies whose conduct you disapprove of? Suppose some clothing company pays its workers in Thailand only a couple of dollars an hour. Should we steal their goods? Would that make them become less exploitive? Do two wrongs actually make a right? One well-known ethical principle is Kant's Categorical Imperative (see Chapter 16), which states you should act in the same way that you want others to act toward you. If you ran a business, would you want people who decide they disapprove of your business to steal from you?

The "information should be free" argument is a common one. At its core is the belief in some sort of entitlement to information, that somehow the existence of the Internet means we have a right to share freely the works of others. In the first place, information does not simply appear; somebody has to create it. It would seem more reasonable to argue that the individual who created the information (music, movies, or video) should be the one to decide if it is free or not. If a musical group thinks that free exposure on the Internet will help them charge more for their concert appearances, they should be able to post their music on Kazaa or other file-sharing systems (many groups have done this). On the other hand, if a group decides that it wants people to pay to hear their music, they should have that right. This is the notion behind the legal doctrine of intellectual property. Suppose you create a clever new video game and share the software with some friends. Suppose further that Microsoft hears about it and offers you a large sum of money to market the game. In the meantime, however, suppose one of your friends, a strong believer in the "information should be free" philosophy, posts your game on the Web and it becomes so popular that Microsoft decides the market is already saturated and withdraws the offer. Should you not have the right to decide what to do with your creation?

The argument about only downloading material that otherwise would not be bought raises an interesting question. In the first place, if you share files, other people who might have otherwise bought the record might download it and not buy it. This would seem to hurt those who created the music. Second, your decision not to buy might have been influenced by the presence of the music for free on the Internet. Who is to say that you might not have a different attitude toward the music if it were not freely available on the Net? Maybe you would buy it after all.

What the last argument is really saying is that the recording industry has yet to come up with a plan to pay artists for their music with which the downloader agrees. The record industry has legitimate downloading systems that a person can subscribe to and use to download music both legally and ethically. Unfortunately, these arrangements are not popular with many file sharers.

Putting aside the various legal arguments about downloading, it would appear that all of the common arguments justifying downloads from Kazaa or other file-sharing systems do not stand up to an ethical analysis. Nonetheless, students and others appear to be unfazed and continue to download. They apparently do not believe that their actions constitute stealing.

Why the ethical disconnect between walking out of store without paying for a CD and downloading a CD without paying? Part of the explanation is the gap between action and consequence. Taking a CD from a store has an immediate and clear effect: The retailer loses the money that he or she paid for the CD. Downloading music from the amorphous and impersonal Web separates the act from its harmful consequence. There is no apparent victim. The record companies and the artists who are harmed by downloading are removed and abstract. Would downloading be as popular if the downloader had a clear idea about how his or her act directly affected the artist?

were disabled. In short, subscribers were renting the music. Installing the proprietary software to download the music was difficult and discouraged many potential users. As of this writing, both MusicNet and Pressplay have yet to become popular.

In mid-2003 Steve Jobs, of Apple Computer fame, introduced another digital music service for Macintosh computer owners. Rather than charging a monthly fee, the Apple system sells individual downloads for 99 cents with no restrictions. Purchasers can keep the music indefinitely and can make copies for personal MP3 or CD players. Apple sold more than a million tracks in the first week of the service, bringing a ray of hope to the industry and perhaps demonstrating what the future might look like.

The industry is also hoping that new formats such as DVD-Audio will increase sales. DVD-Audio is a format designed to provide the highest quality DVD audio. In addition, a DVD-Audio disc can contain video files, song lyrics, and photographs. A conventional DVD player can play a DVD audio disc, but to provide the full range of its sound quality, a special DVD playback unit is necessary.

>> New Security

The recording industry is developing better copy-protection software for CDs. One system enables CD buyers to download tracks to their PC and MP3 players but prevents the files from playing if they are sent out over the Internet or e-mailed. Other security systems prevent the user from making copies of the discs or converting them to MP3 files. Another encodes a noise signal that cannot be heard when the disc is played on a conventional CD player but that sounds dreadful when played on a computer. Consumers have complained that these copy-protected discs do not play in car systems or in combo DVD players. They also complain that the security system prevents them from making a legal backup copy of the disc for personal use.

No matter how sophisticated the copy protection, someone, somewhere will probably find a way to crack it. If just one unprotected disc finds its way onto Kazaa or Grokster, it is only a matter of time before thousands of copies are available for sharing. Technology may never solve the problem.

>> The End of the Recording Business as We Know It?

A more subtle impact of the digital revolution could be the growth of a generation of young people who have never paid for music. Since 1999, when Napster first became popular, it has been possible for a person to build an extensive music collection without ever opening a wallet or purse. What if this becomes a common expectation? Why would anyone pay even 99 cents for a product that can be had for free? What if the music downloaders reject the entire rationale for laws regulating intellectual property and continue the wholesale swapping of music and other copyrighted material? In short, what if the pirates win? This is a disturbing thought for the recording industry. Such a scenario has already played out in Asia, where piracy has ravaged the entertainment industry. In China, where illegal copying accounts for about 90 percent of all CDs available to the public, record companies are reluctant to invest in local talent.

If the free file-sharing programs continue to flourish, there would be little reason for artists to record music (why bother when there is no profit in it) and even less reason for recording companies to invest money promoting the artists. The record labels could conceivably disappear. Rock stars might still make a living from personal appearances and touring (things that cannot be put into digital form), but the age of the millionaire superstar would be over. Retail stores, such as Sam Goody, would close and there would be plenty of open shelf space at Target and Wal-Mart. Granted that this is a Doomsday scenario for the recording industry, but it's one that's probably in the back of the mind of many recording executives.

 ## DEFINING FEATURES OF SOUND RECORDING

Sound recording is a cultural force. Its products help characterize social groups and define movements and trends in American society. Recorded music has been at the center of a great deal of cultural and social controversy. Sound recording helped usher in the Jazz Age during the Roaring Twenties. This new style of music was condemned as corrupting the nation's morals. The same criticisms were heard during the 1950s when rock-and-roll music became the rallying point for a new youth culture. During the 1960s, recorded music joined the counterculture, and big record companies (benefiting from the status quo) made great profits from selling albums that challenged the status quo. In the 1990s, rap music recordings introduced the hip-hop culture to the rest of America. All in all, the sound recording industry has played a major role in shaping modern culture.

Sound recording is also an international enterprise. Five giant companies dominate the business, one in Japan, one in Germany, one in Britain, one in France, and one in the United States. Recording artists sell their music worldwide. Ricky Martin's eponymous album sold 14 million copies worldwide and 7 million in the United States. Celine Dion's greatest-hits album sold 5 million in the United States and 9 million internationally. Recording artists tour all around the globe.

The recording business is a unique blend of business and talent. Recording companies are continually searching for new artists and new sounds that will succeed in the marketplace. The singers and musicians may be the stars, but the recording companies are the star makers. Most hit recordings owe much of their success to the marketing and promotion efforts of their record labels.

 ## ORGANIZATION OF THE RECORDING INDUSTRY

The recording industry consists of the various creative talent and business enterprises that originate, produce, and distribute records to consumers. Rock music accounts for more than 60 percent of the total sales of the record industry; country and rhythm and blues account for another 10 percent each; gospel, jazz, and classical account for the rest. Although this chapter concentrates on rock music, remember that the other music styles are also part of the industry. For our purposes, we will divide the business into four major segments: (1) talent, (2) production, (3) distribution, and (4) retail.

>> **Talent**

The talent segment of the industry consists of all the singers, musicians, songwriters, arrangers, and lyricists who hope to make money by recording and selling their songs. The words "hope to make money" are important because far more performers are laboring in virtual obscurity in and around Detroit, Seattle, Nashville, New York, and Los Angeles than are cashing royalty checks from their recordings. Exactly how many people are "out there" hoping to make it big is impossible to pinpoint.

Figuring out what sells albums may be complicated but Avril Lavigne must have found the answer. Her *Let Go* CD sold more than six million copies.

Performers start out as a beginning act. The initial motivation may be simply personal pleasure. Many begin performing during high school. For example, Bob Dylan (then known as Bob Zimmerman) started out with a high school band in Hibbing, Minnesota.

The novice musician or musical group, if it continues in the business, eventually graduates to being a traveling act, which plays anywhere and everywhere to gain experience, a little money, and maybe some recognition. Traveling acts play in bars and clubs where they are little more than human jukeboxes providing accompaniment or background music. REM played college clubs in Athens, Georgia, while getting its act together. Crossover star Shania Twain spent years singing in bars and lounges before being discovered. Weezer kicked around California for several years, playing in places with names like Club Dump, Al's Bar, and Bob's Frolic Room before finding commercial success. Even Mariah Carey, who debuted on the charts when she was only 20, spent more than two years waiting tables and trying to sell songs before she was discovered.

If the act is talented and lucky, it may be noticed by an A&R (artist and repertoire) scout from a record company, an independent producer, agent, or manager. If things work out right, the act is signed to a contract by a recording company.

❯❯ Production

The recording company brings the act to a recording studio where a large number of songs are recorded. Audio engineers and elaborate sound-mixing facilities are used to get exactly the right sound. Eventually, a single or an album is put together. The company also supplies publicity, advertising, merchandising, and packaging expertise. Promotion, which in the recording industry consists primarily of getting the record played on influential radio stations and getting the music video on TV, is also the responsibility of the company. There are dozens of record companies, but five dominate the business: Sony, AOL Time Warner, Bertelsmann, NBC Vivendi, and EMI.

❯❯ Distribution

There are five main outlets for tape and CD distribution: (1) direct retail, (2) rack jobbers, (3) one-stops, (4) direct consumer sales, and (5) online sales. (See Figure 8–2.) Of these five outlets, retail stores and rack jobbers are most important, accounting for more than 80 percent of all sales.

Direct retail refers to stores that specialize in the sale of CDs, tapes, and related products. Many retail stores are chain operations with several outlets in different parts of the country.

Rack jobbers service the tape and CD racks in variety or large department stores. Wal-Mart and Sears, for example, all have their tape and CD shelves ser-

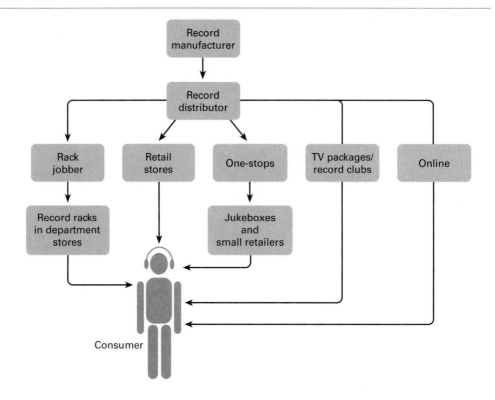

FIGURE 8–2

Record Distribution Channels

viced by rack jobbers. The rack jobber chooses the records that are sold in these locations, thus relieving department store management of the task of keeping up with the latest Eminem CD and such other tasks as reordering and returning unused merchandise.

One-stops purchase records from record companies and resell them to retail stores and jukebox operators. For example, a small, independently owned retail store might not qualify for credit from the record companies and so might purchase its records from a one-stop.

TV packagers and record clubs sell directly to the consumer. You have probably seen TV ads for collections of music (*The Best of Heavy Metal, Connie Francis' Greatest Hits, Zamfir and the Pan Flute*, etc.). Packagers receive licenses from record manufacturers and use TV advertising to market their products. Record clubs depend more on direct-mail advertising and usually offer an attractive introductory deal ("Six CDs for 99 cents") with the stipulation that consumers buy a certain number of offerings in the next year or so.

Online distribution is simple: The consumer deals directly with an online retailer, and the product is delivered to his or her door.

>> Retail

Big chains dominate the retail segment of the industry. The biggest chain is Best Buy, owner of Sam Goody and Media Play, with more than 1,900 locations. Transworld Music is second with about 1,000 outlets. As with the rest of the industry, stores that sell CDs and tapes are struggling through rough economic times. Many stores have closed, and Wherehouse Music filed for bankruptcy in early 2003.

One noticeable trend in retailing has been the increased importance of mass merchandisers, such as Wal-Mart and Target, in selling CDs and tapes. In 1992, according to data from the Recording Industry Association of America, about 25 percent of all purchases were made at mass merchandise stores; in 2003, that percentage had jumped to 42 percent, in part because these stores were offering cheaper prices. Conversely, the percentage of albums and singles sold at media retail chains, such as Best Buy, Media Play, and Borders, has dropped from 60 percent to 43 percent. Sales of recorded music over the Internet accounted for about 4 percent. Record clubs and miscellaneous sources made up the rest.

The digital revolution has also had a major impact on this segment of the business. Retailers are aware that if file sharing and online distribution become the preferred ways of delivering music to consumers, there is little need for a brick-and-mortar retail store. As a result, retailers are offering other products in addition to CDs and tapes. Most retailers also stock DVDs, video games, magazines, books, and maybe even electronic equipment. In addition, a group of retailers, including Best Buy, Borders, and Transworld, started their own online music subscription service to compete with Pressplay and Music Net.

 OWNERSHIP IN THE RECORDING INDUSTRY

The recording industry is one of the most concentrated of all media industries. As shown in Table 8–1, big companies dominate the business, accounting for more than 85 percent of the market. In addition, these companies are multinational conglomerates, with interests in many different industries. In 2003 the ownership structure was reconfigured when General Electric, parent company of NBC, announced plans to acquire Vivendi-Universal's entertainment properties and a group of private investors bought Time Warner's music division.

Company and location	Major labels	Top stars	Other interests
NBC-Vivendi (United States)	Geffen, MCA, Motown	U2, India.Arie, Eminen	Movies, Internet, theme parks, telecommunications
Time Warner* (United States)	Warner Bros., Electra, Atlantic	Madonna, Linkin Park, R.E.M.	Home video, TV, books, movies, Internet
Sony** (Japan)	Columbia, Epic, Legacy	J. Lo., Pearl Jam, Michael Jackson	Electronics, batteries, CD manufacturing
BMG** (Germany)	Arista, RCA, BadBoy	Alicia Keys, Dido, Dave Matthews Band	Printing, book clubs, magazines, TV
EMI (Great Britain)	Virgin, Capitol, Blue Note	Janet Jackson, Radiohead, Garth Brooks	Consumer electronics, information technology

TABLE 8–1

Top Five Recording Companies, 2004

*In 2003 Time Warner sold its music division to a private investment group. The new company retained the Warner Music name.

**Sony and BMG announced merger plans in late 2003.

 PRODUCING RECORDS

There are seven departments within a typical recording company:

1. *Artists and Repertoire (A&R):* This department is the talent scout for the industry. A&R personnel listen to demo tapes sent in by hopefuls and go out on the road to hear a succession of fourth-rate bands (called *garage bands* in the trade) in the hopes of uncovering another B2K or Norah Jones.

2. *Sales and Distribution:* As the name suggests, this department sells the company's products and then makes sure the tapes and CDs get to the stores where consumers can buy them.

3. *Advertising and Merchandising:* This division is responsible for planning media ad campaigns and point-of-purchase displays in sales outlets. The efforts of this department are coordinated with those of the promotion department.

4. *Promotion:* In the recording industry, promotion means getting new releases played on radio stations and music video cable channels. Since many radio stations restrict the music they play to a tightly controlled playlist, the job of the promotion department is challenging. With about 5,000 singles released in the United States each year and only four or five slots open on a given radio station each week to devote to new music, getting a new record on the air can be a frustrating experience.

5. *Business:* This department includes lawyers, accountants, market researchers, financial analysts, and secretarial and clerical staffs. It functions in the recording industry the same way it would function in any other business or industry.

6. *Publicity:* This department attempts to get press coverage for new performers and new releases and also has the job of getting new acts and albums reviewed by influential publications such as *Rolling Stone* and *Billboard*.

7. *Artist Development:* Some of the duties of this department are coordinating tour dates, making sure the act has a well-produced concert show, and arranging for TV appearances.

>> **Making a CD or Tape**

For a performer or group to win a recording contract, they need to convince someone in a record company that they have a sound that will sell. The first step in the process is to produce a demonstration tape, called a **demo,** that can be sent to the appropriate persons. A demo is usually done in a studio with four-track mixing facilities. It does not have to sound as good as the finished product released by the major studios. All the demo has to do is highlight the strengths of the group or performer and capture the attention of recording company executives.

The second step is to sell the demo. Sending an unsolicited tape to a recording company is probably the worst way to sell it. Although there are some exceptions, most of these tapes are never listened to. A better way is to hire a manager or agent to sell the demo for the act. If the agent is successful, step three entails going to the recording studio and making a master tape.

Resembling something you might see at NASA's mission control center, with banks of modern equipment, blinking lights, and digital readouts, the modern recording studio does multitrack recording. Professional studios have machines capable of recording up to 48 different tracks. This means that different instruments and vocals can be recorded on different sections of a disc or tape. A piano might be recorded on one track, drums on another, bass on another, lead vocals on another, background vocals on yet another, and so on. So that one track does not leak onto another, the studio is set up with careful placement of microphones and wooden baffles—soundproof barriers that keep the sound of one instrument from spilling over into the mikes recording the other instruments. Once the session starts, the producer makes most of the creative decisions. The producer decides

A sophisticated mixing board such as this one handles as many as 48 separate sound tracks that contain recordings of instruments and vocals. Note the computer monitors. Computer programs remember previous mixing setups, making the process easier and faster.

when the performers take a break, when the tune has to be played over because of a bad note, when the music should be played back so that the group can hear itself and perhaps make changes in the arrangement, and so on.

The advent of multiple-track recording has revamped the music-making process. Currently, it is not even necessary for band members to record together. The instrumentalists can come in one at a time and "lay down" their tracks, the lead singer or singers can add the vocals later, and everything can be put together at the mixing console.

After the recording session, the next step is the mix down, the technically exacting job of mixing down the multiple tracks onto a two-track stereo master. In the mix down, each track is equalized; echo, overdubbing, or other special effects are added; and certain passages are scheduled for rerecording. If an album is being produced, each track has to be precisely placed on the stereo spectrum. A track can be placed in the left or right speaker or in the center, where it is heard equally in both speakers. Mixing a 16- or 24-track tape down to 2 tracks can take several days. The job has been made somewhat easier in recent years thanks to computerized mixing boards. After the mix is completed, the master is reproduced on tape and disk for manufacture. At the same time, the promotion department is given a preview of the new release, and the advertising and publicity departments begin their efforts.

 ## ECONOMICS

We will approach the topic of economics at two levels. First, we will examine the economic structure of the industry as a whole. Next, we will investigate the financial ups and downs of a typical musical group trying to make it in the recording business.

FIGURE 8–3

Recording Industry Revenues, 1980–2002

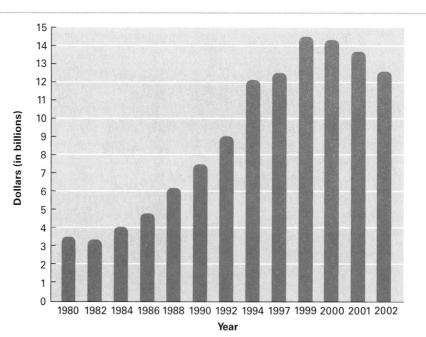

>> Economic Trends

After enjoying nearly two decades of solid economic growth, the recording industry went into a tailspin that started in 2000 and continued through 2003. Figure 8–3 charts the decline. It should also be noted that 2000 was the year when file-sharing programs first gained popularity. Recording industry executives blame illegal file sharing for the decline, and it is easy to see why. Consider these facts: In 2002 consumers bought more blank CDs than recorded CDs. New CDs now experience steep declines in sales the second week of their release, presumably because copies have been uploaded to file-sharing services. Linkin Park's *Hybrid Theory,* the best-selling CD in 2001, sold 4.8 million copies. About the same number of people downloaded it for free. In 2000, the 10 top-selling albums sold 60.5 million copies; in 2002, they sold 33.6 million.

The situation does not look promising. CD burners and 40-gigabyte hard drives are now standard on personal computers, making it easy to store and copy digital music files. More and more people are turning to broadband connections to the Internet that make it easier to download files.

There were, of course, other factors that might have contributed to the decline. An overall weak economy dried up some disposable income that might have been spent on CDs and tapes. Many consumers complained that there was not any good music out there to buy. Others noted that customers were rebelling against what they thought were overpriced CDs. Whatever the reasons, as of early 2004 the industry had yet to come out of its slump, and its future was hard to predict.

One thing is certain. The CD has replaced tape as the preferred medium for recorded music. In 2003, about 90 percent of revenue came from the sales of CDs. Table 8–2 breaks down the typical costs associated with a CD with a list price of $16.98. Keep in mind that the figures in the table are approximate and subject to change.

>> Rock Performers: The Bottom Line

Most of the people who read this book will not go on to be rock stars. Nonetheless, examining the financial arrangements that surround the production of popular music is useful for all readers as it can tell a lot about the economics of the

TABLE 8–2

Cost and Profits of a Typical CD

Manufacturer's costs	
Recording expense	$0.65
Manufacturing expense	1.25
Packaging	1.30
Advertising and promotion	2.00
Artist's royalty	1.60
Freight	0.09
Payment to musicians' trust fund	0.65
Manufacturer's profit	2.94
Distributor's expenses and profit	1.50
Retailer's expenses and profit	5.00
TOTAL	**$16.98**

Courtney Love has been an outspoken critic of the economics of the recording industry.

business. (The examples in this discussion come from Courtney Love's speech to the Digital Hollywood Online entertainment conference in May 2000.)

There are many stories about the fantastic sums of money earned by pop music stars. Some stars do make a lot of money. (R.E.M.'s most recent contract with Time Warner was for $80 million.) Others, however, are not quite as lucky. A new artist or group will receive a royalty rate of about 9 to 12 percent of the suggested retail price of a CD or cassette. A more established act might negotiate a rate that is a little higher, maybe 15 percent. Really successful performers might get 20 percent or more. Royalty rates on singles run about 6 to 9 percent. For simplicity, let us say a hypothetical group of four performers is getting a 20 percent royalty rate and a $1 million advance from their record company (totally unrealistic for a new group, but this is a best-case scenario). They spend half of the advance to record the album, leaving $500,000. They have to pay $100,000 to their manager and $25,000 to their business manager and their lawyer. After $170,000 in taxes, the group has $180,000 to split four ways, or $45,000 a person. The group has to live on that for a year before the album gets released.

Again, let us take a best-case scenario and say that the album sells one million copies. The 20 percent royalty rate works out to about $2 per album, or a total of $2 million in royalties. It sounds good so far.

There are, however, expenses involved. The $1 million advance is recoupable by the record label. The record label spends $300,000 promoting the song; the costs are charged to the band. The band releases two singles and makes two music videos, costing a total of $1 million. A typical contract calls for half of that cost to be charged to the band. In addition, the band goes on tour, and since most tours lose money, the record label kicks in $200,000 in tour support, recoupable from royalties. After all the accounting is done, how much is left for the band? Nothing.

Of course, the band might make a little money from the sale of the singles and from TV appearances, overseas sales, and merchandising. Most artists, however, do not see much money until they have had a couple of back-to-back hits. And even such luck is no guarantee of riches. The group TLC, for example, declared bankruptcy after selling $175 million in CDs.

The truth is that relatively few acts are able to command large sums of money. The riches in the music industry are disproportionately divided, with a small number of artists at the top making most of the money. According to the RIAA, about 27,000 new recordings are released every year. Only 10 percent of them are profitable.

 FEEDBACK

>> *Billboard* Charts

Feedback in the sound recording industry is characterized by stars, triangles, and bullets. These are common symbols used in *Billboard* magazine's charts of popular records. Stars stand for recordings that are movers; they are on their way up in the charts. Bullets go to singles that are one million copy sellers; triangles go to two million sellers. Every week disk jockeys, program directors, and record company executives scan the *Billboard* charts, the most important channel of feedback in the sound recording industry (see Figure 8–4).

What determines the award of stars, triangles, and bullets? How is the *Billboard* chart put together? In general, the *Billboard* charts are based on two components: (1) exposure and (2) sales. To measure sales, *Billboard* relies on Nielsen SoundScan, a data reporting system that keeps track of sales in the United States and Canada. Sales data are collected weekly from about 14,000 retail stores, mass merchandisers, and online outlets.

To measure exposure, *Billboard* uses data from Nielsen Broadcast Data Systems (NBDS). This organization monitors airplay on more than 1,200 radio stations in the United States, Canada, and Puerto Rico that play a variety of formats. NBDS

FIGURE 8–4

Excerpt from a *Billboard* Chart

reports that it detects more than 100 million songs every year. For some of its charts, the Hot 100, for example, *Billboard* combines the two measures and winds up with a single index number for each song and rank orders it accordingly.

Note that another mass medium, radio, plays an important part in the feedback mechanism for sound recording. Radio stations with a music format rely on the *Billboard* charts to determine what songs they should play. Thus, sound recording also functions as a feedback mechanism for radio. This reciprocity is another example of a symbiotic relationship between media (see Chapter 1).

>> Sound Recording Audiences

Information regarding the audience for sound recording (records, tapes, and CDs) is somewhat difficult to uncover, partially because the recording industry is supported by audience purchases and not by advertising. This means that recording companies concentrate on compiling overall sales figures and that detailed demographic information about the audience is typically not sought after. True, some record companies have sponsored market research to find out more about their audiences, but the results of these studies are usually not made available to the general public. We do know that by the turn of the 21st century there were approximately 85 million stereos, with perhaps an equal number of tape playback units and 40 million CD players in use. It has been estimated that more than 90 percent of all the households in the country have some means of playing a record, tape, or CD. In 2000, this audience bought more than a billion tapes and disks.

In general, those people who have a sound system have paid about $500 to $800 for their equipment and have a typical collection of about 70 albums and approximately 30 singles. They listen to disks and tapes about an hour a day.

Record buying is related to age and sex. Older consumers are accounting for more record purchases. In 2003, people over 30 accounted for about 55 percent of the total dollar value spent on prerecorded music, a 25 percent increase from 1988. At the same time, consumer spending by those age 19 and under declined from 32 percent to 21 percent. The percent of the dollar values of all purchases is currently split about evenly between males and females.

THE RECORDING INDUSTRY

Of all the mass media, the recording industry employs the fewest employees. Not counting performers, there are only about 20,000 people in the entire industry.

>> Entry-Level Positions

Basically, there are at least three distinct career paths within the recording business: (1) engineering, (2) creative, and (3) business. We will examine each of these in turn.

Over the past two decades, the technical aspects of sound recording have become tremendously complex. Sometimes it takes two engineers to operate the giant control panel—one to run the machines and the other to do the actual recording. If the engineering side of the industry is of interest to you, it would be of some advantage to study at a college that has its own recording studio so that you can become familiar with the equipment. You could also take courses offered by the Recording Institute of America (RIA) in multitrack engineering and sound production.

If your interests lie more in the creative area and you wish to become a record producer, college courses in mass media, business administration, and music are relevant. You will also need some practical experience in directing a recording session. This can be done by working at a college that has a recording studio or by volunteering your services at a local commercial studio.

If the business side of the profession appeals to you, a college background in business administration and mass media would be most helpful. If you are interested in promotion and sales, you should start out by checking to see if there is a branch office of a major label or independent distributor located nearby. Your goal should be an entry-level position as a local promotion person or a sales representative in a particular market.

The same advice holds for someone interested in advertising and merchandising. A branch office might be able to start you off at a beginning position from which you can move up to the parent company. Those seeking careers in publicity usually have a college background in journalism or public relations.

It is a little more difficult to provide advice on how to get started in the A&R department. Many A&R people come from the promotion department. Others start off as secretaries or clerks and work their way up within the division. A good ear and a knowledge of what will sell and how to sell it are essential for a career in this area.

>> Upward Mobility

There are several paths that lead toward advancement in the recording industry. Beginning audio engineers progress to staff engineers and ultimately to senior supervising engineer. Some engineers do cross over and become record producers, but this is rare. Once you have committed yourself to a technical career in the control room, you will generally stay there.

People who start out as producers advance by becoming staff producers with major labels. The next step up would be the position of executive producer. The executive producer in the record business is analogous to the executive producer in motion pictures or TV. Another upward path is to start off with an established label and then go into independent production. Many independent producers go on to form their own labels.

Those who start off in one of the business departments at a recording company advance by moving up the corporate ladder. The most common route to top management has been through either the production or sales and distribution department.

MAIN POINTS

- Thomas Edison pioneered the development of the phonograph, which was first used as a device to record voice and, later, music. Emile Berliner perfected the modern technique of recording music in a spiral pattern on a disk. By the end of World War I, record players were found in most American homes.

- The coming of radio and the Depression hurt the development of the recording industry, but the business was able to survive because of the popularity of jukeboxes.

- After World War II, the industry grew quickly because of the development of magnetic tape recording and the LP record and, most of all, because radio stations began to play recorded music as part of their formats.

- Rock-and-roll music helped spur record sales and made young people an important part of the market for recorded music.

- File-sharing software such as Kazaa may transform the basic way the music industry conducts business.

- There are four segments in the recording industry: talent, production, distribution, and retail.
- Five big companies, three of them with foreign headquarters, dominate the record business.
- *Billboard* magazine's charts are the most important form of audience feedback for the industry.
- After several years of growth, the recording industry's revenue has declined, due in part to file sharing on the Internet.

QUESTIONS FOR DISCUSSION

1. Trace the various media that have been used to record sound, from Edison's time to the present.
2. How do file-sharing programs such as Kazaa work? Why are they examples of disintermediation?
3. Trace the distribution arrangement in the sound recording business. How many of the distribution channels have you personally used?
4. If the chance of financial success is so small, why do so many people still try to make it in the recording industry?

QUESTIONS FOR CRITICAL THINKING

1. Why did it take the recording industry so long to figure out that radio airplay helped record sales? Will the same be true with file sharing?
2. What are the implications of large corporate ownership in the record business? Are big companies less likely to promote new acts and risky musical styles?
3. What are the ethical implications of downloading and sharing music from services such as Kazaa? If you have ever downloaded music, did you feel guilty doing it? Why or why not?
4. What will be the future of the retail record store in the digital era? If you can download music direct to your computer, why go to a store? Do people go to record stores for purposes other than simply buying an album?

KEY TERMS

phonograph (p. 195)
graphophone (p. 196)
gramophone (p. 196)
nickelodeons (p. 196)

jazz (p. 197)
heavy metal (p. 202)
MP3 (p. 205)
rack jobbers (p. 209)

one-stops (p. 210)
demo (p. 213)
Billboard (p. 217)

INTERNET RESOURCES

Online Learning Center

At the Online Learning Center home page, www.mhhe.com/dominick8, *select* Student Center *and then* Chapter 8.

1. Use the Learning Objectives, Chapter Outline, Main Points, and Time Line sections to review this chapter.
2. Test your knowledge of the chapter using the multiple choice, crossword puzzle, and flashcard features of the site.
3. Expand your knowledge of concepts and topics discussed in the chapter by going to *Suggestions for Further Reading* and *Internet Exercises.*

PowerWeb

At the Mass Communication home page of PowerWeb, www.dushkin.com/powerweb, *log in and select* Mass Communication *as your title. On the next screen, select* Topics *and then quick jump to* Music. *Read Article 4, "I Want Your Sex." Then consider the following questions:*

1. Why all the concern about the sexual content of popular music? Why have magazines or movies not been the focus of all this censorship?

2. What are the cultural dimensions involved in music censorship? Are songs that seem acceptable for one cultural group inappropriate for another?

3. How does the Internet change the situation? Is it possible anymore to suppress songs that have questionable lyrics?

Surfing the Internet

Websites for the recording industry are just as evanescent as the industry itself. The following were current as this book went to press.

www.billboard.com
Billboard magazine's online version. Contains the latest news about the industry plus recent charts.

www.bmg.com
Home of the Bertelsmann Music Group. Lists all of BMG's top artists and has links to the company's various labels.

www.cdnow.com
A retail shopping site. Browse 18 different musical genres (with samples included for many new releases) or search for a particular CD.

www.musicpages.com
One of the most comprehensive sites on the Web. Contains information about the industry, jobs, labels, music dealers, and distributors, 'zines, promotions, and music education.

www.riaa.org
Site of the Recording Industry Association of America. Contains industry data, latest news, and legal information.

MOTION PICTURES

In this chapter you will learn to

- explain how the motion picture industry developed;

- describe how the studios dominated the industry;

- discuss how television affected the film industry and its audience;

- understand the implications that digital moviemaking holds for the industry;

- explain how the digital age is affecting film; and

- describe the components of the movie industry and how a motion picture is produced.

Movie executives fear that films will be traded over file sharing programs, such as Kazaa, just as frequently as music files.

The motion picture industry has seen the digital future and it looks scary.

Films, just like music, can be encoded in digital form and downloaded from the Internet. Just like music, they can be swapped using file-sharing programs such as Kazaa. If the past is any guide to the future, the motion picture industry, just like the music industry, might face some rough times.

There are already some disturbing signs:

- Illegal copies of nearly every major motion picture quickly show up on file-sharing services. Some films have shown up before they were even released to theaters.

- About 400,000 feature films are downloaded illegally every day from the Internet.

- Illegal copying of movies costs the industry about $3 billion a year, according to the Motion Picture Association of America.

In the past, the problem was not so severe since digital movie files were so large that they took hours and hours to download over a typical dial-up connection. In addition, the storage required for movie files was so huge that one movie might take up most of the space on the typical hard drive. (The disk space required for one movie could hold more than 600 music files.) Today,

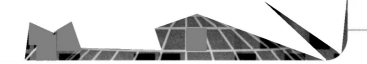

however, more people are signing up for high-speed, broadband Internet connections that make movie downloading more convenient. At the same time, the storage capacity on hard disk drives has increased. New computers typically offer 40 gigabytes or more of space. In addition, personal video recorders that can download content from the Internet have enough space to store about 30 feature films. These developments are more than enough to make movie executives uneasy.

It is unlikely, however, that downloading movies will ever replace the traditional movie theater. After all, moviegoing is still a social experience that cannot be duplicated even in the most advanced home theater. In fact, box office revenue set new records in 2002. The more pressing issue for the movie industry is how much the rental and sales of DVDs and tapes will be affected. As we shall see, DVDs and tapes account for the majority of the revenue earned by films. Will consumers continue to rent and buy when they can get the same stuff for free? That's the scary part.

But we are getting ahead of ourselves. Before we consider the future of the motion picture business, we need to take a look at its past.

HISTORY OF THE MOTION PICTURE

Motion pictures and television are possible because of two quirks of the human perceptual system: the phi phenomenon and persistence of vision. The **phi phenomenon** refers to what happens when a person sees one light source go out while another one close to the original is illuminated. To our eyes, it looks like the light moves from one place to another. In **persistence of vision,** our eyes continue to see an image for a split second after the image has disappeared from view. In the early 19th century, a host of toys that depended on this principle were created in Europe. Bearing fanciful names (the Thaumatrope, the Praxinoscope), these devices made a series of hand-drawn pictures appear to move.

>> The Edison Lab

Before long, some key inventors realized that a series of still photographs on celluloid film could be used with these devices instead of hand drawings. In 1878, a colorful Englishman later turned American, Edward Muybridge, attempted to settle a $25,000 bet over whether the four feet of a galloping horse ever simultaneously left the ground. He arranged a series of 24 cameras alongside a race track to photograph a running horse. Rapidly viewing the series of pictures produced an effect much like that of a motion picture. Muybridge's technique not only settled the bet (the feet did leave the ground simultaneously in certain instances), but also demonstrated, in a backward way, the idea behind motion picture photography. Instead of 24 cameras taking one picture each, what was needed was one camera that would take 24 pictures in rapid order. It was Thomas Edison and his assistant, William Dickson, who finally developed what might have been the first practical motion picture camera and viewing device. Using flexible film, Dickson solved the vexing problem of how to move the film rapidly through the camera by perforating its edge with tiny holes and pulling it along by means of sprockets. In 1889, Dickson had perfected a machine called the **Kinetoscope** and even starred in a brief film demonstrating how it worked.

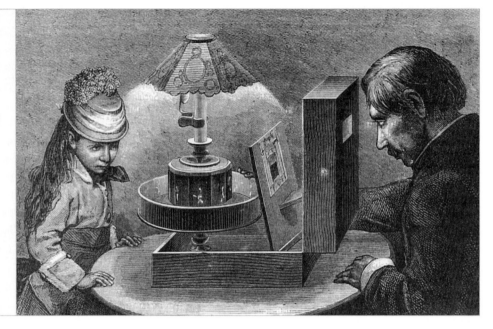

An early version of the Praxinoscope. Later models would be able to project a moving image onto a large screen for many people to view at once.

These early efforts in the Edison lab were not directed at projecting movies to large crowds. Edison thought the device could make money by showing brief films to one person at a time for a penny a look. He built a special studio to produce films for this new invention, and by 1894, Kinetoscope parlors were springing up in major cities. The long-range commercial potential of this invention was lost on Edison. He reasoned that the real money would be made by selling his peep-show machine. If a large number of people were shown the film at the same time, fewer machines would be needed, so he was not interested in adapting the machine for larger audiences.

Developments in Europe proved Edison wrong as inventors there devised large-screen projection devices. Faced with competition, Edison perfected a projector called the Vitascope and unveiled it in New York City in 1896.

Early movies were simple snippets of action—acrobats tumbling, horses running, jugglers juggling, and so on. Eventually, the novelty wore off and films became less of an attraction.

>> The Nickelodeons

Public interest was soon rekindled when early filmmakers discovered that movies could be used to tell a story. In France, Alice Guy Blache produced *The Cabbage Fairy*, a one-minute film about a fairy who produces children in a cabbage patch, and exhibited it at the Paris International Exhibition in 1886. Blache went on to found her own studio in America. Better known is the work of a fellow French filmmaker and magician, Georges Méliès. In 1902, Méliès produced a science fiction film that was the great-great-grandfather of *Star Wars* and *Star Trek;* it was called *A Trip to the Moon.* Méliès, however, did not fully explore the storytelling freedom afforded by film. His films were basically extravagant stage plays photographed by a stationary camera. It was an American, Edwin S. Porter, who in his *Great Train Robbery* first discovered the artistic potential of editing and camera placement. This and other new narrative films were extraordinarily popular with

D. W. Griffith's *Birth of a Nation* was made to commemorate the 50th anniversary of the end of the Civil War. The film was based on a novel entitled *The Clansman.* In 1906, a stage play based on the novel had caused disturbances in Philadelphia when it opened, but Griffith chose to go ahead with his plans to turn the work into a movie.

The story paints the prewar South as a happy and idyllic place whose serenity is disrupted by the war. At the war's conclusion, Southern whites are shown being victimized by coarse renegade African Americans, Northern carpetbaggers, and corrupt politicians. In response, whites form the Ku Klux Klan, which exacts vengeance on black people and restores the prewar utopia.

The NAACP objected to the film when it opened on the West Coast. About 40,000 African Americans demonstrated in California. In response, the San Francisco city censor (several big cities had film censorship boards in this era) ordered a couple of the film's more controversial scenes cut out. A delegation called on the mayor of New York City to stop the premiere but was rebuffed. When the movie opened in Boston, several brawls broke out outside the theater. Unrest was averted in Chicago when the mayor agreed to seat a black man on the city's film censorship board. Griffith, for his part, never understood the feelings of black people toward the film. He responded to these actions by issuing a pamphlet about free speech.

Birth of a Nation is rarely screened today. Modern audiences find the racial depictions unacceptable. The film is remembered not so much for its content as for its technical achievements and because it served notice that motion pictures could exert a political and social force.

audiences and proved to be financially successful. Almost overnight, 50- to 90-seat theaters, called *nickelettes* or *nickelodeons* because of the five-cent admission price, sprang up in converted stores throughout the country.

Nickelodeons depended on audience turnover for their profits. Keeping the audience returning required that films be changed often—sometimes daily—to attract repeat customers. This policy created a tremendous demand for motion pictures, and new production companies were quickly formed. (In these early days, films were regarded as just another mass-produced product; hence, early film studios were called *film factories.*) New York and New Jersey served as the bases for these early film companies.

>> Zukor and Griffith

Adolph Zukor decided to copy European filmmakers who were making longer, more expensive films aimed at a middle-class audience. He acquired the four-reel French film *Queen Elizabeth*, starring Sarah Bernhardt, the most famous actress of the period, and distributed it in the United States at the then-exhorbitant price of a dollar a ticket. His experiment was successful, proving that American audiences would pay more and sit still for longer films. Nevertheless, *Queen Elizabeth* remained essentially the filming of a stage play.

It was an American, D. W. Griffith, who eventually took full advantage of the film medium and established film as its own art form. Although controversial and racist in its depictions (see Media Probe, "Birth of a Controversy"), his brilliant Civil War drama, *Birth of a Nation,* was released in 1915 and became the most expensive American film produced to that date ($110,000). The three-hour movie, which was shot without a script, introduced history as a film topic. Griffith went on to top *Nation's* figures with an even bigger epic, *Intolerance,* a piece comprised of four scenarios dealing with life's injustices. The movie was completed in 1916 at a cost of about $2 million (the same film made in the 2000s would easily cost $90 million to $110 million).

In response to the controversy generated by *Birth of a Nation*, two African American brothers, George and Noble Johnson, made films that presented a more realistic and accurate view of African Americans. The first of these, *The Realization of a Negro's Ambition*, demonstrated that there was an African American audience that would support films that spoke to their community. The Johnsons' company, Lincoln Motion Pictures, stayed in operation until the early 1920s, when lack of capital and an inability to secure bookings at white theaters forced it out of business.

>> Birth of the MPPC

Events in moviemaking during the decade of 1908–1918 had far-reaching effects on the future shape of the film industry. As the basic economic structure of the film industry developed, the center of filmmaking moved to the West Coast, and independent film producers, having survived attempts by the major studios to stamp them out, became an important force in the industry. The tremendous demand for new pictures brought enormous competition into the field. Small film companies cut corners by using bootlegged equipment (for which they paid no royalty fees) and started making films. Competition quickly reached the cutthroat level; lawsuits were filed with alarming frequency. In an effort to bring order to the business (and to cut down legal expenses), the leading manufacturers of films and film equipment banded together, pooled their patents, and formed the **Motion Picture Patents Company (MPPC)** to restrict moviemaking to the nine companies that made up the MPPC. Film exhibitors were brought into line by a two-dollar-per-week tax, which entitled the theaters to use projection equipment patented by the MPPC. Failure to pay this tax meant that the theater owners would no longer be supplied with MPPC-approved films. Eventually, to accommodate the growing industry, a new role, that of film distributor, was created. The film distributor served the function of a wholesaler, acquiring films from the manufacturers and renting them to exhibitors. This three-level structure—production, distribution, and exhibition—is still with us today. The MPPC was quick to take control of film distribution also.

Instead of squelching competition, the MPPC actually encouraged it. Annoyed by the repressive regulations, independent producers began offering films to exhibitors at cheaper rates than MPPC members. Full-length feature films, several reels in length, were imported from Europe. The MPPC declared war. "Outlaw" studios were raided and equipment smashed. In an effort to escape the harassment of the MPPC, independent producers fled New York and New Jersey. They were looking for a location with good weather, interesting geography, low business costs, and proximity to a national border so that the independents could avoid the MPPC's subpoenas. Florida proved to be too humid; Cuba was too inconvenient; Texas was too flat. Finally, they found the perfect environment—a rather sleepy suburb of Los Angeles called Hollywood. By 1913, this new home had so encouraged independent filmmaking that the MPPC could no longer contain its growth. As of 1917, for all practical purposes, the patents organization had lost its power.

>> The Star System

The aura of glamour surrounding Hollywood and its stars might not have emerged if the MPPC had not been so stubborn. Whereas the patents company refused to publicize its performers, the independents quickly recognized that fan interest in film actors and actresses could be used to draw crowds away from the movies offered by the MPPC. Carl Laemmle, an independent producer, shrewdly publicized one of his actresses with a poetic name—Florence Lawrence—until she became what we might call the first movie star. As Florence's fame grew, her pictures brought in more money, spurring other independents to create their own stars to keep pace. The two artists who best exemplified the growth of the star system were Mary Pickford and Charlie Chaplin. In 1913, Chaplin was working in movies for $150 a week, a good salary in those days. Just four years later he was paid a million dollars for making eight pictures. Mary Pickford, nicknamed "America's Sweetheart," was paid $1,000 per week in 1913. By 1918, she was making $15,000 to $20,000 per week in addition to earning a cut of up to 50 percent of her films' profits.

In 1919, the star system reached its natural conclusion. Both Chaplin and Pickford joined with other actors and filmmakers to start their own production company—United Artists. The employees now owned the shop.

The star system had other, more subtle effects. Once stars became popular, the public demanded to see them in longer movies. However, feature-length films that ran one to two hours were more expensive to make. Furthermore, audiences could not be expected to sit for two hours on the wooden benches found in many of the nickelodeons. A need had been created for large, comfortable theaters that could accommodate thousands of patrons and, at the same time, justify higher admission costs. In 1914, the Strand opened in New York. With seats for more than 3,000 people, it occupied a whole city block and had space for an entire symphony orchestra. On the West Coast, Sid Grauman opened his Egyptian Theater (across from the Chinese Theater) in 1922 at a cost of almost a million dollars. His ushers were dressed in Cleopatra costumes. Clearly, the nickel was no longer the symbol of the movies.

Charlie Chaplin, one of the first movie superstars created by the Hollywood star system, delighted film audiences throughout the world. This scene is from one of his earlier works, a 1916 short called *One A.M.*

>> Consolidation and Growth

The increased cost of filmmaking made it imperative for a producer to make sure that a company's movies were booked into enough big, new theaters to turn a profit. Under this economic pressure, the film industry moved in the direction of consolidation. Adolph Zukor, whose company would ultimately become Paramount Pictures, combined the production and distribution of films into one corporate structure. Paramount and its chief rival, Fox, began building their own theaters, and Marcus Loew, owner of a large chain of theaters, purchased his own studio (later to become MGM). Studio owners could exert control over independent exhibitors through another policy known as **block booking.** To receive two or three topflight films from a studio, the theater owner had to agree to show five or six other films of lower quality. Although this policy was not very advantageous to exhibitors, it assured the production companies of steady revenue for their films.

All this was taking place as World War I devastated Europe. When the war ended in 1918, the American film industry was the dominant film force in the world, accounting for upwards of 80 percent of the worldwide market. By the beginning of the 1920s, the major production companies were comfortable and prosperous and enjoyed as firm a lock on the film business as had the old MPPC, which they had replaced only a few years earlier.

>> The Roaring Twenties

The prosperity boom that followed the war exploded in Hollywood with more force than in other business sectors. Profits were up, and extravagance was the watchword as filmmakers endorsed the principle that the only way to make money was to spend money. Between 1914 and 1924, the cost of a feature film increased 1,500 percent. Salaries, sets, costumes, props, and rights to best-sellers all contributed to the mushrooming costs of films. Even the lawyer for United Artists was paid $100,000 a year. By 1927, the average film cost about $200,000, and many films easily topped that. *Ben Hur* (1925) was made for a reported $6 million.

Huge salaries created a boomtown atmosphere in Hollywood, and many people—some still quite young—were unprepared to deal with the temptations that came with sudden wealth. Before long, newspapers were reporting stories about orgiastic parties, prostitution, studio call girls, bootleg whiskey, and drugs. Hollywood was dubbed "Sin City." In 1922, within a few short months, comedian Fatty Arbuckle was involved in a rape case, two female stars were implicated in the murder of a prominent director, and popular actor Wallace Reid died while trying to kick his drug addiction. Public reaction to these revelations was predictable: indignation and outrage. By the end of the year, politicians in 36 states had introduced bills to set up censorship boards for films. The motion picture companies hired a well-respected former postmaster general, Will Hays, to head a new self-regulatory body for the industry. Called the Motion Picture Producers and Distributors Association, this organization was successful in heading off government control, and the basic standards it laid down would be in force for almost four decades.

>> The Coming of Sound

Since optical recording of sound on film had been feasible since 1918, why did Hollywood wait until the late 1920s to introduce sound films? Money.

Business was good during the 1920s, and the major studios did not want to get into costly experimentation with new techniques. Warner Brothers, however, was

Al Jolson in *The Jazz Singer.* This film convinced the industry that audiences wanted to see "talkies," or films with sound, thus ushering in a new era in Hollywood.

not as financially sound as the other studios. Since Warner did not own theaters in the big cities and could not exhibit all its pictures in the most lucrative markets, the company was willing to try anything to get its films into movie theaters. In 1927 Warner released *The Jazz Singer,* in which Al Jolson not only sang but spoke from the screen. Within two years the silent film, for all practical purposes, was dead.

The novelty of sound gave a boost to the film industry, despite the economic effects of the Depression. In 1929, average weekly movie attendance was 80 million; by 1930 it had reached 90 million—a fact that led many to regard filmmaking as a Depression-proof industry. They were quickly proved wrong as attendance dropped in 1931 and again in 1932. The industry generated several innovations to attract audiences. *Becky Sharp* was filmed in the new Technicolor process in 1935. Theaters also began the practice of showing **double features,** two feature films on the same bill. Animated cartoons began to draw sizable audiences. All this new activity called for Hollywood to produce even more films—almost 400 per year during the 1930s—to meet the demands of the market. This high production volume was a boon to major studios since they could churn out larger numbers of films more economically. Moreover, the tremendous amount of money needed to convert to sound and the poor financial conditions created by the Depression forced many small companies out of business, leaving eight major studios with a lock on the film industry.

>> The Studio Years

The 20 years from 1930 to 1950 were the studio years, with MGM, 20th Century Fox, RKO, Warner Brothers, Paramount, Universal, Columbia, and United Artists dominating the industry. These studios created hundreds of acres of back-lot movie sets, constructed elaborate sound stages, and built up showy stables of creative talent, carefully groomed for stardom. Audiences adored and emulated their favorite screen idols, who were presented as larger-than-life gods and goddesses inhabiting a glamorous fantasyland.

Individual studios left their imprint on the films of the period as a studio's products took on a distinct personality. For example, during this period, Warner Brothers became best known for its gangster films, 20th Century Fox for its historical and adventure films, and MGM for its lavish, star-studded musicals.

The most significant period for motion picture achievement were the years from 1939 to 1941. *Gone with the Wind*, which showcased the new Technicolor film process, was released in 1939. In that same year, two other soon-to-become classics, *The Wizard of Oz* and *Stagecoach* (starring John Wayne in his first major role), were released. Just two years later, Orson Welles directed and starred in *Citizen Kane*, which some critics consider the best American film ever made.

The financial backing and diverse holdings of the studio system helped the film industry survive the Depression. Attendance and profits began climbing in 1934 and held steady throughout World War II. During the 1940s, going to a movie was just as much a part of American life as watching television is today. In fact, the all-time peak for filmgoing was 1946, when average weekly attendance reached over 90 million. By 1948, however, all this was to change.

Back in 1938, the Justice Department had filed suit against Paramount and the other major film companies, charging that the industry's vertical control of production, distribution, and exhibition constituted restraint of trade and monopolistic practices. The case had been set aside during the war, but by 1948, the courts had ordered the major studios to get rid of at least one of their holdings in these three areas. Most chose to divest themselves of their theater chains. The court also eliminated the block booking system and thus deprived the studios of guaranteed exhibition for all their films. As a result, the studios had to cut back on film production and reduce costs.

Orson Wells in a scene from the 1941 film *Citizen Kane.* Welles was 25 when he directed, produced, and starred in this film, considered by many critics the best American movie ever made.

>> ## The Film Industry Reacts to TV

When television began building a sizable audience during the late 1940s, it cut into the motion picture industry's profits. The first reaction of the film industry was to fight back. Studios stubbornly refused to advertise their films on TV, and they would not release old films for showing on the newer medium. Many studios wrote clauses into the contracts of their major stars forbidding them to appear on TV. None of their efforts had an appreciable effect on television's growing popularity; more and more Americans bought TV sets, while film attendance slipped.

Hollywood looked for ways to recapture some of its audience from TV. By the early 1950s, the film industry thought it had found the answer—technical wizardry. The first technical gimmick was 3-D (three-dimensional film). The audience wore special polarized glasses to perceive the effect and were treated to the illusion of spears, trains, arrows, knives, birds, and even Jane Russell jumping out at them from the film screen. Unfortunately, the glasses gave some people headaches, and the equipment was too expensive for most theater owners to install. Audiences quickly became bored with the novelty. It was soon apparent that 3-D was not the answer. The second technical gimmick concerned screen size. Cinerama, which involved the use of three projectors and curved screens, surrounded the audience with film. Less expensive techniques that enlarged screen size, such as Cinemascope, Panavision, and Vistavision, were ultimately adopted by the industry but did little to stem Hollywood's loss of money.

The attitude of the movie companies toward TV during those early years was a clear example of shortsightedness. What the film companies failed to see was

One of the problems with 3-D movies was the uncomfortable plastic glasses that audience members had to wear to appreciate the three-dimensional effects.

that they could have played a dominant role in TV's evolution. Because major networks were not eager to supply early television programs, film companies would have been logical sources for television shows. Somewhat belatedly, Hollywood recognized that it was in its best interest to cooperate with television. In the late 1950s, the studios began to release their pre-1948 films to TV and to supply programs to the networks. In 1960, post-1948 theatrical films were made available to the smaller TV screens.

By the 1950s, when it became clear that TV would be a formidable competitor, the film industry cast about for new ways to draw audiences back to the theaters. It tried big-budget, spectacle movies, such as *Cleopatra,* as well as films that addressed more adult subjects, such as adultery and homosexuality, that could not be shown on TV.

>> Realignments: The Film Industry from 1960 to 1990

The 1960s were marked by the waning power of the major studioes and by a closer affiliation with their old competitor, television. The continued rise of the independent producer led to a concomitant loss of power by the studios. As major production houses cut back, they released many actors, writers, and directors who, naturally enough, formed small, independent production companies. Using the big studios for financing and distribution, these independents and the artists they employed frequently took small salaries in exchange for a percentage of a film's profits. By the mid-1960s, roughly 80 percent of all American films were independent productions.

The poor economic climate brought about other changes. Large studios, faced with ever-worsening financial conditions, were absorbed by larger conglomerates. In the early 1970s, both the MGM and 20th Century Fox studios were sold to make room for real estate developers.

The late 1960s also saw a change in the regulatory climate that surrounded films. The Supreme Court issued several decisions that loosened controls on content, and filmmakers were quick to take advantage of their new freedom. In 1968, the Motion Picture Association of America liberalized its attitudes toward self-regulation. Whereas the old production code attempted to regulate content, the new system attempted to regulate audiences by instituting a G-PG-R-X labeling system.

The relationship between film and television became even closer in the 1960s, as movies made expressly for TV appeared in the middle of the decade. In 1974, about 180 of these TV movies were shown on network television. In that same year, the major film companies distributed only 109 films to theaters.

Film history since the early 1970s has been marked by several trends: Revenue has gone up, as have the budgets of many feature films, and several motion pictures have racked up astonishing gross receipts. Foremost among the trends has been a reversal of the slump in box-office receipts that began in 1946 and finally bottomed out in 1971. With the exception of temporary declines in 1973 and 1976, the general trend has been upward. In 1977, total box-office gross came to about $2.4 billion; by 1981, it had risen to nearly $3 billion, although some of this increase could be attributed to inflation.

With more cash flowing into the box office, more money became available for the budgets of feature films. In fact, films of the late 1970s and early 1980s were reminiscent of the extravaganzas of the 1920s. Perhaps the most interesting film phenomenon of the era was the rise of the blockbuster. From 1900 to 1970, only two films (*The Sound of Music* and *Gone with the Wind*) managed to surpass $50 million in film rentals; between 1970 and 1980, 17 films exceeded this mark (see Table 9–1 and Media Probe, "All-Time Box Office Leaders—Another Look" on p. 253).

Rank	Title	Year	Rental (in $ millions)
1	*Titanic*	1997	$601
2	*Star Wars*	1977	461
3	*Star Wars: The Phantom Menace*	1999	431
4	*E.T.*	1982	400
5	*Jurassic Park*	1993	357
6	*Forrest Gump*	1994	330
7	*Harry Potter and the Sorcerer's Stone*	2001	318
8	*Lord of the Rings: The Fellowship of the Ring*	2001	313
9	*The Lion King*	1994	313
10	*Star Wars: Return of the Jedi*	1983	309

On another front, in 1985, the Motion Picture Association of America instituted a new rating category—PG-13. This category was designed for those films for which parental guidance for children under 13 was recommended. Yet another new category, NC-17, replaced the X rating in 1990.

>> Contemporary Trends in Motion Pictures

The past 20 or so years have been favorable to the motion picture industry. Although theater attendance has increased only slightly, high ticket prices have pushed box office revenue to record levels. In addition, sales and rental income from movies on videocassettes and especially DVDs continues to surge. The "aftermarket," rental and sales income, has now far eclipsed the box office as the most important source of industry revenue.

The motion picture industry continues to be dominated by seven big companies: Sony, NBC Universal, Disney, Fox, Warner Brothers, Paramount, and MGM. These companies typically control about 80 percent of the market and are engaged in both motion picture production and distribution.

As far as movie content is concerned, the recent strategy in Hollywood has been to find a story idea that is presold; that is, it has an audience already familiar with it that would probably go see it on the screen. Some examples are sequels (*The Matrix Reloaded*), popular books (*Harry Potter* and *Lord of the Rings*), comic books (*Spider-Man*), video games (*X-Men*), and even amusement park rides (*Pirates of the Caribbean*).

Finally, as mentioned in the opening of the chapter, the movie industry is concerned about "Napsterization," or widespread file sharing of movies on the Internet in the same way music files were traded on Napster and continue to be traded on its successors. The industry is considering several responses to this growing problem.

MOTION PICTURES IN THE DIGITAL AGE

The movie industry officially entered the digital age when Hollywood began to release films on **digital videodisc**, or **DVD**, a digital storage and playback medium. We will consider some of the implications of the move to digital.

Pirates of the Caribbean relied heavily on digital technology to achieve its special effects.

>> Making Movies

Digital moviemaking is already a reality. The special effects in *X2* and *Spider-Man* were digitally created. *Star Wars: Attack of the Clones* was shot entirely with digital cameras. In *Lord of the Rings: The Two Towers*, the character of Gollum was computer-generated using a live actor outfitted with sensors and digital technology. Many production companies are using digital dailies (dailies are the scenes that are shot on a particular day during the making of a film). Rather than wait for motion picture film to be processed and printed, dailies can be converted to digital video and viewed just hours after they are shot. This makes it easier for the studios to correct problems while the actors are still present and the sets still intact.

>> Digital Distribution

Under the current film distribution system, hundreds of copies of a film are duplicated, put into big metal cans, and shipped to various theaters across the country. This is an expensive process since each celluloid copy costs more than $2000 to make, and a film that goes into wide release might need hundreds of copies.

In contrast, digital movies can be distributed much more cheaply. They can be delivered on discs or sent electronically by satellite, by fiber optic line, or even via the Internet. Doing away with the old system of shipping metal containers would save the industry more than $1 billion a year. Along with cost cutting, digital distribution eliminates the scratches and other flaws that come with repeated showings of traditional film. The biggest problem with moving to such a system is that almost all current theaters are not yet equipped to receive or display digital versions of motion pictures. For example, as of 2003, only about 25 of approximately 38,000 movies screens in the United States could receive digital film files over the Internet. Equipping studios and theaters to handle digital distribution will be expensive.

>> Digital Projection

Once the digital movie gets to the theater it has to be shown on a special digital projector. Several companies, including Kodak, have developed digital projectors and are working to improve them, but large-scale manufacturing of the devices is still in the future. One of the problems is making sure that the digital projectors match the same color and sharpness found in traditional celluloid film. A second problem is cost. Equipping each screen with a digital projection system will cost about $150,000. Theater owners, still recovering from a wave of overexpansion, falling profits, and bankruptcies, are not eager to foot the bill. They argue that the studios and the distributors should pick up the tab since they will be the ones saving the most money. For their part, distributors have been reluctant to lead the way. They point out that for several years they will have increased costs because they will have to supply both digital and traditional film versions as the new technology slowly catches on.

The seven big film companies have set up a group, Digital Cinema Initiatives (DCI), to come up with technical standards and copyright projections for the new system. Theater owners are talking with DCI about financial arrangements that might facilitate cost sharing over a number of years. The Boeing Company announced plans to finance the installation of 40 digital systems. Why would Boeing, an aerospace company, be interested in movies? It hopes to convince movies companies to use its satellite technology to distribute digital films.

In another development, a small company, Landmark, whose theaters generally show art and independent films, has announced it will install digital projectors in its 53 theaters by 2004. Keep in mind that it was another small company, Warner Brothers, that pioneered talking movies. Maybe history will repeat itself, and Landmark will start a movement toward digital projection.

>> Preventing Piracy

Piracy consists of making illegal copies of films. This can be done in several ways. The most common is for someone to sneak a camcorder into a special sneak preview and record the entire film. The film is converted to digital files that are then compressed and made available online or copied to tape and DVD. Some sophisticated pirates are able to obtain advance copies of movies that are sent to film executives and stars and make illegal duplicates of them.

Hollywood has launched a multipronged attack on pirates. The first tactic is improved copy protection. Several companies are developing an electronic coding system that would distort copies of a film, rendering them useless for pirates. Another solution being considered is requiring computer makers to build in copy protection on their hard drives, making it impossible to share films over the Internet. For their part, some movie theaters now search customers for concealed camcorders. In China, theater owners use night-vision goggles during film screenings to search for illegal taping. The industry has also been active on the legal front, using the Digital Millennium Copyright Act to close down file-sharing Websites such as Scour and iCrave. As of 2003, lawsuits were also pending against Kazaa and Morpheus, and a couple of people have been arrested for movie piracy.

>> Movielink

Hollywood is also fighting piracy by providing a legal alternative to consumers. In 2002, five major studios launched Movielink, an Internet service through which consumers may download popular films. About 200 films are available, and customers

Steven Spielberg started making movies at age 12 using his father's 8 mm camera. One of his earliest productions was a horror film starring his three younger sisters. He continued to make his own films during his college days, but he graduated with a degree in English because his grades were too low to get him into film school. One of Spielberg's independently made films caught the attention of an executive at Universal Pictures, who hired the young Spielberg to direct episodes of a TV series. The young director eventually wound up directing a made-for-TV movie, *Duel,* which won much critical acclaim.

Steven Spielberg directing *Saving Private Ryan.*

On the basis of his success with *Duel,* Spielberg got approval to direct his first theatrical movie, *The Sugarland Express.* Although praised by critics, the movie did poorly at the box office. Nonetheless, the studio gave him a new assignment: directing the movie version of a best-selling novel about a huge shark. The movie, *Jaws,* released in 1975, marked a significant milestone in movie history. It was the first of the big-budget summer action movies, a strategy that movie studios still follow (consider *Twister, Independence Day,* and *The Patriot*). *Jaws* was also the first of the movie blockbusters, raking in more than $250 million. Hollywood studios quickly adopted a "big budget equals big blockbuster" mentality.

Spielberg also hit upon a formula for making successful pictures that resonated with U.S. moviegoers: Take tried-and-true, classic adventure themes and enhance them with cutting-edge special effects. The *Indiana Jones* trilogy, *Jurassic Park, E.T.,* and *Close Encounters of the Third Kind* are all examples of this formula. Spielberg also tackled more serious themes, as exemplified in *The Color Purple, Schindler's List, Amistad,* and *Saving Private Ryan.*

In a career that has spanned more than a quarter century, Spielberg has won two Oscars and numerous other movie awards. Of the top 25 all-time movie hits, 4 were directed by Steven Spielberg.

---

pay between $2 and $4 to download a movie. A typical film takes about an hour to download over a high-speed broadband connection. After payment is received, a customer has 30 days to watch the film. Once the film is activated, consumers can watch it as many times as they want during the next 24 hours, but they cannot copy the film to a DVD. After 24 hours, the film is no longer available to the consumer.

Movielink has several challenges to overcome before it is successful. It first has to compete against the illegal file-sharing services that offer the same film for free. Movieline is practical only for those with high-speed modems, thus limiting its audience. Finally, unless consumers have a sophisticated system that projects the films on a big-screen TV, they have to watch film on relatively small computer monitors.

DEFINING FEATURES OF MOTION PICTURES

The most noticeable characteristic of motion pictures is their potential cost. Many big-budget Hollywood movies have production expenses that routinely top the $100 million mark. Tack on another $20 million or so for marketing and distribution and you are talking real money. No other media product—book, magazine, TV series, CD—costs as much as motion pictures. (Of course, filmmakers sometimes put together films for much less and sometimes make big money—*My Big Fat Greek Wedding,* for example—but these tend to be rare events.)

Partly because commercial motion picture making is so expensive, the industry has become dominated by big conglomerates. As noted earlier, seven major companies control most of the market. These companies have the financial resources to risk $100 million or so on a few dozen films each year in hopes of finding a blockbuster. Making motion pictures tends to be only one of many media interests in which these conglomerates are involved. Some have holdings in TV and the Internet; others own publishing companies and recording companies.

Film has a strong aesthetic dimension. Of all the media discussed in this book, film is the one most often discussed as an art form. My university library lists 87 entries under the heading "motion picture aesthetics." This characteristic introduces a tension in the field because most big-studio films are produced to make a profit rather than to showcase their artistic merit. Many independent filmmakers, however, make films not because of the bottom line, but because they find their efforts artistically satisfying. Although this chapter discusses primarily mainstream Hollywood moviemaking, keep in mind that thousands of freelance filmmakers work outside the established corporate structure and produce films of varying length on a myriad of topics.

Going to the movies continues to be a social experience. It is the only medium that facilitates audiences gathering in large groups to be exposed to the same message. And, of course, moviegoing is still a popular dating activity. In fact, the social dimension of moviegoing might be the most important.

 ## ORGANIZATION OF THE FILM INDUSTRY

Although film is an art form, the film industry is in business to make a profit. If an occasional moneymaking film also turns out to have artistic merit, so much the better, but the artistic merit is usually a by-product rather than the main focus. Our analysis of the film industry divides its structure into three areas: (1) production, (2) distribution, and (3) exhibition.

>> Production

Films are produced by a variety of organizations and individuals. For many years, the major studios controlled virtually all production, but independent producers have recently become prevalent. The major studios now finance and distribute many films made by independent companies.

Film studios differ in their arrangements but a typical setup involves four main departments: (1) film production, (2) distribution, (3) TV production, and (4) administration. The film production department handles all those elements that actually go into the making of a film, including story development, casting, art, makeup, and sets. The distribution department handles sales and contracts for domestic and worldwide duplication and delivery of films to theaters and to home video. As its name suggests, the TV division develops and produces movies and series for first-run and syndicated television. Sales, financial deals, and legal arrangements are the provinces of the administration department.

After increasing steadily for several years, the number of films released each year declined by 20 percent from 2000 to 2002. Partly behind the decline was a faltering economy as well as a more cautious industry attitude toward greenlighting new films. The major film companies (Sony, Paramount, 20th Century Fox, MGM, Disney, Warner Brothers, NBC Universal) will each produce about 15 to 20 films a year.

At first glance it looked like just another movie premiere: limousines, red carpet, fancily dressed people. But this Hollywood event was not the premiere of a movie. It was the premiere of a video game based on a movie. The crowd was showing up to see the unveiling of *Enter the Matrix.*

In another example of media symbiosis, it is not uncommon to see film producers take in some extra dollars by lending their plots and characters to video game developers. In the case of *Enter the Matrix,* the Wachowski brothers, who wrote and directed *The Matrix Reloaded,* also wrote the video game and shot an hour of original footage with the movie cast so that they might be incorporated into the game.

Some of the biggest video game sellers in 2002 were based on movies: *Spider-Man, Harry Potter, Lord of the Rings,* and *James Bond.* This was not always the case. Before the 1990s, many movie-based games had little to do with the movie. They may have had the title in common, but the characters and the plot lines were unfamiliar. Movie studios eventually came to see that video games could represent another profitable revenue stream, and games were modeled more closely on the movies, and game characters were crafted to resemble actual movie actors. Movie-based game sales jumped.

For example, *Star Wars: Attack of the Clones* spawned several games for personal computers and for Nintendo's Game Boy. *Jurassic Park* has done the same. There are a *Harry Potter and The Sorcerer's Stone* game, a *Harry Potter and the Chamber of Secrets* game, and a *Harry Potter Quidditch World Cup* game for X-Box, Play Station, and Game Cube.

Some games are based on movies that seem inappropriate for amusement. The advertising copy for the game *Black Hawk Down* says you can "gear up with an arsenal of authentically modeled weapons used in the streets of Mogadishu" and "participate in a number of daring and intense raids against oppressive Somali warlords." The plot of the video game based on *The Sum of All Fears* involves leading a three-person squad of an elite antiterrorist team to stop a neo-Nazi conspiracy bent on exploding a nuclear weapon in the United States.

Will this trend continue? Consider the following: In 2002 consumers spent more money on video games than they did going to the movies. Electronic Arts, the biggest publisher of video games, is building a new studio in Hollywood. Action star Vin Diesel plans to set up his own video game studio. Look for more of your favorite movie characters to make the jump to games.

>> Distribution

The distribution arm of the industry is responsible for supplying prints of films to the thousands of theaters located across the United States and around the globe. In recent years, distribution companies have also supplied films to TV networks and to makers of videocassettes and videodiscs. Distribution companies maintain close contact with theater owners all over the world and also provide a transportation and delivery system that ensures that a film will arrive at a theater before its scheduled play date. In addition to booking the film at local movie houses, the distribution company is responsible for making the multiple prints of a film that are necessary when the film goes into general release. They also take care of advertising and promotion for the film. Most of the distribution of motion pictures is handled by the large studios. These companies are firmly entrenched in both the production and distribution aspects of the business.

The nature of film distribution ensures that the large companies will control a large portion of the business. First, it is too expensive for an independent producer or a small distribution company to contact theaters and theater chains spread all over the globe. The big studios already have this communication network set up and can afford to maintain it. Second, the large studios can offer theater owners a steady stream of films that consistently feature big-name stars. A small company could not withstand that competition for long.

Distribution companies also serve as a source of financing for independent producers. These companies lend money to a film's producer to cover all or most of the estimated cost of a film. In this way, the major studios acquire an interest in films that they did not directly produce. This arrangement will be discussed further in the section of this chapter on film economics.

>> Exhibition

The exhibition side of the industry went on a building boom in the late 1990s, constructing new multiscreen theaters with stadium seating and surround sound. By 2000, there were about 37,400 movies screens in the United States, an all-time high. As it turned out, however, theater owners had overexpanded and did not have the cash to pay for this expansion. As a result, several big theater chains, including Carmike, Regal, and Loews, filed for bankruptcy and shut down theaters that were losing money. By 2002, the total number of movie screens had dropped to about 35,300.

Multiplex theaters, featuring 12 or 18 screens clustered around a central concession stand, are still the rule. Most new theaters seat about 200 to 400 patrons. The massive movie palaces of the 1920s and 1930s have not reemerged, but there are noticeable changes inside the motion picture theater as exhibitors go after a slightly older market. Soundproofing to prevent spill from adjoining theaters is now common, and concession stands are putting real butter on popcorn, with a few even offering mineral water, cappuccino, and valet parking.

OWNERSHIP IN THE FILM INDUSTRY

Big conglomerates, many of them mentioned in earlier chapters, dominate the film industry. As of 2004, the top seven were as follows:

1. *The Walt Disney Company:* Headquartered in California, Disney has two movie enterprises: Touchstone, for mature-audience films, and Buena Vista, for general films. Disney has holdings in television, cable, and publishing in addition to its interests in theme parks, hotels, music, real estate, golf courses, and professional hockey (the Mighty Ducks). Disney also makes money licensing Disney characters for use by other companies.

2. *Time Warner:* Warner Brothers is the motion picture arm of this huge conglomerate, which has interests in the Internet, book and magazine publishing, recorded music, motion picture theaters, and cable TV, among other media.

3. *Paramount (Viacom):* In 1994, Viacom acquired Paramount Pictures and the Blockbuster company. In addition to owning and making motion pictures, the company owns CBS, Infinity Broadcasting, video rental stores, cable networks, CD-ROMs, video games, theme parks, motion picture theaters, and publishing companies.

4. *Sony:* Sony Pictures Entertainment is the part of this Japan-based, worldwide conglomerate that manufactures video and audio devices. In addition to producing hardware, Sony has interests in music, video games, movie theaters, and television production.

5. *NBC Universal:* NBC acquired Universal from Vivendi, a French company, in 2003. GE, the parent of NBC, now has interests in cable and broadcast TV, a motion picture studio, and a recording company.

6. *News Corporation:* Rupert Murdoch's Australian-based company owns 20th Century Fox. The company is also involved in satellite broadcasting and publishing and owns a TV network and a cable news channel.

The trend in movie exhibition is big 18- and 24-screen multiplexes. Increased competition and declining profits forced some movie theaters to close during 2000 and 2001.

7. *MGM/UA:* This company was acquired by a French bank in 1992 and was subsequently purchased in 1996 by a consortium that included current management and an Australian TV network. In addition to owning the motion picture studio, the company has interests in home video and leisure-time products.

PRODUCING MOTION PICTURES

>> Preproduction

How does a film get to be a film? The three distinct phases in moviemaking are (1) preproduction, (2) production, and (3) postproduction.

All films begin with an idea. The idea can be sketchy, such as a two-paragraph outline of the plot, or detailed, such as a novel or a Broadway play.

The next step of the preproduction process is writing the screenplay. In general, the route to a finished motion picture script consists of several steps:

1. Step one is called a *treatment*. This is a narrative statement of the plot and descriptions of the main characters and locations; it might even contain sample dialogue.

2. Step two is a first-draft script. This version contains all the dialogue and camera setups and a description of action sequences.

3. The third step is a revised script incorporating changes suggested by the producer, director, actors, and others.

4. Finally, step four is a script polish. This includes adding or subtracting scenes, revising dialogue, and making other minor changes.

While all this is going on, the producer tries to find actors (in the film industry, people who act in films are described by the generic term "talent," whether they have any or not) who will appear in the film. The contracts and deals that are

Jim Carrey's salary made up a substantial percentage of *Bruce Almighty's* $88 million budget.

worked out vary from astronomical to modest. One common arrangement is for the actor to receive a flat fee. These fees have been rising in the past few years and are one of the reasons films cost so much to produce. For example, Bruce Willis received $20 million for *The Sixth Sense*, and Chris Tucker got the same amount for *Rush Hour 2*. At the other end of the scale, the Screen Actors Guild has a contract that spells out the minimum salary that must be paid to talent in minor roles and walk-on parts.

Meanwhile, the producer is also trying to secure financial backing for the picture. We will consider more about the monetary arrangements in film in the section on economics. For now, it is important to remember that the financial arrangements have to be worked out early in the preproduction process.

At the same time, the producer is busy lining up skilled personnel to work behind the camera. Of these people, the film's director is central. When all the elements have been put together, the director will determine what scenes get photographed from what angle and how they will be assembled in the final product. Working closely with the director is the cinematographer (the person responsible for the lighting and filming of the scenes) and the film editor (the person who will cut the film and assemble the scenes in the proper order). A movie crew contains dozens of other skilled people: set designers, makeup specialists, electricians, audio engineers, crane operators, painters, plumbers, carpenters, property masters, set dressers, caterers, first-aid people, and many others.

Shortly after the director has been signed for the project, he or she and the producer scout possible locations for shooting the film. Some sequences may be shot in the sound studio, but others may need the authenticity that only location shooting can provide. As soon as the locations have been chosen, the producer makes the necessary arrangements to secure these sites for filming. Sometimes this entails renting the studios of a major motion picture production company or obtaining permits to shoot in city streets or other places. The producer must also draw up plans to make sure that the filming equipment, talent, and technical crew are all at the same place at the same time.

>> Production

Once all these items have been attended to, the film moves into the actual production phase. Cast and crew assemble at the chosen location, and each scene is shot and reshot until the director is satisfied. The actors and crew then move to another location, and the process starts all over again. Overriding the entire production is the knowledge that all this is costing a great deal of money. Shooting even a moderate-budget film can cost $400,000 to $500,000 *per day*. Therefore, the director tries to plan everything so that each dollar is used efficiently.

The average shooting schedule for the typical film is about 70 days. Each day's shooting (and some days can be 16 hours long) results in an average of fewer than two minutes of usable film.

>> Postproduction

The postproduction phase begins after the filming has been completed. A film editor, working with the director, decides where close-ups should be placed, the angle from which the scene should be shown, and how long each scene should last. The elaborate special effects that some films require are also added during postproduction. Once the scenes have been edited into an acceptable form, postproduction sound can be added. This might include narration, music, sound effects, and original dialogue that, for one reason or another, has to be redone. (About 10 to 15 percent of outside dialogue has to be rerecorded because of interfering noises.) Finally, the edited film, complete with final sound track and special effects, is sent to the laboratory where a release print of the film is made.

 ECONOMICS

Despite a weakening economy at the beginning years of the new century, the motion picture industry continued to see revenue increases at the box office. In 2002, the industry collected about $9.5 billion, up a healthy 23 percent from 2000. Part of this increase was due to higher ticket prices (about $10 in some big cities) and part was due to increased ticket sales. Movie admissions increased 15 percent from 2000 to 2002.

As mentioned earlier, movies are an expensive medium. In 2003, the average film cost about $59 million to produce and another $31 million to advertise and market in the United States and overseas, representing an increase of about 12 percent since 2000. Some films, such as *Pearl Harbor* and *Pirates of the Caribbean*, cost much more. The rising costs of production and marketing have made it difficult for many films to earn a profit for the studio. With many high-budget releases competing for the same audiences during the summer and Christmas holidays it is almost guaranteed that many pictures will fail to break even.

Financial success for a movie is a function of many revenue sources: U.S. and foreign box office revenue, cassette and DVD rental and sales, premium TV channel fees, and cable and broadcast rights plus other sources such as pay-per-view, airline showings, and hotel channels. U.S. box office revenue typically accounts for less than half of the total earnings of a motion picture. To illustrate, *Maid in Manhattan* took in $93 million in the United States, another $40 million overseas, and about $60 million in rental income.

The foreign box office is increasing in importance. Some films do much better around the world than they do in the United States. *Gangs of New York,* for example, took in $77 million at the U.S. box office but more than $110 million overseas. Conversely, some films do not export well. *Adaptation* grossed $22 million domestically but only $7 million overseas.

>> Financing a Film

Where do producers get the enormous sums of money necessary to make a film? Let us take a look at some common financing methods. If a producer has a good track record and a film looks promising, the distributor might lend the producer the entire amount needed to make the film. In return, the distributor gains distribution rights to the film. Moreover, if the distributor also has studio facilities, the producer might agree to rent those facilities from the distributor.

A second method is to arrange for a **pickup.** Under this arrangement a distributor agrees to "pick up" the cost of a finished picture at a later date for a set price. Although this agreement does a producer little immediate good, he or she can take the pickup to a bank to help secure a loan for the cost of the film.

A third method is a **limited partnership,** an arrangement whereby the film is financed through outside investors. Each limited partner puts up a set amount, and his or her personal liability is limited by the amount invested; that is, a partner cannot lose any more money than he or she put up even if the film goes over budget.

A fourth method is a **joint venture.** Under this setup, several companies involved in film production and distribution pool their resources and agree to finance one or more films. Given the increasing cost of motion pictures, this arrangement is becoming more common as several companies share the risk and potential rewards of a movie. *Titanic,* for example, was financed by a joint venture.

The producer and distributor also agree on how to divide the distributor's gross receipts from the film (the money the distributor gets from the theater owners, TV networks, pay-TV operations, and videocassette and videodisc operations that show the film). Since the distributor takes the greatest risk in the venture, the distributor is the first to be paid from the receipts of the film. Distribution companies charge a distribution fee for their efforts. In addition, there are distribution expenses (cost of making multiple prints of the film, advertising, necessary taxes, insurance). Lastly, the actual production cost of the film must be repaid. If the distributor or a bank lent the producer $10 million to make the film, that loan has to be paid off (plus interest). Because of all these expenses, it is estimated that a film must earn two and one-half to three times its production cost before it starts to show a profit for the producers. Hollywood accounting tends to be complicated, however, and sometimes it is hard to determine when a film is profitable.

>> Dealing with the Exhibitor

The distributor is also involved in other financial dealings, specifically with the exhibitors. An exhibition license sets the terms under which the showing of the film will occur. The license specifies the run of the film (the number of weeks the theater must agree to play the picture), holdover rights, the date the picture will be available for showing, and the clearance (the amount of time that must elapse before the film can be shown at a competing theater).

The license also contains the financial terms for the film's showing. There are several common arrangements. The simplest involves a specified percentage split of the money taken in at the box office. The exhibitor agrees to split the money with the distributor according to an agreed-upon formula, perhaps 50/50 the first week, 60/40 the second, 70/30 the third, and so on, with the exhibitor keeping more money the longer the run of the film. Another alternative is the **sliding scale.** Under this setup, as the box-office revenue increases, so does the amount of money that the exhibitor must pay the distributor. For example, if a week's revenue was more than $30,000, the exhibitor would pay the distributor 60 percent; if the revenue was between $25,000 and $29,999, the distributor would receive 50 percent; and so on. Another common approach is the 90/10 deal. Under this method, the movie theater owner first deducts the house allowance (called the *nut*) from the box-office take. The house allowance includes all the operating expenses of the theater (heating, cooling, water, lights, salaries, maintenance, etc.), plus a sum that is pure profit for the theater (this sum is called *air*). From the revenues (if any) that remain, the distributor gets 90 percent and the house 10 percent.

Concession sales are a source of significant income for movie theater owners. According to industry figures, the average moviegoer spends about $4 on popcorn, soda, candy, and other concession munchies. Since slightly more than a billion tickets per year have been sold for the past decade or so, that translates to about $4 billion taken in at the concession stand. At some theaters, 90 percent of the profits come from concessions. (And no wonder—that $2.50 soft drink costs the theater owner less than 50 cents.)

High ticket prices, coupled with large markups at the concession stand, mean that a trip to the movies can be an expensive proposition. For example, consider the costs for two at a theater in Atlanta: admission for two, $15.00; two small boxes of popcorn, $4.50; one package of Twizzlers and one box of Milk Duds, total $4.00; two large Cokes, $5.50. Total tab: $29.00.

>> Promoting a Film

A well-known film executive once said that a film is like a parachute: If it doesn't open, you're dead. The first week that a film is in release is crucial; in fact, since most films open on a weekend, the first three days are even more crucial. Films that open badly seldom do well.

Consequently, a good deal of promotion, marketing, and advertising is targeted to getting people into theaters for that opening weekend. The most common strategy is to launch a media blitz that touts the film weeks before it opens. These campaigns are not inexpensive. Columbia TriStar spent nearly $50 million promoting *Spider-Man*.

Movie studios are relying on the Internet to aid promotion, but their approach has changed over the past three or four years. Up until 2001, most of a film's Internet budget was spent on creating a flashy website. Movie executives then discovered that these websites did not draw nearly as many visitors as did major Internet portals such as Yahoo and MSN and general film websites such as Coming Attractions. Although the studios still create official websites for their films, they now spend more money purchasing ads on Yahoo, AOL, and other portals. Banner ads for films are appearing more often on online movie ticket selling sites such as Fandango. Movie companies are also partnering with online retailers. MGM, for example, linked up with Alloy Online to promote *Legally Blonde*. In short, Hollywood recognizes that the Internet can be an effective marketing tool and continues to search for the optimum way to use it.

Advertising in Movie Theaters: Would You Like an Ad with Your Popcorn?

Maybe this has happened to you. The movie you really want to see is scheduled to start at 7 P.M. You know that you will have to hurry to make it. You rush to the theater, buy an $8 ticket, spend another $8 at the concession stand for a small popcorn and a small drink, and get to your seat just before 7. The house lights go down and pretty soon you are watching . . . commercials. (Note that we are not talking about previews of coming attractions; we are talking about ads for AT&T, Colgate, the U.S. Army . . . real commercials.) This is what you hurried around and paid $16 to see? You could have seen commercials at home on TV for free.

Now showing on about two-thirds of all movie theater screens, premovie ads are becoming increasingly common, and you should only expect to see more of them along with other in-theater marketing techniques in the future.

There are several reasons why movie-theater ads are increasing. First, many movie theaters are in financial difficulty, and several big chains, including Regal and Loews, have filed for bankruptcy. In-theater advertising brings in extra dollars to the theater owners, about $250 million in 2002, and this amount will surely increase in 2003. Second, advertisers know that they have a captive audience. You cannot zap a commercial on the movie screen. Short of leaving the theater, there is no way to avoid them. Third, the moviegoing audience is young and has disposable income—just the target audience that most advertisers are looking for. Finally, they work. A market research survey disclosed that viewer recall of the ads was an amazing 80 percent, much higher than recall for TV spots.

Not everybody is happy with premovie ads. Many feel that ads are simply uninvited guests and argue that they paid their money to see a movie and not commercials. In fact, longtime consumer advocate Ralph Nader has gotten into the act. He is the founder of Commercial Alert, an organization that is pressuring Congress to enact laws to force movie theaters to advertise the time the movie actually begins instead of the time the commercials start. (Such a system is currently used in Europe.) In addition, Commercial Alert is asking audiences to yell, "No Commercials!" when the premovie ads come on. Anticommercial websites instruct moviegoers to stand up during the ads to block the view. A high school teacher from Chicago was so angry over being subjected to the ads that she filed a lawsuit asking that theater owners compensate her and other moviegoers with $75 in damages for their wasted time.

Nonetheless, theater owners continue to make deals with advertisers. Regal Cinemas is partnering with NBC to produce a 20-minute premovie block that consists of a mix of entertainment and ads. The program will use unseen footage from NBC programs such as *The Tonight Show with Jay Leno*. Ads would be targeted to local audiences.

Look for more off-screen marketing as well. Motorola sent around salespeople dressed in 1970s clothing to theater lobbies during the showing of *Austin Powers in Goldmember* to demonstrate the company's new mobile phone. The Department of Defense rents space in many theaters for kiosks that encourage enlistment. Monster.com struck a deal with theater owners that allowed them to park green-colored vehicles outside movie theaters at which patrons could search for new jobs. Target Department Stores bought space on popcorn bags at more than 100 theaters to advertise its 2003 line of back-to-college supplies. All of these deals meant more money for theater owners.

Will movie audiences rebel against his increasing invasion of commercialism? Probably not. People have become used to seeing ads almost everywhere they go. Theater owners want to keep the added revenue. Draw your own conclusion.

 FEEDBACK

>> **Box Office**

Feedback in the movie industry revolves around the weekly box-office figures compiled and reported in various trade publications including *Variety*. Each week *Variety* reports the top grossing films in the American and foreign markets. An example of this listing is reproduced in Figure 9–1.

To compile these data, *Variety*, in cooperation with Nielsen Entertainment Data Incorporated, collects box-office results from 50,000 movie screens in 14 countries, including the United States, Canada, Mexico, and several countries in South America, Europe, and Asia. Most of the column headings in *Variety*'s chart are self-explanatory. Each film's title is listed, followed by the distributor. The remain-

FIGURE 9–1

Variety **Box-Office Revenue Chart**

TITLE/DISTRIBUTOR	Reported Box Office 10/17-10/19 (weekend)	Percent Change in Box Office	Number of Engagements This Week	Last Week	Weeks Avg $ Per Engmnt.	No. Weeks Release	Domestic Box Office Cumulative	Foreign Box Office Cumulative	Worldwide Box Office Cumulative
Texas Chainsaw Massacre (New Line)	$28,094,014	—	3016	—	$9315	1	$28,094,014	$200,259	$28,294,273
Kill Bill Vol. 1 (Miramax)	12,424,841	-44%	3102	3102	4005	2	43,235,778	10,270,000	53,505,778
Runaway Jury (20th/New Regency)	11,836,705	—	2815	—	4205	1	11,836,705	108,000	11,944,705
School of Rock (Par)	11,006,233	-29%	2951	2929	3730	3	54,898,025	—	54,898,025
Mystic River (WB)	10,445,547	+1,530%	1467	13	7120	2	13,532,943	3,252,621	16,785,564
Good Boy! (MGM)	8,932,472	-32%	3225	3225	2770	2	25,713,653	419,000	26,132,653
Intolerable Cruelty (U)	6,515,010	-48%	2570	2564	2535	2	22,720,755	4,863,993	27,584,748
Out of Time (MGM)	4,002,023	-53%	2344	3076	1707	3	35,230,719	440,000	35,670,719
Under the Tuscan Sun (BV)	3,379,245	-31%	1663	1701	2032	4	33,657,195	—	33,657,195
The Rundown (U)	2,780,695	-47%	2099	2823	1325	4	44,518,785	590,689	45,109,474
Lost in Translation (Focus)	1,903,194	-33%	771	882	2468	6	20,964,443	—	20,964,443
Secondhand Lions (New Line)	1,884,995	-43%	1610	2563	1171	5	38,406,515	140,369	38,546,884
House of the Dead (Artisan)	1,763,212	-69%	1540	1520	1145	2	8,811,768	—	8,811,768
The Fighting Temptations (Par)	1,034,764	-46%	867	1168	1193	5	28,773,229	—	28,773,229
Underworld (Sony/Screen Gems)	900,869	-61%	904	1906	997	5	50,503,172	18,000,000	68,503,172
Pirates of the Caribbean: Curse of the Black Pearl (BV)	653,715	-36%	493	801	1326	15	300,557,571	330,000,000	630,557,571
Veronica Guerin (BV)	611,276	—	472	—	1295	1	611,276	6,986,000	7,597,276
Finding Nemo (BV)	511,514	-18%	455	540	1124	21	338,163,432	124,000,000	462,163,432
Luther (RS Entertainment)	378,213	-33%	219	311	1727	4	3,731,329	—	3,731,329
Cold Creek Manor (BV)	280,113	-74%	480	1163	584	5	20,825,290	—	20,825,290

ing columns show box-office revenue, number of screens showing the picture, average revenue per screen, and domestic and foreign revenue estimates. Note that this chart reports only a film's gross earnings; it does not show how much profit, if any, a film has made.

The economic feedback contained in *Variety* is extremely important in the movie industry. One or two blockbuster films can improve the financial position of an entire company. In addition, a film successful at the box office is apt to inspire one or more sequels and several imitators.

>> Market Research

Audience research has become more influential in the movie business because of the tremendous cost of motion pictures. At most studios the first step is concept testing to find promising plotlines. The next step is an analysis of the script. If the script seems promising, the studio will go ahead and film it and make a rough cut. The rough cut is then used by movie researchers in a series of test screenings. In addition, **focus group** sessions are held. A focus group is a small sample (usually about 10 to 15 people) of the target audience that is asked detailed questions about what the viewers liked or did not like. With this information, the studio can add or drop a scene, modify the ending, change the musical score, or make other alterations. Once these changes are completed, the movie is released for a sneak preview. As mentioned earlier, audience members fill out preview cards that summarize their reactions to a film, its characters, and its stars. It is possible for the director to make limited changes in the film in response to this feedback, but it is usually too late to make wholesale changes.

>> **Motion Picture Audiences**

Average weekly attendance has been steady for about the past 20 years (see Figure 9–2). Attendance, however, is nowhere near the levels of the 1930s and 1940s, when film was in its heyday.

The movie audience is a young audience. One out of two moviegoers is under 30. Teenagers are a significant part of the movie audience. Although teens make up only 20 percent of the population, they make up nearly 30 percent of the film audience. The movie audience has changed in recent years. Older fans are now more likely to go out to a theater than they were five years ago. The average U.S. resident attends about five movies a year.

Frequent moviegoers (those who see at least 12 films a year) account for 77 percent of all film admissions. These frequent fans are generally single, within the 16-to-20 age group (going to the movies continues to be a popular dating activity; only 6 percent of the audience goes to a movie alone), more educated, from middle-class families, and from urban areas.

The audience for movies is largest in July and August and smallest in May. The worst two weeks of the year for moviegoing are the first two weeks in December, when attendance drops 30 to 50 percent.

FIGURE 9–2

Average Weekly Film Attendance in the United States

Motion Picture Association of America. Used by permission

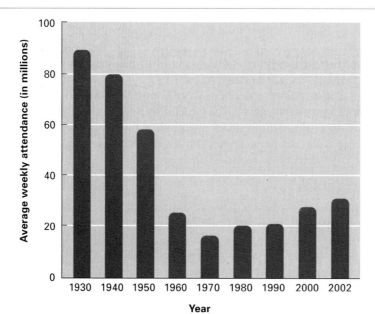

CABLE AND HOME VIDEO: THE HOLLYWOOD CONNECTION

Home video has become Hollywood's biggest revenue source. More than six million Americans rent a video on an average day, about twice as many as go to a movie theater. In 2002, combined income from the sale and rental of DVDs and videocassettes topped the $20 billion mark, more than double the amount taken in at U.S. box offices. Much of the rise in revenue is due to the increasing popularity of DVD players. When they first hit the market in 1997, DVD players cost around $800. In 2003, some were selling for less than $60. This drop in price spurred sales: More than 25,000 units were sold in 2002, quadruple the number sold in 1999. More than 40 percent of U.S. homes now have DVD players. Experts predict that the DVD player will eventually make the VCR obsolete.

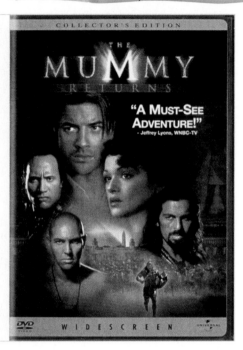

DVDs are reshaping the home-video industry. The DVD of *The Mummy Returns* brought in more than $15 million in DVD rental income.

The home video market, like the theatrical market, is driven by big hits. Movies that were popular on the big screen are almost invariably popular on the home screen. *Spider-Man,* for example, racked up $145 million in DVD sales in just its first week in home video release. At the other end of the continuum, some films that are total box office bombs do better in the home market. *Battlefield Earth,* a flop in theaters, made $20 million in rentals.

Moreover, the DVD is shrinking the amount of time between the release of a movie in theaters and its appearance on disc. Historically, there was a six-month gap between theatrical release and entry into the home video market. That interval has shrunk to just three months thanks to better duplication and distribution facilities that make DVDs easier to manufacture and deliver to retail shelves. In addition, more films are opening on larger numbers of screens, saturating the market much more quickly than before. The shorter interval helps movie studios take advantage of the movie advertising campaigns that are still fresh in consumers' minds.

Pay-per-view (PPV) television provides another revenue stream for movie companies. More than 30 million homes are equipped with PPV, and the number is growing steadily. In addition, the number of channels available on cable and satellite systems is increasing, and many of these new channels are devoted to PPV. Finally, Hollywood gets income from licensing its movies to premium cable channels, such as Home Box Office and Showtime, in addition to receiving money from selling the rights to movies to traditional over-the-air broadcasters. Given these numerous video aftermarkets, it is no surprise that TV generates more revenue for the movie industry than does the box office.

One of the striking figures about the DVD format is that sales of DVDs generate about three times as much revenue as rentals. Tape sales and tape rentals run about equal. Why do people rent tapes but prefer to buy DVDs?

The first reason is that, when people first buy a DVD player, they generally purchase several DVDs to go along with it, usually some of their movie favorites. As long as sales of DVD players continue to rise, so will DVD sales.

A second reason is economic. Taking a family of four to the theater to see *Spider-Man* would cost around $30. The DVD sells for around $18, and the family can watch it as many times as they like without worrying about late fees.

Third, DVDs come with extra features, such as the director's commentary, alternate endings, extra scenes, and interviews with actors. Some movies, such as *Lord of the Rings:*

The Fellowship of the Ring, are released on DVD in longer versions. The rental window might not allow consumers enough time to watch everything on the disc.

Fourth, DVDs are arranged in chapters, making it much easier to find a favorite scene or two. People who buy can watch their favorite scenes again and again without worrying about the rental time clock ticking away.

Finally, consumers are turning to the DVD format to build home film libraries. The slender DVD boxes are easier to store than large and bulky VHS tapes. In addition, many classic films (such as the *Godfather* trilogy) are being released on DVD in special boxed sets, to appeal to collectors.

All of this does not bode well for the VCR or VHS tapes. Many experts predict that the VCR will go the way of the typewriter and the phonograph.

C A R E E R
O U T L O O K

 ## THE FILM INDUSTRY

A young person who has actual experience in films and filmmaking will probably enjoy more success in finding a job. How do you get this experience? In general, there are two ways: (1) taking college courses that deal with film and (2) making your own films.

About 750 colleges and universities now offer courses in film, 227 offer bachelor's degrees, and many offer graduate degrees. The advantages of a university major in film are substantial. In the first place, it provides the student with an opportunity to practice with technical equipment: lights, meters, editing machines, cameras, and so forth. Second, students can take courses in film aesthetics and film history and from these courses can learn how to make their own films by observing how others have made films. Third, students can through such programs take courses in other areas that relate to film, such as art, literature, history, music, and photography. Finally, during the course of his or her studies, a student may have the opportunity to make a film as a final classroom project. This finished film can be shown to potential employers as a sample of the student's capability.

The other approach to gaining experience is to become an independent filmmaker. This method is valuable because it allows a person to gain knowledge of every aspect of filmmaking. Of course, this approach requires that an individual have some money to invest in basic film equipment and the time necessary to devote to the film.

>> **Entry-Level Positions**

Once a person has some experience, the next step is to find an entry-level job. This requires securing a job interview—not an easy task. The common technique of mailing a résumé to a potential employer seldom works in the film industry.

There are three ways to overcome this hurdle. The first is to know somebody. As is the case in most industries, if you have a friend or a friend of a friend in the industry, getting a job interview is less difficult.

The second way is to get yourself noticed. A newcomer accomplishes this by seeking out internships or training programs with production companies. The American Film Institute's *Guide to College Courses in Film and Television* lists such opportunities. Many times, help in finding out about and applying for internships can be secured from teachers or placement offices. Once you have gained entry into an organization, you will have better success in arranging an interview. Another way to get yourself noticed is to enter the many student film festivals. A newcomer who wins one or more awards at these festivals may find getting through the door into the film industry a little easier.

The third way is to be persistent. This is also the hardest way. Make a list of those companies where you wish to work and call on them personally. Take to them a one-page summary of your education and special skills. If you have a completed film that is available for viewing, indicate so in your summary. Do not be discouraged if your first visit is fruitless. Keep checking back. As is the case in television, a film newcomer should be prepared to take practically any job as a starter. Once you are inside the company, your path to more creative and challenging positions is easier to follow.

>> Upward Mobility

Select your first job with an eye toward future advancement. Some routes are best if your ultimate goal is producing and directing. Other avenues are better if top management is your ultimate goal. One early choice an aspiring filmmaker must make is the choice between editing and directing. Although there are some exceptions, most people who start in the editing room stay there, advancing ultimately to the post of supervising film editor. Those interested in producing and directing should begin as production assistants and progress to assistant directors, director, and perhaps producer. To reach high-level management, a person might consider breaking in with the distribution or sales division.

MAIN POINTS

- The motion picture developed in the late 19th century. After being a main attraction in nickelodeons, films moved into bigger theaters, and movie stars quickly became the most important part of the new industry. Sound came to the movies in the mid-1920s.

- Big movie studios dominated the industry until the late 1940s, when a court decision weakened their power. Television captured much of the film audience in the 1950s. By the end of the 1960s, however, Hollywood had adapted to television and was an active producer of TV shows. A major trend in modern movies is the rise of big-budget movies.

- The transition to digital moviemaking may transform the film industry.

- The movie industry consists of production, distribution, and exhibition facets. Large conglomerates control the business. Producing a motion picture starts from a concept, proceeds to the production stage, and ends with the postproduction stage.

- Movie revenues have shown small but steady growth over the past 10 years. Videocassette sales and rentals and foreign box-office receipts are important sources of movie income.

- Movie audiences are getting older, but a significant part of the audience is still the 30-and-under age group.

- Motion picture studios are now using the Internet to promote their products.

QUESTIONS FOR REVIEW

1. What are the defining features of motion pictures?
2. What caused the rise and fall of the Motion Picture Patents Company?
3. How did the film industry react to TV?
4. What are the three main segments of the motion picture industry?
5. What are the various ways films are financed?

QUESTIONS FOR CRITICAL THINKING

1. Suppose the movie industry had never moved to Hollywood, staying instead on the East Coast. How might films be different?
2. What are the potential advantages and disadvantages of big corporations controlling motion picture production?
3. Do filmmakers have an obligation to be socially responsible for what they present on the screen? Why or why not?
4. Will any of the antipiracy tactics adopted by the film industry be effective in stopping the illegal copying and distribution of films? Why? Why not?
5. Someone once said that Hollywood producers don't make films; they make deals. Comment on the validity of this statement and its implications.

KEY TERMS

phi phenomenon (p. 223)
persistence of vision (p. 223)
Kinetoscope (p. 223)
Motion Picture Patents Company (MPPC) (p. 226)
block booking (p. 228)
double features (p. 229)
digital videodisk (DVD) (p. 233)
pickup (p. 244)
limited partnership (p. 244)
joint venture (p. 244)
sliding scale (p. 245)
Variety (p. 246)
focus group (p. 247)
pay-per-view (PPV) (p. 249)

INTERNET RESOURCES

Online Learning Center

At the Online Learning Center home page, www.mhhe.com/dominick8, *select* Student Center *and then* Chapter 9.

1. Use the Learning Objectives, Chapter Outline, Main Points, and Time Line sections to review this chapter.
2. Test your knowledge of the chapter using the multiple choice, crossword puzzle, and flashcard features of the site.
3. Expand your knowledge of concepts and topics discussed in the chapter by going to *Suggestions for Further Reading* and *Internet Exercises*.

PowerWeb

At the Mass Communication home page of PowerWeb, www.dushkin.com/powerweb, *log in and select* Mass Communication *as your title. On the next screen, select* Topics *and then quick jump to Movies. Read Article 50, "The Disc That Saved Hollywood." Then consider the following questions:*

1. From what exactly did the disc save Hollywood?
2. Is a DVD the same as a CD? Explain.
3. What factors caused the rapid rise in popularity of DVDs?

Surfing the Internet

These represent a variety of movie theme sites.

www.imdb.com

The Internet Movie Database. Everything you ever wanted to know about movies. Has information about stars, cast, plot, and box-office performance for just about every movie.

www.mgm.com

MGM Studio's website. View movie trailers for coming attractions, download movie music, see which MGM films are in theaters, and even check out MGM's corporate structure. Comes complete with the MGM lion's roar.

www.mpaa.org

The official website of the Motion Picture Association of America. Contains industry statistics and latest news releases. Has an extensive section that deals with copyright issues.

www.mrcranky.com

An offbeat review page featuring a reviewer who has high standards and a caustic style. Mr. Cranky rates movies by assigning a number of bombs. For example, four bombs means "As good as a poke in the eye with a sharp stick."

www.variety.com

Website of the trade paper that is the bible of the entertainment industry. Includes latest industry news, global box-office charts, film reviews, and a section called a "slanguage dictionary," which translates *Variety's* showbiz language into English. For example, "to ankle" means to walk away from a job; a "sprocket opera" is a film festival.

www.videobusiness.com

Find out the latest trends in home video, satellites, and video-on-demand. Access is free but you have to register.

10

TELEVISION

Walk around the display floor of any big electronics retailer on a fall Sunday afternoon and you are likely to spot a crowd gathered around the television section watching a pro football game on dozens of different TV sets. Starting with the 2003–2004 season, however, you are apt to spot something different. Most of the crowd will be gravitating toward new model TV sets that show the action in super-sharp high definition. **High Definition Television (HDTV)** is one of the technological advances made possible by the shift to digital television. HDTV boasts five times the picture quality of traditional analog TV. It has been around for several years, but it is likely to take off in the near future.

A couple of years ago the first reaction of consumers upon checking out an HDTV set would not have been "Wow, what a picture!" but "Wow, that's really expensive." Prices, however, have dropped 50 percent in the last three years. More and more programming, such as NFL football, the Stanley Cup

CSI is one of a growing number of shows broadcast in HDTV.

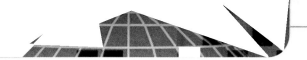

Championships, and some top-rated network programs, is being presented in the HDTV format. Most importantly, more people are finding out about it and want it. When Cox Cable announced plans to offer HDTV in Las Vegas, the next morning there was a line outside their office door waiting to sign up.

HDTV, of course, still faces some hurdles. The sets are still more expensive than traditional TVs, around $1,500 for a basic model. Plus there is a confusing array of formats: HDTV capable, HDTV ready, built-in tuners, set-top converters, and so on. Then a consumer has to choose among projection sets, direct view sets, plasma sets, and liquid crystal displays. Finally, it is a challenge to get an HDTV signal. Some consumers have put up 1950s-style rooftop antennas to get broadcast HDTV. Not many cable systems carry HDTV channels. If you have a satellite, you need a special dish to pick them up.

Despite these obstacles, it is likely that there is an HDTV set somewhere in your future. But we are getting ahead of ourselves. Before we predict TV's future, let us take a look at the past.

HISTORY

HDTV's crisp, clear images are in sharp contrast to the blurry pictures produced by early experiments with television. The two men who developed television in the United States could not have been more different. At the age of 16, Philo Farnsworth diagrammed his idea for a television system on the chalkboard in front of his somewhat amazed high school teacher. Farnsworth, an individualistic and lone-wolf inventor, worked at developing his new device, which he called an *image dissector,* and eventually patented it in 1930. In contrast, Vladimir Zworykin was an organization man, working first with Westinghouse and then with RCA. By 1928, he had perfected a primitive camera tube, the iconoscope.

Picture quality of the early television systems was poor, but technical developments during the 1930s improved performance. RCA, with Zworykin's help and with a patent arrangement that permitted it to use Farnsworth's invention, set out to develop TV's commercial potential. NBC, owned by RCA, gave the first public demonstration of television at the 1939 World's Fair.

The initial public response to TV was lukewarm. Sets were expensive and there were not many programs for people to watch. Even early TV actors were somewhat skeptical about the future of the new medium. They had to wear green makeup to look normal for the TV camera and swallow salt tablets because the intense heat of the lights necessary for TV made them perspire constantly.

World War II interrupted TV's development. When peace returned in 1945, new technology that had been perfected during the war greatly improved TV reception and the working conditions of the performers. New TV cameras required much less light. TV screens were bigger. There were more programs available, and stations were being linked into networks. All the signs pointed to big things for TV. In 1945, there were only eight TV stations and 8,000 homes with TV in the entire United States. Ten years later, there were nearly a hundred stations, and 35 million households, about 67 percent of the country, had TV.

TV's rapid success caught the industry and the FCC off guard. Unless technical standards were worked out, the TV spectrum was in danger of becoming overcrowded and riddled with interference just as had happened with radio 30 years earlier. To guard against this possibility, the FCC imposed a freeze on all new applications for TV stations. The freeze, which went into effect in 1948, would last for four years while the FCC gathered information from engineers and technical experts. When the freeze was lifted in 1952, the FCC had established that 12 VHF and 70 UHF channels (see page 267) were to be devoted to TV. In addition, the commission drew up a list that allocated television channels to the various communities in the United States and specified other rules to minimize interference. Also, thanks largely to the efforts of Frieda Hennock, the first woman to serve on the commission, TV channels were set aside for educational use.

>> The 1950s: Networks, Tape, UHF, and Color

The early television industry was modeled after radio. Local stations served their communities and, in turn, might be affiliated with networks. There were four TV networks during this time period: CBS, NBC, ABC, and DuMont, a smaller network that went out of business in 1956. Also much like early radio networks, TV networks quickly became the primary programming sources for their affiliates. NBC and CBS were usually the most popular networks, with ABC trailing behind. Most early network programs were game shows, sports events, and interviews, with a few comedies and dramas interspersed throughout the schedule.

Most programs were broadcast live from New York or were filmed in California. Live programs, of course, could not be repeated and often had to be performed over again for the West Coast. In 1956, the Ampex Corporation developed videotape, a cheap and efficient way of storing TV programs. By the beginning of the 1960s, most of TV's live programming had switched to tape.

After the FCC-imposed freeze ended, TV stations and TV sets multiplied rapidly. The new UHF channels, however, were not doing well. Few sets equipped with UHF receivers were made during the 1950s. The UHF stations had smaller coverage areas than the VHF stations, and most advertising dollars went to VHF stations. As a result, UHF TV, much like FM radio, started off at a disadvantage.

Color television was introduced during the 1950s. Led by NBC (RCA, the parent company, was manufacturing color TV sets), the networks were broadcasting about two to three hours of color programming per day by 1960.

>> The Golden Age of Television

Many broadcast historians refer to the 1950s as the golden age of TV. Many shows aired during that decade became extremely popular. *Toast of the Town*, hosted by Ed Sullivan, is still regarded as the best example of the variety series.

Mr. Television, Milton Berle, dressed in one of the costumes that were his trademark on *The Texaco Star Theater*.

Texaco Star Theater, starring ex-vaudevillian Milton Berle, prompted many people to buy TV sets just to see what wacky stunts Berle would pull off on his next program.

Live prestige drama was also in prime time. Programs such as *Studio One* featured plays by Rod Serling, Gore Vidal, and Reginald Rose. Broadway stars such as Rex Harrison and Tallulah Bankhead performed in live TV drama. The growing popularity of videotape, however, put an end to these live productions.

By the end of the 1950s, a new genre, the adult Western, in which character and motivation overshadowed gunfights, dominated TV. By 1959, there were 26 Westerns in prime time, including *Gunsmoke, The Life and Legend of Wyatt Earp,* and *Wagon Train.*

>> Coming of Age: Television in the 1960s

By the early 1960s, TV had lost its novelty and became just another part of everyday life. The number of TV stations continued to increase, and by the close of the decade, more than 95 percent of all American households owned at least one TV.

Television journalism came of age during the 1960s. NBC and CBS expanded their nightly newscasts from 15 to 30 minutes in 1963, and ABC followed suit shortly thereafter. In November of that year, TV journalism earned praise for its professionalism during its coverage of the assassination and funeral of President John F. Kennedy. The networks also covered the Civil Rights movement and the growing social unrest across the country. Perhaps the most exciting moment for television news came in 1969 with its live coverage of Neil Armstrong's historic walk on the moon.

Noncommercial broadcasting also evolved during the 1960s. About 69 educational stations were broadcasting by 1965. A report issued by the Carnegie Commission proposed that Congress establish a Corporation for Public Broadcasting. The commission's recommendations were incorporated into the **Public Broadcasting Act of 1967,** which set up the Public Broadcasting Service.

The Beverly Hillbillies was the most popular of the "bucolic" situation comedies. It was the number-one show during the 1961–1962 TV season and spent nine years on the air.

Another segment of the video industry was also experiencing growth during this time period—cable television. We will discuss the history of cable TV later in the chapter.

Television programs popular in the early 1960s included a number of rural comedies, such as *The Beverly Hillbillies* and *Green Acres.* After the Kennedy assassination, however, fantasy and escapist programs dominated prime time. In 1964, for example, some of the shows that premiered included *Bewitched* (about a friendly witch), *My Favorite Martian* (about a friendly Martian), and *My Mother the Car* (self-explanatory).

>> The 1970s: Growing Public Concern

As the 1970s began, public concern over the impact of television programming was growing. A panel of scientists set up by the Surgeon General's office to investigate the impact of exposure to TV violence suggested that TV violence was related in a modest way to aggressive behavior in some young children. We'll explore this topic further in Chapter 18.

The early 1970s were also characterized by the growth of citizen group involvement in Federal Communications Commission (FCC) decisions. Groups such as Action for Children's Television and the Office of Communication of the United Church of Christ and coalitions of minority groups became influential in shaping broadcasting policy.

The three networks continued to dominate the industry during the early to mid-1970s, but by the end of the decade, they were beginning to feel the competition from the growing cable industry. Friction between the traditional over-the-air broadcasters and the cable companies continues today.

The biggest trend in television programming during the early 1970s was the growth of law-and-order programs, such as *The FBI, Charlie's Angels,* and *Mannix.* By the middle of the decade, these shows were replaced by a number of adult situation comedies, shows that dealt with more mature themes. *All in the Family, M*A*S*H,* and *Sanford and Son* typified this trend. By the end of the decade, prime-time soap operas, such as *Dallas* and *Dynasty,* topped the ratings.

>> The 1980s and 1990s: Increased Competition

The biggest trends in the TV industry in the 1980s and 1990s were the continuing erosion of the three big networks' audiences and the increased competition from new networks and cable channels. In the early 1970s the three networks routinely pulled down about 90 percent of the prime-time audience. By the late 1990s, their share had dropped to less than 60 percent. In addition, a fourth network, the Fox

Live TV coverage of the first man landing on the moon in 1969 reached hundreds of millions of viewers.

Broadcasting Company, owned by Rupert Murdoch's News Corporation, started broadcasting in 1987. In the early 1990s, two other networks started up: the United Paramount Network (UPN) and the Warner Broadcasting Network (the WB). Both began with limited schedules but had plans to expand their offerings.

In August 1995, the world of network broadcasting was shaken by two megadeals: The Walt Disney Company acquired CapCities/ABC for $19 billion. The ink was barely dry on that deal when Westinghouse disclosed it was buying CBS for $5.4 billion.

>> ## Cable's Continued Growth

Cable reached more than 68 percent of the population by 2000. As cable systems increased their capacity, new cable programming services rushed to fill the new channels. By 2000, there were six national pay-per-view services, six premium services, including HBO and Showtime, and more than 75 cable networks, including the Sci Fi Channel, Animal Planet, and the Outdoor Channel. Many cable systems were providing more than 100 channels of television to their subscribers. Some new cable networks were having trouble because there was no room left on local systems to carry them. The growing popularity of cable channels further eroded the audiences of the traditional TV networks.

Advertising revenue also grew, topping the $11 billion mark in 1999. By the turn of the century, it was obvious that the cable industry was a full-fledged competitor of traditional broadcasting.

>> ## Zapping, Zipping, Grazing, and DBS

A development that had significant impact on both traditional TV and the cable industry was the spectacular growth of VCRs. Fewer than 5 percent of households had VCRs in 1982. By 2000, that figure was 90 percent. In fact, the VCR has been adopted faster than any other appliance except television. The effects of the VCR abound.

First, the renting of movies on cassettes has become a multibillion-dollar business, with motion picture studios depending on cassettes for a large part of their revenue.

Second, the VCR encourages **time shifting,** playing back programs at times other than when they were aired. Although this has increased total audience by allowing people who might not otherwise view a program to do so, it has caused some new problems for advertisers. Some viewers have special machines that *zap* commercials: The VCR pauses while the commercial is aired and then starts up again when the program is on. Also, when viewers play back programs, many fast-forward, or *zip,* their way through the ads.

Finally, the proliferation of the handheld remote-control device has also caused problems for advertisers and programmers. Remote units are in two-thirds of all households and have encouraged the tendency toward *grazing,* rapidly scanning all the channels during a commercial or dull spot in a program in search of greener pastures.

After a slow start, direct broadcast by satellite (DBS) got a big boost in 1994 when two companies, DirecTV and United States Satellite Broadcasting (USSB), offered subscribers about 150 channels of programming beamed directly to their homes via a small (18-inch diameter) receiver.

On the legal side, the biggest development was the Telecommunications Act of 1996, discussed in Chapter 16, which introduced program ratings and the V-chip,

R. E. "Ted" Turner inherited his family's outdoor advertising company in 1963, when he was 24. The Atlanta-based business was in poor economic shape, but the young Turner managed to turn it around. Six years later Turner learned that a financially troubled UHF television station was for sale. Disregarding the fact that the station's signal was so weak that he could not pick it up on his own home TV set, Turner bought the station, renamed it WTCG, and began to advertise it on his unused billboards around Atlanta. With a skillful programming mix of popular reruns and old movies, the station eventually became one of the few UHF stations in the country at the time to turn a profit. Turner, however, was not content with just turning the station around. He had much bigger plans for it.

One day in 1976 at a meeting of the station's managers, Turner placed a beat-up model of the RCA Satcom I satellite on the table and proclaimed that WTCG would soon be competing with CBS, NBC, and ABC. Turner had decided that he would use the new communication satellites to beam WTCG to cable systems all over the country, making it a national network. Not surprisingly, his managers were incredulous. Almost everybody dismissed Turner's idea as totally impractical.

There were many reasons this bold move would not work. Cable TV had not yet caught on; it was available in only 16 percent of the country, mostly in rural areas. Cable systems relied on terrestrial microwave signals; not many were equipped to receive satellite feeds. The FCC had a rule against leapfrogging that prohibited cable systems from importing signals from distant cities unless they also took the signals of stations closer to their market. Additionally, FCC regulations permitted cable systems to use only expensive 10-meter satellite dishes, which most systems could not afford. Undaunted, Turner pitched his idea to big cable operators. They were not impressed.

As fate would have it, however, two weeks later, the FCC dropped its leapfrogging rules and permitted stations to use smaller and cheaper satellite dishes. All of a sudden, Turner's idea did not seem so far-fetched after all. In December, Turner renamed his station WTBS and started distributing it by satellite, thus creating the first superstation.

WTBS caught on slowly. When it first went on the satellite, the station was received by a grand total of four cable systems. Turner helped its fortunes by purchasing the Atlanta Braves baseball team and making their games available on WTBS. The new superstation continued to grow in popularity, eventually reaching 74 million homes. The success of WTBS inspired the creation of other cable networks and totally changed the cable TV industry. Turner proved that people would subscribe to cable not just to get good reception, but also to get programming.

Turner had other ideas. He had encouraged cable systems to carry WTBS by promising them that he would also provide them with additional cable networks. In 1980, he launched the first of those networks—CNN. Cable operators were lukewarm toward the new project. Most refused to provide money to cover start-up costs. Turner invested $21 million in the new venture, which was immediately derided by competitors for its bargain-basement approach to news. Critics labeled CNN the *Chicken Noodle Network*.

CNN started off losing money, but Turner kept the network alive with the profits from WTBS. Finally, CNN went into the black in 1985. Six years later, during the Gulf War, CNN scooped the other networks by having reporters on the scene in Baghdad when the war broke out. CNN's success spawned several 24-hour news service competitors, including MSNBC and Fox News Channel.

Several other Turner decisions have also paid off. In 1986, he paid more than a billion dollars for the MGM/United Artists film library. Turner used the films to help launch two other cable networks—Turner Network Television and Turner Classic Movies. Turner also bought the Hanna Barbera animation studio and started the Cartoon Network.

However, some of Turner's ventures did not work out so well. After Time Warner merged with AOL, Turner became a vice chairman of the new company. The merger was a disappointment, and AOL Time Warner's stock suffered a huge drop in value. Turner lost millions as a result. In 2003, Turner resigned his position with the company.

Turner has an interest in philanthropy. His United Nations Foundation grants money to organizations that are interested in population control and the environment. His Turner Foundation concentrates on improving life in the United States. The decline in AOL Time Warner's stock, unfortunately, has meant a cutback in funding for both organizations.

Turner has made some good decisions and some that have not been successful. Regardless, his decisions have had an enormous impact on television and have been key contributors to the design of the modern TV industry landscape.

while encouraging competition between cable and phone companies and easing ownership restrictions on TV stations.

TV programming during the mid-1980s marked the return of warm, family-oriented comedies, such as *The Cosby Show* and *Family Ties*. One reason for the popularity of these shows was economic. Family sitcoms did well in the syndication aftermarket (more on syndication later). The biggest programming trend of the early to mid-1990s was the growth of prime-time newsmagazines, such as *60 Minutes, 20/20,* and *Dateline NBC.* At the turn of the century, the success of reality programs, such as *Survivor* and *Big Brother,* surprised many television executives. HBO also enjoyed success with dramatic series such as *The Sopranos* and *Sex and the City.*

 ## CONTEMPORARY TELEVISION

The first years of the new century saw developments in programming, regulation, and technology. For the first time ever during prime time, more people were tuned to cable channels than to the big four broadcast networks. Reality programs continued to proliferate, comprising seven hours of the broadcast networks' prime-time schedule in 2003–2004.

On the regulatory front, the FCC announced changes in its rules regarding ownership of TV stations. One proposed rule increased the national percentage of households reached by stations owned by one organization from 35 percent to 45 percent. Almost immediately, opponents charged that such a move would lead to dangerous ownership concentration in the industry and lobbied against it. Responding to growing anticonsolidation pressure, members of Congress proposed legislation to roll back the cap to its original 35 percent. The FCC vowed to stick to the 45 percent mark. As of this writing, the controversy has not been resolved.

In the technology area, in addition to the developments with HDTV, super-thin television sets that used newly developed plasma or liquid crystal display technology emerged. Their high price tags resulted in limited success. In addition, the number of households receiving their TV from satellites continued to grow, topping the 18 million mark in 2002, an increase of nearly 15 percent over 2001.

S O U N D B Y T E

Digital Makeup?

HDTV creates new challenges for performers and makeup artists. Unlike conventional TV whose lower resolution hides many problems, the super-clear HDTV picture shows every line, blemish, and imperfection on a person's face. What is a performer to do?

Luckily for them, a new makeup technique called *airbrushing* is available. An airbrush pen connected to a small compressor shoots tiny dots or pixels of makeup onto the skin, where it dries to a waterproof finish. The result is that performers are able to put their best face forward.

 ## TELEVISION IN THE DIGITAL AGE

The TV pictures on your set in 2004 are probably using the same technology that was used in 1943—the analog method. A beam of electrons scans an image and creates an electrical signal. At the receiving end, the signal is converted back into a beam of electrons that bombards a fluorescent screen, creating an image. With **digital television (DTV),** the image is still scanned, but the signal is a binary one, assigning bits of code to each pixel on a TV screen that recreates the original image.

Digital TV offers many advantages. Digital pictures are clearer, and the sound quality is better. Digital TV sets also come in a wide-screen format: Instead of employing the 3:4 ratio of regular TV screens, DTVs will be more rectangular and look more like movie screens. Moreover, DTV has more potential than the old analog system. As mentioned at the beginning of the chapter, a broadcaster can use most of the digital channel to broadcast HDTV.

A broadcaster can also subdivide the digital channel and offer several lower-definition programs in the same space. For example, a local TV station might broadcast HDTV during prime time but at other times of the day switch to lower-definition signals and offer four different programs on its single channel. When a viewer tunes in the channel, he or she will see a screen with four small windows. The viewer might be able to choose among the network feed of a soap opera, a local news channel, a weather forecast, and a syndicated show. Moreover, digital TV can send and receive e-mail, provide access to the Internet, and transmit data.

Federal law mandated that all full-power TV stations convert to DTV by the start of 2003. More than 50 percent of broadcast stations, however, failed to meet this deadline and filed for an extension. Nonetheless, by the end of 2003 there were nearly a thousand stations broadcasting a digital signal. Broadcasters are required to broadcast programs in both analog and digital formats until 2007. At that time, if more than 85 percent of viewers in a market can receive the new digital signals, the old analog transmitters will be shut down. If fewer than 85 percent can receive digital, the stations will continue to transmit both analog and digital signals until that figure is reached. Although the digital standards apply only to traditional over-the-air broadcasters, cable companies and satellite systems will support them as well.

The move to digital got a boost in late 2002 when cable systems and electronics companies reached agreement on a technical standard for a "plug and play" connection that would enable most DTV sets to connect directly to a digital cable outlet without a set-top converter. The FCC also helped move the transition along when it ordered that beginning in 2007 all new TV sets have a DTV tuner.

As mentioned earlier, HDTV growth continues to be slow, but there are signs that things may be changing. Set prices keep declining, and more content is being shown in HDTV format. One industry analyst predicts that by 2008 about 15 to 20 percent of U.S. households will be watching HDTV on their digital TV sets.

One thing is certain. Buying a new TV set in the next couple of years will be an interesting if not confusing experience.

MEDIA TALK

The Future of TV

CD 2, Track 16, 5:28 minutes
The technological advances in TV are coming faster and faster. This clip contains demonstrations of those advances and a discussion of their implications. Will interactive TV catch on? Why or why not? What implications do these developments have for TV advertising? How about for programming?

DEFINING FEATURES OF TELEVISION

Like radio, TV is a universal medium. About 99 percent of the homes in the United States have at least one working TV set. In fact, most homes have more than one. Although not quite as portable as radios, miniature TV sets make it possible to take TV anywhere.

Television has become the dominant medium for news and entertainment for Americans. Surveys have consistently revealed that most people choose television as their main source of news. In addition, in the average American household, the TV set is on for about seven hours every day. Prime-time television series may draw an audience of 20 million households. In short, TV has become an important part of our society.

Further, TV, especially network television, is an expensive business. It costs the production company about $1.5 million to produce one episode of a typical one-hour prime-time series. Most series produce about 22 original episodes a year. A little math reveals that the total cost for one season of one prime-time hour for one network is about $33 million. Some more math discloses that the total tab for prime-

Contributed by Kevin Williams
Research Associate, Dowden Center for
New Media Studies, University of Georgia

The concept of Interactive Television seems always to be just around the corner and out of reach, but in reality this new technology may be closer than we think. The first problem of Interactive Television that we must grapple with is how to form a true definition of Interactive Television. Most researchers in this field agree that there is no easy definition and have spent small parts of their careers conceptualizing an encompassing definition. That being said, I would attempt to define it as a form of television that takes advantage of the digital transmission of content (via digital cable, digital satellite, or even over the air) by allowing the viewer to gain extra information from or "interact" with the current programming.

In short, what do you want television to do for you? Advertisers might argue that Interactive Television should allow the viewer to push a button and instantly order whatever product is being pitched on the television at that particular moment. Perhaps while watching *Friends,* a viewer could click on a button on a remote and order the shirt that Chandler is wearing. Television producers may argue that the viewer should be able to access extra information, much like that now offered on DVDs, when viewing favorite programs. Network programmers might want you to be able to search for programs by key word, such as *actor/actress, director, title,* or *genre.*

Some technologies that have been deployed or are currently being developed will serve as a foundation on which to build future interactive capabilities. Perhaps the most overlooked prerequisite to Interactive Television is the Electronic Programming Guide (EPG). Not long ago, viewers had to read *TV Guide* or newspaper "television books" to find out what was showing on TV throughout the week. On screen, viewers may have been able to consult a guide that constantly scrolled, telling what was on television in the next hour or two.

Unfortunately, if the scroll was currently showing what was on channel 2 and you were interested in channel 130, you would have to wait to get your information. EPGs are provided with most digital and cable services today so that the viewer can instantly access programming information.

One of the most promising technologies so far deployed is the personal video recorder (PVR), also known as *digital video recorders* (DVRs). Consumers know these technologies more commonly by their brand names: TiVo or ReplayTV. Some satellite and cable providers have included PVR capabilities in their receiver and converter boxes. PVRs give the user the ability to pause, rewind, and even slow motion or repeat live television. Nearly all of these machines also act as digital VCRs, using their own EPGs to search for and record upcoming shows that the viewer has chosen. Some PVRs go one step further and suggest programs that a viewer may want to record, based on previous recording preferences. One may ask how this device differs from a VCR; both manufacturers and users proclaim that the PVR interface is much more user-friendly.

Media forecasters believe the use of these current technologies could drastically change the way we watch television. With a PVR, a viewer may watch programs whenever he or she chooses. With the multitude of channels available and the ease of searching for shows via EPGs, some forecasters speculate that viewers will not be as loyal to specific channels and will instead jump among channels more frequently to catch different shows (in essence, a highly informed version of channel surfing). Advertisers worry that viewers will use a PVR to fast-forward through commercials. One effect might be product placement or sponsorship of shows as a replacement for the typical 30-second commercial. With the ever-expanding convergence of media, it is not ridiculous to think that the television and computer will soon be fused into an "all-encompassing" box. Soon we may see the dreams of thousands of college students realized when they can order a pizza via their television.

time programming for the four major networks is more than $2 billion. Added to that is the cost of daytime programs and newscasts. TV advertising is also costly, averaging more than $100,000 for a 30-second spot in network prime time.

Finally, over the past several decades, the television industry has watched its audience fragment. Back in 1970, the major networks' share of the audience was about 90 percent. Today, the increase in cable networks, VCR usage, video games, and home video has cut that share in half. The fragmenting audience is most apparent in the cable industry, in which new cable channels are increasingly geared to a small, well-defined audience niche. And even those niche audiences are being divided up. There are two cable networks devoted to health programming, four specializing in women's programs, and five devoted to home and lifestyle topics.

ORGANIZATION OF THE BROADCAST TELEVISION INDUSTRY

The **commercial television** system consists of all those local stations whose income is derived from selling time on their facilities to advertisers. **Noncommercial television** consists of those stations whose income is derived from sources other than the sale of advertising time.

A local TV station is licensed by the Federal Communications Commission to provide TV service to a particular community. In the industry, these communities are customarily referred to as *markets*. There are 210 markets in the United States, ranging from the number-one market, New York City, with about 6.9 million homes, to number 210, Glendive, Montana, with about 4,000 homes. Some of these local TV stations enter into contractual agreements with TV networks. As of 2004, seven commercial networks in the United States supplied programs to local stations: the American Broadcasting Company (ABC), the Columbia Broadcasting System (CBS), the National Broadcasting Company (NBC), the Fox Broadcasting Company (FBC), United Paramount Network (UPN), the Warner Broadcasting Network (The WB), and Paxnet. The Public Broadcasting Service (PBS) serves as a network for noncommercial stations. A local station that signs a contract with one of the networks is an affiliate. ABC, CBS, and NBC have about 200 affiliates scattered across the country; Fox has slightly fewer; and UPN, WB, and Paxnet have still fewer. Local stations that do not have network affiliation are independents.

Much like the film industry, the TV industry is divided into three segments: (1) production, (2) distribution, and (3) exhibition. The production element is responsible for providing the programming that is ultimately viewed by the TV audience. The distribution function is handled by the TV networks, cable, and syndication companies. The exhibition of television programs—the element in the system that most people are most familiar with—is the responsibility of local TV stations.

>> Production

Pretend for a moment that you are the manager of a local TV station in your hometown. Your station must provide 24 hours of programming every day, or approximately 8,800 hours of programming each year. Where does one get all this programming? There are basically three sources:

A local TV news program in Miami. News is the most common form of production at a local TV station and also produces the most revenue.

1. local production,
2. syndicated programming, and
3. for some stations, network programs.

Local production consists of those programs that are produced in the local station's own studio or on location with the use of the station's equipment. The most common local productions are the station's daily newscasts, typically broadcast at noon, in the early evening, and in the late evening. These newscasts attract large audiences, which in turn attract advertisers. As a result, the local news accounts for a major proportion of the ad revenue that is generated by a local station. Not surprisingly, local stations devote a major share of their production budgets to their news shows. Other locally produced programming might consist of local sporting events, early morning interview programs, and public-affairs discussion shows. It would be difficult, however, for a local station to fill its entire schedule with locally produced programming. As a result, most stations turn to programming produced by other sources.

If the station is affiliated with a network (and most stations are), much of its programming problem is solved. Networks typically supply about 65 to 70 percent of the programming carried by their affiliates. Many of the programs supplied by the networks are produced by the networks themselves. News, sports, early-morning talk shows, and an increasing number of prime-time dramas and sitcoms are network productions. Independent production companies or the TV divisions of major motion picture studios supply other programs. Table 10–1 lists some programs and their production companies.

Many independent production companies sell their shows to syndication firms. King World Productions handles *Wheel of Fortune, Jeopardy, The Oprah Winfrey Show,* and *Inside Edition.* Programs that have already played on the networks (called *off-net series*) are also distributed by syndication companies. These programs usually air during the late afternoon or early evening, not in prime time. In addition, packages of movies, made up from some of the 23,000 films that have been released for TV, can be leased from syndication companies.

TABLE 10–1	Production company	Programs
Example of Production Companies and Their Programs for the 2003–2004 Season	*Networks*	
	ABC	*Monday Night Football, 20/20*
	CBS	*CSI, Cold Case*
	NBC	*Will and Grace, Coupling*
	Fox	*24, Arrested Development*
	Independents	
	Wolf Films	*Law and Order, Law and Order Criminal Intent*
	David E. Kelly Productions	*The Practice, The Brotherhood of Poland, N.H.*
	TV divisions of film companies	
	Paramount	*Frasier*
	Warner Brothers	*Friends, I'm with Her*

>> **Distribution**

The three main elements in the distribution segment of television are the broadcast networks, cable networks, and syndication companies. The network distributes programs to its affiliates by transmitting them by satellite. The station then transmits them to its viewers as they are received, or it videotapes them and presents them at a later time. The affiliation contract between a local station and the network is a complicated document. In simplified terms, the station agrees to carry the network's programs, and in return the network agrees to pay the station a certain amount of money for clearing its time so that the network programs can be seen. (Although it may seem contradictory that the network actually pays the station to carry the network's programming, remember that the network is using the local station's facilities to show the network's commercials.) The amount of money paid by the network varies by market size and is influenced by the competition. In general, each of the three older networks pays out about $150 million annually in affiliate compensation. The networks continue to examine their compensation arrangements, and it is likely that affiliates will be receiving less in the future. The network then sells time in its programs to advertisers seeking a national audience.

Cable networks beam their programs via microwaves to satellites where they are, in turn, downlinked to local cable systems. The local system then distributes the programming to its subscribers.

Syndication companies provide another kind of program distribution. These organizations lease taped or filmed programs to local television stations in each local market. Sometimes, as mentioned, the syndication company also produces the program, but more often it distributes programs produced by other firms. Local stations that purchase a syndicated program receive exclusive rights to show that program in their market (a situation complicated by cable TV systems that bring in distant stations). Usually a station buys a package of programs—

Inside a TV control room: The director is the man with glasses toward the upper part of the picture. It is his job to scan the monitors and choose the most appropriate shot. To his left in front of the large control panel, called the *switcher,* is the technical director, who actually pushes the buttons that put the cameras on the air.

perhaps as many as 120 episodes or more—and the contract specifies how many times each program can be repeated.

Syndication companies try to sell their shows in as many TV markets as possible. The greater the coverage of the show, the more appealing it is to national advertisers. Top-rated syndicated shows, such as *Wheel of Fortune* and *Jeopardy,* are seen in nearly all TV markets.

Syndication functions as an important aftermarket for prime-time TV shows. In fact, some prime-time series are produced at a deficit, sometimes $200,000 or more for each one-hour episode. Production companies gamble that they can make back this money in the syndication market. It is a risk, but if a show hits it big in syndication, it might earn half a billion dollars or more. To be attractive in the syndication market, however, a prime-time show must have enough back episodes stockpiled so that stations can run episodes for a long time without showing repeats. Since 100 seems to be the magic number, series usually have a big party to commemorate the production of their hundredth episode. Since only 22 or 24 new shows are produced each season, it is obvious that those series that last four or five years are the best bets for syndication success.

>> Exhibition

At the start of 2004, there were approximately 1,300 commercial TV stations and 380 noncommercial stations in the United States. Some TV stations are licensed to broadcast in the very-high–frequency (**VHF**) band of the electromagnetic spectrum; these stations occupy channels 2 through 13 on the TV set. Other stations broadcast in the ultra-high–frequency (**UHF**) part of the spectrum; these stations are found on channels 14 through 69. As noted earlier, VHF stations have a signal that covers greater distances than UHF stations. Consequently, VHF stations tend to be more desirable to own and operate. These differences will not be as important after the move to digital TV.

As suggested earlier, another important difference among stations concerns their affiliation with national networks. As of 2004, more than 80 percent of all commercial stations were affiliated with CBS, NBC, ABC, or Fox. The two new networks that started broadcasting in 1995, the United Paramount Network (UPN) and the Warner Broadcasting Network (The WB), started their services with significantly fewer stations than the 200 or so stations that are affiliated with each of the older nets. UPN now has 124 affiliates, and The WB has about 180.

Those stations not affiliated with networks are called **independents.** For many years, independents were hampered because most were UHF stations and had less coverage area than VHFs. The emergence of cable, however, gave UHF independents more of a competitive advantage, since unlike the situation with over-the-air signals, with cable both UHF and VHF stations have the same audience reach. Recently, most independent stations signed on with either UPN, WB, or Paxnet. "Pure" independents are now hard to find.

>> TV Online

Promoting their products is the main function of the online sites of TV organizations. Each of the networks maintains at least one website. CBS, for example, previews its nightly program lineup, including the guests on David Letterman's *The Late Show.*

Local stations are well represented on the Web. The website of WCBS-TV in New York, for example, features a weather report, traffic conditions, breaking news stories, and a guide to area cultural events and movies. Many local stations offer live video from their evening newscasts.

Major cable networks also are well represented on the Web. Maybe the most well-known is espn.go.com. CNN and the Discovery Channel also host popular websites, as does premium network HBO.

In addition, many sites are devoted to specific series or stars. Probably a hundred or more sites are devoted to *The Simpsons*. Fans of the 1960s series *Gilligan's Island* have their choice of several dozen sites where they can find (for whatever reason) the lyrics to the theme song, a guide to all 98 episodes, and a full-color cast picture.

OWNERSHIP IN THE TELEVISION INDUSTRY

As of 2000, all the major networks were under the control of large conglomerates:

- NBC Universal is owned by General Electric. In addition to its holdings in nonmedia areas, such as aerospace, aircraft engines, consumer products, and financial properties, GE has interests in TV stations; cable/satellite networks, including CNBC, MSNBC, and Court TV; and a movie studio.

- ABC is owned by the Walt Disney Company, which also owns theme parks, a professional hockey team, a cruise line, retail stores, and media holdings that include daily newspapers, magazines, film production companies, radio networks, record companies, cable networks, and TV stations.

- Fox is controlled by Rupert Murdoch's News Corporation, which owns a major film and TV production company, more than 20 TV stations, cable networks, satellite networks, a record company, newspapers, magazines, and a book publishing company.

- CBS merged with Viacom in 1999. The new corporation has holdings in radio, TV, home video, publishing, theme parks, cable, and motion pictures.

The two newer networks, WB and UPN, are also part of large organizations. WB is owned by the giant Time Warner conglomerate, and UPN is part of the Viacom organization.

At the station level, the Telecommunications Act of 1996 (see Chapter 16) allowed a person or organization to own an unlimited number of TV stations as long as the combined reach of the stations did not exceed 35 percent of the U.S. population. (As mentioned, the FCC announced plans to increase this cap to 45 percent, but the move met with considerable opposition.) By the end of 2003, big groups controlled most of the TV stations in the top 100 markets. Table 10–2 lists the top five group owners.

TABLE 10–2 **Top Five Owners of TV Stations** *Allowed by the FCC to exceed a 35 percent cap, pending review of ownership rules	Group	Percent of U.S. households reached (as calculated by the FCC)
	Viacom*	39.0
	Fox*	37.8
	NBC Universal	33.5
	Paxson	30.9
	Tribune Company	30.0

PRODUCING TELEVISION PROGRAMS

>> **Departments and Staff**

There are many different staffing arrangements in television stations. Some big city stations employ 300 to 400 people and may be divided into a dozen different departments. Small town stations may have 20 to 30 employees and only a few departments.

In one common arrangement, a station manager is ultimately responsible for all station activities. The rest of the station is organized into these departments:

- *Sales department:* Is responsible for selling time to local and national advertisers, scheduling ads, and billing clients.
- *Engineering:* Maintains technical equipment.
- *Production/programming:* Puts together locally produced programming; also acquires programming from outside sources and is responsible for scheduling.
- *News:* Is in charge of producing the station's regularly scheduled news programs.
- *Administration:* Consists of clerical, accounting, and personnel segments that help in the day-to-day running of the station.

At the network level, the divisions are somewhat more complicated. Although the major networks differ in their setups, all seem to have departments that perform the following functions:

1. *Sales:* Handling sale of network commercials and works with advertising agencies.
2. *Entertainment:* Working with producers to develop new programs for the network.
3. *Owned and operated stations:* Administering those stations owned by the networks.
4. *Affiliate relations:* A very important job in the new century; supervising all contracts with stations affiliated with the network (and generally trying to keep the affiliates happy).
5. *News:* Responsibility for all network news and public-affairs programs.
6. *Sports:* Responsibility for all sports programming.
7. *Standards:* Checking all network programs to make sure they do not violate the law or the network's own guidelines for appropriate content.
8. *Operations:* Handling the technical aspects of actually sending programs to affiliates.

>> **Getting TV Programs on the Air**

At the local level, the biggest effort at a TV station goes into the newscast. Almost every station has a studio that contains a set for one or two anchorpeople, a weather forecaster, and a sportscaster. The station's news director assigns stories to reporters and camera crews, who travel to the scene of a story and videotape a report. Back at the station, the newscast producer and news director are planning what stories to air and allotting time to each. In the meantime, the camera crews and reporters return; the reporters write copy and editors prepare videotape segments. When the final script is finished (this may be only a few minutes before airtime), it is given to a director, who is responsible for pulling everything together and putting the newscast on the air.

In addition to the news, the local station might also produce one or two interview programs. Some stations produce a "magazine" program consisting of segments videotaped on location by portable equipment and later edited into final form. Aside from these kinds of shows, most local stations do little other production.

Because they are responsible for filling the hours when the biggest audience is watching (called prime time, 8–11 P.M., Eastern Standard Time), the networks must pay special attention to cultivating new shows. For the moment, we will concentrate on how a prime-time series is produced.

Everything starts with an idea. Network executives receive hundreds of ideas every year; some come from independent producers, some from TV departments of motion picture companies, some from network employees, and a good many from amateurs hoping for a break. From this mass of ideas, the networks select perhaps 50 to 75, usually submitted by established producers or companies, for further attention. After examining plot outlines and background sketches of the leading characters for these 50 to 75 potential series, the networks trim the list once again. For those ideas that survive, the networks request a sample script and a list of possible stories that could be turned into scripts. If the idea still looks promising, the network and producer enter into a contract for a **pilot,** the first episode of a series. In a typical year, perhaps 25 pilots are ordered by each net. If the pilot show gains a respectable audience, the network may order five or six episodes produced and may place the program on its fall schedule. From the hundreds of ideas that are sent to the network, only a few ever make it to prime time.

The process does not stop with the fall season. If a program does well in the ratings, the network will order enough episodes for the rest of the season. If the show does not do well, it will be canceled and another show will replace it. Meanwhile, network executives are sifting through the hundreds of program ideas for the next season, and the cycle begins once again.

 ## ECONOMICS

The television industry has been profitable since 1950, and its total income has increased every year since 1971. In 2002, television advertising revenue amounted to $58 billion. The changing structure of the television industry, however, has had a significant economic impact on both local stations and the networks. We will explore more about this after we look at the traditional sources of television advertising revenue.

>> Commercial Time

Where did the $58 billion in revenue come from? It came from the sale of commercial time by networks, local stations, and cable systems to advertisers. A station, network, or cable system makes available a specified number of minutes per hour that will be offered for sale to advertisers. There are three different types of advertisers who buy time on TV:

1. national advertisers,
2. national spot advertisers, and
3. local advertisers.

Kweisi Mfume, president of the NAACP, speaking at his organization's national convention, criticized the four major TV networks for the lack of diversity in the new shows planned for the 1999–2000 season. He noted that none of the 26 series had a minority person in a leading or starring role. Mfume's criticism marked another chapter in the continuing controversy over the portrayals of minorities in prime time.

During the early years of TV, African American performers were difficult to find. When they did appear, it was usually in a menial or subservient role. In 1965, however, a young Bill Cosby costarred with Robert Culp in *I Spy* and paved the way for more substantial roles for African American performers. By the 1970s, several shows that featured black casts appeared in prime time—most were situation comedies, such as *The Jeffersons.* The number of African American performers increased slowly but steadily during the 1980s. For most of the 1990s, the proportion of black characters seen in prime-time TV was about the same as the percentage of African Americans in the general population. This increase, however, was due in part to the emergence of UPN and WB, two networks that targeted several of their series to African American viewers.

The apparent lack of diversity in the 1999–2000 season was especially troubling to Mfume. The NAACP noted that minorities were hard to find behind the camera as well. Of all the writers who worked on TV sitcoms and dramas, only 6 percent were black. FCC data show that minorities own about 2.8 percent of all broadcast stations.

Mfume threatened a boycott of the networks and their sponsors unless something was done. The networks responded by adding some minority characters to the casts of existing shows. CBS aired *City of Angels,* a drama set in an inner-city hospital, that featured a predominantly black cast and creative team. The networks also planned to increase minority hiring and to appoint executives in charge of their diversity efforts. These moves apparently satisfied Mfume, who called off plans for the boycott.

The 2000–2001 TV season did not spark similar protests. In addition to *City of Angels,* there were several new series with African Americans in major roles, such as *Boston Public.* The situation behind the camera and in minority ownership, however, was unchanged. The situation improved a bit in the 2002 season when there were 43 series featuring multiethnic characters. Back in 1995, there were only 13 such shows on the air.

The diversity issues surfaced again in 2003, but this time the focus was on cable. Members of the Congressional Black Caucus sent a letter to the cable TV industry asking for more minority-themed programs and more minority-owned cable networks.

Why should the networks present a diverse view of society? Many would argue that the networks have a social obligation to present an accurate view of society so that members of minority groups do not feel marginalized or disenfranchised from society. Others would suggest that TV should present role models for all groups. These benevolent reasons aside, it also makes economic sense for the networks to present a diverse menu of programs. The 2000 census will likely show that minorities constitute more than 35 percent of the U.S. population, and their buying power is increasing each year. Presenting shows that appeal to these groups is simply good business.

Further, there are those critics who suggest that paying large amounts of attention to the way the broadcast networks portray minorities overlooks the gains minorities have made in cable. Black Entertainment Television draws a significant audience. Two Spanish-language networks, Galavision and Univision, are aimed at Hispanics.

Finally, consider the opinion of commentator Earl Ofari Hutchinson, who suggests that prime-time TV is not worth fighting for. He charges that the networks have oversaturated the airways with silly sitcoms and action shows designed to appeal to young, affluent whites. These types of programs, he argues, have no relevance for African Americans, who should focus their attention elsewhere. In a similar vein, Cynthia Tucker, the African American editor of the editorial page of the *Atlanta Constitution,* suggests that the NAACP is misplacing its efforts by concentrating on network TV programs. Instead, she argues, the organization should encourage young African Americans to stop watching TV. "Let prime-time TV keep its bland cast of characters," says Tucker. "There are plenty of good books in which black youngsters can find themselves reflected."[1]

---

[1] Quoted in Richard Breyer, "Color TV," *Word and I,* March 2000, 84.

National advertisers are those that sell general-consumption items: soda pop, automobiles, deodorant, hair spray, and so on. These advertisers try to reach the biggest possible audience for their messages and usually purchase commercial time on broadcast network programs or cable networks.

In contrast, other advertisers have products that are used mainly in one region or locale. For example, a manufacturer of snowmobiles would gain little by having his or her ad seen in Miami or New Orleans. Likewise, a manufacturer of farm equipment would probably not find many customers in New York City. These companies turn to national spot buying. The snowmobile manufacturer would buy spots in several northern markets, such as Minneapolis, Minnesota; Fargo, North Dakota; and Butte, Montana. The farm equipment company would place ads in primarily rural markets.

Finally, there are many local businesses that buy advertising time from TV stations. They purchase time on one or more TV stations or cable systems located in a single market. The industrywide figures for 2000 showed the relative importance of these three types of advertising. Network spots (national advertising) accounted for 36 percent of the total amount of advertising dollars, and the remainder was divided about equally between national spot and local advertising.

Revenues depend upon the amount of money a station charges for its commercial time. The larger the audience, the more money a station can charge. The prices for 30- and 60-second commercials are listed on the station's rate card. The cost of an ad will vary tremendously from station to station. A 30-second ad might cost only $100 to $200 in a small market, but the same time would cost thousands in a major market. The same general pricing principles apply at the network level. Shows with high ratings have higher advertising charges than shows with low ratings. For example, in 2002, the average network 30-second spot in prime time cost about $180,000. On top-rated shows, spots were going for about $450,000; on lower-rated shows, the cost was about $85,000. To gain some perspective on how expensive it can get, consider that on the 2004 Super Bowl, a 30-second spot was going for about $2.4 million.

>> Where Did the Money Go?

At the network level, one of the biggest expenses is programming. For example, a typical half-hour sitcom costs around $800,000 to $900,000 to produce. Hit shows such as *Frasier* cost much more. An hour-long show runs about $1.5 million to $1.75 million. ABC spends about $3 million for each *Monday Night Football* telecast.

At the local level, the costs are broken down differently, but the heavy cost of programming is evident there as well. Programming costs account for about 35 to 40 percent of the local station expense dollar, followed by administrative costs and expenses for news.

A 30-second spot on *Everybody Loves Raymond* cost about $450,000 for the 2002–2003 TV season.

PUBLIC BROADCASTING

>> **A Short History**

Public broadcasting in the United States has been in existence for more than 30 years. During its lifetime, its achievements have been considerable, but its evolution has been hampered by political infighting, a lack of a clear purpose, and, most of all, an insufficient amount of money.

Until 1967, noncommercial TV was known as educational television. In 1967, following the recommendations of the Carnegie Commission, Congress passed the Public Broadcasting Act, which authorized money for the construction of new facilities and established the Corporation for Public Broadcasting (CPB) to oversee noncommercial TV and distribute funds for programs. The government also created the Public Broadcasting Service (PBS), whose duties resemble those of commercial networks. Although this arrangement seemed to work well at first, internal disputes soon surfaced concerning which of these two organizations had final control over programming.

In addition, several cable channels began to offer programs that competed for public TV's audience. Many experts felt that much of the traditional programming on public TV would eventually move to cable or to videocassette. On top of this came further reductions in federal funds for public broadcasting.

Then things started to change. Somewhat surprisingly, cable turned out to be more of a friend than a foe to public TV. Since two-thirds of all public stations are in the UHF band, carriage by local cable systems increased their coverage area and helped public TV double its audience from 1980 to 1984. Public TV wound up as the primary cultural channel in the nation, with 90 million viewers every week.

In the mid-1980s, however, the Reagan administration cut funds for public broadcasting and proposed to freeze future funding at current levels. Congress restored some of the cuts, but in 1987 the system was struggling to get along on about the same amount of money it had in 1982. PBS funding became a major political issue again in the early 1990s. Faced with this financial uncertainty, public TV looked to other sources for funding: corporate underwriting, auctions, viewer donations, and sales of program guides.

Public television's problems continued into the new century. PBS's average prime-time ratings were down 23 percent over the past nine years, reaching an all-time low in 2002. More people now watch the cable network Lifetime than watch PBS. To make matters worse PBS's loyal audience is getting older (the average age is in the mid-50s), and younger viewers are not flocking to public TV. Any attempt to attract younger viewers risks alienating public TV's core audience of mature Americans.

Money is still a problem. Public stations are moving to digital transmission, a conversion that will cost millions. Dwindling revenues have meant layoffs at local stations and at the network level. Congressional funding continues to be tight. The 2005 budget for the Corporation for Public Broadcasting totaled $390 million. That is about what ESPN collects every two months in subscriber fees. In short, public TV faces significant challenges if it is to remain a viable alternative for television viewers.

>> **Programming and Financing**

In 1990, the Public Broadcasting Service presented an 11-hour documentary entitled *The Civil War,* which became the highest-rated program in the history of PBS. Although it might be a bit of an exaggeration, much of the history of PBS programming can be described as a civil war between the local public stations and the centralized PBS organization. Each side has scored significant victories in this fray over the years, but most recently the tide has turned in favor of the centralized authority. Let us quickly review how the system used to work and how it has changed.

Before 1990, PBS used a mechanism called the Station Program Cooperative (SPC) to determine which programs were carried by its member stations. The SPC system represented a decentralized decision-making process. Member stations were given a ballot that contained the descriptions of possible programs, and they voted for those they wished to broadcast. After several rounds, the initial list was pared down and stations voted again, but this time each station had to promise that it would help pay for the programs it voted for.

This system encouraged the broadcast of programs that already had some funding or series that could be acquired cheaply. Innovative or daring series that were expensive and had no prior funding commitments were seldom produced. The system also leaned heavily on a few big public TV stations that did the bulk of the production work. Finally, PBS had no cohesive national scheduling system.

In 1990, faced with declining funds and viewers, PBS suspended the SPC and moved toward more centralized programming. An executive vice president for national programming was appointed with the power to develop and schedule new programs. By any measure, the first PBS season under the new centralized system was a success, exemplified by the fact that *The Civil War* series was watched by millions.

Successive seasons, however, were not as successful. For the entire decade of the 1990s, despite being one of the most established TV networks, PBS got an average prime-time rating of 2.0 (of all the TV homes in America, about 2 percent watched PBS in prime time, about the same rating as UPN). In addition, PBS got into trouble with Congress when it was revealed that PBS stations, which are supposed to be politically neutral, were providing Republican and Democratic groups with their donor lists. Political parties might use these lists to solicit money.

Educational programs, such as this one on archaeology, make up a significant part of the PBS schedule.

PBS programs have earned numerous awards and substantial praise from critics. *Sesame Street* revolutionized children's TV by presenting educational content in an entertaining format. *Nova* and

Cosmos introduced millions to the wonders of science. However, PBS programs have also come in for their share of criticism. Many critics have charged that PBS displays a liberal bias, and they have complained about the size of the salaries PBS pays to some of its performers.

Like commercial stations, public TV stations receive licenses from the FCC. As of 2003, there were 350 PBS stations operated by 175 licensees. About half of these licensees are community organizations, another one-third are colleges and universities, about 12 percent are state-operated networks, and the remainder belong to local educational or municipal authorities.

The audience for public TV is substantial. In 2003, more than half the homes in America watched public TV at least once a week. Viewing times, however, are far lower than those for commercial TV. Average household daily viewing time for public TV is about 25 minutes, compared with more than four hours for commercial TV.

In addition to broadcasting, PBS is also active in educational television. It is involved in the Adult Learning Service, which provides college-level courses to about 400,000 students. In addition, PBS operates Teacher Source, which provides instructional programs and educational materials for classroom use in grades K–12.

Unlike commercial TV, public television is funded by a number of sources. In 2002, about one-third of the support for public television came from federal, state, and local governments; about one-fourth came from member contributions; another 15 percent came from corporations; and the rest came from foundation grants, auctions, and other miscellaneous sources.

 ## CABLE TELEVISION

Cable TV marked a milestone in 2002 when, for the first time ever, cable networks attracted more prime-time viewers than did the seven network broadcasters. Original programming, such as *SpongeBob SquarePants, Trading Spaces, The Shield,* and *The World Series of Poker* attracted new viewers to cable and away from the broadcast networks. As cable TV executives like to say, people no longer distinguish between broadcast and cable networks. To the audience, they are both television.

Even with its continued success, cable still faced some problems. The industry still lagged in providing HDTV signals, competition with satellite providers intensified, and many new cable networks found it hard to find space on existing cable systems. Before we discuss in detail the current state of the cable industry, let us take a quick look at its past.

>> ### History

Cable TV began modestly in the 1950s as a device used to bring conventional television signals to areas that could not otherwise receive them. As cable grew, some systems imported signals from distant stations into markets that were already served by one or two local stations. The local stations, as you might imagine, were not pleased, since their audiences were being siphoned off by the imported signals. This situation caused some political maneuverings as stations affected by cable appealed to the FCC and to Congress for help. The FCC vacillated over the question of cable regulation before issuing, in 1965, a set of rules that retarded the

The Meanings of *Dawson's Creek*

Contributed by Amanda S. Hall   Critical-cultural studies are concerned with the relationship between culture and power as examined through experience. Culture is seen as the site of a continuous struggle over meaning in which the media serve as hegemonic outlets for relaying certain messages instead of others. This perspective on media studies seeks to understand why certain groups are represented the way they are and why certain groups' points of view are heard, while others are silenced. Critical-cultural studies also examine how messages, or *texts* as they are commonly called, are produced and consumed by various members of society. Popular culture, at the center of cultural studies, is a key site for the process of making sense of messages.

Television is an ideal subject for the study of popular culture. Since no two viewers of a television program are alike, there is a variety of interpretations of the same message. To comprehend how viewers interpret texts, in one study in-depth interviews were used to discover how teenage females perceived the teenage experience as depicted by the Warner Brothers television show *Dawson's Creek* and to learn how these teenagers incorporated the show's messages into their everyday lives.

The study examined how messages or meaning structures were encoded or produced, by a "technical infrastructure" (the show's production team), and decoded or consumed and subsequently put back into practice in a social system, by viewers. When interpreting critical-cultural data, it is important to look for themes but avoid making generalizing statements. The analysis of the study participants' decoding processes revealed several themes.

First, *Dawson's Creek*'s view of the teenage world coincides with that of the participants, many of whom felt the show complimented them by treating them as older and more mature than other shows. Participants frequently mentioned the advanced vocabulary the characters use, which according to Ann[1] confirms that "Teenagers aren't stupid and they don't say 'dude' or whatever all the time." Due to its treatment of teenage life, viewers remain loyal to the show because they feel it "understands" the complexity of the teenage experience.

In fact, the show strikes such a chord with viewers in its portrayal of the teenage experience that several of the study's participants formed fan clubs, perceived similarities between characters and themselves or their friends, and tried incorporating character mannerisms and vocabulary into their everyday lives. Two of the participants in the study designed T-shirts that read, "Eat. Sleep. Watch *Dawson's Creek.*" For those participants, the show is more than just an hour of entertainment; it is a way of life. Dawson, Joey, Jen, and Jack are not just characters on the show; they are friends to many of these study participants, and as such, these viewers care about what happens to each of them.

Second, the show plays several roles in participants' lives: providing a "blueprint" for viewers on how to "be" and behave as a teenager and serving as a surrogate parent by addressing tough problems teenagers face and are not comfortable discussing with their parents (e.g., drug use/abuse and sexual behavior). Most participants mentioned they had distant relationships with their parents and relied on the show to help them through problems that occurred in their lives. Jessica, for instance, talked about her experience of almost losing a friend to a drug overdose and about the fact that one of the show's characters, Andy, almost died from an overdose. Amanda explained, "It's really weird to see how it works out in real life and how it works out on TV 'cause it's usually the same."

Third, even though watching *Dawson's Creek* is an individual experience, it is also a social experience. Teenagers watch the show with friends and/or family members. Study participants also communicated with their friends during commercial breaks and after the show by telephone or e-mail or at their schools the next day. Through these social interactions—viewer/television screen, viewer/friends, and viewer/families—the show contributed to the ongoing project of defining the teenage reality and identity.

1. Why did *Dawson's Creek* strike a nerve with teenage females when other teen-oriented shows (e.g., *Roswell*) failed?

2. What potential problems may arise when teens rely on a TV show for advice on handling real-life problems?

3. Some teens reported watching *Dawson's Creek* in groups. How does the viewing situation influence the interpretation of what's on the screen?

---

[1]Pseudonyms are used in place of participants' actual names.

growth of cable in large markets. In 1972, the FCC enacted a new set of less restrictive rules for cable. By 1980, in a move toward deregulation, the FCC dropped virtually all rules governing cable.

This deregulation move helped systems grow as cable companies scrambled to acquire exclusive franchises in communities across the nation (see Figure 10–1). Some companies made extravagant promises to win these contracts: 100 or more channels, local-access channels, community channels, shopping and banking at home, two-way services—and all at bargain prices. After the smoke cleared, the industry recognized economic reality dictated that its performance would fall short of promises.

Cable quickly recovered from these setbacks and continued to grow. As of 1991, 7,500 cable systems served about 55 million households. Keep in mind that this growth occurred despite the fact that cable companies generally avoided expensive urban installations. The growth rate slowed somewhat during the mid-1990s, but by 2002, about 72 million households subscribed to cable.

Cable also scored several programming coups. ESPN signed a three-year deal with the National Football League to carry prime-time pro football games. CNN's coverage of the Gulf War, the O. J. Simpson trial, and the Clinton scandal demonstrated that it could be a formidable competitor to network news. Big-ticket network series bypassed the traditional syndication route and premiered first on cable.

FIGURE 10–1

Growth Within the U.S. Cable TV Industry

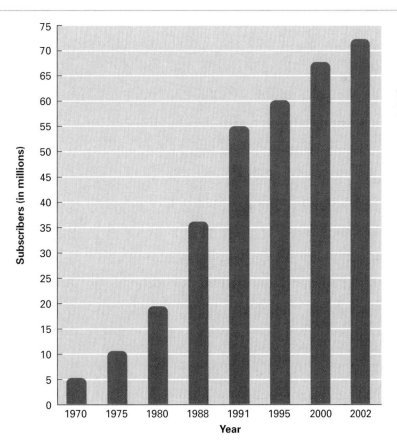

For many of you reading this, Judy McGrath would seem to have the ultimate dream job: She is the president of the MTV Networks Music Group and is responsible for MTV, MTV2, VH1, CMT, and all of the company's digital media services. Under her direction, MTV has grown from a small niche cable network to an international brand that symbolizes a unique attitude and lifestyle.

Always a music fan, McGrath first tried to get a job writing for *Rolling Stone*. When her efforts proved unsuccessful, she turned to writing advertising copy and then went to work for *Mademoiselle* and *Glamour*. In 1981, she heard about a new cable channel launched by Warner Entertainment that would be devoted to rock music. Despite the fact that she could not even get the channel on her home TV, McGrath joined the newly created MTV as a copywriter and on-air promotion person. (She was one of the ones responsible for using all the space film footage to promote the channel.) To the surprise of many people, MTV was successful in attracting 16 to 24 year olds, an audience coveted by advertisers. MTV became part of the huge Viacom conglomerate, and McGrath quickly moved up the ranks to creative director, executive vice president, and eventually president. Under her direction, MTV expanded all over the world.

When the music video novelty began to wear off in the mid-1980s and ratings started to sag, McGrath introduced programs that became popular culture icons: *Beavis and Butt-Head, The Real World, The MTV Music Awards, MTV Unplugged,* and *Total Request Live.* She also introduced political coverage to MTV and was instrumental in the development of the 1992 *Choose or Lose* get-out-the-vote campaign. More recently, McGrath has led MTV into other media: movies, books, and the Internet.

What does she see in MTV's future? Since a high proportion of MTV viewers are also Web surfers and spend a good deal of time on MTV.com, look for more integration of the music on MTV and MTV2 with the website. MTV.com will be used to highlight some of the artists or genres featured on the cable channels. In addition, plans are underway for more international expansion, particularly in Asia. Finally, it is likely McGrath will continue to provide special programming that deals with important social issues, such as the 17 hours the channel devoted to hate crimes. And, of course, there will always be music videos.

On the economic side, cable advertising revenues exceeded $2 billion in 1990 and rose to about $12 billion by 2002. Although still small in comparison with the ad revenues generated by traditional television, the 2002 figure represents an increase of more than 27 percent over that of 1999.

The most significant developments in the cable industry in the last two decades have been legal ones. In 1984, Congress deregulated the rates cable systems could charge consumers. Eight years later, in response to subscriber complaints, Congress reregulated the industry by passing the Cable Television Consumer Protection and Competition Act, which caused about a 17 percent reduction in rates and mandated that broadcasters choose between *must carry* (the local cable system had to carry the station's signal) and *retransmission consent* (the local station had the right to negotiate compensation for carriage of their signal). Most broadcasters opted for consent and were compensated with promotional time on the system or were granted space for their own existing or planned cable networks.

The next major piece of legislation was the Telecommunications Act of 1996 (discussed in more detail in Chapter 15). The new law gave telephone companies the right to enter the cable business and gave cable companies the right to provide telephone services. In addition, both telephone and cable companies could own competing systems in the same community. Finally, the act allowed most cable companies to once again set their own rates. The competition between phone companies and cable companies made possible by the act did not materialize to any significant degree. Most customers still receive basic telephone services from phone companies and receive cable television from cable TV companies. After being deregulated by the 1996 act, cable television subscription fees increased. As of 2003, there were indications that Congress was considering a review of the 1996 legislation.

The biggest competitor to cable turned out to be satellite television. DBS providers such as EchoStar and the Dish Network attracted 2.1 million more subscribers from 2001 to 2002. Almost 20 percent of U.S. households now get their TV via satellite.

Cable was also experiencing problems resulting from its own growth. There were more cable networks around than available space on local systems. Some cable systems were making room for only those channels that would pay the systems to carry their signals. Cable networks that lacked deep financial resources were having problems gaining access to local systems. In addition, like the broadcast networks, cable TV was becoming a victim of audience fragmentation.

Despite these difficulties, the long-range outlook seems positive. Cable continues to draw viewers away from the broadcast TV networks. In addition, thanks to their existing coaxial cable and optical fiber facilities, cable companies can offer subscribers high-speed Internet connections.

>> Ownership

The ownership trend in the cable industry, as in other media, has been one of consolidation. Comcast acquired the assets of ATT Broadband in 2002 to become the nation's largest cable provider. Comcast and number-two company Time Warner serve nearly 45 percent of all cable customers. The five largest cable systems are listed in Table 10–3.

>> Structure

Cable systems are structured differently from those of conventional TV. There are three main components in a cable system (see Figure 10–2):

1. the head end,
2. the distribution system, and
3. the house drop.

The **head end** consists of the antenna and related equipment that receive signals from distant TV stations or other programming services and process these signals so that they may be sent to subscribers' homes. Some cable systems also originate their own programming, ranging from local newscasts to weather dials, and their studios may also be located at the head end.

The **distribution system** consists of the actual cables that deliver the signals to subscribers. The cables can be buried or hung on telephone poles. In most

TABLE 10–3	Company	Number of subscribers (in millions)
Five Largest Cable System Operators, 2003	Comcast	21.3
	Time Warner	10.9
	Charter Communications	6.5
	Cox Communications	6.3
	Adelphia Communications	5.8

FIGURE 10–2

Diagram of the transmission of HBO programming from videotape studios, via satellite, to the pay subscriber's television set.

At the head end, the signal is assigned to a cable TV channel before being sent on its way to the subscriber's home.

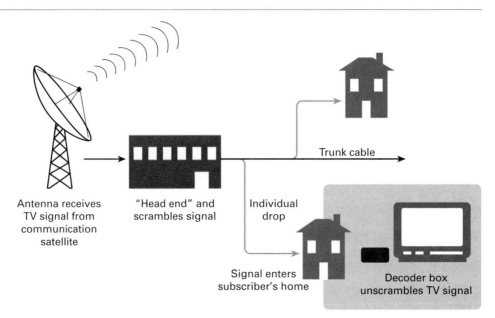

Antenna receives TV signal from communication satellite

"Head end" and scrambles signal

Individual drop

Trunk cable

Signal enters subscriber's home

Decoder box unscrambles TV signal

systems, the main cable (called the *trunk*) has several feeder cables, which travel down side streets or to other outlying areas. Finally, special amplifiers installed along the distribution system boost the strength of the signal as it comes from the head end.

The **house drop** is that section of the cable that connects the feeder cable to the subscriber's TV set. Drops can be one-way (the signal travels in only one direction—from the head end to the house) or two-way (the signal can also be sent back to the head end by the subscriber). Fiber-optic cables make it possible to carry 500 or more channels.

>> Programming and Financing

We will examine these topics from two perspectives: (1) that of a local cable system operator and (2) that of a national cable network.

Local Operators   The sources of programming for a local system are as follows:

1. *Local origination:* This programming might include local news, high school football, and discussions. A local government channel may carry city council meetings or zoning board hearings. Some systems have set aside public-access channels for anyone to use for a modest fee.

2. *Local broadcast television stations:* Some cable systems carry signals from nearby cities in addition to local channels.

3. *Superstations:* These are local stations whose signals are carried by many systems nationwide. There are six major superstations: WGN, Chicago; KTLA, Los Angeles; WPIX and WWOR, New York; KWGN, Denver; and WSBK, Boston. The original superstation, WTBS, Atlanta, changed its status in 1998 to that of a cable network.

4. *Special cable networks:* These are services distributed by satellite to cable systems. Most of these networks are advertiser supported. Examples include

MTV, The Weather Channel, the USA Network, Black Entertainment Television, and the noncommercial C-SPAN (which covers Congress).

5. *Pay services:* These are commercial-free channels that typically provide theatrical movies and original programming. HBO, Showtime, The Movie Channel, and Cinemax are examples.

6. *Pay-per-view:* These are channels set aside for the showing of recently released theatrical films and special sports and entertainment events. Subscribers receive the programs for a specified price. Movies, for example, might cost $4.95; special events, such as Wrestlemania, might run $20 to $30.

A local cable system has two basic sources of income: (1) subscription fees from consumers and (2) local advertising. Most systems charge a fee for local stations, superstations, and special cable networks. In addition, consumers might pay an additional fee to receive one or more pay channels. Cable is a capital-intensive industry: It takes a lot of money to start a system. The operating costs of a typical system are more reasonable. A good part of the basic cable monthly subscription fee goes to cover construction and maintenance costs.

Cable systems must also pay for their programming. In the case of pay services, the consumer fee is split between the cable system and the cable network. There has been a recent shift in the composition of cable system revenue. Pay-cable and pay-per-view receipts now account for more than half of cable operators' income. Local advertising on cable represents another source of income for operators. This sum is growing, but it still represents less than 20 percent of total income for local systems. In addition, cable systems that carry home shopping networks generally receive a percentage of the sales revenue generated in their market.

National Operators   At the national level, cable networks draw upon three major sources for their programming: (1) original production, (2) movies, and (3) syndicated programs. The all-news channel, CNN, relies upon original production for virtually all its content. Most of ESPN's programming is also original, as is C-SPAN's. Movies make up most of the content on HBO and Showtime. Superstations program a mix of all three sources, while channels such as the USA Network and Lifetime depend heavily upon syndicated programs.

There are three main revenue sources for national cable services: advertising, carriage fees, and subscription fees. Pay-TV channels such as Showtime and HBO make their money from subscription fees paid by the consumer. Some cable networks, such as MTV and ESPN, charge local operators a **carriage fee** (also called an *affiliation fee*) that ranges from about 10 cents to a few dollars per subscriber. Some channels, such as C-SPAN, support themselves entirely from this money. Other networks will sell advertising in addition to the carriage fee, and still others,

C-SPAN carried the debate between candidates Mark Pryor and Tim Hutchinson in the 2002 Arkansas senatorial election. Special-interest channels such as C-SPAN have fragmented the cable TV audience.

such as TNN, support themselves almost entirely through ads. As mentioned earlier, advertising revenues for cable are growing, but cable still accounts for only a small percentage of the total TV ad dollars. Table 10–4 lists the top cable channels.

>> **Pay-per-View (PPV)**

PPV makes most of its money from sporting events, mainly high-profile boxing matches, movies, concerts, and adult content. Subscribers pay fees ranging from $5 to $50 to see these events. After racking up impressive revenue figures during the late 1990s, PPV has fallen on difficult times. Increasing competition from video-on-demand (see Media Probe, "Video on Demand") and digital cable channels has forced many cable system operators to reexamine the long-range future of this service. Still, the potential for big money exists. The 2002 Lennox Lewis–Mike Tyson boxing match brought in $106 million and was the biggest moneymaker in PPV history.

 HOME VIDEO

The home video industry came into existence because of the tremendous growth of VCR sales. By 2003, about 92 percent of homes in the United States were equipped with the device. Recently, the VCR was joined by DVD (digital videodisc) players. DVD offers better pictures and sound than videotape; can contain additional video material, such as outtakes and interviews with a director; and can feature multiple-language soundtracks. DVD sales have skyrocketed; it is estimated that there are now more than 50 million in U.S. homes.

Both VCRs and DVD players are used to play back prerecorded cassettes and discs that can be purchased or rented from video stores such as Blockbuster. There are more than 35,000 prerecorded cassette and disc titles on the market, and many more are introduced each month. In addition, VCRs are also used to time shift, to record TV shows for playback at a more convenient time. (Regular DVD players cannot be used to time shift because they cannot record. Newer DVD players, however, will have this capability.)

A new entry in the home video market is the **personal video recorder (PVR),** such as TiVo, which allows a viewer to record television programs on a hard drive. Sales of PVRs were slow in the beginning years of the new century, but experts predict these new devices will become popular once more people are aware of what they can do (see Social Issues, "TiVo: The End of TV Advertising as We Know It?").

Like most other businesses, home video can be divided into three segments: production, distribution, and retail. The production side of the industry consists of

TABLE 10–4	Network	Number of subscriber households (in millions)*
Top Cable Services, 2003	TBS	87.4
	CNN & CNN Headline News	86.3
*Includes cable and satellite homes	Discovery	86.3
	ESPN	86.3
	USA	86.0

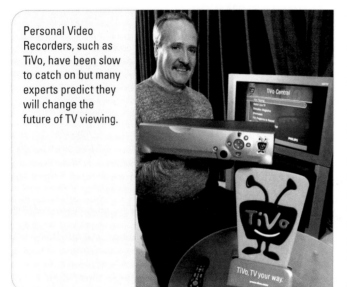

Personal Video Recorders, such as TiVo, have been slow to catch on but many experts predict they will change the future of TV viewing.

those companies that produce prerecorded cassettes and discs. Since much of the home video market consists of movies, many of the large motion picture studios also dominate the cassette/disc business.

These companies sell to distributors, who form the bridge between production and retail. Currently, some 90 distributors in the United States handle videocassettes. Major companies include Disney, Fox, Columbia, and Paramount. Moreover, the cassette/disc distribution business now resembles record distribution as a new breed of rack jobber is making it easy for many retail and department stores to get into the video renting business.

The retail side of the industry is the most volatile. It was estimated that in 2000 there were about 30,000 video rental/sales stores in the United States, in addition to the thousands of tape counters at grocery stores. The typical large retail store carries a library of about 3,000 to 5,000 different titles, representing a balance of current hits with other titles that have a longer shelf life. In contrast, other outlets stock only 200 to 500 titles, most of them current hits.

Large chains, such as Blockbuster and Hollywood Video, dominate the video rental business. Blockbuster alone accounts for around 30 percent of all tape/disc rentals and sales.

Sales and rentals are big business. Consumers spent more than $20 billion on cassettes and discs in 2003. DVDs are quickly replacing videocassettes as the preferred rental/sales vehicle. Many experts predict it will not be long before videotape becomes obsolete. Retailers are concerned about the competition posed by video on demand and the growing number of premium movies available through direct broadcast satellites.

DIRECT BROADCAST SATELLITES

Subscribers to **direct broadcast satellite (DBS)** systems have access to dozens of movie channels as well as pay-per-view. As of 2003, about 18 million households were equipped for DBS, and market research suggested that these consumers were not only canceling their cable subscriptions but also were making fewer trips to the video store. It will take a few years, however, before the ultimate impact of DBS can be determined.

A satellite dish uses digital technology to produce sharp pictures and CD-quality sound. When it was first introduced in 1994, the dish retailed for about $700; by 2003, dishes were selling for less than $200.

Subscriber growth was slow at first, partly because DBS systems were prohibited by law from carrying local television stations. In 1999, however, the Satellite Home Viewer Improvement Act granted satellite companies the right to retransmit the signals of some local broadcast stations. More subscribers signed on in the wake of this development.

Imagine sitting in your favorite chair and being able to watch any movie ever made any time you want to watch it. That is the goal of **video on demand (VOD),** the couch potato's ultimate dream.

Here is how it works. The digital revolution makes it possible to store movies as computer files on a server. A searchable index contains the files of all the movies available. These files can be transmitted over regular cable TV lines. One server can deliver the same movie to about 20,000 different cable subscribers. Viewers need a special set-top box to be able to decode the movies. The boxes enable consumers to pause, stop, fast-forward, and rewind. They simply choose a movie, pay for it, and sit back and watch. No trips to the video store and no late fees required.

Video on demand has been progressing slowly, but that pace looks as if it is about to change. The service was launched in New York and Philadelphia in late 2002. Current estimates suggest that about seven million homes now have access to some form of video on demand. By 2006, industry experts are predicting that this number will rise to more than 35 million, enabling the VOD industry to generate nearly $3 billion in revenue. Some think this forecast is overly optimistic, but only time will tell.

Cable operators are betting heavily on the new technology. It is one technology in which cable has an advantage over its satellite competitors. VOD requires a two-way connection. DirecTV and EchoStar are strictly one-way services. The cable industry, of course, is also hoping that VOD eats into the money now going to Blockbuster and other video rental stores.

Cable systems are experimenting with various pricing schemes. Some arrangements charge a separate fee for every movie or TV program that is viewed. Other systems offer a flat monthly fee for which the consumer may watch as many movies or programs as he or she wants. One large cable system is even considering a free version of VOD in which programming from various cable and broadcast networks is available at any time of the day.

Some problems still need to be worked out. Hollywood studios have to make their films available. Viacom, for example, owns both Paramount and Blockbuster and, not surprisingly, has been cool to the VOD arrangement. Plus the studios would have to rearrange their release schedules. To be competitive, VOD would have to get the movies at the same time that they are made available at video rental stores. Currently, movies go first to stores and then to cable.

It is unclear what the future of VOD will be. However, whatever happens, VOD will mean more choices and more convenience for the home TV viewer.

Two companies dominate the DBS business: DirecTV and EchoStar. The two announced plans for a merger in 2002, but the FCC vetoed the plan. In the wake of the failed merger, media mogul Rupert Murdoch purchased a controlling stake in DirecTV. If it passes regulatory review, Murdoch's takeover of DirecTV means that his company will operate satellites that reach 33 million subscribers all over the world. Like cable systems, DBS companies are upgrading for the digital age by offering HDTV, high-speed Internet access, and interactive television to their subscribers.

 FEEDBACK

>> Measuring TV Viewing

Let us examine how the ratings for both network programs and local stations are determined.

Network Ratings   Nielsen Media Research, serving the United States and Canada, provides the networks with audience data through its Nielsen Television Index (NTI). To compile these ratings, Nielsen uses a device called a People Meter, introduced in the late 1980s. The People Meter consists of an apparatus about the size

TiVo has been around for only a few years, but it has already had an impact. In the first place, it introduced a new verb into the language: to *TiVo,* as in "Did you watch *ER* last night?" "No, but I TiVoed it." More importantly, TiVo and other personal video recorders (PVRs) have changed the way some Americans watch TV. A PVR such as TiVo digitally stores up to 80 hours of TV programs on a hard disk for later playback. TiVo enables you to pause live TV, makes recording a program as easy as pushing one button on a remote control, and allows you to record a whole season worth of programs with a couple of button pushes. TiVo can also learn what you like to watch and can record programs that it thinks you would be interested in. Finally, PVRs have a fast-forward button that permits the user to zip right through TV ads. Replay TV, another brand of PVR, has a "quick skip" button that jumps ahead 30 seconds—which just happens to be the length of the typical TV ad.

The commercial-zapping feature is the one that has television executives running scared. People with PVRs are less likely to watch commercials. One survey found that about 70 percent of owners skipped over the ads while they were viewing. Fewer people watching TV ads translates into decreased revenue for the TV industry and more challenges for advertisers seeking to reach a mass audience. As of 2003, PVRs were being used in only 1 percent of U.S. households, but some experts are predicting that the PVR will end traditional TV advertising as we know it. Most agree that PVR penetration has nowhere to go but up. Satellite TV companies are now offering PVRs already built into their converter boxes; many cable companies are following suit. One study predicts that PVRs will be in more than 50 million homes by 2008.

The TV industry has responded in several ways. A half-dozen media companies filed a lawsuit in 2002 against one PVR manufacturer, arguing that PVRs encourage copyright infringement because they make it possible to swap digitally recorded programs over the Internet. Jamie Kellner, former chair of the Turner Broadcast System, hinted that people who zapped commercials were stealing the programming. He suggested that PVR owners should pay an extra $250 per year for ad-free TV.

Programmers are scrambling to find TiVo-proof programs. Look for more TV programs to steal a page from movies and counteract zapping by using product placements. A 2003 *Alias* episode, for example, prominently featured Ford automobiles and featured a scene in which two of the characters talked about buying a Ford. Some shows are integrating advertiser logos into their sets. An example is Fox Sports Net's *Best Damn Sports Show,* whose set prominently features the Labatt's beer label. *American Idol* does the same with Coke cups. The creator of *Who Wants to Be a Millionaire* has planned a new show called *Live from Tomorrow* that will not have any interruptions for traditional 30-second TV ads. Instead, advertising messages will be incorporated into the show's content, such as by having a singer perform on a stage with the Pepsi logo in the background. (Students of TV history will quickly point out that this was a technique used back in the 1940s and 1950s.)

Ironically, even the folks who make PVRs are reexamining their stance toward advertising. PVR companies do not stress the ad-zapping capability in their own advertising. Indeed, as of mid-2003, TiVo was examining ways to incorporate advertising into its service. One plan called for electronics retailer Best Buy to embed an electronic tag visible only to TiVo users into a commercial featuring singer Sheryl Crow running on MTV. Those who clicked on the tag would see a 12-minute segment that featured more of Crow and ads for Best Buy while TiVo continued to record MTV.

In summary, PVRs will likely change the shape of TV advertising. It is, nevertheless, unlikely that they will cause its demise.

of a clock radio that sits on top of a TV set and a handheld device that resembles a TV remote-control unit. Demographic data are gathered from each household member, and then each is assigned a number. While watching TV, each family member is supposed periodically to punch in his or her number on the handheld device to indicate viewing. People Meters can be used to tabulate all viewing— network, syndicated shows, and cable—and can even tabulate VCR playbacks. There are about 5,000 households in the Nielsen People Meter sample, and usable data are obtained from more than 90 percent of the meters. The sample is replaced every two years. The People Meter service is not cheap. Networks pay millions of dollars annually for the service.

Nielsen is also testing other systems. The most ambitious plan uses a passive meter and remote image recognition. Families agreeing to participate in this arrangement will be photographed and their facial features stored digitally in a black box atop the TV. At prearranged intervals, a tiny camera located in the black box takes a picture of a 120-degree arc in front of the TV and matches the faces of anyone watching the set with the faces stored in its memory.

Local-Market TV Ratings   Nielsen surveys more than 200 markets in the United States at least four times a year, using a combination of diary and electronic meter techniques. A computer selects phone numbers at random from all telephone directories in the area. The households selected into the sample are asked to keep a diary record of their television viewing.

Households that agree to participate receive one diary for every working TV in the household. The diary provides a space for entering the viewing of the head of the household as well as that of other family members or visitors. Participants are asked to record their viewing every quarter hour. In addition, the respondents are asked to record the sex and age of all those who are watching. At the back of the diary are questions concerning family size, the city where the household is located, and whether the family subscribes to cable. Diaries are kept for seven days and then returned to the ratings company. Nielsen reports that it is able to use approximately 40 to 50 percent of all the diaries it sends out.

In about 50 markets, Nielsen has electronic meters that record any time a sample household's TV is turned on or off and what channel is viewed. The meters also record VCR usage. Data from this sample are compiled overnight and sent to subscribers early the next morning. These local meter data are augmented by information from the diary sample. Nielsen's long-term plans call for replacing these electronic meters with People Meters.

>> Ratings Reporting

Television viewing data for TV are reported essentially the same way as for radio. The following formula is used to calculate the **rating** for a TV program in a local market:

$$\text{Rating} = \frac{\text{Number of households watching a program}}{\text{Number of TV HH}}$$

where "TV HH" equals the number of households in a given market equipped with television.

Similarly, the **share of the audience** is found by using the following formula:

$$\text{Share of audience} = \frac{\text{Number of households watching a program}}{\text{Number of HUT}}$$

where "HUT" equals the number of households using (watching) television at a particular time.

Figure 10–3 reproduces a sample page from a local Nielsen ratings book. As can be seen, Nielsen reports shares, ratings, and an estimate of the number of people in the audience in various demographic categories for different areas in the market.

Four times every year (February, May, July, and November), Nielsen conducts a "sweep" period during which every local television market in the entire country is measured. Local stations rely on these ratings to set their advertising rates. Naturally enough, affiliated stations pressure the networks for special programming that will attract large audiences. All three networks generally go along with

FIGURE 10–3

Sample Page from a Nielsen TV Ratings Book

CHARLESTON, SC

WK1 1/30-2/05 WK2 2/06-2/12 WK3 2/13-2/19 WK4 2/20-2/26

MONDAY-FRIDAY 12:30PM - 4:30PM

METRO HH				DMA HOUSEHOLD									DMA RATINGS																										
				RATINGS WEEKS				MULTI-WEEK AVG		SHARE TREND			PERSONS											WOMEN							MEN						TNS	CHILD	
RTG	SHR	STATION	PROGRAM	1	2	3	4	RTG	SHR	NOV '02	MAY '02	FEB '02	2+	18+	12-24	12-34	18-34	18-49	21-49	25-54	35+	35-64	50+	18+	12-24	18-34	18-49	25-49	25-54	WKG	18+	18-34	18-49	21-49	25-49	25-54	12-17	2-11	6-11
1	2			3	4	5	6	7	8	11	12	13	15	16	17	18	19	20	21	22	23	24	25	26	27	28	29	31	32	34	35	36	37	38	39	40	41	42	43
2			*R.S.E. THRESHOLDS 25+%*	*7*	*7*	*7*	*7*	*2*					*1*	*2*	*6*	*4*	*4*	*3*	*3*	*2*	*2*	*2*	*2*	*2*	*10*	*9*	*4*	*4*	*3*	*3*	*2*	*10*	*4*	*5*	*5*	*4*	*13*	*9*	*13*
1			*(1 S.E.) 4 WK AVG 50+%*	*2*	*2*	*2*	*2*	*LT*					*LT*	*LT*	*1*	*1*	*1*	*1*	*1*	*LT*	*LT*	*1*	*LT*	*LT*	*2*	*2*	*1*	*1*	*1*	*1*	*1*	*2*	*1*	*1*	*1*	*1*	*3*	*2*	*3*
		12:30PM																																					
2	9	WCBD	AVG. ALL WKS	2	3	4	1	3	9	6	8	6	1	2	2	2	2	2	1	2	1	1	1	2	2	3	2	2	2	1	1	1	1			1			
2	7		#PASSIONS-NBC	2				2	10				1	1		2	3	2	2	2	1	1		2			3						1	1					
3	10		PASSIONS-NBC		3	4	1	3	9				1	2	2	2	2	1	1	1	1	2	2	2	3	3	2	1	2		1	2	1			1			
1	2	WCIV	AVG. ALL WKS	1	<<	<<	<<	1	2	3	5	3																											
1	4		#PORT CHRLS-ABC	1	<<			1	4												1		1	1						1									
<<			PORT CHRLS-ABC		<<	<<	<<	<<																															
10	37	WCSC	AVG. ALL WKS	6	8	15	13	11	39	42	45	37	5	6	2	3	4	4	4	5	7	5	9	10	4	8	7	7	8	5	2	1	1	1	1	1		1	
7	27		#YOUNG&RESTLESS	6	8			7	29				3	4	1	1	2	2	2	3	5	4	7	6	2	4	4	3	5	3	2		1	1	1	1			
13	47		YOUNG&RESTLESS			15	13	14	47				6	8	4	5	7	6	6	6	9	7	11	13	6	12	11	11	10	8	2	1	1	1	1	1	1	1	1
1	2	WITV	CAILLOU	1	<<	<<	<<	<<			2	5																											
<<		WMMP	GOOD DAY LIVE	<<	<<	<<	<<	<<																															
2	8	WTAT	MAURY POVICH	1	2	3	1	2	6	6X	9	7	1	1	2	1	2	1	1	1	1	1	1	2	3	3	2	1	1	1	1	1	1		1	1			1
<<		ABLN	CELBRTY JSTC B	<<	<<	<<	<<	<<																															
26			HUT/PUT/TOTALS*	23	26	31	28	27		23	26	23	12	15	9	10	12	12	11	12	17	14	21	21	14	19	18	18	19	11	9	5	5	4	4	6	4	4	2
		1:00PM																																					
3	10	WCBD	AVG. ALL WKS	3	1	4	1	3	10	14	12	10	1	1		1	1	1	1	1	1	1	2	2	1	3	2	2	2	1	1					1			
4	17		#DAYS-OUR LIVES	3				3	15				2	2		2	3	2	3	3	2	1	2	3			4				1		1	1					
2	8		DAYS-OUR LIVES		1	4	1	2	8				1	1	1	1	1	1		1	1	1	1	2	1	2	1	1	1										
3	13	WCIV	AVG. ALL WKS	2	3	4	2	3	11	5	11	13	1	2	1	1	1	1	1	2	2	2	3	3	1	1	2	2	2	2	1	2	1			1			
3	13		#ALL-CHILDREN	2		5		3	11				1	2		1	1	1	1	2	2	2	3	2		1	2	2	3	3	1	1				1			
3	13		ALL-CHILDREN		3	4	2	3	11				2	2	2	2	2	2	1	1	2	2	2	3	2	2	2	2	2	1	1	2	1			1			
9	34	WCSC	AVG. ALL WKS	5	7	14	11	9	36	36	41	34	4	5	2	3	4	4	4	5	6	5	7	9	4	8	7	7	8	5	1	1	1	1	1	1		1	
6	26		#YOUNG&RESTLESS	5				5	24				2	3		2	2	1	2	3	3	3	5	4			2				1		1	1					
9	36		YOUNG&RESTLESS		7	14	11	11	40				5	6	3	4	5	5	5	5	7	6	8	10	5	9	9	9	9	6	2	1	1	1	1	1		1	
<<		WITV	TELTUBBIES-PTV	<<	<<	<<	<<	<<		X	3	3																											
1	3	WMMP	JUDGE HATCHETT	2	<<	1	<<	1	3		3	2									1	1	1	1			1	1	1	1									
<<		WTAT	BEYOND JVP	<<	<<	<<	<<	<<			2	3														1													
<<		ABLN	TEXAS JUSTC R	<<	<<	<<	<<	<<																															
25			HUT/PUT/TOTALS*	22	26	32	24	26		23	24	25	12	15	8	10	12	12	12	13	16	14	19	21	13	19	18	18	19	12	8	5	5	5	5	6	3	4	2
		1:30PM																																					

the affiliates' desires. As a result, blockbuster movies and specials are scheduled in competing time slots, leaving many viewers to wonder why all the good programs on TV always come at once.

Determining the Accuracy of Ratings Because the numbers in the rating books are the basis for spending vast amounts of money, it is important that they be as accurate and reliable as possible. During the early 1960s, in the wake of quiz show and payola scandals, Congress took a close look at the broadcasting industry. In response to one congressional committee's criticism of audience-measurement techniques, advertising and broadcasting leaders founded the Electronic Media Ratings Council (EMRC). The task of the EMRC is basically threefold. It monitors, audits, and accredits broadcast measurement services. The council monitors performance of ratings companies by making sure that reported results meet the minimum standards of performance set up by the EMRC. Audits are performed on a continuing basis. If the ratings company passes the audit, it is accredited and is allowed to display the EMRC's seal of approval on its ratings reports.

Despite the EMRC's work, broadcast ratings are still subject to widespread criticism. One common complaint, voiced by many who evidently do not understand the statistical theory that underlies sampling, is directed at Nielsen's national survey. How can a sample of only 5,000 homes, these critics ask, accurately reflect the viewing of 100 million television households? In actuality, this sample size will generate tolerably accurate results within a specified margin of error. Other criticisms, however, deserve closer attention.

First, it is possible that the type of person who agrees to participate may have viewing habits different from those of the viewer who declines to participate. Second, in the case of the Nielsen reports (based on about 55 percent of the diaries sent out), it is possible that "returners" behave differently from "nonreturners." Third, people who know that their viewing is being measured may change their behavior. Fourth, ratings companies admit that they have a problem measuring the viewing of certain groups. For example, minorities—particularly blacks and Hispanics—may be underrepresented in the ratings companies' samples. Last, the stations that are being measured can distort the measurement process by engaging in contests and special promotions or by running unusual or sensational programs in an attempt to "hype" the ratings. The distinction between hype and legitimate programming, however, is somewhat fuzzy. Clearly, the ratings are not perfect. Nonetheless, despite all their flaws, they present useful information at an affordable price to advertisers and to the television industry. As long as the United States has a commercial broadcasting system, some form of the ratings will always be around.

>> Questionnaires, Concept Testing, and Pilot Testing

In addition to ratings, the TV networks gather three special types of feedback from the audience to help them predict what television shows will be popular with viewers. The first kind of research consists of questionnaires that attempt to measure audience tastes, opinions, and beliefs. Perhaps as many as 100,000 people per year are questioned in person or over the phone as the networks try to identify what situations and topics might be acceptable for programs.

A second form is called **concept testing.** In concept testing, a one- or two-paragraph description of an idea for a new series is presented to a sample of viewers who are asked for their reactions. Show ideas that do well in concept testing have an increased chance of getting on the air.

The third form is **pilot testing,** which consists of placing a group of viewers in a special test theater and showing them an entire program. The audience usually sits in chairs equipped with dials or buttons that are used to indicate the degree to which audience members like or dislike what is shown. For example, the audience might be told to press a green button when they see something on screen that they like and a red button when they see something they dislike.

The networks currently test pilots on cable TV systems since that is the closest thing to real TV viewing. In a cable test, several hundred cable subscribers in a certain community are telephoned and are asked to participate in the test. They watch the show on an unused channel of their cable system and then respond by telephone to a questionnaire that asks them about plot, character, relationships, and so on.

>> Television Audiences

The TV set has become firmly entrenched in the life of Americans. As of 2000, some 99 percent of all homes in the country had at least one working television set. About 75 percent had more than one. Cable television had more than 72 million subscribers in 2003, roughly 68 percent of all TV households.

The set in the average household is on for about seven hours a day, with each individual watching an average of more than three hours daily. The TV audience changes throughout the day, steadily growing from 7 A.M. until it reaches a peak from 8 to 11 P.M., Eastern Standard Time. After 11 P.M., the audience drops off dramatically. Figure 10–4 details this pattern of audience viewing.

FIGURE 10–4

Household Viewing of Television at Various Times of the Day

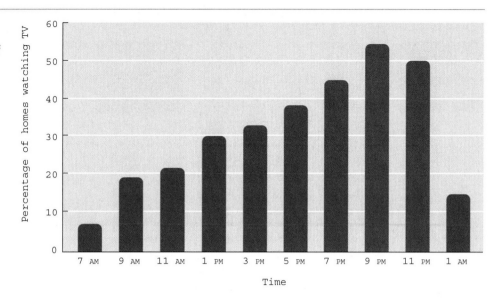

Not surprisingly, the television audience is largest during the winter months and smallest during July and August, when people spend more time outdoors. The composition of the television audience changes during the day. Preschool and female viewers tend to predominate during the daytime hours from Monday to Friday. On Saturday mornings, most of the audience is under 13. Prime time is dominated by those in the 18- to 49-year-old age group.

Various demographic factors, such as age, sex, social class, and education, affect viewership. For example, teenagers watch the least. People in low-income homes generally watch more television than their middle-income counterparts. People with more education tend to watch less, and women watch more often than men. Cable subscribers are younger, have more children, and are more affluent than the average viewer. They also are dissatisfied with traditional television and want more program variety. Subscribers to the pay-cable channels have younger heads of households, are more affluent, and watch more TV than families in noncable homes.

CAREER OUTLOOK

THE TELEVISION INDUSTRY

Someone hunting for a job in TV quickly discovers that it is a relatively small industry. According to recent figures provided by the FCC, about 110,000 people are employed in commercial TV; 100,000 in CATV; 10,000 in noncommercial television; and about 16,000 at TV networks.

>> Entry-Level Positions

Here are some general hints on job hunting in TV:

1. *Think small.* As in radio, in TV small-market stations offer more employment potential than larger-market stations. Moreover, at a small station, you have a chance to do more and learn more than you might at a larger station.

2. *Do not be afraid to start at the bottom.* Once you get in, it is easier to move upward into a position that might be more to your liking. Many successful people in TV started in the mailroom, secretarial pool, or shipping department.

3. *Be prepared to move.* Your first job will probably not be a lifetime commitment. Frequently, the road to advancement in TV consists of moving about and up—from a small station to a large station, from an independent station to a network affiliate, from the station to the network.

>> Upward Mobility

Those interested in producing TV shows might consider looking for a job as a camera operator, floor manager (the person who gives cues to the talent and makes sure everything in the studio goes smoothly during the telecast), or production assistant (a person who handles all the odd jobs that need to be done during a show). From there a person might progress upward to become an assistant director or assistant producer or perhaps a writer. Eventually, he or she would hope to become a full-fledged director or producer.

If you are interested in being an on-camera news reporter, your best bet might be to find a general reporting job at a small station. If your interests lie behind the camera, you can start out as a newswriter or news researcher or even a cameraperson or tape editor. Most people interested in performing before the camera generally stay in that capacity. Upward mobility for general-assignment reporters consists of moving into the anchor position. For anchors, it consists of moving to bigger and more lucrative markets. For those behind the scenes, the first move up will probably be to the assistant news director slot and then on to the news director position.

Sales is the division that offers the most upward mobility. Most stations prefer people who have had some experience in selling (many move from radio sales to TV sales). Once a salesperson is established, however, his or her monetary rewards can be substantial. Salespeople advance their careers by moving to larger markets or by moving up to the sales manager position.

The highest level a person can reach at the local level is the general manager's position. In the past, most general managers came from the sales department. This trend is likely to continue, but it is also probable that more people who start off in the news departments will move into management, since news is becoming more of a moneymaker.

>> **Other Opportunities**

A television station is not the only place to look for employment. As cable provides more local programming and adds more channels, the industry will need more people in promotion, publicity, performance, marketing, and community relations. Allied with cable are the pay-TV services (HBO, Showtime, etc.). These organizations will also need skilled personnel.

Another emerging employment source is home video. The production of prerecorded cassettes and videodiscs represents another area with opportunities. In addition, many large companies, such as IBM and Microsoft, use TV to produce employee training programs and to fill other internal communication needs. Although not as visible as some other parts of the industry, this is an important source of employment for a large number of people.

MAIN POINTS

- Electronic television developed during the 1930s. After World War II, it quickly grew in popularity and replaced radio as the main information and entertainment medium.

- The three networks—NBC, CBS, and ABC— dominated early TV. Live drama, variety, and quiz and game shows were popular during the 1950s.

- Television matured in the 1960s, and its content became more professional. The public television network began in 1967. Cable TV grew slowly during this decade.

- The 1970s saw TV programs criticized for excessive violence.

- In the 1980s and 1990s, the three traditional TV nets lost viewers to cable and to VCRs. The Fox network became a major competitor.

- The Telecommunications Act of 1996 had a significant impact on TV-station ownership and also introduced program content ratings. Rules for the eventual conversion to digital TV were announced in 1997.

- Changing from analog to digital signals will mean better pictures and sound. Consumers will have to buy a new TV set or a converter to receive the new signals. TV stations may use the digital signal to broadcast high-definition television or lower-definition programs among which viewers may choose.

- TV is universal, dominant, and expensive. Its audience is currently fragmenting into smaller segments.

- The broadcast TV industry consists of program suppliers, distributors, and local stations.

- Big conglomerates own the major TV networks, and large group owners control most of the stations in large markets.

- Public broadcasting relies less on tax revenues and more on private sources of funding.

- Cable TV had reached maturity by the turn of the century and was facing problems associated with its rapid growth. The Telecommunications Act of 1996 permitted cable and phone companies to compete with one another.

- The costs and revenues connected with a cable system are different from those of a broadcast station.

- Home video is dominated by the major motion picture studios. Retailers are concerned about the eventual impact of direct broadcast satellite systems (DBS) and video on demand on their business.

- DBS systems started slowly but have become more widespread in the last two to three years.

- The Nielsen company compiles both network and local-station television ratings.

QUESTIONS FOR REVIEW

1. What are the defining features of the TV medium?
2. What are some of the advantages of being an affiliate of a major TV network?
3. Who owns the TV networks?
4. Trace the evolution of U.S. noncommercial TV programming.
5. What companies control the cable TV industry?
6. Compare and contrast Nielsen's method of measuring network TV viewers with its technique for measuring local-market TV viewing.

QUESTIONS FOR CRITICAL THINKING

1. How will HDTV change the TV industry?
2. What should be the goal of public television? Should the government support public broadcasting?
3. Large companies control both the broadcast and cable television industries. What are some of the good points and bad points of large corporate ownership?
4. The major broadcast networks have been losing viewers for the past two decades or so. Will they still be around 10 to 15 years from now? Why or why not?
5. In addition to the Nielsen People Meter, what are some ways that television viewing can be measured?

KEY TERMS

High Definition Television (HDTV) (p. 254)
Public Broadcasting Act of 1967 (p. 257)
time shifting (p. 259)
digital television (DTV) (p. 261)
commercial television (p. 264)
noncommercial television (p. 264)
VHF (p. 267)
UHF (p. 267)
independents (p. 267)
pilot (p. 270)
head end (p. 279)
distribution system (p. 279)
house drop (p. 280)
carriage fee (p. 281)
personal video recorder (PVR) (p. 282)
video on demand (VOD) (p. 284)
direct broadcast satellite (DBS) (p. 283)
rating (p. 286)
share of the audience (p. 286)
concept testing (p. 288)
pilot testing (p. 288)

INTERNET RESOURCES

Online Learning Center

At the Online Learning Center home page, www.mhhe.com/dominick8, *select* Student Center *and then* Chapter 10.

1. Use the Learning Objectives, Chapter Outline, Main Points, and Time Line sections to review this chapter.
2. Test your knowledge of the chapter using the multiple choice, crossword puzzle, and flashcard features of the site.
3. Expand your knowledge of concepts and topics discussed in the chapter by going to *Suggestions for Further Reading* and *Internet Exercises*.

PowerWeb

At the Mass Communication home page of PowerWeb, www.dushkin.com/powerweb, *log in and select* Mass Communication *as your title. On the next screen, select* Topics *and then quick jump to* Television. *Read Article 47, "The Evolution of Gendercasting." Then consider the following questions:*

1. A new "gendercasting" cable network, Spike TV, debuted in 2003. Compare the programming on Spike to the programming on Lifetime. What do you conclude?

2. Does gendercasting promote gender stereotypes? For example, does Lifetime carry sports programming? Shows about fishing? Car repair?

3. Do you agree that female audiences are now "better served" by targeted cable networks than they were with traditional broadcast TV?

Now read Article 53, "HD Production Gets the Last Laugh."

1. What is the future of traditional celluloid film now that HDTV is becoming more affordable?

2. Will increased sports programming help HDTV become more popular? Why or why not?

Surfing the Internet

www.historychannel.com/
The History Channel's home page. Has more about history than it does about its cable network, but it has good examples of interactivity and streaming video.

www.howstuffworks.com/hdtv.htm
A basic, easy-to-understand explanation of HDTV technology.

www.mtr.org/
Those interested in the history of television should visit the home page of the Museum of Television and Radio. Site contains a guided tour of the museum's New York and Los Angeles locations.

www.mtv.com
MTV online. Detailed site that contains links to just about everything on MTV.

www.netreach.net/~kaufman/
The "Kill Your Television" home page. If you do not like TV, this is the site for you. Includes a page that suggests things to do instead of watching TV.

www.nielsenmedia.com
Information about Nielsen Media Research, the firm that rates TV programs. Check out the Ratings 101 link for a basic description of how the TV audience is measured.

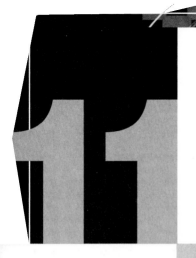

THE INTERNET AND THE WORLD WIDE WEB

This chapter will prepare you to

- describe how computers were invented;

- explain how the Internet and the World Wide Web were developed;

- understand the advantages of broadband Internet access;

- recognize the economic impact of the Internet; and

- discuss the social concerns raised by the Internet.

It may seem hard to believe but in 2002 the FBI estimated that more than 2500 Americans fell for the Nigerian e-mail scam or one of its hundreds of variations,

How lucky can a guy be? I was browsing through my e-mail the other day and found a message from a member of Nigeria's Audit Committee informing me that he had found a forgotten account from some now-defunct corrupt oil company with $15 million in it and all he needed to get the money was a foreign-based intermediary. He was asking me to be his partner, for which he would give me one-third of the loot, or $5 million! All I had to do was supply him with the name of my bank and my bank account number.

But it got better. Another e-mail was from the personal assistant of a rich farmer in Zimbabwe. The local political situation was apparently becoming hostile to rich landowners, and this particular farmer had managed to send about $30 million out of the country, but then he died. So his assistant was asking me to help him find a safe haven for the money. All I had to do was give him my bank name and bank account number, and he would give me one-third of the loot, or $10 million! For just providing a little information! What had I done to get so lucky?

Actually, I had done nothing. I was just one of millions of others who were contacted. As you may have already realized, these examples are just two of the many scams that are circulating via e-mail on the Internet. In the past, confidence artists would spend a long

---

E-mail – Message

To: Dominick, Joseph
Subject: Request for urgent business relationship

REQUEST FOR URGENT BUSINESS RELATIONSHIP

FIRST, I MUST SOLICIT YOUR STRICTEST CONFIDENCE IN THIS TRANSACTION. THIS IS BY VIRTUE OF ITS NATURE AS BEING UTTERLY CONFIDENTIAL AND 'TOP SECRET'. I AM SURE AND HAVE CONFIDENCE OF YOUR ABILITY AND RELIABILITY TO PROSECUTE A TRANSACTION OF THIS GREAT MAGNITUDE INVOLVING A PENDING TRANSACTION REQUIRING MAXIIMUM CONFIDENCE.

WE ARE TOP OFFICIAL OF THE FEDERAL GOVERNMENT CONTRACT REVIEW PANEL WHO ARE INTERESTED IN IMPORATION OF GOODS INTO OUR

time researching and selecting potential victims. Now, with e-mail, they can simply send mass messages and hope that some suckers will bite. Is anybody actually so dumb as to fall for one of these schemes? Apparently so. The U.S. Secret Service estimated that the scammers collected about $100 million in 2002. As a matter of fact, Internet fraud ranks among the top five industries in Nigeria. Faced with international pressure, the Nigerian government has recently cracked down on those who conduct these rip-offs.

On a more general level, these schemes illustrate that the Internet has brought us both positive and negative consequences. On the one hand, it entertains us, informs us, links us with friends and family, provides us with the world's greatest reference library, and stimulates commerce. On the other hand, it opens up whole new areas of concern: identity theft, fraud, deceptive advertising, pornography, and invasion of privacy.

For better or for worse, the Internet has become firmly embedded in the nation's communication repertoire. It is hard to imagine how we ever got along without e-mail, e-commerce, e-dating, and eBay. This chapter examines how the computer turned into a communication medium, how the Internet developed, the coming of broadband, e-business, the growing online audience, the Internet's role in blurring the distinction between mass and interpersonal communication, and some of the social implications of this new medium.

A BRIEF HISTORY OF THE COMPUTER

The earliest versions of the computer were basically adding machines designed to take the drudgery out of repetitive arithmetical calculations. In the 17th century, French mathematician and philosopher Blaise Pascal (a modern computer language was named for him) created the *arithmatique*, a machine the size of a shoebox filled with interconnected 10-toothed wheels that could add numbers up to one million. A few decades later, the German mathematician Gottfried Wilhelm von Leibniz explored the subject of binary arithmetic, a system with just two possible values, 0 and 1. The binary system is the one used by modern computers.

During the 19th century, English inventor Charles Babbage, working with Augusta Ada Byron, the daughter of Lord Byron, the English poet, worked out plans for an "analytical engine," a steam-powered device about the size of a football field, that would quickly perform complicated mathematical operations. The existing technology, however, was not sufficient to build this machine, and after 19 years of trying, Babbage and Byron gave up.

In America, Herman Hollerith developed a tabulating machine to help process data collected in the census of 1880. His machine used punched cards and electrical circuits to do calculations and worked so well that businesses all over the country clamored for it, prompting him to start his own company, International Business Machines (IBM).

In 1940, a Harvard University mathematician, Howard Aiken, made the next major breakthrough when he created a digital computer—one that worked with binary numbers, 0 and 1, or in Aiken's case, switch closed or switch open. Aiken's computer, the Mark I, was 50 feet long and 8 feet tall and had 750,000 parts. When it was running, it sounded like thousands of knitting needles clicking together. A few years later, researchers at the University of Pennsylvania constructed the first all-electronic computer, ENIAC. Although ENIAC was much faster than any previous mechanical computer, its size was a drawback—it stood two stories tall, weighed 30 tons, and used about 18,000 vacuum tubes.

The invention of the transistor in the 1950s led to new electronic computers that were smaller, cheaper, and easier to maintain. Integrated circuits made it possible for many transistors to be embedded in a tiny silicon chip, which paved the way for the microprocessor. These advances opened up new markets for computer manufacturers. In the late 1970s, personal computers (PCs), using packaged software, appeared in new computer stores. Designed for home use, these computers were used primarily for word processing, financial management, and game playing.

A few years later, developments in hardware and software expanded the communication function of the computer. The **modem,** from *mod*ulate and *dem*odulate, enabled PCs to converse with one another and with larger computers located in other places over telephone lines. New communications software facilitated the development of local area networks (LANs), which linked several computers into a network. As miniaturization continued, laptop computers and wireless modems became more common.

The 1990s saw an explosion in computer communication that continues today. Every day more than 500 million pieces of electronic mail (e-mail) are carried over the Internet. Every night thousands of individuals log on to computerized chat

ENIAC, completed in the late 1940s, was the world's first general-purpose, digital all-electronic computer. The device took up most of the space in a good-sized room. ENIAC is a far cry from today's laptop computers.

lines, check bulletin boards, visit websites, shop, read the news, play trivia and other games, engage in online conferences, and transfer information files. Perhaps the biggest reason for this surge in online communication has been the development of the Internet.

 THE INTERNET

The Internet is a network of computer networks. Think of it as a system that combines computers from all over the world into one big computer that you can operate from your own PC. Some computers are run by government agencies (like the National Aeronautics and Space Administration), some are run by universities, some by libraries, some by school systems, some by businesses, and so on. The connections among these networks can be ordinary phone lines, microwaves, optical fibers, or wires built specially for this purpose. A related example might be the phone system. When you call somebody in Cleveland, the call is routed through several different phone networks in different parts of the country. You really do not care what route it takes or what companies handle it as long as your call gets there. So, too, with the Internet. When you search for information, send mail, or chat online, several different networks may handle your messages. Just as there is no one phone company, there is also no one Internet company.

The Internet's seemingly chaotic structure arose from its somewhat fractured history. A little background will help to clarify.

>> **From ARPANET to Internet**

Back in the early 1970s, when the cold war was still raging, the U.S. Department of Defense was concerned about the vulnerability of its computer network to nuclear attack. The Pentagon did not want to lose all its computing and communication ability to one well-placed atomic bomb. Consequently, defense computer experts decentralized the whole system by creating an interconnected web of computer networks. The net was designed so that every computer could talk to every other computer. Information was bundled in a packet, called an Internet Protocol packet, which contained the destination address of the target computer. The computers themselves then figured out how to send the packet. Thus, if one portion of the network happened to be disabled, the rest of the network could still function normally. The system that the Pentagon eventually developed was called ARPANET.

At about the same time, companies developed software that enabled computers to be linked to local area networks (LANs) that also contained the Internet Protocol programs. Not surprisingly, many of these LANs were also connected to ARPANET, causing the network to grow even more.

The users of this early network were primarily scientists and computer experts, and most observers thought it would continue to be of interest only to high-tech types. (The network was once uncharitably labeled a "Disneyland for geeks.") In the late 1980s, however, the National Science Foundation, whose own network was already connected to the net, created supercomputing centers at U.S. universities. Since they were so expensive, only five could be built. This meant that they had to be shared and interconnected. The ARPANET seemed like the obvious choice for interconnection, but there were too many problems involved. Instead, the National Science Foundation built its own system using the Internet Protocol and hooked together chains of regional networks that were eventually linked to a supercomputer. Thus the Internet, or Net, was born.

Now that students, scientists, government workers, and others had access to supercomputers, the amount of information at their disposal increased tremendously. The Internet also served as a communications link that enabled scientists from all over the country to share data. Doctors, lawyers, journalists, authors, and business owners recognized the potential of the Net, and traffic increased.

The Internet was still used by only a small fraction of computer owners. Three developments, however, contributed to a meteoric rise in the Internet's popularity. The first was the development of the World Wide Web (WWW, or Web) in 1990. Engineers working at a physics laboratory in Switzerland created an interconnected set of computers on the Net that all used the same communications program. This communications program took advantage of **hypertext,** a navigational tool that linked one electronic document, either text or graphics, with another, thus creating a virtual web of pages. The Web started off as an electronic information resource for scientists but was quickly discovered and utilized by the entire Internet community. Any organization or individual could create a page on the Web as long as the person or organization used the communication rules developed in Switzerland. It was not long before conventional media companies, businesses, organizations, and individuals got involved with the Web. By 1998, it was estimated that there were more than a million websites in operation.

The second development made it easier for consumers to find what they were looking for on the Web. This happened in 1993 with the creation of user-friendly navigation tools that helped further spur the growth of the World Wide Web. The first of these **browsers,** called Mosaic, was able to retrieve data, determine what it was, and configure it for display. Mosaic created a graphical display for users that simplified navigating the Internet. In 1994, one of the developers of Mosaic formed a commercial company that was eventually named Netscape. Software giant Microsoft introduced its own browser, Internet Explorer, a few years later.

The third development was the **search engine,** a utility that scans the Internet for terms selected by the user and displays the results according to some predetermined criterion, such as relevance. Some well-known search engines are Google, Alta Vista, and Excite. These advances helped users make sense of the Internet and turned it into a useful information tool.

At the end of 2003, more than 200 million host computers were connected to the Net. Two of every three adults in the United States were online. Obviously, the Internet had grown into a powerful mass communication medium.

 ## STRUCTURE AND FEATURES OF THE INTERNET

As mentioned earlier, the Internet is a global network of computer networks. In more technical terms, this means that a group of two or more networks is electronically connected and able to communicate with one another. Together, they act as a single network. For this to work, however, the computers have to speak a common language. The common language, called a **protocol** by computer programmers, that was developed for the Internet is called the TCP/IP protocol. TCP/IP stands for Transmission Control Protocol/Internet Protocol. It is actually a set of protocols that govern how data travel from one machine to another over networks. IP is sort of like the address on an envelope. It tells a computer where to send a particular message. TCP breaks up the information into packets that can be transmitted efficiently and then reassembles them at their destination.

Figure 11–1 presents a schematic view of the Internet and some of its major elements. At the bottom of the diagram is the audience, the people who provide content for and access content from the Internet. They gain access to the Internet in one of two ways:

1. through an Internet Service Provider (ISP), a company that connects a subscriber to the Net and usually charges a fee (many companies, including some local phone companies, function as ISPs), or

2. through an Online Service Provider (OSP) such as America Online or Prodigy.

Technically speaking, the difference between an ISP and an OSP is that OSPs typically offer exclusive content or services to their subscribers, and ISPs simply connect the user directly to the Internet. Many ISPs, however, offer exclusive browser software and other features so that the distinction between these two services is becoming blurred.

Once connected to the Internet, an individual can make use of a variety of tools for information, entertainment, and communication. Some of the more popular applications are e-mail, newsgroups, and the World Wide Web.

>> E-Mail

Millions of people are connected to the Internet, and you can send mail to one of them or to many of them. **E-mail** works on the client/server arrangement. To send and read e-mail, users (clients) must access another computer (the server), where their mailbox resides. E-mail messages are not limited to text. Attachments, such as graphics or spreadsheets, can also be sent.

E-mail is usually fast, cheap, and reliable. It is the most widely used Internet resource. In 2000, more than six trillion e-mail messages moved through the Net.

FIGURE 11–1

Structure of the Internet

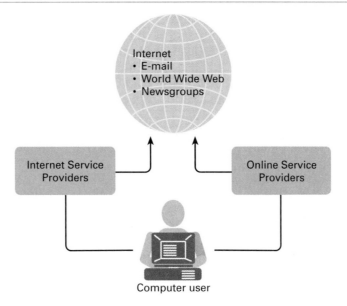

It is not surprising that the computer and the Internet have raised many new ethical questions. Computer experts at the Computer Ethics Institute have developed the Ten Commandments for Computer Ethics. The commandments are rather general and noncontroversial, such as "Thou shalt not use a computer to steal" and "Thou shalt not use a computer program for which you have not paid." There are other areas, however, where the issues are not so clear.

One such area involves anonymity. In the offline world, a person has to make an extra effort to remain anonymous. Hiding your true identity might require an unlisted phone number, a fake ID, and a disguise. On the Internet, however, anonymity is the default condition. User names generally are generic and say little about the true identity of the user. A person has to make an extra effort to establish his or her *real* identity.

Anonymity is not necessarily bad. For example, it disguises differences in race, sex, age, and physical appearance. To the extent that these items interfere with fairness, anonymity may serve as an equalizer. Further, people may be encouraged to reveal their true feelings if they know their identity will not be revealed. Battered spouses, for instance, might be better able to ask for help.

Conversely, anonymity creates problems. People are more apt to behave in undesirable ways when they act anonymously. They may send inflammatory or racist messages, post offensive material, and snoop into the affairs of others. It is also easy for a person to claim to be someone he or she is not or to become multiple persons with multiple identities. The best illustration of this is the case of a man who pretended to be a woman and participated in an online discussion group that dealt with women's issues. Is such behavior ethical? What if the man used his online female persona to arrange a date between his true self and a woman in the group?

Anonymity can undermine trust. In the offline world, people establish a history of dealing with other people and can decide whether a person is to be trusted. This is far more difficult in the online world where the same person might have multiple identities or the same identity might be used by more than one person. You have trouble developing a history because you are never sure about whom you are dealing with.

Are there ethical principles (see Chapter 16) that can be applied to anonymity on the Net? One possibility is situational ethics. There may be some situations in which no one expects others to reveal their true identities. Adult-oriented chat rooms, for example, might call for a high level of anonymity (in which everybody assumes that everybody else is not who they purport to be). On the other hand, it would be unethical to participate in a discussion group about the consequences of child abuse by falsely claiming to be an abuse victim. As the popularity of the Net continues to grow, much more attention will be paid to issues such as these.

E-mail is helpful, but it also has some drawbacks. First, it is not as formal as a printed letter, so there may be some tasks for which it is inappropriate (like telling someone he or she has been fired). Second, e-mail is not as private as a letter in an envelope. Your message may travel through several computers where others might have access to it. At some companies employee e-mail might also be available to management. Third, e-mail comes with the ever-present nuisance called **spam.** Spam, the cyber equivalent of junk mail, includes unsolicited messages touting get-rich-quick schemes, low mortgage rates, porno sites, and miracle cures; clogs up people's mailboxes; and takes time to delete. Spam is on the increase; one Internet consulting firm predicts that by the end of 2004 there will be more spam messages than legitimate e-mail. If that were not bad enough, the same firm found that one in every 200 spam messages contained a virus. Fourth, there is the problem of information overload. In many businesses, memos that used to go to a small group of people now get sent to everybody, and every decision—no matter how small—gets circulated via e-mail. As a result, the average worker at a Fortune 500 company sends and receives nearly 200 messages every day, taking up a big chunk of the workday.

>> Newsgroups

Newsgroups are collections of electronic bulletin boards, arranged according to topic, where people can read and post messages. Some newsgroups are devoted to current events, but the *news* in *newsgroups* refers to topical discussion groups, not news in the traditional sense. The information or "articles" that make up the news are written by people interested in the topic. Others can read the articles and comment on them. The newsgroups exist on a special network called Usenet, one component of the Internet.

Newsgroup categories are organized in a systematic hierarchy that moves from the general to the specific. For example, two general categories of newsgroups end in the suffixes *alt* and *sci*. One subtopic in one of the alt categories is *algebra,* and a subtopic under that entry is *help.* Looking at the messages on this board reveals that they are about how to solve various equations. Under the sci category is a listing for *materials* and another subtopic for *ceramics.* This bulletin board contains many articles about the tiles on the space shuttle.

There are more than 40,000 different newsgroups, with topics ranging from the highly intellectual to the downright weird. Each newsgroup is made up of messages about the topic. If one or more people reply to a message, those messages are grouped into a thread. For example, suppose you were browsing through the Elvis newsgroup. You might come upon one message asking about details of Elvis's performances in Las Vegas. Six people might have replied to that message, creating a thread seven messages long.

>> World Wide Web

As mentioned earlier, the **World Wide Web (WWW)** is a network of information sources incorporating hypertext that allows the user to link one piece of information to another. Note that the Web is *part* of the Internet; the two terms are not synonymous. The Web is nonlinear. This means that the user does not have to follow a hierarchical path from one piece of information to another. A user can jump from the middle of one document into the middle of another. In addition, the Web incorporates text, graphics, sound, and motion.

Some terminology might be useful at this point. The structure of the Web is based on the Web server, a computer connected to the Internet that facilitates the transfer of hypertext pages. One server can hold thousands of hypertext pages. A **website** is a complete set of hypertext pages linked to each other that contains information about a common topic. A **Web page** is a hypertext page that is contained within a website. The home page of a website is the entry or doorway to the site that might contain links to other pages or to various sections of the site.

The protocols for navigating the Web assign each Web page a uniform resource locator (URL) and an Internet address. URLs are structured as follows:

protocol://server.subdomain.top-level domain/directory/filename

For example, the URL for the McGraw-Hill Publishing Company's Communication page (which has links to the latest updates of this book and other interesting materials) is

http://www.mhhe.com/catalogs/hss/comm

This means that the page is in the hypertext transfer protocol, the server is linked to the WWW, the subdomain name is *mhhe,* the top-level domain is *com,* the directory name is *catalogs,* the file name is *hss,* and the specific file is *comm.* Not every URL will have a directory and a file name.

The tremendous variety of sites and the motives behind them make it difficult to describe websites in general terms. There are sites maintained by big media companies, such as the *New York Times* and the Walt Disney Company, that are used to promote their traditional media products and to build an audience for the online content as well. Other companies, such as Nissan and the Miller Brewing Company, use their websites to advertise their product lines. Government agencies, such as the IRS and the Department of Agriculture, have designed websites to serve their constituents and to promote good public relations. Professional organizations, such as the Association for Education in Journalism and Mass Communication, use their sites to share information among their members. Groups with special interests, such as the American Diabetes Association, use their sites to disseminate information. Professors set up pages where they post syllabi, readings, and other resources for their classes. Some sites are on the Web to make a profit; they sell advertising or charge a subscription fee. Some sites are simply search engines that enable the user to search other sites.

Many websites function as **portals.** A portal, as the name suggests, is an entryway, the first page a person looks at before zooming off into the Web. The strategy behind a successful portal is to offer visitors useful information, such as news headlines, weather, stock information, chat rooms, and bargains, so that he or she does not go looking for these items at some other site. The longer a person stays at the portal, the greater the chance that he or she might see some of the advertising on the site. Some of the best-known portals are those provided by Yahoo!, Excite, MSNBC, and Netscape.

Finally, some Web pages are published by individuals. Many of you reading this may already have your own Web page.

How big is the World Wide Web? The answer is hard to come by because the Web grows every day. As of 2003, the search engine Google estimated that there were about 3.3 billion unique pages on the Web. However, although it is called the *World Wide Web,* it is primarily a Web for industrialized nations. About 85 percent of the pages on the Web are in English, Japanese, French, or German.

>> Online Service Providers

Started back in the 1980s, Online Service Providers (OSPs) provide their subscribers with exclusive information and entertainment as well as access to the Internet. As of 2003, there were three major OSPs:

1. *America Online (AOL):* The biggest OSP, AOL also owns Compuserve, giving it a total of about 27 million subscribers. AOL has recently seen its fortunes wane. Its merger with Time Warner was a disappointment, and it continues to lose subscribers to other ISPs that offer more economical high-speed Internet connections. In addition, AOL suffers from a problem with churn. Many of its users take advantage of a free trial period but quit the service when the free period is over. One source estimated that, at any given time, more than three million of AOL's subscribers are nonpaying customers.

2. *Microsoft Network (MSN):* With more than seven million subscribers, MSN runs a distant second to AOL, but the gap has been closing over the past two years. MSN launched a massive $300 million ad campaign in 2003 featuring the MSN butterfly and emphasizing MSN's new parental control feature.

3. *SBC Yahoo!:* SBC Communications acquired OSP Prodigy in 2001. The next year SBC struck a deal with Yahoo! to start the new SBC Yahoo! The new service has a subscriber base of about three million.

All three of these companies are concerned about the future. To keep their subscriber count growing, the OSPs offer special features such as message filters, exclusive content, spam controls, and instant messages and chatting. Moreover, all are trying to entice conventional dial-up subscribers to switch to their more expensive high-speed connections.

THE EVOLVING INTERNET

The Internet changes so fast that it is hard to predict its future. Nonetheless, here are several trends that most experts agree will significantly affect the Net in the next few years.

>> Broadband

Most Americans still access the Net through a dial-up phone connection and a 56 K modem. This arrangement works fine for text, but it is painfully slow for sending audio or graphics, and it is not at all practical for video. The phone line does not have enough bandwidth to handle the tremendous amount of information used for multimedia.

The answer to this problem is broadband. **Broadband** refers to any of the several ways to connect to the Internet that carry information many times faster than conventional dial-up modems. The tremendous gain in speed makes it possible to send huge files in much less time. Downloading a typical music file might take more than half an hour with a dial-up modem but only a minute or so with a broadband connection. In addition, broadband makes it practical to send video over the Internet.

Currently, consumers can access broadband through three main sources:

1. *Satellite:* Satellite connections to the Internet transmit data about seven or eight times faster than conventional modems. Subscribers, of course, must have a satellite dish. Cost is about $30 to $100 per month, depending on use.

2. *Cable modem:* Download speeds with a cable modem, provided by companies that also carry cable TV, can be as fast as 1 megabyte per second. Subscribers

with cable modems share bandwidth. If many users are online at the same time, speed is reduced. Also, if your cable TV service goes out, so does your modem. Cost is about $50 to $75 per month.

3. *Digital subscriber line (DSL):* A DSL line piggybacks Internet service on a regular phone line. Speeds range from 640k per second to several megabytes per second, depending upon the modem and the wiring used to connect the modem to the computer. DSL works only if you are 3 miles or less from a central telephone office (a central office is a building where the local switching equipment is housed), which makes it more practical for urban and suburban dwellers. Cost ranges from $45 to $150 per month.

Technology experts have touted broadband for many years as the wave of the Internet future. In addition to facilitating high-speed Internet access, broadband makes possible many other desirable things, including video on demand, interactive television, live streaming video, and downloadable movies. As mentioned previously, it was the promise of broadband services that was a prime factor behind the megamerger of AOL and Time Warner.

Despite all the hype, broadband has been slow to catch on in the United States. Many people are unwilling to pay the extra monthly fees for broadband. Recognizing this, some ISPs are offering special pricing plans, and some have introduced a cheaper, reduced-speed broadband service. Despite these developments, as of 2003, only about 20 percent of American homes had some form of broadband. Most analysts suggest that this number will grow slowly over the next five years or so.

Interestingly enough, the United States is behind other countries in the adoption of broadband. In Hong Kong and South Korea, for example, more than 50 percent of households are equipped with broadband. The United States is lagging primarily because local phone companies have not pushed broadband as aggressively as their counterparts in other countries. In addition, in some countries the government has partially financed the broadband conversion.

Those who do subscribe to broadband like it. A study done by the National Association of Broadcasters found that people with broadband connections spend about two and one-half hours online every day compared with one hour a day for those with dial-up modems.

≫ The Wireless Web

As described earlier, wireless technology will become more and more common during the next decade. Not surprisingly, the Internet will reflect this growing trend. There were about 15 million laptop computers with wireless Net access in use in 2003 along with about 22 million cell-phone subscribers and PDA users who reported using their devices to connect to the Net. Improved color screens and easier-to-use interfaces will probably increase this number in the near future. Pretty soon, the Internet will be available everywhere.

What makes all of this possible is the development of **wireless fidelity,** or **WiFi,** technology. WiFi uses low-power radio signals to connect devices to one another and to the Internet. A base station serves as a transmitter, and PDAs, computers, and cell phone customers can use special hardware and software to hook into the system.

Many WiFi public access locations or "hot spots" have sprung up all over the country, in airport waiting rooms, cafes, and even parks. People who frequent these

Contributed by Scott Shamp
Director, New Media Institute, University of Georgia

The Internet gave us our first true taste of on-demand information. With our connected computer we can access information from around the world at any time of the day or night. But any information at any time is not enough. Now we want that information anywhere we are—in the car, at the coffee shop, in the classroom.

Wireless technologies now allow untethered access to the Internet. Basically, all wireless systems utilize basic radio technology. And, although there are many different types of systems, two have emerged as the leading wireless options.

The first system, 3G, is built on the same principles as cellular telephone service. Like cellular telephone service, 3G divides geographic areas into cells (or zones). Towers equipped with transmitting antennas are strategically placed to provide connectivity to all areas of the cell. The size of the cells differs according to the topology of the land and man-made features such as buildings. Cells are typically measured in kilometers. The biggest limitation on 3G is its transmission speed. It would take a little over a minute to download the average MP3 file on a 3G network. Today, 3G networks are more a goal than a mature service. 3G networks exist on a limited scale in Japan and Europe but are slowly coming online in the United States.

WiFi (wireless fidelity) provides a very different approach to wireless data transmission. WiFi was originally designed as a wireless local area network for laptop and desktop computers. But today WiFi is being used to deliver connectivity to a range of other types of devices. In a WiFi network, a small low-powered device called an *access point* (AP) about the size of this textbook handles transmission to and from the computers. The AP then relays the data to the Internet, typically through a broadband wired connection. WiFi is a short-range technology with a typical coverage area of about a city block. It operates in a portion of the electromagnetic spectrum that governments have set aside for amateur use. Therefore, no license is required to operate a WiFi network. The result has been a proliferation of WiFi networks, or "hot spots," where users can connect for a small fee or even for free. The primary advantage of WiFi is its higher transmission speeds. With speeds 28 times faster than existing 3G networks, a three-minute MP3 would take less than three seconds to download using WiFi.

Today, these systems are distinct and incompatible. 3G networks are sending data over larger areas at slower speeds, typically to increasingly smaller handheld phones. WiFi networks offer higher bandwidth but in much smaller areas, mainly for laptop computers or PDAs (personal digital assistants). Wireless will become even more powerful when 3G and WiFi become compatible, allowing the user to connect to the best wireless system available.

hot spots can link up with the Internet at no cost. Experts estimate that there are tens of thousands of WiFi public locations in the United States. Those not fortunate enough to find a free hot spot can purchase WiFi access for about $50 or more a month. (For more information on WiFi, see Media Probe, "The Internet Unleashed.")

>> Streaming Video

The switch to broadband will make **streaming video** much more popular. When video files first showed up on the Web, a user had to download the entire file onto his or her computer's hard drive and then play it back. Since even relatively small video files could be several megabytes in size, downloading required the patience of a saint. Streaming video, in effect, enables the user to watch the beginning of a video file while the rest is still downloading. The first part of the video file is stored in a buffer and then played back while another portion is downloaded, making for a seamless stream of information.

During the heady times of the dot-com boom, several companies tried to turn streaming video into a competitor with traditional TV. The economic downturn forced most of these companies out of business. One that survived was RealNetworks. As of 2003, its RealOne service had about 600,000 subscribers paying for streaming replays of ABC newscasts, entertainment news from E!, sports news from Fox, forecasts from the Weather Channel, and original short films.

Entertainment websites make frequent use of streaming video by providing short video clips of movies or music videos to visitors. The major online news providers also offer streaming video clips of news events. The biggest increase, however, in the use of streaming video has come from the business sector. After the September 11 terrorist attacks, many companies turned to streaming video conferences instead of having employees travel by air to face-to-face meetings. Additionally, many large U.S. corporations have integrated streaming video into their training operations.

>> Microcasting

When the Brookwood High School Marching Bronco Band of Snellville, Georgia, spent a few days at band camp in South Carolina, parents back in Georgia could check up on their progress thanks to a Web cam that sent video of their practices over the Internet. Newlyweds Dusty and Fernando of Austin, Texas, put streaming video of their wedding on their website so that people who could not attend in person could see the ceremony. At the other end of the spectrum, more than 60 funeral parlors nationwide offer webcasts of funerals.

The word *broadcasting,* as first used with early radio and then TV, meant sending a message to a large, heterogeneous group of people. When format radio and cable TV networks came into being, the word *narrowcasting* was coined for targeting your message to appeal to a small, well-defined subsegment of the total audience. Top 40 radio stations, for example, narrowcast to 12 to 22 year olds; ESPN narrowcasts primarily to male sports fans; C-SPAN, to aficionados of politics. Video sent over the Internet takes this process one step further by making possible *microcasting,* sending a message to a small group of interested people. This is another example of the "few-to-few" model of communication mentioned in Chapter 1.

Although many experts think that the Internet will ultimately become a mass communication medium and that audiences will watch TV shows and Hollywood movies over their broadband connections, all appearances are that the Internet is evolving in the other direction. The most successful applications, such as instant messaging, online auctions, and peer-to-peer file sharing, have been inspired by the end users and not by big mass communication conglomerates. Microcasting is yet another example of this trend.

Fergerson Funeral Home microcasts funerals on the Web. *(Fergerson Funeral Home, Inc.)*

Before long Internet-capable cell phones will be equipped with video cameras. When that happens, the possibilities of Web microcasts will become endless. Dad could microcast Scott's and Buffy's soccer games or band recitals to the grandparents in another state. High schools could microcast the prom to interested parents. How about video of the local Little League games? Microcasting, of

Even Better Than Cliffs Notes?

Don't have time to read all those novels for your English class? Never fear, the Web is here. Check out rinkworks.com and its Book-a-Minute link for a really bare-bones summary of a plot. For example, with apologies to Charlotte Brontë, here is *Jane Eyre:*

People are mean to Jane Eyre.

Edward Rochester: I have a dark secret. Will you
                         stay with me no matter what?
Jane Eyre: Yes.
Edward Rochester: My secret is that I have a
                         lunatic wife.
Jane Eyre: Bye.

Jane Eyre leaves. Somebody dies. Jane Eyre returns.

Or how about Twain's *Huckleberry Finn:* Goes rafting. Goes home.

course, will raise all sorts of questions about privacy that will have to be resolved in the near future.

 ## ECONOMICS

We will now look at the general impact of the Internet on the national economy, examine the impact of e-commerce, and then focus on the finances of individual websites.

>> The Internet and the National Economy

After a boom period from 1998 to mid-2000, Internet-related businesses found hard times in the new century. At the beginning of 2001, it was estimated that stocks of Internet companies had lost more than $1.7 trillion in value. Many dotcom companies folded, and thousands of jobs were lost.

The bust, however, may have a silver lining. The dot-com companies that survived the fallout are those that have sound business plans and good cash flow. At the end of 2002 about 40 percent of publicly traded Internet companies were profitable, including such familiar companies as eBay, Expedia, and Ask Jeeves. Further, traditional companies have become more skilled at using the Net. Many companies have integrated their once-independent Internet divisions back under the corporate umbrella. Banking giant Citigroup, for example, started e-Citi in an attempt to create a dominant Web presence. Consumers were lukewarm to the new service, and Citigroup eventually folded it back into the parent company, after which it saw its online customers greatly increase.

More traditional brick-and-mortar stores, such as Wal-Mart and Home Depot, use the Internet as an additional revenue stream. Other corporations are turning to the Net as a business tool, using it to buy parts, handle customer relations, and facilitate worker teamwork. In short, the final economic impact of the Net is yet to be determined, but the long-term outlook seems positive.

>> E-Commerce

E-commerce is the term used to describe the selling of goods, products, and services online. There are two kinds of e-commerce: the better-known type in which companies sell directly to consumers and a less-visible kind called *B2B* or *e-business* in which companies sell to each other. We will look at consumer e-commerce first.

Statistics reveal the scope of e-commerce. From being nonexistent in the early 1990s, global e-commerce came to account for approximately $110 billion in online spending in 2002. About 10 million consumers purchase something online every week. A 2002 survey of 1,000 businesses revealed that 90 percent had some form of online e-commerce. The products and services that account for most of e-commerce are travel, computer hardware and software, apparel, books, and music.

Impressive as these numbers might be, they pale in comparison to B2B e-commerce. In 2002, the B2B online market accounted for about $500 billion in

One way to make money with a website is to sell merchandise online as does ecost.com. *(eCOST.com)*

sales. Experts think that this number will exceed the trillion-dollar mark in a few years. The Internet enables businesses to deal directly with one another, sometimes eliminating the middleperson (another example of disintermediation), making the process more efficient. Commerce One, for example, is a B2B site that helps buyers connect with sellers in industries ranging from auto parts sales to soft-drink bottling. Experts predict that B2B will save American businesses billions of dollars in the years to come.

Now let us take a more specific look at the financial side of individual websites.

>> Website Economics

The tremendous variation in the kinds of people and organizations found on the Internet makes it hard to summarize its economic arrangements. Suffice it to say that the profit motive matters more to some than to others. A company that sells merchandise over the Internet is probably much more concerned with generating revenue than is a government agency or university that maintains a site as a service to its clients. Likewise, Uncle Max is probably not worried whether his personal Web page ever generates a profit.

The rest of this section examines those online operations for which making money is an important consideration. There are three basic ways to make a profit over the Internet.

The first is to create a site with content so compelling that people will pay to see it. One type of company that follows this model offers specialized information that has value for a large number of customers. As we saw in Chapter 4, many newspapers have adopted this model. The *Wall Street Journal,* one such example, charges a subscription fee to access its online edition. Other news sites seem to be following suit. CNN now charges people to see its streaming video; ABC News and Fox Sports have adopted subscription charges for much of their video. *Consumer Reports* offers access to its product evaluations for $24 a year. Web portals, such as Yahoo!, have also instituted charges for such services as game playing, personals, and enhanced e-mail. It seems likely that individuals eventually will be paying for much of the content that used to be free on the Web.

The other type of business that uses this pay-for-content model is pornography. At last count there were thousands of these sites, and some were among the most profitable on the Web. Sex sells, even on the Internet.

The second way to make money on the Net is to sell merchandise or services online. Amazon.com, the site that sells everything from laptops to lawn mowers, is the best example of this business model. Although many online retailers went bust in the early years of the new century, many of those that remain are profitable. For example, eBay had a profit of more than $300 million in 2002.

The third moneymaking method is for the site to sell advertising, consisting of ads that appear on the page or that pop up under the page (see Chapter 14). Online advertising has not lived up to expectations, and only those websites that draw large numbers of visitors (such as Google or Yahoo!) can use this method to generate a profit.

Of course, some Websites use some combination of one or more of these techniques. For instance, eBay charges for its services, sells advertising, and markets its own customized merchandise.

 FEEDBACK

As with the other industries mentioned in Part III, independent companies provide information about the Internet audience. Reliable data about audience size are important for advertisers who want to place banner ads on websites. The two

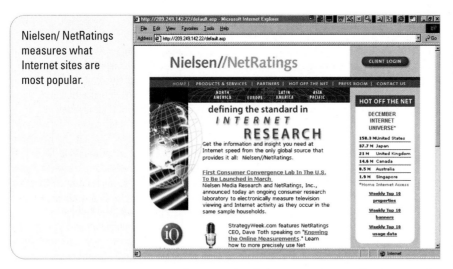

Nielsen/ NetRatings measures what Internet sites are most popular.

companies that dominate the audience measurement field are Media Metrix and Nielsen/ NetRatings. Both organizations use a panel of consumers to generate their data. Media Metrix samples about 60,000 people in the United States, using software that works with a computer's operating system to monitor Internet activity at home and at work. Nielsen uses a similar setup with a sample of about 68,000 people. Both services issue periodic reports that list the most popular websites. For example, in October 2003 Nielsen reported that Microsoft, AOL, Yahoo!, Google, and eBay were the parent companies of the top five websites.

>> Audiences

The Internet audience is changing rapidly. When the Internet first started, mostly young, affluent males were surfing the Web. As of 2003, the audience was split nearly 50–50 between males and females, and the percentage of adults above the age of 50 had grown by 50 percent. In short, the Internet audience is becoming more like the general population. More than 150 million people regularly use the Internet, with the typical user spending about 10 to 15 hours online per week. The main reasons for going online are to send e-mail or to find a specific piece of information.

 ## SOCIAL IMPLICATIONS

Now that you know some of the details about the Internet, let us discuss some of its social implications. In the first place, the Internet supplements the surveillance function of traditional mass media. When a news event occurs, interested parties can post Web logs for others to read. During the 2003 Iraq War, military personnel posted blogs describing their experiences during the campaign. In that same year, dozens of blogs reported happenings during the California recall election. This represents a shift from traditional journalism in which decisions are made by editors and flow from the top down. Now the news can start at the bottom and is generated by people close to or with an interest in a topic.

>> Lack of Gatekeepers

As mentioned in Chapter 1, traditional mass media have a number of gatekeepers. On the Internet, however, there are none. This situation has several implications.

First, the risk of overloading the system with unwanted, trivial, worthless, or inconsequential messages is increased. Suppose I posted this chapter on every active message board on the Internet and e-mailed it to everybody on every mailing list I could get. Suppose everybody did that with everything they thought was important. The system would get bogged down by all the excess traffic.

Second, gatekeepers also function as evaluators of information. Newspaper editors and television news directors consider the authenticity and credibility of potential news sources. If the system works properly, bogus news tips, unsubstantiated rumors, and false information are filtered out before they are published or broadcast. Information obtained on the Internet, however, comes without a guarantee. Some of it might be accurate; some of it you must use at your own risk. For example, the UFO-related newsgroups contain several accounts of UFO sightings and abductions by aliens. How credible these reports are is anybody's guess.

Third, having no gatekeepers means having no censorship. The Internet is like a huge city. There are some streets where the whole family feels comfortable, and other streets where you probably would not want to take your children.

>> Information Overload

The Internet represents an information retrieval tool that is unparalleled—provided a person knows how to use and understand it. In the days before the Net, students doing research would have to look things up in a text, reference book, or encyclopedia—sources that had some recognized authority. Today, students can post a request for information with a relevant newsgroup or use a search engine to look for the topic. The credibility of responses on a newsgroup, however, is open to debate. A Web search indiscriminately displays a list of "sources," which may number in the thousands. Every source on the screen seems to have the same credibility, even though some may be scientific documents and others comic books.

For example, while doing research, I used Google to look for references to "virtual reality." My search turned up 3,890,000 matches, including some that were about virtual reality games, quite a few that were XXX-rated, a large number from multimedia companies that produce virtual reality software, some that described technical background, and one about the use of virtual reality techniques for law enforcement and explosive ordinance training. (Of course, I might have narrowed my search using some advanced techniques, but the fact remains: There is so much on the Web that it is sometimes more overwhelming than useful.) Further, other than making a reasoned guess from the titles, I had no clue as to which sources were more authoritative than the others. (Students doing a conventional search would also have to assess the credibility of their sources, but the profuseness of information and the sheer size of the Net make this extremely difficult to do.)

>> Privacy Concerns

The Internet also raises a number of privacy concerns. Maintaining a person's privacy in the electronic age is not a new problem, but before the advent of the Internet, compiling a detailed dossier on someone required days or even weeks of searching through records scattered in dozens of places. Today, computerized databases enable a person to accomplish the same things with only a couple of clicks of a mouse. What follows are some illustrations of this growing problem:

■ In 2002, as part of its efforts to combat terrorism, the Pentagon announced the Total Information Awareness project, which would allow the government to search online databases for information about an individual's credit card purchases, travel arrangements, and personal data. Complaints from civil rights activists forced the Pentagon to reexamine the project.

■ Some states have put the names and addresses of sex offenders on websites. Although the motives behind this practice may be understandable, the potential for harm due to incorrect or outdated information is substantial. In North Carolina, a family was harassed because their address was listed online as the home of a known sex offender. The sex offender had actually moved away many months earlier, but the entry was never removed from the database. Many companies now charge as much as $150 to do online searches that will disclose someone's current address, Social Security number, bank account number, any criminal records, and a work history.

■ Another growing concern is identity theft. A person can obtain someone's name, Social Security number, and date of birth from the Internet and can then apply for credit cards, get loans, and even commit crimes under another name. Even more unsettling is the fact that the victim may not even know what has been done in his or her name. In California, a young man could not figure out why he was always turned down when he applied for retail jobs. He finally learned that someone had stolen his identity using the Internet and had been convicted of shoplifting. Whenever a potential employer ran a background check on the young man, the shoplifting conviction wrongly appeared on his record.

For the past few years, the government has wrestled with this privacy problem, and several bills have been introduced in state legislatures as well as the U.S. Congress that would restrict the availability of personal information. The issue is complicated because many are concerned that government regulation would be so rigid that legitimate searches for information would be difficult. Many prefer voluntary guidelines to laws.

›› Escapism and Isolation

Finally, does the Internet detach people from other people? Many individuals already spend lots of time engaging in sending e-mail, instant messaging, online chatting, game playing, online shopping, and maybe even cyber sex. As more and more attractions go online, will we spend even more of our lives staring at computer screens? Some psychologists have identified a condition known as *Internet addiction,* similar to drug or alcohol addiction. Early studies of Internet users revealed that those who spend many hours online also show signs of isolation and depression. Subsequent studies, however, have not found such a link.

THE FUTURE: THE EVERNET

Computers and computer chips keep shrinking. Before long tiny computers will be part of our household appliances, maybe even our clothes. These devices will be so small we probably will not even realize they are there. Moreover, experts predict that in the next 10 years advances in technology will enable these microcomputers to carry Web addresses and be connected constantly to the Internet. Imagine a furnace that automatically orders new filters over the Internet whenever it senses that the old ones are dirty. Imagine wearing a tiny computer that automatically unlocks your car, opens your garage door, pays your toll and parking fees, and reminds you that your tires need to be rotated. If you can imagine all of this, you have some idea what the **Evernet,** the successor to the Internet, will be like.

The Evernet (also called the Supranet or Internet II) will mark the convergence of wireless, broadband, and other devices, resulting in a person being connected

Back in the good old days, when your author was in college, if a professor assigned a term paper it meant that students would spend a lot of time in the library, searching for sources, finding relevant information, evaluating its credibility, summarizing it on index cards, and finally organizing the information into a coherent paper. These days, alas, when a research paper is assigned, few students venture into the library. Why go, they ask, when everything you need is available on the Internet?

Most professors will probably agree that when it comes to higher education, the Internet has been a mixed blessing. On the plus side, the Net has made huge amounts of information readily accessible to students. Further, today's students are highly skilled in using the Net quickly to track down facts and figures. Web search engines also help students find many disparate sources of information and encourage them to make connections that were not easily seen before the advent of the Internet.

But there is a downside. My colleagues and I have had the following experience many times. After a research paper is assigned, one or two students will come to us and complain that they cannot find any information on the topic. When asked where they searched, they reply, "Online." When asked if they considered searching in the library, they almost always say no. For many students, if information is not online, it does not exist. Some students are amazed to discover that informa-

tion specialists report that only about 15 percent of all information can be found online.

Then there is the problem of students cutting and pasting material from the Web into their own research papers. This situation was more severe a few years ago when many students simply downloaded huge chunks of information and pasted it verbatim into papers. Most now realize that professors have antiplagiarism software that can detect this wholesale borrowing. More common today is the practice of lifting a few sentences, changing a word here, cutting a word there, adding a couple of words at the end, and passing off the result as an original thought.

Perhaps most disturbing is the hopscotch nature of information gathering on the Web. So many possible sources show up that students simply jump from one to another, seldom spending much time digesting the contents of one article before going to the next. As a result, students have trouble constructing a valid argument from premise to conclusion and presenting a logical, coherent framework of supporting evidence. The facts are there, but there is not much of an indication that students have thought much about them.

Well, enough ranting. In closing, I would urge all who read this to go to the library and actually touch books. You might be surprised by how much you enjoy and get from the experience.

---

continuously to the Internet anywhere using any information device. You will no longer have to "log on" to the Net; you and all of the other devices that have computer chips will be automatically "online" all the time and all connected to one another. The Evernet will merge the virtual world with the physical world.

The implications of the Evernet are staggering. A person could send or access information instantly from anywhere in the world. What does that mean for consumers? You could order anything from anywhere at any time. Impulse buying would take on a whole new meaning. Further, shoppers could access price comparison search engines and find out if there was a better deal across the street. What about the implications for business? A manufacturer's assembly lines could be connected to cash registers all over the country. When sales go up, the assembly line works overtime.

What about daily living? "Smart houses" that run themselves would be possible. A smart house would inform you about your daily appointments and chores, monitor security systems, schedule maintenance and repairs, order food when supplies are low, regulate temperature and lighting, start the coffee brewing, and even run a hot bath.

What about health? People wearing pacemakers could have their heart rate and other medical data transmitted continuously to their physicians. If something were amiss, a person would get a call from his or her doctor's computer: "Your blood pressure is too high. Are you taking your pills?"

Granted, all of this sounds a bit like science fiction, and there is always the possibility that new technology will not impress consumers. Nonetheless, just 30 years ago the Internet also sounded a lot like science fiction.

C A R E E R
O U T L O O K

THE INTERNET AND THE WEB

The Internet and the Web are so new that it is difficult to define career paths in these areas. Some careers that involve the Internet have been mentioned earlier—such as online journalism—and others, such as online advertising, will be discussed in subsequent chapters. The rest of this section examines general career opportunities for those interested in the online area. Keep in mind, however, that the economic crunch that hit many Internet companies has made job prospects somewhat bleak.

One typical entry-level job would be a Web developer (also called a *Web designer* or *Web publisher*). Web developers are responsible for the actual creation of a website. They consult with the appropriate people about the content of the site and put together the content that will appear. Once the content has been assembled, the Web developer converts the documents into hypertext and scans the text, graphics, and pictures into the server. Since many sites now incorporate multimedia, the developer might also include prerecorded or live audio and video. Developers also upgrade sites and make sure that the sites are easy to use.

The next step up from a Web developer is a Web master. This is a managerial position that involves working closely with Web developers and members of an organization that sponsors the site. Web masters consult with staff members from departments such as engineering, customer support, and public relations. Web masters are responsible for all aspects of a website. They design the overall look of a site and approve all materials that are published on the site. Webmasters make sure the site is performing as expected and is meeting the needs of users and the sponsoring organization.

As of this writing, there is no established curriculum that prepares students for online jobs. However, some colleges now offer courses in Web page design or related topics. In addition to these, you should probably take courses in computer science, graphic design, journalism, public relations, and English and be on the lookout for those jobs that have not yet been invented.

MAIN POINTS

- The computer's ancestors were machines that performed mathematical calculations.
- By the 1970s, personal computers using packaged software were on the market.
- The Internet is a network of computer networks. It was started by the U.S. Department of Defense and in its early years was used primarily by scientists. The current Internet started in the 1980s thanks to the efforts of the National Science Foundation.
- The main features of the Internet are e-mail, newsgroups, and the World Wide Web.
- AOL, Yahoo!, and Microsoft Network are three companies that operate online information systems.

- The introduction of broadband Internet connections will encourage the growth of streaming video and microcasting.
- Despite recent economic troubles, the Internet has had a beneficial impact on the national economy, and e-commerce continues to grow.
- Many more websites are becoming profitable.
- The Internet has created social concerns about lack of gatekeepers, information overload, lack of privacy, and isolation.
- The Evernet may be the successor to the Internet.

QUESTIONS FOR REVIEW

1. How did the Internet come into being?
2. Distinguish between a website, a web page, and a portal.
3. What is broadband? How will it affect the Internet?
4. What's the difference between e-commerce and B2B Net commerce?
5. What are some of the social implications of the Internet?

QUESTIONS FOR CRITICAL THINKING

1. Check out some of the newsgroups available on the Net. Should there be some authority that controls what content is available?
2. Do a Web search for your name. See how much personal information you can find out about yourself on the Web. How easy was it for you to find the information? Could others have found it as well?
3. Rank the following media in terms of how credible each is as a news source: TV, newspapers, Internet, radio. Why did you rank them the way you did?
4. Some critics (Roger Ebert among them) have suggested that the era of free information on the Internet is about over and that, ultimately, we will pay for most of the content we get over the Net. Do you agree? Would you pay to access a search engine? Or a website such as CNN.com?
5. Speculate on some of the implications of the Evernet.

KEY TERMS

modem (p. 296)
hypertext (p. 298)
browsers (p. 298)
search engine (p. 298)
protocol (p. 298)
e-mail (p. 299)

spam (p. 300)
newsgroups (p. 300)
World Wide Web (WWW) (p. 301)
website (p. 301)
web page (p. 301)
portals (p. 302)

broadband (p. 303)
wireless fidelity (WiFi) (p. 304)
streaming video (p. 305)
Evernet (p. 312)

INTERNET RESOURCES

Online Learning Center

At the Online Learning Center home page, www.mhhe.com/dominick8, *select* Student Center *and then* Chapter 11.

1. Use the Learning Objectives, Chapter Outline, Main Points, and Time Line sections to review this chapter.

2. Test your knowledge of the chapter using the multiple choice, crossword puzzle, and flashcard features of the site.

3. Expand your knowledge of concepts and topics discussed in the chapter by going to *Suggestions for Further Reading* and *Internet Exercises.*

PowerWeb

At the Mass Communication home page of PowerWeb, www.dushkin.com/powerweb, *log in and select* Mass Communication *as your title. On the next screen, select* Topics *and then quick jump to* Internet. *Read Article 52, "The Great Wi-Fi Hope." Then consider the following questions:*

1. Is WiFi something that most consumers want or is it something that will appeal only to those who are technically sophisticated?

2. Why did WiFi develop? What was the motivation for developing such a system?

Now look at Article 56, "Broadband's Coming Attractions," and reflect on the following:

1. The author thinks that streaming video will never be as good as traditional video and will never threaten mainstream cable and TV broadcasters. Do you agree?

2. Compare the economics of traditional television broadcasting with the economics of streaming video.

Surfing the Internet

http://www.excite.com
The address of one of the many popular Web portals.

http://www.fcc.gov/broadband
The Federal Communications Commission site, which deals with the progress of broadband in the United States. Some of the information is highly technical.

http://www.isoc.org/internet/history
Contains links to various sites that detail the growth and history of the Internet.

www.rossiterandco.com/streamingvideo-intro.htm
Contains numerous examples of streaming video.

www.vivalasvegasweddings.com/live_internet_weddings.htm
One site that microcasts weddings over the Web. You might even be lucky enough to see one live.

SPECIFIC
MEDIA
PROFESSIONS

12

NEWS GATHERING AND REPORTING

This chapter will prepare you to

- describe the qualities that characterize news;

- identify the three main types of news stories;

- distinguish the role of the gatekeeper among broadcast, print, and online news;

- recognize the wire services that provide national and international news;

- discuss the strengths and weaknesses of broadcast, print, and online journalism; and

- explain how the Internet and new digital media have changed news reporting.

In early April, during the opening days of Operation Iraqi Freedom, those watching CNN were able to see live pictures of the Third Infantry Division as it raced toward Baghdad. Embedded reporter Walter Rodgers told viewers that his unit had been under attack for nearly two hours. As he was talking, the camera showed scenes of tanks rumbling by, burning vehicles by the side of the road, and columns of black smoke in the distance. Viewers were able to see this real-time portrait of war thanks to advances in digital technology that have transformed the way reporters cover breaking news events.

In Rodgers's case, a small digital camera captured the images that were then compressed and sent via videophone to a satellite that relayed the live pictures to CNN. Other reporters plugged their microphones and digital cameras into a suitcase-sized device that used a built-in global positioning system to find the nearest communications satellite. Some correspondents shot digital video footage that was edited on a laptop computer and then sent via e-mail or

NBC's David Bloom was one of hundreds of reporters embedded with U.S. military units during Operation Iraqi Freedom. Bloom later died from a blood clot that blocked an artery in his lungs, a condition aggravated by his working conditions in the field.

LIVE

DAVID BLOOM
WITH THE THIRD INFANTRY DIVISION
IN IRAQ

satellite phone back to the United States. Cell phones were also used for audio reports from the battlefield.

Although this new generation of technology is impressive, we need to remember that it is simply a tool to improve reporting. High-tech equipment does not alter the basic principles of journalism. Reporters must still be aware of the qualities that characterize a news story, the types of news that exist, and the differences in the way various media cover news. This chapter examines these topics and looks at the process of news gathering and news reporting in the digital age.

DECIDING WHAT IS NEWS

From the millions of events that happen every day, print, broadcast, and online journalists decide which few are worth reporting. Deciding what is newsworthy is not an exact science. News values are formed by tradition, technology, organizational policy, and, increasingly, economics. Nonetheless, most journalists agree that there are common elements that characterize newsworthy events:

1. **Timeliness:** Put glibly, news is new. Yesterday's news is old news. A consumer who picks up the evening paper or turns on the afternoon news expects to be told what happened earlier that same day. News is perishable, and stale news is not interesting.

2. **Proximity:** News happens close by. Readers and viewers want to learn about their neighborhood, town, or country. A train derailment in France, for example, is less likely to be reported than a similar derailment in the local train yard. Proximity, however, means more than a simple measure of distance. Psychological proximity is also important. Subway riders in San Francisco might show interest in a story about rising vigilantism on the New York subways, even though the story is happening 3,000 miles away.

3. **Prominence:** The more important a person, the more valuable he or she is as a news source. Thus, activities of the president, other heads of state, and sports and entertainment figures attract tremendous media attention. Even the infamous have news value. The past lives and recent exploits of many criminals are frequently given media coverage.

4. **Consequence:** Events that affect a great many people have built-in news value. The 2003 power failure in the Northeast, for example, was a huge news event because it affected more than 50 million people.

5. **Human interest:** These are stories that arouse some emotion in the audience—stories that are ironic, bizarre, uplifting, or dramatic. Typically, these items concern ordinary people who find themselves in circumstances with which the audience can identify. Thus, when the winner of the state lottery gives half his winnings to the elderly man who sold him the ticket, the story becomes newsworthy.

In addition to these five traditional elements of news value, economics plays a large role. First, some stories cost more to cover than others. It is cheaper to send a reporter or a camera crew to the city council meeting than to assign a team of reporters to investigate city council corruption. Some news operations might not be willing to pay the price for such a story. Conversely, after spending a large sum of money pursuing a story, the news organization might run it, even if it has little traditional news value, simply to justify its cost to management.

By the same token, the cost of new technology is reflected in the types of stories that are covered. When TV stations went to electronic news gathering (ENG), stories that could be covered live became more important. In fact, many organizations, conscious of the scheduling of TV news programs, planned their meetings and/or demonstrations during newscasts to enhance their chances of receiving TV coverage. Further, after helicopters became an expensive investment at many large TV stations, traffic jams, fires, beautiful sunsets, and other stories that lent themselves to airborne journalism suddenly became newsworthy.

Newspapers are not immune to the pervasive influence of the bottom line. As more corporations and large newspaper chains dominate the business, more businesspeople than journalists are becoming newspaper executives. The topics of greatest interest to this new breed of manager are marketing surveys, budget plans, organizational goals, and strategic planning—not the news-gathering process. This new orientation usually shows up in the newspaper's pages. The paper's "look" improves—more color, better graphics, an appealing design—and there are more features—food sections, personal finance columns, entertainment guides, and reviews. The paper becomes a slickly packaged product. At the same time, however, the amount of space devoted to local news decreases, reporters are discouraged from going after expensive investigative stories, and aggressive pieces about the local business community tend to disappear.

Economics alters news values in other, more subtle, ways. Ben Bagdikian, in *The Media Monopoly,* noted that the rise of media conglomerates (large corporations that own newspapers, broadcasting stations, and other properties) poses a problem for journalism. Can a newspaper or TV station adequately cover the actions of its parent company? For example, could ABC news objectively report the activities of the Disney Company if it were involved in some alleged wrongdoing? Or could a Gannett-owned paper adequately cover events at *USA Today,* another Gannett property?

The media cover Arnold Schwarzenegger's first press conference after becoming governor-elect of California.

The 2003 Iraq War marked a new era in the sometimes flinty history of the relationship between the military and the press. The Pentagon provided about 800 members of the press access to the action by "embedding" them with various ground, air, and naval units throughout the combat zone.

Controversy cropped up as soon as the plan was announced. First, opponents of the plan accused the Pentagon of using the press as a propaganda tool to popularize the war. As one critic put it, the media will be "in bed" rather than embedded with the military. Embedding was seen, not as an attempt to improve reporting, but rather as a ploy to improve the military's image with the U.S. public.

Second, how would it be possible, asked some observers, for reporters to maintain their objectivity when they were eating with, sleeping with, and even facing danger with the people they were supposed to be reporting about?

The third criticism arose after the reports started coming in from the war zone. Having embedded reporters in the field prompted the networks to rely heavily on them for news. Some argued that this resulted in overcoverage of the troops and undercoverage of war-related civilian hardships in Baghdad and Basra, where no reporters were present. Embedded reporters could, and often did, present vivid and moving accounts of the war as it affected their units, but their reporting showed only small slices of the total picture. Too often, said some analysts, these narrow viewpoints did not fully represent the total scope of the campaign.

Fourth, many objected to the tone of the coverage, calling embedded reporters "cheerleaders" for the military. An article in *The Nation* charged that the embedded reporters were not sending back balanced and objective reports but instead were creating a "myth" that was used to justify war and boost civilian morale. Some opponents pointed out that most of the embedded reports sanitized the conflict and did not show dead Iraqi soldiers or civilians.

Despite such criticisms, many of the embedded reporters felt that being embedded with the military did not affect their objectivity. A reporter for the *Atlanta Journal-Constitution* noted that the journalists covering the war were for the most part professionals whose basic values were not easily compromised.

Overall, it seems that the opinion that many people had about embedded journalists hinged upon their attitude toward the war in general. Many who supported the war found the coverage to be fair. Those opposed to the war found the coverage biased because it did not focus enough on the horrors of combat or the suffering of civilians. All would probably agree, however, that the embedded reporters provided a live, firsthand, unprecedented close-up view of combat.

CATEGORIES OF NEWS AND REPORTING

Generally, news can be broken down into three broad categories: (1) hard news; (2) features, or soft news; and (3) investigative reports.

>> Hard News

Hard news stories make up the bulk of news reporting. They typically embody the first four of the five traditional news values discussed. Hard news consists of basic facts: who, what, when, where, how. It is news of important public events, such as government actions, international happenings, social conditions, the economy, crime, environment, and science. Hard news has significance for large numbers of people. The front sections of a newspaper or magazine and the lead stories of a radio or TV newscast are usually filled with hard news.

Print Media   There is a standard technique used to report hard news. In the print media, it is the traditional inverted pyramid form. The main facts of the story are delivered in the first sentence (called the *lead*) in an unvarnished, no-nonsense style. Less important facts come next, with the least important and most expendable facts at the end. This structure aids the reporter (who uses it to compose facts quickly), the editor (who can lop off the last few paragraphs of a story to make it fit the page without doing wholesale damage to the sense of the story), and the reader (who can tell at a glance if he or she is interested in all, some, or none of the story). This format has been criticized for being predictable and old-fashioned.

More literary writing styles have been suggested as alternatives, but the inverted pyramid has survived and will probably serve as the model for online reporting as well.

Broadcast Media   In the broadcast media, with the added considerations of limited time, sound, and video, broadcast reporting follows a square format. The information level stays about the same throughout the story. There is usually no time for the less important facts that would come in the last paragraphs of a newspaper story. TV and radio news stories use either a "hard" or a "soft" lead. A hard lead contains the most important information, the basic facts of the story. For example, "The city council has rejected a plan to build the Fifth Street overpass." A soft lead is used to get the viewers' attention; it may not convey much information: "That proposed Fifth Street overpass is in the news again." The lead is then supported by the body of the story, which introduces new information and amplifies the lead. The summation, the final few sentences in the report, can be used to personalize the main point ("This means that the price you pay for gasoline is likely to go up"), introduce another fact, or discuss future developments.

The writing style of broadcast news is completely different from that of print news: It is more informal, conversational, and simple. In addition, it is designed to complement sound bites (recorded comments of the newsmaker) or videotape segments.

>> **Soft News**

Soft news, or features, covers a wide territory. The one thing that all soft news has in common is that it interests the audience. Features typically rely on human interest for their news value. They appeal to people's curiosity, sympathy, skepticism, or amazement. They can be about places, people, animals, topics, events, or products. Some stories that would be classified as soft news are the birth of a kangaroo at the local zoo, a personality sketch of a local resident who has a small part in an upcoming movie, a cook who moonlights as a stand-up comedian, and a teenager who mistakenly gets a tax refund check for $400,000 instead of $40.

Features are entertaining, and the audience likes them. Many television and print vehicles are based primarily on soft content (*Entertainment Tonight; E!*, the cable entertainment network; *People; Life Styles of the Rich and Famous; Us* magazine; the "Life" section of *USA Today*). Even prime-time newsmagazines such as *60 Minutes* and *20/20* have substantial amounts of soft news. Likewise, the fiercely competitive early morning network TV shows are turning more to soft news.

The techniques for reporting features are as varied as the features themselves. In the print media, features seldom follow the inverted pyramid pattern. The main point of the feature is often withheld to the end, much like the punch line to a joke. Some features are written in chronological order. Others start with a shocking statement, such as "Your secrets just might kill you," and then proceed with an explanation: "If you have a medical problem, you should wear a Medic-Alert bracelet." Still other features are structured in the question-and-answer format.

TV features are more common than radio features. In some large TV markets, one or more reporters cover nothing but features. Almost all stations have a feature file where story ideas are catalogued. If a local sta-

MEDIA TALK

Investigative Journalism

CD 2, Track 9, 2:25 minutes
The clip talks about a group of Northwestern University students who practice investigative journalism as part of a college class. Their efforts have apparently called into doubt the verdicts in many death penalty cases. Is it a good idea for nonprofessionals to look into convicted killers' cases for new evidence or technicalities?

tion does not have the resources to produce local features, it can look to syndication companies that provide general-interest features for a fee. Broadcast features also use a variety of formats. Humorous leads and delaying the main point until the end sometimes work well, a technique often used by Andy Rooney in his features for *60 Minutes.* Other times a simple narrative structure, used in everyday storytelling, is quite effective. The interview format is also popular, particularly when the feature is about a well-known personality.

>> Investigative Reports

Investigative reports unearth significant information about matters of public importance through the use of nonroutine information-gathering methods. Since the Watergate affair was uncovered by a pair of Washington newspaper reporters, investigative reporting has been perceived as primarily concerned with exposing corruption in high places. This connotation is somewhat unfortunate for at least two reasons. In the first place, it encouraged a few short-sighted reporters to look upon themselves as self-appointed guardians of the public good and to indiscriminately pursue all public officials, sometimes using questionable techniques in the hope of uncovering some indiscretion. Much of this investigative journalism turned out to be insignificant. In the second place, this emphasis on exposing political corruption distracted attention from the fact that investigative reporting can concentrate on other topics and perform a valuable public service.

Stone Phillips, host of NBC's *Dateline,* poses with former co-host Jane Pauley. *Dateline* has aired a number of award-winning investigative reports since it went on the air in 1992.

Investigative reports require a good deal of time and money. Because of this heavy investment, they are generally longer than the typical print or broadcast news item. Broadcast investigative reports are usually packaged in documentaries, or in 10- to 15-minute segments of a newsmagazine program (such as *Dateline NBC* or *60 Minutes*). Print investigative pieces are usually run as a series of articles.

The mechanics of investigative reporting are similar in the print and broadcasting media. First, a reporter gets a tip or a lead on a story from one of his or her sources. The next phase consists of gathering facts and cultivating news sources. Eventually, a thick file of information on the topic is developed. These facts are then organized into a coherent piece that is easily digested by the audience. Here the differences between print and broadcast reporting techniques become apparent. The print journalist can spend a good deal of time providing background and relating past events to the topic. Additionally, the print investigative reporter can draw heavily upon published documents and public records. In television and radio, the investigative reporter usually has less time to explore background issues. Documents and records are hard to portray on TV, so less emphasis is placed on them. Instead, the TV reporter must come up with interviews and other visual aspects that will illustrate the story. Moreover, the length of the TV report will sometimes dictate its form.

Some noteworthy examples of recent investigative reports are a Peabody Award–winning report by WISN-TV in Milwaukee, Wisconsin, about the need for family escape plans in case of fire and a 2002 Pulitzer Prize–winning series of stories in the *Washington Post* about the neglect of children placed in protective care.

 THE NEWS FLOW

As mentioned in Chapter 1, one of the characteristics of traditional mass communication is the presence of a large number of gatekeepers. This fact is seen in the gathering and reporting of news for conventional print and broadcast media. Reporting is a team effort, and quite a few members of the team serve as gatekeepers. Online reporting, in contrast, may have only one or a few gatekeepers. This section will first examine the news flow in the traditional print and broadcast media and then look at online media.

>> Print Media

There are two main sources of news for a newspaper: staff reports and the wire services. Other, less important sources include feature syndicates and handouts and releases from various sources.

Let us first examine how news is gathered by newspaper personnel. The city editor is the captain of the news-reporting team. He or she assigns stories to reporters and supervises their work. There are two types of reporters: Beat reporters cover some topics on a regular basis, such as the police beat or the city hall beat; general-assignment reporters cover whatever assignments come up. A typical day for the general-assignment reporter might consist of covering an auto accident, a speech by a visiting politician, and a rock concert. Stories from the reporters are passed along to the city editor, where they are approved and sent to the copy desk for further editing. The managing editor and assistant managing editor are also part of the news team. They are responsible for the overall daily preparation of the paper.

Let us review the news flow and the various gatekeepers in the process. The city editor can decide not to cover a story in the first place or not to run a story even if the event is covered. The reporter has a wide latitude of judgment over what he or she chooses to include in the story. The copyeditor can change the story as needed, and the managing editor has the power to emphasize or de-emphasize the story to fit the day's needs.

>> Broadcast Media

The sources of news for the broadcast media are similar to those for the newspaper. Special wire services cater to television and radio stations, and local reporters are assigned to cover nearby events. In addition, many broadcast newsrooms subscribe to syndicated news services or, if affiliated with a network, have access to the network's news feeds.

The broadcast newsroom is organized along different lines from its print counterpart. At the local station, the news director is in charge of the overall news operation. In large stations, most news directors spend their time on administrative work—personnel, budgets, equipment, and so on. In smaller stations, most news directors perform other functions (such as being the anchorperson) as well. Next in command is the executive producer. This person supervises all the producers in the newsroom. Typically, producers are assigned to the early-morning, noon, evening, or late-night newscasts. In addition to looking after the other producers, the executive producer might produce the evening news, typically the station's most important program. Here are some of the things that a news producer does:

1. decide which stories are covered, who covers them, and how they are covered;
2. decide the order in which stories appear in the newscast;
3. determine the amount of time each story is given;
4. write copy for some stories; and
5. integrate live reports into the newscasts.

The assignment editor, who assigns and monitors the activities of reporters, camera crews, and other people in the field, works closely with the news producer. Since speed is important in broadcast news, there is great pressure on the assignment editor to get the crews to the story in the shortest amount of time.

Then, of course, there are the "glamour" jobs—on-air reporters and anchors. Most reporters in broadcast news function as general-assignment reporters, although the large-market stations might have one or two regularly assigned to a beat, such as the entertainment scene. In many stations, anchors occasionally do field reports, but most of the time they perform their work in the studio, preparing for the upcoming newscast. In addition to the people seen on camera, there are quite a few workers whom no one ever sees or hears. Photographers accompany reporters to shoot the video. Tape editors trim the footage into segments that fit within the time allotted to the story. Big stations also have newswriters and production assistants who pull slides and arrange other visuals needed during the newscast.

Obviously, the chain of gatekeepers in broadcast news is a long and complicated one. Starting with the assignment editor and ending with the anchor, usually more than a half-dozen people have some say-so over the final shape of the newscast. Sometimes, the way a story ends up might be drastically different from the way it started at the beginning of the gatekeeper chain. It is not unusual for a reporter to work all day on a story and then be told by a producer that the story will get only 40 seconds of airtime.

Everybody is pretty familiar with "shopping bots," those price comparison programs that search the Net and display the best prices for whatever you want to buy. Imagine that your newspaper's website sets up such a service for its readers. Also imagine that the shopping bot is rigged to display results only from those companies that advertise in the paper. Is this ethical or not?

This is just one of several new ethical dilemmas that the Internet has raised for journalists. Some problems are solved easily; others are not. In our example, most ethical experts would probably suggest that rigging the shopping bot was unethical. At the least, the website should warn users that the results would be limited only to advertisers.

But what if a journalist used an assumed identity in a chat room to gather information about a story? Is such deception permissible? One might argue that there is a "user beware" principle in place in chat rooms, and chatters should not expect everybody to be truthful. It is categorically imperative that if you do not want to be deceived yourself, you should not practice deception, even if the circumstances treat deception as routine. Could a reporter simply "lurk" in the background unidentified? A utilitarian view would suggest that lurking would be permissible, if the benefits were significant.

Can a reporter take quotes from a chat room or a bulletin board and publish them without permission? Aside from the legal problem that might arise if such a practice violated a site's terms and conditions, there are some ethical problems. Common ethical practice suggests that a reporter on the street should identify him- or herself to a news source and ask permission before printing quotes. The same principle would seem to apply to chat rooms and message boards. Cultural ethics advocate that the reporter get permission before publishing the material.

>> **Online Media**

The news flow in an online news department is similar to that in the traditional media. Top executives decide how the site will be structured and how many specialty areas (e.g., sports, financial, weather, entertainment) it will contain. Editors decide what content will be used on the website, which stories will have additional audio and video files, where the stories will be placed, and how often they will be updated. Staff members skilled in website design take care of the technical side. Online news departments that are affiliated with a broadcast or cable network, such as CNN or MSNBC, will use the audio and video that appeared on the parent network but may edit it differently. Other stories may be rewritten from wire copy or from copy that has appeared in print or on the air. Not all online news, however, is recycled. Most online news staffs also employ reporters who do original reporting for the website.

 TECHNOLOGY

Two technological developments that have had a tremendous impact on TV news are **electronic news gathering (ENG)** and **satellite news gathering (SNG)**. The development of small, lightweight video cameras in the 1970s meant that pictures could get on the air much faster. Advances in satellite and microwave technology also made it possible to broadcast live from the scene of a major story. This development brought both benefits and problems. ENG enabled TV news to take advantage of the immediacy of its live reports and added another dimension to its coverage. On the other hand, immediate coverage is unedited coverage, and this raises the probability that inaccuracies will make it on the air. Also, live reports run the risk of violating the standards of ethics or good taste.

SNG uses a van or truck equipped with satellite links that enable reporters to send back pictures and audio from any location. More than 250 stations, most of

A news reporter in action: Lightweight cameras and video-tape recorders as well as electronic news-gathering (ENG) technology make it easy to broadcast from the scene of a news event.

them in large markets, now possess SNG capability. SNG enables local stations to cover national and international stories that used to be covered only by the networks. Most local stations like the local angle and the additional prestige that go along with SNG coverage.

A third technological development, digital technology, uses a videophone about the size of a lunchbox to stream audio and video over a satellite phone connection. Mini-TV stations, called *flyaways,* can be set up in a short amount of time to enable live broadcasts to originate from almost anywhere. Tiny digital cameras can be connected to laptop computers that can edit their video. The eerie, green-tinged night-vision footage so common during the coverage of the Iraq War was also transmitted via digital video.

THE WIRE SERVICES

The next time you read your local newspaper, notice how many stories have the initials AP or UPI in the datelines. *AP* stands for Associated Press; *UPI,* for United Press International. These two organizations are called *wire services,* and together they provide you with much of the news about what is going on outside your local community.

In simplified form, here is how the wire services work. A correspondent covers a local news event, such as a fire. He or she reports the event to the bureau chief of the local wire service. If the bureau chief thinks the story is newsworthy enough, the chief will send it on to the state bureau to go out on the state or regional wire. The state bureau chief then decides whether to send it on for inclusion on the national wire. All in all, the wire services are the eyes and ears for local papers and broadcasting stations that cannot afford to have people stationed all over the country.

The AP has about 242 bureaus around the world. Members of the association pay for this service according to their size and circulation. A large paper, such as the *New York Times,* will pay more than a small-town paper. United Press International also has dozens of domestic bureaus and a large number of foreign offices. As with the AP, member payment is based on the subscriber's size and audience.

Local papers and broadcast stations rely on the wire services for national and international stories to which they would otherwise not have access. Shown here is the newsroom at UPI headquarters in New York City.

In 2000, the AP had about 15,000 customers worldwide, including about 1,700 member newspapers. It serves about 5,000 radio and TV stations, plus more than 500 cable systems. The AP offers a wide range of services to its clients, encompassing a weather wire, a sports wire, and a financial wire along with a broadcast wire used by TV and radio stations.

In the past few years, UPI has been plagued by financial difficulties. The company was bailed out of bankruptcy in 1992 when it was bought by the Middle Eastern Broadcasting Company, which, in turn, sold it to News World Communications (the publisher of the *Washington Times*) in 2000. As a result of its economic troubles, UPI restructured itself in 2003 to concentrate on two main products: news commentary and analysis and brief news stories tailored for wireless devices, such as PDAs and cell phones, or for websites.

AP and UPI are not without competition. Major newspapers, such as the *New York Times,* the *Los Angeles Times,* and the *Washington Post,* offer supplemental news stories generally not covered by other services. Some newspaper groups, such as Gannett, have their own wire services. There is competition overseas as well. The British-based Reuters agency has about 30 bureaus in North America. Agence-France-Press is another formidable worldwide service.

 ## MEDIA DIFFERENCES IN NEWS COVERAGE

It does not take a genius to see that broadcast journalism is different from print journalism and that both are different from Web journalism. Over the years these differences have led many people to argue about which type of journalism is "best." Proponents of print journalism correctly point out that the script of a typical network evening newscast would fill up less than one page of a typical newspaper. They argue that the print media have the potential to conduct in-depth reporting and lengthy analysis, elements that are usually missing from broadcast news because of time pressure. Moreover, some critics have taken to disparaging broadcast journalism as showbiz and commenting on its shallowness. The supporters of broadcast news answer that measuring a network newscast by comparing its word count with that of a newspaper is using the wrong yardstick. They suggest it is more appropriate to ask how many pages of a newspaper it would take to print the thousands of different visuals that regularly accompany a TV newscast. The emergence of 24-hour news channels and late-night newscasts, say these proponents, now makes it possible to cover news in depth. Print journalism is criticized for being slow, old-fashioned, and dull.

Critics of online journalism suggest that many Web journalists are too quick to post stories and do not check their facts as thoroughly as do traditional journalists. They also note that many online news sites are slow to post corrections. Moreover, critics note that the line between reporting and commerce is blurry at many online sites. For example, online music and book reviews include links to sites where readers can buy the music and books online, with part of the profits going to the online news site. Such an arrangement can increase pressure for good reviews. Finally, many people have a problem with how easy it is for someone to become an "online journalist." All that is needed is a website; no professional training or credentials are required.

And so the debate goes. Unfortunately, the argument covers up an essential fact: Print, online, and broadcast journalism have their own unique strengths and weaknesses. One should not be considered better than another. All play an important role in informing the public.

>> Words and Pictures

The inherent characteristics of all three media have an impact on what news gets covered and how it gets covered. In the first place, print and online journalism are organized in space; TV journalism is organized in time. Hence, the newspaper or online site can contain far more stories than the typical TV newscast and can provide more details about any one story. Given the time constraints of broadcasting (even on all-news channels), it is hard for television to provide more than a headline service and a brief look at a few stories. Even if a topic is treated in depth, the amount of information and detail included is typically much less than what is contained in the newspaper or online. Some observers have said that TV is better at transmitting experience or impressions, while the newspaper and online sites are better at providing facts and information. In any case, lengthy analysis and complicated interpretation tend to be better suited to the print or online media.

Second, print and online news have more permanence than broadcast news. A reader can go back and reread difficult and complicated parts as many times as necessary for understanding. Viewers of broadcast news do not have this luxury. TV newscasts are written to be understood with a single exposure. This means that complicated and complex stories are sometimes difficult to cover in the electronic media.

Third, television news has the advantage of the visual dimension. TV news directors ask if a story has action, visual appeal, something that can be seen. Faced with a choice between two events that are of equal importance, the television news organization will cover the one that has better pictures available. Obviously, the visual dimension is important and represents a powerful weapon in the arsenal of TV reporting. Some of the visuals carried by TV news are deeply ingrained in the national memory: students fleeing Columbine High School and the destruction of the World Trade Center. Nonetheless, it is easy for TV news to needlessly cater to the visual and run news items that have little news value other than their potential for dramatic pictures. There have been many examples of a small,

relatively insignificant fire leading a local newscast simply because good pictures were available. This is not to say that print and online reporters do not like a visual story. Quite the opposite. The advent of good color reproduction in newspapers and magazines and the ability of online sites to feature streaming video mean that good visuals can accompany print and online stories. It is fair to say, however, that the print and online media are less likely to be influenced by the visual nature of a story.

>> Print, Online, and Broadcast Journalists

Another key difference among types of media has to do with the fact that, in TV news, the appearance and personality of the reporter are an important part of the process. This situation is in direct contrast to print and online journalism, in which the reporter stays relatively anonymous, with perhaps only a byline for identification. (Bob Woodward and Carl Bernstein, the newspaper reporters who broke the Watergate story, and Matt Drudge, the online reporter who broke the Lewinsky–Clinton scandal, are exceptions.) In TV, the person reading or reporting the news is part of the story. Repeated exposure of newscasters at the local and network levels has turned many of them into celebrities. Some viewers evidently develop what amounts to a personal relationship or a sense of empathy with reporters and anchors. *Today Show* host Matt Lauer probably received more comments about his new haircut than about any of the stories he covered.

>> News Consultants

Yet another difference among print, online, and broadcast journalism is the amount of control that outside news consultants have on the news itself. Market research consultants are employed by both newspaper and broadcasting organizations, but their activities are most noticeable at local TV stations. Consultants introduced the audience survey to local stations, making recommendations to management about coverage based on what the public said they wanted to see in local news, not on what journalists thought should be in the newscasts. This caused a fundamental shift in the traditional definition of *news*.

Recently, local TV newscasts have returned to a more traditional approach to covering the news. This does not mean that consultants have disappeared; they are still a strong force in local TV news. It is easy to see their influence, particularly if you travel across the country. The local TV news in Anchorage looks very much like the local TV news in Atlanta. Newscast formats, styles, and even the anchorpeople all seem quite familiar—a direct result of stations all over the country using the same consultants. (Compare this development with the format homogenization trend in radio; see Chapter 7.)

>> Similarities Among the News Media

Although there are significant differences among print, online, and broadcast journalism, there are many similarities as well. All journalists share the same basic values and journalistic principles.

Honesty in news reporting is crucial for television, online, and newspaper reporters. Stories must be as truthful as possible. The print or online journalist should not invent fictional characters or make up quotations and attribute them to news makers. Broadcast journalists should not stage news events or rearrange the questions and answers in a taped interview.

Another shared value is accuracy. Checking facts takes time, but it is something that a professional reporter must do for every story.

A third common value is balance. Every story has two or more sides. All journalists must make sure that they do not publicize or promote just one of them. Information should be offered on all sides of a story.

Print, online, and broadcast reporters also share the value of objectivity. Objectivity means that the reporter tries to transmit the news untainted by conscious bias and without personal comment or coloration. Of course, complete and total objectivity is not possible because the process of reporting itself requires countless judgments, each influenced in some way by the reporter's value system. Nonetheless, journalists have traditionally respected the truth, refused to distort facts deliberately, and consciously detached themselves as much as possible from what they were reporting.

Finally, online, print, and broadcast reporters must maintain credibility with their audiences. The news media periodically undergo crises of confidence, during which people begin to doubt the integrity of journalists. Sometimes these crises occur because of excesses in reporting, as occurred during the coverage of the Bill Clinton–Monica Lewinsky scandal. They may arise following disclosure of violations of journalistic values, as happened in 2003 when it was revealed that a *New York Times* reporter had plagiarized the work of others and invented "facts" for his stories. Whenever public opinion polls reveal that the news media have slipped another notch or two in credibility, journalists try to regain the lost confidence. After much soul-searching, the crisis usually passes. Credibility, however, is not something that should be examined only during journalistic crises. If a

An investigator examines part of the wreckage of the space shuttle *Columbia*. Some images, such as the videotape of the crash, are replayed so many times that it's impossible to forget them.

The relationship between the press and the authorities has always been complicated. Police are interested in catching criminals. Reporters want to tell the public how they do it. Sometimes the two entities use each other. The police want to get a message out to the criminals, so they use the press. Reporters like scoops, so they use sources in the police department who conveniently leak facts. However, sometimes they work against one another. The police want to keep certain information secret; reporters do their best to publicize that information.

This complicated relationship and the ethical problems that go with it were plainly demonstrated in the coverage of the Washington, D.C., area sniper attacks during the closing months of 2002. Not surprisingly, the police were reluctant to release details of the crimes. In the absence of hard information, many news media, the 24-hour cable networks in particular, turned to profilers, people whose expertise is generating a psychological and physical profile of a criminal based on information from the crimes, and pundits, people with relevant experience, such as with serial killers. On the one hand, it can be argued that these profilers and pundits served some purpose. They put the crimes in some context and provided a perspective that perhaps eased some of the tension being felt by D.C.–area residents. As it turned out, most of the speculation by these experts was totally incorrect. All predicted the killer was white; some thought the killer was a man in his 30s; some said middle-aged; others predicted teenage boys. Some speculated the killer was married. Most believed the killer was a long-term resident of the Washington area. As it turned out, the two suspects convicted in the case were both African American males, one in his 40s and the other a teen. The pair were drifters, with no roots in the area.

Did the speculation of the profilers and pundits cause any harm? This is a question that may never be answered conclusively. However, all of the conjecture might have led people to pay special attention to white males who had lived in the area for many years and perhaps blinded them to other possibilities. Would such speculation have stopped if the police had been more forthcoming with information? Probably not. The 24-hour news channels had a lot of time to fill. It is likely that they would have filled the time with expert opinions, no matter how much information the police released.

A more direct ethical dilemma surfaced near the end of the case. Law enforcement officers were looking for a blue Chevy Caprice with New Jersey plate number NDA-21Z. They decided not to release this information to the press for fear that the suspects might find out that the police had identified their car. Nonetheless, someone leaked the description and tag number to a reporter, and soon all of the major TV and cable news networks were broadcasting it. Was this an ethically responsible decision? In the end, the publication of this information helped catch the sniper suspects. A truck driver spotted the car at a rest stop, and the suspected snipers were arrested without incident.

What if the suspects had been closely monitoring press coverage of the story and learned that the police had identified their car? On the alert, they might have decided to ditch their car and find another one. Would the killings have gone on for days or weeks longer?

---

reader or a viewer loses trust or stops believing what is being reported, the fundamental contract between audience and reporter is undermined, and the news organization cannot survive. It matters little if the news organization is a newspaper, magazine, radio, online site, or TV station; its credibility is paramount to its viability.

 ## READERSHIP AND VIEWERSHIP

In September 2002, the Pew Charitable Trusts Research Center released results of a survey examining how Americans use the news media. The most significant finding of this survey was the fact that the Internet is quickly becoming a significant source of news. About 35 percent of Americans go online for news at least once a week, compared with 20 percent in 1998. The number of people reporting that they watch network and local TV news has been declining. The survey revealed that the number of people who regularly get their news from cable news channels or from the print media has also been declining.

Although broadcast TV news viewership is declining, the Pew survey disclosed that TV is still the medium the audience believes the most. Print media (newspapers and magazines) ranked next in credibility. Online news sources varied widely in their credibility ratings. The major news sites (CNN.com, ABCNews.com, MSNBC.com) rated on a par with or slightly higher than their TV counterparts, while the credibility ratings of the news found on portals such as Yahoo! and Excite ranked below those of the print media. Table 12–1 lists the top online news sites.

 ## NEWS ONLINE

Online news operations are relatively young and are still evolving. After the dot-com crash in 2000–2001, some online news operations ceased operations, and others cut back on staff and services. Moreover, as mentioned in Chapter 11, making online news profitable is still a challenge. Many online sites, particularly those associated with newspapers, have begun to charge for certain information, and others are requiring visitors to register and provide personal information in order to make the site more attractive to advertisers.

In general, there are three types of online news sources. The first is a mainstream general news site, such as CNN.com or usatoday.com, which offers text, audio, and video in several topic areas such as world news, national news, technology, sports, and politics. The second type is a news aggregator, such as Google or Yahoo!, which offers a digest of news from several different sources and links to news sites in the first category. Google's news site, for example, browses 4,500 different news sources and continually updates breaking stories. The third type is a specialized news source, which offers editorial content with a tight focus. Some examples would be the *Wall Street Journal*'s website, specializing in financial news, and ESPN.com for sports news.

Let us take a look at some of the implications of the growing importance of online news. We will first take the perspective of someone in the audience, then we will look at online news from the perspective of the journalist, and finally we will consider it from the viewpoint of the news-gathering organization and the profession.

❯❯ The Audience Perspective

For those who consume news, the Internet has meant an increase in the number of news sources available. General news sites and news aggregators appear to be the most frequently visited. Further, audience members can customize their news.

TABLE 12–1	Site	Number of unique visitors per month (in millions)
Top Online Sites for News, 2003	CNN	6.3
	MSNBC	6.0
Compiled by author using data from Jupiter Media Metrix.	Yahoo	5.3
	New York Times	2.9
	AOL News	2.8

A news council is an independent body composed of journalists and private citizens that unofficially hears and adjudicates disputes over press conduct. People and organizations who feel that they have been wronged by news coverage but lack the time, energy, and money to pursue a libel case turn to news councils to help set the record straight. Those who bring complaints before a news council waive the right to file a lawsuit. Staff members look into complaints, and the council holds hearings on those cases that raise significant issues. The council then votes on whether it thinks the complaint should be upheld. Councils have no legal power to enforce their decisions or to impose penalties. Their power stems from the publicity they bring to the case.

News councils are not a new idea. Wisconsin and Colorado had them; Minnesota and Hawaii still do. There was even a national news council that operated from 1973 to 1984 but was discontinued because of lack of money and lack of cooperation from influential media organizations. The idea of news councils resurfaced in 1997 when *60 Minutes* correspondent Mike Wallace suggested that the creation of a news council would help counter public skepticism and the negative feelings that members of the public have about the press. After the program was broadcast, residents from a number of states called the Minnesota News Council to ask how they could start their own news councils. In mid-2000, a news council started operation in the state of Washington, and another was being planned in Oregon.

Most members of the news media do not share Wallace's enthusiasm for news councils. They make several arguments to support their view. The argument heard most often is that news councils are the first step toward government regulation. One of the reasons the *New York Times* refused to cooperate with the National News Council was its belief that the council would encourage an atmosphere of regulation in which government intervention might gain public support. Many journalists think that lawmakers would use the public complaints to justify more regulation of the press. A second argument is that news councils would discourage hard-hitting stories. Journalists might be fearful of being unfairly targeted and forced to defend their decisions in controversial stories. If a council decision goes against a reporter, he or she might be afraid of doing any more such stories. Another argument contends that news councils substitute the judgments of people who do not know much about journalism for the judgments of professionals. How, ask the critics, can laypeople question the merits of a story when they do not know what went into producing it? In short, journalism should be left to the journalists. As one longtime journalist put it, "They have no damn business meddling in our business."

Supporters of the council idea first note that councils can prevent long and costly lawsuits. For example, they could give the principals in a defamation suit another forum in which to present the worthiness of their cases. Proponents also note that councils promote media fairness by making news outlets publicly accountable. Moreover, the councils give news media the chance to explain the reasons behind the choices they made and why they believed their decisions were proper. Such a discussion helps educate the public about some of the problems involved in the everyday practice of journalism and may help the public have a greater appreciation for the profession.

Supporters also contend that the press sees no problems in holding up other professions to public scrutiny but is unwilling to subject itself to the same treatment. They also note that there is wide public support for such an idea. Public opinion polls show that 85 percent of the general public likes the idea.

All things considered, the notion of a news council will be a hard sell to members of the news-gathering profession. Many media outlets are adamantly opposed to the notion. Journalists have never been leading supporters of self-criticism. As Edward R. Murrow once said, when it comes to criticism, "The press is not thin-skinned. It is no-skinned."

There may be signs, however, that things are changing. Although the *New York Times* is still not backing the idea of a news council, in the aftermath of the Jayson Blair scandal, the *Times* did agree to appoint a "public editor," a person who would monitor performance at the paper and look into reader complaints.

Yahoo!, for example, offers visitors a number of different news configurations from which to choose. CNN offers an e-mail service that alerts subscribers to breaking news stories. Finally, audience members can benefit from the "memory" of online news sites. Most have online archives that are searchable, providing the consumer with an opportunity to look for more information on a topic.

>> **The Journalist's Perspective**

From a journalist's point of view, the Internet has provided a new set of tools for news reporting. As pointed out by Randy Reddick and Elliot King in their book *The Online Journ@list,* in the past elite media organizations would send reporters to power centers and other locations where news happened to cover news events. Today, the reporter can sit at his or her desk and instantly access documents, databases, government records, and expert sources. Journalists can now bring to their desks the information they previously went out to look for.

The Internet can be a tremendous benefit, but journalists must learn new skills to be able to take full advantage of it. Today's reporters must know how to perform Web searches, download files, construct e-mail attachments, set up list-servs, navigate news-groups, and analyze databases. These skills are sometimes lumped under the general name of **computer-assisted reporting (CAR).**

The CNN website is one of the leading sources for online news. Each visitor spends an average of 18 minutes on the site.

A new term, the **backpack journalist,** has been coined to describe the next generation of digital reporters. A backpack journalist is a "do it all" reporter who carries around a small digital camera that can record audio and video, a laptop computer, and a satellite phone. In theory, he or she can write the text of a story, shoot video, record audio, pull still pictures from the video, add relevant graphics, and post the finished package on a Web page or perform a stand-up report for a TV station.

Some professionals think that the backpack journalist sounds good in theory, but in reality there are few reporters who are willing to undergo the training in the various technologies necessary to be able to do all that is required. The old adage "Jack of all trades, master of none" has been revived to describe this new phenomenon. Other journalists believe that backpack journalism is just a way for companies to save money by having one person do the work of several.

Proponents argue that the training required will become less burdensome as the technology progresses and the various tasks become easier to learn. Preston Mendenhall, a reporter for MSNBC.com, demonstrated the potential of backpack journalism during the 2003 Iraq War by sending text, photos, and TV reports during the conflict. Developments in the next few years will probably decide if the backpack journalist is here to stay for a while.

>> The Perspective of the Profession

On a more general level, the growth of online news raises some fundamental questions for the profession, not the least of which is "Who exactly is a journalist?" Before the Internet, it was relatively easy to identify journalists. They worked for formal organizations, such as the local paper, a local TV station, a national TV network, or a national magazine. As mentioned in Chapter 1, only companies with enough money to start and sustain a newspaper, magazine, or broadcast channel could reach a mass audience. The barriers to entry were formidable. Further, these organizations had chains of command. Journalists had editors; editors had managers. There were people who supervised the reporting process.

The Internet has changed all of that. Today, anybody with a computer and a connection to the Internet can set up a website and call herself or himself a journalist. No formal organization is needed; no editors or managers supervise what gets published. This development has both good and bad implications. On the one hand, the Internet makes it possible for a single journalist to become influential and make a difference.

Cyber journalist Matt Drudge demonstrated that big media organizations no longer have a monopoly on news.

The expanded access provided by the Internet encourages lively debate between the public and members of the journalism profession. When Matt Drudge's website published reports based on questionable sources, the traditional news media were inspired to take a hard look at their own standards of credibility.

Starting a Web news site requires no formal journalistic education, no apprenticeship, and no exposure to the norms and ethics of the profession. Not surprisingly, many online news operations have been criticized for a lack of standards in their reporting. Will shoddy online journalism drive out the good?

Further, online journalists may have little investment in their sites and thus take more liberties with the truth because they do not have much to lose. A traditional news operation has large sums of money invested in its reputation. If a newspaper, magazine, or broadcast news organization repeatedly makes misstatements of fact or distorts the truth, the resulting loss in credibility might cause the organization to lose large sums of money and maybe even go out of business, losing its entire investment. As a result, traditional news organizations normally pay close attention to what they report. A single person sitting at a computer has much less to risk from reporting untruths. In fact, he or she might even gain some notoriety if what is published is sensational enough.

Will the news-consuming public be able to differentiate between legitimate journalism and the reporting of gossip and rumors that is found on some websites? If they cannot, the public might simply become cynical toward all news reporting and eventually tune out everybody.

In early 2002, CNN and Fox were battling for viewers, particularly young viewers in the coveted 18- to 49-year-old demographic group. In an attempt to change its rather staid and stuffy image, CNN revamped its Headline News Channel and brought in former *NYPD Blue* actress Andrea Thompson as an anchor. CNN also managed to lure Paula Zahn, a photogenic reporter and anchor with more than 20 years of journalistic experience, from Fox. She was scheduled to host her own morning show, *American Morning with Paula Zahn*. Naturally, her debut was heavily promoted.

One of the promos featured a narrator who said, "Where can you find a morning news anchor who's provocative, super-smart . . . and just a little sexy?" A picture of Zahn then filled the screen. The sound of a zipper could clearly be heard as the narrator said the word *sexy*.

Along with many female TV journalists, Zahn was offended when she saw the ad. Embarrassed by a wave of negative publicity, CNN claimed that the ad was put together by a woman in its promotions department and was never approved by top management. The promo was quickly pulled from the schedule. (A cynical observer might argue that the CNN executives arranged the whole controversy. The resulting flap gave Zahn far more publicity than she would have had otherwise.)

The whole episode once again opened up the debate about the relative importance of looks versus professional ability in TV news. It is not a new debate, nor is it limited to just female news professionals. Arthur Kent was dubbed the "scud stud" during his reporting of the Gulf War. During the war in Afghanistan, CNN's Nic Robertson was named *People* magazine's sexiest correspondent. MSNBC's correspondent Ashleigh Banfield was nicknamed "the Osama mama" during that same conflict. Fox's anchor Laurie Dhue has also received much attention because of her looks.

In a perfect world, it would seem that the qualities that would be most in demand for a TV journalist would be skill and competence. Television, however, is a star-making medium (see the discussion of status conferral in Chapter 2), and on-camera talent are highly paid and treated with celebrity status. Thus, it is not surprising that they are perceived in the same way as movie or TV stars. And, as is fairly obvious, movie and TV stars are generally pretty good looking.

Did the flap help Paula Zahn? She was moved from her morning show into prime time during the 2003 Iraq War. Her show's ratings, however, were actually lower than the program she replaced, *Connie Chung Tonight*. What cable news program had the highest ratings in the time period? *The O'Reilly Factor*, with Bill O'Reilly, whose promos never described him as even "a little sexy."

C A R E E R

O U T L O O K

NEWS GATHERING AND REPORTING

The weak economy during the first few years of the new century has made it more difficult for aspiring journalists to find employment. Many newspapers and magazines have reduced their staffs and cut back on hiring. One 2002 survey found that after six to eight months, only half of journalism and mass communication graduates were working in the field, the lowest percentage since 1992.

Conditions are also rough in broadcast journalism. Most radio stations, aside from all-news stations in major markets, have drastically reduced or even eliminated their news operations, making the job market bleak. In TV, the situation is not much better. The glamour jobs of anchor and on-camera reporter continue to have far more applicants than there are available positions. The only bright note is that the growth of all-news national and local cable networks and the emergence of two-hour newscasts at large market stations have created some opportunities for those who want to work behind the camera as producers and videographers. The prospects for online journalists are also discouraging. Cutbacks and layoffs have reduced the number of available jobs.

As the economy improves, however, the job situation should become more favorable. For the time being, it would be advisable for newcomers to look for their first jobs at small-market newspapers or TV stations and then work their way into larger markets.

MAIN POINTS

- The qualities that characterize news are timeliness, proximity, prominence, consequence, and human interest. Economics is also important.
- There are three main types of news stories: hard, soft, and investigative.
- Traditional print and broadcast news media have many gatekeepers. In contrast, online news media have only a few.
- The Associated Press and United Press International are two wire services that provide stories to print and broadcast journalists.
- Print, broadcast, and online journalism have their unique strengths and weaknesses.

- All forms of news media strive for credibility.
- Online news enables audience members to select from more news sources and customize their news.
- Computer-assisted reporting using the Internet is a powerful news tool for reporters.
- New digital devices have made possible the backpack journalist, a reporter who is skilled at reporting for multiple media.
- Online news reporting raises fundamental issues about the journalism profession.

QUESTIONS FOR REVIEW

1. What are the characteristics that determine newsworthiness? Should others be added to the list?
2. What is the difference between hard and soft news? Is it possible to do a hard news report on a soft news topic, such as entertainment?
3. How does online news reporting differ from traditional print and broadcast reporting?
4. How is online news reporting similar to traditional print and broadcast reporting?
5. What is backpack journalism?

QUESTIONS FOR CRITICAL THINKING

1. Should news be what the audience wants to know or what the audience needs to know? Who should decide?
2. Where do you get most of your news about what is going on in the world? Why?
3. What news medium is most believable? Print? TV? Online? Why?
4. Will the growth of online news help or hurt traditional news reporting?

KEY TERMS

timeliness (p. 319)
proximity (p. 319)
prominence (p. 319)
consequence (p. 319)
human interest (p. 319)

hard news (p. 321)
soft news (p. 322)
investigative reports (p. 323)
electronic news gathering (ENG)
   (p. 326)

satellite news gathering (SNG)
   (p. 326)
computer-assisted reporting
   (CAR) (p. 335)
backpack journalist (p. 335)

INTERNET RESOURCES

Online Learning Center

At the Online Learning Center home page, www.mhhe.com/dominick8, *select* Student Center *and then* Chapter 13.

1. Use the Learning Objectives, Chapter Outline, Main Points, and Time Line sections to review this chapter.

2. Test your knowledge of the chapter using the multiple choice, crossword puzzle, and flashcard features of the site.

3. Expand your knowledge of concepts and topics discussed in the chapter by going to *Suggestions for Further Reading* and *Internet Exercises*.

PowerWeb

At the Mass Communication home page of PowerWeb, www.dushkin.com/powerweb, *log in and select* Mass Communication *as your title. On the next screen, select* Topics *and then quick jump to* Journalism. *Read Article 20, "Where TV Has Teeth." Then consider the following questions:*

1. What is the difference between investigative reporting and in-depth reporting?

2. Almost all of the examples cited in the article took place at the major networks or at TV stations in

large markets. Can you think of an example of investigative journalism that was done by any TV stations in your area?

Now read Article 28, "The Priest Scandal."

1. Why did investigative TV reporters not break this story?

2. Why did it take so long before this story achieved the "critical mass" necessary to get it the attention of the mainstream media?

Surfing the Internet

There are hundreds of sites that have a connection to journalism. Only a few are listed here.

www.aim.org
Media watchdog group Accuracy in Media's site, which critiques the operation of the news media.

www.cnn.com
CNN Interactive's site. A good example of an online news service. Contains international and national spot news plus links for political, scientific, health, travel, financial, and entertainment news.

www.freedomforum.org
The Freedom Forum is an organization dedicated to exploring and improving journalism. This site has links to the First Amendment Center, Media Studies Center, and the Newseum.

www.mediachannel.org
Nonprofit site that offers criticism, interviews with journalists, and a discussion forum devoted to news reporting.

www.newslink.org
Has links to other media sources as well as research tools.

www.ojr.org
Home of the *Online Journalism Review,* at the Annenberg School of Communications at the University of Southern California. The single best resource for information concerning online journalism.

www.trib.com
A good example of online journalism as practiced by a local paper—the Casper, Wyoming, *Star-Tribune.*

PUBLIC RELATIONS

This chapter will prepare you to

- distinguish among *public relations, publicity, press agentry,* and *advertising;*

- understand the background of modern public relations;

- discuss the major areas in which public relations is practiced;

- explain the steps involved in developing a public relations campaign; and

- recognize the impact of the Internet on public relations.

In the aftermath of the September 11 terrorist attacks, the Kingdom of Saudi Arabia faced a huge political problem in the United States. The country was home to 15 of the 19 hijackers as well as Osama bin-Laden, the mastermind behind it all. How did the Saudis respond? With an expensive public relations campaign.

The Saudis hired a Washington, D.C., public relations firm, Qorvis Communications, to improve their image. Helped by a $200,000-a-month retainer, Qorvis developed a $10 million ad campaign. Television and radio spots ran in all of the major markets in the United States, and print ads appeared in newspapers and in major magazines. One TV ad showed the American and Saudi flags hoisted together as a narrator reminded viewers that the two countries had been allies for more than 60 years. Another spot showed film clips of Saudi leaders meeting with U.S. presidents from Franklin Roosevelt to George W. Bush.

In addition, Qorvis arranged for Adel Al-Jubeir, an articulate, urbane, well-educated Saudi diplomat, to be interviewed by Ted Koppel, Barbara Walters, Paula Zahn, and other high-profile media figures. Al-Jubeir adroitly defended his country's efforts in the war on terror and stressed the close cooperation between his country and the United States.

Saudi spokesperson Adel Al-Jubeir figured prominently in the public relations efforts of the Saudi Arabian government.

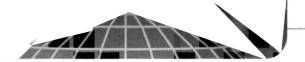

Nonetheless, after spending a record $14 million on public relations in a six-month period in 2002, American public opinion decreased sharply. One poll revealed that the number of people having a negative opinion of Saudi Arabia increased from 50 percent to 63 percent after the massive public relations effort. Another poll found that the number of people who considered Saudi Arabia to be an ally dropped from 19 percent in 2000 to 10 percent in 2002. A more recent 2003 poll reported that 70 percent of its respondents thought Saudi Arabia was a country that supported terrorism.

What can we learn about public relations from this apparently unsuccessful effort? First, performance overrides public relations. No matter how slick the ads or how smooth the spokesperson's presentation, if events do not support the message, the campaign will fail. In the Saudi case, the impact of the message was diminished by a Congressional hearing that examined allegations that Saudi men were kidnapping their American-born children and taking them back to the kingdom with the apparent cooperation of the Saudi government. Further, it was revealed that the charitable donation made by the wife of a Saudi diplomat ultimately wound up in the bank accounts of two of the hijackers. Lastly, it did not help the public relations effort when a Saudi prince declared that Israel was actually behind the September 11 attacks in an attempt to spark an American war against

Islam. In sum, there may be some things that public relations cannot do.

Second, public relations is often part of controversial issues. Many public relations practitioners endorse the attorney model that holds that public relations professionals, like lawyers, have an obligation to represent clients even if a client's cause may be unpopular or contentious. (Qorvis seems to be a good example of this viewpoint. Its clients have included the Arctic Power Company, which espoused the environmentally unpopular cause of drilling for oil in the Arctic National Wildlife Refuge, and the American Institute of Certified Public Accountants, a group that opposed accounting-reform legislation drafted in the aftermath of the Enron accounting scandals.)

Third, ethical problems often accompany controversy. Is it proper for a public relations company to put a positive spin on the actions of a country whose national interests may be at odds with those of the United States? Are there exceptions to the attorney model mentioned? Would it be proper for a public relations company to represent the Ku Klux Klan?

Finally, the Saudi case illustrates the growing importance of favorable public relations in the political setting. Public relations has become an accepted tool for lobbyists, candidates, administrations, political parties, and even countries. In this chapter, we explore the role of public relations in contemporary society.

 DEFINING PUBLIC RELATIONS

Before we investigate what public relations is, it may be helpful to compare it with other facets of mass communication. There are, for example, similarities between advertising and public relations. Both are attempts at persuasion, and both involve using the mass media. Public relations, however, is a management function; advertising is a marketing function. Another difference is that advertising uses the mass media and machine-assisted communication settings; unlike PR, it does not involve interpersonal communications. A third difference is seen in the fact that advertising is normally sponsored. Public relations messages appear as features, news stories, or editorials, and the space or time involved is not paid for. In many instances, advertising, particularly corporate advertising, is used to help further a public relations program.

A concept that is sometimes confused with public relations is press agentry. Press agentry involves staging events or planning enterprises that attract media or public attention to a person, product, organization, or cause. Although press agents are useful in some PR campaigns, public relations encompasses a much broader area and involves more than just attracting attention.

Another concept that is sometimes confused with public relations is **publicity,** the placing of stories in the mass media. Publicity is a tool in the public relations process, but it is not equivalent to PR. For example, it is perfectly possible for a firm to have extensive publicity and bad public relations. Further, publicity is primarily one-way communication; public relations is two-way.

Having examined what public relations is *not,* we may now turn to what it *is.* The term *public relations* has many interpretations and meanings. One PR veteran has compiled 500 different ones, ranging from the concise, "PR is doing good and getting credit for it," to the 100-word definition in the *Encyclopaedia Britannica.* Most of the leading textbooks on PR usually lead off with a chapter that attempts to define exactly what public relations is or is not. Rather than catalog these many definitions, we may find it more useful to define PR by examining what PR people do:

1. *Public relations involves working with public opinion.* On the one hand, PR professionals attempt to influence public opinion in a way that is positive to the client. For example, in the Saudi episode, the public relations campaign was designed to improve Americans' attitudes toward Saudi Arabia.

2. *Public relations is concerned with communication.* Most people are interested in what an organization is doing to meet their concerns and interests. It is the function of the public relations professional to explain the organization's actions to various **publics** involved with the organization. Public relations communication is two-way communication. The PR professional also pays close attention to the thoughts and feelings of the organization's publics. Some experts refer to public relations as a two-way conduit between an organization and its publics.

   Note that the word *publics* in the preceding section is plural. This is because an organization typically deals with many different publics in its day-to-day operations. Several PR scholars divide these groups into internal and external publics. *Internal* publics include employees, managers, labor unions, and stockholders. *External* publics consist of consumers, the government, dealers, suppliers, members of the community, and the mass media. Public relations serves as the link for all these publics.

3. *Public relations is a management function.* It is designed to help a company set its goals and adapt to a changing environment. Public relations practitioners regularly counsel top management. Inherent in the specification of public

Imagine that your PR firm has been offered a sizable fee to represent Seven-Eleven Limited, a big conglomerate that owns gambling casinos in several states. A state referendum legalizing casino gambling is planned in your state. The casino group wants you to organize a grass roots citizens' organization called Citizens for Economic Growth that will campaign in favor of legalizing casino gambling. Seven-Eleven Limited has conducted economic studies that have indeed shown that your state's treasury would benefit from legal gambling. They have ample funds available to set up and finance the operations of the citizens' group. There is one condition, however. The casino group does not want to be connected with Citizens for Economic Growth. They think that revealing the connection would hurt their chances in the referendum. Do you accept the assignment? Is it ethical to conceal information that might have an impact on the results of a public relations campaign?

On the one hand, there would be positive results if your firm took the assignment. Your firm would make a profit, and employees would be happy. Moreover, as the research suggests, casino gambling might in fact benefit the residents of your state. More jobs would be created and more tax revenue generated.

On the other hand, a deception is involved. If a reporter subsequently discovered the casino group's involvement in the campaign, it would hurt the credibility of your firm and maybe hurt the overall credibility of the public relations profession. In addition, the public would be voting on an issue without having all of the relevant facts before them.

The deception may never be uncovered, and the deception might serve a good cause. Is it worth doing?

The Code of Ethics of the Public Relations Association of America offers some guidance. It states, in part, that open communication is necessary for informed decision making. All information that might influence a decision should be revealed: "Be accurate and honest in all communications.... Avoid deceptive practices."

relations is a planned activity. It is organized and directed toward specific goals and objectives.

Of course, public relations involves much more than just the three functions mentioned. Perhaps it would be easier, for our purposes, to use the following definition approved by the World Assembly of Public Relations:

Public relations is the art and social science of analyzing trends, predicting their consequences, counseling organization leaders, and implementing planned programs of action that serve both the organization's and the public's interest.

 ## A SHORT HISTORY OF PUBLIC RELATIONS

If the term *public relations* is interpreted broadly enough, its practice can be traced back to ancient times. The military reports and commentaries prepared by Julius Caesar can be viewed as a triumph in personal and political public relations. During medieval times, both the church and the guilds practiced rudimentary forms of public relations.

It was not until the American Revolution that more recognizable public relations activities became evident. The early patriots were aware that public opinion would play an important role in the war with England, and they planned their activities accordingly. For example, they staged events, such as the Boston Tea Party, to gain public attention. They also used symbols, such as the Liberty Tree and the Minutemen, that were easily recognized and helped portray their cause in a positive light. Skillful writers such as Samuel Adams, Thomas Paine, Abigail Adams, and Benjamin Franklin used political propaganda to swing public opinion to their side. As a case in point, note that the altercation between an angry mob and British soldiers became known as the "Boston Massacre," an interpretation well suited to the rebel cause.

The Boston Tea Party was a PR move calculated to gain support for the Revolution. Such an event today would be done in daylight so that TV news crews would have an easier time covering it.

Later, the Industrial Revolution and the resulting growth of mass production and mass consumption led to the growth of big business. Giant monopolies were formed in the railroad, steel, and oil businesses. Many big corporations tended to disregard the interests of the consumer in their quest for more profits. In fact, many executives felt that the less the public knew about their practices and operations, the better. Around the turn of the century, however, public hostility was aroused against unscrupulous business practices. Muckrakers (see Chapter 5) filled the nation's magazines with exposés of industrial corruption and ruthless business tactics. Faced with these attacks, corporations hired communications experts, many of them former newspaper writers, to counteract the effect of these stories. These specialists tried to combat negative publicity by making sure the industry's side of the issue was also presented. These practitioners were the prototypes of what we might call *press agents* or *publicists*.

The debut of modern public relations techniques dates back to the first decade of the 1900s. Most historians agree that the first real public relations pioneer was a man named Ivy Lee. In 1903, Lee and George Parker opened a publicity office. A few years later, Lee became the press representative for the anthracite coal operators and the Pennsylvania Railroad. When these industries were confronted with a strike in the coal industry, Lee issued a "Declaration of Principles." This statement endorsed the concepts of openness and honesty in dealing with the public; it also marked the shift from 19th-century press agentry to 20th-century public relations. Lee went on to have a successful career counseling people such as John D. Rockefeller Jr. Among other achievements, Lee is credited with humanizing business and demonstrating that public relations is most effective when it affects employees, customers, and members of the community. Moreover, Lee would not carry out a public relations program unless it was endorsed and supported by top management.

The government got involved in public relations during World War I when President Woodrow Wilson set up the Creel committee (named for its chair, journalist George Creel). Creel enlisted the top figures in the public relations field to mount a campaign that persuaded newspapers and magazines to donate space for ads that urged Americans to save food and to buy war bonds. Creel advised Wilson on communication strategies and was instrumental in publicizing Wilson's war goal "to make the world safe for democracy." The work of the Creel committee was significant because it demonstrated the power of a well-planned and well-executed public relations campaign. In addition, it helped legitimize the field of public relations.

Following World War I, two more public relations pioneers, Carl Byoir and Edward L. Bernays, appeared on the scene. Bernays is credited with writing the first book on public relations, *Crystallizing Public Opinion*, published in 1923. In

Public relations pioneer Ivy Lee.

1930, Byoir organized a public relations firm that was one of the world's largest.

The Depression caused many Americans to look toward business with suspicion and distrust. In an attempt to regain public favor, many large corporations established their own public relations departments. The federal government, in its attempt to cope with the bad economic climate, also used good public relations practices to its advantage. Franklin Roosevelt introduced his New Deal reform program complete with promotional campaigns to win public acceptance. Roosevelt also recognized the tremendous potential of radio in shaping public opinion, and his radio-broadcasted fireside chats were memorable examples of personal public relations. The government intensified its public relations efforts during World War II with the creation of the Office of War Information.

During the second half of the 20th century, changes in American society created an atmosphere in which public relations grew tremendously in importance. What are some of the reasons behind the recent surge in this area?

1. Many corporations have recognized that they have a social responsibility to serve the public. Finding the means of fulfilling this responsibility is the task of the public relations department.

2. A growing tide of consumerism has caused many corporations and government agencies to be more responsive to and communicative with their customers or clients, a function served by the public relations department.

3. The growing complexity of modern corporations and government agencies has made it difficult for them to get their messages to the public without a department that is specifically assigned that task.

4. Increasing population growth along with more specialization and job mobility have made it necessary for companies to employ communication specialists whose task it is to interpret the needs of the audience for the organization.

All these trends have combined to make the past 50 years or so the "era of public relations." The profession grew from about 19,000 members in 1950 to more than 300,000 people in 2003. Along with this growth has come increased professionalization among public relations practitioners. The Public Relations Society of America, founded in 1947, adopted a code of standards in 1954. Public relations education has also made great strides. Recent estimates suggest that about 400 colleges across the country offer courses in public relations. In 1967, the Public Relations Student Society of America was founded. It now has 220 chapters and 6,500 members.

The past decade has seen public relations become even more important. Spin doctors, specialists in political public relations, have assumed prominence in political campaigns and government activities. The Bush administration used public relations extensively to gather public support for Operation Iraqi Freedom

The code of conduct of the Public Relations Society of America states in part, "We adhere to the highest standards of accuracy and truth in advancing the interests of those we represent and in communicating with the public." It goes on to state that a member shall "be honest and accurate in all communications." These statements seem fairly straightforward, but is there room for interpretation of what constitutes the *truth* and *accuracy*?

An example used by Thomas Schick in the winter 1994/ 1995 issue of *Public Relations Quarterly* illustrates some of the issues associated with this question. Suppose you are the PR director for an historical park. The park recreates the home life, crafts, costumes, and general ambience of 19th-century life. The biggest attraction at the park is a restored antique train that visitors can ride around the park. Many people come to the park simply to ride the train. This year, however, the train is undergoing repairs and will not be operating.

The time has come for you to write a press release promoting the park for the upcoming season. What do you do?

A. Write the release stressing the benefits of visiting the park's other attractions and not mentioning the train repairs.

B. Write the release and include the fact that the train will not be operating.

Suppose you chose *A*. There is nothing inaccurate in what you have prepared; you simply withheld some information. Is there an ethical difference between telling a lie and withholding a truth? How might you analyze this course of action? One method of ethical analysis suggests that a person weigh the good that would result from a decision against the bad. Let us try that method on this particular case.

You might argue that, if you mentioned that the train would not be operating, many people would stay away and would miss out on the educational benefits of all the other exhibits. You might also argue that mentioning the train's absence would decrease the number of visitors to the park and hurt the park's finances so much that it might be forced to close, therefore denying everybody the educational experience of visiting the park. Thus, there seem to be some good reasons for withholding the truth.

On the other hand, not mentioning the train's unavailability seems calculated to deceive the public. In the absence of other information, most reasonable people would expect the train to be operating. Some people would be inconvenienced if they made a long trip solely to ride the train, and they might leave when they found it was not operating. Others would suffer disappointment when they found the train was not operating. Many might never come back. This could cost the park in the long run.

Moreover, by issuing a press release, the PR director would have placed the message in the news media. The audience has a high expectation that information appearing in the news media is accurate and complete. By not telling the whole story, the PR director would also have harmed the credibility of the news media and might have jeopardized future relationships with them. Editors might view any subsequent news releases with great skepticism and perhaps not run them.

In sum, it seems that the short-term gains realized by not telling the whole truth are outweighed by the long-term losses. In this case, telling the whole truth might be the best policy.

in 2003. One facet of this program was the "embedding" of more than 500 journalists with military units to provide firsthand accounts of the action (see Social Issues, "Can a Reporter Be Embedded and Objective?" on page 321). In the business sector, the accounting scandals at major corporations such as Enron, Global Crossing, and Arthur Andersen increased the need for better public relations in order to restore confidence in a company's financial reports and to make top executives more responsible to their employees and shareholders. Despite lost revenue from the dot-com bust, according to the Bureau of Labor Statistics the PR industry is still one of the fastest growing professions in the United States.

 ## ORGANIZATION OF THE PUBLIC RELATIONS INDUSTRY

Public relations activities are generally handled in two ways. Many organizations have their own public relations departments that work with the managers of all other departments. About 85 percent of the 1,500 largest U.S. companies have such departments. In many companies, these departments are part of top management, and the PR director is responsible to the president of the company. For example, General Motors and AT&T both employ more than 100 people in their U.S. PR departments. Other organizations hire an external public relations counsel to give advice on press, government, and consumer relations. In business and industry, about one-third of the PR activity is handled by outside counseling firms. Many major corporations retain an outside agency in addition to their own internal public relations department.

Each of these arrangements has its particular advantages and disadvantages. An in-house department can be at work on short notice and has in-depth knowledge about the company; in addition, its operations tend to be less costly. On the other hand, it is hard for a corporate PR team to take an objective view of the company. Further, internal PR departments tend to have trouble coming up with fresh ideas unless new personnel are frequently added. An outside agency offers more services to its clients than does an internal department. Additionally, external counselors have the advantage of being objective observers, and many firms like the prestige associated with being a client of a respected PR firm. On the other side of the coin, outside agencies are expensive, it takes time for them to learn the inner workings of their client's operations, and their involvement may cause resentment and morale problems among the staff of the client's organization.

Internal or external, public relations professionals perform a wide range of services. These include counseling management, preparing annual reports, handling news releases and other forms of media coverage, supervising employee and other internal communications, managing promotions and special events, fundraising, lobbying, handling community relations, and writing speeches.

Public relations is practiced in a variety of settings. Although the general principles are the same, the actual duties of the PR practitioner will vary according to the setting. Following are brief descriptions of the major areas in which public relations is practiced:

1. *Business:* Public relations helps the marketing process by instilling in the consumer a positive attitude toward the company. Public relations also helps promote healthy employee-management relations and serves as a major liaison between the firm and government regulators. Last, all businesses have to be located somewhere, and the PR department makes sure the company is a good citizen in its community.

2. *Government and politics:* Many government agencies hire public relations specialists to help them explain their activities to citizens and to assist the news media in their coverage of the different agencies. These same specialists also communicate the opinions of the public back to the agency. Government PR is big business; its total expenditures on public information rival the budgets of the four major TV networks. The Department of Defense, for instance, produces thousands of films and TV programs every year. The Department of Agriculture sends out thousands of news releases annually. Political public relations is another growing field. A growing number of candidates for public office hire PR experts to help them get their message across to voters.

3. *Education:* PR personnel work in both elementary and higher education. The most visible area of practice in elementary and high school concerns facilitating communication between educators and parents. Other tasks, however, are no less important. In many school systems, the PR person also handles relations with the school board, local and state legislative bodies, and the news media. Public relations at the college and university level, although less concerned with parental relations, has its own agenda of tasks. Fund-raising, legislative relations, community relations, and internal relations with faculty and students would be concerns of most college PR departments.

4. *Hospitals:* The rising cost of health care and greater public expectations of the medical profession have given increased visibility to the public relations departments in our nation's hospitals. Some of the publics that hospital PR staffs have to deal with are patients, patients' families, consumers, state insurance commissions, physicians, nurses, and other staff members. Despite

This billboard is an example of a public-service PR campaign with a tie-in to a grocery chain.

the increasing importance of hospital public relations, many hospitals do not have a full-time PR staff. Consequently, this is one area that will see significant growth in the future.

5. *Nonprofit organizations:* The United Way, the Girl Scouts, the American Red Cross, and the Salvation Army are just a few of the organizations that need PR professionals. Probably the biggest PR goal in organizations such as these is fund-raising. Other objectives include encouraging volunteer participation, informing contributors how their money is spent, and working with the individuals served by an organization.

6. *Professional associations:* Organizations such as the American Medical Association, the American Dairy Association, and the American Bar Association employ PR practitioners. In addition to providing news and information to the association's members, other duties of the PR staff are recruiting new members, planning national conferences, influencing government decisions, and working with the news media.

7. *Entertainment and sports:* A significant number of PR experts work for established and would-be celebrities in the entertainment and sports worlds. A practitioner handling this type of client has two major responsibilities: Get the client favorable media coverage and protect the client from bad publicity. Additionally, many sports and entertainment events (e.g., the Super Bowl, a motion picture premiere) have PR campaigns associated with them.

8. *International PR:* Corporations with branches throughout the world, global news media such as CNN, an interrelated world economy, the shifting political scene in Europe—all these factors have combined to make this area one of the fastest growing in public relations. International PR specialists provide businesses operating in other countries with aid and information about local customs, language problems, cultural difficulties, and legal dilemmas.

9. *Investor relations:* This area (called IR for convenience) entails building a favorable image for a company and keeping shareholders happy. A public company needs to communicate information, both positive and negative, that might have an impact on its stock price to the financial community in general and shareholders in particular. To do this effectively, IR professionals must know the workings of the financial press as well as the various channels used to communicate with shareholders, such as annual reports, quarterly reports, and annual meetings. As more and more Americans invest in the stock and bond markets and as financial markets become more global, the importance of IR will surely increase.

10. *Politics:* The importance of public relations in political campaigns increases with every election. Building the right personal image, putting the proper

spin on the interpretation of events, and responding to the charges of other candidates are all part of the job of a political PR specialist. Many public relations firms specialize in political campaigns.

11. *Crisis management:* Probably the ultimate test for the PR practitioner is dealing with a crisis. Such crises arise infrequently, but poor handling of a crisis can have long-term negative effects that might cripple a company and/or ruin the reputation of a PR firm. Pepsi-Cola faced a crisis when reports about hypodermic syringes in Pepsi cans began to surface. Pepsi used its PR departments to cope successfully with its predicament. In a crisis, the public seeks out more information and the organization involved in the crisis is subjected to increased scrutiny by both the media and the public. Experts in crisis management PR generally counsel their clients to accomplish three goals: terminate the crisis, limit damage, and restore credibility.

From the above list, it appears that the profession requires PR specialists as well as generalists. In the next section, we will see how the PR function is typically organized and what jobs PR professionals perform.

 ## DEPARTMENTS AND STAFF

At the outset, remember that no two companies have the same exact departmental structure. In one common arrangement for an internal corporate PR department, the director of public relations reports directly to the president of the company. Since PR affects every department, its supervision by the person who runs the entire organization makes sense. The PR department is further subdivided into three main divisions that are designed to communicate with both internal and external publics: (1) corporate communications, (2) community relations, and (3) press relations. The corporate communications division handles communications with internal publics (workers, shareholders, unions), and the community relations division deals with external publics (community residents, customers, the government, etc.). As its name suggests, the press relations division deal with the news media.

The organization of an external PR agency is more complex. One possible arrangement consists of five departments:

1. *creative services:* is responsible for ideas and production of press releases and audio/video media;
2. *research:* supervises survey research, focus groups, and data collection;
3. *publicity and marketing:* takes charge of merchandising and sales promotions;
4. *accounts:* oversees and coordinates relations with clients; and
5. *administration:* is responsible for the day-to-day personnel, clerical, legal, and financial tasks that keep a business running.

 ## THE PUBLIC RELATIONS PROGRAM

Imagine you are the public relations director for a leading auto company. The company is entering into an agreement with a foreign car manufacturer to produce a foreign model in the United States. Unfortunately, to increase efficiency and centralize its operations, the company will have to close one of its plants located in a Midwestern city. About a thousand employees will have to be trans-

Media Probe Whom Do You Trust?

The National Credibility Index was started by PR professionals to measure how the American public perceives its leaders and public figures as believable sources of information. Fifty different sources of information were measured. As of 2000, these were the top five most credible sources:

1. Supreme Court justice,
2. teacher,
3. national expert,
4. member of armed forces, and
5. local business owner.

These were the bottom five:

46. head of a national interest group,
47. political party leader,
48. public relations specialist,
49. entertainer, and
50. radio or TV talk show host.

ferred or find new jobs, and the community will face a significant economic blow. It will be the job of the public relations department to communicate this decision to the community.

The thorny problem just outlined is a typical one for the public relations professional. Handling it requires a planned, organized, and efficient public relations program. This section will trace the four main steps involved in developing a typical PR campaign:

1. information gathering,
2. planning,
3. communication, and
4. evaluation.

>> Information Gathering

The information-gathering stage is an important one because what is learned from it will influence the remaining stages. **Information gathering** can be achieved through several means. Organizational records, trade journals, public records, and reference books serve as valuable sources for data. Personal contacts, mail to the company, advisory committees, and personnel reports represent other sources of information. If more formal research methods are required, they might be carried out by the PR department or by an outside agency that specializes in public opinion polling or survey research. Return to our example. The PR director at the auto company will need to gather a great deal of information. How much will the company save by its reorganization? Exactly how many workers will be transferred? Will the company help find new jobs for the workers who will be unemployed? What will be the precise economic impact on the community? What will become of the empty buildings that will be left behind? Will the employees believe what the company tells them? What do people expect from the company? Will the company's image be hurt in other areas of the United States?

>> Planning

Phase two is the planning stage. There are two general types of planning: **strategic** and **tactical.** Strategic plans involve long-range, general goals that the organization wishes to achieve. Top management usually formulates an organization's strategic plans. Tactical plans are more specific. They detail the tasks that must be accomplished by every department in the organization to achieve the strategic goals. Some plans that are drawn up might be used only once; others might serve as standing plans that set general organizational policy.

Planning is a vital part of the PR program. Some of the items involved in a PR campaign are framing the objectives, considering the alternatives, assessing the risks and benefits involved in each alternative, deciding on a course of action, figuring out the budget, and securing the necessary approvals from within the organization. In recent years, many PR practitioners have endorsed a technique known as **management by objectives (MBO).** Simply put, MBO means that the organization sets observable and measurable goals for itself and allocates its resources to meet those objectives. For example, a corporation might set as a goal increasing sales by 25 percent over the next two years. When the time had elapsed, it would be easy to see if the goal had been achieved. This approach is becoming more popular in PR because top management typically thinks in these terms, and if PR practitioners speak the same language as chief executives, they can communicate more effectively with them. It also keeps the department on target in solving PR problems, and it provides concrete feedback about the efficiency of the PR process. In our hypothetical example, some objectives might be informing more than 50 percent of the community about the reasons for the move and making sure community and national attitudes about the company are not adversely affected.

>> Communication

Phase three is the communication phase. After gathering facts and making plans, the organization assumes the role of the source of communication. Several key decisions are made at this stage concerning the nature of the messages and the types of media to be used. Because mass communication media are usually important channels in a PR program, it is necessary for public relations practitioners to have a thorough knowledge of the various media and their strengths and weaknesses. Moreover, PR professionals should know the various production techniques for the print and broadcast media. Some common ways of publicizing a message through the mass media are press releases, video news releases, press kits, photographs, paid advertising, films, videotapes, press conferences, and interviews.

Public relations also makes use of other channels to get messages to its publics. These include both the interpersonal and the machine-assisted settings. House publications, brochures, faxes, letters, bulletins, posters, websites, e-mail, billboards, and bulletin boards are communication channels used by a company to reach its own employees. On a more personal level, public meetings, speeches, demonstrations, staged events, open houses, and tours are other possibilities.

In the hypothetical example, our PR director would probably use a variety of messages and media. News conferences, ads, news releases, and public meetings would be appropriate vehicles for explaining the company's position to its external public. Meanwhile, house publications, bulletin boards, speeches, and letters could be used to reach its internal public.

>> Evaluation

The last phase concerns **evaluation** of the PR program. How well did it work? The importance of evaluation in public relations is increasing through the use of MBO techniques. If a measurable goal was proposed for the PR program, then an evaluation technique should be able to measure success in reaching that goal. Several different aspects might be measured. One easy method is simply to gauge the volume of coverage that the campaign generated. The number of press releases sent out, letters mailed, speeches made, and so on, are simple to compute. In like manner, press clippings and mentions in TV and radio news can be tabulated. It is important to remember, however, that volume does not equal results. A million press clippings mean nothing if they are not read by the audience. Measuring the impact of a campaign on the audience requires more sophisticated techniques of analysis. Some common techniques are questionnaires distributed to random samples of the audience, telephone surveys, panels, reader-interest studies, and the use of experimental campaigns. It is likely that our hypothetical PR director would use many of these techniques.

Before closing, we should note that we have been talking about these four steps as though they were distinct stages. In actuality, the PR program is a continuous process, and one phase blends into the next. The results learned in the evaluation stage, for example, are also part of the information-gathering phase of the next cycle of the PR program. In our continuing car company example, the PR department would use the results of surveys and focus groups to determine whether the company's image had suffered, how much credibility the company had with consumers, and if there were any change in customer loyalty. These findings would help in planning the goals of the next PR campaign.

 ECONOMICS

Companies, nonprofit groups, and government agencies spend large sums of money on public relations. After record years for PR in 1999 and 2000, a weak economy caused revenues to decline in 2001 and 2002. The total amount of money spent on corporate PR activities is hard to measure, but some information is available about the revenues of PR agencies. In 2002, the top 50 PR firms in the United States collected more than $2 billion in fee income.

The industry is dominated by giant PR firms owned by ad agencies. As of 2003, the biggest PR companies with ad agency parent companies were the Omnicom Group (including Porter-Novelli and Fleishman-Hillard) and the WPP group (including Hill & Knowlton and Burson-Marsteller). The two largest independent PR companies were Edelman PR Worldwide and Ruder Finn. The PR business can be volatile, especially for smaller agencies, whose fee income might vary by 40 to 80 percent from year to year.

PR agencies earn their money in a number of ways. Some perform a specific project for a fixed fee. An annual report, for instance, might cost $5,000. Some charge their clients a retainer every month, which might range from a few hundred to a few thousand dollars. Hill & Knowlton, for example, has a minimum monthly fee of $7,500. Other firms keep track of the time spent on various projects and charge clients an hourly rate. Still others bill for time plus for extra services and materials.

PR ONLINE

The Internet has added a dimension to public relations. It provides new tools for PR practitioners to use and opens up new channels of communication with the public and the media. Some of the PR uses of the Internet are predictable; others are rather innovative.

First, as might be expected, e-mail has replaced the traditional paper-mail channel that was used for press releases. E-mail rather than the telephone has become the preferred means of communication between practitioners and journalists. Furthermore, the Web has become an important instrument in distributing information to the media. PR Newswire's website, for example, collects information from PR agencies and PR departments and makes this information available to newsrooms across the country.

Additionally, corporate websites have become more than just flashy sites that try to sell a product or service. They have become the first line of communication

The online home of PR Newswire. More than 40,000 journalists can access press releases through this web site.

for consumers, shareholders, and reporters. In addition to featuring chat rooms, news releases, and message boards, corporate websites can be used to help an organization react quickly to a crisis or a controversy. The website of Saudi Arabia (www.saudinf.com), for example, contains a section describing the official Saudi reaction to the September 11 attacks.

Finally, it is not surprising that PR agencies use the Web for feedback on companies, products, and issues. Some companies, such as eWatch, monitor online news media and related sites for mentions of specific organizations. Other companies monitor websites, newsgroups, chat rooms, and Web logs for references to specific businesses.

One of the more inventive uses of the Web for PR is the Web-based video conference. After September 11, many firms cut back on travel to traditional in-person conferences and meetings and turned instead to virtual meetings using streaming Web video. Many companies discovered that Webcasts attract a larger audience of journalists than do traditional face-to-face meetings since they save reporters the need to travel to cover the event.

Another development is the online pressroom. This is a website designed to be used by reporters who need information for a story. It contains basic company information, recent and past press releases, a searchable archive, photos, video clips, information about the organization, and a list of contacts for reporters who need other information. Online newsrooms have the advantage of being available 24 hours a day, seven days a week. They also save organizations the cost of printing and shipping information kits to the various media.

Finally, the Intranet, sort of an Internet within a particular company that contains information not available to the general public, has become a widely used tool for internal communication. An Intranet might contain training tutorials, a newsletter, and company workplace policies.

CAREER
OUTLOOK

 ## PUBLIC RELATIONS

Newcomers to the public relations field typically begin their work in the corporate area, with most people starting off in the public relations department of a medium-sized to large organization. A smaller number go directly into PR counseling firms. Others follow a different career path into the profession by first working at a newspaper or a broadcasting station and then moving into public relations. In any case, those in the PR industry recommend that prospective job seekers have excellent communications skills, particularly in writing, since many entry-level jobs entail writing and editing news releases, reports, employee publications, and speeches. Other qualifications that are desirable are a knowledge of public opinion research techniques, business practices, law, the social sciences, and computer-related skills.

New employees in the PR department are expected to perform a wide range of duties. More specifically, a newcomer is expected to write news releases; update mailing lists; research materials for speeches; provide material for an organization's website; edit company publications; arrange special events; produce special reports, films, and tapes; and give public speeches.

One way to gain initial entry into the profession is to secure an internship with a public relations firm while you are still in college. A survey of recent graduates now working in public relations revealed that undergraduate internships turned into full-time jobs for about one-fifth of those surveyed. Internships may carry a modest salary, or they may involve no pay at all; some internships carry college credit, others do not. In any event, all internships can be valuable training experience.

As in other media-related work, the job applicant should not be too choosy about his or her first job. Most counselors recommend taking any job that is available, even if it lacks the glamour and the salary that the applicant was hoping for. Once you are inside the firm, it is much easier to move to those positions that are more attractive.

MAIN POINTS

- *Public relations* is difficult to define, but most practitioners agree that PR involves counseling management about communication strategies that can improve public opinion about an organization.
- Modern public relations began around the turn of the 20th century and has steadily increased in importance.

- PR is practiced in numerous settings, including business, government, and the nonprofit sector.
- A PR campaign consists of the following stages: information gathering, planning, communication, and evaluation.
- The Internet is an important part of PR. It is used to provide information to the public and to obtain background information for PR professionals.

QUESTIONS FOR REVIEW

1. Define *public relations*.
2. What are some of the major areas that make use of public relations?

3. What are the stages in a public relations campaign?
4. How has the Internet changed the practice of public relations?

QUESTIONS FOR CRITICAL THINKING

1. Can you think of any examples of your using PR in your personal life (like putting the best spin on a bad grade in a course)?
2. Why is the term *public relations* so hard to define? Is it important to have a definition that everybody agrees on?

3. Which model of public relations, the attorney model or the social responsibility model, do you support? Why?
4. Many journalists look with disfavor on the field of public relations. What might account for this attitude?

KEY TERMS

publicity (p. 342)

publics (p. 342)

information gathering (p. 351)

strategic (planning) (p. 351)

tactical (planning) (p. 351)

management by objectives (MBO)
 (p. 352)

evaluation (p. 352)

INTERNET RESOURCES

Online Learning Center

At the Online Learning Center home page, www.mhhe.com/dominick8, *select* Student Center *and then* Chapter 13.

1. Use the Learning Objectives, Chapter Outline, Main Points, and Time Line sections to review this chapter.

2. Test your knowledge of the chapter using the multiple choice, crossword puzzle, and flashcard features of the site.

3. Expand your knowledge of concepts and topics discussed in the chapter by going to *Suggestions for Further Reading* and *Internet Exercises.*

PowerWeb

At the Mass Communication home page of PowerWeb, www.dushkin.com/powerweb, *log in and select* Mass Communication *as your title. On the next screen, select* Topics *and then quick jump to* Agenda Setting. *Read Article 27, "On Message: A Theater of War at the Pentagon." Then reflect on the following questions:*

1. Why does the author of this article use the term *theater* in the title?

2. In this context, what does *on message* mean?

3. What is the proper relationship between the press and the military's public relations apparatus? Will there always be tension?

Surfing the Internet

Some of these sites are mentioned in the text. Others appear first on this list. Remember that the Web is always changing. Some sites move, some change their focus, and others simply evaporate.

www.ewatch.com
The Internet monitoring service. Its promotional text says, "Safeguard stakeholder value, protect corporate reputation, monitor competition, identify trends, and pinpoint corporate activism." Includes sound bites from satisfied customers of companies such as Heinz and Mrs. Fields.

www.ketchum.com
The home page of Ketchum Public Relations Worldwide. Includes a description of the company, a list of the worldwide offices, and case studies.

www.prnewswire.com
A source of news about corporations for reporters and investors. Lists the day's top business stories and offers links to specialized news about entertainment, autos, finance, and leisure activities.

www.prmuseum.com
A museum of public relations. Contains extensive information on the pioneers of PR.

www.prsa.org
The home page of the Public Relations Society of America. Includes general information about the society, a list of relevant publications, and a link to the PR student society. A recently added feature enables members to post their résumés in cyberspace.

14

ADVERTISING

Is there anybody who has not heard about the X10 miniature surveillance camera—the tiny wireless video camera that broadcasts color videos directly to your PC, television, or VCR? The one you can use for security? Or to capture "special moments"? Well, if you don't know about the X10, don't blame the Seattle-based company that manufactures this tiny camera. In 2002, it placed more than 1.3 *billion* pop-up ads for this product on various websites throughout the Internet.

The X10 campaign was the first significant use of a relatively new form of Internet advertising: the pop-up or the pop-under ad. These are ads that launch a separate window behind (or in front of) your main page when you visit a site. Unlike the banner ads that are part of a Web page, these ads must be clicked on in the little box at the top of the window before they will go away.

When the Internet first arrived, advertisers thought it would be a perfect medium for advertising. Consumers

The miniature X-10 surveillance camera was one of the first products to make use of a massive Internet pop-up ad campaign.

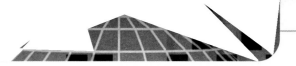

would see an ad on a website, click on it, and be taken to another site where they could learn more about the product and even order it. Plus, it would be easy to track which banner ads were most effective and which websites produced the most traffic. As it turned out, not many people paid attention to banner ads. Only a microscopic segment of the audience clicked on them, and fewer still used them to buy products. Advertisers had to find some other way to get their messages across. Enter the pop-up ad. The pop-up ads and their spawn are just one of several innovations that have marked advertising's entry into the digital age. We will take a closer look at online advertising as we examine the structure, history, operations, and social effects of this ever-changing enterprise.

 ## DEFINING ADVERTISING

Simply defined, *advertising* is any form of nonpersonal presentation and promotion of ideas, goods, and services usually paid for by an identified sponsor. Note three key terms in this definition. First, advertising is "nonpersonal"; it is directed toward a large group of anonymous people. Even direct-mail advertising, which may be addressed to a specific person, is prepared by a computer and signed by a machine. Second, advertising typically is "paid for." This fact differentiates advertising from publicity, which is not usually purchased. Sponsors such as Coke and Delta pay for the time and the space they use to get their message across. (Nonprofit organizations, such as the Red Cross or the United Way, advertise but do not pay for time or space. Broadcast stations, newspapers, and magazines run these ads free as a public service.) Third, for obvious reasons, the sponsor of the ad is "identified." In fact, in most instances, identifying the sponsor is the prime purpose behind the ad—otherwise, why advertise? Perhaps the only type of advertising in which the identity of the advertiser may not be self-evident is political advertising. Because of this, broadcasters and publishers will not accept a political ad without a statement identifying those responsible for it.

>> Functions of Advertising

Advertising fulfills four basic functions in society. First, it serves a marketing function by helping companies that provide products or services sell their products. Personal selling, sales promotions, and advertising work together to help market the product. Second, advertising is educational. People learn about new products and services, or improvements in existing ones, through advertising. Third, advertising plays an economic role. The ability to advertise enables new competitors to enter the business arena. Competition, in turn, encourages product improvements and can lead to lower prices. Fourth, advertising reaches a mass audience, thus greatly reducing the cost of personal selling and distribution. Finally, advertising performs a definite social function. By vividly displaying the material and cultural opportunities available in a free-enterprise society, advertising helps increase productivity and raises the standard of living.

>> **Types of Advertising**

Advertising can be classified in several ways. One useful division is to distinguish the **target audience**—the specific segment of the population for whom the product or service has a definite appeal. Many target audiences can be defined; the most general are consumers and business. **Consumer advertising,** as the name suggests, is targeted at the people who buy goods and services for personal use. For example, Campbell's (known for its soups) uses consumer advertising to direct its ads to the adults and children most likely to buy soup at the grocery store. Most of the advertising that people are exposed to falls into this category. **Business-to-business advertising** is aimed at people who buy products for business use. Industrial, trade, and professional—as well as agricultural—advertising are all part of this category. Consumer advertising is the focus of most of this chapter, but we will also take a brief look at business-to-business advertising.

Geographic focus is another way to classify advertising. International advertising is employed for products and services that are used all over the globe. Coca-Cola and McDonald's, for example, advertise in dozens of countries and in many different languages. National advertising is advertising in many different regions of the same country. Delta, Wal-Mart, and Sprint, for example, run ads on TV networks and in national magazines to reach customers in many different markets across the United States. International advertisers, of course, also use national ads. Retail or local advertising is done within one specific market. The neighborhood restaurant or car dealership typically relies on local ads.

Yet a third way to categorize advertising is by purpose. Some ads are for distinct products or services, such as frozen pizzas or muffler repairs, while others try to improve a company's image or influence public opinion on an issue, such as the ads run by oil companies describing their efforts to keep down fuel costs. Another distinction involves primary demand and selective demand ads. A **primary demand ad** has as its purpose the promotion of a particular product category rather than a specific brand. The campaign to encourage milk drinking that shows various celebrities with milk moustaches is an example of this type. A **selective demand ad** is used by an individual company to sell its particular brand, such as a certain brand of milk. Finally, ads can be classified as direct action and indirect action. A **direct action ad** usually contains a toll-free number, coupon, e-mail address, or some similar device to enable the advertiser to see results quickly. In contrast, an **indirect action ad** works over the long run to build a company's image and increase consumer awareness.

Advertising is part of the overall marketing process. Broadly defined, **marketing** consists of the

An example of a primary demand ad. The "got milk?" campaign was designed to promote milk drinking, not the purchase of a particular brand of milk.

The most outspoken critics of advertising charge that it stimulates greed, envy, and avarice—three of the seven deadly sins—a claim that can be made by no other industry. Specifically, foes of advertising claim that it causes people to buy things that they otherwise would not. Flashy ads for new-model cars prompt people to trade in perfectly good older models simply for the prestige and status of owning new ones. Even though the old DVD works fine, run out and buy the latest version with new bells and whistles. Still wearing last year's clothes? Shame on you. Go out and buy the latest fashions as seen in print and TV ads. In short, advertising *creates* needs and makes people buy things they do not *really* need or want.

In reply to this criticism, advertising practitioners point out that humans have a variety of needs; some are biological (the need for food) and basic (the need for a safe place to live). Others are more complicated (the need for self-esteem and self-actualization). Advertising, say its supporters, caters to a wide variety of needs, not just basic ones. There is nothing wrong with buying a new car every year if it helps a person's self-esteem. Buying the latest fashions can help a person on a quest for self-actualization. Advertising is directed at many forms of need fulfillment, some of them subtle and personal. It is presumptuous of critics to tell consumers what they need or do not need. In this argument, advertising is pictured as catering to a variety of needs that are already present in consumers; it does little to create new ones. As further support for this argument, advertisers point out that many heavily advertised products fail, and there is no evidence to suggest that advertising can compel people to purchase things they do not want.

A second line of criticism holds that advertising promotes materialistic values and lifestyles. Advertising persuades us to evaluate others not by who they are, but by what they possess. Material objects are portrayed as desirable goals. The people whom advertising presents as models to be emulated are not those who possess admirable personal qualities. Instead, we are compelled to emulate people who drive fancy or powerful cars, wear expensive jewelry, write with the best pen, wear the trendiest clothes, or watch TV on the biggest set. Advertising encourages people to spend and acquire and makes consumption the most important activity in life. Critics go on to point out that this aspect of advertising is particularly disruptive for those with low incomes who do not have the means to attain the material goals portrayed in ads.

In response to this argument, supporters of advertising point out that advertising did not create the emphasis on materialism in American life. Writings about rampant materialism in American culture were present as early as 1830. Major holidays in the United States celebrate consumption and materialism. Christmas, for example, encourages gift giving; Thanksgiving, eating. Our basic economic system of capitalism stresses the production and consumption of economic goods. Advertising simply reflects the larger values of U.S. society and should not be blamed for portraying them.

Finally, advertising is criticized for its intrusiveness. The typical American is the most advertised-to person in the world. U.S. companies spend more than $500 per person on advertising, more than companies in any other country. According to *Business Week,* we are exposed to about 3,000 commercial messages a day. In addition to the ubiquitous commercials on radio, on TV, and in print, advertising is now piped into supermarkets, airports, and doctors' offices; plastered on bathroom walls; splashed on the sides of race cars; snuck into the plots of feature films; displayed on blimps; and printed on the sides of hot dogs. Plans are even in the works to put ads in outer space. The avalanche of ads has made it difficult for advertisers to get consumers to notice their ads, let alone remember them. This causes additional pressure to find new channels and new attention-getting techniques and results in even more intrusiveness.

Even advertising's supporters agree that advertising is hard to avoid. But they go on to point out that this is a small price to pay for the social and economic benefits that it provides for society. Without advertising, television and radio would not be free, and magazines and newspapers would cost at least twice as much. Advertising that appears on the sides of buses helps keep fares down. The uniforms worn by Little League teams are often given for free in return for plastering the advertiser's name on the back. Would you mind seeing ads for Coke in this textbook if it meant the price was $10 cheaper?

Obviously, these are complicated issues, made even more difficult because there is no simple way to sort out the effects of advertising from the effects of all the other factors in modern life. Nonetheless, because of its high visibility and its role in the well-being of consumers, advertising will continue to be subjected to intense social scrutiny.

development, pricing, distribution, and promotion of ideas, goods, and services. Advertising is part of the general promotion process, along with personal selling, sales promotions, and public relations. It is an important element in marketing, but it is not the only element.

 A BRIEF HISTORY OF ADVERTISING

Advertising's beginnings are impossible to pinpoint, but several examples date back thousands of years. Clay tablets traced to ancient Babylon have been found with messages that touted an ointment dealer and a shoemaker. The town crier was an important advertising medium throughout England and other countries in Europe during the medieval period.

In more recent times, the history of advertising is inextricably entwined with changing social conditions and advances in media technology. For instance, Gutenberg's invention of printing using movable type made possible several new advertising media: posters, handbills, and newspaper ads. The first printed advertisement in English, produced about 1480, was a handbill that announced a prayer book for sale. Its author, evidently wise in the ways of outdoor advertising, tacked his ad to church doors all over England. By the late 1600s, ads were common sights in London newspapers.

Advertising made its way to the American colonies along with the early settlers from England. Ben Franklin, a pioneer of early advertising, made his ads more attractive by using large headlines and considerable white space. From Franklin's time to the early 19th century, newspaper ads resembled what today are called *classified ads*.

The Industrial Revolution caused major changes in American society and in American advertising. Manufacturers, with the aid of newly invented machines, were able to mass-produce their products. Mass production, however, also required mass consumption and a mass market. Advertising was a tremendous aid in reaching this new mass audience.

The impact of increasing industrialization was most apparent in the period from the end of the Civil War (1865) to the beginning of the 20th century. In little more than three decades, the following occurred:

1. The railroad linked all parts of the country, making it possible for Eastern manufacturers to distribute their goods to the growing Western markets.
2. The population of the United States doubled between 1870 and 1900. More people meant larger markets for manufacturers.
3. The invention of new communication media—the telephone, typewriter, high-speed printing press, phonograph, motion pictures, photography, rural mail delivery—made it easier for people to communicate with one another.
4. Economic production increased dramatically, and people had more disposable income to spend on new products.

This improved economic and communication climate helped advertising thrive. Magazines were distributed from coast to coast and made possible truly national advertising. The development of the halftone method for reproducing photographs meant that magazine advertisers could portray their products more vividly. By 1900, it was not unusual for the leading magazines of the period (*Harper's, Cosmopolitan, McClure's*) to run 75 to 100 pages of ads in a typical issue.

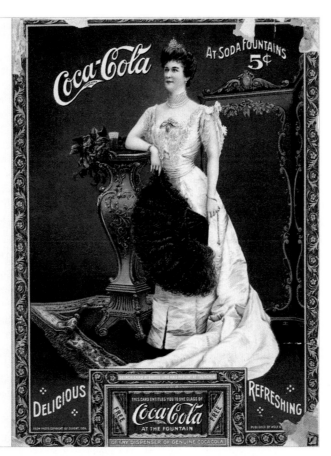

An ad from the 1900s for Coca-Cola. Included at the bottom is a coupon for a free Coke.

It is not surprising that the increased importance of advertising in the marketing process led to the birth of the **advertising agency,** an organization that specializes in providing advertising services to its clients. The roots of the modern-day agency can be traced to Volney B. Palmer of Philadelphia. In 1842, Palmer bought large amounts of space in various newspapers at a discount and then resold the space at higher rates to advertisers. The actual ad—the copy, layout, and artwork—was still prepared by the company wishing to advertise; in effect, Palmer was a space broker. That situation changed in the late 19th century when the advertising agency of N. W. Ayer & Son was founded.

Ayer & Son offered to plan, create, and execute complete advertising campaigns for its customers. By 1900, the advertising agency became the focal point of creative planning, and advertising was firmly established as a profession.

The 1920s saw the beginning of radio as an advertising medium (see Chapter 7). Network broadcasting made radio an attractive vehicle for national advertisers; by 1930 about $27 million was spent on network advertising, and many of the most popular shows of the day were produced by advertising agencies. However, the stock market crash of 1929 had a disastrous effect on the U.S. economy, and total dollars spent on advertising dropped from $2.8 billion in 1929 to $1.7 billion in 1935. It would take a decade for the industry to recover. During World War II, many civilian firms cut back on their advertising budgets. Others simply changed the content of their ads and, instead of selling their products, instructed consumers on how to make their products last until after the war.

World War II was followed by the Cold War, when Americans were concerned about the rise of communism. Despite growth in mass consumption and economic prosperity, the prevailing mood of the country was one of fear and apprehension as many people were afraid that communists were secretly taking over the government and subverting the American way of life. This mood also had an impact on public opinion about advertising. After the Korean War (1950–1953), many stories surfaced about brainwashing and mind control of American prisoners. It was not long before advertising was indicted as a form of mind control that seduced people by subtle appeals to deep, subconscious urges. A best-seller called *The*

CRITICAL / CULTURAL ISSUES

Cultural Meaning and Trade Characters

Tony the Tiger, Mr. Clean, the Maytag repairman, Ronald McDonald, the Jolly Green Giant, Betty Crocker, the Keebler Elves—these are examples of trade characters, fictional beings, played by actors or animated, created to help sell a product, service, or idea. Like slogans, trade characters are popular because they are an effective way of linking the product and its advertising so that consumers can easily remember the message. But trade characters do more than slogans; they give a product personality, style, and depth by creating an image with a clear cultural meaning with which the audience can identify.

Created by the Leo Burnett Agency, the Jolly Green Giant has been ho-ho-ho-ing for more than 30 years.

An article by Barbara Phillips in a 1996 issue of the *Journal of Popular Culture* examines the role of trade characters in American culture. Phillips notes that mass-produced products have little cultural meaning. A Duracell battery is hard to distinguish from an Eveready battery, and neither is likely to arouse any emotional response. Trade characters, however, give meaning and significance to otherwise indistinguishable products by linking a product to an image that has a cultural meaning. One way that trade characters create this meaning is by employing commonly accepted mythical symbols—images that convey cultural meaning. Take the Jolly Green Giant, for example. The giant is a common mythical symbol whose size connotes strength, power, and authority. His green color is associated with freshness, while his hearty "ho-ho-ho" imparts warmth and humor. The giant's image on a can of peas makes the product less remote and more friendly.

The use of mythical symbols gives trade characters another quality: They communicate messages without having explicitly to state them. Mr. Clean, for example, immaculate in his all-white costume, symbolizes cleanliness and purity. His image suggests that using his product will produce these results, but he never actually says so. In contrast, an ad that proclaims "Our cleaner will leave your countertop spotless and pure" might be met with some degree of doubt. Since trade characters do not directly state that a product has specific attributes, their "claims" are less likely to be rejected.

There are, of course, some drawbacks to the use of trade characters. Cultural meanings shift over time, and advertisers must be careful to monitor changing attitudes in society. Perhaps the best example of this potential is Aunt Jemima. The Quaker Oats Company started using this trade character in 1889. Over the years, however, the image became an unacceptable stereotype. In 1968, during the Civil Rights movement, her image changed: She lost 100 pounds and became younger; her red bandana was replaced by a headband. In 1990, she was made over again into an image that was the black equivalent of Betty Crocker, an image the company hoped was more positive. Some trade characters may be entirely inappropriate. Joe Camel, for example, was the subject of much criticism because the cartoon character seemed designed to encourage children to smoke. Camel eventually phased him out.

Trade characters have become an established part of American culture. Their ranks will undoubtedly increase in the future.

1. Why do marketers want us to have emotional connections to mass-produced products, and how might their efforts affect our society? Those peas are not warm and friendly after all; why do we like it better when we think they are?

2. Besides the Aunt Jemima example (which in itself is worthy of further consideration), how else are expectations and stereotypes of race and gender reflected in trade characters?

3. If you can, look through some magazines from the 1950s, or even earlier. How do the trade characters you see there compare to the ones you see today, and what might that tell us about how (and whether) society has changed?

in a few big cities, such as New York, Chicago, and Los Angeles. That trend has changed, however, and many of the more memorable ad campaigns of recent years have been put together by agencies located far from Madison Avenue. When it comes to total income, however, the big-city agencies still dominate.

The last few years in the agency business have seen the spawning of super-agencies, or mega-agencies, resulting from the merger and consolidation of several large ad agencies. In addition, the business has been globalized, since these new mega-agencies have branches all over the world. The five mega-agencies listed in Table 14–1 dominated the industry at the close of 2002.

The global reach of advertising is apparent in the agency business as in many other media. Three of the megagroups in Table 14–1 are foreign-owned.

Agencies can be classified by the range of services they offer. In general terms, there are three main types: (1) full-service agencies, (2) media buying services, and (3) creative boutiques.

As the name implies, a **full-service agency** handles all phases of the advertising process for its clients; it plans, creates, produces, and places ads. In addition, it might also provide other marketing services, such as sales promotions, trade show exhibits, newsletters, and annual reports. In theory, at least, there is no need for the client to deal with any other company for help promoting its product.

A **media buying service** specializes in buying radio and television time and reselling it to advertisers and advertising agencies. The service sells time to the advertiser, orders the spots on the various stations, and monitors the stations to see if the ads actually run.

A **creative boutique** (the name was coined during the 1960s and has hung on to the present) is an organization that specializes in the actual creation of ads. In general, boutiques create imaginative and distinctive advertising themes and produce innovative and original ads. A company that uses a creative boutique would have to employ another agency to perform the planning, buying, and administrative functions connected with advertising.

What does a full-service ad agency do for a client? To begin with, the agency studies the product or service and determines its marketable characteristics and how it relates to the competition. At the same time, the agency studies the potential market, possible distribution plans, and likely advertising media. The agency then makes a formal presentation to the client detailing its findings and its recommended advertising strategy. If the client agrees, the agency then launches the execution phase. This phase entails writing and producing the ads, buying space and time in various media, delivering the ads to the appropriate media, and verifying that all ads actually appear. Finally, the agency works closely with the client's salespeople to make sure they get the greatest possible benefit from the ads.

TABLE 14–1	Company	Headquarters	2002 income (in billions)
Top Five Advertising Agencies, 2002	Omnicom Group	New York	$7.54
	Interpublic Group	New York	$6.20
	WPP Group	London	$5.78
	Publicis Group	Paris	$2.71
	Dentsu	Tokyo	$2.06

>> Media

The last part of the advertising industry consists of the mass media. The media serve as the connection between a company and its customers. The media that are available for advertising include some obvious ones—radio, TV, newspapers, magazines, the Internet—and others that are not so obvious, such as direct mail, billboards, transit cards (bus and car cards), stadium scoreboard ads, and point-of-purchase ads. Chapters 4, 5, 7, 10, and 11 presented an overview of the mainstream mass media and discussed their dependence on various kinds of advertising. This section examines these media from the perspective of an advertiser.

Even the slickest and most imaginative advertising message will fail if it is delivered to the wrong people. To make sure that this does not happen, advertisers employ highly skilled media planners to help them place and schedule their ads.

Advertising specialists evaluate media along four dimensions:

1. *Reach:* How many people can get the message?
2. *Frequency:* How often will the message be received?
3. *Selectivity:* Does the medium actually reach potential customers?
4. *Efficiency:* How much does it cost to reach a certain number of people? (This is usually expressed as cost per thousand people.)

Table 14–2 summarizes how the various media rate on these dimensions.

In addition to considering these factors, advertisers have to take into account many others before deciding on which medium to use. An important part of any decision involves considering the creative limitations imposed by the physical properties of each medium. Television, for example, enables the advertiser to show the product in action. On the other hand, TV ads are short and cannot be used to present a great deal of technical information. A magazine ad can be in full color and can present a large amount of data, but it might not have the same impact as a TV ad. All in all, choosing which media to use in the final advertising mix is a difficult decision.

TABLE 14–2

Characteristics of Various Media

CHARACTERISTICS			MEDIUM				
	Newspapers	Magazines	Radio	TV	Outdoor	Direct mail	Internet
Reach	High	Low	High	High	High	High	Medium
Frequency	High	Low	High	High	High	Medium	Medium
Selectivity	Low	High	High	Medium	Low	High	High
Efficiency	Medium	Medium	Low	High	High	High	Medium

Here Is Another Way to Use Your Head

Advertisers have always had a tough time reaching college students. A British marketing company has come up with a novel way to advertise to this age group: The company wants to rent space on students' foreheads. Students who agree to participate will have the logos of prominent companies semipermanently tattooed on their foreheads. They will be paid about $2.50 for every hour they are out in public displaying their tattoos.

No word yet as to the company's plans to rent space on other body parts.

ADVERTISING ONLINE

Online advertising began in 1994 when HotWired, the digital counterpart to the techno-hip *Wired* magazine, started a website with about a dozen sponsors who paid to have advertising banners embedded throughout the site. Since that time, online advertising has gone through a number of changes.

Helped by an infusion of ad dollars from dot-com companies and the good economic times of the late 1990s and early 2000s, online advertising boomed. When the bubble burst, however, revenues shrank. By 2004, there were signs that online advertising was picking up again. There were several reasons behind this revival:

- Lower prices for online ads made them more attractive for advertisers.
- Innovative technologies, including streaming video and full-motion graphics, made ads more memorable.
- Surveys indicated that people were spending more time online and less time with TV. Advertisers followed the audience and spent more on Internet ads.
- Advertisers discovered that some online techniques were more effective than traditional banner advertising. Although they might be annoying, those pop-up and pop-under ads generated five times more click-throughs than banner ads. At the other end of the spectrum, advertisers discovered that those unobtrusive ads that appear above or next to Google or Yahoo! search results were also effective in generating traffic.

Even if online advertising picks up, the amount spent on Internet advertising is small compared to the amount spent in other media. In 2002, online ads accounted for only about 3 percent of all U.S. advertising dollars. The most optimistic forecasts suggest that online advertising will grow relatively slowly, perhaps accounting for 5 to 6 percent of U.S. ad dollars by 2006–2007.

Furthermore, there are some problem spots on the horizon. Internet advertising is becoming increasingly intrusive and annoying as spam, pop-ups, and pop-unders become more common. Advertisers are also becoming more sophisticated about purchasing online ads. Some are no longer paying a fixed price for an ad but are basing their payments on the number of people who actually click on the ad or who actually buy the advertised product. As a result, poorly executed online campaigns or campaigns for unsuccessful products might bring next to nothing for the websites that run the ads.

>> Categories of Internet Advertising

Banner ads, pop-ups, and pop-unders are still the most common forms of online ads, but other configurations are gaining popularity. You have probably seen the following:

An example of an Internet banner ad.

abc**7NEWS** ● **ONLINE** **KMGH DENVER**   The Reason to Watch

NetFlix is just one of many companies who use pop-up ads. Pop-ups are economical and advertisers think they are effective.

- Splash pages are Web advertising pages that appear before a Web page loads and then disappear a short while later.
- A skyscraper is an elongated vertical banner ad that borders one side of a Web page.
- A floating ad is one in which an object moves across the page on a preset course or moves up and down a page as the user scrolls.
- Mousetrapping occurs when the user closes one ad that is then replaced by a slew of others that keep popping up.

Advertisers, of course, have other ways of getting their message across online. Some advertisers sponsor chat rooms that are related to the product they are selling. AT&T, for example, sponsors a chat room where business travelers can discuss the best places to dine or shop in various cities. The AT&T business calling card is featured prominently on the page.

Finally, websites devoted to a product or company are another form of Web advertising. Companies spend a good deal of time and money creating the site that is most appropriate for their product. To illustrate, Gap.com divided its website into sections that mirror those of their retail stores: men's clothes, women's clothes, boys' clothes, and so on. Pictures of the products are laid out in a simple manner to aid online shoppers.

 PRODUCING ADVERTISING

>> Departments and Staff

There are typically four major departments in a big advertising agency:

- creative services,
- account services,
- marketing services, and
- administration.

The creative department, as the name implies, actually produces the ad. The people in this department write the advertising **copy** (the headline and message of the ad), choose the illustrations, prepare artwork, and/or supervise the scripting and production of radio and TV commercials.

The account services department is responsible for the relationship between the agency and the client. Because the advertising agency is an organization outside the firm doing the advertising, it is necessary to appoint someone, usually called an *account executive* (AE), to promote communication and understanding between client and agency. The AE must represent the viewpoint of the agency to the client but at the same time keep abreast of the needs of the advertiser. Since the AE tends to be the person in the middle, his or her job is obviously an important one in the agency.

The marketing services department is responsible for advising the client as to what media to use for his or her messages. Typically, this department makes extensive use of the data collected by the Audit Bureau of Circulations, Arbitron, Nielsen, MediaMetrix, and the other audience research services mentioned in earlier chapters. This department is also in charge of any sales promotions that are done in connection with the advertising. These may include such things as coupons, premiums, and other aids to dealers.

Finally, like any other business, the advertising agency needs a department to take care of the day-to-day administration of the agency. This department is in charge of office management, clerical functions, accounting, personnel, and training of new employees.

>> The Advertising Campaign

The best way to illustrate how ads get produced is to present a general discussion of an advertising campaign for a national product. A **campaign** consists of a large number of advertisements, all stressing the same major theme or appeal, that appear in a number of media over a specified time. Following is a discussion, greatly simplified, of the six phases of a typical campaign:

Many advertisers like to use well-known celebrities in their ad campaigns. Jerry Seinfeld , for example, has appeared in American Express commercials for nearly ten years.

1. choosing the marketing strategy,
2. selecting the main appeal or theme,
3. translating the theme into the various media,
4. producing the ads,
5. buying space and time, and
6. executing and evaluating the campaign.

In the first phase, a great deal of research is done to determine the target audience, the marketing objective, the appropriate price for the product or service, and the advertising budget. It is during this phase that the word **positioning** is often heard. Positioning has

Perhaps you are one of the many who saw a TV spot for Miller Lite beer created by the Ogilvy & Mather ad agency entitled "Catfight." In the 30-second ad, two voluptuous models get into a "tastes great" vs. "less filling" argument about Miller Lite. The argument intensifies until the two rip off each other's clothes. The quarrel ends with the two women in their underwear wallowing around in a trough of wet cement. (The quarrel had a slightly racier ending in the version shown on cable networks.)

At that point the audience learns that the fight was just the fantasy of two guys dreaming up their perfect beer ad. "Who wouldn't want to see an ad like that?" asks one of the men. The camera then pans to their apparent girlfriends, who are obviously two of the people who would not want to see such an ad.

The two girlfriends were not the only ones who did not think much of the ad. The beer company received more than 2,500 calls and e-mails complaining about the spot. Not surprisingly, the biggest complaint was that the ad promoted sexism. It degraded women, portrayed them as sexual objects, and encouraged attitudes harmful to women. Moreover, the ad ran during the NFL playoffs when a large number of children were in the audience; many parents complained that the ad was not appropriate for children. Some men objected to the ad because it made men look like idiots who think only about mud-wrestling females.

Of course, it should be noted that beer advertising has never been an arena in which women's liberation and sexual enlightenment have thrived. A few years ago Old Milwaukee ran a campaign featuring the "Swedish Bikini Team." The ads were so offensive that Old Milwaukee's own female employees sued to stop the spots from being aired.

Furthermore, the fact that a beer company would run such a provocative ad is not surprising given that the current media scene is populated by the likes of Howard Stern, Victoria's Secret TV specials, *Maxim* magazine, and *The Man Show*. Like everybody else, beer advertisers are pushing the envelope in order to get their message across.

The response of Miller Lite to the criticism generated by its ad was that everybody should lighten up. One Miller Lite executive called the ad merely "a lighthearted spoof" of guys' fantasies that was meant neither to be taken seriously nor to offend anybody. He went on to describe the ad as "over the top," "silly," and "ridiculous."

In addition, Miller Lite had little to lose by running the ad. The target market for light beer is 21- to 31-year-old single males. Not surprisingly, market research suggested that this group liked the spot. Most of the opposition came from married females over the age of 40, a group that does not drink much beer.

Although not everybody agreed about the message in the ad, one thing was certain: It generated a lot of media attention. The spot was debated on CNN's *Crossfire, The O'Reilly Factor, Good Morning America,* and *The Rush Limbaugh Show*. The beer company estimated that the media coverage had exposed about 80 million consumers to the ad. That kind of free publicity is the kind that advertisers dream about. It will come as no surprise to learn that Miller Lite plans to run seven or eight sequels to the ad, one starring former *Baywatch* star Pamela Anderson and a couple that will feature male models. Stay tuned.

many interpretations, but in general it means fitting a product or service to one or more segments of the broad market in such a way as to set it apart from the competition without making any change in the product.

For example, in 2003, the McDonald's Corporation signed ex–N-Sync member Justin Timberlake to appear in its new "I'm Lovin' It" campaign. The company announced that the new ad effort was designed to reposition McDonald's as "hip, contemporary, and today" and make the company "in sync" with modern pop culture.

The restaurant chain Huddle House also launched a 2003 ad campaign designed to change its image as a "breakfast only" restaurant and to reposition itself as a place for lunch and dinner. New TV commercials featured satisfied customers praising the variety of menu items.

Sometimes positioning does not work. Minute Maid orange juice failed in its attempt to reposition its product from simply a breakfast drink to an all-purpose beverage. Despite an $18 million campaign that featured the slogan "Not just for breakfast anymore," sales of orange juice remained flat as customers failed to respond.

After the product or service has been positioned, an overall theme for the campaign is developed. Nissan, for example, launched a multimillion-dollar ad campaign in 2002 based on its new theme "Shift." The idea behind the theme was to demonstrate to consumers that Nissan did not accept the status quo. Ads included the word *shift* linked to various other words, as in "Shift_desire," "Shift_dreams," and "Shift_passion."

The next phase involves translating the theme into print and broadcast ads. Advertisers try to achieve variety in their ads but with a consistency of approach that will help consumers remember and recognize their product. To illustrate, Saab produced six TV spots, five radio spots, and four print ads all based on its new theme, "state of independence." All of the TV spots showed shots of Saab automobiles traveling down curvy mountain roads intercut with shots of spinning wheels and smiling drivers. All of the spots ended with a tag line: "Saabs are made in the state of independence. . . ."

The actual production of the ad is done in much the same way that other media content is produced. In the print media, the copy, the headline, subheads, any accompanying illustrations, and the layout are first prepared in rough form. The initial step is usually just a thumbnail sketch that can be used to experiment with different arrangements within the ad. The headline might be moved down, the copy moved from right to left, and so on. Next a **rough layout,** a drawing that is the actual size of the ad, is constructed. Usually, several layouts are prepared, and the best are used to produce the **comprehensive layout,** the one that will be used to produce the ad. Many agencies use outside art studios and printers to help them put together print ads and billboards.

Radio commercials are written and created in much the same way that early radio drama shows were produced. A script is prepared in which dialogue, sound effects, and music are combined to produce whatever effect is desired. The commercial is then either produced in the sound studio or recorded live on location. In either case, postproduction editing adds any desired special effects, and eventually, a master tape is prepared for duplication and distribution.

The beginning step in the preparation of a television commercial is a **story-board,** a series of drawings depicting the key scenes of the planned ad. Storyboards are usually shown to the client before production begins. If the client has any objections or suggestions, changes can be made to the script before production. Once the storyboards are approved, the commercial is ready to go into production. Most TV commercials are shot on film (although some are now switching to videotape). Television commercials are the most expensive ads to produce. A 30-second commercial can easily cost $350,000. Special effects, particularly animation, can drive the costs even higher. In an effort to keep costs down, much of the time spent producing TV commercials consists of planning and rehearsing. As with the print media, many agencies hire outside production specialists to produce their commercials.

While the creative department is putting together print and broadcast ads, the marketing department is buying time in those media judged to be appropriate for the campaign. If the product is seasonal (e.g., suntan lotion, snowmobiles), the ads are scheduled to reflect the calendar, appearing slightly before and during the time people begin buying such items. Other products and services might call for a program of steady advertising throughout the year.

Advertisers know that many people who watch TV actively avoid the commercials. Using the remote control to channel surf during commercials has become something close to a national pastime. If that were not enough of a problem for advertisers, consumers can now buy personal video recorders, such as TiVo, that make it easy to fast-forward through commercials.

Advertisers are not taking this lying down. They have responded with "product integration," placing their merchandise within the fabric of a program so that viewers cannot help but notice it. The idea is not new. Back in the 1950s, Phillip Morris sponsored the popular *I Love Lucy* sitcom. The stars of the show were frequently shown smoking Phillip Morris cigarettes. Modern product integration is different only in degree: There is a whole lot more of it now. Consider these recent examples:

- The star of the series *Monk* constantly cleaned items with Lysol before he touched them.
- Nokia cell phones are prominently featured in the action-adventure series *Alias.*
- Coca-Cola products were ubiquitous on *American Idol.*
- Crest Whitestrips and Disaronno Originale Amaretto show up frequently in Bravo's *Queer Eye for the Straight Guy.*

This is just a short list from a large number of examples. Perhaps the ultimate in product placement was achieved with NBC's 2003 summer series *The Restaurant.* The concept for the show came from a company that specialized in product placement. The company did not try to sell the series primarily as entertainment but as the perfect vehicle for product placement. As a result, people who ordered beer at the restaurant were served Coors (paid product placement) and paid their bills with the American Express Card (paid product placement) while the restaurant manager was off driving his new Mitsubishi (paid product placement).

Despite its seeming popularity, product placement carries with it some unique drawbacks for advertisers. First, it only works with recognizable brands. Unfamiliar products would probably not be noticed by viewers. Second, there is no way to measure its effectiveness. The final drawback is product placement paradox. If the product placement is too obvious, people become resentful and wind up with bad feelings about the product. On the other hand, if the product placement is too subtle, people will not see it, and the placement becomes worthless. Even with these shortcomings, the trend seems to be toward more products appearing in more shows.

The last phase of the campaign consists of the running of the ads. Testing is done during and after this phase to see if consumers saw and remembered the ads. In addition, sales data are carefully monitored to determine if the campaign had the desired effect on sales.

>> ### Advertising Research

Advertising research, which takes place during all phases of the campaign, helps agencies and their clients make informed decisions about their strategy and tactics. **Formative research** is done before the campaign begins to help guide the creative effort. It can take several forms. One is audience definition—identifying the target market, such as "females 18 to 34" or "all adults." After this is accomplished, audience profiling is done to discover as much as possible about how the target market lives—what they think, what their attitudes are, how they decide to buy.

The next phase, **message research,** involves pretesting the messages that have been developed for the campaign. At its most basic level, pretesting determines if the audience can actually understand the ads. This type of testing guards against possible double meanings or overlooked sexual connotations that might have eluded the creative staff. In a second type of pretest, researchers show mock-ups of magazines that contain the prototype of the print ad and rough cuts of TV ads to test audiences. Consumers are tested to see whether they recall the main points of the ad and whether their attitude toward the product has shown any change. Some advertising campaigns go through pilot tests in actual markets. A split-cable transmission can show one version of an ad to one group of people and a second version to a similar group. The ads are compared to see which did a better job. A split-run of a magazine uses the same strategy.

Tracking studies examine how the ads perform during or after the actual campaign. Samples of consumers are studied to see if they recall the ads, if their attitudes about the product have changed, and if they have bought the product or used the service advertised.

 ECONOMICS

In this section we will examine the economics of advertising on two levels. First, we will look at the total industry and trace expenditures in various media. Second, we will narrow our focus and examine how an agency makes money.

>> Advertising Volume in Various Media

About $218 billion was spent on advertising in the United States in 2002. Figure 14–1 shows how this money was divided among the various media. Since 1960, newspapers have seen a decrease in their relative share of advertising volumes—as have magazines. Television has shown a significant increase, while radio, outdoor advertising, and direct mail have shown modest growth. The Internet will probably account for more of the pie in the future.

>> Agency Compensation

How an advertising agency makes money is not well known outside the agency and media community. In this section we will explore three common methods: (1) media commissions, (2) agency charges, and (3) fees.

Historically, the major mass media have allowed advertising agencies a 15 percent commission on the time and space they purchase. Recently, however, the commission system has been declining in popularity. Many advertisers have struck pay-for-performance deals with ad agencies. Payments to ad agencies are based on sales or some other measure of performance. If sales go up, the ad agency gets more money. Other companies pay agencies a fixed fee, and still others use a combination of a flat fee plus performance-based incentives.

FIGURE 14–1

Advertising Expenditures in Various Media, 2002

(Dollar figures are in billions.)

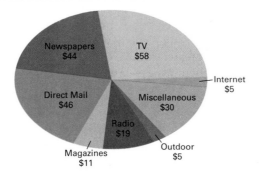

The medium of outdoor advertising has grown rapidly over the past decade. Modern billboards use striking new designs and graphics.

 ## BUSINESS-TO-BUSINESS ADVERTISING

As its name suggests, business-to-business advertising is designed to sell products and services not to general consumers but to other businesses, typically via specialized trade publications, direct mail, professional journals, and display advertising at trade shows. Recently, however, some business-to-business ads have turned up in the mass media. There are four main categories of business-to-business advertising:

- *Trade:* Advertising goods and services to wholesalers and retailers who, in turn, resell these items to a more general audience.
- *Industrial:* Advertising those items that are used in the further production of goods and services, such as copy machines, forklifts, and drill presses.
- *Professional:* Advertising aimed at doctors, lawyers, architects, nurses, and others who might influence the buying process or use the product in their profession.
- *Agricultural:* Advertising aimed at farmers and possibly including products such as feed, fertilizer, seed, and chemicals.

Although its visibility might not be high, business-to-business advertising is big business, ringing up more than $150 billion in revenue in 2002. Some people overlook the potential for a career in business-to-business advertising because they feel it is not as glamorous as consumer advertising. There may be some truth to this: Ads for a chemical solvent, bench-top fermenter, or blast furnace usually are not as flashy as campaigns for sleek new sports cars. In its own way, though, business advertising poses greater creative challenges. Coming up with a theme to sell the sports car is probably much easier than coming up with a winning idea for the chemical solvent.

>> Consumer versus Business-to-Business Advertising
There are some obvious differences between advertising directed at consumers and business advertising. In this section we will consider four.

First, the target audience in business advertising is much smaller. In some industries, the audience may number in the hundreds. Companies that manufacture storage tanks for petroleum products have determined that there are only 400 people in the United States authorized to purchase their product. In other areas, the audience may be in the thousands. This means, of course, that the media used to reach the target market must be selected carefully. In the nuclear reactor business, everyone in the market may read one or two publications.

Second, most of the products that are advertised tend to be technical, complicated, and high priced. For the advertiser, this means that the ads will probably contain a great deal of technical information and will stress accuracy.

Third, the buyers are professionals: purchasing agents whose only job is to acquire products and services for their company. Generally speaking, the decisions of the purchasing agent are based on reason and research. An error of a penny or two on a large purchase might cost a company thousands of dollars. Consequently, business advertising typically uses the rational approach. Additionally, it is important for advertisers to know exactly who makes buying decisions, since most purchases in large business are generally made in consultation with others in a company.

Fourth, personal selling plays a greater role in the business arena, and advertising is frequently used to support the sales staff in the field. As a result, ad budgets in the business sector may not be as high as those of their consumer counterparts.

>> Media

The media mix for business advertising is also different from that of consumer advertising. Since the target audience tends to be small, personalized media are best. Business publications tend to be the mainstay of campaigns. One study suggested that about 60 percent of industrial advertising dollars went to business and trade publications. Trade publications can be horizontal, dealing with a job function without regard to industry (such as *Purchasing Agent*), or vertical, covering all job types in an entire industry (such as *LP/Gas*).

Direct mail is also a valuable business advertising tool. Highly differentiated mailing lists can be prepared and ads sent to the most likely prospects. Research

An example of business-to-business advertising. This ad for Caterpillar industrial equipment contains far more technical information than would be found in a consumer ad.

Exceeding Your Expectations

has shown that direct mail is perhaps more effective among business-people than among consumers. Whereas a large percentage of direct-mail material is thrown out unopened by the general public, about three-quarters of all businesspeople, according to a survey done in the early 1980s, read or at least scan their direct-mail ads.

Advertising in trade catalogs is particularly important to companies that sell through distributors rather than via their own sales staff. Since a catalog is a direct reflection of a company, extra care is taken to make sure it is up-to-date, accurate, and visually appealing.

Business-to-business advertising in the mass media used to be rare, but some large companies, such as Federal Express, IBM, and Xerox, have used it to great effect. Federal Express, for example, found that its business increased more than 40 percent after it started to advertise in consumer media. Purchasing time and space in the mass media must be done skillfully because of the expense and the chance of wasted coverage if the right decision makers are not in the audience. Specialized cable channels have made it possible for many business-to-business advertisers to use more general media with reduced chances of wasted coverage. CNN's *MoneyLine* and several shows on CNBC, for example, attract an audience that contains many business decision makers. General newsmagazines, such as *Time* and *Newsweek,* along with *Forbes, Business Week,* and *Fortune,* are rather obvious choices for this type of advertising.

>> Appeals

Close attention is paid to the copy in business-to-business advertising. Many consumer ads depend on impression and style to carry their messages. The copy tends to be brief and can cater to the emotions. Business copy tends to be longer, more detailed, and more factual. A premium is placed on accuracy and completeness. If the ad contains technical inaccuracies or exaggerations, the credibility of the product is compromised. Some of the most-used formats in business advertising are testimonials, case histories, new-product news, and demonstrations.

Ethical Issues   Advertising and Kids

There is no doubt that advertisers have zeroed in on the child audience. The last few years have seen the growth of kid-specific media: Nickelodeon, websites, kid-oriented magazines, movie tie-ins, and even hamburger wrappers. From 1993 to 1999, advertising in these media increased more than 50 percent, to $1.5 billion per year.

Part of the reason behind this increase is the fact that kids have become important factors in family buying decisions. First, they have more money to spend. The under-14 set gets allowances, earns money, and receives gifts to the tune of about $20 billion per year. In addition, kids probably infuence another $200 billion worth of shopping decisions. Second, the increase in single-parent families and dual-career families means that kids are now making some of the purchasing decisions that were once left to Mom and Dad.

It is not surprising, then, to find that companies are intensifying their efforts to reach this market segment. And it is not just traditional toymakers, cereal companies, and fast-food restaurants that are in the mix. General Motors, for example, placed ads for its new minivan in *Sports Illustrated for Kids* and sent prototype vans to shopping malls where they showed previews of Disney's *Hercules* on a VCR inside the van. GM does not expect many six-year-olds to go out and buy a van, but the company knows through its research that kids can play an influential role in the decision about which van to buy. In that connection, United Air Lines keeps its younger travelers happy by serving McDonald's Happy Meals.

Market research that examines children's psychology has been used to help sell goods. Researchers know that seven and eight year olds like to collect things. This urge used to be satisfied by bottle caps, seashells, and baseball cards. More recently, the maker of Beanie Babies cashed in on this urge by creating a large number of different animals to collect, limiting production and discontinuing models to create artificial scarcity.

The marketing even extends into schools. Companies donate money, equipment, and educational materials to schools in return for the opportunity to advertise their products. It all started with Channel One, a news program for students. In return for a donation of electronic equipment, schools agreed to show a newscast that contained commercials. Other companies did not take long to follow Channel One. Nike, for example, mailed out shoe-assembly kits to schools. Teachers were supposed to help kids make the sneakers while teaching a lesson on environmentally safe manufacturing (presumably by companies like Nike). McDonald's sponsored a seven-week curriculum on how to build a McDonald's restaurant and how to interview for a job there. Some school districts, hard up for cash, have sold advertising space on the sides of school buses and in school hallways.

There are many who feel that all this selling to children is not right. They argue that children are an unsophisticated audience and are vulnerable to the flashy, persuasive techniques of the advertising industry. Not many parents would allow a salesperson to come into their home and talk to their kids; why, then, should they allow TV to target their children? Additionally, critics contend that advertising teaches values that are undesirable. Advertising focuses on the superficial and the material, and it glorifies consumption. Finally, critics contend that advertising creates conflicts between parents and children by encouraging kids to pester their parents for all the products they see advertised. Parents must continually say no and run the risk of possible strife. There is some evidence to support these positions (as discussed in Chapter 18). Even without this support, however, many people feel that advertising to kids is just plain wrong.

The advertisers reply that these critics do not give kids enough credit. They feel that kids are more sophisticated consumers than people realize and learn very quickly to see through the hype and manipulation that may be found in some ads. Additionally, the marketing community points out that kids are going to live in a world saturated by advertising. Coming into contact with it at an early age may help them learn how to deal with it when they become adults. Finally, they argue that kids get valuable information about new products and services from advertising, information that improves their lives.

The issue, of course, has legal as well as ethical overtones. To date, the government has weighed in on the side of kids. The Children's Television Act limits the amount of commercial minutes in TV shows that can be directed at children. The government and the tobacco industry worked out an agreement that prohibited the Camel cigarette company from using the cartoon character Joe Camel in its ads because the character appealed to children. There have been proposals to ban or limit beer, wine, and liquor advertising. Despite these efforts, it is clear that parents will be the ones to confront this issue head-on.

This is not to say, however, that all industrial ads should be stodgy and dull. In recent years, several ad agencies specializing in business ads have introduced warmth, humor, and creativity into their messages. The philosophy behind this movement is that businesspeople are also consumers and that they respond as consumers to business and trade ads. For example, Teddi, a California company that makes women's sportswear, placed special cover wraps on hundreds of copies of *Forbes* magazine that went to clothing retailers. The wraps featured Teddi clothes with headlines such as "As seen in *Cosmo.* Cosmopolis, Washington," or "As seen in *Harpers.* Harper's Ferry, West Virginia."

C   A   R   E   E   R ADVERTISING
O   U   T   L   O   O   K

After a couple of hard years, the advertising business showed signs of recovery in 2003, but employment prospects looked only a little bit brighter. Employment at U.S. advertising agencies was down more than 16 percent from 2000 as was employment in other advertising sectors of the media. Long-term prospects are tied to the general economy; a rebound will mean more advertising jobs.

>> **Entry-Level Positions**

A job applicant must make some basic decisions early in his or her professional training. Probably the first decision is whether to concentrate on the creative or the business side of the industry.

The creative side, as mentioned earlier, consists of the copywriters, art directors, graphic artists, photographers, and broadcast production specialists who put the ads together. Entry-level jobs include junior copywriter, creative trainee, junior art director, and production assistant. In most of these positions, a college degree in advertising or the visual arts is helpful, with a secondary concentration in marketing, English, sociology, or psychology also a benefit. Good Web skills are also a plus.

The business side of the industry offers careers as account executives, media planners, market researchers, or business managers. Proper preparation for these careers includes extensive course work in both advertising and business, with particular emphasis on marketing. Common entry-level positions in these fields are assistant media buyer, research assistant, junior account executive, or account service trainee.

>> **Upward Mobility**

Opportunities for advancement in advertising are excellent. Outstanding performance is rewarded quickly, and many young people progress swiftly through the ranks. Beginning creative people typically become senior copywriters or senior art directors. Eventually, some may progress to creative director, the person in charge of all creative services. On the business side, research assistants and assistant buyers can hope to become research directors and media directors. Account trainees, if they perform according to expectations, move up to account executives and later may become management supervisors. The climb to success can occur rapidly; many agencies are run by people who achieved top status before they reached age 40.

MAIN POINTS

- Advertising is any form of nonpersonal presentation and promotion of ideas, goods, and services paid for by an identified sponsor.
- Advertising can be classified by target audience, geographic focus, and purpose.
- Modern advertising began in the late 19th century and grew during the early 20th century as magazines and radio became mass advertising media.
- After World War II, advertising grew at a fast rate, particularly when TV came on the scene.
- The past two decades have seen the start of new channels for advertising, including cable TV and the Internet. Online advertising has grown in the past few years. It consists of banner ads, pop-ups, and websites.
- The three main components of the advertising industry are advertisers, agencies, and the media.
- Advertising agencies put together large-scale campaigns for clients, consisting of a market strategy, theme, ads, media time/space, and evaluation.
- Although not as visible as consumer advertising, business-to-business advertising makes up a significant portion of the industry.

QUESTIONS FOR REVIEW

1. What are the three defining characteristics of advertising?
2. Briefly describe the three main components of the advertising industry.
3. Describe the main types of online advertising.
4. What is positioning? Why is it important to advertisers?
5. How does consumer advertising differ from business-to-business advertising?

QUESTIONS FOR CRITICAL THINKING

1. What would society be like without advertising?
2. Is it right to advertise to children? If you think it is appropriate to advertise to children, what special considerations, if any, should be applied to such ads?
3. Check the national media for ongoing advertising campaigns. What are some themes that are currently running?
4. How can you tell if an advertising campaign has been effective?
5. What will be the future of online advertising?

KEY TERMS

target audience (p. 360)
consumer advertising (p. 360)
business-to-business advertising (p. 360)
primary demand ad (p. 360)
selective demand ad (p. 360)
direct action ad (p. 360)
indirect action ad (p. 360)
marketing (p. 360)
advertising agency (p. 363)
national advertisers (p. 366)
retail advertisers (p. 366)
agency (p. 366)
full-service agency (p. 367)
media buying service (p. 367)
creative boutique (p. 367)
copy (p. 370)
campaign (p. 371)
positioning (p. 371)
rough layout (p. 373)
comprehensive layout (p. 373)
storyboard (p. 373)
formative research (p. 374)
message research (p. 374)
tracking studies (p. 375)

INTERNET RESOURCES

Online Learning Center

At the Online Learning Center home page, www.mhhe.com/dominick8, *select* Student Center *and then* Chapter 14.

1. Use the Learning Objectives, Chapter Outline, Main Points, and Time Line sections to review this chapter.

2. Test your knowledge of the chapter using the multiple choice, crossword puzzle, and flashcard features of the site.

3. Expand your knowledge of concepts and topics discussed in the chapter by going to *Suggestions for Further Reading* and *Internet Exercises.*

PowerWeb

At the Mass Communication home page of PowerWeb, www.dushkin.com/powerweb, *log in and select* Mass Communication *as your title. On the next screen, select* Topics *and then quick jump to* Advertising. *Read Article 46, "Virtual Product Placement." Then reflect on the following questions:*

1. Is it ethical for advertisers to change reality by inserting virtual ads? Would you want virtual ads intruding into your viewing experience? Are there limits? Suppose a golf ball manufacturer digitally inserted its logo onto the green during a televised golf tournament?

2. Will viewers learn to accept product placement in the same way they have come to accept 30-second spots?

Now look at Article 49, "A Tough Sell," and answer the following questions:

1. This article appeared in June of 2000. How has the situation changed since then?

2. This quote appears in the last paragraph of the story: ". . . Internet advertising has more in common with direct mail advertising than with TV or print advertising." Do you agree?

Surfing the Internet

The following sites represent just a small sample of the hundreds and hundreds of sites that are relevant to this chapter. All were current as of late 2003. Keep in mind, however, that ad sites change rapidly.

www.aaaa.org
Home of the American Association of Advertising Agencies. Contains agency news, career information, and awards programs.

www.adage.com
Advertising Age is the leading trade publication for the industry. Its Web page has current news, useful statistics, and critiques of website advertising.

www.chiatday.com
Chiat Day is an ad agency that handles Nissan and Apple. At first glance the site does not look like that of an ad agency, but do not let it fool you. A sampling of the agency's current and past award-winning work is available.

www.clioawards.com
The Clios are advertising's counterparts to the Oscars. This site has a listing of winners and a searchable archive.

www.donnakaran.com
The fashion designer's website is a good example of consistency of execution. The tone and feel of this company's advertising are carried over to the website. Plus it has some pretty neat clothes.

www.X10.com
If you really need a tiny surveillance camera . . .

REGULATION
OF THE MASS
MEDIA

15

FORMAL CONTROLS: LAWS, RULES, REGULATIONS

For purposes of this chapter, formal controls over the media include laws, court decisions that refine those laws, and rules and regulations administered by government agencies. We will discuss six different areas in which these formal controls are important: (1) the controversy over a free system of mass communication, (2) copyright, (3) restrictions on obscenity and pornography, (4) regulation of radio and television, (5) regulation of the Internet, and (6) regulation of advertising. Unfortunately, many students have the idea that the field of mass communication law and regulations is dull and boring. Nothing could be further from the truth. In what other textbook could you read about raunchy magazines, the CIA, mass murderers, women in men's locker rooms, juicy divorces, and a man who owned a submarine?

Over the years court decisions have had a major impact on the operations of the mass media.

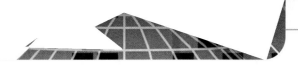

>> A Free Press

As noted in Chapter 4, the idea of a free press did not catch on at first in America. The early colonial papers had problems if they were not "published by authority"; that is, if they were not open to censorship by the Crown. Through the Stamp Act, the British government attempted to suppress hostile opinion by taxing printed matter. Recognizing these dangers to a free press, the framers of the Constitution added an amendment (the **First Amendment**) that stated in part that "Congress shall make no law . . . abridging the freedom of speech, or of the press." The precise meaning and interpretation of these words, however, have been open to some debate. Let us examine some key instances in which press and government have come into conflict.

>> Prior Restraint

When the government censors the press by restraining it from publishing or broadcasting material, that act is called **prior restraint.** Attempts at prior restraint have been relatively rare. Nonetheless, this area does illustrate that the provisions in the First Amendment are not absolute. The Supreme Court has ruled that, under certain circumstances, prior restraint or censorship of the press is permitted, but the government faces a difficult task in proving that the restraint is justified. There are some obvious examples of legal censorship. During wartime, say, a newspaper could be prevented from publishing the sailing schedules of troop transports; a radio station could be prohibited from broadcasting the location and numbers of soldiers on the front lines. Other attempts at prior restraint have not been particularly successful; the Supreme Court has generally upheld the right of the press. There are two seminal cases in this area that are beneficial for us to examine. One is not widely known; the other made the front pages.

The Near Case　During the 1920s, the Minnesota legislature passed a law under which newspapers that were considered public nuisances could be curtailed by means of an **injunction** (an order from a court that requires somebody to do something or refrain from doing something). The motives behind this law may have been praiseworthy because it appears to have been designed to prevent abusive attacks on minority groups. Using this public nuisance law, a county attorney sought an injunction against the *Saturday Press* and the paper's manager, J. M. Near, on the grounds that the paper had printed malicious statements about city officials in connection with gangland activities allegedly controlled by minority groups. In 1931, the Supreme Court ruled that the Minnesota law was unconstitutional. Said the Court,

> *The fact that for approximately 150 years there has been almost an entire absence of attempts to impose previous restraints upon publications relating to the malfeasance of public officers is significant of the deep-seated conviction that such restraints would violate constitutional rights.*

This issue would not be raised again for 40 years.

The Pentagon Papers　U.S. Attorney General John Mitchell was eager to see the Sunday, June 13, 1971, edition of the *New York Times*. Mitchell had attended the wedding of President Richard Nixon's daughter Tricia the day before, and he

The first installment of the Pentagon Papers appeared in the *New York Times*. Attempts by the government to halt further publication ended when the Supreme Court ruled in favor of the *Times*. (© 1971 by the New York Times Company)

wanted to see how the *Times* had covered it. On the left side of page 1, Mitchell saw a flattering picture of the president with his daughter on his arm. Next to the wedding picture, another story caught Mitchell's eyes: "Vietnam Archive: Pentagon Study Traces 3 Decades of Growing U.S. Involvement." As Mitchell read further, he realized that the *Times* article was sure to cause problems.

The basis for the story in the *Times* began three years earlier when Secretary of Defense Robert McNamara became disillusioned with the Vietnam War and ordered a massive study of its origins. This study, known eventually as the Pentagon Papers, was put together by 36 different people and ran for more than 7,000 pages. The final report was classified "Top Secret—Sensitive." During April 1971, one of those Pentagon staff members who compiled the report leaked a copy to a reporter for the *New York Times*. After much study and secrecy, the paper was ready to publish the story in nine installments. The U.S. Justice Department, under John Mitchell's direction, asked a U.S. district court judge to halt publication of the stories on the grounds that they would "cause irreparable injury to the defense interests of the United States." The order was granted, and for the first time in history, a U.S. paper was ordered by the courts to suppress a specific story. By then, however, other newspapers had obtained copies of some or all of the Pentagon documents and started publishing them. The Justice Department sought more restraining orders, but as soon as one paper was ordered to stop publishing, another newspaper in another part of the country would pick up the series. It was obvious that the Supreme Court would eventually have to intervene.

The Court did intervene and with uncharacteristic haste. On June 30, 1971, only 17 days after the story first appeared and only four days after hearing oral arguments on the case, the Court decided in favor of the newspapers' right to publish the information. Naturally, the staff at the *New York Times* was delighted. The paper called the decision a "ringing victory for freedom under law." Upon closer examination, however, the victory was not quite as ringing as it was made out to be. The Court did not state that prior restraint could never be invoked against the press. Instead, it pointed out that the government "carries a heavy burden of showing justification" for imposing restraint. The government, in the opinion of the Court, had not shown sufficient grounds for doing this. The government was free, if it wished, to bring other prior restraint cases to the courts to establish exactly how much justification it needed to stifle publication. In addition, each of the nine judges wrote a separate opinion that highlighted the ambiguities and complexities surrounding this topic.

More Recent Cases After the release of the Pentagon Papers, the prior restraint issue cropped up several times in cases involving ex–CIA agents. In one case, the CIA was successful in having portions of a book deleted because they revealed classified information.

In the 1991 Gulf War, two news organizations challenged the Defense Department's restrictive rules on coverage, but the war ended before the lawsuit could be heard. The Pentagon's policy of embedding reporters with military units during Operation Iraqi Freedom in 2003 apparently forestalled any lawsuits in connection with that action.

In 1999, a ruling by a district court judge held that the prohibition against prior restraint also included websites. The creator of a website devoted to news about the Ford Motor Company had posted documents obtained from Ford employees. The company had obtained a ruling that prevented the documents from being posted, but the ruling by the district court judge overturned that prohibition.

Finally, in 2003, an appeals court ruled that a Florida law that restricted billboards on interstate highways did not constitute prior restraint.

In sum, there is a strong constitutional case against prior restraint, but gray areas exist in which censorship might be legal. These areas will probably remain ambiguous until further court cases help define the limits of government authority in this area. It is likely, however, that the barriers against prior restraint will remain formidable.

 PROTECTING NEWS SOURCES

Before we begin an examination of this topic, it is important to consider that the issues are fairly complicated. Conflicting interests are involved. Reporters argue that, if they are forced to disclose confidential sources, those sources will dry up and the public's right to know will be adversely affected. Government arguments cite the need for the administration of justice and the rights of an individual to a fair trial.

Perhaps a hypothetical example will help bring these issues into focus. Suppose you are a reporter for a campus newspaper. One of your sources calls you late one night and informs you that several students have started a drug ring that has monopolized the sale of illegal drugs on campus. To check the accuracy of this report, you call another one of your sources, one who in the past has given you reliable information on campus drug dealing. This second source confirms what your caller told you and adds more details. For obvious reasons, both of your sources ask not to be identified, and you agree. On the basis of these reports and some additional research, you publish a lengthy article in the campus newspaper about the drug ring. A few days later you are summoned before a grand jury that is investigating criminal drug dealings. You are asked to reveal your sources. If you refuse, you will be charged with contempt and possibly fined or sent to jail. What do you do?

>> The Reporter's Privilege

Other reporters have found themselves in the same fix. One was Paul Branzburg. In 1969, Branzburg wrote a story for the *Louisville Courier-Journal* in which he described how two local residents were synthesizing hashish from marijuana. His article stated that he had promised not to reveal their identities. Shortly thereafter, Branzburg was subpoenaed (ordered to appear) by the county grand jury. He refused to answer questions about his sources, claiming, in part, that to do so would violate the First Amendment provision for freedom of the press. The case ultimately reached the Supreme Court, which ruled that the First Amendment did not protect reporters from the obligation to testify before grand juries to answer questions concerning a criminal investigation.

Initially, this ruling was viewed as a setback for reporters' rights. However, the Court did suggest some situations in which the reporter's claim to privilege would be valid. These included harassment of news reporters, instances in which grand juries do not operate in good faith, and situations in which there is only a remote connection between the investigation and the information sought. Additionally, the Court suggested that Congress and the states could further define the rights of a reporter to protect sources by enacting legislation (called **shield laws**) to that effect.

After the Branzburg decision, state courts were somewhat inconsistent in their rulings. On the one hand, several cases upheld the reporter's right to keep his or her sources secret. In Florida, Lucy Ware Morgan, a reporter for the *St. Petersburg*

Times, refused to disclose her source for a story about a grand jury report on corruption in city government. She was promptly convicted of contempt of court and received a 90-day jail sentence. In 1976, however, the Florida Supreme Court overturned the conviction. Using the Branzburg decision as a guideline, the court concluded that the name of her source was not relevant to the investigation of a crime and that the contempt charge was designed to harass her.

Other decisions have narrowly defined the test of relevancy between the case at hand and the reporter's sources. In Virginia, a newspaper reporter refused to identify a source during testimony at a 1978 murder trial. The lawyer for the accused argued that the source's name was needed to question the credibility of a prosecution witness. The Virginia Supreme Court ruled in favor of the reporter and stated that a reporter's privilege must yield only when the defendant's need for the information is essential. To be essential, said the court, the information had to (1) relate directly to the defendant's guilt or innocence, (2) bear on the reduction of an offense, or (3) concern the mitigation of a sentence.

Just because these cases are taken from the 1970s, do not get the idea that reporters no longer go to jail or get fined. From 1999 to 2000, three reporters in California, a state with what many experts consider the strongest shield law in the country, got into legal trouble when they failed to reveal confidential information. One journalist went to jail for five days, and another was fined $1,000 a day for every day he refused to testify. Fortunately for the reporters, either the sanctions were overturned on appeal or the original requests were dropped. Finally, there is the complicated case of Vanessa Leggett, a freelance writer who was jailed for 168 days in 2001–2002 for refusing to disclose confidential materials she compiled while doing research for a planned book. The Leggett case raised important issues that were never resolved (see Social Issues, "Who's a Journalist?").

As of 2003, 31 states and the District of Columbia had shield laws. Journalists generally recognize these laws as helpful, but most realize that they are not the powerful protectors of the press that many had hoped for. In addition, the laws themselves represent a bewildering collection of provisions, qualifications, and exceptions. Some states protect only confidential material; some protect the reporter from revealing the name of a source but do not protect the information obtained from sources. Other state laws confer less protection if the reporter is involved in a libel case. In some states, shield laws do not apply to reporters subpoenaed by a grand jury. Further, many courts are interpreting the shield laws on a case-by-case basis and ignoring or limiting the interpretation of judgments contained in the law.

>> Search and Seizure

Finally, there is the troublesome question of protecting notes and other records that might disclose sources. In this regard, the courts have offered little protection. Three particular cases have disturbed the news media.

In the first case, in 1971, four police officers entered the offices of the *Stanford Daily*, the campus newspaper of Stanford University, and produced a search warrant authorizing them to search for photographs of a clash between demonstrators and police that the *Daily* had covered the day before. The newspaper brought suit against the authorities, charging that its First Amendment rights had been violated. In 1978, the Supreme Court ruled that the search was legal. (In 1980, however, Congress extended some protection to newsrooms by passing a bill that

Vanessa Leggett was intrigued by a 1997 murder case in Houston, Texas. She planned to write a book about the case, so she interviewed many of the principals involved, including one person accused of the crime who later apparently committed suicide in prison while awaiting trial. A second person eventually went to trial and was acquitted. After the state trial, the federal government started investigating the case for possible interstate conspiracy charges.

A federal grand jury subpoenaed Leggett for her notes, tapes, and other documents. The government argued that she was not a journalist (and therefore not entitled to a qualified privilege that would allow her to protect her sources) and that, even if she were, there is no federal shield law that protects journalists. Leggett refused to turn over her material and was jailed.

She appealed, but an appeals court ruled that, as long as there was no proof of government harassment, journalistic privilege could not be used to avoid a grand jury subpoena. The court did not rule as to whether Leggett was a journalist. Leggett stayed in jail for 168 days, the longest jail stay on record for someone who refused to turn over material to a grand jury. She was finally released when the term of the grand jury expired, but she still faced the possibility of being subpoenaed again if the case went to trial.

Still unresolved is the vexing question of who decides who is a journalist and therefore entitled to protection under state law. Would you consider Leggett a journalist? She had no formal training in journalism. She had never worked for a newspaper or magazine. She had no contract for a book. Her only publications were articles in two FBI manuals. She had edited a couple of crime novels for a Houston publisher. The government concluded she was not a journalist.

Regardless, should the government decide who is a journalist? It is easy to imagine a government with a hostile attitude toward the press using this decision as a tool to suppress criticism. Further, does not the First Amendment apply to beginning journalists without a track record as well as to veteran reporters who have published hundreds of articles? As an editorial in the *New York Times* put it,

> Integral to our freedom of the press is the notion that the First Amendment protects those who are engaged in journalism, not those certified as journalists by the government. If the government refuses to recognize a fledgling freelancer as a real journalist, it may next decree that someone who works for a small newspaper also fails to make the grade.

This argument sounds reasonable but does it mean then that anyone can legitimately claim to be a journalist? How about people who publish Web logs? Are they journalists? They report on day-to-day events and publish their work. Can they claim journalistic privilege if called before a grand jury? How about students doing research for a term paper? Are they protected?

The argument that journalists deserve some kind of privilege is based on the fact that they are individuals who represent the public and keep the public informed. Forcing them to reveal sources hampers their credibility and ultimately makes it difficult for them to gather and report information, which in turn harms the public interest. Does such an argument apply to Leggett? Was she representing the public in this case? It might be argued that she was doing the research in order to get a book contract. Maybe she was only representing her own self-interest. On the other hand, it would not be too difficult to develop an argument for why a book on a murder case *could* represent the public interest.

would require the government to secure a subpoena to obtain records held by reporters. The scope of a subpoena is somewhat more limited than that of a search warrant. In addition, a subpoena can be challenged.)

In the second case, the U.S. Court of Appeals in the District of Columbia decided another case that further eroded reporters' rights to protect sources. In 1974, the Reporters Committee for Freedom of the Press filed suit against the American Telephone and Telegraph Company (AT&T) because the company would not pledge to keep records of reporters' toll calls safe from government scrutiny. (An analysis of these calls might help locate a reporter's source of information.) The court of appeals ruled that it was legal for the government to examine such records without a reporter's knowledge or consent.

The third case involved *New York Times* reporter Myron Farber. During 1976, Farber had been reporting the investigation into mysterious deaths at a New Jersey hospital. The stories led to the indictment of a prominent physician on charges of poisoning five patients. Defense lawyers ultimately subpoenaed notes and documents pertaining to the case that were held by Farber and the *Times*. Both Farber and the paper refused to provide the documents, and both were convicted of contempt of court. Farber was sentenced to six months in jail and a $1,000 fine; the *Times* was slapped with a $100,000 fine and was ordered to pay $5,000 every day until it complied with the court's order. The *Times* ultimately turned over its files, but a judge ruled that the paper had "sanitized" them by removing some relevant material, so it reinstated the fine. Farber, meanwhile, had spent 27 days in jail. Eventually, Farber wound up spending 40 days in jail, and the *Times* paid $285,000 in fines. All penalties finally ended with the jury's verdict that the physician was innocent.

The privacy of computer-stored messages and e-mail received protection from the Electronic Communication Privacy Act, which requires the government to obtain a search warrant before examining online or stored messages intended to be private.

Perhaps the safest conclusion that we can draw is that a reporter's privilege in protecting sources and notes is not absolute. Even those decisions that have favored journalists have been qualified. It also appears that further developments in this area will be put together on a piece-by-piece basis by lower courts unless the Supreme Court generates a precise decision or the legislature passes a comprehensive law. As for reporters, they must carefully consider these issues when they promise confidentiality to a news source.

 ## COVERING THE COURTS

On the one hand, the Sixth Amendment guarantees a defendant the right to a trial before an impartial jury; on the other, the First Amendment guarantees freedom of

High-profile criminal cases can illustrate the tension between the First and the Sixth Amendment. The trial of Scott Peterson was moved to a different city because of pre-trial publicity.

the press. Trial judges are responsible for the administration of justice; reporters are responsible for informing the public about the workings of the legal system. Sometimes these responsibilities clash.

>> Publicity Before and During a Trial

If a potential jury member has read, seen, or heard stories in the news media about a defendant that appear to indicate that person's guilt, it is possible that the defendant will not receive a fair trial. Although research has not produced definitive evidence linking pretrial publicity to prejudice, this concern has been at the heart of several court decisions that have castigated the news media for trying cases in the newspaper or on television instead of in the courtroom.

The 1960s saw a flurry of cases suggesting that the Supreme Court was taking a close look at pretrial publicity. In 1961, the Court for the first time reversed a criminal conviction entirely because pretrial publicity had made it impossible to select an impartial jury. The case concerned Leslie Irvin, a rather unsavory character who was arrested and charged with six murders. Newspapers carried police-issued press releases that said "Mad Dog" Irvin had confessed to all six killings. The local media seized upon this story with a vengeance, and many stories referred to Irvin as the "confessed slayer of six." Of the 430 potential jurors examined by attorneys, 90 percent had formed opinions about Irvin's guilt—opinions that ranged from suspicion to absolute certainty that he was guilty. Irvin was convicted—hardly a surprise—and sentenced to death. After six years of complicated legal maneuvers, made even more complicated by Irvin's escape from prison, the case went before the Supreme Court. The Court ruled that the pretrial publicity had ruined the defendant's chances for a fair trial and sent the case back to be retried. (Irvin, who had been recaptured, was again found guilty, but this time was sentenced to life imprisonment.)

Perhaps the most famous case of pretrial publicity concerned an Ohio physician. On July 4, 1954, the wife of Cleveland-area osteopath Dr. Sam Sheppard was found slain in the couple's home. Sheppard became a prime suspect, and the news media, especially the Cleveland newspapers, were impatient for his arrest. "Why Isn't Sam Sheppard in Jail?" and "Why Don't Police Quiz Top Suspect?" were headlines that appeared over page-one editorials. News reports carried the results of alleged scientific tests that cast doubt on Sheppard's version of the crime (these tests were never brought up at the trial). Articles stressed Sheppard's extramarital affairs as a possible motive for the crime. After his arrest, the news stories and editorials continued. There were enough of them with headlines such as "Dr. Sam Faces Quiz at Jail on Marilyn's Fear of Him" and "Blood Is Found in Garage" to fill five scrapbooks. Every juror but one admitted to reading about the story in the newspapers. The sensationalized coverage continued during the trial itself, which produced a guilty verdict. Twelve years later the Supreme Court reversed Sheppard's conviction because of the extremely prejudicial publicity. This case assumed added importance because the Court listed six safeguards that judges might invoke to prevent undue influence from publicity. These safeguards included sequestering the jury (i.e., moving them into seclusion), moving the case to another county, and placing restrictions on statements made by lawyers, witnesses, or others who might divulge damaging information.

>> Gag Rules

Some judges have issued restrictive orders, or **gag rules,** that restrain the participants in a trial (attorneys, witnesses, defendants) from giving information to the media or that restrain media coverage of events that occur in court. For example, a superior court judge in a Washington murder trial ordered reporters to report only on events that occurred in front of a jury. Two reporters violated this rule by writing about events that took place in the courtroom while the jury was not present; they were subsequently charged with contempt. The Washington Supreme Court refused to review this ruling.

The whole question of gag rules reached the Supreme Court in 1976. A Nebraska judge had prohibited reporters from revealing certain information about a mass murder case. The Nebraska Press Association appealed the order to the Supreme Court. The Court ruled on the side of the press association and held that reporting of judicial proceedings in open court cannot be prohibited. Once again, upon first examination, this rule appeared to be a significant victory for the press. As time passed, however, it became apparent that the Nebraska decision had left the way open for court-ordered restrictions on what the trial participants could say to the press. It seemed to indicate that some legal proceedings, primarily those that take place before the actual trial begins, might be legitimately closed to the public. By the early 1980s, this was exactly what was happening. Although the press was left free to report what it chose, its news sources were muzzled by judicial order. During the late 1970s, judges began holding pretrial hearings in private to limit pretrial publicity. A 1979 Supreme Court decision held this practice to be constitutional. In 1980, the Court did go on record as stating that the press did, in fact, have a constitutional right to attend criminal trials. *Pretrial* events, however, might still be closed. Because many criminal cases are settled out of court, these pretrial hearings are often the only public hearings held.

In the 1980s, the press gained wider access to court proceedings. In 1984, the Supreme Court ruled that the jury selection process should be open to the press except in extreme circumstances, and it established standards that judges must meet before they can close a pretrial hearing. A 1986 Supreme Court decision, however, gave the press a major victory in its efforts to secure access to pretrial proceedings. The Court held that preliminary trial proceedings must be open to the press unless the judge could demonstrate a "substantial probability that the defendant's right to a fair trial would be violated." Additionally, lower courts have held that the First Amendment right of access to trials also extends to documents used as evidence. Also in 1986, the Supreme Court ruled that the jury selection process, as well as the trial itself, must ordinarily be open to the public. The Court also provided a set of strict guidelines that would justify a private selection of a jury.

A 2002 case raised questions about journalists' access to jurors after a trial is concluded. After a murder trial ended with a hung jury, a New Jersey judge ruled that reporters could not interview jurors for fear that the jury pool might be tainted in the event of a retrial. Reporters from the *Philadelphia Inquirer* defied the judge's rule and were convicted of contempt of court. The newspaper appealed but was turned down by the New Jersey Supreme Court. In 2003, 12 news organizations petitioned the U.S. Supreme Court to review the case.

In summary, Supreme Court decisions do not give the press an absolute right of access to all court proceedings. Some parts of trials and pretrial hearings may still be closed if the judge can fulfill the Court's guidelines regarding closure. Further, the recent Court decisions have not changed the legal status surrounding the privacy of grand jury hearings—they continue to have the right to secrecy. All in all, it might be safe to conclude that the press has been given a green light to report matters that occur in open court with little fear of reprisal. But gag orders on news sources and the closing of various legal proceedings threaten to be areas of tension between the press and the judiciary for some time to come.

>> Cameras and Microphones in the Courtroom

For many years, the legal profession looked with disfavor on the idea of cameras and microphones in the courtroom. There was a time when this attitude may have been entirely justified. The whole problem seems to have begun in 1935 when

Bruno Hauptmann was put on trial for the kidnapping and murder of the son of national hero Charles Lindbergh. Remember that news photography and radio journalism were still young in 1935, and this fact may have contributed to some of the abuses that occurred during this trial (see Media Probe, "Canon 35 and the Hauptmann Trial"). After the trial, the American Bar Association added Canon 35 to its Canons of Professional Ethics. This provision stated that the taking of photographs in the courtroom and the broadcasting (later amended to include telecasting) of court proceedings should not be permitted. Although Canon 35 was not law, its language or some variation of it was adopted as law by every state except Colorado and Texas.

In 1965 the Supreme Court entered the picture when it ruled on the Billie Sol Estes case. Estes was on trial in Texas for allegedly swindling several farmers. The trial judge, over Estes's objections, had allowed the televising of the trial. Estes was found guilty, but he soon appealed that decision to the Supreme Court on the grounds that the presence of television had deprived him of a fair trial. The high court agreed with Estes and argued for the prohibition of television cameras in the courtroom. The decision said that broadcasting a trial would have a prejudicial impact on jurors, would distract witnesses, and would burden the trial judge with new responsibilities. However, the Court went on, there might come a day when broadcast technology would become portable and unobtrusive and television coverage so commonplace that trials might be broadcast. Thus, the decision in the Estes case was not a blanket provision against the televising of trials.

Since 1965, the trend has been toward a general relaxation of the tension between the legal profession and the electronic press. In 1972, the American Bar Association adopted a new code of professional responsibility. Canon 3A(7) of this document superseded the old Canon 35. Canon 3A(7) still maintained the ban on taking photographs and broadcasting in the courtroom, but it did allow the judge the discretion to permit televising a trial to a pressroom or to another courtroom to accommodate an overflow crowd. In 1981, the Supreme Court ruled that broadcast coverage of a criminal trial is not inherently prejudicial, thereby clearing the way for the presence of radio and TV in the courtroom. The Court left it up to the states to devise their own systems for implementing such coverage.

As of 2003, all 50 states allowed some form of coverage. The rules for coverage vary state by state. In Georgia, for example, the judge may permit one television camera in the courtroom. In Ohio trial courts, coverage of nonconsenting victims and witnesses is prohibited. Cameras are not allowed in federal district courts or at Supreme Court proceedings.

REPORTERS' ACCESS TO INFORMATION

>> Government Information

Reporting the doings of the government can be a frustrating task if the government insists that information about its activities be kept secret. After World War II, many members of the press complained that government secrecy was becoming a major problem. Reporters were being restricted from meetings, and access to many government documents was difficult to obtain. In the midst of continuing pressure from journalists and consumer groups, Congress passed the **Freedom of Information Act (FOIA)** in 1966. This law gave the public the right to discover what the federal government was up to—with certain exceptions. The law states that every federal executive-branch agency must publish instructions on what methods a member of the public should follow to get information. If information is improperly withheld, a court can force the agency to disclose what is sought. There are nine areas of exemptions covering material that does not have to be made public. Some of these exemptions are trade secrets, files of law enforcement investigations, and maps of oil wells.

In 1996, the Electronic Freedom of Information Act (EFOIA) was passed to make more information available on the Internet. Currently, many government agency websites contain a variety of information, ranging from statistics to press releases, that can be accessed via website visit rather than through an FOIA request. Nonetheless, many agencies have been slow to fully implement the requirements of the EFOIA.

A "Sunshine Act" ensures that regular meetings of approximately 50 federal government agencies will be open to the public. There are, however, 10 different situations that might permit an agency to meet behind closed doors, so the right of access to meetings is far from absolute. In addition, many states have their own versions of laws pertaining to information access and open meetings. The degree of compliance with these laws varies widely from state to state.

In the aftermath of the September 11 terrorist attacks, concerns about safety and security came into conflict with guarantees of press freedom. The **Patriot Act,** passed in October of 2001, gave the government more power to access e-mail and telephone records. This increased monitoring power could be used not only to track terrorists but also to eavesdrop on journalists. In addition, the new law made it easier for the government to restrict access to official records, and another provision prevented the press from finding out about FBI searches of books bought in bookstores or borrowed from libraries by those suspected of terrorist activities. The press, naturally, chafed under these new restrictions and editorialized against a 2003 bill that would further expand the Patriot Act.

>> Access to News Scenes

We have already examined this issue in our discussion of the right of the press to attend certain judicial proceedings. But what about the reporters' right of access to news settings outside the courtroom? The law here appears to be in the developmental stage. In the few decisions that have been handed down, the courts have given little support to the notion that the First Amendment guarantees a right of access. In separate rulings, the courts have declared that journalists may be sued for invasion of privacy, for trespassing on private property, and for disobeying a police officer's legitimate command to clear the way at the scene of a serious automobile accident. Three of the most relevant Supreme Court opinions have focused on the question of access to prisons and prisoners. In these cases, the courts have ruled that reporters do not have the right to visit specific parts of a prison, to speak to specific prisoners, or to bring cameras inside. In general, the Court seems to be saying that the access rights of the press are not different from the access rights of the general public. When the public is not admitted, neither is the press.

Some rulings, however, have recognized a limited right of access. A Florida decision said that journalists who are customarily invited by police onto private property to view a news scene cannot be prosecuted for trespassing. The courts have also allowed access to news settings in order to halt discrimination among journalists. For example, in one case it was ruled that a female journalist could not be barred from entering a baseball team's locker room if male reporters had been admitted. In sum, the final words on this topic have yet to be written by the courts. A case as influential as the Branzburg or Estes decision has yet to be adjudicated in the area of press access. It is a good bet, however, that such a test will not be long in surfacing.

 DEFAMATION

The preceding discussions make it clear that in its news-gathering activities, the press often collides with the government. In addition, the right of free speech and the rights of a free press sometimes come into conflict with the right of an individual to protect his or her reputation. Protection for a person's reputation is found under the laws that deal with **defamation.**

To understand this somewhat complicated area, let us start with some general definitions:

- **Libel:** Libel is written defamation that tends to injure a person's reputation or good name or that diminishes the esteem, respect, or goodwill due a person.
- **Slander:** This is spoken defamation. (In many states, if a defamatory statement is broadcast, it is considered libel even though technically the words are not written. Libel is considered more harmful and usually carries more serious penalties than does slander.)
- **Libel per se:** Some words are always libelous. Falsely written accusations, such as labeling a person a "thief" or a "swindler," automatically constitute libel.
- **Libel per quod:** Words that seem perfectly innocent in themselves can become libelous under certain circumstances. Erroneously reporting that Mr. Smith was seen eating a steak dinner last night may seem harmless unless Mr. Smith happens to be the president of the Worldwide Vegetarian Society.

For someone to win a libel suit brought against the media, that person must prove five things: (1) that he or she has actually been defamed and harmed by the statements; (2) that he or she has been identified (although not necessarily by name); (3) that the defamatory statements have been published; (4) that the media were at fault; and (5) in most instances, that what was published or broadcast was false.

Not every mistake that finds its way into publication is libelous. To report that James Arthur will lead the Fourth of July parade when in fact Arthur James will lead it is probably not libelous because it is improbable that leading a parade will cause harm to a person's reputation. (Courts have even ruled that it is not necessarily libelous to report incorrectly that a person died. Death, said the courts, is no disgrace.) Actual harm might be substantiated by showing that defamatory remarks led to physical discomfort (such as sleepless nights) or loss of income or increased difficulty in performing a job.

Identification need not be by name. If a paper erroneously reports that the professor who teaches Psych 101 at 10 A.M. in Quadrangle Hall is taking bribes from his students, that would be sufficient.

Publication, for our purposes, pertains to a statement's appearance in a mass medium and is self-explanatory.

Fault is a little more complicated. To win a libel suit, some degree of fault or carelessness on the part of the media organization must be shown. As we shall see, the degree of fault that must be established depends on several things: (1) the person who is suing, (2) the subject matter of the suit, and (3) the particular state's laws that are being applied.

A 1986 Supreme Court decision held that private persons (as opposed to public figures) suing for libel must prove that the statements at issue are false, at least when the statements involve matters of public concern. For all practical purposes, however, proving that the media were at fault also involves proving the falsity of what was broadcast or published, so that virtually everyone who brings a libel suit must show the wrongfulness of what was published.

It should be emphasized that a mass medium is responsible for what it carries. It usually cannot hide behind the fact that it only repeated what someone else said. In most situations, a magazine could not defend itself against a libel suit by claiming that it simply quoted a hospital worker who said a colleague was stealing drugs. If, in fact, the hospital worker's colleague was not stealing drugs, the magazine would have to look to some other defense against libel.

>> **Defenses Against Libel Suits**
What are some of the defenses that can be used? There are three.

The first is truth. If what was reported is proved to be true, there is no libel. This defense, however, is rarely used since it is extremely difficult to prove the truth of a statement. In addition, since the Supreme Court's decision placed the burden of proving the falsity of a statement on the person bringing the libel suit, the defense of truth has become even less attractive.

A second defense is privilege. There are certain situations in which the courts have held that the public's right to know comes before a person's right to preserve a reputation. Judicial proceedings, arrest warrants, grand jury indictments, legislative proceedings, and public city council sessions are examples of situations that are generally acknowledged to be privileged. If a reporter gives a fair and accurate report of these events, no lawsuits can result, even if what is reported contains a libelous statement.

The third defense is fair comment and criticism. Any person who thrusts himself or herself into the public eye or is at the center of public attention is open to fair criticism. This means that public officials, professional sports figures, cartoonists, artists, columnists, playwrights, and all those who invite public attention are fair game for comment. This defense applies only to opinion and criticism, not to misrepresentations of fact. You can report that a certain director's new movie stank to high heaven without fear of a lawsuit, but you could not report falsely that the director embezzled funds from the company and expect protection under fair criticism. However, criticism can be quite severe and caustic and still be protected from lawsuit. In 1990, the Supreme Court ruled that expressions of opinion are not automatically exempt from charges of libel. Opinions that contain an assertion of fact that can be proved false might trigger a defamation suit.

The dividing line between opinion and fact is a blurry one. In 2002 an appeals court ruled in favor of ABC's *Prime Time Live* in a case that involved a cardiac surgeon. In a hidden camera interview the surgeon told employees of ABC that he ranked somewhere in the middle of a list of cardiac surgeons ranked by surgical mortality. In reality, the surgeon ranked 103 out of 112. The ABC reporter stated that the surgeon "wasn't representing where he had finished" and had not been "up front" about his ranking. After the surgeon sued for defamation, the court ruled that the reporter's statements represented an opinion and not fact.

In 1964, the Supreme Court, in the *New York Times* v. *Sullivan* case, significantly expanded the opportunity for comments on the actions of public officials and also changed the nature of the law governing defamation. The case involved the *Times* and an official of the Montgomery, Alabama, police department, L. B. Sullivan, and took place during the Civil Rights struggle of the early 1960s. A Civil Rights group published an ad in the *Times* concerning a protest in Montgomery that Sullivan claimed libeled him. Testimony in the case revealed that, indeed, several statements in the ad were false. An Alabama court awarded him $500,000, but the *Times* appealed the case to the Supreme Court.

The Court reversed the Alabama decision and enumerated three major principles that would affect future decisions concerning defamation:

1. Editorial advertising is protected by the First Amendment.
2. Even statements that are false might qualify for First Amendment protection if they concern the public conduct of public officials.
3. To win a libel suit, public officials must prove that false and defamatory statements were made with actual malice.

The Court also clarified what is meant by *actual malice*—publishing a statement with the knowledge that it is false or publishing a statement in "reckless disre-

Many people are confused by the meaning of the phrase *actual malice* as it applies to defamation. Some individuals mistakenly think that a person who is defamed has to prove evil motives, spite, or ill will on the part of the person or medium that allegedly committed the defamation. Not so. In the famous *New York Times* v. *Sullivan* case, the Supreme Court defined *actual malice* as (1) publishing something that is known to be false ("I know what I'm publishing is not true but I'm going to publish it anyway") or (2) publishing something with reckless disregard for whether it is true or not ("I have good reason to doubt that what I'm publishing is true, but I'm going to publish it anyway").

A recent libel case involving CBS, Inc., and Walter Jacobson, a news anchor and commentator at WBBM-TV (the CBS affiliate) in Chicago, illustrates this definition. The Brown & Williamson Tobacco Corporation (maker of Viceroy cigarettes) claimed that Jacobson libeled their company when he charged during a TV commentary that Viceroy was using an ad campaign to persuade children to smoke. Viceroy, said Jacobson, was equating cigarette smoking with "wine, beer, shaving, or wearing a bra . . . a declaration of independence and striving for self-identity . . . a basic symbol of the growing-up process." The commentary cited as evidence a Federal Trade Commission report that claimed the company had been advised by its advertising agency to launch such a campaign. Brown & Williamson, forced to prove actual malice

on the part of Jacobson because of the company's position as a public figure, denied ever having launched such a campaign. In fact, company lawyers argued that Brown & Williamson was so outraged by its ad agency's advice that it fired the advertising firm. Further, Brown & Williamson argued that Jacobson knew this fact before he broadcast his commentary. In court, one of the officials for the tobacco company testified that a researcher for Jacobson had been told that the ad agency had been fired and that the campaign was not used. During the trial, Jacobson said that he had rejected a suggestion from this researcher that a disclaimer should be included in the commentary stating that Brown & Williamson had not used the campaign. Evidently, this fact was enough to convince the jury that Jacobson knew that what he was saying was false—thus establishing actual malice. The jury found in favor of the tobacco company and awarded Brown & Williamson more than $5 million in damages.

For their part, Jacobson and CBS still maintain that the commentary was an accurate summary of the Federal Trade Commission report and that Brown & Williamson had a strategy directed toward children, even if the company did not fully implement it. In late 1985, CBS announced plans to appeal the decision. The appeal was decided in 1988 in favor of the tobacco company. CBS was ordered to pay $3.05 million in damages.

gard" of whether it is false or not. A few years later, the Court expanded this protection to include statements made about public figures as well as public officials. In 1971, it appeared that the Supreme Court would even require private individuals who become involved in events of public concern to prove actual malice before collecting for a libel suit. Three years later, the Court seemed to retreat a little from this position when it held that a lawyer involved in a civil lawsuit was not a public figure, that he was not involved in an event of public interest, and that he did not have to prove actual malice.

Even more protection was extended to the private citizen in 1976 in a case concerning the divorce of Mary Alice Firestone from her husband, tire heir Russell Firestone Jr. The trial lasted 17 months and received large amounts of media coverage. Ms. Firestone even called several press conferences while the trial was taking place. When *Time* magazine erroneously reported that the divorce had been granted on the grounds of extreme cruelty and adultery, Ms. Firestone sued for libel. (Her husband had charged her with adultery, but adultery was not cited as grounds for the divorce.) *Time* argued that she was a public figure and contended that Ms. Firestone had to show not only that the magazine was inaccurate but also that it acted with malice. The Supreme Court ruled that she was not a public figure, despite all the attendant press coverage, and drew a distinction between legitimate public controversies and those controversies that merely interest the public. The latter, said the Court, are not protected, and actual malice need not be proved.

The Court affirmed this distinction in 1979 by noting that the fact that someone is involved in a "newsworthy" event does not make the person a public figure. When a U.S. senator presented a scientist with a satirical award used to denote wasteful spending of government funds, the scientist sued for defamation. The Court ruled that even though the scientist became the subject of media attention, his public prominence before receiving the satirical award did not merit labeling him a public figure. Therefore, he did not have to meet the actual malice standard. Private citizens, however, do have to show some degree of fault or negligence by the media. In many states, this means showing that the media did not exercise ordinary care in publishing a story. Establishing this will allow a private citizen to collect compensation for any actual damages that stem from the libel. The big bucks, however, come from punitive damages assessed against the media. These awards are designed to punish the media for their past transgressions and serve as a reminder not to misbehave again. To collect punitive damages, even private citizens must show actual malice.

The amount of money that juries award to the winners of libel cases can be substantial. Awards of $1 million or more have become common. Singer Wayne Newton, for example, received a $20 million judgment against NBC. On the other hand, most libel cases are appealed, and about 75 percent are either reversed or have the monetary awards substantially reduced. For example, the Wayne Newton verdict was eventually reversed.

The difficulty that public figures face in successfully bringing a libel suit against the media has prompted some news subjects to look for other remedies. In the past decade, several subjects of news stories sued the news media for the way they gathered the news rather than on the content of the story. Lawsuits concerning trespass and invasion of privacy by the media have become more common.

>> Defamation and the Internet

The Internet has created new problems with regard to defamation. One problem involves who can be sued for defamation. Suppose you post a defamatory message on an AOL message board. Can someone sue both you and AOL? Congress addressed this issue in the Communications Decency Act of 1996. The law states that Internet service providers such as AOL are not liable for the content that they carry unless they (the providers) are the actual authors of the content.

A second vexing question involves jurisdiction. Since the online versions of newspapers, magazines, and newsletters are available all over the world at the click of the mouse, where should a lawsuit be filed? This is an important question because laws governing defamation vary by state. In one recent case, online newspapers in Connecticut published a story about prison conditions in Virginia. A court ruled that the warden of a Virginia prison could sue the newspapers for libel in Virginia because the publications were accessible in that state. In a similar ruling, a court in Australia ruled that the Dow Jones Company, based in New Jersey, could be sued for defamation in Australia because the online version of one its magazines was available for downloading in Australia. Both of these decisions have been appealed but, if the decisions stand, it means that newspapers and magazines that provide an online version open themselves up to lawsuits in other states and even other countries.

For a private citizen to prevail in a defamation case, he or she must prove some degree of negligence on the part of the media. The standards for determining what constitutes negligence vary from state to state, and as with the actual malice standard, negligence is determined on a case-by-case basis. Nonetheless, some general statements can be made.

A common legal definition of negligence states that it is conduct that creates an unreasonable risk of harm. The standard of conduct that the possible negligence is measured against is whether a reasonable person under the same circumstances would behave in the same way. As far as the media are concerned, employees are to be judged against the appropriate practices and customs for their profession. Thus, in many cases, the issue of negligence boils down to whether the reporter or editor exercised reasonable care and followed the accepted practices of the profession in determining whether a story was true or false.

Some specific factors might also be taken into account. First, was the story prepared under deadline? If sufficient time and opportunity were available, then reasonable care might require more checking of facts. Second, what was the interest being promoted by the story? Stories covering heated political debates have greater merit than gossip, but gossip can be extremely harmful. Hence, greater care should be exercised in the latter situation.

A concrete example might help illustrate negligence and show how it differs from actual malice. In a 1975 case in Massachusetts, a rookie reporter had been covering a drug trial. The reporter was unaware that a table in the front of the courtroom was reserved for the press. Consequently, he sat in the back, where he had trouble hearing the testimony. One of the defendants was the 20-year-old son of a man named John Stone. John Stone ran the lunchrooms in a public school. When the prosecutor asked a marshal the question of who had the drugs, the reporter thought he heard the marshal say, "Mr. Stone" and assumed he meant John Stone, the only "Mr. Stone" that the reporter knew. He wrote in his story that John Stone had possession of the drugs. When questioned by his editor, who knew John Stone personally and had a hard time believing that he could have possessed illegal drugs, the reporter said he had heard the name in court. In fact, the marshal was talking about Jeffrey Stone, the son of John Stone. John Stone, naturally enough, sued for libel.

The court found that the reporter was guilty of negligence because he did not sit where he could properly hear and did not check with another source to confirm who the "Mr. Stone" was—two practices that were in keeping with the accepted procedures of journalism. By contrast, the reporter's conduct did not constitute actual malice since he was new in town and did not have reason to doubt that the Stone mentioned in court was the only Stone he knew.

But what about the editor? The one who knew Mr. Stone personally and had trouble believing the story? The editor had reason to doubt the story but did not even make a phone call to check its accuracy. The court ruled that he had acted with reckless disregard for the truth of the report, which was enough to constitute actual malice.

 ## INVASION OF PRIVACY

>> ### The Right to Privacy

Closely related to libel is the right to privacy. In fact, a single publication will often prompt both types of suits. The big difference between the two is that libel protects a person's reputation, but the right of privacy protects a person's peace of mind and feelings. A second difference is that libel involves the publication of false information; invasion of privacy might be triggered by disclosing the truth.

There are four different ways that the mass media can invade someone's right to privacy.

Intrusion upon Solitude The first is intruding upon a person's solitude or seclusion. This generally occurs when reporters wrongfully use microphones, surveillance cameras, and other forms of eavesdropping to record someone's private activities. A TV news crew hiding in a van outside your room and secretly taping your activities while you are inside would probably constitute a situation of intrusion.

The use of tiny, hidden cameras and microphones by reporters in their quest for news has raised special problems in this area. In a 1999 decision, the California Supreme Court ruled that an ABC reporter committed an invasion of privacy when she went to work for a psychic hot line and secretly videotaped a conversation with a co-worker. Even though the conversation took place in an open office and was overheard by others, the court ruled that the co-worker had a reasonable expectation that a reporter would not secretly videotape his conversations. This decision suggests that reporters should give extra thought to the use of hidden recordings in their news-gathering activities.

Unauthorized Release of Private Information The second occasion is the unauthorized release of private information. A newspaper's publishing private medical records that reveal that a person has a dread disease is an example in this area. The courts allowed a suit claiming invasion of privacy to be filed when a newspaper published information about a person's sex-change operation without the person's consent.

Creating a False Impression A third method is publicizing people in a false light or creating a false impression of them. This invasion is most closely related to libel because falsity is also involved. Some TV stations get into trouble in this area through the practice of putting new narration over some stock tape footage, which sometimes creates a false impression. For example, a Chicago TV station was sued when it ran stock footage taken three years earlier of a doctor performing a gynecological exam with a story describing how another doctor allegedly used an AIDS-infected swab during a similar exam. The face of the doctor in the stock footage was readily identifiable and she sued the station, claiming the story made it appear that she had performed the allegedly negligent procedure. (The station settled the suit out-of-court and paid the doctor an undisclosed amount of money.)

Appropriation of Identity The last means of invading privacy is through appropriation of a person's name or likeness for commercial purposes. This commonly involves stars and celebrities who find their names or images used without their permission in some business or promotional activity. Model Christy Brinkley, for example, successfully filed suit to stop poster stores from selling her picture without her permission. The not-so-famous are also protected against appropriation. One man sued because he found that a camera company had used his picture without permission in its instruction manual.

>> Trespass

Trespass, defined as unauthorized entry into someone else's territory, is a concept that is closely related to invasion of privacy. The close of the 20th century saw a significant increase in the number of trespass cases brought against the news media. These cases highlighted a fundamental question for news reporting: Do journalists have a special First Amendment privilege to break the law in pursuit of a legitimate news story that will advance the public interest? Several recent court decisions suggest the answer to this question is no.

In one case, a Wisconsin court found that a TV photojournalist who had entered private property with permission of a police officer responding to a call was guilty of trespassing. Similarly, a 1999 circuit court ruling found that journalists who enter a private home with law enforcement officers but without consent of the homeowner could be sued for trespass. In another case, reporters who followed antinuclear demonstrators through a fence onto the property of a utility company were found guilty of trespassing. A related 1999 Supreme Court case found that law enforcement officers who permitted the news media to accompany them across the threshold of a home when serving a search warrant were violating the Fourth Amendment's provisions against unreasonable searches.

Finally, consider the 1996 case of *Food Lion* v. *ABC*. Reporters for the newsmagazine *Prime Time Live* faked résumés to get jobs at a Food Lion supermarket and used hidden cameras to shoot video to document their story. After the program aired, Food Lion brought suit against the network not for defamation, but for fraud and trespass. Outside the courtroom, lawyers for Food Lion explained that they thought the story was libelous, but they thought they had a better chance of winning on the basis of the trespass and fraud charges. A jury found in favor of Food Lion and awarded the supermarket chain a whopping $5.5 million in damages. A district court judge reduced this amount to $350,000. Eventually, the circuit court of appeals dismissed most of the case, but it did uphold the trespass decision. The original jury awarded Food Lion only $1 in damages for the trespass, but now that the precedent has been set, it is possible that future lawsuits will seek far greater sums for trespass violations.

 COPYRIGHT

Copyright protects an author against unfair appropriation of his or her work. Although its roots go back to English common law, the basic copyright law of the United States was first enacted in 1909. In 1976, faced with copyright problems raised by the new communications technologies, Congress passed legislation covering literary, dramatic, and musical works, as well as motion pictures, television programs, and sound recordings. The law also states what is not covered. For example, an idea cannot be copyrighted, nor can a news event or a discovery or a procedure.

For works created on or after January 1, 1978, copyright protection lasts for the life of the author plus 70 years. Works published before that date are eligible for copyright protection for a total of 95 years. To obtain full copyright protection, it is necessary to send a special form, copies of the work, and a small fee to the Register of Copyrights. The owner of a copyrighted work can then reproduce, sell, display, or perform the property.

It is important to note that copyright protection extends only to copying the work in question. If a person independently creates a similar work, there is no copyright violation. As a result, one of the things that a person who brings a copyright suit must prove is that the other person had access to the work under consideration. Thus, if you contend that a hit Hollywood movie was actually based on a pirated script that you had submitted to the company, you must show that the people responsible for the movie had access to your work. (To guard against copyright suits, most production companies will not open the envelopes of what look like unsolicited scripts.) Note, however, that you do not have to prove that someone intentionally or even consciously copied your work.

In addition, the law provides that people can make fair use of copyrighted materials without violating the provisions of the Copyright Act. Fair use means that copies of a protected work can be made for such legitimate activities as teaching, research, news reporting, and criticism without penalty. The following factors are taken into consideration in determining fair use:

1. the purpose of the use (whether for profit or for nonprofit education),
2. the nature of the copyrighted work,
3. the amount reproduced in proportion to the copyrighted work as a whole, and
4. the effect of the use on the potential market value of the copyrighted work.

Thus, a teacher who reproduces a passage from a long novel to illustrate writing style to an English class will probably not have to worry about copyright. On the other hand, if a commercial magazine reproduces verbatim a series of articles published in a not-for-profit magazine, it is likely that the copyright statute will be determined to have been violated.

Recent cases involving copyright law have dealt with the new communication media. In what is popularly known as the "Betamax case," the Supreme Court ruled in 1984 that viewers who own videocassette recorders could copy programs off the air for later personal viewing without violating the Copyright Act. Such taping, ruled the court, was a fair use of the material. In 1991, a federal court ruled that commercial copying companies, such as Kinko's, had to get permission from the publishers before copying and selling copyrighted articles and book excerpts used for college courses.

The most recent issue concerning copyright has to do with the Internet. Copyright laws *do* apply to the online world. A 1995 Presidential Task Force concluded that materials on the Internet are protected by current copyright laws. This was firmly demonstrated in the famous Napster case. In 1999 the recording industry filed suit against the file-sharing service. Napster argued that its activities were protected by the "fair use" provision of copyright law: Making copies of a song for noncommercial, personal use was the same as videotaping a TV program off the air for personal use. The recording industry argued that Napster was knowingly facilitating the illegal distribution of copyrighted material.

The courts sided with the recording industry and ordered that Napster remove all copyrighted material from its system. The decision spelled the end for Napster, and the service filed for bankruptcy in 2002. Napster's demise, however, did not put an end to file sharing. New, harder to shut down services, such as Kazaa and Grokster, took its place. By 2003, more people were downloading and sharing music than during Napster's heyday.

The recording industry responded by filing copyright infringement lawsuits against more than 250 individuals for sharing music files on the Internet. Those targeted first were those who had more than 1,000 songs stored on their hard drives, but the industry hinted that more lawsuits were in the works. The family of one 12 year old who was sued settled their case by paying the recording industry $2,000. It remains to be seen if such legal tactics are successful.

Copyright issues have also had an impact on Internet radio stations. The Digital Millennium Copyright Act ordered that recording companies and artists be paid an additional royalty when their songs are played on Internet stations. The initial fee set by the Copyright Office seemed like a small amount, but it was enough to put many Internet stations out of business. After much discussion, Congress passed a bill in 2002 that gave stations some relief by allowing them to negotiate fees based on their revenues or expenses.

OBSCENITY AND PORNOGRAPHY

Obscenity is not protected by the First Amendment; that much is clear. Unfortunately, nobody has yet come up with a definition of *obscenity* that satisfies everybody. Let us take a brief look at how the definition of this term has changed over the years. (If, when we are done, you are a little confused about this whole issue, do not feel bad. You are not alone.)

For many years, the test of whether something was obscene was the **Hicklin rule,** a standard that judged a book (or any other item) by whether isolated passages had a tendency to deprave or corrupt the mind of the most susceptible person. If one paragraph of a 500-page book tended to deprave or corrupt the mind of the most susceptible person (a 12-year-old child, a dirty old man, etc.), then the entire book was obscene. The standard was written in the 1860s and widely used for the next 80 years.

In a 1957 case, *Roth* v. *United States,* the Supreme Court tried its hand at writing a new definition. The new test for detecting obscenity would be the following: whether to the average person, applying contemporary standards, the dominant theme of the material taken as a whole appealed to prurient interests. (*Prurient* means "lewd" or "tending to incite lust.") The Roth test differed from the earlier rule in two significant ways. Not only did the entire work, rather than a single passage, have to be taken into consideration, but the material had to offend the average person, not simply anyone who saw it. Obviously, this standard was less restrictive than the Hicklin rule, but fuzzy spots remained. Should the community standards be local or national? How exactly would prurient interest be measured?

The next few years produced more obscenity cases to plague the High Court. Other decisions added that the material had to be "patently offensive" and "utterly without redeeming social value" to be obscene. During the 1960s, the Supreme Court began considering the conduct of the seller or distributor in addition to the character of the material in question. For example, even if material was not considered hard-core pornography, it could be banned if sold to minors, thrust upon an unwilling audience, or advertised as erotic to titillate customers. A 1969 ruling introduced the concept of "variable obscenity" when it stated that certain magazines were obscene when sold to minors but not obscene when sold to adults.

By 1973, so many legal problems were cropping up under the Roth guidelines that something had to be done. Consequently, the Supreme Court attempted to close up loopholes in the case of *Miller* v. *California*. This decision did away with the "utterly without redeeming social value" test and stated that the "community standards" used in defining obscenity could be local standards, which, presumably, would be determined by local juries. The new test of obscenity would include these principles:

1. whether the average person, applying contemporary community standards, would find that the work as a whole appealed to prurient interests;
2. whether the work depicted or described in a patently offensive way certain sexual conduct that was specifically spelled out by a state law; and
3. whether the whole work lacked serious literary, artistic, political, or scientific value.

Despite this new attempt, problems were not long in coming. The language of the decision appeared to permit a certain amount of local discretion in determining what was obscene. The question of how far a local community can go in setting standards continues to be troublesome. The Supreme Court has since ruled that the motion picture *Carnal Knowledge* is not obscene, even though a state court said that it was. The Court has also said that *Screw* magazine and the *Illustrated Presidential Report of the Commission on Obscenity and Pornography* are obscene no matter what community's standards are invoked. The Court further clarified the third of the *Miller* guidelines in a 1987 case when it ruled that judges and juries must assess the literary, artistic, political, or scientific value of allegedly obscene material from the viewpoint of a "reasonable person" rather than applying community standards. These issues could be decided with the help of experts who would testify about the value of a work. The first two guidelines, however, would still be decided with reference to contemporary community standards.

Over the years, the Court has taken a somewhat more lenient view as to what constitutes obscenity. The Miller case suggests that the Court is encouraging the states to deal with the problem at the local level. Given the long history of controversy that surrounds this topic, however, it is unlikely that this predicament will end soon. In fact, the whole issue surfaced again in 1986 when the Justice Department released a report on pornography. The report, which had strong political overtones, called for more stringent laws concerning pornography. One such law, the Child Protection and Obscenity Enforcement Act, took effect in 1988.

More recent problems have concerned the Internet. Child pornography is illegal on the Internet just as it is in other media. The 1988 act specifically mentions computers as one of the channels through which this illegal material might be circulated. Sexual "stalking" over the Net is also prohibited. In an effort to keep pornographic material from children, Congress passed the Communications Decency Act in 1996. Part of the act made it illegal to use a computer to create, solicit, or transmit any obscene, lewd, lascivious, filthy, or indecent communication. The Supreme Court eventually found the act to be unconstitutional and ruled that the Internet should be given the highest level of First Amendment protection, similar to that given to books and newspapers, rather than the more limited rights of broadcasting and cable, where regulation is more common. The Court noted that even though the government had a legitimate interest in trying to protect children from harmful content, this interest does not justify broad suppression of materials directed at adults.

A second attempt at protecting children from pornography also ran into legal difficulty. The Child Online Protection Act required commercial websites to demand proof of age before delivering material that might be harmful to minors. In 2000, an appeals court upheld an injunction that blocked implementation of the act, ruling that the act raised serious First Amendment problems. As a result, the act has never been enforced.

A similar measure, the Children's Internet Protection Act, required libraries that receive federal funds to use filters to block access to pornographic images on their computers. The American Library Association challenged the act, but in 2003 the Supreme Court ruled that the act was constitutional.

As is probably apparent by now, the Internet brings new challenges along with its benefits.

 ## REGULATING BROADCASTING

The formal controls surrounding broadcasting represent a special case. Not only are broadcasters affected by the laws and rulings previously discussed, but they are also subject to additional controls because of broadcasting's unique position and character. When broadcasting was first developed in the early 20th century, it became clear that more people wanted to operate a broadcasting station than there were suitable frequencies available. As a result, the early broadcasters asked the U.S. Congress to step into the picture. Congress passed the Radio Act of 1927, which held that the airwaves belonged to the public and that broadcasters who wished to use this resource had to be licensed to serve in the public interest. A regulatory body, called the Federal Radio Commission (later known as the Federal Communications Commission), was set up to determine who should get a license and whether those who had a license should keep it. Because of this licensing provision, radio and television are subject to more regulations than are newspapers, magazines, films, and sound recording.

>> The Federal Communications Commission

The Federal Communications Commission (FCC) does not make law; it interprets the law. One of its big jobs is to interpret the meaning of the phrase "public interest." For example, the FCC may write rules and regulations to implement the Communications Act of 1934 if these rules serve the public interest. Moreover, the

The home page of the FCC. In addition to television and radio, the FCC also regulates telephone, telegraph and personal communication devices.

FCC awards and renews licenses if the award or renewal is in the public interest. Over the years, several significant FCC rulings have shed some light on this rather ambiguous concept. One of the first things the commission established was that it would examine programming and determine whether the public interest was being served. It was not enough for a station to adhere to the technical operating requirements of its license. It would also have to provide a "well-rounded" program structure. In its 1929 Great Lakes decision, the commission also put broadcasters on notice that the broadcasting of programs that tended to injure the public—fraudulent advertising, attacks on ethnic groups, attacks on religions—would not be in the public interest.

What can the FCC do to stations that do not operate in the public interest? It can take several official actions. At the mildest level, it can fine a station up to $250,000. The next level of severity is to renew a station's license only for a probationary period (usually a year). This action typically puts the station on notice that it has to improve its performance or face even more serious consequences. The most severe form of official action is the revoking or nonrenewal of a license. Revocation/nonrenewal is more of a threat, however, than a reality. From 1934 to 1978, the FCC took away the licenses of only 142 stations. This figure should be weighed against the thousands of renewals that the commission granted each of those years. In fact, it has been calculated that 99.8 percent of all licenses are renewed. Nonetheless, the threat of revocation is a potent one that is universally feared among broadcasters.

During the 1980s, as was the case in many industries, the prevailing philosophy that governed broadcasting was one of deregulation. The FCC and Congress had eliminated literally dozens of rules and regulations, including the controversial Fairness Doctrine (see the section devoted specifically to this doctrine). The rush to deregulation slowed during the 1990s as the FCC and Congress established new rules and regulations for broadcasting and cable.

Congress passed the Children's Television Act, which required that TV stations present programs designed to meet the educational and informational needs of young persons through the age of 16. The bill also created a $2 million endowment to fund children's educational programs. Additionally, the act limited the amount of commercial time during children's programming to 10 1/2 minutes per hour on weekends and 12 minutes per hour on weekdays, a limit that applies to both broadcasters and cable operators. Stations and systems that violate these standards could be subject to a fine. In response to a provision in the law that instructed the FCC to encourage children's programming, the commission mandated that stations devote three hours per week to informational and educational programs for children.

≫ Indecent Content

When it comes to regulating indecent content, the FCC finds itself caught between the wishes of Congress and the rulings of the federal court system. A 1978 Supreme Court ruling gave the FCC the right to regulate indecency because the pervasive presence of broadcasting made it easily accessible to children. In the late 1980s, after many radio stations began to air raunchy content, Congress passed legislation that instructed the FCC to ban indecent programming 24 hours a day. A federal court declared that this ban was unconstitutional and ordered the FCC to establish a "safe harbor," a time when indecent material could be aired without much chance of reaching children. The FCC responded by banning indecent content between the hours of 6 A.M. and 8 P.M.. This did not satisfy Congress (there is some political benefit to be derived from being against indecency), which passed a law banning indecency before midnight. This law was ruled unconstitutional, and finally, a law that banned indecent content between 6 A.M. and 10 P.M. was approved. As should be clear by now, trying to protect children from indecency while protecting the First Amendment rights of adults is an exasperating task. Meanwhile, the FCC continues to be on guard against indecent programming. Radio stations carrying Howard Stern's talk show have been fined more than $2 million for airing indecent content.

≫ The Equal Opportunities Rule

The **Equal Opportunities rule** is contained in Section 315 of the Communications Act and is thus federal law. Section 315 deals with the ability of bona fide candidates for public office to gain access to a broadcast medium during political campaigns. Stated in simple terms, this section says that if a station permits one candidate for a specific office to appear on the air, it must offer the same opportunity to all other candidates for that office. If a station gives a free minute to one candidate, all other legally qualified candidates for that office are also entitled to a free minute. If a station sells a candidate a minute for $100, it must make the same offer to all other candidates. Congress has made some exceptions to this law, the most notable of which are legitimate newscasts and on-the-scene coverage of authentic news events.

≫ The Fairness Doctrine

The **Fairness Doctrine** no longer exists. The FCC repealed it in 1987. That does not mean, however, that it is dead and buried. There were several proposals in Congress to revive it, the most recent attempt in 1994.

When it was still in force, the Fairness Doctrine provided that broadcasters had to seek out and present contrasting viewpoints on controversial matters of public importance. On any issue, broadcasters had to make a good-faith effort to cover all the opposing viewpoints. This did not have to take place in one program, but the broadcaster was expected to achieve balance over time. Note that the Fairness Doctrine never said that opposing views were entitled to equal time. It simply mandated that some reasonable amount of time be granted.

 ## REGULATING CABLE TV

The regulatory philosophy of the FCC and Congress toward cable has shown wide variation over the years. In the 1950s, the FCC ruled that it had no jurisdiction over cable. This notion changed in the 1960s when the commission exerted control over the new medium and wrote a series of regulations governing its growth. By 1972, a comprehensive set of rules governing cable was on the FCC's books. The growth of cable during the 1970s led to successful lobbying efforts by the industry to ease many of these restrictions. In the 1980s, in line with the deregulatory philosophy of the Reagan administration, almost all the FCC rules concerning cable were dropped. Moreover, Congress passed the Cable Communications Policy Act in 1984, which gave cable operators great freedom in setting rates and deciding what channels they could carry on their systems. The law also allowed state and local governments the right to grant cable **franchises** (a franchise is an exclusive right to operate in a given territory).

In the years following the passage of this act, many consumers complained that their cable system raised rates and was insensitive to the needs of its customers. Consequently, in 1992, Congress enacted the Cable TV Act, which gave the FCC the authority to regulate the rates of most cable systems, required that cable systems carry the signals of any broadcast station with significant viewing in their market, and allowed commercial broadcast stations to waive their right to be carried in exchange for appropriate compensation from the cable system.

Two provisions in this law had important consequences. First, most consumers saw their monthly cable bills go down as the FCC instituted rate reductions of about 17 percent. Second, the provision requiring cable systems to carry the signals of broadcast stations was challenged in federal court as a violation of the First Amendment rights of cable operators. In 1994 the Supreme Court ruled that cable operators deserved more First Amendment protection from government regulation than did broadcasters but not as much as newspapers and magazines. Consequently, the Court declared that it was constitutional for Congress to pass laws to guarantee that the free flow of information not be restricted by a private company that controlled the means of transmission.

The issue of the constitutionality of the specific rules about which stations must be carried by cable systems was decided in 1997 when the Supreme Court ruled in favor of the "must carry" provision.

 ## THE TELECOMMUNICATIONS ACT OF 1996

While all this was going on, Congress was wrestling with the regulatory problems caused by convergence and the information superhighway. The result of this struggle was the **Telecommunications Act of 1996,** the first major overhaul of communication laws in more than 60 years. The Telecommunications Act contained provisions that affected traditional broadcasters, cable companies, and telephone companies. The following are among the key provisions of the law:

- It removed limits on the number of radio stations that can be owned by one person or organization. Up to eight stations may be owned in a single market. (See Chapter 7.)
- It removed limits on the number of television stations that can be owned as long as stations do not reach more than 35 percent of the nation's TV homes.
- It extended the term of broadcast licenses to eight years.
- It allowed telephone companies to enter the cable television business.
- It allowed cable TV companies to enter the telephone business.
- It deregulated the rates of many cable systems.
- It mandated that newly manufactured TV sets come with the ability to block unwanted programming based on an electronically encoded rating (popularly called the **V-Chip;** see Chapter 16).
- It mandated that the TV industry come up with a voluntary ratings system for violence, sex, and other indecent materials.

Now that the 1996 Telecommunications Act has been in force for several years, we can see evidence of its impact. As mentioned earlier, the removal of the cap on radio station ownership unleashed a wave of consolidation in the industry. The deregulation of cable rates has led to a general increase in cable subscribers' bills. In one area, however, the anticipated results have yet to occur. One of the major goals behind the act was to increase competition between cable companies and telephone companies by allowing each to cross over into the other's business. It was hoped this competition would result in better service and lower prices for consumers. As of 2003, however, there was little change in the situation. Most Americans still get their phone service from phone companies and their cable TV from cable companies.

 REGULATING ADVERTISING

>> **Deceptive Advertising**

The problem of deceptive and potentially harmful advertising has been around a long time. The philosophy of *caveat emptor* (let the buyer beware) was dominant until the early 1900s. Exaggerated claims and outright deception characterized many early advertisements, especially those for patent medicines. Spurred on by the muckrakers (see Chapter 5), the government took steps to deal with the problem when it created the Federal Trade Commission in 1914. In the early years of its existence, the commission was concerned with encouraging competition through the regulation of questionable business practices, such as bribery, false advertising, and mislabeling of products; protecting the consumer was not the main focus. The consumer started to receive some protection in 1938 with the Wheeler-Lea Act, which gave the FTC the power to prevent deceptive advertising that harmed the public, whether or not the advertising had any bad effects on the competition.

Like the Federal Communications Commission, the Federal Trade Commission has several enforcement techniques available to it. First of all, it can issue trade regulations that suggest guidelines for the industry to follow. In 1965, for example, it ruled that auto ads must contain both the city and highway estimates of gas mileage. The FTC also uses the **consent order.** In a consent order, the advertiser agrees to halt a certain advertising practice, but at the same time, the advertiser does not admit to any violation of the law; there is only an agreement not to continue. Somewhat stronger is a **cease-and-desist order.** This order follows a hearing by the commission that determines that a certain advertising practice does indeed violate the law. Violation of a consent order and failure to comply with a cease-and-desist order can result in fines being levied against the advertiser.

In the late 1960s and the 1970s, the FTC took a more active role in the regulation of advertising. The rising tide of interest in the rights of the consumer and the emergence of consumer activist groups (such as Ralph Nader's Raiders) were probably behind this new direction. A flurry of activity took place. First, the FTC wanted documentation for claims. If Brand Y claimed to be more effective in relieving pain than Brand X, the advertiser was now required to have proof for that claim. The FTC also ordered "corrective advertising" in which some advertisers were required to clarify some of their past claims.

More recently, the FTC has been concerned about advertising inappropriately directed toward children. In 1997, the FTC issued an unfair advertising complaint against the R. J. Reynolds Tobacco Company. The FTC argued that ads featuring Joe Camel, the company's cartoon character, encouraged children to start smoking. In response, Reynolds announced it would no longer use the controversial camel in its ads.

In 2000, the FTC targeted the film industry for marketing R-rated movies to persons under 17. An FTC report found that marketing plans for 28 R-rated films included strategies for reaching children as young as 10. The report criticized Hollywood for routinely aiming its advertising at children for movies that its own rating system labels inappropriate. In response, eight movie studios announced plans to reform their promotional efforts. More recently, the FTC has cracked down on deceptive advertising claims for diet products.

>> Commercial Speech under the First Amendment

The 1970s marked a change in judicial thinking about the amount of protection that advertising, or *commercial speech,* as it is called, receives under the First Amendment. Before the 1970s, advertising had little claim to free-speech protection. In the 1940s, F. J. Chrestensen found this out the hard way. Chrestensen owned a former U.S. submarine. There is not much that a private individual can do with a submarine, aside from charging admission to view it. This was Chrestensen's idea, and he wanted to distribute handbills advertising the sub. No way, said the New York City police commissioner. The city's sanitation code did not allow the distribution of advertising matter in the streets. However, handbills of information or of public protest were allowed. Inspired, Chrestensen put his submarine advertising message on one side of the handbill, while the other side was printed with a protest against the City Dock Department. Sorry, said the city, the protest message could be handed out, but the advertising on the other side would have to go. Chrestensen appealed, and two years later the Supreme Court ruled against him and agreed with the city of New York that advertising merited no First Amendment protection.

In the 1940s and 1950s, much cigarette advertising promoted the health benefits of smoking. This ad for Camels suggests that doctors endorse not only this brand of cigarette but smoking in general.

Since that time, however, the Supreme Court has retreated from this view. In 1964, in the *New York Times* v. *Sullivan* case, it extended First Amendment protection to ads that dealt with important social matters. Seven years later, the Court further extended this protection when a Virginia newspaper ran an ad for an abortion clinic located in New York and thus violated a Virginia law against such advertising. The Supreme Court ruled that the ad contained material in the public interest and merited constitutional protection. More recent cases suggest that, in many instances, commercial speech falls under the protection of the First Amendment.

In a 1980 ruling concerning advertising by an electric utility company, commonly called the Central Hudson Case, the Supreme Court enunciated a four-part test for determining the constitutional protection of commercial speech. First, commercial speech that involves an unlawful activity or advertising that is false or misleading is not protected. Second, the government must have a substantial interest in regulating the commercial speech. Third, the state's regulation must actually advance the government interest involved. Fourth, the state's regulations may be only as broad as necessary to promote the state's interest.

A 1984 ruling illustrated the use of these principles: The Court upheld a prohibition against posting signs on city property. The Court first noted that, although the advertising was for a lawful activity and not misleading, the government has a substantial interest in reducing "visual blight" and that the ordinance directly advanced that interest and was not overly broad. Further, the Court affirmed that corporations also have the right of free speech and granted lawyers, doctors, and professionals the right to advertise their prices. Although all the questions surrounding this issue have not been answered, it seems safe to conclude that at least some commercial speech is entitled to First Amendment protection. Its status, however, is less than that given to political and other forms of noncommercial expression (see Social Issues, "The Limits of Commercial Speech").

A 1996 CBS News report contained charges that the Nike Corporation operated sweatshops in Southeast Asia at which its workers were poorly paid, subject to abuse, and exposed to harmful chemicals. In response, Nike launched a public relations campaign designed to counter the accusations. Using news releases, pamphlets, and op-ed columns in newspapers, the company argued that its workers were treated well and paid a reasonable wage.

A consumer activist in San Francisco sued Nike under California's false advertising law, asserting that Nike's statements were fraudulent. Nike maintained that the comments were not advertising and therefore not subject to California's law. The case eventually found its way to the California Supreme Court, which ruled that the Nike messages were aimed at consumers of their products and not protected by the First Amendment.

This decision set off alarm bells among companies and the public relations companies that represented them. If commercial speech can be defined that broadly, would any corporation dare to speak out on a public issue if every statement it made could be challenged under consumer protection laws? If an opposing group wanted to intimidate a company to make it stop speaking out, it could do so by filing a flurry of lawsuits forcing the company to defend the truth of every statement it made. Opponents could freely level criticism, no matter how inaccurate or frivolous, while the corporation could be put at legal risk if it responded. (One animal rights group in California sued the California Milk Advisory Board because its advertising and public relations messages portrayed happy cows. The group charged that the messages were misleading because the cows in California are not happy.)

Nike appealed the decision to the U.S. Supreme Court, asking it to rule that the First Amendment protected its responses to the charges. Forty newspapers, professional organizations, and media companies filed briefs in support of Nike. The Court, however, declined to review the case on procedural grounds and sent it back to California for further action. Rather than pursue the case further, Nike settled the case out of court and agreed to pay $1.5 million to a workers' rights group.

The core issue still remains. What are the boundaries of commercial speech? If the California decision becomes accepted nationwide, will the public be deprived of vital information? Or as one lawyer put it, should a company be impeded from entering the marketplace of ideas just because it operates in the marketplace of goods?

 CONCLUSION

The term *half-life* is a useful concept in physics. It refers to the length of time in which one-half of the radioactive atoms present in a substance will decay. We might borrow this term and reshape its meaning so that it is relevant to this book. The half-life of a chapter in this text is the time it takes for half the information contained in the chapter to become obsolete. With that in mind, it is likely that the half-life of this chapter may be among the shortest of any in this book. Laws are constantly changing; new court decisions are frequently handed down, and new rules and regulations are written all the time. All this activity means that what is written in this chapter will need frequent updating. In addition, it means that mass media professionals must continually refresh their understanding of the law. Of course, this also means that there will be a continuing stream of colorful characters, intriguing stories, and high drama as the courts and regulatory agencies further wrestle with the issues and problems involved in mass communication regulation.

MAIN POINTS

- There is a strong constitutional case against prior restraint of the press.
- Reporters have special privileges that protect them in some instances from having to reveal the names of their news sources. These privileges, however, are not absolute.
- Reporters can cover matters that occur in open court with little fear of reprisal. Some pretrial proceedings can still be closed to the press.
- All but two states now allow cameras in the courtroom on a permanent or experimental basis. Cameras and microphones are still barred from federal trial courts and from the Supreme Court.
- Defamation can be either libel or slander. To prevail in a defamation suit, a public figure must show that the published material was false and harmful and that the media acted with actual malice when they published the information. A private citizen must also show that the material was false and harmful and that the media involved acted with negligence.
- Invasion of privacy can occur when the media intrude upon a person's solitude, release private information, create a false impression, or wrongfully appropriate a person's name or likeness.
- Copyright law protects authors from unfair use of their work. There are instances, however, when portions of copyrighted material can be reproduced for legitimate purposes.
- Online file-sharing systems have raised serious questions about copyrights in a digital medium.
- Obscenity is not protected by the First Amendment. To be legally obscene, a work must appeal to prurient interests, depict or describe certain sexual conduct spelled out by state law, and lack serious literary, artistic, political, or scientific value.
- Special regulations and laws apply to broadcasting. The FCC is charged with administering the rules and regulations that deal with cable, TV, and radio. The Telecommunications Act of 1996 had a major impact on the electronic media.
- The Federal Trade Commission oversees advertising. Commercial speech has recently been given more First Amendment protection.

QUESTIONS FOR REVIEW

1. Whom do shield laws protect?
2. Whom do gag orders gag?
3. What is the Freedom of Information Act? How have reporters used it?
4. What is the difference between libel and slander?
5. What factors determine fair use?
6. Briefly explain the significance of the following court cases:
   a. The Betamax case
   b. The Pentagon Papers case
   c. *New York Times* v. *Sullivan*
   d. *Miller* v. *California*

QUESTIONS FOR CRITICAL THINKING

1. Why should reporters have special privileges when other professionals, such as architects, nurses, and accountants, have none?
2. Libel suits can be long and expensive for both sides. What are some other methods of conflict resolution that might cut down the time and the cost but still provide satisfaction for both sides?
3. Why are broadcasting and cable not entitled to the same amount of First Amendment protection as newspapers and magazines? Do you agree with this type of differentiation?
4. Do you think the recording industry's efforts to stop illegal file sharing by suing individuals will be successful?
5. How can children be protected from exposure to adult-oriented content on the Internet?

KEY TERMS

First Amendment (p. 385)
prior restraint (p. 385)
injunction (p. 385)
shield laws (p. 388)
gag rules (p. 392)
Freedom of Information Act
   (FOIA) (p. 395)
Patriot Act (p. 395)
defamation (p. 396)

libel (p. 396)
slander (p. 396)
libel per se (p. 396)
libel per quod (p. 396)
trespass (p. 402)
Hicklin rule (p. 405)
Equal Opportunities rule (p. 409)
Fairness Doctrine (p. 409)

franchises (p. 410)
Telecommunications Act of 1996
   (p. 410)
V-Chip (p. 411)
consent order (p. 412)
cease-and-desist order (p. 412)

INTERNET RESOURCES

Online Learning Center

At the Online Learning Center home page, www.mhhe.com/dominick8, *select* Student Center *and then* Chapter 15.

1. Use the Learning Objectives, Chapter Outline, Main Points, and Time Line sections to review this chapter.

2. Test your knowledge of the chapter using the multiple choice, crossword puzzle, and flashcard features of the site.

3. Expand your knowledge of concepts and topics discussed in the chapter by going to *Suggestions for Further Reading* and *Internet Exercises.*

PowerWeb

At the Mass Communication home page of PowerWeb, www.dushkin.com/powerweb, *log in and select* Mass Communication *as your title. On the next screen, select* Topics *and then quick jump to* Regulatory Policy. *Read Article 35, "The Children's Television Act in Its Second Year." Then consider the following questions:*

1. Why is it necessary to pass a law to require broadcasters to provide programs that educate and inform children? Why do they not do it voluntarily?

2. Take a look at the current children's programming on the major networks. Have things changed much since this article was published?

Now go to Federal Communications Commision *and read Article 29, "Media Mergers: The Dangers Remain." Then answer the following questions:*

1. What are the dangers of big media companies controlling much of what we see and hear?

2. What does *diversity* mean in the media ownership context? How important is it?

3. The proposals talked about in this article raised a great deal of controversy, and the Senate even passed a bill demanding their rollback. Why was there so much opposition?

Surfing the Internet

Many websites deal with legal matters. The ones listed here seem most helpful for students.

www.fcc.gov/
The FCC's home page. Site contains an archive of recent speeches, a search engine, and consumer information along with more technical data.

www.freedomforum.org
Site contains a summary of recent First Amendment court decisions, relevant law articles, a First Amendment time line, and a full text of relevant Supreme Court rulings.

www.rcfp.org
The Reporters Committee for Freedom of the Press maintains this site, which contains recent court decisions, legal news, and a link to their publication, *The News Media and the Law.*

www.rtnda.org
Home page of the Radio and Television News Directors Association. The site has information about covering the courts, libel, copyright, and other legal issues.

16

ETHICS AND OTHER INFORMAL CONTROLS

This chapter will prepare you to

- distinguish among the types of informal controls on the media;

- explain the most important ethical principles;

- explain what the standards department and performance codes are;

- discuss the relationship between the media and their advertisers vis-à-vis ethical practices; and

- understand the pros and cons of pressure groups.

Laws and regulations are not the only controls on the mass media. Informal controls, stemming from within the media themselves or shaped by the workings of external forces such as pressure groups, consumers, and advertisers, are also important. The following hypothetical examples illustrate some situations in which these controls might spring up:

1. You are the program director for the campus radio station. You get a call one morning from the promotion department of a major record company offering you a free trip to California, a tour of the record company's studios, a ticket to a concert featuring all the company's biggest stars, and an invitation to an exclusive party where you will get to meet all the performers. The company representative explains that this is simply a courtesy to you so that you will better appreciate the quality of her company's products. Do you accept?

Like a winding road, the path to an ethical decision needs to be carefully navigated.

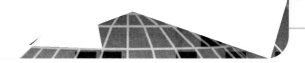

2. You are a reporter for the local campus newspaper. The star of the football team, who also happens to be the president of the Campus Crusade for Morality, has been involved in a minor traffic accident, and you have been assigned to cover the story. When you get to the accident scene, you examine the football player's car and find a half-dozen pornographic magazines strewn across the backseat. You have a deadline in 30 minutes; what details do you include in your story?

3. You are the editor of the campus newspaper. One of your reporters has just written a series of articles describing apparent health-code violations in a popular off-campus restaurant. This particular restaurant regularly buys full-page ads in your paper. After you run the first story in the series, the restaurant owner calls and threatens to cancel all her ads unless you stop printing the series. What do you do?

4. You are doing your first story for the campus paper. A local businessperson has promised to donate $5 million to your university so that it can buy new equipment for its mass communication and journalism programs. While putting together a background story on this benefactor, you discover that he was convicted of armed robbery at age 18 and avoided prison only by volunteering for military duty during the closing months of World War II. In the more than 50 years that have passed since then, his record has been spotless. He refuses to talk about the incident, claims his wife and his closest friends do not know about it, and threatens to withdraw his donation if you print the story. Naturally, university officials are concerned and urge you not to mention this fact. Do you go ahead and include the incident as simply one element in your overall profile? Do you take the position that the arrest information is not pertinent and not use it? Do you wait until the university has the money and then print the story?

We could go on listing examples, but by now the point is probably clear. There are many situations in the everyday operation of the mass media in which thorny questions about what to do or not to do have to be faced. Most of these situations do not involve laws or regulations but instead deal with the tougher questions of what is right or what is proper. Informal controls over the media usually assert themselves in these circumstances. In this chapter we will discuss the following examples of informal controls: personal ethics; performance codes; internal controls, such as organizational policies, self-criticism, and professional self-regulation; and outside pressures.

PERSONAL ETHICS

Ethics are rules of conduct or principles of morality that point us toward the right or best way to act in a situation. Over the years, philosophers have developed a number of general ethical principles that serve as guidelines for evaluating our behavior. We will briefly examine five principles that have particular relevance to those working in the mass media professions. Before we begin, however, please note that these principles do not contain magic answers to every ethical dilemma.

In fact, different ethical principles often suggest different and conflicting courses of action. There is no perfect answer to every problem. Also, these ethical principles are based on Western thought. Other cultures may have developed totally different systems. Nonetheless, these principles can provide a framework for analyzing what is proper in examining choices and justifying our actions.

>> Ethical Principles

The Principle of the Golden Mean   Moral virtue lies between two extremes. This philosophical position is typically associated with Aristotle, who, as a biologist, noted that too much food as well as too little food spoils health. Moderation is the key. Likewise, in ethical dilemmas, the proper way of behaving lies between doing too much and doing too little. For instance, in the restaurant example mentioned earlier, one extreme would be to cancel the story as requested by the restaurant owner. The other extreme would be to run the series as is. Perhaps a compromise between the two would be to run the series but also give the restaurant owner a chance to reply. Or perhaps the story might contain information about how the restaurant has improved conditions or other tempering remarks.

Examples of the **golden mean** are often found in media practices. For example, when news organizations cover civil disorders, they try to exercise moderation. They balance the necessity of informing the public with the need to preserve public safety by not inflaming the audience.

The Categorical Imperative   What is right for one is right for all. German philosopher Immanuel Kant is identified with this ethical guideline. To measure the correctness of our behavior, Kant suggested that we act according to rules that we would want to see universally applied. In Kant's formulation, *categorical* means unconditional—no extenuating circumstances, no exceptions. Right is right and should be done, no matter what the consequences. The individual's conscience plays a large part in Kant's thinking. A **categorical imperative** is discovered by an examination of conscience; the conscience informs us what is right. If, after performing an act, we feel uneasy or guilty, we have probably violated our conscience. Applied to mass communication, a categorical imperative might be that all forms of deception in news gathering are wrong and must be avoided. No one wants deception to become a universal practice. Therefore, for example, a reporter should not represent himself or herself as anything other than a reporter when gathering information for a story.

The Principle of Utility   Utility is defined as the greatest benefit for the greatest number. Modern utilitarian thinking originated with the 19th-century philosophers Jeremy Bentham and John Stuart Mill. The basic tenet in their formulations is that we are to determine what is right or wrong by considering what will yield the best ratio of good to bad for the general society. Utilitarians ask how much good is promoted and how much evil is restrained by different courses of behavior. Utilitarianism provides a clear method for evaluating ethical choices: (1) calculate all the consequences, both good and bad, that would result from each of our options; then (2) choose the alternative that maximizes value or minimizes loss.

Looking at the mass communication area, we can easily see several examples of utilitarian philosophy. In 1971, the *New York Times* and other papers printed stolen government documents known as the Pentagon Papers (see Chapter 15). Obviously, the newspapers involved thought that the good that would be achieved by printing these papers far outweighed the harm that would be done. (Note that the Kantian perspective would suggest a different course of action. Theft is bad. Newspapers do not want the government stealing their property, so they should not condone or promote the theft of government property.) Or take the case of a small Midwestern paper that chose to report the death of a local teenager who had left town, had turned to prostitution and drugs, and was murdered. The paper decided that the potential benefits of this story as a warning to other parents outweighed the grief it would cause the murder victim's family.

The Veil of Ignorance Justice is blind. Philosopher John Rawls argued that justice emerges when everyone is treated without social differentiations. Everybody doing the same job equally well should receive equal pay. Everybody who got an 80 on the test should get the same grade. Rawls advocated that all parties in a problem situation should be placed behind a barrier, the **veil of ignorance,** that conceals roles and social differentiations and that each participant be treated as an equal member of society as a whole. Rawls's veil of ignorance suggests that we structure our actions to protect the most vulnerable members of society. It is easy to see the relevance of this principle to the workings of the mass media. If we applied the veil of ignorance to the problem of hammering out the proper relationship between politicians and journalists, Rawls would argue that the blatant adversarial relationship so often found between the groups should disappear. Behind the veil, all newsmakers would be the same. Inherent cynicism and abrasiveness on the part of the press would disappear, as well as mistrust and suspicion on the part of the politicians. On a more specific level, consider the case of a financial reporter who frequently gets tips and inside information on deals and mergers that affect the prices of stocks and passes these tips on to personal friends who use this information for their own profit. The veil of ignorance suggests that the reporter must treat all audience members the same. Personal friends should not benefit from inside information.

Principle of Self-Determination Do not treat people as means to an end. This principle, closely associated with the Judeo-Christian ethic and also discussed by Kant, might be summarized as "Love your neighbor as yourself." Human beings have unconditional value apart from any and all circumstances. Their basic right to **self-determination** should not be violated by using them as simply a means to accomplish a goal. A corollary to this principle is that no one should allow himself or herself to be treated as a means to someone else's ends. Suppose that sources inside a government investigation on political corruption leak to the press the names of some people suspected of taking bribes, and the press, in turn, publishes the allegations and the names of the suspects. The principle of self-determination suggests that the press is being used by those who leaked the story as a means to accomplish their goal. Perhaps those involved in the investigation wanted to turn public opinion against those named or simply to earn some favorable publicity for their efforts. In any case, the press should resist being used in these circumstances. The rights, values, and decisions of others must always be respected.

>> A Model for Individual Ethical Decisions

In numerous situations personal ethical decisions have to be made about what should be or should not be included in media content or what should be or should not be done. Every day reporters, editors, station managers, and other media professionals have to make these decisions. Too often, however, these decisions

A recent case involving a newspaper in Washington State vividly illustrates an ethical dilemma concerning journalistic responsibility. The bizarre case involved a man who had been convicted of murdering his wife and was serving a 60-year sentence in the Washington State Penitentiary. The man was apparently plotting revenge against his former mother-in-law, who maintained that he had killed her daughter. The man wanted his cell mate, who was soon to be released, to burn down his former mother-in-law's house in return for about $17,000 in jewelry that the convicted murderer had hidden away. The man demanded that his cell mate show proof of the arson by mailing him a newspaper clipping about the fire.

Upon his release, the cell mate went to the police, and the police arranged to stage a fake fire. The police also asked a local paper to carry a news story about the faked fire. The newspaper complied and published a seven-sentence story that reported the details of the fire and that it apparently was the work of an arsonist. The paper's cooperation helped the authorities file charges against the inmate.

Did the newspaper behave ethically? Is it proper for a newspaper to run a fake story in order to help authorities? The paper's editor argued that the first responsibility a newspaper has is to the safety of its community. Publishing the fake story may have prevented future acts of revenge orchestrated by the inmate and may have saved lives. (In fact, authorities reported that the inmate hinted his next target might be the deputy prosecutor who put him behind bars.)

Others were not sure about the paper's reasoning. One journalist maintained that the primary responsibility of a newspaper to its community is to tell the truth. Publishing a falsehood, no matter how noble the purpose, erodes the foundation of trust that readers have in a newspaper and, in the long run, may cripple the paper's credibility.

Note how this case illustrates the conflict between two of the ethical theories discussed in this chapter. The newspaper editor endorses a utilitarian view: The good accomplished by the story eclipses the possible harm to the paper's credibility. The opponents endorse the categorical imperative: Publishing a falsehood is always wrong.

Was there another way for the newspaper to handle this situation that would satisfy the authorities and raise fewer ethical questions? Would it have been possible to print a single copy of the paper, one designed only for the inmate to read, that contained the false story? Or does this alternative also raise problems? As the chapter suggests, ethical decisions can be difficult.

are made haphazardly and without proper analysis of the ethical dimensions involved. This section presents a model that media professionals can use to evaluate and examine their decisions. This model is adapted from the work of Ralph Potter[1]:

$$DEFINITIONS \rightarrow VALUES \rightarrow PRINCIPLES \rightarrow LOYALTIES \rightarrow ACTION$$

In short, the model asks the individual to consider four aspects of the situation before taking action. First, define the situation. What are the pertinent facts involved? What are the possible actions? Second, determine what values are involved. Which values are more relevant to deciding a course of action? Third, establish what ethical principles apply. We have discussed five that might be involved. There may be others. Fourth, decide where our loyalties lie. To whom do we owe a moral duty? It is possible that we might owe a duty to ourselves, clients, business organizations, the profession, or society in general. To whom is our obligation most important?

Let us examine how this model would work in a real-life situation. During the summer of 2003, pro basketball superstar Kobe Bryant was accused of and later indicted for sexual assault. The case reopened the ethical questions surrounding the privacy of alleged victims of rape or sexual assault. In the past, mainstream media have been reluctant to identify the accuser in such cases. They have adopted this policy because the added stress and trauma of publicity might discourage others from reporting such crimes.

---

[1]Ralph Potter, "The Logic of Moral Argument," in *Toward a Discipline of Social Ethics*, P. Deats, ed. (Boston: Boston University Press, 1972).

Covering sensational trials, such as the Kobe Bryant sexual assault case, can raise serious ethical questions for journalists.

- *Establish the facts:* The facts of the situation are simple. A 19-year-old woman accused Bryant of sexual assault. Reporters and editors knew her name. There is no law that prohibits the press from naming the victim in such a case, but the media generally refrain from doing so without the alleged victim's consent. Not surprisingly, the name and a photograph of the accuser were published on several websites. The host of a Los Angeles radio talk show also identified her. Should newspaper and television reporters continue to keep her name confidential?

- *Clarify values:* There are conflicting values in such a case. First, journalists support the notion of fairness in reporting. The young woman made a serious allegation against someone who was then subjected to intense media scrutiny. Is it fair to let the accuser hide behind anonymity? In addition, withholding the name is paternalistic and stigmatizes the accuser. On the other hand, violating the privacy of the accuser is not to be taken lightly. Naming the alleged victim might cause emotional trauma and subject the person to additional distress. In the case of a popular figure, such as Bryant, identifying the accuser might bring her scorn, ridicule, and perhaps threats.

- *State principles:* A person who endorses the categorical imperative would argue that it is the job of journalists to disseminate information rather than suppress it. No matter how embarrassing or traumatic the news might be to the person involved, the news should still be published. A utilitarian might argue that any benefit that is gained by naming the accuser should be weighed against the potential harm to the individual involved. The principle of self-determination would seem to suggest that reporters should not name the victim simply to increase their circulation or their ratings.

- *Loyalties:* Journalists have a loyalty to their audiences to report fully the facts of a story, but they also have an obligation to follow the standards of their profession, and in this case professional standards suggested that the name not be revealed. Are these standards obsolete in the age of the Internet and talk radio when it seems impossible to keep the names of the accusers from the public record? Many professionals felt that the standards were still relevant. As one put it, "We can't be driven by what the Internet . . . does." Said another, "If you have a policy . . . you cannot be influenced by what others do."

What actions resulted from this incident? The major news media continued to withhold the name of Bryant's accuser. This decision seemed peculiar since many news outlets were quick to publish stories that revealed details of her life, where she went to college, and information about her previous emotional problems. The woman's friends and relatives were also named in many news reports, making it easy to deduce the woman's identity. Whatever might happen in this case, this episode illustrates some of the difficult questions reporters must face while trying to behave in an ethical manner.

Most of the time, ethical decisions are made in good faith with a sincere desire to serve the public, and the decisions reflect positively on the profession. Sometimes, however, ethical judgments may be adversely affected by other influences.

>> Acculturation

One of the factors that influence the judgment of some reporters is a phenomenon known as **acculturation.** Simply defined, *acculturation* in a media context means the tendency of reporters or other media professionals to accept the ideas, attitudes, and opinions of the group that they cover or with whom they have a great deal of contact. Many political reporters, for instance, come to share the views of the politicians they cover. So do many police-beat reporters. Publishers and station managers who spend a great deal of time with business leaders might come to adopt the point of view of industry. A 1977 study of reporters and legislators in Colorado revealed that political reporters and politicians held quite similar views. The study also revealed that many reporters identified with legislators, felt a sense of kinship with them, and actually considered themselves part of the legislative process. In the Potter model, these individuals have confused their loyalties. They see their duty to the group they are covering as more important than their duty to the profession of journalism.

Acculturation is not necessarily bad; it can cause concern, however, when it begins to affect judgment. Recently, a California newspaper learned that several off-duty police officers had terrorized a bar and had gotten into fistfights with some of its patrons. The disturbance was so serious that the chief of police recommended that three of the officers be dismissed. The paper, however, sat on the story for almost six weeks. It turned out that in the past, the police and the paper had developed an easy sense of cooperation. Police officers had been given the OK to look at the paper's files; in turn, the officers would give the paper mug shots if the paper needed a picture of a suspect. It is possible that this close and cooperative atmosphere led some journalists to identify with the police officers, which affected their news judgment in handling this particular story.

Some critics have argued that the reporters embedded with military units during Operation Iraqi Freedom were also influenced by acculturation.

PERFORMANCE CODES

Many ethical decisions have to be made within minutes or hours, without the luxury of lengthy philosophical reflection. In this regard, media professionals are not very different from other professionals, such as doctors and lawyers. In these professions, codes of conduct or of ethics have been standardized to help individuals make decisions. If a doctor or a lawyer violates one of the tenets of these codes, he or she may be barred from practice by a decision of a panel of colleagues who oversee the profession. Here the similarity with the mass media ends. Media professionals, thoroughly committed to the notion of free speech, have no professional review boards that grant and revoke licenses. Media codes of performance and methods of self-regulation are less precise and less stringent than those of other organizations. But many of the ethical principles discussed are incorporated into these codes.

>> The Print Media

During the colorful and turbulent age of jazz journalism (see Chapter 4), several journalists, apparently reacting against the excesses of some tabloids, founded the American Society of Newspaper Editors. This group voluntarily adopted the Canons of Journalism in 1923 without any public or governmental pressure. There were seven canons: responsibility, freedom of the press, independence, accuracy, impartiality, fair play, and decency. By and large, the canons are prescriptive (telling what ought to be done) rather than proscriptive (telling what ought to be avoided). Some of the canons are general and vague, with a great deal of room for individual interpretation. Under *responsibility,* for example, it is stated that "the use a newspaper makes of the share of public attention it gains serves to determine its sense of responsibility, which it shares with every member of its staff." This is a noble thought, but it is of little guidance when it comes to deciding if a newspaper should include the detail about the pornographic magazines in the star football player's car. Other statements seem simplistic. Under *accuracy,* for example, one learns that "headlines should be fully warranted by the contents of the article they surmount." Before you get the wrong idea, it should be pointed out that these canons should not be dismissed as mere platitudes and empty rhetoric. They do represent the first concrete attempt by journalists to strive for professionalism in their field.

When the canons were first released, *Time* magazine held out grandiose hopes for the future of the profession: "The American Society of Newspaper Editors (ASNE) aims to be to journalism what the American Bar Association is to the legal fraternity." *Time* was overly optimistic. The legal fraternity, through its powerful bar associations, has the power to revoke a member's license to practice. Journalists have fiercely resisted any idea that resembles licensing as a restriction on their First Amendment rights. The ASNE has never proposed licensing or certifying journalists for this reason. In fact, the ASNE has never expelled a member in its history, even though it has had ample reason to do so. For example, just one year after the canons were adopted, Fred Bonfils of the *Denver Post* testified that he had accepted $250,000 to suppress stories about the Teapot Dome oil-lease scandal that was then plaguing the administration of President Warren G. Harding. (Ironically, Harding himself was a former newspaper editor.) Rather than expelling Bonfils, the ASNE decided to stress voluntary compliance with its canons.

The Society of Professional Journalists (SPJ; formerly Sigma Delta Chi) adopted its code at about the same time as the ASNE. The code was designed to guide journalists working in all media. The SPJ code was unchanged for more than 45 years, but as journalistic ethics became more problematic, the code was revised in 1973, 1984, 1987, and again in 1996. The newly adopted SPJ code is organized around four main principles:

1. *Seek the truth and report it.* Journalists should be honest, fair, and courageous in reporting the news.
2. *Minimize harm.* Journalists should treat sources, subjects, and colleagues as human beings deserving of respect.
3. *Act independently.* Journalists should be free of obligation to any interest other than the public's right to know.
4. *Be accountable.* Journalists should be accountable to their audience and to each other.

In 1975, the Associated Press Managing Editors (APME) association adopted a code that also discussed responsibility, accuracy, integrity, and independence. Revised in 1995, the APME code covers such issues as plagiarism and diversity. As with the ASNE's canons, adherence to the code is voluntary. Neither the SPJ nor the ASNE has developed procedures to enforce its codes.

In late 1999, the Gannett Company became the first newspaper chain to spell out ethical principles for its papers. Other newspaper chains have companywide guidelines covering general issues, but individual papers can set policy in their own newsrooms. The Gannett guidelines are the first to be newsroom-specific. The decision to establish guidelines stemmed from a growing public distrust of the media and a desire to reassure readers about the fairness and accuracy of newspaper content. The new guidelines forbid, among other things, lying to get a story, fabricating news, and publishing misleading alterations of photographs. The full text of the guidelines can be found at the company website (www.gannett.com).

>> Broadcasting

For many years, radio and television broadcasters followed the National Association of Broadcasters (NAB) Code of Good Practice. This code first appeared in 1929 and was revised periodically over the years. It was divided into two parts, one covering advertising and the other covering general program practices. In 1982, however, a court ruled that the code placed undue limitations on advertising, and the NAB suspended the advertising part of its code. The next year, to forestall more legal pressure, the NAB officially dissolved the code in its entirety.

Although the code is gone, its impact lingers on. In 1990 the NAB issued voluntary programming principles that addressed four key areas: children's TV, indecency, violence, and drug and substance abuse. The new guidelines were stated in a broad and general way: "Glamorization of drug use and substance abuse should be avoided." "Violence . . . should only be portrayed in a responsible manner and should not be used exploitatively." To stay out of trouble with the Justice Department, the NAB declared that there would be no interpretation or enforcement of these provisions and that the standards were not designed to inhibit creativity.

Trying to resurrect a code for broadcasters is a favorite activity among politicians. In 1997, four U.S. senators introduced a bill that would exempt the broadcasting and cable industries from antitrust laws so that they could develop a new code. Other bills that urged broadcasters to develop a voluntary code of conduct were introduced in Congress in 1998 and 1999. More recently, Senators Joseph Lieberman and John McCain offered a bill to the 2000 Congress that would urge media companies to create a "uniform rating system" that would apply to video games, TV, movies, and music. None of these bills was enacted into law.

In the broadcast journalism area, the Radio and Television News Directors Association has an 11-part code that covers everything from cameras in the courtroom to invasion of privacy.

The V-Chip and its companion ratings system represent an interesting interaction between formal and informal controls. The nuts and bolts of this arrangement are discussed in Chapter 15 as part of the Telecommunications Act of 1996. For purposes of this section, it is important to point out that the V-Chip represents an example of the government's pressuring the video industry to adopt "voluntary" guidelines that categorize programming. If the industry failed to develop its own program ratings to work with the V-Chip, Congress left the door open for the FCC to do it for them. The threat of government action has been used before to prod broadcasters into reforms that they were reluctant to make on their own. In fact, scholars who have studied the FCC have even given this phenomenon a name: the "raised eyebrow" technique. The V-Chip legislation is a bit stronger than the raised eyebrow, but its end result is the same.

>> Motion Pictures

Codes of conduct in the motion picture industry emerged during the 1920s. Scandals were racking Hollywood at that time (see Chapter 9), and many states had passed or were considering censorship laws that would control the content of movies. In an attempt to save itself from being tarred and feathered, the industry invited Will Hays, a former postmaster general and elder of the Presbyterian church, to head a new organization that would clean up films. Hays became the president, chairman of the board, and chairman of the executive committee of a new organization, the Motion Picture Producers and Distributors of America (MPPDA). In 1930, the Motion Picture Production Code was adopted by the new group. The code was mainly proscriptive; it described what should be avoided in order for filmmakers to get their movies past existing censorship boards and listed what topics should be handled carefully so as not to rile existing pressure groups. The 1930 code is remarkable for its specificity; it rambles on for nearly 20 printed pages. The following are some excerpts:

> The presentation of scenes, episodes, plots, etc. which are deliberately meant to excite [sex and passion] on the part of the audience is always wrong, is subversive to the interest of society, and is a peril to the human race.
>
> The more intimate parts of the human body are the male and female organs and the breasts of a woman.
>
> a. They should never be uncovered.
> b. They should not be covered with transparent or translucent material.
> c. They should not be clearly and unmistakably outlined by garments. . . .
>
> There must be no display at any time of machine guns, sub-machine guns or other weapons generally classified as illegal weapons. . . .
>
> Obscene dances are those: which represent sexual actions, whether performed solo or with two or more, which are designed to excite an audience, arouse passion, or cause physical excitement.

A few years after the Production Code was drafted, a Roman Catholic organization, the Legion of Decency (see Media Probe, "The Legion of Decency"), pressured the industry to put teeth into its code enforcement. The MPPDA ruled that no company belonging to its organization would distribute or release any film unless it bore the Production Code Administration's seal of approval. In addition, a $25,000 fine could be levied against a firm that violated this rule. Because of the hammerlock that the major studios had over the movie industry at this time, it was virtually impossible for an independent producer to make or exhibit a film without the aid of a member company. As a result, the Production Code turned out to be more restrictive than many of the local censorship laws it was designed to avoid.

The Production Code was a meaningful force in the film industry for about 20 years. During the late 1940s, however, changes that would ultimately alter the basic structure of the motion picture industry also scuttled the code. In 1948, the Paramount case ended producer-distributor control of theaters, thus allowing independent producers to market a film without the Production Code seal. In addition, economic competition from television prompted films to tackle more mature subjects. The industry responded during the 1950s by liberalizing the

After World War I, during the roaringest part of the Roaring Twenties, the films that grossed the most money had titles like *Red Hot Romance, She Could Not Help It, Her Purchase Price,* and *Plaything of Broadway.* One movie ad of the period boasted breathlessly, "brilliant men, beautiful jazz babies, champagne baths, midnight revels, petting parties in the purple dawn." Before long public opposition to such sensational movies began to form. The appointment of Will Hays, the creation of the Motion Picture Producers and Distributors of America, and the adoption of the Motion Picture Production Code were designed, in part, to forestall this public criticism.

Much of the code was suggested by a Roman Catholic layman, Martin Quigley, and a Roman Catholic priest, Father Daniel Lord. Despite the existence of the code, however, sensational films still appeared in significant numbers. This trend was disturbing to many segments in society, particularly the Catholic Church. Keep in mind that at this time the United States was in the midst of a severe economic depression. Many individuals, including prominent Catholics, connected the country's economic poverty with the nation's moral bankruptcy as evidenced by the films of the period. Additionally, an Apostolic Delegate from Rome took the film industry to task in a blistering speech before the Catholic Charities Convention in New York.

In April of 1934, a committee composed of American bishops responded to the speech and to the general tenor of the period by announcing the organization of a nationwide Legion of Decency, whose members were to fight for better films. The legion threatened to boycott those theaters that exhibited objectionable films, and it sometimes made good on its threats. The Chicago chapter of the legion enrolled half a million members in a matter of days and was matched by equal enrollment in Brooklyn. Detroit Catholics affixed "We Demand Clean Movies" bumper stickers to their cars. Other religious groups joined the legion—Jewish clergy in New York, Lutherans in Missouri. Pope Pius XI praised the legion as an "excellent experiment" and called upon bishops all over the world to imitate it.

There were 20 million Catholics in the United States in 1934, and naturally, the film industry took this group seriously. The Production Code Administration was set up with the power to slap a $25,000 fine on films released without the administration's seal of approval. The Legion of Decency's boycotts hurt enough at the box office to force many theaters to book only films that the legion approved. In Albuquerque, New Mexico, 17 of 21 theaters agreed not to book a film condemned by the legion. In Albany, New York, Catholics pledged to avoid for six months each theater that had screened the condemned film *Baby Doll.* Producers, frightened by this display of economic power, began meeting with legion members to make sure there were no potentially inflamatory elements in their films.

By the 1960s, however, the Legion of Decency was losing most of its clout. The restructuring of the film industry allowed independent producers to market their films without code approval. Many producers did just that and demonstrated that some films could make money even without the legion and Production Code approval. The increasingly permissive mood of the country encouraged an avalanche of more mature and controversial films. Moreover, the legion, renamed the National Catholic Office for Motion Pictures, painted itself into a corner when it condemned such artistically worthwhile films as Bergman's *The Silence* and Antonioni's *Blowup,* and endorsed such films as *Godzilla vs. the Thing* and *Goliath and the Sins of Babylon.* By the 1970s, this group had effectively lost all its power; it was essentially disbanded in 1980. Nonetheless, during its prime, the Legion of Decency was the single most effective private influence on the film industry.

---

code; despite this easing of restrictions, more and more producers began to ignore them. Nonetheless, the code, outdated and unenforceable, persisted into the 1960s. A 1966 revision that tried to keep pace with changing social attitudes proved to be too little too late.

In 1968, the motion picture industry entered into a new phase of self-regulation when the Production Code seal of approval was dropped and a new motion picture rating system was established. Operated under the auspices of the Motion Picture Association of America (successor to the MPPDA), the National Association of Theater Owners, and the Independent Film Importers and Distributors of America, this new system, commonly referred to as the **MPAA rating system,** places films into one of five categories:

G: Suitable for general audiences.

PG: Parental guidance suggested.

PG-13: Some content may be objectionable for children under 13 (a new category added in 1984).

R: Restricted to persons over age 17 unless accompanied by parent or adult guardian.

NC-17: No children under 17 admitted. (This category replaced the X rating in 1990. The MPAA made the change in response to several producers who argued that adult-themed, daring, but nonpornographic films should not be lumped into the same category as porno films.)

Unlike the old Production Code, which regulated film content, the new system leaves producers pretty much free to include whatever scenes they like as long as they realize that, by so doing, they may restrict the size of their potential audience. One possible repercussion of this system may be the steady decline in the number of G-rated films released each year. Producers evidently feel that movies in this category will be perceived as children's films and will not be attractive to a more mature audience. During the first 11 years of the rating system's existence, the percentage of films in the G category dropped, while the percentage of films in the R category increased. X-rated or NC-17–rated films have never accounted for more than 10 percent of the total number of films submitted for review (of course, many low-budget, hard-core pornographic films are never submitted for classification).

The PG-13 rating is being given to an increasing number of films. In 2002, 65 percent of the top 20 moneymaking films were rated PG-13. The remaining 35 percent were rated G or PG. No R film was among the top 20 moneymakers.

In order for the MPAA rating system to work, producers, distributors, theater owners, and parents must all cooperate. There is no governmental involvement in the classification system; there are no fines involved. Moviemakers are not required to submit a film for rating. People evidently think that the system is a good idea. An industry survey done in 2002 disclosed that 74 percent of the adults surveyed considered the ratings "very useful" guides for children's attendance.

The MPAA ratings system came under scrutiny once again in 2000 after it was revealed that movie companies were marketing R-rated films to children under 17. In response to this, the MPAA instituted new guidelines that included withholding all preview trailers for films rated R for violence from playing before any G-rated films. In addition, the organization urged movie theaters to enforce the age guidelines more conscientiously and actually check IDs of young people who attempt to see an R-rated movie without an adult.

The Motion Picture Association of America's rating is a prominent part of this movie marquee.

>> The Advertising Industry

In the advertising industry, several professional organizations have drafted codes of performance. The American Association of Advertising Agencies first adopted its Standards of Practice in 1924. This code, which covers contracts, credit extension, unfair tactics, and the creative side of advertising, contains provisions prohibiting misleading price claims, offensive statements, and the circulation of harmful rumors about a competitor. The Advertising Code of American Business, developed and distributed by the American Advertising Federation and the Association of Better Business Bureaus International, covers much the same ground. Memberships in these organizations and adherence to the codes are voluntary. In public relations, the Public Relations Society of America adopted its first code in 1954 and revised it during the 1980s. As with the other codes, enforcement is essentially voluntary, and the society has no control over a practitioner who is not a member.

INTERNAL CONTROLS

Codes established by professional organizations and individual ethics are not the only informal controls on media behavior. Most media organizations have other internal controls that frequently come into play. Written statements of policy can be found in most newspaper, television, radio, and motion picture organizations. In advertising, a professional organization for self-regulation has existed since 1971.

>> **Organizational Policy: Television Networks' Standards and Practices**

For many years, each major network maintained a large department that was usually labeled "standards and practices" or something similar. Staff members in these departments would make literally thousands of decisions each season on the acceptability of dialogue, plotlines, and visual portrayals. During the late 1980s, however, network budget cuts took their toll, and most of these departments were scaled back dramatically. As criticism of television content increased during the 1990s, these departments were enlarged somewhat but still have far fewer people working in them than they did in the early 1980s. The departments at Fox, NBC, and ABC review everything their networks air, including commercials. At CBS, the standards department reviews children's programs, docudramas, ads, new shows, and about a dozen existing series. The efforts devoted to monitoring standards vary greatly among cable networks. MTV, for example, closely monitors all its programs; the Discovery Channel rarely has problems regarding taste. Pay channels, such as HBO, have more liberal standards.

The broadcast and cable networks are also relying more and more on the judgment of series producers to determine standards of acceptability. Producers, for their part, have a general notion about how far they can go without raising network displeasure. The networks will generally closely monitor the first few episodes of a series that may cause problems. After that, they will put more trust in the producers' standards.

It is probably obvious to any casual observer of broadcast television that network standards have become more liberal over the years. *NYPD Blue* shows partial nudity and routinely uses street language that would not have been acceptable 10 years ago. Characters on *The Practice* and *Boston Public* make direct references to oral sex. *Will and Grace* has a gay character as a star.

There are several reasons behind these changes. First, society has become more open-minded. Subjects that were once taboo, such as male impotence, are now discussed routinely in commercials. Second, the broadcast networks have to compete with the more permissive cable networks on which shows such as *Sex and the City* have pushed the envelope of acceptability even further. Finally, the sex scan-

Although it lasted only a few episodes before cancellation, NBC's *Coupling,* pushed the boundaries of what was acceptable in prime time.

dal involving President Bill Clinton and Monica Lewinsky put sexual topics on the evening newscasts and immediately eliminated many taboos.

Despite this liberalization, the networks' standards and practices departments still exercise some caution. Same-sex kissing scenes are still, with some exceptions, generally frowned upon. Offensive stereotypes are not allowed. Networks traditionally have not aired ads for abortion clinics, contraceptives (some local stations have aired contraceptive ads), or massage parlors.

In addition to the networks, local stations also exercise self-regulation. Occasionally a local station will decide that a network show is inappropriate for its audience and decline to show it or broadcast it at a later time. For example, a TV station in Augusta, Georgia, decided to show NBC's half-hour version of *Queer Eye for the Straight Guy* at 2:30 A.M. rather than in the early evening. More than 20 local stations refused to air *Maxim's Hot 100,* a one-hour special that featured scantily clad females.

Local stations also construct a **policy book.** This book typically spells out philosophy and standards of operation and identifies which practices are encouraged or discouraged. For example, most television and radio stations have a policy against newsroom personnel functioning as commercial spokespersons. Radio stations typically have a policy against airing "homemade" tapes and records. Other stations may have rules against playing songs that are drug oriented or too suggestive. Commercials that make extravagant claims or ads for questionable products and services might also be prohibited under local station policy.

>> Organizational Policy: Newspapers and Magazines

Newspapers and magazines create policy statements that take two distinct forms. **Operating policies** cover the everyday problems and situations that crop up during the normal functioning of the paper or magazine. **Editorial policies** are guidelines that the newspaper or magazine follows to persuade the public on certain issues or to achieve specific goals.

Operating policies vary from one paper or magazine to another. In general, however, these policies cover such matters as accepting freebies, using deception to gather information, paying newsmakers for a story or exclusive interview (checkbook journalism), taking junkets, conducting electronic surveillance, using stolen documents, accepting advertising for X-rated films, and deciding whether to publish the names of rape victims. Also covered are outside employment of reporters and editors and conflicts of interest. Here, for example, are excerpts from *Rules and Guidelines* used by the *Milwaukee Journal:*

> *Free tickets or passes to sports events, movies, theatrical productions, circuses, ice shows, or other entertainment may not be accepted or solicited by staff members.*
>
> *A gift that exceeds token value should be returned promptly with an explanation that it is against our policy. If it is impractical to return it, the company will donate it to a charity.*

The digital revolution in photography has made it possible to alter images with just a couple of mouse clicks. The retouched images are extremely difficult if not impossible to detect. This development has both positive and negative aspects. On the one hand, as most people who have experimented with digital photography are aware, software programs such as Photoshop make it possible to correct for poor lighting conditions, remove the annoying "red eye" effect, and in general tweak an image so that it looks better. On the other hand, digital photography has raised some perplexing issues for photojournalists. How much alteration is ethically acceptable in a news photo?

This dilemma has surfaced several times. Probably the most prominent example occurred during the O. J. Simpson murder trial when *Time* magazine published an altered photo in which his face was darkened and the background was lightened, alterations that made Simpson look more menacing. In the aftermath of this event, all major newsmagazines and newspapers reaffirmed policies that forbade any alteration of news photos.

A more recent example occurred during the 2003 Iraq War when Brian Walski, a photographer for the *Los Angeles Times,* was fired for digitally altering a photo of a British soldier and a group of Iraqi civilians. In order to improve composition and make the crowd of civilians look larger, Walski combined elements of two separate pictures into a composite. A close look at the picture reveals that the images of some Iraqis were copied from one photo and digitally pasted on another.

Walski's behavior raises several issues, not the least of which is why he would do something like this. He was not a novice photojournalist. He had worked for the *Times* for about five years and had won several awards from the California Press Photographers Association for his Afghan War photos. Is this a case of a photojournalist working for a major paper being under so much pressure to produce great photos and beat the competition that he overlooks basic journalistic ethics?

Even more puzzling is the fact that the composite photo is not that much different from the originals. Why risk a career over what appears to be a minor improvement in the aesthetics of the picture? Might members of a profession be motivated more by a desire to impress their editors and other photojournalists than they are by ethics?

On a more general level, is it ethically correct to do any kind of alteration to a news photo? What about changing the dark and light tones in a photo to make it more printable in a newspaper or magazine? The content of the photo is the same; it just looks better. What about blurring the foreground and the background in a photo to make the main subject stand out? Again, the content stays the same; it is just that some parts are a little fuzzy. In a technique called *reverse cropping* a person can lengthen a photo either vertically or horizontally by extending elements of the existing photo. The information in the photo stays basically the same.

Perhaps the results of an audience survey published in a 2001 issue of *Journalism and Communication Monographs* might help journalists establish some cultural norms for these new digital techniques. Almost all of the respondents thought that adjusting the tones in a photo to make it print better was an acceptable practice. Blurring the background and reverse cropping were less acceptable in news photos. Only about one in four respondents approved of this process. The digital techniques that almost all respondents felt were unethical were changing the tone of a photograph for dramatic effect, eliminating persons and other distracting items from the background of a photo, and creating composite photos by adding people or objects not in the original.

Most newspaper and magazine editors agree with these respondents, as demonstrated by the existence of many ethics policies, such as the one at the *Los Angeles Times,* that forbid the alteration of news photos. The logic behind such policies is easy to understand. If it is revealed that one news photo is a fake, doubt is cast on all the other photos that have been published. As one contributor to a Web forum for photojournalists put it, "I'll never be able to look at another one of Walski's award-winning photographs without wondering whether or not it is a fake."

Participating in politics at any level is not allowed, either for pay or as a volunteer. Public relations and publicity work in fields outside the Journal should be avoided.

Some newspapers and magazines are liberal; some are conservative. Some support Democratic candidates; others support Republicans. Some are in favor of nuclear energy; others against. These and other attitudes are generally expressed in the editorial pages of the newspaper. Editorial policy is generally clear at most publications. The *Chicago Tribune* has traditionally expressed a conservative point of view. The *New York Times* has a more liberal policy. The editorial policy of a paper will exert a certain amount of control over the material that is printed on its editorial pages. This, of course, the paper has a perfect right to do. There may be

Following are selected results from a study done by the Parents Television Council that compared violence, sex, and profanity in four weeks of the 1989 TV season with four weeks of the 1999 TV season. As is obvious, standards are different now.

References to	1989	1999	Percent increase per hour of programming
Oral sex	0	20	
Masturbation	2	17	700
Homosexuality	4	125	2,650
Genitalia	10	92	650
Kinky sex	13	60	357
Pornography	7	28	300

times, however, when the editorial policy of the paper spills over onto its news pages, and this might cause a problem for the paper's reputation for objectivity, responsibility, and integrity.

One problem that crops up periodically is called *boosterism*, a procommunity philosophy that sometimes causes not-so-good news to go unreported. In Flint, Michigan, when the local Fisher Body plant closed, TV networks and newspapers across the country announced the bad news that Flint was about to lose 3,600 jobs. The local Flint paper did not mention the job loss until the 11th paragraph on an inside page. "Good news," however, got prominent play: A story about new shrubs being planted at the local Buick facility earned front-page coverage.

Owners and publishers can exert editorial control over news policy in several ways. They can hire only those people who agree with their editorial views. (For example, the *New Orleans Times-Picayune* ran an ad in a trade magazine for a business reporter. One of the qualifications was a "probusiness philosophy.") They can also fire people who produce stories that the owner does not like, or they can issue orders to downplay some topics while paying large amounts of attention to others.

What is the significance of these examples for the news-consuming public? For one thing, the sample cases are probably exceptions to the norm rather than the norm itself. Nonetheless, they do illustrate the potential hazards of relying on only one source for news. The intelligent consumer of news and information should rely on several different media to get a more complete picture.

>> Self-Criticism

Some informal control over media content and practices comes from within. Although the amount of internal media criticism has grown in the past few years, it is still small when compared with the amount of investigative reporting and critical analyses that newspapers, magazines, television, and radio conduct about other facets of society. Many newspapers and magazines have media critics and media reporters. The amount of meaningful critical writing done by these journalists, however, is highly variable. Some of the more well-known critics in the print media are Ken Auletta of *The New Yorker*, Howard Kurtz of the *Washington Post*, and Tom Shales of *Television Week*.

Several journalism reviews regularly criticize media performance. The *Columbia Journalism Review* is the best known, but its circulation is only about 35,000. Others that are important are the *American Journalism Review* and the *Media Studies Journal*.

The Internet has opened up a new channel for media self-criticism. The Media Channel (www.mediachannel.org), for example, contains news, analysis of issues, and criticism about media across the globe. Journalist Jim Romenesko maintains a similar site at www.poynter.org. The impact of these and similar sites is yet to be determined.

Cable and broadcast television networks usually offer few programs with serious criticism of the media. Newspapers do a bit more in this area; *The Wall Street Journal* has occasionally run an in-depth study of the problems facing the newspaper industry. In film, the industry newspaper *Variety* has sometimes published an

article critical of the film industry. *Billboard,* the trade publication of the sound-recording industry, has run analytical, if not critical, pieces on the recording industry.

Some newspapers and other media organizations have tried to incorporate an idea from Scandinavia into their operations to provide some internal criticism. An **ombudsperson** is employed by the company to handle complaints from audience members who feel they have gotten a raw deal. The ombudsperson also criticizes in general the performance of the organization's personnel. Although the number of ombudspersons in the United States remains small, interest in the position has grown in recent years primarily because news organizations are worried that they are losing credibility with their audiences. There are about 40 ombudspersons in the United States, just about all at newspapers. The position is almost nonexistent in TV newsrooms. (One of the reasons may be the difficult-to-pronounce title "ombudsperson." At one newspaper, letters were addressed to the "Omnibus person" or to "Dear Omnipotent.")

>> Professional Self-Regulation in Advertising

In 1971, the leading advertising professional organizations—the Council of Better Business Bureaus, the American Advertising Federation, the American Association of Advertising Industries, and the Association of National Advertisers—formed the National Advertising Review Council. Its objective is to sustain high standards of truth and accuracy in advertising. The council itself is composed of two divisions: the National Advertising Division (NAD) and the National Advertising Review Board (NARB). When a complaint about an ad is made by a consumer or competitor, the complaint goes first to the NAD, which evaluates it. The NAD can dismiss the complaint as unfounded or trivial, or it can contact the advertiser for an explanation or further substantiation. If the NAD is satisfied that the ad in question is accurate, it will dismiss the complaint. If the NAD is not satisfied with the explanation, it can ask the advertiser to change the ad or discontinue the message.

If the advertiser disagrees, the case goes to the NARB, which functions as a court of appeals. Ultimately, if the case does not reach an acceptable solution, the NARB may call it to the attention of the Federal Trade Commission or other appropriate agencies. Sending a case to the FTC happens rarely. In 1993, the board turned over to the FTC the first fraudulent advertising case in the NARB's 22-year history. Most advertisers generally comply with the NAD's wishes. In 2002, for example, the NAD recommended that Rembrandt Plus toothpaste modify its ad that claimed that brushing with the product would make teeth "five" shades whiter. The NAD noted that the ad did not point out that it would take six months of daily brushing to achieve those results. Rembrandt's manufacturer agreed to take the recommendation into account in future ads.

Industry groups also exert control over advertising for their products. For example, the Distilled Spirits Council of the United States in 1996 ended a decades-old, self-imposed ban on advertising distilled liquor on television and radio. The major television networks declined to air any liquor ads, but many local stations accepted them. On the other side of the coin, the Miller Brewing Company and the Anheuser-Busch Company voluntarily agreed to remove their ads from MTV because they did not want to appear to be encouraging underage drinking.

▰ OUTSIDE INFLUENCES

The larger context that surrounds a media organization often contains factors that have an influence on media performance. In this section we will discuss four: economics, pressure groups, press councils, and education.

>> Economic Pressures

Money is a potent influence on media gatekeepers. In commercial media, the loss of revenue can be an important consideration in controlling what gets filmed, published, or broadcast. Economic controls come in many shapes and forms. Pressure can be brought to bear by advertisers, by the medium's own business policy, by the general economic structure of the industry, and by consumer groups.

Pressure from Advertisers   The recording industry gets its revenue from the purchase of individual tapes and discs. Consequently, it earns virtually no money from advertisers and is generally immune to their pressures. The film industry makes most of its money from the sale of individual tickets. Advertisers have some limited influence through what is called *product placement*—an arrangement whereby an advertiser pays a movie studio to include its product in a film (*Die Another Day*, for example, was filled with scenes of Ford products). Nonetheless, in relative terms, advertisers have only modest influence over motion picture content. In the print media, on the other hand, newspapers depend on advertising for about 75 percent of their income, while magazines derive 50 percent of their revenues from ads. Radio and television, of course, depend on ads for almost all their income.

The actual amount of control that an advertiser has over media content and behavior is difficult to determine. It is probably fair to say, however, that most news stories and most television and radio programs are put together without much thought as to what advertisers will say about them.

Occasionally, however, you may find examples of pressure:

- *Esquire* killed a 1997 story about a gay college student because the Chrysler Corporation apparently expressed concern about placing advertising in that issue.
- Executives at the *Boston Herald* suspended a reporter who wrote columns critical of a merger between two big Boston banks. One of the banks was a big advertiser in the newspaper and held the mortgage on the newspaper's building. (Management eventually relented and reinstated the journalist.)

Finally, a 2000 poll conducted by the *Columbia Journalism Review* found that about one in three reporters said they avoided stories that would be detrimental to advertisers.

Business Policies   Economic pressure on media content is sometimes encouraged by the business practices of the media themselves. When the Supreme Court of Massachusetts ruled that a creditor could be sued for harassing those who owed money, the Boston newspapers declined to identify the retail store involved in the suit. The store in question was a big newspaper advertiser. In San Francisco, a newspaper killed a column that criticized the Nike Company. It so happened that Nike was the sponsor of the paper's "Bay to Breakers" race.

Trading news coverage for advertising time or space is a common problem. A TV station in south Florida sent a flyer to its advertisers offering to do a news story on them in return for $5,000. While trying to negotiate a contract to carry live drawings for the New York State Lottery, a TV station promised lottery officials

Zapme! was a company that offered school systems across the country a computer lab, 15 Pentium computers with built-in software, a printer, and a broadband Internet connection all for free. What was the catch? When students used the computers to surf the Net, they saw advertisements in the lower left-hand corner of the screen. And therein was the problem that led to Zapme! getting zapped.

For a while it looked like a great idea. By late 2000, Zapme! was providing service to about 1.2 million students at 1,200 schools. Big advertisers such as Kodak, Frito-Lay, and Xerox bought time on the service. Then a problem surfaced. Citizens groups, including Ralph Nader's Washington-based Commercial Alert, attacked ZapMe! for commercializing the classroom. Nader called Zapme! a "corporate predator" that was trying to take control away from parents over their children's experiences. Opponents charged that Zapme! was taking advantage of taxpayer-funded classrooms by using them as a channel for corporate advertising.

The controversy scared off potential advertisers and hurt Zapme!'s stock value. Its price went from $17 a share down to $2. Faced with these developments, Zapme! pulled the plug on the project. The company notified schools that they could buy the computers or the company would take them back. Schools that were slated for Zapme!'s computers were out of luck.

Many had spent money rewiring and remodeling rooms for the expected computers. Teachers who had planned their classes assuming the computers would be available now had to start from scratch.

This event illustrates how two disparate groups used different ethical standards to support their actions. School systems that needed the computers endorsed a utilitarian view. The benefits of having such modern technology available for students who otherwise might not have had access to it outweighed any potential harm that might have come from exposure to advertising. As one teacher put it, "If the price of 15 computers is a small strip of ad space, it's worth it." On the other hand, opponents endorsed the categorical imperative. They believed that advertising, no matter what the positive benefits, does not belong in the classroom. The fact that many educators and students were eager to get the technology and willing to accept the ads did not affect their viewpoint: No advertising in classrooms, period.

Is society better off now that Zapme! is gone? Would you be willing to accept advertising in your classroom if it lowered the cost of tuition and brought you improved facilities? What about advertising in a third-grade classroom? Is there an optimal ethical solution to this problem?

positive news coverage of lottery events. In both instances, the stations withdrew the offers when their breach of ethics was revealed.

Then there is the problem of revenue-related reading matter. This issue crops up when a new shopping center or discount store opens in a community and gets heavy news coverage, maybe more than is justified by ordinary journalistic standards, in return for advertising revenue. Recently in Waco, Texas, the local newspaper devoted half its front page and two inside pages (with seven color photographs) to the opening of a new supermarket. Not surprisingly, supermarkets spend a lot on newspaper ads.

These examples are not meant to criticize or impugn the reputation of any medium or profession. There are probably countless, less-publicized examples of newspapers, magazines, television, and radio stations resisting advertising and economic pressure. What you should learn from this section is the nature of the close relationship that can sometimes exist between advertisers and media and the pressures that can result. Most of the time, this relationship causes few problems. When professional judgment is compromised by the dollar sign, however, then perhaps the economic pressures are performing a dysfunction for the media.

>> Pressure Groups

Various segments of the audience can band together and try to exert control over the operation of mass-media organizations. These groups sometimes use the threat of economic pressure (boycotts) or simply rely on the negative effects of bad publicity to achieve their goals. In radio and television, pressure groups (or *citi-*

zens' groups, as they are often called) can resort to applying legal pressure during the license-renewal process. Because of broadcasting's unique legal position, it has been the focus of a great deal of pressure-group attention. In 1964, for example, a group of black citizens working with the Office of Communication of the United Church of Christ formed a pressure group and attempted to deny the license renewal of a TV station in Jackson, Mississippi, because of alleged discrimination on the part of station management. After a long and complicated legal battle, the citizens' group succeeded in its efforts. This success probably encouraged the formation of other groups. John Banzhaf III headed an organization called ASH (Action for Smoking and Health), for example, which was instrumental in convincing Congress to ban cigarette advertising from radio and television. At about the same time, perhaps the most influential of all the pressure groups interested in broadcasting was formed: Action for Children's Television (ACT). From a modest start, this group was successful in achieving the following:

1. persuading the networks to appoint a supervisor for children's programming,
2. eliminating drug and vitamin ads from kids' shows,
3. instituting a ban on the host's selling in children's programs,
4. reducing the amount of advertising during Saturday morning programs, and
5. helping a bill concerning children's TV pass Congress in 1990.

ACT disbanded in 1992. In its final press release, the organization said its major goal had been achieved with the passage of the 1990 Children's Television Act and that people who want better television for kids now "have Congress on their side."

In the mid-1970s, other self-interest groups whose primary interest was not broadcasting began to get involved in television programming. The American Medical Association and the National Parent Teachers Association both criticized TV violence. The National Organization for Women campaigned for more representative portrayals of women in the mass media. The American-Arab Anti-Discrimination Committee protested that Disney's *Aladdin* featured a song whose lyrics contained a slur against Arabs. Protests by gays and lesbians against the 2000 launch of Dr. Laura Schlessinger's TV show prompted many advertisers to back out from sponsoring the show and several stations to drop it altogether. Dr. Laura eventually apologized for some of her antigay remarks.

Pressure groups organized along political lines have also exerted control over media content and practices. One particularly vicious example occurred in the 1950s during the Cold War period, when a massive communist scare ran throughout the country. A self-appointed group called Aware, Inc., tried to point out what it thought were communist influences in the broadcasting industry. Performers whose background was thought to be even the least bit questionable were blacklisted by the organization and were unable to find employment in the industry until they "rehabilitated" themselves by going through a rigid 12-step process. The blacklist went to the heart of the commercial broadcasting system. Its founders threatened to boycott the products of advertisers who sponsored shows with suspected communists. The investigation techniques of Aware, Inc., were slipshod and deficient. Many innocent persons were put on the blacklist and had their careers permanently damaged.

More recent examples of pressure groups are easy to find. The public interest group Center for a Digital Democracy campaigned in 2003 against a proposed merger of ABC and CNN and threatened legal action if such a move was made. A

American television operates in a system that encourages producers to provide content that satisfies the largest number of viewers. This is the notion behind cultural democracy. By watching a certain program on a certain channel at a certain time, we "vote" for that program. As a result, the content that gets the highest rating is the content that endures and is imitated. This approach assumes that heeding the majority opinion of the TV audience is the best way to decide what content is of value.

This approach has intuitive appeal and seems consistent with the democratic ideals behind American society. It should come as no surprise that the cultural democracy concept is endorsed by many in the industry. But is it the best way to decide what programming gets aired? Do producers have an ethical duty to look beyond the numbers?

First, cultural democracy will inevitably lead to the lowest common denominator in programming. Shows that titillate and excite will draw bigger ratings than shows that make people contemplate. Perhaps programmers have a duty to society at large to present content of value that may not get the highest ratings.

Second, how can viewers register their dissatisfaction with current programming? Parents who think that certain programs are not desirable for their children can choose not to watch, but this action may not communicate their feelings to program producers. Dissatisfied viewers can write letters of protest and form watchdog groups (actions most viewers do not take); otherwise, cultural democracy allows little room for dissent.

Finally, cultural democracy makes it difficult for society to distinguish between content that is popular yet trivial and content that is important but lacks mass appeal. If value and worth are associated with popularity, then the unpopular will be perceived as valueless no matter what its intrinsic merit.

In today's ratings-driven television environment, it is easy to justify scheduling another clone of *American Idol* or *CSI* because that is what the public wants. Popularity, however, may not equal significance.

year earlier, Mothers Against Drunk Driving fought against a decision by NBC to air hard liquor ads. NBC eventually reversed itself and decided not to carry the ads. The Center for Media Education is active in monitoring how well local stations follow the FCC's regulations concerning children's broadcasting.

We can sum up by saying that there are both positive and negative aspects to the activities of these citizens' groups. On the one hand, they probably have made some media organizations more responsive to community needs and more sensitive to the problems of minorities and other disadvantaged groups. Citizen-group involvement with media organizations probably has also increased the feedback between audience and the media industry. On the other hand, these groups are self-appointed guardians of special interests. They are not elected by anyone, and their wishes may not be at all representative of those of the larger population. In addition, many of these groups have exerted unreasonable power, and some extremist groups, like Aware, may actually abuse their influence and do more harm than good.

>> Press Councils

Some of the general issues surrounding press councils, also called *news councils*, were discussed in Chapter 12. The idea of a press council originated in Europe. A press council is an independent agency whose job is to monitor the performance of the media on a day-to-day basis. In Great Britain, for example, the council consists of people with media experience and some lay members. It examines complaints from the public about erroneous or deficient press coverage. The council has no enforcement powers; if it finds an example of poor performance, the council issues a report to that effect. Unfavorable publicity is the only sanction the council can bring to bear.

The idea of a press council has not been popular in the United States. As mentioned in Chapter 12, a National News Council existed in the United States from

1973 to 1984 but was hampered by lack of media cooperation. There are, however, a few local news councils in operation. The most active one is in Minnesota.

>> **Education**

Education also exerts informal control over the media. Ethics and professionalism are topics that are gaining more and more attention at colleges and universities. In fact, there has been a recent upsurge of interest in teaching ethics at many schools of journalism and mass communication. About 40 percent of the schools in the United States offer a special ethics course to their students. More than half of the approximately 40 books specifically devoted to mass media ethics have been published since 1980. Numerous workshops and conferences on how to teach ethics were held during the 1990s. Most of the experts in this area agreed that instead of teaching specific codes of ethics to students, a systematic way of thinking about ethics should be stressed, so that individuals can consider issues and arrive at decisions rationally. In the wake of the Jayson Blair episode at the *New York Times* (see Chapter 4), it is likely that the emphasis on ethics training will increase even more.

Even this book can be thought of as a means of informal control. The hope is that, after reading it, you will bring a more advanced level of critical thinking and a more sensitive and informed outlook to your media profession or to your role as media consumer.

MAIN POINTS

- There are several types of informal controls on the mass media, including ethics, performance codes, organizational policies, self-criticism, and outside pressures.

- The most important ethical principles that provide guidance in this area are the golden mean, the categorical imperative, the principle of utility, the veil of ignorance, and the principle of self-determination.

- All the media have performance codes that guide professional behavior.

- Many media organizations have standards departments that monitor the content that is published or broadcast.

- The National Advertising Review Council is the main organization that supervises self-regulation in advertising.

- Outside pressures from advertisers can sometimes influence media conduct.

- Special interest groups, such as Action for Children's Television, have been successful in modifying the content and practices of the TV industry.

- Although they exist in many foreign countries, only a few press councils operate in the United States.

QUESTIONS FOR REVIEW

1. What are the main ethical principles discussed in the chapter?

2. Why was the NAB Code of Good Practice discontinued?

3. What is the difference between editorial policies and operating policies?

4. What is an ombudsperson? What does he or she do?

5. What are some ways advertisers can influence news content?

QUESTIONS FOR CRITICAL THINKING

1. How would you handle each of the examples mentioned in the introduction to the chapter?

2. What are some of the advantages and disadvantages of written codes of conduct?

3. Do special interest groups exert too much power over the media?

4. Do advertisers have too much power over the media?

5. Is it ever ethically correct to use deception to gather information for a news story? How would each of the ethical principles discussed in this chapter apply to this question?

KEY TERMS

golden mean (p. 420)
categorical imperative (p. 420)
utility (p. 420)
veil of ignorance (p. 421)

self-determination (p. 421)
acculturation (p. 424)
MPAA rating system (p. 429)
policy book (p. 433)

operating policies (p. 433)
editorial policies (p. 433)
ombudsperson (p. 435)

INTERNET RESOURCES

Online Learning Center

At the Online Learning Center home page, www.mhhe.com/dominick8, *select* Student Center *and then* Chapter 16.

1. Use the Learning Objectives, Chapter Outline, Main Points, and Time Line sections to review this chapter.

2. Test your knowledge of the chapter using the multiple choice, crossword puzzle, and flashcard features of the site.

3. Expand your knowledge of concepts and topics discussed in the chapter by going to *Suggestions for Further Reading* and *Internet Exercises.*

PowerWeb

At the Mass Communication home page of PowerWeb, www.dushkin.com/powerweb, *log in and select* Mass Communication *as your title. On the next screen, select* Topics *and then quick jump to* Ethical Issues. *Read Article 37, "Ethically Challenged." Then consider the following questions:*

1. If you were the managing editor of a newspaper, what would be your policy toward using material from other sources?

2. How has the Internet contributed to the problem of plagiarism?

3. How would a personal code of ethics be helpful in this area?

Surfing the Internet

There are few websites that deal with the topics discussed in this chapter, but the ones listed here are relevant.

http://jmme.byu.edu/
The home page of the *Journal of Mass Media Ethics.* Contains scholarly articles regarding issues of mass media and morality.

www.asne.org/ideas/codes/codes.htm
The American Society of Newspaper Editors has collected codes of ethics from about three dozen media organizations.

www.cme.org
This colorful site is the home page of the Center for Media Education, one of the special interest groups mentioned in the text. Contains a detailed description of the group's efforts in the area of children's television.

www.mpaa.org/caramap
Information about the MPAA movie rating system. Contains a database that lists the ratings of all recently released films.

www.poynter.org/classes/ethics.htm
The Poynter Institute's ethics page. Good for finding out the most current ethical issues.

www.spj.org/ethics/index.htm
The ethics page of the Society of Professional Journalists. Contains the latest ethics news and an "Ethics Hotline" that you can call for advice.

IMPACT OF
THE MEDIA

THE GLOBAL VILLAGE: INTERNATIONAL AND COMPARATIVE MEDIA SYSTEMS

This chapter will prepare you to

- recognize the global leaders in newspapers, radio, and television;

- distinguish among the four main theories of government-press relationships;

- categorize media systems by ownership patterns and the degree of government control;

- understand how politics, culture, geography, history, and economics affect a country's media system; and

- explain the media systems in Japan, Mexico, and China.

The crowd of cheering teenagers starts forming early in the afternoon. Many hold signs and banners. Some are dressed in outrageous costumes; a few have bought baked goods. All are clamoring for a chance to get into a broadcast of MTV's *Total Request Live*, or *TRL* as just about everybody calls it. This, however, is not just a typical weekday scene outside MTV's Time Square Studios. The signs and banners are in Italian, and just around the corner from the crowd of cheering teens is the Duomo, a huge Gothic cathedral that was built around the 14th century. These young people are trying to get into MTV's Italia studios in Milan where the local version of *TRL* is being televised to an audience of about 12 million Italians.

Environmentalist Rene Dubois is credited with coming up with the phrase "think globally, act locally" in the 1970s. He probably never envisioned that MTV would follow his advice on the way to becoming the world's biggest global television network.

MTV International has 38 channels, including MTV Italia, MTV India, MTV Latin America, MTV Russia, and MTV China. The programs go to 166 different countries in 18 languages.

Dave Berry is the host of the British version of *Total Request Live* broadcast from central London.

In combination with its sister networks, Nickelodeon and VH-1, MTV reaches about 1 billion 10 to 34 year olds; that is about one of every three people in the world in that age group. No other network even comes close to those numbers. (CNN International has an audience less than half of MTV's.) During the early years of the new century when almost all other media companies were struggling, MTV International saw profits soar.

How did MTV become so successful? It blended a global concept (popular music has universal appeal) with a local angle. To be sure, MTV promotes its share of American rock stars from J. Lo to Beyonce, but it also recognizes that audiences in other countries want to hear local talent. The VJs are drawn locally, and local artists are regularly featured. Taiwanese pop star Jolin Tsai, for example, has become a favorite on MTV China. MTV Russia is credited with launching the career of Tatu, two teens who have become favorites in Eastern Europe. In India, MTV plays the romantic soundtracks of local Indian movies. Nonmusic shows are also customized. MTV Italia runs *MTV Kitchen* on which rock stars talk about their music while cooking their favorite recipes. MTV Brasil televises *Rockgol,* a series of soccer matches between rock stars and executives from the recording industry.

About 40 years ago, media guru Marshall McLuhan predicted that mass communication would turn the world into a global village. Communication satellites, 24-hour global news channels, the Internet, and networks such as MTV have indeed made national borders blurry. But even if McLuhan's prediction about the global village is coming true, international success stories such as MTV's remind us that the villagers are still interested in their own local village.

This chapter first looks at international media systems, like MTV, that are designed to be distributed to other countries. Next, we will examine media systems as they exist in other nations.

INTERNATIONAL MEDIA SYSTEMS

The study of international mass media systems focuses on those media that cross national boundaries. Some media may be deliberately designed for other countries (as is the case with the Voice of Russia, the Voice of America, and the international edition of *Newsweek*); other media simply spill over from one country to its neighbors (as happens between the United States and Canada). Let us look first at those media designed for international consumption.

>> Global Print Media

Many newspapers provide foreign-language or international editions. The popular ones fall into two categories: general newspapers and financial newspapers. As far as United States– and British-based publications are concerned, the following were the leaders at the close of 2003:

- *The International Herald Tribune,* published by the *New York Times* and headquartered in France, has a worldwide circulation of more than 250,000, most of it in Europe. The paper, which recently celebrated its 100th anniversary, is printed in 19 cities around the world, including New York, Singapore, and Tokyo.

- *USA Today International* is a newcomer to the scene, with a circulation of about 300,000, again mostly in Europe. The Gannett-owned paper is printed in London, Frankfurt, Milan, and Hong Kong. Most of its readers are U.S. citizens traveling abroad. *USA Today* recently became available in Russia.

- *WorldPaper,* published by the World Times Company in Boston, is distributed as a newspaper supplement primarily in Latin America, Asia, and the Middle East. It is printed in 25 different countries and boasts a circulation of more than 1 million.

- *The Financial Times of London,* as its name suggests, specializes in economic news and has a circulation of about 300,000.

- *The Economist,* also based in London, carries financial news and analysis. Readily available in the United States, the weekly is printed in Virginia, London, and Singapore. It reaches about 800,000 readers.

- *The Wall Street Journal*'s international editions reach about 1 million people, mainly in Europe, Asia, and South America.

Other papers that enjoy international status are the *New York Times, Le Monde* (France), *El País* (Spain), *The Times* (Great Britain), *The Statesman* (India), and *Al Ahram* (Egypt).

The international flow of news is dominated by global news agencies. Reuters, Associated Press, Agence France-Presse, and ITAR-TASS are the biggest, but in recent years more specialized news organizations, such as the New York Times Syndicate and the Los Angeles Times Syndicate, have also become important.

As far as magazines are concerned, *Reader's Digest* publishes more than 45 international editions that are distributed to about 28 million readers in nearly 200 countries. Time Warner, in addition to publishing the international edition of *Time,* which is distributed in about 190 countries, also publishes *Asiaweek* and a newsweekly in Chinese. The international edition of *Newsweek* reaches about a half-million readers. Hearst Magazines International oversees the distribution of eight major titles—including *Cosmopolitan, Good Housekeeping,* and *Redbook*—in more than 100 countries. *Cosmopolitan* alone is sold in 31 countries, including Japan, Poland, and Russia.

Smaller special-interest magazines are also growing internationally. A Spanish-language version of *Popular Mechanics* is sold throughout Latin America. *Men's Health* publishes a British edition as well as one for South America (where it is called *Hombre Saludable*). Many business magazines, including *Business Week* and *Fortune,* also have significant foreign readership.

>> Global Broadcasting

About 150 countries engage in some form of international broadcasting. Many of these services are government run or at least government supervised. Others, like WRMI, Miami, are private operations supported by the sale of commercial time.

In the past, international radio broadcasting was done exclusively in the short-wave part of the radio spectrum (see Chapter 7). Although it goes a long distance, shortwave radio is hard to pick up and prone to interference problems. In an attempt to improve technical quality, major international broadcasters have been striking partnerships with locally operated FM stations. The Voice of America, for instance, has a network of 400 local stations in Latin America that rebroadcast its signal. Further, many international radio services are available in digital form on the Web or carried by satellite.

On the set of CNN International. During its news broadcasts, CNN International links together anchorpersons from CNN bureaus all over the world.

Listed here are the leading global broadcasters as of 2003:

- The World Service of the British Broadcasting Corporation (BBC) has a worldwide reputation for accurate and impartial newscasts because, in theory at least, it is independent of government ownership. Along with its news, the BBC also carries an impressive lineup of music, drama, comedy, sports, and light features. The BBC pioneered the international radio call-in show in which prominent people, such as Prime Minister Tony Blair, answer calls from listeners around the globe. The BBC broadcasts 1,120 hours per week in 43 languages and has about 140 million worldwide listeners.

- Voice of America (VOA), now in its fifth decade of operation, broadcasts 870 weekly hours of news, editorials, and features in more than 50 languages to an audience of about 95 million people, about half of them in Russia and Eastern Europe. The United States also operates Radio Free Europe and Radio Liberty. With the end of the Cold War, however, the long-term future of these two services is in doubt. The VOA is part of the International Broadcasting Bureau, which also includes Radio Martí, a special AM service beamed at Cuba; its TV counterpart, TV Martí; and the Worldnet TV service.

- Radio China International transmits about 1,400 hours of programming weekly in 43 foreign languages. Radio China International carried strident anti-American propaganda until the early 1970s, when improved relations led to a mellowing of its tone. Most of Radio China International's programming consists of news, analysis, commentary, and cultural information about China.

- Deutsche Welle (DW), "German Wave," broadcasts about 1,000 hours per week in 36 languages. DW's transmitters are located in Germany, Africa, and Asia. It has a large audience, particularly in Africa.

- Radio France International (RFI) broadcasts more than 300 hours a week to 45 million listeners, many on the African continent, in 20 languages. RFI programming consists of a blend of music, news, commentary, and locally produced features.

The biggest change in international broadcasting in recent years has been the proliferation of global news, sports, and music channels. The pioneer in this area was CNN, which now reaches thousands of hotel rooms and numerous cable systems in Europe, Africa, and Asia. CNN International (CNNI), started in 1990, reaches more than 150 million homes in about 200 countries. CNN International has been regionalized into four networks: CNNI for Europe, Africa, and the Middle East; CNNI for Asia; CNNI for Latin America; and CNNI U.S. CNN International has also started broadcasting newscasts in several local languages as well as in English. CNBC offers 24-hour business news to 147 million households in 70 countries worldwide. In addition, BBC World, a full-time news channel, is available in Europe, Asia, Africa, and some U.S. locations.

Sports and music channels also have audiences all over the world. As mentioned earlier, MTV is available almost everywhere, reaching more than

Rupert Murdoch's News Corporation is a vivid example of the international reach of one company. Table 17–1 is a partial list of the properties owned by the News Corporation grouped by geography.

Table 17–1   News Corporation Properties Throughout the World

	United States	Australia	Latin America	United Kingdom	Asia	Japan
Film	20th Century Fox	Fox Studios Australia	Fox Studios Baja			
TV	Fox Broadcasting Company	Fox Sports Australia	Sky Latin America	British Sky Broadcasting	Star Satellite Broadcasting	Sky Movies
Cable TV	Fox News Channel				Taiwan Cable	
Newspapers	New York Post	The Australian		The Sun	Fiji Times	
Magazines	TV Guide	Inside Out				
Book publishing	Harper Collins U.S.	Harper Collins Australia		Harper Collins U.K.		

In addition to the holdings in Table 17–1, the News Corporation has interests in the Los Angeles Dodgers baseball team, an Australian rugby league, the Staples Center in Los Angeles, a marketing company, a recording label (Festival Mushroom Records—the home of Dashboard Confessional), and a company that makes hardware for pay-TV systems. Once again, this listing is only a fraction of the total holdings of this company. In the global village it seems as if Rupert Murdoch is everybody's neighbor.

400 million households. ESPN International (ESPNi) is the biggest global provider of sports programming. Launched in 1988, the service is seen in more than 140 countries and territories and reaches about 90 million households. ESPNi serves Canada, Asia, Latin America, the Pacific Rim, Africa, and the Middle East. The News Corporation also operates satellite services that beam news and sports programming to more than 180 million viewers in Europe and Asia. The Cartoon Network, TNT, and the WB also have large global audiences.

>> Film and TV

American films still dominate the box offices of many foreign countries. Exporting films is big business. In 2002, film rentals from foreign countries amounted to more than $7 billion. About half of the revenue for an average film comes from the foreign box office. Some films even do better overseas than they do in the United States. *Terminator 3,* for example, made $148 million in the United States and $216 million overseas.

In addition, a good deal of electronic media traffic consists of films on video cassettes and DVDs that are shipped from one country to another and rented or sold to individuals for home viewing. In 2002 consumers outside the United States

MEDIA TALK

Why Is the United States Viewed So Poorly in the Arab World?

CD 2, Track 18, 2:32

This interview with *New York Times* reporter and Middle East expert Thomas Friedman was conducted in 2002. In the wake of the Iraq War and the continuing violence in Israel, how successful has the United States been in getting its message across? How could the United States improve its image in the Arab world?

spent about $20 billion on videocassettes and DVDs. This added revenue can add a significant amount to a film's bottom line.

The United States still dominates the international TV program market, but its influence is declining. Locally produced programs are becoming more popular. Plenty of American shows are popular worldwide, but they typically appear during the day or late at night. In a growing number of countries, prime time is dominated by local fare. Moreover, American shows do not do as well in the ratings as homegrown products. In Great Britain, for example, *Friends* gets an audience of about 2 million people, but the British-produced *Coronation Street* is typically seen by 15 million.

As more countries produce their own TV content, many U.S. production companies, especially those that produce game and reality shows, have concentrated on licensing formats to overseas producers who turn them into local versions. There are dozens of foreign variations of *Wheel of Fortune, Jeopardy, Who Wants to Be a Millionaire,* and *Temptation Island.* Many reality programs that have been successful on American TV originally came from other countries. *Big Brother* and *Fear Factor* came from the Netherlands, and *Survivor* first aired in Sweden.

Another aspect of international media is the problem of cross-border spillover. TV signals, of course, know no national boundaries, and the programs of one nation can be received easily in another country. The problem has caused some friction between the United States and Canada. Shows on ABC, NBC, and CBS are just as popular in Canada as they are in the United States, and they take away audiences from Canadian channels. Fearful of a cultural invasion of U.S. values and aware of the potential loss of advertising revenue to U.S. stations, the Canadian government has instituted content regulations that specify the minimum amount of Canadian content that must be carried by Canadian stations. Not surprisingly, spillover is also a problem on the crowded European continent. More than a third of TV viewing time in Finland, Ireland, and Belgium is spent watching programs from another country's TV service. In Switzerland, 60 percent of viewing is "out-of-country."

WORLD MEDIA ONLINE

The Internet has come the closest to fulfilling McLuhan's global village concept. The World Wide Web provides access to worldwide media on a scale never before possible. Radio stations in other countries, for example, are available on the Net. A scan of websites in early 2003 found stations in Japan, the Philippines, Hong Kong, Russia, Brazil, Great Britain, and many other countries broadcasting on the Net. Live TV programs from other countries have yet to become common on the Web, but the major international and domestic TV systems in many countries have websites that contain general information and programming highlights as well as live video.

Individuals who want to read newspapers or magazines from other countries now have a wide selection at their disposal. In addition to the U.S. papers that have an international readership, such as the *New York Times* and *The Wall Street Journal,* papers from France (*Le Monde*), Germany (*Die Welt*), Great Britain (*London Times*), Japan (*Asahi Shimbun*), Australia (*Sydney Morning Herald*), and many other

News from Russia is easily available on the Web. Interfax Russia has subscribers in more than 100 countries.

countries make available online versions as well. International magazines that have established websites include *Asia Week, Asia Online, New Woman* (Great Britain), *Beat* (Australia), *Der Spiegel* (Germany), *Playmen* (Italian equivalent of *Playboy*), *Tokyo Journal* (Japan), and *Art Bin* (Sweden).

Furthermore, e-mail has made it possible to send messages across the globe in seconds. Many newsgroups are devoted to news about international events and other cultures, and people all over the world have web pages that can be visited directly.

We need to keep in mind, however, that although it is called the *World Wide Web*, this new medium is far from globally accessible. In 2003, it was estimated that around 600 million people were online. This sounds like a large number, but it represents less than 10 percent of the world's population. The global village is most accessible to those in the developed countries. More than 180 million are online in North America compared to just 4 million in Africa.

 COMPARATIVE MEDIA SYSTEMS

Let us now turn our attention to media systems as they exist in individual nations. Before we start, we should note that the media system that exists in a country is directly related to the political system in that country. The political system determines the exact relationship between the media and the government. Over the years, several theories have developed concerning this relationship. In the sections that follow are examples of these theories in operation.

>> Theories of the Press

Since the 16th century, scholars and philosophers have attempted to describe the relationship between the government and the media and its implications with regard to freedom and control. Over the years, as political, economic, and social conditions have changed, various theories of the press have developed to articulate and explain this relationship. All theories, however, fall somewhere between two "isms" that reflect polar opposites in the amount of control the government exerts over the media—authoritarianism and libertarianism (see Figure 17–1). Current theories of the press represent modifications of these two fundamental principles. Let us look at each of them.

The **authoritarian theory** arose in 16th-century England about the same time as the introduction of the printing press in that country. Under the authoritarian system, the prevailing belief was that the ruling elite should guide the masses, whose intellectual ability was held in low esteem. Public dissent and criticism were considered harmful to both the government and the people and were not tolerated. Authoritarians used various devices to force compliance of the press, including licensing, censorship of material before publication, the granting of exclusive printing rights to favored elements of the press, and the swift, harsh punishment of government critics.

The **libertarian theory** is directly opposed to authoritarianism. Libertarians assume that human beings are rational and capable of making their own decisions and that governments exist to serve the individual. Libertarians believe that the common citizen has a right to hear all sides of an issue to distinguish truth from falsehood. Since any government restriction on the expression of ideas infringes upon the rights of the citizen, the government can best serve the people by not interfering with the media. In short, the press must be free from control.

The libertarian theory fit well with the freewheeling political climate and rugged individualism of early America. By the mid-20th century, however, two world wars and a depression had changed world politics, media industries had become big business, and broadcasting had made it possible to reach millions of people instantaneously. As a result, new theories of the press emerged. In 1956, a book entitled *Four Theories of the Press* reexamined the libertarian and authoritarian philosophies and described two more modern approaches. The **social responsibility theory** (also referred to as the *Western concept*) incorporates part of the original libertarian approach but introduces some new elements as well. This approach holds that the press has a right to criticize government and other institutions, but it also has a responsibility to preserve democracy by properly informing the public and by responding to society's needs and interests. The press does not have the freedom to do as it pleases; it is obligated to respond to society's requirements. The government may involve itself in media operations by issuing regulations if the public interest is not being adequately served. The regulation of broadcasting by the Federal Communications Commission is a good example of this latter provision. The United States, Japan, Britain, and many other European countries are examples of countries that subscribe to this theory.

FIGURE 17–1

Theories of Media-Government Relationships

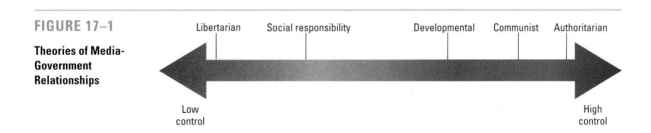

Libertarian | Social responsibility | Developmental | Communist | Authoritarian

Low control

High control

"The Repeal, or the Funeral Procession, of Miss-Americ-Stamp." Colonial newspapers operated under an authoritarian philosophy as practiced by the British government. This English cartoon, published in 1766, satirized the repeal of the Stamp Act, an attempt to suppress hostile opinion by placing a tax on the pages of colonial newspapers.

The other theory spelled out in *Four Theories of the Press* is the **communist theory.** This theory is a variant on the authoritarian scheme. The media are "owned" by the people as represented by the state. Their purpose is to support the Marxist system and to achieve the goals of the state as expressed through the Communist Party. Recent history has shown the communist approach to the press works best in a closed society in which information is tightly controlled by the government. Once information is available from competing sources, people give little credibility to the official media.

This fact was illustrated by events in Russia and Eastern Europe at the end of the 1980s. The British Broadcasting Corporation (BBC), Voice of America, CNN, Radio Liberty, and Radio Free Europe unraveled the Communist Party's media monopoly. TV viewers in Eastern Europe saw Western TV shows beamed from West Germany or sent via satellite. Hollywood movies on videocassette were widely available. The people of Eastern Europe and Russia saw the shortcomings of their political and economic systems and clamored for change. As a result, the communist theory of the press has few proponents today. China, Cuba, and North Korea are about the only places where it can be found, and even in those countries the official version of the theory often bears little resemblance to the actual practices of the media. In short, the communist theory has been rendered obsolete by events.

A more recent formulation is the **developmental theory,** which would fall more toward the authoritarian side of the spectrum. In this ideology, the government mobilizes the media to serve national goals in economic and social development. Information is considered a scarce natural resource and must be carefully managed by the government to achieve national goals. Some of the goals the media are expected to help achieve include political integration, literacy, economic self-sufficiency, and the eradication of disease. The notion of developmental journalism was one of the central issues in the debate about the New World Information Order.

Until recently, many emerging countries espoused the developmental approach, but changing economic and political conditions have made it less prevalent. Many emerging countries, such as Brazil, Chile, and Pakistan, have replaced dictatorships with democracies, and democracies typically look with disfavor upon government control over the media. In addition, even in those countries where democracy has yet to appear, such as Kenya, the government has either privatized the formerly state-run media or allowed competition from independent channels. Consequently, the government has less control over the flow of information and is less able to pro-mote the developmental approach. All in all, the growth of democracy and the growing popularity of free marketplace economics have resulted in more countries endorsing the social responsibility approach.

>> Control and Ownership of the Media

One helpful way of distinguishing among the various media systems throughout the world is to classify them along the dimensions of (1) ownership and (2) con-trol. Finnish Professor Osmo Wiio has developed a useful analysis scheme, pre-sented in Figure 17–2. As can be seen, ownership can range from private to public (*public ownership* usually means some form of government ownership), and con-trol can range from centralized to decentralized. Note that this typology is an oversimplification. In many countries, there are mixed media systems in which part of the broadcasting system is owned by the government and part by private interests. In some countries, the print media could be placed in one cell of the matrix and the broadcasting system in another. Nonetheless, this model is helpful for displaying some of the major differences among systems.

In the upper-left cell are type A systems. These represent decentralized control and public ownership, a type best illustrated by the broadcasting systems in European countries such as France, Denmark, and Italy. Some of the broadcasting media are publicly owned, but no single political or special interest group can con-trol their messages. In Great Britain, for example, the British Broadcasting Corporation is a government-chartered, publicly owned corporation that is rela-tively immune to government censorship and interference. Private broadcasting systems also operate in these countries.

FIGURE 17–2

Typology of Media Ownership and Control

From "The Mass Media Role in the Western World" by Osmo A. Wiio in *Comparative Mass Media Systems* by L. John Martin and Anju Grover Chaudhary. Copyright © 1983 by Longman Inc. Reprinted by permission of Allyn and Bacon.

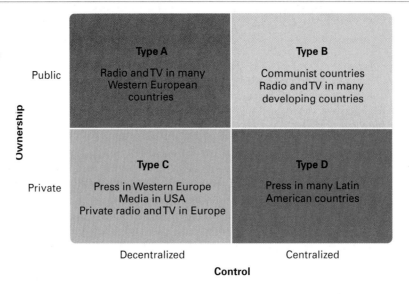

In the upper-right cell are type B systems. This arrangement is typical of communist or socialist countries in which the media are publicly owned and controlled by the dominant political party. China is an example.

In the lower-left cell is the decentralized-control, private-ownership model. This is the system that currently operates in the United States and in many European countries. The media are owned by private companies, and there is little, if any, centralized control.

The lower-right cell is the centralized-control, privately owned system. In many countries, particularly the developing countries of Africa and Latin America, the media are owned by private organizations but are firmly controlled by the government.

Far fewer countries today would fall into cell B of the matrix than would have five years ago. Only a handful of nations still exemplify the communist or socialist media model. (Cuba, China, and North Korea are examples.) In these countries the ruling party exercises control, and freedom of the press belongs to the state, not to the media. Communist countries feel that it is necessary to speak with one voice, and antigovernment or antiparty criticism is forbidden.

Press control is exercised in several ways. First, the government controls the source. Printing and broadcasting equipment are given only to approved organizations. In Cuba, for example, there is a newsprint shortage and only the government newspaper is supplied with it. Next, journalists are state trained and state approved. Finally, news agencies are state owned and news sources state controlled.

Those countries that have abandoned the communist philosophy have generally moved into cells A and C of the matrix. The state-run media organizations have seen much of their control taken away, and private media outlets are permitted. Individual media outlets are given much more freedom to criticize the government.

The most significant trend in those countries that fall into cell A of the matrix has been a move toward pluralism in their broadcasting systems. State-owned monopolies in many countries, including France, Italy, Greece, Spain, and some of the Scandinavian countries, have given way to privately owned and commercially sponsored broadcasting systems. In addition, cable promises to bring even more video diversity to these countries.

>> Role of the Media in Various Countries

The role of a mass media system in a given country will differ according to its place in the typology. For example, as mentioned, in many developing countries where there is strong centralized control over the media, the principal role of mass communication is to help develop and build the nation. It is not surprising that many less-developed countries are concerned primarily with economic and political development. This concern is translated into a rather focused definition of the role of mass media. In general, the media are expected to help further modernization or other national goals. In fact, a new term, *developmental journalism*, has been coined to describe this philosophy. In short, **developmental journalism** means that the role of the media is to support national interests for economic and social development and to support objectives such as national unity, stability, and cultural integrity.

On the one hand, developmental journalism entails finding ways to make abstract stories about commodity pricing, agriculture, and educational goals understandable to readers and to highlight the developmental goals achieved by the nation. On the other hand, developmental journalism can also mean that the press refrains totally from any criticism of the government and prints only what the government deems helpful to its cause. The philosophy of many Asian, Latin American, and African developing nations falls somewhere between these two conceptions of developmental journalism.

The role of the media under the communist theory is straightforward: They are tools of propaganda, persuasion, and education. They function only secondarily as sources of information and entertainment. This philosophy dates all the way back to Lenin, who decreed that the communist press was to help further the revolution.

As we saw in Chapter 2, Western media inform and entertain, but their content is somewhat different from that of communist and less-developed nations' media. Most of the information carried by the media in the Western democracies is geared to the specific political and economic needs of the audience. An examination of the press in the United States and Canada, for example, would reveal a large amount of news about the local and national government, some of it unfavorable and critical. The role of government watchdog, based on the ideas presented in the social responsibility theory, is a function that would be unsettling to many of the countries in cells B and D of the matrix in Figure 17–2. Moreover, a great deal of content in the Western media is consumer oriented, consisting of advertising, news, and entertainment. Further, there is, relatively speaking, little regulation of the content of the entertainment media. Aside from some regulations governing pornography and prohibitions against certain content on the broadcasting media, the government takes little interest in entertainment content.

It is the interpretation or editorial function in which the biggest differences are found. The United States and other Western countries have a tradition of press freedom that recognizes the right of the media to present ideas to try to persuade the audience to some point of view. The philosophy of the **free marketplace of**

ideas is endorsed by most countries in cells A and C of Figure 17–2. All relevant ideas concerning an issue are examined in the media, and a "self-righting" process occurs. Given the autonomous nature of the Western media, it would be difficult for the government to mobilize the media to support some national goal, as is typically done in developing and communist countries. There is a built-in tension and adversarial relationship between press and government that makes such efforts rare.

>> Economic Differences

In the United States, advertising plays a key role in media support (see Chapter 14). Newspapers, magazines, radio, and television all derive a significant amount of their total income from the sale of advertising time or space. Direct government subsidy or support of the media is minimal, limited to the funds given to public broadcasting. (Of course, the government also indirectly helps support the media by buying a lot of advertising.) In Western Europe, several countries provide indirect subsidies to the media, such as cheaper mailing privileges and tax concessions. Some Scandinavian countries have a system whereby newspapers controlled by various political parties are given direct financial assistance. Several different systems are used to support broadcasting. In the United Kingdom, for example, the British Broadcasting Corporation (BBC) is state chartered and gets its operating funds from an annual license fee paid by the owners of TV sets. At the same time, the independent TV networks make their money from the sale of advertising time, in much the same way their U.S. counterparts do. Many other Western countries follow this same model.

It is difficult to generalize about the means of economic support for media in less-developed countries. Where the print media are privately owned, money comes from circulation fees and advertising. Publishers are generally free to keep all profits, but in many countries space must be provided free of charge for government announcements. Advertising and license fees are the two major sources of income for broadcasting.

In those few communist countries that still exist, most economic support for the media comes directly from the government. Since the media are state owned, money for their operation is simply set aside from the government's budget. Because of this subsidy, the single-copy costs of newspapers and magazines tend to be cheap. Advertising used to be a minuscule source of income in communist countries, but recently communist governments welcomed it as an important revenue stream.

EXAMPLES OF OTHER SYSTEMS

Let us now take a more detailed look at the mass media in three different countries. One is an industrialized nation, Japan. The second is Mexico, a developing nation, and the third is China, a communist country.

>> Japan

More than 127 million people live on this nation of islands. Japan's geography, culture, history, and economy have shaped its current media system. Education is highly valued in Japan, where the literacy rate is nearly 100 percent. This has helped the country develop a strong print media industry.

CRITICAL / CULTURAL ISSUES

Cultural Imperialism?

Cultural domination refers to the process in which national cultures are overwhelmed by the importing of news and entertainment from other countries—mainly from the United States and other industrialized nations. Residents of many countries are concerned that their national and local heritage will be replaced by one global culture dominated by U.S. values. They point out that American music, books, TV shows, and films are popular around the world. Many are fearful that audiences will become persuaded to adopt the values portrayed in this content—capitalism, materialism, consumption, and so forth. As a result, many countries, including Canada, Spain, and France, have placed quotas on the amount of foreign material that can be carried on their broadcasting systems.

The notion of cultural domination also spills over into the news area. For many years, the representatives of many developing nations have been arguing for a New World Information Order. They point out that the existing flow of news is one way: from the industrialized West to the developing nations, sometimes referred to as the *Third World*. Under such a system, say the developing countries, news from the Third World is scant, and what news there is reflects unfavorably upon the developing nations. For example, what do you know about South America? Most people will mention two things—revolutions and drugs—the two topics that dominate the news coverage. Most know little else about the whole continent. To remedy this imbalance, developing countries have advocated controls over the news and content that come across their borders. A resolution reflecting this philosophy was passed by the United Nations Educational, Scientific, and Cultural Organization (UNESCO) in the 1980s. The United States looked with disfavor on this proposal, and it was one of the factors that prompted the United States to withdraw from UNESCO back in the mid-1980s.

Is this charge of cultural imperialism a valid one? One claim of those who urge a New World Information Order has substance. News coverage of Third World nations is unbalanced. In response, the Western media have attempted to report more non-Western news and have started programs to train journalists of former Third World countries. In addition, several other alternative news agencies have developed—including the Inter Press Third World News Agency, the South North News Service, and the Pan African News Agency— that supplement and enlarge the coverage of the major Western news organizations.

Any consideration of this debate must also acknowledge that the whole controversy has economic implications. Those who champion the free flow of information across borders also champion their right to profit from the sale of their products across borders. Those who advocate controls in the name of avoiding cultural domination are also assuring themselves of less competition in the marketplace. If a country limits foreign television programs to 30 percent of its schedule, the other 70 percent must be produced locally. How much of the cultural imperialism debate is based on principle and how much on cash is hard to determine.

The cultural imperialism argument seems to assume that people in other countries are weak and simply absorb and accept cultural messages. One of the key things that the critical/cultural analysts point out is that the audience is anything but passive. It is likely that audiences in other cultures pin their own meanings and interpretations on media content. Those in other countries will reinterpret what they receive in light of their own culture and personal experiences.

The changing world political scene and the increasing trend toward market-driven economies and less oppressive governments have increased support for the Western model. The proponents of the New World Information Order received considerable backing from the Soviet Union and the communist countries of Eastern Europe. Now that these countries have changed governments, there is less support for the notion of increased media control. Consumers the world over seem to welcome the changes.

Those who campaign against cultural imperialism contend that American values are becoming dominant. This raises the question of exactly what American values are. The United States is currently experiencing a wave of multiculturalism, and the heritages of many ethnic and racial groups have influenced the cultural tastes and values of the entire country. In the music area, for example, reggae—which came from Jamaica—found a following among white Americans and went on to influence the development of African-American rap music. Is the global popularity of rap a manifestation of Jamaican, African-American, or white American values?

1. To what extent do you agree that American media products can influence the traditional values held in other societies?

2. If you were a political leader in another country, would you favor quotas on the amount of foreign material that could be broadcast? Why or why not? Does it depend on what country you are thinking about? Why or why not?

3. What foreign content have you seen in/on American media, and what have you learned about other cultures from that content?

There are more than 120 newspapers in Japan with a combined circulation of about 70 million, a total that exceeds that of U.S. papers. Japan has more than 10 newspapers with circulation above the million mark, and the United States has three. Some of the major national newspapers are *Yomiuri Shimbun, Asahi Shimbun,* and *Mainichi Shimbum.* (As you may have deduced by now, *shimbun* is the Japanese word for newspaper.) The *Yomiuri Shimbun* has a daily circulation of about 14 million, making it the world leader. For comparison, *USA Today* has a circulation of about 2 million. Along with the national papers, Japan supports many other regional and local dailies. Tokyo alone has a dozen newspapers, several of them in English.

As in other countries, however, newspaper readership is declining, especially among younger readers. Competition from the Internet, video games, cell phones, and television has made it difficult for newspapers to attract a younger audience. Again, much like their counterparts in the United States, the major Japanese newspapers have websites that have contributed little to the bottom line.

Japan also has two newsmagazines and an influential business magazine. Leisure and lifestyle publications are popular. Asian editions of familiar publications such as *Time, Forbes,* and *Reader's Digest* are widely available. Comic books in Japan sell millions of copies every year. These publications, although they bear a surface resemblance to American comics, are deeply rooted in Japanese culture and are read by young and old.

Broadcasting in Japan started in the 1920s when the Japanese government adopted the British model of a noncommercial system headed by a public corporation. Commercial broadcasting started after World War II, a result in part of the influence of the American forces who occupied the country. Japan's economy has helped it become one of the world's leaders in the development of electronic media, and Japan has one of the most technologically advanced broadcasting systems in the world.

The state-run noncommercial Japan Broadcasting Corporation (*Nippon Hoso Kyokai,* or NHK) is patterned after the BBC. It has an annual budget of more than a billion dollars, all of which comes from a license fee imposed on all TV sets in Japan—$50 a year for a color TV and $30 for a black-and-white set. Competing with the three NHK channels are five commercial TV networks and two satellite channels. (The most viewed networks are commercial ones: Fuji Television, Nippon TV, and the Tokyo Broadcasting System, but NHK is not far behind.) TV and radio reach virtually 100 percent of the population as 11,000 transmitters blanket the country. Almost all the programs on Japanese TV are locally produced. American series do not do well in Japan. About 28 percent of all Japanese homes are equipped for cable. At present, however, cable is used to retransmit regular TV into areas that suffer poor TV reception. About 85 percent of all homes have VCRs or DVD players, and the video software business is booming.

Because of its mountainous terrain, Japan pioneered the development of a direct broadcast satellite (DBS) system. NHK has spent about $2 billion in DBS research and now operates two satellite channels that beam entertainment, sports, movies, music, and specials direct from satellite to living room. NHK's system has about four million subscribers, but other privately operated satellite systems are struggling to stay in the black. Japan was one of the pioneers of HDTV. However, NHK backed an analog system of HDTV, which has since been surpassed by the digital version (see Chapter 10). In early 1997, NHK finally announced that it too was backing a new digital system.

After many years of growth, commercial TV broadcasters in Japan ran into problems in 2002 and 2003. On top of a long recession that hurt advertising revenue, the commercial TV industry was faced with mounting costs connected with a planned conversion from analog to digital TV. Interestingly enough, NHK, the public broadcasting organization, was doing fine thanks to its guaranteed annual income from the license fee.

American films tend to dominate the Japanese box office, but recently some locally produced movies have provided some unexpected competition. Sony, the huge Japan-based conglomerate, is heavily involved in making Hollywood movies through its Sony Pictures Entertainment unit. *Bad Boys II* and *Charlie's Angels: Full Throttle* are two of the studio's recent releases.

Japan has been a leader in developing new technologies. As we have already discussed, cell phone use, especially text messaging, is extremely popular in Japan, and many people rely on their cell phones to connect to the Internet. Speaking of the Internet, 73 companies provide Internet service to about 56 million Japanese, about 45 percent of the population. The comparable figure for the United States is about 60 percent.

Clearly, the digital revolution has come to Japan. Newspapers and magazines are searching for ways to make money from their online versions; TV networks are struggling with the transition from analog to digital, and the influence of the Internet and mobile media is growing. In sum, Japan is a media-rich country whose media industries face many of the same problems and challenges found in Great Britain and the United States.

>> Mexico

The media situation in Mexico is typical of that of many developing countries. It demonstrates some of the many challenges faced by nations as they strive to form indigenous systems. The media system in Mexico has been influenced by economics, politics, and geography. A country with 104 million inhabitants and a literacy rate of 90 percent, Mexico has been saddled with massive foreign debt and high inflation. Sharp divisions exist between the rich and the poor. Many urban areas are characterized by relative prosperity, and some rural areas are mired in poverty. Literacy is higher in the cities than in the countryside. Moreover, various governments have taken different attitudes toward the media, vacillating between strict control and relative leniency. Finally, Mexico's media system always operates in the shadow of its neighbor to the north, the United States.

Mexico has approximately 300 daily newspapers. Total daily circulation is about 10 million. For many years the *Excelsior,* published in Mexico City, was the country's leading newspaper. Ownership and labor problems, however, have plagued the newspaper in the last two or three years. Some provincial newspapers, such as *El Norte* in Monterrey are also influential. Most large newspapers have their own websites.

Mexico publishes more than 200 periodicals. Media conglomerate Televisa is the world's largest publisher of Spanish-language magazines, including many that are aimed at Hispanics living in the United States. Televisa's best known publication is the women's magazine *Vanidades.*

Freedom of the press has a checkered history in Mexico. For many years the government kept the press in check by controlling the national supply of newsprint. Publications that were critical of the government often found their supply of paper cut off. The government also controlled broadcasting permits and could force radio and TV stations off the air if their reports offended the regime. Finally, the government and ruling political party exerted power by bribing journalists.

After the turn of the century, however, the situation seems to be changing. A new political party came into power and promised press freedoms. A survey by the World Association of Newspapers, a group that monitors press freedom, found that government reforms had improved the situation but that there was still more reform needed.

Radio broadcasting developed in Mexico about the same time as it did in the United States. An official broadcast service signed on in 1923, and the model followed was heavily influenced by the U.S. system. In addition to state-run educational and cultural services, a system of private ownership of stations and commercial support was instituted. During the 1950s, the state sold most of its stations to private interests. Today, there are more than 800 commercial radio stations and only 50 noncommercial stations, along with a dozen commercial networks.

Television broadcasting was modeled directly on the U.S. system. It began as a commercially supported private enterprise, but a 1960 law dictated that TV had to perform certain social functions, such as fulfilling moral principles and preserving human dignity. Government became more involved in TV during the 1970s when an agreement with station owners set aside 12.5 percent of the broadcast day for government-produced programs. The government also acquired a Mexico City station as an outlet for its programs.

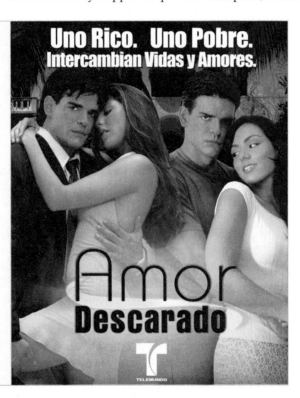

A typical scene from one of the steamy *telenovelas* popular in Mexico and other Spanish-speaking countries.

The private television and radio sector is dominated by Televisa, which controls about 70 of the 120 TV stations in the country. Televisa is the parent company of Univision, a U.S. Spanish TV network, and Televisa produces and exports *telenovelas*, the Spanish versions of U.S. soap operas, which are tremendously popular throughout Latin America.

For most of its existence, Televisa held a virtual monopoly on TV broadcasting, sometimes reaching 95 percent of all Mexican TV homes. In the past few years, however, it has faced competition from TV Azteca, which was government owned until it was sold to a private firm in the mid-1990s. Broadcasting a program lineup that featured racy *telenovelas*, TV Azteca attracted about 20 percent of the audience in 2002, and some big advertisers were abandoning Televisa in favor of the younger network.

Some U.S. TV programming is popular in Mexico, but, as in many other countries, the top-rated shows are generally Mexican productions of situation comedies or telenovelas. Some American shows that were carried by Mexican TV in

2002 are *The Simpsons, Sabrina the Teenage Witch,* and *Charmed.* Reality programs came late to Mexico with a local version of *Big Brother* premiering in 2003.

VCR and DVD player penetration tops 60 percent, one of the highest figures in Latin America. About 18,000 different video releases are available in video rental stores. Like many developing countries, Mexico has a problem with pirated video-tapes and DVDs. One authority calculated that about 25 percent of all videos for rent in Mexico City are pirated copies.

U.S. films do well in Mexico. The *Harry Potter* and *Lord of the Rings* series of films were box office leaders in 2002 and 2003. Some recent films made in Mexico, such as *El Crimen del Padre Amaro* and *Y Tu Mamá Tambien* got favorable critical reviews and were also box office successes in the United States. The Televisa con-glomerate also has interests in the Mexican film industry through its efforts in financing and producing films. The company also owns a chain of movie theaters.

The growth of new media has been slow in Mexico. About 3 percent of the population has access to the Internet. Cell phones have been adopted more rapidly, but as of 2003 they were in the hands of less than 20 percent of the population. Nonetheless, cell phone use is expected to grow rapidly.

In sum, the media scene in Mexico is changing. More competition is present and long-time giant Televisa is losing a little of its dominance. In addition, Mexico's proximity to the United States has had many effects. Although a good deal of news and entertainment content flows from the United States to Mexico, there is now a significant flow in the other direction. The large Mexican-American population in the United States constitutes an enthusiastic audience for Mexico's media. In fact, although hard figures are difficult to find, it is likely that Mexico exports more media content to the United States than does any other nation. This trend is likely to continue.

>> China

The media in China have been expanding rapidly, particularly in the past 20 to 25 years. The past decade or so, with some exceptions, has seen a trend toward less government control and a more diverse media landscape. This trend is due in part to China's move toward a free-market economy and a greater dependence on advertising to support the media. Owners of many print and broadcast outlets are responsive to profit-and-loss considerations and act accordingly. As a result, the marketplace rather than the Communist Party is now the major influence on the content of Chinese media.

The country has about 2,000 newspapers, many started since 1980, with a combined circulation of more than 200 million. China has five national newspapers. The party-controlled *People's Daily* once dominated newspaper circulation, but since 1980 its circulation has dropped from 7 million to 2 million. Three other papers, *Xinmin Evening News, Yangcheng Evening News,* and the *Yangzi Evening News,* boast circulations of more than 1 million. One English-language paper, *China Daily,* is aimed at foreigners living in China and interested foreigners living in America and Europe. Business and sports publications have proliferated, and China now publishes more than 100 financial newspapers. Xinhua, the Chinese state-run news service, has 80 overseas bureaus and transmits more than 50,000 words every day to Chinese media.

For decades state-owned newspapers enjoyed a captive audience. People who worked for the Chinese government, a large number of the workforce, were forced to subscribe to government publications. Recent reforms have done away with

Newspapers in China are sometimes posted in public places for passersby to read. *(Stone/Dave Saunders)*

this practice, and it is expected that the *People's Daily,* the official newspaper of the Communist Party, will see its circulation tumble even more. Additionally, there is a proposal to change the current status of China's newspapers and magazines from cultural units administered by the government into independent legal entities that depend on profits to continue operations.

The relaxation of government media control has prompted many independent newspapers to start operation. The government's more liberal attitude toward the press was demonstrated during the SARS virus outbreak in 2003. After some initial hesitation, Beijing encouraged newspapers to pursue the story aggressively and many did just that. This renewed spirit has helped these publications succeed in attracting both readers and advertising revenue. In 2003, newspaper advertising revenue topped the $2.5 billion mark.

The total number of magazines published in China is probably somewhere near 10,000. *Look* and *How,* the two most popular magazines, attract significant advertising revenue. In addition, Chinese editions of popular titles, such as *Elle China* and *Business Week China*, are best-sellers.

Most Chinese live in rural areas where literacy rates are lower than in cities. Consequently, many people rely on radio for news and entertainment. The country's 600 radio stations reach more than 95 percent of the population. China National Radio administers two national radio networks that broadcast on the AM, FM, and shortwave bands, and a third national network provides an FM-only service. Many local communities also have their own FM stations.

Television in China showed remarkable growth during the 1980s and the 1990s. As of 2003, TV penetration was around 90 percent, or about 325 million households, making China the largest television market in the world. China Central Television provides 11 channels with 200 hours of programming every day. CCTV-1, the primary service, broadcasts news, entertainment, and special events. The other channels are more specialized, featuring science, children's programming, and music. In addition to CCTV, there are several thousand local and regional TV stations.

The trend toward a free market economy has encouraged the growth of TV advertising. Commercials are now a common sight on Chinese TV, and experts

The students in Iran who demonstrated against the country's government in the summer of 2003 were mobilized by an unlikely source: TV stations in Los Angeles.

Four Iranian TV stations in L.A. beam satellite broadcasts into Iranian homes. The government tightly controls the media in Iran, and the only news that the people receive is filtered through the ruling regime. The authorities do their best to keep out opposing viewpoints. Owning a satellite dish is forbidden in Iran. Many have been arrested for receiving foreign news programs, and the Iranian government has tried repeatedly to jam the signals of the L.A. stations. Nonetheless, it is estimated that about 25 million Iranians, about one of every three people, have access to the outlawed stations. The L.A.–based programming is often recorded on videotape and distributed on the Internet.

The stations offer a wide range of programs. Newscasts that focus on the situation in Iran, not surprisingly, are favorites. But the stations also broadcast music, commentary, and even an occasional comedy skit that makes fun of the mullahs who rule the country. During the uprisings in Teheran, the four stations aired live phone calls from people in Iran describing the demonstrations and urging other Iranians to protest against the government.

For their part, the rulers in Iran see the L.A. stations as subversive and dangerous. They label them tools of the CIA and urge Iranians not to watch. The Iranian minister of information charged that America was waging psychological warfare against Iran.

What should be the official position of the United States toward such activity? The situation in which privately owned broadcast stations in the United States directly encourage subversive activity in another country is unprecedented. U.S. lawmakers have voiced strong support for the democracy movement in Iran but have declined to pass legislation for money to help support the broadcasts. The United States does support Radio Farda, a Persian-language station that broadcasts into Iran, but like the VOA, Radio Farda's charter mandates it to be factual and to refrain from stirring local unrest. Should the United States channel money to support these stations? Do they serve a national interest? Or do these stations simply make it more difficult for traditional diplomacy to succeed? How would the United States react if a foreign country used the satellite to broadcast programs urging civil unrest to various minority groups in the United States? These are just some of the problems that crop up in the global village.

---

predict that advertising revenue will continue to grow thanks to China's entry into the World Trade Organization and the Beijing Olympics scheduled for 2008.

Despite its more liberal attitudes, the Chinese government occasionally takes steps to limit what can be shown in the country. State regulations limit local stations to no more than 25 percent imported programming. Foreign news programs are typically not allowed to be shown in China. Moreover, the government can take over TV networks if they violate local rules. The government also controls the installation of satellite dishes that can receive Western programs.

China has a fairly active motion picture industry, much of it centered in Hong Kong. In 2002, about 100 movies made in China were released. Competition from foreign films is limited by a quota that allows no more than 20 films to be imported per year. Despite this restriction, most of the top Hollywood films are shown in China. An occasional Chinese film, such as *Crouching Tiger, Hidden Dragon,* co-produced with Sony, is successful in the United States.

Internet penetration is low in China, about 4 percent in 2002, but this figure is misleading because many Chinese access the Internet through cybercafes. The Chinese government has maintained a cautious attitude toward the new medium. On the one hand, China needs the Internet if it wants to continue its economic growth. On the other, the Internet has the potential to give Chinese citizens access to information that the government thinks is undesirable. As a result, China periodically cracks down on Internet users. In 2001, for example, the government closed down more than 17,000 cybercafes because the cafes did not block Internet access to sites the government labeled subversive.

Mobile media are also slowly becoming popular. About 10 percent of the population has a cell phone. Despite their small numbers, cell phones have played an important role in communication. The earliest news of the SARS outbreak in China was not carried by the mainstream media but was spread by individuals sending text messages on their cell phones.

In the years to come, it is likely that the trend toward a free marketplace economy will continue to have an impact on China's mass media. In turn, the mass media may also influence the country's political climate.

In sum, the media systems in these three countries illustrate the varying influences that economics, culture, geography, and politics have on the development of mass communication systems. Because of these and other factors, each nation will create a media system that is best suited to its own needs.

MAIN POINTS

- Communications across international boundaries have increased in the past two decades.

- Newspapers designed for international consumption include the *International Herald Tribune*, *USA Today International*, and financial papers. Many magazines also have international editions.

- Global radio broadcasters include the Voice of America, the BBC, Radio China International, Deutsche Welle, and RFI.

- The leaders in global television are CNN, MTV, ESPN, BBC World, and CNBC.

- Comparative analysis of media systems allows us to view alternative ways of structuring the mass media.

- The four main theories of government-press relationships are authoritarian, libertarian, social responsibility, and developmental.

- Media systems can be categorized by examining ownership patterns and degree of government control.

- The development of media systems in various countries is influenced by politics, culture, geography, history, and economics.

- The media systems in Japan, Mexico, and China illustrate how the theories of government-press relationships have operated in other countries and how numerous factors have affected those systems.

QUESTIONS FOR REVIEW

1. Name the major international newspapers and broadcasting services.
2. Compare and contrast the four major theories of the press.
3. Distinguish between public and private ownership of mass media.
4. What is developmental journalism?
5. How has geography shaped the mass communication systems in Japan, Mexico, and China?

QUESTIONS FOR CRITICAL THINKING

1. Why has MTV become such an international phenomenon? What factors influence the international success of a television program?

2. Strictly speaking, the term *global village* is an oxymoron. What are some ways today's international communication system is different from that of a traditional village? Is there another metaphor that is more appropriate?

3. Given the ubiquity of the Internet, is it possible for any nation today to use the authoritarian approach?

4. American media products are easily available in other countries. What media products from other countries are easily available here? Why is there such a difference?

5. As China moves more and more toward a free-market economy, what will happen to the country's media system?

KEY TERMS

authoritarian theory (p. 449)
libertarian theory (p. 449)
social responsibility theory (p. 449)

communist theory (p. 450)
developmental theory (p. 450)

developmental journalism (p. 453)
free marketplace of ideas (p. 453)

INTERNET RESOURCES

Online Learning Center

At the Online Learning Center home page, www.mhhe.com/dominick8, *select* Student Center *and then* Chapter 17.

1. Use the Learning Objectives, Chapter Outline, Main Points, and Time Line sections to review this chapter.

2. Test your knowledge of the chapter using the multiple choice, crossword puzzle, and flashcard features of the site.

3. Expand your knowledge of concepts and topics discussed in the chapter by going to *Suggestions for Further Reading* and *Internet Exercises.*

PowerWeb

At the Mass Communication home page of PowerWeb, www.dushkin.com/powerweb, *log in and select* Mass Communication *as your title. On the next screen, select* Topics *and then quick jump to* International News. *Read Article 13, "The View from Abroad." Then consider the following questions:*

1. Why do U.S. media give so little attention to foreign news?

2. Is it possible to cover objectively a conflict in which your own country is involved?

3. Have you ever sought out foreign news media to see how the news is reported in the rest of the world? Why or why not?

Surfing the Internet

Many sites deal with international mass communication in general, and many others are the home pages of international media. Those listed here are a sampling of both.

www.aib.org.uk
The home page of the Association for International Broadcasting. Contains links to many international broadcasting stations.

www.bbc.co.uk/worldwide/television/html
BBC Worldwide Television handles the international operations of the BBC. This is part of the general BBC website.

www.cctv.com/english/
Home page of China Central Television. Includes a program schedule.

www.iht.com
Home of the *International Herald Tribune,* "The World's Daily Newspaper."

www.ipl.org/reading/news/
The Internet Public Library has links to online papers in every region of the globe.

www.mtv.com/mtvinternational/
Check out the various configurations of all the foreign MTV networks. Find out what is the number-one music video in India and generally keep up-to-date with this website.

www.tvradioworld.com
A directory of Internet radio and TV stations that includes the major international outlets.

18

SOCIAL EFFECTS OF MASS COMMUNICATION

This chapter will prepare you to

- explain how scientists use surveys and experiments to study the effects of mass communication;

- describe how the media can serve as an agent of socialization;

- explain why advertisers need to show special consideration for children;

- discuss the impact of televised violence;

- define the *agenda-setting effect* and *agenda building;*

- explain how the media can help crystallize a viewer's political choices; and

- describe how the Internet may affect social involvement.

Early one Sunday morning in July 2003, three teenagers dressed in black outfits and armed with machetes, rifles, shotguns, and more than 2,000 rounds of ammunition tried to hijack a car in the Philadelphia suburb of Oaklyn, New Jersey. Despite their armament, the carjack attempt failed, and their intended victim called the police, who captured the trio without incident. Subsequent interrogation of the teens revealed that they had planned to "execute" three students from a local school and then go on a random shooting spree.

Further investigation uncovered that the three teens were big fans of the *Matrix* movies, and their black outfits were patterned after the one worn by Keanu Reeves in the films. The leader of the trio was fascinated with the movie and often wore his hair slicked back and referred to himself as Neo, in reference to the main character. The storyline of the three films in the *Matrix* trilogy posits that reality is an illusion created by machines that have taken over the world. A few select humans, including Neo, have become aware of the illusion, which is a computer program called *The Matrix,* and by entering the program consciously they undertake a violent fight for survival against the machines.

The Matrix has been blamed for several acts of imitative violence.

This was not the first time the *Matrix* films had been linked to violent behavior. In February of the same year, a 19-year-old Virginia resident, who also owned an outfit similar to Neo's and kept a poster of him on the wall of his room, bought a shotgun similar to the one Neo uses in the film and shot to death his father and mother. He then calmly called the police. Lawyers for the teenager said that he believed he was living inside the Matrix.

In Ohio a woman killed her landlady because she thought the landlady was drugging her and invading her dreams in an attempt to suck her into the Matrix. The movie might also have played a part in the string of sniper killings in the Washington, D.C., area in 2002. Suspect Lee Boyd Malvo apparently was obsessed with the movie and kept a journal in his jail cell in which he wrote, "Free your mind, you are a slave to the matrix control. Free yourself of the matrix control."

These incidents set off another round of debate about the antisocial effects of media violence. The controversy is not new. In 1993 a young child was killed when a 5 year old, apparently inspired by episodes of *Beavis and Butthead,* set fire to the family house. In 1999, a fan of the violent computer game "Duke Nukem" killed three people in a local movie theater in an apparent recreation of a scene in the game.

These examples (and these are only the recent ones; there are more that span five decades) highlight the dramatic power that the media sometime possess. Typically, of course, the effects are not that strong. Millions watched the *Matrix* movies and did not commit acts of violence; not everybody who plays "Duke Nukem" commits murder. Nonetheless, the media have the potential to influence what the audience knows, thinks, and does. Accordingly, this chapter concentrates on the social effects of mass communication. The first part looks at the impact of media on people's attitudes, knowledge, and perceptions. The second part examines how the media affect the way people behave. Before we discuss these effects, however, we need to examine how they have been investigated.

INVESTIGATING MASS COMMUNICATION EFFECTS

There are many ways to investigate what is or is not an effect of mass communication. Some people claim that personal observation is the best way to establish proof. As we noted in Chapter 2, the critical/cultural analysts focus on the various meanings that audience members construct from specific texts. Others rely on expert opinions and evaluations; still others point to common sense when they wish to support their views. All these methods are valuable, but this chapter will focus on the results of scientific studies of the media's impact on individuals. Keep in mind, however, that the scientific approach is only one of many ways to examine this topic.

When it comes to gathering information about media effects, scientists have typically used two main methods:

1. A **survey** is carried out in the real world. It usually consists of a large group of individuals answering questions put to them via a questionnaire. Although the survey is usually not sufficient proof of cause and effect, it does help establish associations. A special kind of survey, a **panel study,** enables

researchers to be more confident about attributing patterns of cause and effect in survey data. The panel study collects data from the same people at two or more different points in time. As a result, it is possible, for example, using sophisticated techniques that control the effects of other variables, to determine if viewing televised violence at an early age is related to aggressive behavior at a later date. Panel studies are expensive and take a long time to complete.

2. An **experiment** is performed in a laboratory and usually consists of the controlled manipulation of a single factor to determine its impact on another factor. A special kind of experiment, a **field experiment,** is conducted in a real-life setting. Experiments are useful because they help establish causality.

In the remainder of this chapter, we will focus on scientific findings about the effects of media on knowledge, attitudes, perceptions, and behavior.

EFFECTS ON KNOWLEDGE AND ATTITUDES

The dividing line between attitudes and behaviors is fuzzy. In many instances, we can only infer that an attitude or perception exists by observing relevant behavior. Thus, many of the studies mentioned in this section involve the measurement of *both* behavior and attitudes.

We will examine five topics that have generated the most research interest:

1. the role of the media in socialization,
2. cultivation analysis,
3. the impact of TV advertising on children,
4. agenda setting, and
5. media exposure and cognitive skills.

>> Media and Socialization

In Chapter 2, we defined *socialization* as the ways in which an individual comes to adopt the behavior and values of a group. In this section, we will concentrate on the socialization of children. Socialization is a complex process extending over a number of years and involving various people and organizations, called **agencies of socialization,** who contribute in some degree to the socialization process. Figure 18–1 presents a simplified diagram of some of the more common agencies.

FIGURE 18–1

Agencies of Socialization

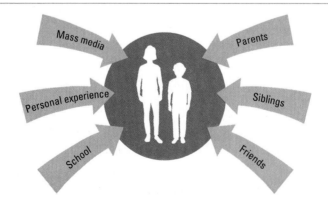

Could a media celebrity, such as Britney Spears, serve as an agency of socialization for young women? Could she influence their attitudes about what body type is desirable and what behaviors are appropriate for teens?

In many situations, the media's contribution to socialization will be slight. Parents might have greater influence ("Eat your spinach; it's good for you"). So might friends ("Don't be a tattletale"). So might direct experience ("I'd better not take my sister's stuff because the last time I did, she popped me one").

On the other hand, the media, especially television, may play an important role in socialization when it comes to certain topics. Let us now look at evidence pinpointing some of these areas.

≫ The Media as a Primary Source of Information

Learning is an important part of the socialization process, and the media serve as important sources of information for a wide range of topics, especially politics and public affairs. For example, a survey of sixth and seventh graders found that 80 percent named a mass medium as the source of most information about the president and vice president, 60 percent named a mass medium as the primary source of information about Congress, and half named a mass medium as the chief information source about the Supreme Court.

Other research has shown that the media, primarily TV, serve as primary information sources for many age groups about a wide range of topics. More than 90 percent of Americans cited television as their primary source of information about the September 11 terrorist attacks. Television is the source of most information for local and congressional elections. This phenomenon is not limited to political and public-affairs information. There is reason to believe that media presentations, including those in entertainment programs, are important sources of information on topics such as occupations, crime, law enforcement, alcohol and drug usage, the environment, and minorities. One recent study of high school students, for example, found that about 2 in 10 students listed rock music as an important source of information about moral values and that 1 of 4 specified it as an important source of information about interpersonal relationships.

≫ Shaping Attitudes, Perceptions, and Beliefs

The mass media also play an important role in the transmission of attitudes, perceptions, and beliefs. Several writers have suggested that, under certain conditions, the media (especially TV) may become important socialization agencies in determining the attitudes of young people. Specifically, TV will be an influential force when the following factors are operative:

1.   The same ideas, people, or behaviors recur consistently from program to program; that is, they are presented in a stereotyped manner.

For a number of years, social scientists have been studying the way communication channels function during momentous news events. Research that examined how Americans learned about the death of President Franklin D. Roosevelt, the assassination of President John F. Kennedy, and the explosion of the space shuttle *Challenger* has led scientists to draw conclusions about how news spreads or diffuses across society in times of social trauma.

Surveys focusing on the diffusion of news about the terrorist attacks of September 11, 2001, have contributed new information about the process. Consistent with prior studies, these surveys found that interpersonal channels were important when it came to first hearing about the event. Surveys conducted shortly after September 11 disclosed that between 30 and 50 percent of the audience first learned about the attacks from another person, either by telephone, by e-mail, or in person. Only about 5 percent of the audience would hear about typical news events from another person.

Not surprisingly, television is the mass medium that was the initial source of information for most people. Between 40 and 50 percent first heard the news from TV. Radio was the first source for about 20 percent. Only a few people first read about the news on the Internet.

The news diffused quickly. One survey found that almost everybody had heard about the attacks within two hours after they occurred. News about the Kennedy assassination spread at approximately the same speed.

After learning of the attacks, about 8 of 10 people turned to television for further information, spending about seven hours watching news about the events. The Internet played a secondary role to television as a source of additional information. One reason for this was the fact that some people had trouble accessing the Internet due to the increased traffic sparked by the attacks. About 25 percent of those with Internet access went online after the incident, and most of those spent fewer than 30 minutes online.

Once the news of the attacks had sunk in, the interpersonal channels opened up again as people apparently felt the need to talk with others about what was happening. One survey found that about half of their sample phoned family members, and another reported that about the same number sent e-mail messages after the attack.

In sum, these results indicate that in times of national trauma both the mass and interpersonal channels function as important sources of information for the audience. (For more information about this topic, see Bradley Greenberg (Ed.), *Communication and Terrorism: Public and Media Responses to 9/11*, Cresskill, N.J.: Hampton Press, 2002.)

2. A child is heavily exposed to TV content.
3. A child has limited interaction with parents and other socializing agents and lacks an alternative set of beliefs to serve as a standard against which to assess media portrayals.

All this means that, under certain conditions, TV will be an influential force in shaping what children think about certain topics. Complicated though the task is, some researchers have identified some of the conditions, the topics, and the children to which this theory applies. Moreover, they have specified some of the effects that may result when television does the socializing.

Creating Stereotypes   In the study of media socialization, it is helpful to identify consistent themes or stereotypes present in media content. For instance, consider how television programs typically portray law enforcement and crime. Programs about crime and law enforcement are a staple of prime-time television; between 20 and 35 percent of all program time consists of shows dealing with cops and criminals. However, the large percentage of law enforcement characters portrayed on TV does not accurately reflect the actual percentage employed in this capacity in real life. Furthermore—on television, at least—crime doesn't pay. One study found that some 90 percent of TV crimes were solved; real-life law enforcement agencies are not nearly as effective.

Television also overrepresents violent crimes, such as murder, rape, and armed robbery. One study found that violent crime accounted for about 60 percent of all TV crimes in one week of programming. To put this figure in perspective, consider that only 10 percent of crimes in the real world are violent. Last, television emphasizes certain aspects of the legal system (ask a young fan of any police show to name an arrested suspect's rights) but ignores others (ask that same young fan what happens at an arraignment or what the functions of a grand jury are).

The war in the Persian Gulf and the September 11 attacks focused attention on the way Arabs had been portrayed in the mass media. Content analyses of TV revealed that Arab men were typically portrayed via three main negative stereotypes: (1) terrorist, (2) oil sheik, and (3) Bedouin. Arab women were rarely seen and, when they appeared at all, were shown as belly dancers or members of a harem (harems were never common and none exist today). And how many Arab children have you seen on *Sesame Street?*

In summary, there appears to be evidence that the TV world often presents images that are at odds with reality. Stereotyping has also characterized, in addition to police dramas, sex-role portrayals, the depiction of occupations, methods of problem solving, portrayals of scientists, and the depiction of mental illness.

The Effects of Heavy Viewing   It seems probable that youngsters who are heavy TV viewers would display a pattern of beliefs and perceptions consistent with media portrayals. The earliest research in this area, completed in the 1930s, found that frequent viewing of crime and gangster movies could change attitudes on topics such as capital punishment and prison reform. More recently, other researchers have noted a connection between heavy viewing of violent TV programs and favorable attitudes toward the use of violence in real life. Further, children who are heavy viewers of cops-and-robbers TV programs are likely to believe that police are more successful in apprehending criminals than are children who are not fans of these shows.

Do TV programs such as *The Bernie Mac Show* represent the most important source of information about African American families for white viewers? Mass media researchers are interested in how television influences socialization.

In other areas, several studies have linked high levels of television viewing with attitudes favoring traditional sex roles. In other words, children who are heavily exposed to television are more likely to feel, among other things, that men make better doctors and that women make better nurses or that raising children is a job for women rather than men.

To be fair, we must again stress that this type of research *assumes* but does not necessarily *prove* that the mass media play a significant part in creating the attitudes held by these youngsters. Surveys can only highlight associations, not prove causality. Although some experimental evidence points to the media as the cause of certain attitudes, we cannot entirely rule out other interpretations. Nevertheless, it is likely that the link between media exposure and certain attitudes demonstrates reciprocal causation. What this means is best shown by an example. Watching violent TV shows might cause a youngster to hold favorable attitudes toward aggression. These favorable attitudes might then prompt him or her to watch more violent TV, which, in turn, might encourage more aggressive attitudes, and so on. The two factors might be said to be mutually causing one another.

The Absence of Alternative Information   Although research evidence is less consistent in this area than in others, it appears that, under some circumstances, television can affect young people's attitudes about matters for which the environment fails to provide firsthand experience or alternative sources of information. One survey that examined the potential impact of TV on dating behavior found that teenagers are more likely to turn to TV for guidance when they have limited real-life experience with dating.

Where media influence is indirect, it is difficult to pinpoint. This is particularly true when the media operate simultaneously with other agencies of socialization and when interpersonal channels outweigh media channels in forming attitudes and opinions. In the area of politics, for instance, the media probably supply youngsters with information and viewpoints that are subsequently commented on by parents and friends. Political beliefs and attitudes evolve out of this double context. In such cases, the socializing impact of parents and other interpersonal sources is more important than that of the media. One study dealing with attitudes toward police found that, although children spend a great deal of time watching TV cop shows, friends and family are the important socializing agents. The point is this: The media play a significant role in socialization. Sometimes this role is easy to detect; sometimes it is indirect and harder to see; at still other times it is apparently slight. Clearly, numerous factors are influential in determining how a child comes to perceive the world. The media (and television, in particular), however, have become important factors in the socialization process.

>> Cultivation Analysis

Directly related to socialization is an area of research called **cultivation analysis.** Developed by George Gerbner and his colleagues at the University of Pennsylvania, cultivation analysis suggests that heavy TV viewing "cultivates" perceptions of reality consistent with the view of the world presented in television programs. Cultivation analysis concentrates on the long-term effects of exposure— on both adults and children—rather than on the short-term impact on attitudes and opinions.

Methodology   The first stage in cultivation analysis is a careful study of television content to identify predominant themes and messages. Not surprisingly, television portrays a rather idiosyncratic world that is unlike reality along many dimensions. For example, television's world is usually populated by a preponderance of males: Two-thirds to three-quarters of all leading characters are men. Moreover, television overemphasizes the professions of—and, as previously mentioned, overrepresents the proportion of workers engaged in—law enforcement and the detection of crime. Last, the TV world is a violent one—around 60 to 80 percent of all programs contain at least one instance of violence.

Step two examines what, if anything, viewers absorb from heavy exposure to the world of television. Respondents are presented with questions concerning social reality and are asked to check one of two possible answers. One of these answers (the "TV answer") is in line with the way things are portrayed on television; the other (the "real-world answer") resembles actual life. Here is an example:

> *What percentage of all males who have jobs work in law enforcement and crime detection? Is it*
>
> _____ *1 percent or* _____ *10 percent?*

On television, about 12 percent of all male characters hold such jobs. Thus 10 percent would be the TV answer. In reality, about 1 percent are employed in law enforcement; thus, 1 percent is the real-world answer. The responses of a large sample of heavy TV viewers are then compared with those of light TV viewers. If heavy viewers show a definite tendency to choose TV answers, we would have evidence that a cultivation effect is occurring.

Research Findings   Is there evidence to suggest such an effect? Most findings suggest that among some people, TV cultivates distorted perceptions of the real world. In one survey of approximately 450 New Jersey schoolchildren, 73 percent of heavy viewers compared with 62 percent of light viewers gave the TV answer to a question about the number of people involved in violence in a typical week. Youngsters who were heavy viewers were also more fearful about walking alone at night in a city. They overestimated how many people commit serious crimes, how often police find it necessary to use force, and how frequently police have to shoot at fleeing suspects.

Other cultivation research has focused specifically on college students. In one study, students' exposure to pornography was examined to see if stereotyped perceptions were being cultivated. Among males, those who were heavy users of pornography were more apt to report that they had less confidence in females doing certain jobs (e.g., mechanic, mayor). They also tended to agree more with stereotypes of sexuality ("Men have stronger sexual urges than women; women say 'no' to sex when they don't really mean it") than did light users. These relationships stood up even after rigorous statistical controls removed possible influences of other factors. Women showed no such effects from exposure. A 1993 study found that college students who had high exposure to televised portrayals of sexual behavior thought those behaviors happened more frequently in real life than did students with lower levels of exposure.

How many real-life high school principals are like the principal in *Boston Public?* Cultivation analysis would suggest that for some heavy viewers, TV portrayals might influence their perceptions of real-life events.

The island nation of Fiji did not get television until 1995, when a local TV station began broadcasting shows such as *ER*, *Seinfeld*, and *Melrose Place*. In the years that followed, there was an increase in bulimia and other eating disorders among young Fijian girls, disorders that were rare before the arrival of TV. In addition, there was a big jump in the number of females dissatisfied with their body image. A 1998 survey turned up the fact that three of four female teens on the island reported feeling too big or too fat.

An anthropologist who has studied the Fijian culture since 1998 attributed these changes to the influence of television. The traditional Fijian female body type has been one that has been described as "robust" and "well muscled."

American TV shows, however, portray the ideal body type as thin and wispy. Fijian teen girls apparently believed that this body type was the one that was preferred in the modern world and tried to emulate it.

The Fiji case illustrates that TV shows contain more than just entertainment; they also embody the social values of the nation that produces them. As this book went to press, no follow-up anthropological study had been published that updated these research findings. An updated study would be interesting because the following shows were available on Fiji TV in late 2003: *Scrubs* (featuring Heather Locklear), *Baywatch,* and *Sex and the City.*

Although the results of cultivation-analysis studies are evocative and fascinating, conclusions are clouded by three problems. First, it is difficult to determine cause and effect. For example, does heavy TV viewing cause people to be fearful of walking alone at night, or does being fearful cause them to stay home and watch more TV?

The second problem concerns the fact that people differ in ways other than their TV viewing habits. Consequently, factors other than TV watching might affect the differences in perceptions and attitudes between heavy and light viewers. When certain factors that appear relevant to the cause-and-effect relationship (such as age, sex, and education) are statistically controlled, one factor at a time, the association between TV watching and perceptions is evident but somewhat weakened. When two or more factors are controlled simultaneously (e.g., examining the relationship between TV viewing and anxiety while simultaneously controlling for effects of both sex and age), some overall relationships disappear. We cannot conclude, however, that a relationship does not exist. In fact, recent research indicates certain subgroups will show a cultivation effect and others will not.

Gerbner and his associates, for example, have detected a phenomenon they have labeled **mainstreaming,** whereby differences apparently due to cultural and social factors tend to diminish among heavy–TV-viewing persons. They have also found evidence for what they call **resonance,** a situation in which the respondent's real-life experiences are congruent with those of the television world, thereby leading to a greater cultivation effect.

Third, technical decisions about the way TV viewing and attitudes are measured can have a significant impact on findings. For example, the precise wording of the questions has been shown to be important. In addition, some researchers argue that exposure to a particular kind of program (e.g., violent shows) gives a more accurate picture of cultivation than simply measuring overall TV viewing. Others note that deciding on the number of hours of viewing that differentiates high and low viewers has a bearing on the magnitude of cultivation.

Perhaps the most comprehensive summary of cultivation research is a 1997 review of more than 5,600 findings collected over two decades. The authors of this review found that there was evidence of a small but persistent cultivation effect that may have significance for the social, cultural, and political climate. As the authors concluded, "Certainly not all of the [cultivation] issues are resolved, but, taken as a whole, the data show that cultivation theory has amply demonstrated the nature, importance, and resilience of its findings."[1]

To sum up and perhaps oversimplify, we can say that, although not all mass communication scholars are totally convinced by the reasoning underlying cultivation analysis, a growing body of evidence suggests that the cultivation effect is indeed real for many people.

>> Children and Television Advertising

If you have ever watched Saturday morning television, you are probably familiar with Tony the Tiger, Captain Crunch, Count Chocula, Ronald McDonald, and Snap, Crackle, and Pop. This is not surprising because, by the time you graduated from high school, you had already seen about 350,000 TV commercials. A typical child will see about 20,000 commercials every year, mostly for toys, cereals, candies, and fast-food restaurants. During the 1970s, the citizens' group Action for Children's Television brought this issue to the attention of the Federal Communications Commission (FCC) and the Federal Trade Commission (FTC). By the early part of the 1980s, most people had accepted the notion that children deserve special consideration from television advertisers, for the following reasons:

1. Children are a vulnerable audience and should not be exploited by TV advertising.
2. Children, especially younger children, might be deceived by TV techniques that make products appear more desirable than they really are.
3. The long-term effects of exposure to TV ads might have a negative effect on a child's socialization as a future consumer.

Using this threefold division, we will examine some of the many research studies that have investigated the effects of TV advertising on children.

Vulnerability of the Audience   Adults can easily distinguish commercials from regular TV programs, but what about children? Research suggests that children from 5 to 8 years of age can separate ads from the rest of a program, but they have little idea as to the purpose of the ads. Older children (from 9 to 12) are better able to identify ads and are aware that their purpose is to persuade people to buy things. Partly as a result of these findings, in 1974, the FCC concluded that some device was needed to clearly separate commercials from programs. Current programs aimed at children use such signals as "We will return after these messages" or "We now return to [name of show]." Experiments have shown that these program separators are not effective with kids under the age of 5 but are somewhat effective with older children.

Effects of Special Selling Techniques   When you were much younger, you may have had an experience like the following. On Saturday morning, while watching your favorite cartoon show, you saw an ad for a toy, perhaps a plastic model truck called "Toughie." In the ad, the truck, with headlights flashing and horn blowing, was shown dumping a load of sand in the middle of a miniature construction site,

---

[1]This review was done by Michael Morgan and James Shanahan and appears on pages 1–46 of *Communication Yearbook,* edited by Brant Burleson and published by Sage.

The typical child sees up to 20,000 commercials in a year, many for popular games and toys. The impact of television advertising and its role in consumer socialization is a popular research topic.

surrounded by miniature construction workers. The truck was then shown close up, practically dwarfing the young child in the background. Excited, you told your parents that Toughie was the one thing you wanted most for Christmas. When Christmas arrived and you were lucky enough to find Toughie under the tree, you were disillusioned to find that the actual truck was much smaller than it had appeared to be on TV. The headlights did not flash and the horn did not blow because batteries were not included with the truck. There was no sand, no miniature construction site, no tiny construction workers. Somehow, it was not the same toy that you remembered.

It is obvious that toys and other products designed for children can be made to look more appealing through the use of special camera angles, lenses, advertising copy, sound effects, animation, and special lighting techniques. The ability of children to distinguish the illusion created by these techniques from the real object has been an area of continuing interest among policymakers and mass communication researchers. Recently, in response to tighter industry guidelines, commercials directed toward children have included disclaimers, messages such as "Some assembly required" or "Batteries not included" or "Accessories sold separately," which are read by an announcer and/or flashed on the screen. Some critics have argued that these disclaimers are not understood by children, and several research studies have examined this area.

The effects of these special selling techniques on children are hard to summarize. At least one study found that children who saw a commercial that purposely exaggerated the appeal of a building-block game were more disappointed with the game than were children who saw an ad with a more realistic depiction. Other research has shown that the wording of product disclaimers is an important factor. Young children, for example, were far more likely to understand that a toy required some assembly when they heard a disclaimer that said "You have to put it together" than when they heard the standard "Some assembly required" disclaimer.

Consumer Socialization Consumer socialization includes all those processes by which children learn behaviors and attitudes relevant to their future behavior as consumers. Research in this area is not clear-cut, but we can make some generalizations. First, as children get older, they tend to distrust commercials and even become cynical about them. One study revealed that the percentage of youngsters who believed commercials declined to only 7 percent by the fifth grade. Second, exposure to TV commercials is not related to consumer skills, such as price comparisons. Watching a lot of commercials on TV does not make a person an intelligent consumer.

We have seen in this brief review that some criticisms voiced by public-interest groups such as Action for Children's Television appear to be supported by research. Some children, especially younger ones, have trouble understanding the basic intent of advertising. As a child matures, repeated exposure to commercials evidently results in disillusionment and cynicism about the merits of advertising. This whole topic raises questions about regulation. Ideally, organizations such as the Federal Trade Commission and the Federal Communications Commission will construct a public policy on advertising for children in the near future.

>> Agenda Setting

One influence of mass media that has turned up in many studies of mass communication is the **agenda-setting effect.** (An agenda is a list of things to be considered or acted upon.) When we say that the media have an impact on agenda setting, we mean that they have the ability to choose and emphasize certain topics, thereby causing the public to perceive these issues as important. To paraphrase Bernard Cohen in his book *The Press and Foreign Policy,* we can say that the media may not always be successful in telling people what to think, but they are usually successful in telling people what to think about.

Agenda-setting studies typically concern themselves with information media: newsmagazines, newspapers, television, and radio. Much of the research on agenda setting has been carried out during political campaigns. There are two

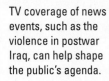
TV coverage of news events, such as the violence in postwar Iraq, can help shape the public's agenda.

reasons for this. First, messages generated by political campaigns are usually designed to set agendas (politicians call this tactic "emphasizing the issues"). Second, political campaigns have a clear-cut beginning and end, thus making the time period for study unambiguous.

One typical agenda-setting study was an investigation of the 1968 presidential election, which asked a sample of voters to rank what they believed to be the key issues of the campaign. While this was going on, researchers examined newsmagazines, newspapers, and television newscasts, and they prepared a ranking of campaign issues according to the time and space the media devoted to each issue. When the media's ranking was compared with the voters' ranking, there was a strikingly high degree of correspondence. In other words, the voters perceived as important those issues that the media judged important, as evidenced by the amount of coverage they received. Similar studies of more recent elections have found similar results. Although such studies strongly suggest a relationship between personal agendas and media agendas, they do not address the question of causation, an issue that we have encountered before.

Some studies indicate that there are situations in which the direction of cause and effect is unclear—or will even depend on the medium under consideration. At least two studies report that newspapers exert a greater agenda-setting effect than does television. In fact, one survey found that, during a political campaign, television appeared to alter its coverage to conform to voter interest, and newspapers appeared to shape the voters' agendas.

Recent reviews published in scholarly journals noted two new directions of research interest. The first pertains to the notion of **framing,** the general way a news topic is treated by the media. This line of research posits that not only do the media tell us what to think about, they also tell us how to think about it by the way the story is framed. For example, suppose Congress is considering changes in the food stamp program. One way the media might frame this story is by concentrating on both the increased efficiency that might result from the changes and the savings to taxpayers. Alternatively, the media might choose to emphasize the hardships that might be experienced by people who will no longer qualify for the program. The particular choice of frames will affect the saliency of the story and our attitudes toward the revised program.

A second direction concerns **agenda building.** Research on this topic examines how the media build their agenda of newsworthy items. Some factors that seem to have an impact are presidential press conferences, congressional hearings, and public relations efforts. One recent study, for example, found that a public relations effort by the Christian Coalition was influential in shaping the media agenda some three months later. Another recent study suggested that a journalist's own personal agenda (the issues that he or she considers important) might also have an impact on the media agenda.

MEDIA EFFECTS ON BEHAVIOR: A SHORT HISTORY

The political effects of the mass media, especially radio, prompted much of the early research. Many people feared that a skilled political demagogue might use the new medium of radio to gain political power. As a result, large-scale studies were conducted during the 1940s to gauge the extent of media influence. Somewhat surprisingly, these early surveys found that the media had little direct effect on political decision making. Personal influence was more important, and individuals labeled "opinion leaders" were thought to be more important in transmitting political orientations.

The explosive growth of TV during the 1950s and 1960s shifted the research focus to young people. Early large-scale surveys noted that television could influence children's values and perceptions of the world. In addition, the new medium might adversely affect social relationships and skills necessary for success in school. The impact of media portrayals of violence was of special concern as evidenced by Senate subcommittee hearings on the topic in 1961 and 1964. In 1967, a national commission concluded that a steady diet of media violence had "an adverse effect on human character and attitudes."

The topic was revisited again in 1970 when the United States Surgeon General issued a report that linked exposure to TV violence with antisocial behavior. A 1982 follow-up study reinforced the conclusions of the original report. Media violence remained the center of attention during the 1990s. As mentioned in previous chapters, the Telecommunications Act of 1996 contained provisions for program ratings and a V-Chip that enabled parents to block violent and other unwanted programming from their TVs. In the wake of the 1999 shootings at Columbine High School, several bills to regulate TV and movie violence were introduced into Congress, but none became law.

Franklin D. Roosevelt used radio effectively as a political communications tool during his "fireside chats" with the nation. The increasing importance of radio as a tool prompted several large-scale studies during the 1940s.

We will next examine more closely some of the topics mentioned in the summary, beginning with the topic that has generated the most research attention, the effects of TV violence.

THE IMPACT OF TELEVISED VIOLENCE

Does television viewing prompt violent or other antisocial behaviors on the part of the viewer? As we have just seen, this question has been debated for the better part of four decades. It is a complicated issue, and the absolute answer has not yet been found. Nonetheless, enough evidence has been gathered so that we can begin to point to some preliminary conclusions. To arrive at these conclusions, we must examine research data from surveys and from experiments.

>> Survey Results

Table 18–1 contains abbreviated and modified questionnaire items taken from surveys designed to analyze the viewing of TV violence and aggressive behavior.

As you can see, with measures such as the ones in the table (assuming, of course, a questionnaire that was much longer), it would be possible to index a person's viewing of programs that generally contain violence. It would also be possible to measure that same person's tendency to report his or her willingness to use violence in everyday situations. If viewing violent TV does affect behavior, we would expect to find some relationship between reported heavy viewing of violence and an individual's own self-report of aggressive tendencies. If we do not find such a link, we might assume that exposure to media violence has no impact on subsequent aggressive tendencies. If, however, we do find a connection, we might suspect that media violence actually causes aggression. We could not be sure, however, because survey data alone are not sufficient to establish a cause-and-effect relationship. We must also keep in mind that there are different ways of measuring exposure to TV violence and aggressive tendencies.

Viewed as a whole, surveys compiled over the years are difficult to summarize. Perhaps the most concise generalization is one that appears in a recent summary of television research findings. After carefully analyzing all survey results, the authors of this summary "conclude that the evidence to date indicates that there is a significant correlation between the viewing of violent television programs and aggressive behavior in day-to-day life."

Nevertheless, as already mentioned, a relationship is not necessarily evidence of cause and effect. Remember, however, that the special survey technique known as a *panel study* gives us a little more confidence in making cause-and-effect statements based on survey data. However, since panel studies cost a lot and sometimes take years to complete, not many exist. Further, the results from those that are available are not as clear as we might like them to be. One panel study whose

TABLE 18–1

Questionnaire Items

	Almost always	Often	Sometimes	Never
The Sopranos	_____	_____	_____	_____
Malcolm in the Middle	_____	_____	_____	_____
NYPD Blue	_____		_____	_____
Will and Grace	_____	_____	_____	_____
CSI	_____	_____	_____	_____
Law & Order	_____	_____	_____	_____

1. About how often do you watch the following TV programs?
2. Next, what would you do if these things happened to you?
    a. Pretend somebody you know took something from you and would not give it back. What would you do?

_____ Hit the other person and take my property back.

_____ Call the police.

_____ Ask the person to return it.

_____ Nothing.

    b. Pretend somebody was telling lies about you. What would you do?

    _____ Hit the person and make the person stop.

    _____ Ask the person to stop telling lies.

    _____ Nothing.

methods might have been stronger was included in the 1972 Surgeon General's report on television and social behavior. It found evidence that viewing violent TV shows at an early age was a cause of aggression in later life.

Additional survey evidence appeared in 1982 with the publication of *Television and Aggression: A Panel Study.* This book reported the results of a three-year research project sponsored by the NBC television network. Data on aggression, TV viewing, and a large number of sociological variables were collected on six different occasions from children in two Midwestern cities. Eventually, about 1,200 boys in grades two through six participated in the main survey.

Lengthy and detailed analysis of the data suggested that there was no relationship between the viewing of TV violence and subsequent aggressive behavior. Later, other researchers were given the opportunity to reanalyze the NBC data. One reexamination did find some partial evidence of a causal relationship between TV violence and aggression, but its impact was tiny. In sum, if a causal relationship was present in the NBC data, it was extremely weak and hard to find.

In 1986, an international team of scientists reported the results of panel studies done in five countries: the United States, Finland, Australia, Israel, and Poland. The U.S. study and the Polish study found that early TV viewing was significantly related to later aggression. The Finnish study reached a similar conclusion for boys but not for girls. In Israel, viewing TV violence seemed to be a cause of subsequent aggression among boys and girls who lived in urban areas but not among those

What makes some children imitate the violent acts they see on TV? Scientists have been studying this question since the early 1950s.

who lived in rural areas. The panel study done in Australia was not able to find a causal relationship. Despite these differences, the five panels were consistent in at least two findings. First, the relationship between the viewing of violence and aggression tended to be somewhat weak. Second, there was a pattern of circularity in causation. Viewing violent TV caused some children to become more aggressive. Being aggressive, in turn, caused some children to watch more violent TV.

The results of an extensive panel survey reported in 2002 found that teens who watched more than one hour of TV a day were more likely to commit violent acts in later years than were teens who watched less. The survey tracked 707 children for more than 17 years. The researchers interviewed the participants several times and also checked arrest records to document violent behavior. The relationship between TV viewing and aggressive acts was still evident after other factors such as low family income and a prior history of violence were controlled statistically. The results of the study were weakened, however, by the fact that the researchers measured the total amount of TV exposure rather than exposure to violent content. It is difficult to explain why general TV exposure, much of it to nonviolent programs, would be related to aggression.

What are we to make of all these panel studies? On the whole, they seem to suggest that there is a mutual causal connection between watching TV violence and performing aggressive acts. This connection, however, is small and influenced by individual and cultural factors. At this point, we will turn to the results of laboratory studies to aid us further in forming a conclusion about what causes what.

>> Experimental Results

Imagine that it is a cold winter night. As part of the requirements of Psychology 100, a course in which you are enrolled, you are required to serve as a subject in three hours of research. Tonight is your night to fulfill part of your obligation. Thus, you find yourself trudging across campus to the Psychology Building. Upon arriving, you join several dozen other students in a large auditorium. Before long, an individual enters the room, introduces himself as Professor So-and-so, and tells you that you are about to begin your first experiment of the evening.

Professor So-and-so has a new IQ test that he is trying to develop, and he needs your cooperation. The test booklet is passed out, and you are told to begin. As soon as you start the test, you realize that it is unlike any IQ test you have ever seen before. There are questions about advanced calculus, early Greek architecture, and organic chemistry, which you have no idea how to answer. In a few minutes, Professor So-and-so starts making sarcastic comments: "You'll never finish college if this simple test takes you so long"; "It looks as if this group will certainly flunk out"; "High school students have finished this test by now." Finally, with an air of exasperation, the professor says, "There's no hope for you. Hand in the papers. Since most of you won't be in school after this semester's grades, let me say good-bye to you now." With that, the professor storms out of the room.

A few minutes go by, and then another individual enters the room and calls out two lists of names. Each group is assigned to another room down the hall. When you report to your assigned room, you find another professor already there. She tells you that this is the second experiment you will participate in tonight. It is a study to see how much people remember from films. You are going to be shown a brief excerpt from a film, and then you will be asked questions about it. The lights go out, and all of a sudden you are watching an eight-minute fight scene from a Kirk Douglas film called *The Champion*. In the movie, Douglas, playing a boxer, gets the stuffing beaten out of him as he competes for the championship. (Unknown to you, that other group of students is also seeing a film. At the same time you are watching Douglas get battered, they are viewing a totally different scene from *Canal Boats in Venice*.) When the film ends, you are asked several memory questions about its content.

Video games are becoming more popular. A recent survey done by the Kaiser Family Foundation found that almost three-quarters of respondents had at least one video game platform (Sega, Nintendo, etc.) available in their homes. The survey also disclosed that preteen and teenage boys spend nearly 45 minutes a day playing these games. Many popular games, such as "Grand Theft Auto," "Duke Nukem," and "Return to Castle Wolfenstein," feature violent themes. A study published in the March 2003 issue of the *Journal of Broadcasting & Electronic Media* documented just how much violence these games contained.

Based on available sales figures, the researchers selected the 20 most popular games for each of the three leading game platforms. They next played each game for 10 minutes, resulting in a sample of 10 hours of game play.

They found that more than two-thirds of the games they examined had one or more instances of violence. The average number of violent acts in all of the games worked out to be more than two per minute. If an average child spends about 45 minutes a day playing these games, he or she would be exposed to about 90 violent acts a day or about 2,700 acts a month. This number far exceeds the amount of violent acts that would be seen on TV during the same amount of time.

Further, the researchers found that games that were rated T or M (suitable for teens and adults) were far more violent than video games rated E or K-A (suitable for ages 6 and up). Games rated T or M were more likely to contain repeated acts of violence and were also characterized by more graphic displays of blood and gore. More than half of the T or M games contained blood and gore compared to only 4 percent of the general audience games. Moreover, about one-fifth of the games were "first person shooters," in which the player takes the role of the perpetrator of the violence.

In short, many parents would find these results disturbing. As concluded by the researchers, "[V]ideo games . . . are saturated with violence and feature elements that pose risk for development of aggressive scripts for social problem solving."

You are then directed to yet another room. Once in this cubicle, you are told that the third and last experiment is to begin. You are seated in front of a rather strange-looking machine with a dial that can be moved from a setting of 1 to 11. You also notice a button and a light connected to something behind the machine. The researcher explains that you are to be part of an experiment designed to investigate memory. In another room, but wired up to this same machine, is a student who is learning a word-association test. Every time this other student makes a mistake, you are to punish him by giving him a shock. The dial on your panel determines the intensity of the shock; when you press the button, it will be administered. You can choose any level you like; you can hold the button down as long as you like. The experimenter then gives you a level-2 shock to show you what it feels like. You jump and wonder why you did not take Botany instead of Psych. Your thoughts are interrupted, however, when the little light on the panel flashes on. The other student has made a mistake. It is your job to administer punishment. Your hand reaches for the dial. . . .

>> The Catharsis versus Stimulation Debate

This is an abstracted, simplified, and condensed version of the prototype experimental design used in several key studies to investigate the impact of media violence. The idea behind this experiment is to test two rival theories about the effects of watching violence. The first theory is thousands of years old; it is called the **catharsis theory** and can be traced back to Aristotle. This theory holds that viewing scenes of aggression can actually purge the viewer's own aggressive feelings. Thus, a person who sees a violent television program or movie might end up less likely to commit violence. The other theory, called the **stimulation theory,** argues just the opposite. It suggests that seeing scenes of violence will actually stimulate an individual to behave more violently afterward.

As you may have understood, in the hypothetical experiment, everybody was first insulted and presumably angered (this part of the experiment gave you some hostility to be purged); one group saw a violent film, and the other saw a nonviolent film. Both groups were then given a turn at the punishment machine. If catharsis was at work, then the group that saw *The Champion* would have given less intense shocks; if stimulation was at work, then *The Champion* group would have given more intense shocks.

The catharsis versus stimulation debate was one of the earliest to surface in the study of mass media's effects. One early study seemed to point to catharsis, but a series of studies carried out by psychologist Leonard Berkowitz and his colleagues at the University of Wisconsin found strong support for the stimulation hypothesis. Since that time, the bulk of the evidence seems consistent: Watching media violence tends to stimulate aggressive behavior on the part of the viewer. There is little evidence for catharsis.

≫ Bandura's Experiment

The catharsis versus stimulation question was only one of several topics that sparked early experimental work in the investigation of the effects of the media. Another controversy arose over the possibility that TV and movies were serving as a school for violence. Would children imitate violent behavior they had just observed in films or TV programs? A series of experiments conducted by psychologist Albert Bandura and his colleagues during the 1960s indicated that, in fact, films and TV might teach aggressive behaviors.

Preschool children were shown films in which a model reacted violently to a large rubber doll (called a Bobo doll). When children were placed in a play situation similar to the one they had just observed, they mimicked the behaviors they had seen, performing far more aggressively toward the unfortunate Bobo doll

A series of still photographs of the famous study by Bandura, Ross, and Ross (1961). In this experiment, children watched adults act aggressively toward a Bobo doll. When allowed to play in the same room, these children imitated the behavior of the adult models.

than did children who had not seen the film. It was further determined that children would behave more aggressively if they were rewarded for doing so or if they saw the model in the film rewarded. Of course, there is a big difference between hitting an inanimate doll and hitting a human being. To account for this, more recent studies have substituted a human being dressed as a clown for the faithful Bobo doll. Although more children were willing to hit the rubber doll, a large number also physically assaulted the human clown. This reaction did not occur among children who had not seen the violent film.

>> Complicating Factors

Of course, many complicating factors might influence the results of such experiments. To begin with, many of these studies used specially made films and videotapes. In laboratory situations, the experimental "program" may not duplicate the impact of actual TV or films. In those films and tapes produced especially for laboratory use, the violence is concentrated in a short period; there is usually a clear connection between the violence and its motivations and consequences. Films and TV shows are not this direct, and violence is usually embedded in a larger story line. Punishment for violence may not occur until the end of the program. Motives may be mixed or unclear.

Further, it is likely that a person's age, sex, social class, and prior level of aggression influence the ultimate effect of viewing televised violence. Boys, for example, tend to be more affected by TV violence than are girls. Children who come from homes in which there are no explicit guidelines condemning violence also seem to be strongly affected. It also appears that a similarity between the circumstances surrounding televised violence and the situation in which a person finds himself or herself immediately after viewing it is an important factor. The more alike the two settings, the more aggressively the person is likely to behave.

Finally, the reactions of other people directly influence aggression. If children watch an aggressive film in the company of an adult who makes positive comments about the media violence, they act more aggressively than do children who view the aggression with a silent adult. Conversely, children who hear the on-screen aggression condemned commit fewer aggressive acts. It has also been shown that children who view violence in pairs act more aggressively than do children who are alone.

>> Field Experiments

In field experiments, people are studied in their typical environment, where they probably react more naturally than they do in the lab. Field experiments are therefore subject to the contaminating influences of outside events.

At least two field experiments done in the early 1970s revealed no link between TV and aggression. On the other hand, five field experiments have yielded data consistent with the survey and lab data. Their main conclusion is that people who watch a steady diet of violent programs tend to exhibit more antisocial or aggressive behavior.

One of the more elaborate field experiments involved a Canadian town that did not receive a TV signal until 1974. Two similar towns were selected for comparison—one could get only Canadian TV, and the other could get Canadian and U.S. channels. The research team gathered data from all three towns in 1974 and again two years later. Children in the town that had recently received access to U.S. TV showed an increase in their rate of aggressive acts that was more than three times higher than that of children living in the other two towns. Taken as a whole, the results from the field experiments tend to support the notion that viewing TV violence fosters aggressive behavior.

>> What Can We Conclude?

Let us now try to summarize the results of these surveys and experiments. Although no single survey or experiment can provide a conclusive answer, and although every study has certain shortcomings, there appears to be a thread of consistency running throughout these studies. Surveys and panel studies have shown a relationship between the viewing of violent programs and aggressive behavior. Lab and field experiments also have shown that watching violence increases the possibility of behaving aggressively. Taken as a whole, these results encourage a tentative acceptance of the proposition that watching violence on television increases aggressiveness on the part of at least some viewers.

However, viewing TV violence is only one of many factors that might prompt a person to behave aggressively, and in relative terms its influence is not particularly strong. But is a weak relationship an inconsequential relationship? Much of the recent debate about TV violence has centered on this question. In statistical terms, researchers gauge the strength of any relationship by the amount of variability in one measure that is accounted for by the other. For example, height and weight are two factors that are related. If I know how tall you are, I can make a better guess about your weight than if I do not know your height. I may not get your weight exactly right, but at least I will be closer to the correct figure. Consequently, height "explains" some of the variability associated with weight. If two factors are perfectly related, one explains 100 percent of the variability of the other. If two factors are not related (for example, weight and IQ), one explains 0 percent of the variability of the other. Exposure to TV violence typically explains from about 2 percent to 9 percent of the variability of aggression. In other words, about 91 percent to 98 percent of the variability in aggression is due to something else. Given these figures, can we conclude that the impact of TV violence is really that important?

The answer to that question is more political and philosophical than scientific, but research does provide some benchmarks for comparison. In psychology, the relationship between undergoing psychotherapy and being "cured" of your mental ailment is only slightly stronger than that between TV violence and aggression. Further, the effect size for TV violence's impact on antisocial behavior is only slightly less than that of the effect size between viewing *Sesame Street* and readiness for school. *Sesame Street,* of course, was regarded as a great success. Lastly, the Food and Drug Administration has released for general use several drugs whose therapeutic effect is about as great or even less than the size of the effect between TV violence and aggression. Thus, although the effect might be small, it is not necessarily trivial.

ENCOURAGING PROSOCIAL BEHAVIOR

Most early research into the effects of mass communication dealt with the negative or antisocial effects of the media. Toward the end of the 1960s, however, sparked perhaps by the success of public television's *Sesame Street,* researchers rec-

The lovable Blue from *Blue's Clues,* a program with obvious prosocial messages.

ognized that positive behaviors could be promoted by television programs. (These behaviors are generally referred to by the umbrella term **prosocial behavior** and can include actions such as sharing, cooperating, developing self-control, and helping.)

>> Experiments

Lab experiments have shown that films and TV programs can affect the performance of prosocial behavior, including such things as self-control, cooperation, sharing, and helping. These experiments typically show a brief segment from a television program demonstrating one of these behaviors to one group of children and show a different program or no program at all to another group. After watching the segment, the children are given a chance to exercise self-control (such as by following directions from the experimenter) or to share (such as by winning money in a game and giving some to charity).

>> Surveys

There is little survey data about prosocial behavior. One study noted that children who watched *Sesame Street* were able to identify prosocial messages contained in the programs. Do prosocial messages actually influence day-to-day behavior? At least two surveys found little relationship between viewing prosocial programs and prosocial behavior.

Judging from these studies, we can say that the relationship between viewing and prosocial behavior is much weaker than that between viewing and aggressive behavior. Closer examination indicates why this should be the case. Violent behaviors as portrayed on TV and in films are blatant, easy to see, and physical; prosocial behaviors are subtle, sometimes complicated, and largely verbal. Because children learn better from simple, direct, and active presentations, aggressive behaviors may be learned more easily from media content. Further, since most children are taught early in life that they should be friendly, helpful, and cooperative, media content may only reinforce what children already know. On the other hand, aggressive behavior is usually punished at home and at school, and frequent viewing of it on TV might serve to overcome children's inhibitions against performing this discouraged behavior. It appears that much more research is necessary before the total impact of the media on prosocial behavior is known.

 OTHER BEHAVIOR EFFECTS

>> Political Behavior

Trying to summarize the many studies that have been conducted about the influences of the media on politics would require far more space than we have available. Consequently, we will restrict our discussion to the more central findings. At

Sesame Street is probably the most successful educational television program ever produced. After its debut in 1969, the show was showered with praise from critics, parents, teachers, and children. Initial projects indicated that the program was accomplishing its educational goals. However, *Sesame Street* did not succeed without generating some criticism.

Seven years after its inception, *Sesame Street* had established itself as an international favorite. The program was viewed regularly in more than 40 countries around the world, and Big Bird, Cookie Monster, and Oscar had become household names. Children in Latin America watched *Plaza Sesamo,* in Germany, *Sesamstrasse,* and in Holland, *Sesamstraat.*

With international prominence came international problems. The Spanish-language version, *Plaza Sesamo,* was faced with the difficult task of producing a program that would adequately reflect the diverse subcultures of 22 million Latin American preschoolers. The program ignored the language variations in favor of a standardized approach. Further, although Latin America has many varietes of folk music, the first series of *Plaza Sesamo* contained only one Latin American selection per program; other selections consisted of American rock. Soon critics of the program charged that *Plaza Sesamo* was submerging local culture and substituting a standardized American-influenced culture in its place.

Despite good intentions, *Sesame Street* ran into political problems. A joint Palestinian-Israeli version of the show that debuted in 1998 quickly ran into trouble. Both the Israelis and the Palestinians criticized the show for perpetuating stereotypes. Production on the series was subsequently halted. A proposed South African version of the show had to use 11 official languages to satisfy political concerns.

Another criticism that emerged closer to home was that *Sesame Street* was teaching too well. One of the program's original goals was to aid the intellectual growth of disadvantaged children, and the show was clearly meeting this goal.

However, advantaged children were also watching *Sesame Street* and learning from it, sometimes at a faster pace than their disadvantaged counterparts. As a result, *Sesame Street* had done little to narrow the gap between the two groups and, in fact, might even have widened it. Other educators criticized the program's fast-paced format, which contrasted dramatically with the slower-paced classroom environment. Such a frenetic format, these educators claimed, might contribute to hyperactivity and other behavioral problems.

One recent criticism had to do with the increasing trend toward commercializing the *Sesame Street* characters. Dolls and other figures based on the characters have always been popular (consider "Tickle Me Elmo"), but the latest trend has seen the program form partnerships with well-known companies. In 2000 the Keebler Company introduced a Cookie Monster line of cookies (chocolate chips with a *C* on one side and the Cookie Monster's likeness on the other). They will be joined by Elmo Tickles and Bert and Ernie Cookie Pals. In addition, Kmart has introduced *Sesame Street* clothing. One of its TV commercials ends with the line, "This is brought to you by the letter *K*—for Kmart." Or should that be *K* for Keebler? Is *Sesame Street* teaching kids that learning and consuming go hand in hand?

Another criticism centered on the decision to include an HIV-positive muppet in the South African version of *Sesame Street.* When an executive at the Sesame Workshop, the organization that produces the program, hinted that the character might also appear in the U.S. version, members of Congress reacted with alarm, arguing that the character was inappropriate for a show that reached 2- to 4-year-old viewers. The HIV-positive muppet never made it to U.S. TV, but the possibility raised some troublesome issues. Should *Sesame Street* just stick to numbers and letters or should it tackle complicated social problems? If so, who decides what social problems should be addressed?

the core of our current discussion will be an examination of the individual's most important political behavior, the ultimate payoff in any political campaign— namely, voting behavior.

Studies of Voter Turnout Voter turnout in presidential elections generally increased from 1924 to 1960 (if we exclude the war years). From that time, however, the trend has been reversed, and fewer people have voted in presidential elections. Have the media had an impact in this area? The data are not conclusive, and many people have different viewpoints. At least one political scientist has argued that part of the increased voter turnout from 1930 to 1940 was due to the impact of radio. As this new medium reached those who were less educated, less politically involved, and beyond the reach of printed media, it apparently stimulated greater interest in politics and increased the tendency to vote. The parallel emergence of TV did not have such an impact, although many argued that the visual dimension of TV would make the political process more vivid and so further increase participation. But turnout has decreased, starting with the 1964 election (the first election in which the first "TV generation" would be eligible to vote). A current explanation for this drop holds the unique characteristics of TV news partly responsible. TV news, it is argued, presents the news in such a way that it is hard to avoid messages about the opposition. Seeing an opponent making a good case for his or her position rarely converts a voter, but it might make that voter less sure of his or her own views and more confused. As a result, these voters might simply tune out and become less interested in politics and voting.

Recent political campaigns have centered attention on *negative political advertising*. Although there is no standard definition of this term, most political experts interpret it as a personal attack on the opposing candidate or an attack on what the opposing candidate stands for. There was much speculation that negative advertising would turn off voters, make them distrustful of politics, and make them less inclined to participate in the political process. Both survey and laboratory research suggested that most of these fears were unfounded. When compared with those who did not view negative ads, voters who were exposed to negative ads were just as likely to vote, were just as involved, and showed little difference in the amount of trust they placed in the political system. There was a tendency, however, for negative advertising to be related to more polarized attitudes, but this polarization did not seem to have much impact on political behavior.

More recent surveys indicate that those candidates who use a lot of negative advertising tend to receive a lower proportion of the vote. This does not necessarily mean that negative ads are ineffective; it may be that candidates who are behind in preelection polls turn to negative advertising since they have little to lose. (For a summary of the rather voluminous literature on negative advertising, read Chapter 5 in *Television: What's On, Who's Watching, and What It Means*, by George Comstock and Erica Scharrer.)

Effects of the Mass Media on Voter Choice   A person's decision to vote for a particular candidate is affected by not only the mass media but also many other factors, both social and psychological. Still, some tentative generalizations can be made.

It would appear that conversion (changing your vote from Republican to Democrat, for example) is unlikely to result from media exposure, because it is difficult for the media to persuade someone whose mind is already made up to change and because most people (roughly two-thirds) have already made up their minds before the campaign begins. Far more common are two effects that have a direct bearing on voter choice: **reinforcement** and **crystallization.** *Reinforcement* means the strengthening or support of existing attitudes and opinions. *Crystallization* means the sharpening and elaboration of vaguely held attitudes or predispositions. If a person approaches a campaign undecided or neutral, then crystallization is likely to occur. If the person has already made up his or her mind, then reinforcement will probably take place.

In recent national elections, there has been an increase in ticket splitting (supporting one party's candidate for president and another's for governor, for example).

This phenomenon may be due to crystallization, which in turn results from exposure to mass media. The flow of information during the campaign evidently crystallizes a voter's vague intention, and, in many instances, these new choices do not square with party loyalty. On the other hand, when partisan voters are exposed to the media, reinforcement is likely.

These findings do not necessarily mean that the media are not influential. A key factor in winning any election is to keep the party faithful loyal (reinforcement) and to persuade enough of the undecideds to vote for your side (crystallization). Thus, even though widespread conversion is not usually seen, the media are still influential. Even more important, the media may have significant indirect influence on the electorate. By serving as important sources of political news, by structuring "political reality," and by creating an image of candidates and issues, the media may have a potent effect on a person's attitudes about the political system. Furthermore, our discussion has been mainly concerned with the effects of the media in national elections. Local elections present a somewhat different picture. Most research evidence indicates that the media, especially local newspapers, might be highly influential in affecting voter choice in a city, county, or district election.

Effects of Televised Debates.   The first series of presidential debates between John Kennedy and Richard Nixon during the 1960 election prompted more than 30 different studies. Most concluded that the main effect of the debates was reinforcement, since most people had made up their minds before the debates. There was also evidence of a crystallization effect as independent voters shifted to the Kennedy camp. Although the crystallization effect was small, the 1960 election was decided by a tenth of a percentage point, suggesting that even small effects can have significant results.

The reinforcement effect was found again during the 1984 and 1988 debates. In 1996, the debates between Bill Clinton and Bob Dole seemed to have little impact on voter choice. Any effect of the debates between Al Gore and George W. Bush in the 2000 election was difficult to detect. The audience for these debates was the smallest ever due to competition from sporting events and entertainment programs.

Television and the Political Behavior of Politicians   On a general level, it is clear that the emergence of television has affected the political behavior of politicians and political campaigns. A comparison of pre-TV practices with those occurring after TV's adoption reveals the following:

1. Nominating conventions are now planned with television in mind. They are designed not so much to select a candidate as to make a favorable impression on public opinion.
2. Television has increased the cost of campaigning.
3. Television has become the medium around which most campaigns are organized.
4. Campaign staffs now typically include one or more television consultants whose job it is to advise the candidate on his or her television image.

>> Effects of Obscenity and Pornography

The results of research into the effects of obscene and pornographic material are not conclusive, but some consistencies have begun to emerge. Several studies conducted in the 1980s found a disturbing link between exposure to pornography and feelings of callousness toward women. One study found that men who were exposed to a heavy diet of pornography had less compassion for female rape victims and were less supportive of women's rights than were men who were exposed to lesser amounts of pornographic material.

The most recent debate in this area is over the relative effects of violent versus nonviolent pornography. Several studies have noted a link between exposure to films that are both violent and pornographic and feelings of sexual callousness toward women. But is it the violence or the pornography that is the cause? At least one study has found the same result of viewing nonviolent pornography, but others have failed to replicate this finding.

In 1995, a comprehensive review of 30 experiments in this area produced some interesting conclusions. The authors found that exposure to erotic materials that contained only nudity was actually related to diminished subsequent aggressive behavior. There was also a relatively small connection between exposure to nonviolent pornography and aggression and a somewhat stronger link between violent pornography and subsequent aggressive behavior. In short, viewing pornography, whether violent or nonviolent, tended to increase aggressive behavior, at least as measured in the laboratory.

 RESEARCH ABOUT THE SOCIAL EFFECTS OF THE INTERNET

For obvious reasons, research concerning the effects of spending time on the Internet is still in a formative stage. Nonetheless, we can already identify two major trends in Net studies:

1. the impact of Internet use on other media and
2. the relationship between Internet use and social involvement.

The Internet seems to have had the most impact on television usage. This is not surprising since much Internet use takes place during the evening—the same time that most TV viewing generally takes place. Magazine and newspaper reading, radio listening, and moviegoing seem not to have been significantly affected.

As mentioned in Chapter 12, the Internet is becoming more important as a source of news. At the same time, there has been a decline in the number of people who rely on broadcast TV and newspapers as their main sources of news. At the moment, however, online news sources are no threat to replace traditional TV and print journalism.

Early studies that looked at the Internet and social involvement suggested that people who were heavy users of the Internet were also those who reported greater feelings of loneliness and social isolation. More recent surveys, however, have found just the opposite. One survey found that Internet use was related to more social involvement in the local community; another found that those who spent a great deal of time on the Internet were more politically involved and had more contacts than those who did not spend time online. Yet another found that

Internet users were the ones with the most social contacts. Apparently, both the audiences and the Internet have changed over the last few years and innovations such as instant messaging encourage greater social contact.

All in all, surveys that have studied people's Internet use supported the "rich get richer" model. Extroverted people were the ones who gained the most social contacts through the Internet. To them, it was just another channel to use to link up with friends. Conversely, introverted people who went online tended to shy away from social contacts.

 ## COMMUNICATION IN THE FUTURE: SOCIAL IMPACT

Let us close this chapter (and this book) with an examination of some of the relevant questions about the impact of the new communications technology on society. Advances in media technology usually have an upside and a downside. The telephone, for example, made communication at a distance much more convenient. It also meant that we could be interrupted, awakened, or bothered at any hour of the day or night. Radio and television brought immediate access to information and entertainment but also encouraged the proliferation of couch potatoes. What might the future bring?

>> Privacy

Computers have opened up threats to privacy. Some systems enable supervisors to monitor every keystroke of their employees to observe productivity. E-mail, no matter how personal, can be read by anyone with access to the system. Consumers who subscribe to computerized data services run the risk of having their personal files examined by unauthorized persons.

In the past, spying on our personal habits was made difficult simply because information was scattered about in different places. Now computers store huge amounts of information about us in one centralized place, the computer's memory, that is easily accessed from anywhere over phone lines. We willingly provide much of this information when we apply for a credit card, buy a car or a house, take out insurance, file a lawsuit, claim unemployment benefits, and so on. What many consumers do not know is that much of this information is sold to other organizations for other purposes. This is one of the reasons many of us are hit with barrages of spam from organizations we have never heard of.

Computer scanning systems used at the checkout counters of supermarkets and drug and discount stores now record your every purchase. Such information is invaluable to marketers. The makers of Mylanta can offer discounts to people who regularly buy Tums to get them to switch to their product. Bumblebee Tuna can send free samples to Chicken of the Sea buyers. Although this is great for marketing purposes, it is troubling for consumers. If you are like the rest of us, there are some purchases you make that you might like to keep private. Do you want everybody to know what kind of birth control method you use?

>> Fragmentation and Isolation

The mass media are increasingly serving the needs of more specialized audiences. Magazines, radio stations, and cable TV networks, with their highly targeted niche audiences, are the best examples of this trend, but the other media are moving in this direction. The media are increasingly directing individuals toward

CRITICAL / CULTURAL ISSUES

Beers and *Cheers*

Although this particular chapter spotlights the traditional effects-oriented model of mass communication research, the critical approach can also be a valuable tool in analyzing media impact. A good example of this method can be found in an article by Dr. Heather Hundley in a 1995 issue of the *Journal of Broadcasting and Electronic Media*, "The Naturalization of Beer on 'Cheers.'" Her analysis suggests that beer drinking on *Cheers* was portrayed as normal, acceptable behavior with little evidence of any harmful effects. In effect, it was shown as the natural, normal, and desirable thing to do.

To support her thesis, Dr. Hundley analyzed approximately 25 hours of *Cheers* episodes from its last season on the air. She identified three methods by which beer drinking was naturalized. First, jokes associated with beer drinking were common. For example, after taste-testing 22 different beers, Norm goes to *Cheers* to drink a few beers as his lunch. Even while suffering a hangover, Norm asks for a beer. Connecting humor to drinking distracts the audience from thinking about its potential negative effects and shows it as a harmless activity. A second method was camaraderie. People are brought together over beer, and beer drinking is connected to sociability and male bonding. For example, when Frasier first appears on the program, he orders Manhattans. He is not accepted as one of the boys until he switches to beer. The final method was detoxification. *Cheers* depicted characters who can seemingly drink beer all night and show no aftereffects. Norm, for example, consumes copious amounts of lager but never shows any evidence of drunkenness. Interestingly, the apparently harmless nature of beer drinking is contrasted with the harmful effects of drinking "hard" liquor. Norm's hangover, mentioned previously, came about as the result of consuming mixed drinks. In short, the show depicted the drinking of beer as being as harmless as drinking water.

In reality, of course, alcohol consumption is related to many social problems, and many problem drinkers start out at a young age by consuming beer. The nonrealistic depiction of beer drinking in *Cheers* seems to exacerbate this problem.

Who benefits from such a portrayal? The beer industry spends almost a billion dollars on advertising each year. TV networks get a significant chunk of that. As Dr. Hundley concludes, the *Cheers* message serves the economic and ideological interests of both beer producers and the television networks.

1. Some people respond to arguments such as this by saying, "Lighten up! It's only TV!" But is it "only TV"? How much do we learn from what we see, even when the producers are "only" trying to entertain us?

2. What else might *Cheers* have taught us? How did the show portray women and people of color?

3. What responsibilities do producers have to let the audience know, for example, that heavy drinking (even of beer) is not normal, desirable, or harmless?

---

more selective content exposure. If this trend continues, it might result in a generation of consumers fragmented into smaller and smaller interest groups with little in common with the rest of society. If people are overspecialized in their interests, they may run the risk of being ignorant about the rest of the world.

This phenomenon has been labeled the *cocoon effect* by sociologists. From their perspective, it refers to the process, already evident in the 1990s, whereby people surround themselves with only the political and social information that they find comforting, appealing, or acceptable. It is as though people retreat into their informational cocoon to escape some of the uncertainty of modern life and to help reduce the multitude of choices that have to be made in today's society. It seems possible that this cocooning could generalize into cultural and recreational use of knowledge as well.

Moreover, as telecommuting becomes more popular, more and more people will stay at home. The computer will enable people to work, bank, shop, and be entertained at home. Books, groceries, flowers, movies, meals, medicines, diapers, and deodorants can be delivered directly to a consumer's door. With worries over personal safety mounting daily, will people decide to just stay at home?

Will the home computer increase isolation as more people interact online and not in person?

>> Escape

The issue of escape has been around almost since the time that the mass media were invented. Many parents and educators were worried that young people would much prefer to spend time in the media world instead of the real world. Social critics have painted bleak pictures of mesmerized children attending to various forms of media: radio, movies, TV, video games, and Net surfing. In the future, this concern might have more validity since the media realities that are available are becoming more and more like life outside the media. Home theaters that duplicate the theater experience are already on the market. Big-screen HDTV sets with stereo sound and interactive features are also available. Manufacturers of video games are experimenting with ways to make their displays three-dimensional. And who knows what advances will be made in the virtual reality area? What happens when it is far more fun to be in some media-generated reality than in real life? In fact, virtual reality simulations raise the question "What exactly is 'real' life anyway?" Will large numbers of us abandon socially relevant pursuits for a romp in the media world?

And what happens farther down the road? In William Gibson's 1984 novel *Neuromancer,* people plug computer chips, called *stims,* directly into their brains. Stims provide experiences for all the senses and are usually preprogrammed, but there is also the possibility of becoming a *rider,* traveling through the world computer matrix (which bears an eerie resemblance to the Internet) or even shifting yourself into another person's reality and experiencing the world as the other person experiences it. Could this be the ultimate media experience? Alternate realities hardwired into the cerebral cortex? You decide.

MAIN POINTS

- Surveys and experiments are the two main quantitative techniques used to study the effects of mass communication.

- Media can serve as socialization forces when they are the primary sources of information about a topic and that information is presented in a consistent manner.

- Media can cultivate false perceptions of reality among some heavy users.

- TV ads directed at children can influence attitudes and perceptions about certain products.

- The media can set the priority of certain issues for the public.

- TV violence shows a small but persistent correlation with antisocial behavior among heavy viewers.

- Experiments have shown that TV can produce prosocial behavior, but little evidence of this effect has been found in surveys.

- Television has had little effect on voter turnout. The media are more effective in reinforcing or crystallizing a person's voting choice. TV has had

- significant impact on the conduct of politicians and political campaigns.

- Exposure to pornography has been linked to feelings of sexual callousness.

- The main topics of research concerning the Internet are its effects on the usage of other media and the relationship between social isolation and online media use.

- Other concerns about the effects of mass communications focus on the areas of privacy, isolation, and escape.

QUESTIONS FOR REVIEW

1. What are the two main methods that social scientists use to investigate media effects?

2. What gets cultivated in a cultivation analysis?

3. Summarize the catharsis versus stimulation debate. What viewpoint does research evidence favor?

4. What is the difference between the public's agenda and the media's agenda?

5. How do the media influence the voting choices of the audience?

QUESTIONS FOR CRITICAL THINKING

1. Why is it difficult to establish the effects of mass communication?

2. Young children are not the only ones who go through a socialization period. College students have to be socialized as well. What were the main socialization agencies that prepared you to fit into college life? How important were the media?

3. How are college students portrayed on prime-time TV? Do these portrayals perpetuate any stereotypes?

4. Why has the debate over media violence gone on so long? Will scientists ever amass enough evidence to satisfy everybody? Why or why not?

5. What sorts of research projects should be developed to study the social impact of the Internet?

KEY TERMS

survey (p. 465)
panel study (p. 465)
experiment (p. 466)
field experiment (p. 466)
agencies of socialization (p. 466)
cultivation analysis (p. 470)

mainstreaming (p. 472)
resonance (p. 472)
agenda-setting effect (p. 475)
framing (p. 476)
agenda building (p. 476)
catharsis theory (p. 481)

stimulation theory (p. 481)
prosocial behavior (p. 485)
reinforcement (p. 487)
crystallization (p. 487)

INTERNET RESOURCES

Online Learning Center

At the Online Learning Center home page, www.mhhe.com/dominick8, *select* Student Center *and then* Chapter 18.

1. Use the Learning Objectives, Chapter Outline, Main Points, and Time Line sections to review this chapter.

2. Test your knowledge of the chapter using the multiple choice, crossword puzzle, and flashcard features of the site.

3. Expand your knowledge of concepts and topics discussed in the chapter by going to *Suggestions for Further Reading* and *Internet Exercises.*

PowerWeb

At the Mass Communication home page of PowerWeb, www.dushkin.com/powerweb, *log in and select* Mass
Communication *as your title. On the next screen, select* Topics *and then quick jump to* Prosocial Effects. *Read
Article 7, "Ozzy Without Harriet." Then consider the following questions:*

1. Is the author serious in his contention that
   The Osbournes is an antidrug program?

2. What is the "culture war" that the article talks
   about?

3. How much, if any, impact do the mass media
   have on culture? Why?

Surfing the Internet

*In addition to websites, several newsgroups and listservs are useful to those interested in mass media effects. The listings that
follow represent only a small sample.*

www.aejmc-mcs.org
Home page of the Mass Communication and
Society division of the Association for Education
in Journalism and Mass Communication. Contains
a link to various news groups.

www.gsu.edu/~wwwcom/content
Site devoted to content analysis of communication
messages. Contains summaries of studies of media
content, some of which deal with violence and
stereotyping.

http://tvnews.vanderbilt.edu
Home page of the Vanderbilt University Television
News Archive. Researchers can examine abstracts of
network news programs dating back to 1968.

www.uiowa.edu/~commstud/resources
Contains links to resources in all areas of mass media
effects.

>> Glossary

acculturation In a media context, the tendency of reporters or other media professionals to adopt the ideas and attitudes of the groups they cover or with which they have a great deal of contact.

advertising agency A company that handles both the creative and the business side of an advertising campaign for its clients.

agencies of socialization The various people or organizations that contribute to the socialization of an individual.

agency An organization that handles basic needs of advertisers.

agenda building The ways the media decide what is newsworthy.

agenda-setting effect The influence of the mass media created by emphasizing certain topics, thus causing people to perceive those same issues as important.

alphabet A group of letters used to symbolize each of the sounds that make up a word.

AM Amplitude modulation of radio waves.

Arbitron The professional research organization that measures radio audiences.

Audit Bureau of Circulations (ABC) An organization formed by advertisers and publishers in 1914 to establish ground rules for counting circulation data.

authoritarian theory The prevailing belief that a ruling elite should guide the intellectually inferior masses.

backpack journalist A reporter who can prepare news stories for print, electronic, and online media.

best-seller lists The ranking of best-selling books based on retail sales.

beware surveillance A media function that occurs when the media inform the public of short-term, long-term, or chronic threats.

Billboard The sound-recording industry trade publication that tabulates record popularity.

block booking A policy of major film studios that required theater owners to show several of a studio's low-quality films before they could receive the same studio's top-quality films.

broadband Increased bandwidth for Internet connections, which speeds up downloads.

browsers A type of software that enables individuals to search for content on the World Wide Web.

business-to-business advertising Advertising directed not at the general public but at other businesses.

campaign In advertising, a large number of ads that stress the same theme and appear over a specified length of time.

carriage fee A fee paid by cable systems to carry a cable network.

categorical imperative The ethical principle that people should behave as they wish all others would behave.

catharsis A release of pent-up emotion or energy.

catharsis theory A theory that suggests viewing aggression will purge the viewer's aggressive feelings.

cease-and-desist order A Federal Trade Commission order notifying an advertiser that a certain practice violates the law; failure to comply with a cease-and-desist order can result in fines being levied against the advertiser.

channels Pathways by which a message travels from sender to receiver.

circulation The total number of copies of a publication delivered to newsstands, vending machines, and subscribers.

clock hour A radio format that specifies every element of the program.

commercial television Television programs broadcast by local stations whose income is derived from selling time on their facilities to advertisers.

Communications Act of 1934 An act of Congress creating the Federal Communications Commission.

communist theory A theory of the press that holds the media should promote the goals of the ruling political party.

comprehensive layout The finished model of a print ad.

computer-assisted reporting (CAR) Skills involved in using the Internet to aid reporting.

concept testing A type of feedback in which a one- or two-paragraph description for a new series is presented to a sample of viewers for their reactions.

consent order A Federal Trade Commission order in which the advertiser agrees to halt a certain advertising practice without admitting any violation of the law.

consequence The importance or weightiness of a news story.

consumer advertising Advertising directed at the general public.

controlled circulation A type of circulation in which publications are sent free or distributed to a select readership, such as airline passengers or motel guests.

convergence The blending of communication technologies, operations, or businesses.

conversational currency Topic material presented by the media that provides a common ground for social conversations.

copy The headlines and message in an ad.

corporate convergence The merging of companies with holdings in one medium with companies that have assets in other media.

creative boutique An advertising organization that specializes in the creative side of advertising.

credibility The trust that the audience holds for media that perform surveillance functions.

critical/cultural approach An analytical technique that examines power relationships in society and focuses on meanings people find in texts.

crystallization The sharpening and elaboration of a vaguely held attitude or predisposition.

cultivation analysis An area of research that examines whether television and other media encourage perceptions of reality that are more consistent with media portrayals than with actuality.

culture Common values, behaviors, attitudes, and beliefs that bind a society together.

custom magazines Free magazines published by corporations for current and prospective customers.

cycle In all-news radio, the amount of time that elapses before the program order is repeated.

decoding The activity in the communication process by which physical messages are translated into a form that has eventual meaning for the receiver.

defamation The act of harming the reputation of another by publishing false information.

demo A demonstration tape used to sell a musical performer or group.

developmental journalism A type of journalism, practiced by many less-developed countries, that stresses national goals and economic development.

developmental theory The assumption that government uses media to further national, economic, and social goals.

device convergence The tendency for functions once served by separate machines to be merged into a single device.

digital technology A system that encodes information—sound, text, data, video—into a series of on and off pulses that are usually denoted as zeros and ones.

digital television (DTV) Television signals consisting of binary signals that enable improved picture quality.

digital videodisk (DVD) A disk that stores audio, movies, video, and graphics in a digital format that is compatible with DVD players and home computers.

direct action ad An ad that contains a direct response item (such as a toll-free number) that enables advertisers to see results quickly.

direct broadcast satellite (DBS) A system in which a home TV set receives a signal directly from an orbiting satellite.

disintermediation The process of delivering a product or service directly to the consumer.

distribution system The cables that deliver the signals to subscribers.

double features The practice started by theaters in the 1930s of showing two feature films on the same bill.

dummy A rough version of a magazine that is used for planning how the final version will look.

dysfunctions Consequences that are undesirable from the point of view of the welfare of society.

e-book A digital version of a book, which can be read by using a computer or a special reader.

editorial policies Guidelines the print media follow to persuade the public on certain issues or to achieve specific goals.

electronic news gathering (ENG) Producing and airing field reports using small, lightweight portable TV equipment.

e-mail Electronic messages sent from computer to computer.

encoding The activity in the communication process by which thoughts and ideas from the source are translated into a form that may be perceived by the senses.

Equal Opportunities rule   Part of the Communications Act of 1934; Section 315 allows bona fide candidates for public office to gain access to a broadcast medium during political campaigns.

evaluation   Research done to measure the effectiveness of an advertising or a public relations campaign.

Evernet   The successor to the Internet; an arrangement by which an individual is constantly connected to the Internet using various information devices.

experiment   A research technique that stresses controlled conditions and manipulates variables.

Fairness Doctrine   A now defunct FCC doctrine that required broadcast stations to provide various points of view on a controversial issue.

Federal Communications Commission (FCC)   A regulatory agency, composed of five individuals appointed by the president, whose responsibilities include broadcast and wire regulation.

feedback   The responses of the receiver that shape and alter subsequent messages from the source.

field experiment   An experiment that is conducted in a natural setting as opposed to a laboratory.

First Amendment   The first amendment of the Bill of Rights, stating that Congress shall make no law abridging the freedom of speech or of the press.

FM   Frequency modulation of radio waves.

focus group   A group of 10 to 15 people led by a moderator that discusses predetermined topics.

format   Consistent programming designed to appeal to a certain segment of the audience.

format wheel   A visual aid that helps radio programmers plan what events happen during a given time period.

formative research   Advertising research done before developing a campaign.

framing   The general way a news medium treats a topic.

franchises   Exclusive rights to operate a business in a given territory.

Freedom of Information Act (FOIA)   A law stating that every federal executive-branch agency must publish instructions on the methods a member of the public should follow to get information.

free marketplace of ideas   A press philosophy that endorses the free flow of information.

full-service agency   An ad agency that handles all phases of advertising for its clients.

functional approach   A methodology that holds that something is best understood by examining how it is used.

gag rules   Judicial orders that restrict trial participants from giving information to the media or that restrain media coverage of events that occur in court.

gatekeepers   Individuals who decide whether a given message will be distributed by a mass medium.

golden mean   An ethical principle that states that moderation is the key to virtue.

gramophone   A "talking machine" patented in 1887 by Emile Berliner that utilized a disk instead of a cylinder.

graphophone   A recording device similar to the phonograph but utilizing a wax cylinder rather than tinfoil.

hard news   Timely stories with significance for many people.

head end   The antenna and related equipment of the cable system that receives and processes distant television signals so that they can be sent to subscribers' homes.

heavy metal   A counterculture musical trend of the 1960s–1970s, characterized by a vaguely threatening style and heavy use of amplification and electronic equipment.

hegemony   The dominance of one entity over another.

Hicklin rule   A long-standing obscenity standard based upon whether a book or other item contains isolated passages that might deprave or corrupt the mind of the most susceptible person.

HDTV   A supersharp television system that delivers about twice the resolution of traditional TV.

house drop   The section of the cable that connects the feeder cable to the subscriber's TV set.

human interest   A news value that emphasizes the emotional, bizarre, offbeat, or uplifting nature of a news story.

hypertext   A digital navigational tool that links one electronic document to another.

IBOC   A digital radio broadcasting system that is also compatible with current analog radio.

ideology A particular set of beliefs or ideas.

independents Radio or TV stations unaffiliated with any network.

indirect action ad An advertisement that works over the long run to build a company's image.

information gathering A phase of a public relations campaign in which pertinent data are collected.

injunction A court order that requires an individual to do something or to stop doing something.

instrumental surveillance A media function that occurs when the media transmit information that is useful and helpful in everyday life.

interpersonal communication A method of communication in which one person (or group) interacts with another person (or group) without the aid of a mechanical device.

investigative reports News reporting that requires extraordinary efforts to gather information about matters of public importance.

jazz A form of popular music that emerged during the Roaring Twenties and was noted for its spontaneity and disdain of convention.

jazz journalism Journalism of the Roaring Twenties that was characterized by a lively style and a richly illustrated tabloid format.

joint-operating agreement (JOA) An agreement, intended to preserve editorial competition, in which two newspapers merge their business and printing operations but maintain separate newsrooms.

joint venture A method of movie financing in which several companies pool resources to finance films.

Kinetoscope The first practical motion picture camera and viewing device, developed by William Dickson in 1889.

libel Written defamation that tends to injure a person's reputation or good name or that diminishes the esteem, respect, or goodwill due a person.

libel per quod Written material that becomes libelous under certain circumstances.

libel per se Falsely written accusations (such as labeling a person a "thief" or a "swindler") that automatically constitute libel.

libertarian theory The assumption that all human beings are rational decision makers and that governments exist to serve the individual.

limited partnership A method of movie financing in which a number of investors put up a specified amount of money for a film.

linkage The ability of the mass media to join different elements of society that are not directly connected by interpersonal channels.

machine-assisted interpersonal communication A method of communication involving one or more persons and a mechanical device (or devices) with one or more receivers.

macroanalysis A sociological perspective that considers the functions performed by a system (e.g., mass media) for the entire society.

magazines Printed publications that contain an assortment of materials that appear on a regular basis.

mainstreaming In cultivation analysis, the tendency of differences to disappear among heavy–TV-viewing people, apparently because of cultural and social factors.

management by objectives (MBO) A management technique that sets observable, measurable goals for an organization to achieve.

marketing Developing, pricing, distributing, and promoting an idea, a good, or a service.

mass communication The process by which a complex organization, with the aid of one or more machines, produces and transmits public messages that are directed at large, heterogeneous, and scattered audiences.

mass media The channels and the institutions of mass communication.

meaning The interpretation an audience makes of text.

media buying service An organization that specializes in buying media time to resell to advertisers.

Mediamark Research Inc. (MRI) A company that measures magazine readership.

media vehicle A single component of a mass medium, such as a newspaper or TV network.

message The actual physical product in the communication process that the source encodes.

message research Pretesting messages in an ad campaign.

microanalysis A sociological perspective that considers the functions performed by a system (e.g., mass media) for the individual.

mobile parenting   An arrangement by which parents keep track of children by using cell phones and pagers.

modem   A device that enables computers to communicate via phone lines.

Motion Picture Patents Company (MPPC)   An organization formed by the nine leading film and film equipment manufacturers in 1908 for the purpose of controlling the motion picture industry.

MP3   A digital method of encoding sound files on the Internet.

MPAA rating system   The G, PG, PG-13, R, NC-17 rating system for movies administered by the Motion Picture Association of America.

muckrakers   A term coined by Theodore Roosevelt to describe the reform movement undertaken by leading magazines in the 1890s to expose corrupt practices of business and government to the general public.

national advertisers   Advertisers who sell a product all across the country.

National Public Radio (NPR)   A noncommercial U.S. radio network.

network   An organization composed of interconnecting broadcasting stations that cuts costs by airing the same programs.

newsgroups   A section of the Internet devoted to message boards that are organized according to topic.

newshole   The amount of space available each day in a newspaper for news.

nickelodeons   Popular name for the many penny arcades and amusement centers that emerged around the beginning of the 20th century and specialized in recordings and film.

noise   In communication, anything that interferes with the delivery of a message.

noncommercial television   Television programs broadcast by those stations whose income is derived from sources other than the sale of advertising time.

nonduplication rule   An FCC rule passed in 1965, stating that an AM-FM combination may not duplicate its AM content on its FM channel for more than 50 percent of the time.

ombudsperson   An individual in a media organization assigned to handle complaints from audience members.

one-stops   Individuals who sell records to retail stores and jukebox operators who are not in a position to buy directly from the record company.

operating policies   Guidelines that cover the everyday problems and situations that crop up during the operation of a media organization.

operational convergence   A system used in media organizations whereby one staff produces content for two media.

paid circulation   A type of circulation in which the reader must purchase a magazine through a subscription or at a newsstand.

panel study   A research method in which data are collected from the same individuals at different points in time.

paradigm   A model used for analysis.

parasocial relationship   A situation whereby audience members develop a sense of kinship or friendship with media personalities.

pass-along audience   That portion of a magazine's total audience composed of individuals who pick up copies of a magazine while at the doctor's office, at work, while traveling, and so on.

Patriot Act   A law that gave the government increased powers of surveillance.

payola   Bribes of gifts and money paid to DJs by record companies in order to gain favorable airplay for their releases.

pay-per-view (PPV)   A system that enables cable TV subscribers to pay a one-time fee to view one specific program or movie.

penny press   The mass-appeal press of the early 19th century.

persistence of vision   The quality of the human eye that enables it to retain an image for a split second after the image has disappeared.

personal digital assistants (PDAs)   Digital devices that keep track of addresses, schedules, and other useful information.

personal video recorder (PVR)   A device such as TiVo that records television content on a hard disk.

phi phenomenon   The tendency of the human perceptual system to perceive continuous motion between two stationary points of light that blink on and off; the basis for the illusion of motion in motion pictures.

phonograph   A "talking machine" developed by Thomas Edison in the late 1870s; the hand-cranked device preserved sound on a tinfoil-wrapped cylinder.

photojournalism   Journalism in which written text is secondary to photographs in news stories.

pickup   A technique of financing a motion picture.

pilot   The first episode of a projected television series.

pilot testing   A process that involves showing a sample audience an entire episode of a show and recording their reactions.

policy book   At radio and TV stations, a book that spells out philosophy and standards of operation and identifies practices that are encouraged or discouraged.

political press   Newspapers and magazines of the 1790–1820 era that specialized in publishing partisan political articles.

polysemic   Having many meanings.

portals   First pages a person sees when opening an Internet browser.

positioning   In advertising, stressing the unique selling point of a product or service to differentiate it from the competition.

primary audience   That portion of a magazine's total audience made up of subscribers or those who buy it at the newsstand.

primary demand ad   An advertisement that promotes a specific product category, such as milk.

printing on demand   One-at-a-time printing of books that exist in a digital database.

prior restraint   An attempt by the government to censor the press by restraining it from publishing or broadcasting material.

prominence   News value that stresses the importance of the person involved in the event.

protocol   A common language accepted by computer programmers.

proximity   News value based on the location of a news event.

Public Broadcasting Act of 1967   A congressional act that established the Public Broadcasting Service.

publicity   The placing of stories in the mass media.

publics   The various audience served by public relations.

publishers   A segment of the print media industry responsible for the creation of content.

rack jobbers   Individuals who service record racks located in variety and large department stores by choosing the records to be sold in each location.

Radio Act of 1927   A congressional act establishing the Federal Radio Commission, a regulatory body that would issue broadcasting licenses and organize operating times and frequencies.

rate base   The number of buyers guaranteed by a magazine and used to compute advertising rates.

rating   The ratio of listeners to a particular radio station to all people in the market; the ratio of viewers of a particular TV program to the number of households in the market equipped with TV.

receiver   The target of the message in the communication process.

reinforcement   Support of existing attitudes and opinions by certain messages.

resonance   In cultivation analysis, the situation in which a respondent's life experiences are reinforced by what is seen on TV, thus reinforcing the effect of TV content.

retail advertisers   Businesses that have customers in only one trading area.

rough layout   An early version of a print ad.

satellite news gathering (SNG)   Using specially equipped vans and trucks to transmit live stories from any location via satellite.

search engine   Software that enables users to search the Internet for specific information.

selective demand ad   An ad that stresses a particular brand.

self-determination   The ethical principle that human beings deserve respect for their decisions.

share of the audience   The ratio of listeners to a particular radio station to the total number of listeners in the market; the ratio of the number of households watching a particular TV program to the number of households watching TV at that time.

shield laws   Legislation that defines the rights of a reporter to protect sources.

slander   Spoken defamation; in many states, if a defamatory statement is broadcast, it is considered libel, even though technically the words are not written; libel is considered more harmful and usually carries more serious penalties than does slander.

sliding scale   An arrangement between a motion picture exhibitor and a distributor that details how much box office revenue will be kept by the movie theater.

social responsibility theory   The belief that the press has a responsibility to preserve democracy by properly informing the public and by responding to society's needs.

social utility   The media function that addresses an individual's need to affiliate with family, friends, and others in society.

socialization   The ways an individual comes to adopt the behavior and values of a group.

soft news   Features that rely on human interest for their news value.

source   A person who initiates communication.

spam   The electronic equivalent of junk mail.

status conferral   A process by which media attention bestows a degree of prominence on certain issues or individuals.

stimulation theory   A theory that suggests viewing violence will actually stimulate an individual to behave more violently.

storyboard   A series of drawings depicting the key scenes in a TV ad.

strategic planning   A management technique that sets long-range, general goals.

streaming video   A method of sending TV over the Internet.

subsidiary rights   Rights given by a publisher to others, allowing them to reproduce certain content.

surveillance   The news and information function of the mass media.

survey   A technique of gathering data that typically uses a questionnaire.

tablet PC   A small, lightweight personal computer that can display text and graphics and connect to the Internet.

tabloids   Heavily illustrated publications usually half the size of a normal newspaper page.

tactical planning   A management technique that sets short-range, specific goals.

target audience   In advertising, the segment of the population for whom the product or service has an appeal.

technological determinism   The theory that contends technology drives historical change.

Telecommunications Act of 1996   A major revision of U.S. communication laws that affected broadcasting, cable, and telephone industries.

text   The object of analysis in the critical/cultural approach.

timeliness   News value that stresses when an event occurred.

time shifting   Recording programs and playing them back at times other than when they are aired.

tracking studies   Studies that examine how ads perform during or after a campaign.

trespass   Illegal entry onto another's property.

UHF   The ultra–high-frequency band of the electromagnetic spectrum; channels 14 through 69 on the TV set.

underground press   A type of specialized reporting that emerged in the mid- to late 1960s, with emphasis on politically liberal news and opinion and cultural topics such as music, art, and film.

uses-and-gratifications model   A model proposing that audience members have certain needs or drives that are satisfied by using both nonmedia and media sources.

utility   The ethical principle that stresses the greatest good for the greatest number.

Variety   The entertainment industry trade publication.

V-Chip   A device installed in a TV set that restricts the reception of violent or objectionable material.

veil of ignorance   The ethical principle that everyone should be treated equally.

VHF   The very–high-frequency band of the electromagnetic spectrum; channels 2 through 13 on the TV set.

video on demand   A system by which a cable TV system can provide movies to customers at times of the customers' choosing.

voice tracking   A technique in radio in which a disc jockey prerecords the voice portion of a shift that is later broadcast on several stations.

Web page   A hypertext page contained within a website.

website   A set of hypertext pages linked to each other that contain information about a common topic.

wireless fidelity (WiFi)   A system by which personal computers and other information devices connect to the Internet without wires.

World Wide Web (WWW)   A network of information sources that uses hypertext to link one piece of information to another.

yellow journalism   Sensationalized journalism, appearing during the 1890s, noted for its emphasis on sex, murder, popularized medicine, pseudoscience, self-promotion, and human-interest stories.

zoned editions   Newspapers that have special sections for specific geographic areas.

>> Photo Credits

Chapter 15

p. 384, © Corbis; p. 386, © 2003 by The New York Times Co. Reprinted by permission; p. 391, © Reuters NewMedia Inc./Corbis; p. 413, PAR Archive

Chapter 16

p. 418, © Corbis; p. 423, © AP/Wide World Photos; p. 429, © Alán Gallegos/AG Photograph; p. 431, © NBC/Courtesy Everett Collection

Chapter 17

p. 442, © 2003 MTV Networks Europe; p. 445, © The CNN Inc.; p. 450, © The Granger Collection, New York; p. 458, Courtesy Telemundo; p. 460, © Dave Saunders/Stone/Getty Images

Chapter 18

p. 464, © Warner Brothers/Courtesy Everett Collection; p. 467, © AP/Wide World Photos; pp. 469, 471 © 20th Century Fox Film Corp. All rights reserved. Courtesy Everett Collection; p. 474, © B. Glover/Index Stock Imagery; p. 476, © AP/Wide World Photos; p. 477, © Bettmann/Corbis; p. 479, © Edouard Berne/Getty Images/Stone; p. 482, © Albert Bandura; p. 485, © Ted Thai/Timepix; p. 492, © Mark Richards/PhotoEdit

» Text & Illustration Credits

Figure 1.1: Map of impact of "Slammer" worm from David Moore, Vern Paxson, Stefan Savage, Colleen Shannon, Stuart Staniford, and Nicholas Weaver, "The Spread of the Sapphire/Slammer Worm," www.cs.berkeley.edu~nweaver/sapphire/. Reprinted by permission.

Figure 4.7: *El Diario*, front page for November 4, 2003. http://www.eldiariony.com/noticias/portada.aspx. Reprinted with permission.

LA Times.com registration screen. Reprinted with the permission of Tribune Media Services.

Figure 5.5: Zinio.com home page, www.zinio.com. Reprinted with permission.

"Hot 100" from *Billboard* (November 1, 2003). Copyright © 2003 by VNU Business Publications. Reprinted with the permission of VNU Business Publications.

Figure 9.1: Kazaa home page, www.kazaa.com. Reprinted with the permission of Sharman Networks.

"Box Office" from *Variety* (October 27-November 1, 2003). Copyright © 2003 by Reed Business Information. Reprinted with the permission of Reed Business Information.

Excerpt from *Nielsen Station Index, Viewers in Profile* (February 2003). Copyright © 2003 by Nielsen Media Research. Reprinted with the permission of Nielsen Media Research, a division of VNU Business Publications.

Figure 11.1: The Urban Legend Reference Pages (www.snopes.com), excerpt from "Nigerian scam" letter. Reprinted by permission of Snopes.com.

Figure 11.5: Nielsen//NetRatings, screen capture of Net View Usage Metrics screen, www.netratings.com/news.jsp?section=dat_to. Copyright © 2004 by NetRatings, Inc. Reprinted with permission.

Figure 12.7: CNN.com, screen capture of CNN.com homepage (November 3, 2003).

Figure 13.5: PR Newswire, screen capture of News & Information screen, www.prnewswire.com/news (November 5, 2003). Reprinted with permission.

Figure 14.1: X10 Home Solutions, screen capture of Welcome screen showing miniature wireless video camera, www.X10.com/techtoysab11.htm. Reprinted with the permission of X10 Wireless Technology, Inc.

Figure 14.2: Screen capture of Netflix pop-up ad, http://images.trafficmp.com/tmpad/content/netflix/pop3.html. Reprinted with permission.

Figure 17.2: "Typology of Media Ownership and Control" from L. John Martin and Anju Grover Chaudhary, *Comparative Mass Media Systems.* Published by Allyn & Bacon, Boston, MA. Copyright © 1983 by Pearson Education. Reprinted by permission of the publisher.

Figure 17.3: Interfax, screen capture of Interfax home page (English version), www.interfax.ru/e/0/0/0.html (November 3, 2003). Reprinted with the permission of Interfax America Inc.

>> Index